INDIANS OF THE GREAT PLAINS

Daniel J. Gelo

University of Texas at San Antonio

PEARSON

Boston   Columbus   Indianapolis   New York   San Francisco   Upper Saddle River
Amsterdam   Cape Town   Dubai   London   Madrid   Milan   Munich   Paris   Montreal   Toronto
Delhi   Mexico City   Sao Paulo   Sydney   Hong Kong   Seoul   Singapore   Taipei   Tokyo

Editorial Director: Craig Campanella
Editor in Chief: Dickson Musslewhite
Publisher: Nancy Roberts
Project Manager, Editorial: Kate Fernandes
Editorial Assistant: Nart Varoqua
Director of Marketing: Brandy Dawson
Senior Marketing Manager: Laura Lee Manley
Managing Editor: Maureen Richardson
Project Manager, Production: Shelly Kupperman
Senior Operations Supervisor: Mary Fischer

Senior Operations Specialist: Sherry Lewis
Director, Cover Design: Jayne Conte
Cover Designer: Bruce Kenselaar
Cover Art: William III/Photo Researchers, Inc.
Cartographer: Alice Thiede
Digital Media Editor: Rachel Comerford
Full-Service Project Management and Composition:
  Integra Software Services Pvt. Ltd.
Printer/Binder: R.R. Donnelley & Sons
Cover Printer: R.R. Donnelley & Sons

Credits and acknowledgments borrowed from other sources and reproduced, with permission, in this textbook appear on page 375 within text.

Library of Congress Cataloging-in-Publication Data
Gelo, Daniel J.,
  Indians of the Great Plains / Daniel J. Gelo.—1st ed.
    p. cm.
  Includes bibliographical references and index.
  ISBN-13: 978-0-13-177389-9 (alk. paper)
  ISBN-10: 0-13-177389-5 (alk. paper)
  1. Indians of North America—Great Plains—Textbooks. I. Title.
E78.G73G45 2011
978.004'97—dc22
                              2010053159

10 9 8 7 6 5 4 3 2 1

ISBN 13: 978-0-13-177389-9
ISBN 10:   0-13-177389-5

BRIEF CONTENTS

CONTENTS

PREFACE

The idea for this book came most directly out of a conversation with Charles Hudson, who gave me the modest and deceptively simple advice, "why don't you expand on your class notes, that's what I did," referring to his outstanding text *The Southeast Indians*. In this kindly way, Charles provided both a model for the modern regional survey of Indian cultures and the needed assurance that something similar could and should be attempted for the Plains.

As a teacher of a college course on the Indians of the Great Plains, I have long been troubled by the lack of a suitable text. Those that exist I found to be dated or needing lots of supplementation. The first purpose of this book is to provide a contemporary rendering based on recent scholarship. Secondly, I seek to bring readers up to date with historical and cultural developments of the twentieth and twenty-first centuries and emphasize that Plains societies and cultures are continuing, living entities. Along

the way I attempt to present wide and balanced coverage of the many different tribal groups, with more than the usual attention to Canadian and southern populations along with the famous and populous Sioux and their close neighbors. I was also intent on providing a single text that could support undergraduate lecture course instruction with, if desired, few or no supplementary readings and with an organization that lends itself to the usual weekly topical explorations in a semester survey. Lastly, I hope that this book will function as a reference for general readers that in its comprehensiveness and level of detail sits comfortably and usefully among the myriad journal articles, scholarly monographs, popular press books, and encyclopedias on Plains Indians and derivative subjects.

The outlook and aim of this work is anthropological, and readers will no doubt perceive in it all of the reputed virtues and vices of this disciplinary approach. I am not a Native American and would claim a privileged perspective only so far as I have spent time, during and after long training in cross-cultural theory and method, living in and talking with members of Indian communities fairly steadily for the past 29 years. During this time I have been adopted into a Comanche family and initiated into a Comanche tribal association, was designated an Ambassador to the Comanche Nation by proclamation of the Tribal Chairman, and learned to speak, sing, and dance in Comanche idioms (all quite imperfectly). Through the years I have also enjoyed interviews, casual conversations, and quiet times with members of the Kiowa, Plains Apache, Southern Cheyenne, Ponca, Omaha, Osage, Pawnee, and Lakota tribes. I have been especially close with the late Comanche elders Margaret Thomas and Carney Saupitty, Sr., and their families. The additional Indian people who have helped me learn about their cultures are too numerous to all thank here, and I must be satisfied in having recognized several of them in other publications. Though proud of these relationships, I fully recognize the limits of my own expertise. So I have made an effort to include the personal identities, voices, and viewpoints of Native American people, along with material in Native languages, wherever possible in this text.

This volume also depends on dozens of other researchers and Native consultants whose knowledge is available in printed sources. Most properly each fact or idea presented in the text would be immediately supported with citations from the literature through footnoting or parenthetical referencing. But for a work of this kind, I felt that readability was paramount and therefore, except where there are direct quotations or key concepts, the sources are simply collected at the ends of chapters. In most cases the background documentation for each topic should be evident from the titles of the works listed in the sources section and cited fully in the bibliography. When multiple editions of a source existed, rather than automatically citing the earliest ones I chose to cite those most likely to be available widely in university and public libraries. For similar reasons I have not shied away from citing edited volumes and anthologies that conveniently synthesize materials in such areas as archaeology and mythology. I hope readers, and students in particular, will contemplate what I present critically and follow the trail traces deeper into the supporting literature.

I take sole responsibility for any weaknesses or errors in this work, but several organizations and people must be credited for its completion and whatever good may come of it. I am forever grateful to the Wenner-Gren Foundation for Anthropological Research, Inc. for funding my initial Plains fieldwork with a student grant-in-aid. Bill and Marla Powers were and remain the best teachers, mentors, and friends a budding and former (or, rather, continuing) student could have hoped for. David P. McAllester was also monumentally supportive. I am also deeply indebted to my other professors at Rutgers, my colleagues and correspondents in the fields of Plains and Great Basin anthropology, and my former or current companions in the University of Texas at San Antonio (UTSA) Anthropology Department, especially Robert M. Hill II, James H. McDonald, and Laura J. Levi. Five administrators at UTSA have been unfailingly encouraging and generous in allowing me some semblance of a research and writing schedule amid decanal duties: Guy Bailey, David R. Johnson, Rosalie Ambrosino, Julius Gribou, and John H. Frederick. Steve Tomka and Bruce Moses at the UTSA Center for Archaeological Research provided artifact images. At the UTSA Institute of Texan Cultures, Patrick Lemelle was cheerful and prompt in helping to locate photos. Sharon A. Silengo at the State Historical Society of North Dakota also lent critical support. UTSA graduate students Robert Flourney, Ruth Matthews, Deborah Wagner, and Maria-Raquel Weaver assisted in the research for this book by obtaining and synopsizing reference materials. My wife M. Gabrielle Gelo and our sons Terence and

Thomas were most understanding of all the many hours of travel, reading, and writing, over several years, necessary to finish the volume. Nor would the work have been at all possible without the initial encouragement of Bill Stinner Trimble, the unendingly patient vision and guidance of Nancy E. Roberts, and the skillful assistance of Kate Fernandes, all of Pearson. George Jacob of Integra did masterly editorial work. Finally, I am beholden to eight reviewers for the press, who offered many helpful suggestions that improved the accuracy, clarity, and relevance of the text: Robert M. Hill II, Tulane University; Clarence R. Geier, James Madison University; James Berry, University of Evansville; Janet O. Frost, Eastern New Mexico University; Christine L. Fry, Loyola University Chicago; Richard A. Krause, The University of Alabama; Kathleen Pickering, Colorado State University; Betty A. Smith, Kennesaw State University. I offer my heartfelt thanks to all of these friends for their help.

Much controversy still attends the question of what to call the earliest inhabitants of North America and their descendants. Despite scholarly and popular fashions and government practices, the people I have spent time with in the Plains communities almost always refer to themselves as "Indians." In the spirit of the sagacious peace chief, this book will use "(American) Indian" and "Native (American)" interchangeably, as well as "First Nations" for groups of Canada, as preferred there.

Daniel J. Gelo
University of Texas at San Antonio

CHAPTER 1

THE GREAT PLAINS

The land is great.
When man travels on it
    he will never reach land's end;
But because there is a prize offered
To test a man to go as far as he dares,
He goes because he wants to discover
  his limits.

That wind, that wind
Shakes my tipi, shakes my tipi
And sings a song to me.
And sings a song to me.

—*Kiowa Gomda Dawgyah* ("Wind Songs")
as sung by Sallie Hokeah Bointy (Boyd
1981:18, 19)

THE PLAINS LANDSCAPE

Knowledge of the environment must be the basis for any discussion of Plains Indian culture. In Plains landforms, weather, animals, and plants, we see the origins of Indian adaptive regimes and material culture, migration patterns and tools, and hunting practice and house styles; and it is not too much to say that language, cognition, and religious symbolism—elements often included under the term "worldview"—are also influenced by natural surroundings.

The early Plains anthropologist Clark Wissler (1870–1947) noted that culture "approaches geographical boundaries with its hat in its hand." Recognizing the influence of geography or environment on culture requires caution, however. It would be a mistake to accept the notion that surroundings strictly determine the cultural development and customs of a people, when humans show great adaptability and their prior customs can exist under new circumstances. Another pitfall is the concept that certain people have a unique relationship to nature that is the product of some exclusive mystical or spiritual disposition. It is possible to appreciate Indian knowledge and respect for nature without regarding their sensitivities as superhuman. Like any environment, the Plains region presents a distinct set of opportunities and limits to the humans who encounter it. Exploring the physical characteristics of the region is a good way to start understanding its inhabitants.

Where and what are the Plains? There have been several attempts to determine the boundaries of the region in geographic and ecological terms.

A good starting point is the outline offered by the historian Walter Prescott Webb in his classic work *The Great Plains* (1981; orig. 1931). Webb tells us that a plains environment has three characteristics: it is a comparatively level surface of great extent, it is unforested, and its rainfall is not sufficient for ordinary intensive agriculture. In North America, a level surface extends for the most part between the Appalachian and Rocky Mountains. The unforested area of the continent, though, is mostly west of the Mississippi. It begins at the timber line, an artificial boundary where deep woods yield to brush and grass, running on the east generally between the 94th and 98th meridians (east Texas and Oklahoma, western Missouri and Minnesota) but veering east to the 87th meridian around 40°N, or the area around Iowa and Illinois. Discounting the timber of the Rocky Mountains, this unforested zone extends west to the Sierras and Coast ranges of California, Oregon, and Washington. The dry zone of the continent extends from the 20-inch rainfall line, the so-called "humid line" running roughly along the 98th meridian, again west to the Pacific ranges excepting the Rockies.

The area where all three key characteristics come together—the dry, untimbered, level land between the 98th meridian and the Rockies—is known as the Great Plains. The wetter untimbered level land east of the 98th meridian is also of interest as a zone showing related Indian cultural adaptations; this area is referred to as the Central Plains, Central Lowland, or simply the Prairie. Both the Great Plains and the Prairie are considered in this book (see Map 1.1). Elevation as well as moisture distinguishes the Great Plains from the Prairie, with the Lowland rising no more than 1,500–2,000 feet above sea level and the Great Plains rising from this elevation to around 5,500 feet at the foot of the Rockies. Thus, another name for Great Plains is "High Plains." Transition between Lowlands and High Plains is gradual, but abrupt between the Plains and Rocky Mountains.

The entire Great Plains grassland region is bounded on the north by the boreal forests and lakes of subarctic Canada, and the conventional boundary on the south is the Rio Grande.

The most noticeable difference between the Great Plains and Prairie is in the kinds of grasses that are dominant in the groundcover under natural conditions. Short-grass species are characteristic in the Plains. Short grasses often form a mat of intertwined roots, though this sod gives way to separate tufts or "bunch grass" toward the drier west. Blue grama and various other types of grama and buffalo grasses are common, along with little bluestem, western wheatgrass, galleta, needle-and-thread grass, mesquite grass, and three-awn grass. The Prairie, by contrast, contains taller grasses, some growing to 6 feet or more by autumn: big bluestem, little bluestem, Indian grass, switch grass, and needle grass. Dense sod develops in the moister east, and a square yard of Prairie turf contains literally miles of tangled roots. The transition between tall and short grasses is actually gradual, and many ecologists see at the heart of the mid-continental grasslands a mixed-grass zone featuring the medium-sized little bluestem plus shorter species. The main grass types in any area coexist with one another and several others in a number of patterns depending on local conditions. Tall-grass outliers have been found far to the west, while rivers, pond areas, and sand hills harbor atypical communities. Each grass community has its own character as well because of the particular forbs (broad-leaved weeds and wildflowers) that it hosts.

One of the reasons tall grass thrives toward the east is that the soil is deeper and richer there. Mid-continental soils lay on a foundation of marine rock sheets which are uplifted to varying degrees and which generally slant toward the east. One can see in road cuts in central Texas, for example, thick limestone beds chock full of oceanic fossils, mere inches below the topsoil. At a macro level,

MAP 1.1 The Great Plains.

the soils have been deposited on the rock sheets through the millennia as streams from the eroding Rockies carry mineral and organic debris eastward and, losing energy along the way, drop their sediments in alluvial fans. These huge deltas have spread, overlapped, and clogged their streams and been re-cut in a continuous process. In addition, till left by Ice Age glaciers is found in parts of Montana and the Dakotas, and silts from the Appalachians have been washed westward onto the eastern Prairie. Wind and local runoff further distribute the soils, and they are enhanced

FIGURE 1.1 Short grass and playa on the vast, level Staked Plains near Amarillo, Texas.

with decaying plant matter. These workings have combined to produce a relatively barren Great Plains and a Prairie region with some of the richest dirt on the planet.

The western soils based on soluble limestone drain quickly and dry out, though water may be held deep below. Sedimentary sandstone, siltstone, shale, and gypsum all occur in formations on a local and regional scale. There are also remnants of ancient volcanic activity—granite, quartzite, rhyolite—on the High Plains. Huge deposits of soft coal of various grades underlie sections of the Dakotas, Montana, Wyoming, Colorado, and New Mexico. Oil and natural gas are widespread, with important producing areas around Williston, North Dakota, Denver, and the Permian Basin of West Texas. Metals are absent, with one important exception: gold is mined in

southwestern South Dakota, and its discovery there in the 1870s sparked U.S. government efforts to seize the area from Native peoples. The Homestake Mine near Deadwood is the site of the greatest known U.S. gold reserves.

Toward the west, in the shadows of the Rockies, where erosive forces are greatest, and in other transitional areas the land surface is heavily scarred, with solitary hills and plateaus, large canyons, and narrower ravines that are known regionally as "arroyos," "gulches," or "draws." An old saying of the Comancheros, the Hispanic traders in the Texas Panhandle, had it that "There are mountains below the Plains," describing the effect of coming to the edge of a large canyon like Palo Duro and seeing within it a range of hills whose crests were below the horizon. Areas of monumental erosion such as those occurring

FIGURE 1.2   Tall-grass prairie in Minnesota.

FIGURE 1.3   Badlands in South Dakota.

where one geologic zone gives way to another are often termed "badlands" or "breaks."

Weather works on the landforms and soil, and works with these features to determine the course of life. The meteorological forces shaping the Plains are among the most remarkable anywhere. Webb noted long ago that the wind blows harder and more constantly on the Plains than any place in the United States except for some Pacific Coast areas. Winds prevail from the west with average hourly speeds of as much as 10–14 miles per hour (mph), comparable to the Outer Banks of the North Carolina shore and twice the rate found in the intermontane west. The winds are of high velocity, with special erosive power resulting from the abrasive sediments they carry.

The wind is everywhere, and the humming telephone wires and waving grass can be more ominous than comforting for those who know the power of its aberrant forms. The chinook is a warm, dry wind plunging from the east slopes of the Rockies at 70–100 mph that can raise the temperature by 40°F within a day. The chinook may moderate harsh winter conditions, exposing grass for hungry grazing animals, but the rapid thawing of snow and flash flooding can be dangerous as well as helpful. Polar air masses descending in winter toward the southern Plains, called "northers," cause temperatures to plummet rapidly. Blizzards, intense snowstorms characterized by snowdrifts and sub-zero temperatures, are another winter weather hazard. During drought the wind blows yellow and then black with dust, producing "rollers" or enormous clouds that inundate and sandblast the landscape. Dust storms are most prevalent after spotty rainfall has promoted the buildup of loose sediments. Dust carried by a Great Plains storm can be deposited 1,800 miles away.

The most dramatic windstorms are the tornados. These whirlwinds occur mainly in the spring and summer, in the imaginary 500-mile-wide

FIGURE 1.4 A huge wall of dust races in front of a supercell thunderstorm in Parmer Country, Texas.

corridor called "tornado alley," running from Texas to the Dakotas or Illinois, depending on the yearly pattern. Southwestern Oklahoma sees the greatest frequency. Winds rotating to form the tornado funnel reach speeds of 100–300 mph. The funnel can be very capricious in the way it does damage, removing the roof from a house without upsetting the breakfast dishes, imploding the house next door, and missing the next house altogether. Most tornados run briefly across open lands, but about 20 every year do significant damage to communities. In their artwork and stories, the Kiowas still vividly recall the twister that flattened much of Snyder, Oklahoma, on May 10, 1905, claiming at least 97 lives. Three tornadoes that dropped from the sky near Wichita Falls, Texas, on April 10, 1979 cut paths as much as a mile wide and 60 miles long, killing 56 people, injuring 1,916, and causing losses for 7,759 families. Prior to dense Euro-American settlement, tornados would not have exacted such a heavy toll, but they must still have appeared awesome to Plains inhabitants. Even their smaller cousins, the dust devils that arise in the midday sun, are often regarded as dangerous spirits in traditional Indian belief.

Winter on the Plains in general is bitterly cold, producing some of the continent's lowest temperatures, as low as –60°F. An old saying on the Plains is that there is nothing between Texas and the North Pole but some barbed wire. There is no relief to block the descent of polar air masses or large bodies of water to moderate continental cooling. The daily average temperature in January is between 0°F in the Canadian provinces to 50°F in Texas. Summers are also extreme, with daily average temperatures in July ranging from 60°F in Canada to 85°F in Texas and record highs of 120°F. The normal absence of cloud cover allows radiational cooling at night, and low humidity (except in Texas) also helps make the heat tolerable. But the overall picture is one of wide seasonal variation in temperature. North Dakota experienced the record high and record low in a single year, 1936, and has a greater spread of monthly average temperatures (89.5°F) than any state but Alaska.

Dryness is the most critical Great Plains weather characteristic, as understood by the Anglo settlers who called the region "the Great American Desert." Rainfall ranges between 24 and 16 inches annually (for comparison, 128 inches is the heaviest annual rainfall in North America, occurring in the Pacific Northwest). The effects of low rainfall are magnified because a good part of the yearly rain total may come in only a few storms. Also, high wind speeds and little cloud cover in the region mean a high rate of evaporation, so the effective moisture is even less than the rainfall rate might suggest.

Dryness promoted the wildfires that roared over the grasslands periodically in former times, blackening sometimes thousands of square miles. Pioneers describe the blast of superheated air, choking smoke, and a rain of blazing tinder that could trap anyone trying to outrun the inferno. Normally started by lightning or a stray campfire spark, prairie fires were sometimes also intentionally set by Indians to flush out the enemy during battle (a legend common to several tribes tells of the "Black Legs" or "Burned Thighs," warriors who bravely withstood such a blaze). Whatever the cause, fire was an integral factor in the balanced succession of plant and animal species and, at least to some extent, responsible for the continuing dominance of grasses in the landscape. Flames cleared the weakened sod-bound grasses and killed off saplings intruding into the prairies from the forest margins. New grass would sprout from protected roots and rhizomes. Prairie dogs, mice, and rats, with their underground refuges and food supplies, then took the lead in reclaiming the land for animal life. Scientists now realize that burned prairie produces twice the biomass of unburned grassland.

Trees and shrubs nevertheless make their stands along streams and sheltered scarps. Aspen and ponderosa pine intrude from the west in the hills of the northern Plains. The juniper known as red cedar is common in uplands and overgrazed areas, and pinion is found along with cedar on the volcanic mesas. Post oak, blackjack oak, and mesquite are common in the south. Chokecherry, sand plum, and haw are among several shrubs that provide edible fruit. Willow, elm, ash, walnut, and hackberry are common floodplain species, along with the cottonwood, which is the archetypal Plains tree. In some Indian languages "tree" and "cottonwood" are simply the same word.

Rivers of the Plains rise in or toward the Rockies (see Map 1.2). They have several characteristic features. Since they flow over low gradients, they tend to meander and clog with their own silt; they often become "braided," with multiple channels crisscrossing over the sediments. The soft banks are liable to cave in, taking along entire trees that are carried downstream as driftwood. Sometimes huge logjams develop, and these can divert the flow to create lakes, swamps, and floodplain. The Great Raft was a solid entanglement of cottonwood, cedar, and cypress logs, 30–40 feet deep, which in 1806 stretched for nearly 100 miles along the Red River in northwest Louisiana. Quicksand is found on the Arkansas River, as trader Josiah Gregg noted in 1844, and along many other streambeds. The sands and gravels forming a Plains riverbed may be 40–60 feet deep, with water flowing through them even when the surface is dry, and travelers have long known it is possible to find water by digging in a "dry" riverbed. And indeed, rivers can run dry for part or much of the year, especially in the south, although flash flooding is also common. In all, the rivers are unpredictable, periodically difficult to cross, and generally not good for shipping or as sources of drinking water.

Looking from north to south, major rivers include the Saskatchewan, Qu'Appelle–Assiniboine, Red River of the North, the Missouri, Yellowstone, Cheyenne, Niobrara, Platte, Republican, Kansas, Arkansas, Cimarron, Canadian, Red, Brazos, Colorado, Guadalupe, Pecos, and Rio Grande. The Saskatchewan, Assiniboine, and Red of the North drain into Lake Winnipeg and Hudson Bay; otherwise, Plains rivers drain into the Gulf of Mexico, either through the Mississippi–Missouri system or, in Texas, directly. One effect of this arrangement is that riparian zones extend like fingers westward into the Plains, hosting grasses, trees, and animal life more characteristic of areas to the east. These river corridors are also friendlier to agriculture, and so have been especially important as avenues of human occupation.

Perhaps the most important water on the Plains is underground. The High Plains aquifer system made up of the Ogallala, Arikaree, and Brule formations underlies about 174,000 square miles from lower South Dakota far into the Texas

FIGURE 1.5   Platte River, Nebraska.

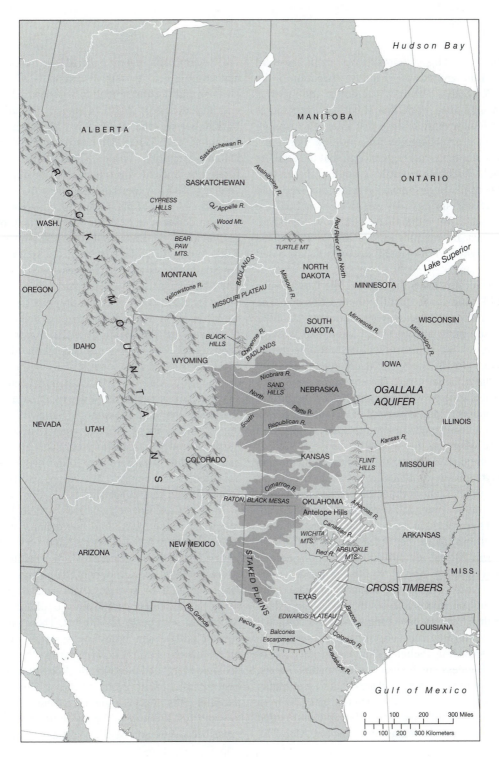

MAP 1.2 Plains Natural Features and Landmarks.

Panhandle. This system supplies about one-third of all the groundwater used for irrigation in the United States. The draw rate on the aquifers was low until after World War II but has increased as much as sevenfold since that time, outstripping the rate of recharge by precipitation. Formerly, the water table was high enough that the aquifers would discharge from the ground at the eastern edge of the High Plains, but numerous seeps and paradisaic springs that would have marked the landscape in Indian days are now vanished. Modern Indian populations are among those vulnerable to projected declines in irrigated Plains land.

Ironically, given the dryness, the Great Plains and Prairie are frequently likened to a sea. The vast rolling ground, waving motion of the taller grasses, immense sky, steady wind, and sense of openness and vulnerability all contribute to this picture. Josiah Gregg and many others remarked on the oceanic vistas. The covered wagons that carried settlers west became known as prairie schooners. Many observers have commented on what a visual environment the open country is, a place where, as on the sea, the sense of sight is paramount. Yet in order to understand human adaptations to the Plains, it is best to move past the image of a uniform ocean of grass and appreciate the diversity of environments and the landmarks presented in the lands under consideration. Oklahoma alone has been divided into nine distinct natural regions on the basis of geology and vegetation. And if "sea" is apt image in one sense, then "islands" are bound to be significant.

The anomalous features that today are valued for their scenery have long served as ecological islands, hosting unusual plant and animal species and providing shelter for human groups. There are countless small sites, such as buttes, knolls, and springs, that were and are of interest to Indian people; here it will do to mention, in order from north to south, a number of larger features that give variety to the Plains landscape (see Map 1.2).

The north has several isolated low mountains appearing in belts or singly, such as the Cypress Hills straddling the border in southern Alberta and Saskatchewan, Wood Mountain in southern Saskatchewan, the Bear Paw Mountains in Montana, and Turtle Mountain on the North Dakota–Manitoba border. These hills were formed by ancient volcanic activity or uplifting and they rise a few thousand feet above the plains. The general area of plains and hills covering the western Dakotas and eastern Montana is known as the Missouri Plateau. Peaks reaching over 7,000 feet occur in the Black Hills of southwestern South Dakota and nearby areas of Wyoming. The Black Hills catch rain and thus feature heavy pine forest and many streams; the hills figure in the history of several tribes as a refuge and sacred place and are the location of the major gold deposits previously mentioned. Around the Black Hills to the east, south, and west is an area of heavily eroded clay beds cut into beautiful shapes, part of which is now protected as the Badlands National Monument. Sand hills and dunes cover about 24,000 square miles of northern and west-central Nebraska, and less extensive dune areas are also found in southern Saskatchewan, central Wyoming, northeast Colorado, and central Kansas.

Mesas of resilient volcanic rock such as Black Mesa and Raton Mesa mark the country where Colorado, New Mexico, Texas, and Oklahoma join. Oklahoma also contains the distinctive Antelope Hills area and two Plains mountain ranges of note: the Wichitas, with isolated peaks rising up to 1,000 feet over the plains, and Arbuckles, with peaks to 400 feet. These eroded ancient granite and limestone systems are the oldest on the Plains, deriving from the same geologic events and predating the Rockies. Further east, in eastern Kansas and northeast Oklahoma, the Flint Hills present a low ridge running north to south for 220 miles. The shore of an ancient ocean became the soil base for a band of dense oak thickets called the Cross Timbers, 5–30 miles wide and running north–south for 400 miles through Oklahoma and into north-central Texas.

The Llano Estacado or Staked Plain(s) is a remarkably bare and flat region in the Texas Panhandle and eastern New Mexico. Escarpments bounding the Staked Plains on the west and east may have given rise to the name, which suggests palisade walls, although an improbable legend says that Coronado marked his path across the treeless wastes with sticks. Seasonal ponds called *playas* dot the Plains in this region. To the southeast lies the Edwards Plateau of central Texas, featuring limestone uplands with little overlaying soil. The Edwards is treated as part of the Great Plains, but has more relief, more trees, and milder winters than the rest of the region; it was a significant foraging area for prehistoric peoples and a retreat for horse Indians and their herds. The Edwards Plateau gives way to the coastal plains at the Balcones Escarpment.

These many subregions have hosted a fascinating variety of wild animals. Aside from the bison, which will be discussed separately because of its central role in Indian life, five other ungulates populated the Plains. The wapiti or American elk formerly was abundant as far south as the Red River. Two deer species occupied the region—the mule deer of the west extending its range into the High Plains in the northwest and Oklahoma/Texas panhandles and the smaller whitetail deer of the eastern forests covering the whole area. The huge numbers of pronghorn in former days rivaled those of the buffalo. This "American antelope-goat" (*Antilocarpa americana*) was found throughout the region. With an ability to graze on the coarsest plants and its great speed (it is the fastest of all American mammals, reaching speeds of 55 mph), the pronghorn was well suited to its surroundings. All four animals were essential in supporting human life, providing meat and skins, and were nearly eradicated by 1900. Since then, whitetail deer have returned in great numbers, mule deer

have retreated to upland areas, pronghorns have made a moderate comeback, and elk persisted in the north and were reintroduced to reserves in Oklahoma. A race of bighorn sheep also grazed in the grasslands and hills of the Dakotas and western Nebraska, but by the start of the twentieth century hunters and livestock diseases killed it off.

Wolves were the main animal predators on the Plains. The gray wolf depended on small game for some of its diet, but also worked in packs to isolate and attack the weak members of bison, deer, elk, and pronghorn herds. When the packs turned to domestic stock, the American wolf felt full bore a legacy of hatred that was part of Euro-American culture, and commercial wolfers cleared the Plains states of the animals with their rifles, traps, and strychnine between 1865 and 1895. The wolf's smaller, adaptable relative, the coyote, remains resilient despite similar bounty campaigns and has even spread beyond the Plains in recent decades. Other large carnivores that were present on the Plains had more restricted habitats. The black bear and the larger, more aggressive grizzly were most common in forested bottomlands and broken country. Mountain lions, favoring remote, high areas, were probably never plentiful; now they are protected in most areas and are making a comeback on the western and southern Plains fringes. More usual, but seldom seen, are bobcats. Jaguars and ocelots occasionally ranged north into the Southern Plains in earlier times.

Several small animals are notable either because of their unusual character or because they have been important to humans. The badger is a small but tough carnivore burrowing on the open Plains, where it preys on prairie dogs and other ground squirrels. Prairie dog "towns" or burrow systems attract a great number of other species, and their eradication by farmers has altered the animal life of the Plains and caused the near extinction of one prairie-dog predator, the black-footed ferret. Red, gray, and swift foxes remain, along with raccoons, ringtails, and three kinds of skunk: striped, spotted, and hog-nosed. Beaver, muskrat, otter, and mink are common around water. Cottontails and jackrabbits are plentiful, and there are many mouse and rat species such as the hispid cotton rat and prairie vole. Josiah Gregg reported in 1844 that rattlesnakes were "proverbially abundant upon all these prairies." States in the region have inventoried from 50 to 135 fish species, a surprising variety for arid country and just one example of how Plains animal life can be complex beyond expectation.

Bird life on the Plains is diverse and of special interest because of the use of feathers and bird forms in Indian symbolism. The whooping crane lingers on the verge of extinction, the 130 or so remaining wild ones migrating over the Plains between the Canadian bogs where they breed and wintering grounds on the Texas coast. At 5 feet tall with a $7 \frac{1}{2}$-foot wingspan, the whooper is the tallest North American bird. The great blue heron and sandhill crane are among the more common waders, sharing the prairie potholes and river margins with various ducks and geese. Ground-dwelling prairie chickens and grouse hold courtship rituals at "booming grounds" where the males pose, strut, hop, fan their feathers, and drum the air with rapid wing beats. Turkey vultures, and black vultures in the south, wheel in the sky looking for carrion. The burrowing owl is a daytime hunter of mice, lizards, and grasshoppers; larger nocturnal owls are also common. Other birds of prey include several kinds of hawks, such as the Swainson's and ferruginous hawks, which are primarily Plains species, and the bald and golden eagles, the latter considered the preeminent animal in Indian belief.

Plains animal life of earlier days was bound to capture the imagination. Josiah Gregg wrote of the animals as "companions" who constituted "the society of the traveler" crossing the lonely grasslands. Lewis and Clark were less genial in describing the first of their chronic encounters with awesome grizzly bears. Their expedition also named the prairie dog as such because of its bark, but it is of course a marmot. This tendency of Plains animals to wind up with misleading names was noted by Webb, who notes "buffalo" for bison, "jackrabbit" (from "jackass rabbit") for a large hare, and "antelope" for the pronghorn; we could add "horned toad" for the squat lizard, and others. In these names, we see how pioneers from the east struggled to make the strange familiar. Indians were far more familiar, but equally fascinated, by these life forms.

Animals no longer furnish quite so much companionship, for the present mid-continental landscape shows dramatic alterations, most in the name of intensive agriculture and ranching. Native grasses have been either eliminated or eaten short. In particular, less than 1 percent of the original tall-grass prairie vegetation remains, mostly in small, isolated patches. The only larger tract left is a strip 2×50 miles long in the Flint Hills of Kansas and Oklahoma. As a functioning ecosystem, the tall-grass prairie is extinct. Much of the Cross Timbers foliage has also been cleared away. Fire is kept under control. Rivers are channeled and impounded, and the water table drawn down, to water towns and fields. Rock outcrops have been quarried flat for building stone and road material.

Today, the landscape might be best understood as a mosaic of agricultural land use patterns. Spring wheat, planted in spring and harvested in the fall, is planted in the Dakotas; winter wheat, planted in fall and harvested in late spring, dominates from south Nebraska to the Texas Panhandle. Barley is raised in the wheat areas too. In the eastern part of the former grasslands the main crop is corn grown to feed cattle and hogs. South of this "corn belt" is a "cotton belt." Alfalfa for livestock feed is grown under irrigation in the drier west, and the driest areas are given over to pasturing cattle, sheep, and goats. Other important crops include flax and sugar beets in the north and peanuts in the south.

Despite the often high productivity of farms on the Plains, it remains questionable whether agriculture is really sustainable there. The region has always been subject to sharp boom and bust cycles. Economic downturns hit in the 1890s, the Dust Bowl 1930s, and the 1980s, an era of foreclosures and "Farm Aid" benefit concerts. In the past century many Plains towns have lost more than 50 percent of their population; entire counties have been virtually abandoned; bank failures, poverty rates, and dependence on federal subsidies have increased. Regardless of some recent upturns, many analysts think there is an inevitable trend toward the failure of agriculture and depopulation of the Plains.

Two Rutgers University social scientists, Frank and Deborah Popper, a land-use planner and geographer, respectively, have recommended a radical solution: abandon farming and the market towns that support it and let the Plains revert to their natural state. In their controversial "Buffalo Commons" concept, sections of 10 states would compose an enormous nature preserve managed by the federal government. Bison, elk, and wolves would be restocked; wildlife and solitude would be the commodities in a mixed-use economy of recreation, tourism, and retirement. The reintroduction of wildlife is not a purely romantic gesture, but a matter of efficiency. Bison, for example, have a slightly more efficient digestion rate than cattle and can live on coarser plants. The fate of American Indians under this plan is not clear, but it is suggested that they might receive parts of the new commons in payment for tribal land claims or at least enjoy preference of employment as stewards and guides. While it remains doubtful that all of the Plains agricultural infrastructure will be undone purposefully, there are in fact already many small experiments throughout the Plains in reversion. These include preserved areas of vegetation such as the national grasslands (reclaimed from farmlands abandoned during the Dust Bowl), protected Indian sacred sites, and reintroduced buffalo herds.

THE PLAINS CULTURE AREA

The Plains constitutes a particular cultural setting as well as a distinctive natural environment. It is one of the major culture areas that anthropologists recognize in North America. "[A] culture area is a geographical area within the boundaries of which similar cultures or life styles are found" (Howard 1975:22). More technically, "[c]ulture areas are geographical territories in which characteristic culture patterns are recognizable through repeated associations of specific traits and, usually, through one or more modes of subsistence that are related to the particular environment" (Ehrich and Henderson 1968:563).

A complete listing of North American culture areas might look like this (there are multiple variants of this scheme but all are similar):

Woodlands: Southern Maine and Ontario to Florida, westward to the Mississippi and eastern Texas. This region encompasses coastal plains and swamps, the Piedmont, Appalachian Mountains, Great Lakes region, and easternmost tall-grass prairies, but the overarching factor is forested land, in contrast to open grasslands or desert. It is often subdivided into Northeastern and Southeastern areas.

Plains: The dry, short-grass High Plains extending west of the 98th meridian to the Rocky Mountains. This area runs from the southern Prairie Provinces of Canada (Manitoba, Saskatchewan, and Alberta) southward to Texas and is wider in the north than in the south. This area sometimes also includes the tall-grass prairies east of the High Plains—in Minnesota, Iowa, and Missouri—which are otherwise assigned to the Woodlands area.

Basin and Plateau: Includes the Rocky Mountains and neighboring ranges and intermountain deserts. The Great Basin includes most of Utah, Nevada, western Colorado, western Wyoming, southern Idaho, and southeastern

California. The Plateau covers most of Idaho, western Montana, eastern Oregon and Washington, and interior British Columbia. These two are often treated as separate areas.

Southwest: Corresponds to the Chihuahuan and Sonoran deserts in New Mexico and Arizona and closely adjacent parts of Utah, Colorado, Texas, and Mexico.

California: Corresponds to the modern state excepting the extreme northwest and southeast. Landforms include the Sierras and Coast Ranges, Central Valley, northern lava fields, and coasts.

Northwest Coast: A long narrow culture area between the coastal mountain ranges and shores, plus islands, extending from northern California through Oregon, Washington, British Columbia, and the Alaskan Panhandle.

Subarctic: The lands spanning the north of the continent from Northern Maine and Newfoundland to interior Alaska, composed of coniferous forests, bogs, lakes, and taiga, and excepting the Arctic coast.

Arctic: The strip of land 100–200 miles wide, and islands, along the coast of the Arctic Ocean from Labrador to Alaska.

Each of these areas has a characteristic (if easily oversimplified) array of Native American cultural adaptations. For example, the temperate Woodlands features a mixture of forest hunting and gardening of corn, beans, and squash in cleared plots, villages of wigwams and longhouses (pole frame, bark-covered dwellings), pottery, birch or hickory bark canoes and containers, soft-soled moccasins, and so on. The dry, rugged Great Basin area necessitated dependence on rabbits and seeds, residence in small mobile groups for much of the year, baskets but virtually no pottery. The rainy Northwest Coast is an area of large rectangular timber and plank houses, totem poles, long ocean-going dugout canoes, abundant salmon, and whale hunting.

The Plains culture area is customarily distinguished by the following traits:

- dependence on bison hunting
- lack of agriculture
- limited use of gathered foods
- nomadism
- dependence on the horse for riding and traction
- dogs for traction
- travois (wood frame for dragging possessions)
- tipi (moveable skin dwelling)
- general lack of boats and fishing
- lack of or only simple pottery and weaving
- bison skin and deerskin clothing
- highly developed work in skins and rawhide
- little work in wood, stone, or bone
- beadwork
- geometrical art
- bilateral descent (tracing ancestors and relatives through both mother and father)
- band-level social organization
- warfare
- sodalities (men's and women's clubs)
- Sun Dance (major religious ceremony)
- sign language
- platform burials

These traits pertain to the High Plains subarea specifically. Since this volume includes populations living east of the High Plains in its definition of the Plains culture area, the following traits relevant to those groups are also noted:

- corn horticulture
- semi-permanent settlements
- horses, dogs, and travois
- occasional bison hunts
- symbiotic relations with High Plains nomads
- massive sod houses (north) or large grass houses (south)
- tipi used for hunting trips
- hand-molded pottery
- some fishing

- large calendrical ceremonies
- elaborate celestial mythology
- clan social structure

Although this book is entirely predicated on the existence of the Plains culture area, it is important to question the validity and utility of this construct. We should consider the history of the idea and the pros and cons of its application in understanding Native peoples.

The culture area concept grew out of two related intellectual trends: the rise of scientific classification and the development of modern museums. An early museum was apt to look like an eccentric person's attic—a hodgepodge of curiosities with little apparent rhyme or reason. The emerging standards of science, however, required above all else classification, the grouping of items according to similarities and differences. The first published classifications of North American tribes *circa* 1830–1880, such as Albert Gallatin's *Synopsis of Indian Tribes* (Gallatin 1973; orig. 1836), grouped them according to shared linguistic backgrounds, though this procedure did not yield a distinct Plains area. Then, during the latter nineteenth century major museums such as the Peabody Museum in Cambridge, Massachusetts, the American Museum of Natural History in New York, the Smithsonian Institution in Washington, D.C., and the Columbian Exhibition (1893 Chicago World's Fair) began grouping objects in exhibits according to didactic themes, such as item type, patterns of evolution in technology development, geographic origin, or linguistic stock of the makers. Principal advocates of organized exhibits in the United States were Otis T. Mason (1838–1908) of the Smithsonian; Clark Wissler and Pliny Earl Goddard (1869–1928); and Franz Boas (1858–1942), all associated with the American Museum. Each of these scholar-curators was interested in what Mason called the "Influences of Environment upon Human Industries or Arts" (Mason 1896), and soon the dominant rationale for display became the correlation of environmental region and material culture. The idea of culture areas such as the Woodlands and Plains stemmed most directly from this practice of grouping material objects to suggest consistent environmental conditions and patterned cultural adaptations to those conditions.

As anthropologists, historians, and other researchers tried to make sense of the large variety of Indian cultural practices, they found comfort in this classificatory framework. The Plains culture area, among others, became the subject of much attention and attempts at refinement. When patterned variations became apparent within the proposed areas, the areas were subdivided to reflect them. Wissler sought a center for Plains Indian culture from which the archetypal traits diffused, and he defined a core High Plains area with two secondary areas to the east and one to the west. Alfred Kroeber (1876–1960) was more exacting, proposing eight subareas with names like "Northern Plains," "Central Prairie," and "Red River." Kroeber, however, noted the inadequacy of such categories and suggested that the best approach would be a color map showing the intensity and shadings of the definitional culture. These early efforts focused on environments and material items when weighing the similarities and differences between tribes. George Peter Murdock (1897–1985) looked instead for clusters of social and linguistic traits and proposed seven major subareas that differed from prior classifications and produced a less unified image of the Plains. Harold E. Driver (b. 1907) and associates sought statistical correlations among 35 groups previously identified as "Plains" tribes, using an index of similarity called the phi coefficient. A phi coefficient of 1 between two tribes would mean they were identical, and lesser numbers indicated degree of difference. Across all 35 tribes Murdock found a phi coefficient of .35. This was about the same degree of difference evident across all of North America, suggesting a weak case for internal consistency in the Plains culture area. Driver did, however, find higher coefficients, in the .50s and .60s, within four proposed subareas: the (High) Plains, Prairie, Northeastern Canadian Plains, and Shoshonean area west of the High Plains.

The culture area approach does offer benefits for study. It simplifies our learning about numerous, diverse cultural groups. One can gain a good degree of knowledge about Native people of the Plains by learning the general features of the culture area, without having to study every tribe and every ceremony. And culture areas illustrate the broad patterns of human adaptation to particular environments.

There are, however, also many drawbacks to a reliance on culture areas. The basic problem is that the areas are ultimately arbitrary. The term "area" suggests a fixed and bounded territory, but culture areas are theoretical constructs with no strict borders. Disagreement can occur not only about the centers and boundaries of areas, but about which cultural traits should be considered essential in defining them. The choice of diagnostic traits determines the apparent degree of similarity between tribes. Thus, there is never a single indisputable scheme of culture areas, but rather different possibilities that claim researchers' allegiance. Adherence to one or another scheme may cause researchers to overlook, ignore, or misinterpret information that does not readily fit with expectations. Another problem is that culture areas are static concepts that assume long stability of populations and cultural practices and do not reveal processes of culture change. Furthermore, they are asynchronous. North American culture areas generally refer to the time of early Indian–white contact, and since this time was different across the continent, the areas taken together do not form a simultaneous picture; even within the Plains area, contact times varied significantly. A final and perhaps obvious weakness is that the standard culture areas tell us very little about the realities of contemporary Indian life.

Anthropologist James H. Howard (1925– 1982) mounted the most cogent criticism of the culture area approach. Howard, who worked among several Plains tribes, called the approach "a foul deed," perpetrated upon Indian people by members of the anthropological profession. Though useful as a crude rule of thumb, Howard wrote, culture areas had become so pervasive in general discussions, in textbooks and grade school instruction, that non-Indians and even many Indians alike had come to believe that Native cultures were fixed in these rigid categories. This rigidity contradicted what Indian people knew from their own tribal traditions about the continuous mixing and blending of cultures. The insistence of non-Indians on fixed categories can cause stress for living members of Indian cultures, such as the contemporary man of a Woodlands tribe who was reproached for wearing a Plains-style feather war bonnet because it was not from his own culture area. Also, Howard noted, because they are based on the presence of particular traits, culture areas amount to a set of requirements such that tribal groups having numerous prescribed traits are proper members of the area while those with fewer traits are considered "marginal" and hence less authentic or worthy of consideration.

The culture area concept therefore must be used advisedly, though it is both convenient and so ingrained as to be unavoidable. In defining the member tribes of the Plains area, this work follows the practice set forth in the *Handbook of North American Indians* (Sturtevant 2001). It includes social units of both the High Plains and Prairie. Discussions will also occasionally include other groups that ventured onto or influenced the Plains area, especially the Shoshones and Utes centered just west of the High Plains who are often assigned to the Great Basin culture area, the Apache groups living southwest of the High Plains, and the Caddos living just southeast of the Plains in Texas and Louisiana, frequently considered a Southeast Woodlands group. The area and tribes covered in this volume are shown in Map 1.3. The dynamic origins of these social units are explored in the next chapter.

MAP 1.3 Plains Culture Area with Neighboring Tribes.

Sources: Allan and Warren (1993); Baumgartner and Baumgartner (1992); Beck and Haase (1989); Boyd (1981); Caire et al. (1989); Callenbach (1996); Chadwick (1995); Costello (1969); DeMallie (2001); Driver (1962); Driver and Coffin (1975); Driver et al. (1972); Ehrich and Henderson (1968); Flores (1984, 1990); Gallatin (1973); Gelo (1993, 1994, 2000); Gilbert (1980); Gregg (1967); Horgan (1979); Howard (1975); Kroeber (1939); Lynch (1970); Mason (1896, 1907); Murdock (1967); Pirkle and Yoho (1985); Popper (1992); Popper and Popper (1987, 1988); Scaglion (1980); Sturtevant (2001); U.S. Department of Commerce (1980); Webb (1981); Weeks et al. (1988); and Wissler (1917).

CHAPTER SUMMARY

Knowledge of the Great Plains landscape is critical to the understanding of Plains Indian culture. The Plains environment presents a unique set of limits and opportunities for human occupation. The region considered in this book encompasses lands between the Mississippi River and Rocky Mountains and between the Canadian subarctic and Rio Grande. It is a region of comparatively level grasslands, including the tall-grass Prairie and short-grass High Plains. Within the grasslands are geologic features that contribute to habitat diversity, and a series of rivers flowing from west to east. Peculiarities of climate, weather, vegetation, and animal life also add to the distinctive character of the Great Plains. The region encouraged development of a human adaptive regime involving bison hunting, horsemanship, and other traits related to a mobile lifestyle. In eastern parts of the region, gardening and fixed villages were also possible. Indians of the region are said to belong to the Plains culture area. The idea of the Plains as a uniform cultural area is helpful to learning but must be used carefully so as not to mask significant variation.

QUESTIONS FOR REVIEW

1. What factors have traditionally been used to define the Great Plains as a natural area? How does each factor mesh with the others to produce a workable definition?
2. Describe the natural features of the Great Plains, including climate and weather, anomalous surface features, and plant and animal life, that have contributed to the region's distinctive character.
3. What are the characteristic traits of the Plains culture area? How does this area differ from adjacent ones? What traits are associated with the Prairie rather than the High Plains?
4. Explain the origin of the culture area concept, and comment on the strengths and weaknesses of this concept.

CHAPTER 2

PLAINS PREHISTORY

The era of the horse Indians was but a small moment within the grand sweep of human life on the Plains, which spanned 11,000 years or more. The 10 generations or so of people who led the classic equestrian life participated in a drama of cultural adaptation that extended deep into the past. This story unfolded prior to the written observations of non-Indians; it is therefore not historic, but prehistoric. The prehistoric record is revealed through the excavation and examination of artifacts and human physical remains conducted by archaeologists and physical anthropologists, in the analysis of Indian languages which shows ancient connections, and in the oral traditions and picture writing of Native peoples. This chapter will focus on the Plains Indian past as it is reconstructed by anthropologists.

THE ARCHAEOLOGICAL RECORD

Archaeologists, most of whom see themselves as members of a field within the larger discipline of anthropology, study human life in the past, usually the remote past. Their hallmark research technique is excavation—digging for buried evidence of human existence. Objects that result from human activity are called *artifacts*. Common artifacts include tools shaped from stone or bone, but also such traces as chips of bone from butchering, fireplaces, middens (human-made piles of rock, bone, or shell), pottery shards, woven plant fibers, and even the stains left in the soil from rotted house frame posts. Artifacts should not be confused with *fossils*. A fossil is the hardened remains or imprint of an ancient plant or animal. Paleontology is the branch of science dealing with fossils. Fossils are sometimes found in relation to human evidence but are not the prime focus of archaeological inquiry.

There is far more, however, to archaeological research besides digging. The analysis of any artifacts discovered, by themselves and in relation to other artifacts from the same site and others already kept in collections, is essential. Of prime concern is the dating of artifacts, either absolutely or at least relative to other artifacts. Stratigraphic dating is an indirect method in which artifacts are dated according to the layer of earth in which they are found. Normally the layer-cake deposits are assumed to be newest at the surface and older proceeding downward; however, vagaries of water and wind action and volcanism, along with disturbances from human activity, produce variations in the local stratigraphy that must be reconstructed carefully before dates can be posited. Other dating methods apply directly to the artifact and are conducted in the laboratory. Each available method has limits of application and dependability. Most well known is radiocarbon or carbon-14 (^{14}C) dating, which measures the amount of an unstable isotope of carbon present in the artifact. Since carbon-14 decays at a fixed rate, the amount found indicates elapsed time. Carbon-14 is only present in organic matter and its amount eventually diminishes beyond measurability, so the method is limited to materials such as bone and charcoal deposited up to about 40,000 years ago. Several other dating methods are available to calculate elapsed time from changes owing to radioactive decay or magnetism in certain artifact materials or the surrounding mineral deposits. In order to arrive at confident dates, archaeologists must often combine the results from multiple and alternate tests.

Many other procedures allow refinement of the archaeological record. Human skeletal remains can be checked for evidence of diet, disease, and trauma. For example, increased tooth decay correlates with a shift from meat-eating to plant foods, and analysis of human bone for stable isotopes of carbon (^{12}C and ^{13}C) can reveal the amount of maize in the diet. On these questions archaeologists work alongside physical anthropologists (including forensic anthropologists), scientists trained to determine sex, age, ethnicity, facial features, body build, diet, health, and cause of death from human remains. Study of the soil chemistry at sites is sometimes needed because of its possible effects on bone and artifacts. Lithic sourcing is a technique that relies on trace element analysis of stone artifacts to determine the place of origin for the stone, which might be hundreds of miles from where the artifact is found, showing human migration or trade of either raw materials or finished products. Traces of plants (pollen, leaf impressions) and animals (feces, bone) from a site, sometimes called *ecofacts*, are subject to floral and faunal analysis to paint a picture of the environment in the past and the food types available to humans; and, plant and animal remains in turn lend clues about the climate during past times. Electronic technology is also highly useful. Computer modeling enables all sorts of hypotheses to be tested without actually handling large quantities of artifacts. Remote sensing instruments including aerial infrared cameras, radar, and thermal radiation scanners may detect large land-use features such as ancient monuments, roads, or settlements that are not easily seen from the ground. Computers synthesize the data from remote sensing devices into usable images. In addition to what can be found through these technical approaches, some archaeologists are interested in the symbolic meaning of those artifacts, such as glyphs and rock paintings, which lend themselves to interpretation.

The original purpose of archaeology was to reconstruct culture history, that is, the backgrounds of different cultural groups prior to written records and the origins and spread of major human inventions such as fire use and pottery. By the mid-twentieth century, though, emphasis shifted to the processes of cultural change and the formulation of scientific laws that governed these processes. In this "new archaeology" the testing of hypotheses about local evolutionary forces and results became central. Attention focused on the relation between technology and the environment, ancient peoples' means of getting food and shelter, their social organization, and the reasons for migration and settlement. By the late twentieth century, however, some archaeologists, inspired by cultural anthropology and literary studies, voiced disappointment in the limitations of what could be known via the "new archaeology" and began to specialize instead in recreating the ideologies, motives, and sentiments of ancient peoples through the examination of cultural remains. And all through these times a good deal of archaeological research was not preoccupied with historical or theoretical questions at all, but instead concentrated simply on the preservation of the artifact record before sites were destroyed by roads, dams, and other forms of development; this work has been known as "relief" or "salvage" archaeology and more recently as cultural resource management. All of these schools are apparent in the research on prehistoric peoples of the Great Plains.

Archaeologists have defined sequential time periods, within which artifacts and adaptations are similar, and across which change is evident. These periods, which are continually being refined, are essential for classifying artifacts and understanding the life ways of their makers. The three broad Prehistoric periods that are applicable across North America are called, in reference to the Plains in particular, the Paleoindian Period (11,500 to 8,000 years ago), the Archaic Period (8,000 to 2,000 years ago), and the Late Prehistoric (2,000 to 500 years ago). Immediately, however, some qualifications must be added. The dates presented here are rough and variable according to subregion. Periods are subdivided into more specific time spans and artifact patterns by referring to phases, traditions, complexes, foci, aspects, components, horizons, and ultimately, to individual sites and occupations of sites. Such smaller, more localized units are more meaningful to specialists striving for a precise picture of the past, and consequently, archaeologists have proposed time schemes for different parts of the Plains that diverge from each other and from the general tripartite scheme. Also, new discoveries are constantly being made, and the overall picture is continually under revision. Coverage of all the current frameworks is beyond the scope of an introduction. A review of the three broad North American periods as they are manifested on the Plains must suffice.

The Paleoindians

According to scientists the present human species, *Homo sapiens*, which includes all people today and for the last 100,000 years, originated in Africa and spread from there. The date at which humans first arrived in the Americas has been a matter of sometimes bitter debate. Until the mid-1800s a literal interpretation of the Bible, in which the human generations might be counted backward to Adam and Eve, held sway among scientists; the earth was therefore thought to be 6,000 years old and the human race not more than that. By around 1860 accumulated evidence for long geological processes and the obvious ancientness of certain human artifacts, such as stone points found with the remains of extinct animals, forced the conclusion that the earth and its human inhabitants were much older. Scientists then recognized an Old Stone Age or Paleolithic cultural period in Europe, when humans lived alongside giant bison, mammoths, and mastodons in the shadow of Ice Age glaciers. Evidence for a similar period in North America was slower in coming.

On the night of August 27, 1908 a massive rainstorm flooded the town of Folsom in northeastern New Mexico. Some time afterward, on the nearby Crowfoot Ranch, a cowboy and former slave named George McJunkin found some curious bones washing out of a gully. McJunkin was a learned amateur naturalist and he got museum people and investors interested in his find. It was only in 1926 that excavations were started at the site, which soon yielded numerous skeletons of an extinct and yet unknown form of bison, as well as distinctive stone spear points about 2–3 inches long with large areas of fluting (hollowing on the sides to receive the notched end of a shaft). The following year some of these so-called Folsom points were found lodged in the bison skeletons, ending any doubt that they dated to the same time as the extinct animals. The Folsom discovery established that humans

©1988 DMNH

FIGURE 2.1   The first Folsom point found in situ, among extinct bison ribs.

lived on the Great Plains around 11,000 years ago, during the reign of extinct megafauna, in a period analogous to the European Paleolithic. These early inhabitants have since been termed *Paleoindians*.

In the 1930s, an even older form of Paleoindian projectile point was first excavated about 150 miles south of Folsom, in Blackwater Draw between Clovis and Portales, New Mexico. Clovis points are larger than Folsom points, about

3–4 inches long, with a relatively smaller area of fluting, but similar in shape and in their fine crafting. These points were sometimes found among the bones of mammoths, and the Clovis culture has been dated as far back as 13,000 years ago. Subsequently, Clovis points and other related stone and bone tools have been found in many places across the United States, Mexico, Central America, and northern South America. Clovis is considered ancestral to the Folsom tradition as well as to later unfluted Paleoindian point types called Plainview, Scottsbluff, and Eden.

Together these finds evince a widespread and mostly uniform Paleoindian way of life. Big game hunting was the main means of survival. The Paleoindians pursued mammoths, mastodons, giant bison, camels, musk oxen, bears, deer, antelope, and early forms of the horse, all of which ranged in the cool, moist parklands (mixed grassland and evergreen forests) spanning North America below the line of polar ice, which at the time extended into what is now the northern United States. The exquisite craftsmanship of Paleo points, chipped and ground from fine chert, jasper, and quartzite, chosen for its working qualities, and often sourced from distant locations, bears witness to Paleoindian skill and intelligence. They hafted their points to wooden shafts to form long spears or shorter darts flung with an atlatl (throwing lever). These weapons allowed them to kill large animals from safe distances. They also fashioned stone knives and scrapers for butchering. Hunts were group efforts conducted by small mobile family bands that knew how to take advantage of the landscape and their prey's natural herding instincts when stalking and ambushing. They might drive a mammoth into a bog and surround it or chase bison up a blind canyon and attack from behind and above. A favorite technique was to chase the lead animals of a herd over a cliff edge, causing the entire herd to follow. Then, the hunters gathered at the foot of the precipice to finish off and butcher their victims, yielding enormous amounts of meat. Remains of these massive "jump-kills" have been found at several Plains locations. Paleoindian hunters were also probably proficient stalkers and individual kills were much more common than the dramatic mass slaughters.

Other aspects of Paleoindian culture are not revealed to us to any great degree. It seems clear that they existed in low population densities, though sites at Lindenmeier, Colorado, and along Crowley's Ridge, Arkansas, tell that they had regular camping places near fresh water or chert sources where they built fires and prepared tools and meat. But we don't know exactly what kind of shelters they built. We cannot know the languages they spoke or whether they formed ethnic units, and their ritual life can only be imagined. It bears repeating, however, that the Paleoindians were fully modern humans from an anatomical standpoint. They were clearly ancestors to American Indians of later time periods, up to the present.

Between 12,000 and 7,000 years ago the glaciers receded northward for good. In geologic terms, there was a transition from the Pleistocene or Ice Age to the warmer Holocene or "recent" (i.e., post-glacial) epoch. Climates and vegetation became more varied, and distinctive grasslands, forests, and deserts arose where once there had been tundra and parkland. Over 100 species of mammals became extinct during this period of intense environmental change. The huge herbivores and their fearsome animal predators, such as the saber-toothed cat and dire wolf, were most prone to disappearance, and smaller mammals inherited the environment.

The Paleoindians were apparently very productive hunters, and moreover, their heyday corresponds to the disappearance of the huge prehistoric herbivores. Could it be that they caused the extinctions? This idea was first offered by Paul S. Martin and is known as the Pleistocene Overkill Hypothesis. Later reconstructions have challenged or moderated such claims, implicating dramatic climate change or disease instead of, or in combination with, Paleoindian hunting to explain the great extinctions. In the later stages of the Paleoindian

FIGURE 2.2   Artist's rendering of Paleoindians with Pleistocene megafauna in northwest Oklahoma.

Period we see populations begin adapting to more varied vegetative landscapes with an emphasis on sundry smaller game. This shift is indicated by more specialized toolkits, with a greater variety of stone tools meant for specific tasks.

Origins and Antiquity

The question remains, where did these earliest known Americans come from? The most commonly accepted theory for the origin of humans in the Western Hemisphere is that they migrated from Asia. Paleoindians and modern Native Americans alike share a trait known as *sinodonty* with populations in northern China and Japan. This is a particular pattern of tooth structure, most notably a shovel shape to the incisors, which is lacking in other human populations. American Indians also frequently manifest the Mongoloid spot, a concentration of pigment on the lower back at birth that is otherwise characteristic of Asians; and some Indian and Asian populations share the epicanthic fold, skin of the upper eyelid covering the inner corner of the eye. Other lines of evidence are provided by biological and genetic testing, which shows, for example, that there is a particular variant of blood serum protein present in both Siberians and American Indians. There are also numerous resemblances between the languages and religious concepts of peoples in Siberia and North America that suggest a past connection.

The prevailing thinking for a long time was that Asian migrants entered the Americas by walking across a strip of land, which scientists named Beringia, that once connected Siberia and Alaska, and into the interior of the continent. This "land bridge" scenario often also entailed the idea that there were ice-free corridors through the inland glaciers of Northwest North America that would have allowed passage. These arguments in turn required particular reconstructions of the regional geology and climatic cycles, most of which are debatable. More recently the proposition that people migrated along the coast, perhaps using boats or rafts, has gained some acceptance. The 1997 authentication of a human settlement site far to the south in Monte Verde, Chile, which was discovered in 1975 and dated to 14,500 years ago, lends support to the coastal migration hypothesis. Artifact evidence for this picture, however, is difficult to assemble because the prehistoric coastline is today underwater. In either case, the migration was probably not a purposeful mass colonization but simply the result of small hunting parties exploring new territory.

How and when the migration took place are related questions. Clovis culture was long regarded as the earliest consistent expression of human presence in the Americas, suggesting human entry perhaps 13,000 years ago. Wide acceptance of the Monte Verde dates has many scientists now open to the possibility of earlier dates. Other "pre-Clovis" site dates, some radically earlier than those confirmed at Monte Verde thus far, have been proposed for sites in Pennsylvania, Virginia, and South Carolina, and time will prove if they are supportable. Meanwhile, analysis of the mitochondrial DNA of contemporary Indian people throughout North and South America is indicating that there were three major migration episodes. The first of these is posited to have taken place at or prior to the appearance of Clovis culture, and to have been the wellspring for most of the population of the Americas. A second wave came about 9,000 years ago and brought the forerunners of the present-day Athapaskans or Na-Dene, a linguistic family found from Alaska to the U.S. Southwest and including the Navajos and Apaches. The third episode brought the Aleuts and Eskimos, only around 4,000 years ago. Other episodes still could have occurred and are just no longer reflected in

the modern gene pool, or perhaps they may become apparent as the genome is studied further.

Some archaeologists think it probable that people also migrated into northeastern North America from northwestern Europe, pointing, for example, to the resemblance between Solutrean stone tools from Paleolithic France and late Clovis points from the eastern United States. The Solutrean possibility, however, has been vigorously contradicted by those who point out that the Solutrean Period ends long before Clovis begins, and there is no evidence that Solutrean people would have had skills in maritime hunting and navigation needed for the proposed migration, or a convenient "jumping off" point from Europe to North America.

In addition to the overall antiquity of humans in the Western Hemisphere, the length of time that humans have been present on the Plains is another vital question. Although local archaeologists had been unearthing artifact evidence of prehistoric occupation since the 1880s, the earliest professional anthropologists such as Lewis Henry Morgan, Clark Wissler, and Alfred Kroeber believed the Plains were pretty much uninhabited before the Historic Period. Their "empty Plains theory" gave undue heed to ethnographic evidence, which indicated that many of the historically known tribes had migrated into the territory only in the 1700s, upon adopting the horse. But the Folsom discovery in 1926 made it clear that humans were present on the Plains far earlier, and a paper by William Duncan Strong, an archaeologist working in Nebraska, "The Plains Culture Area in the Light of Archaeology" (Strong 1933) clinched the argument by tying together existing lines of evidence.

Strong's conclusions were especially persuasive because of his use of the *direct historical approach.* In this approach, archaeologists study historically known ethnic groups and then project backward to make sense of the prehistoric artifact evidence. Such studies may demonstrate culture continuity and change over long periods or determine the ethnicity of a prehistoric population. The method was well suited to the area of western Nebraska where Strong worked. The historical inhabitants there were the Pawnees, and archaeological evidence of the forerunners of the Pawnees could be found in the same area, sometimes buried directly beneath the sites of historical Pawnee villages. Like the Pawnees, the earlier people pursued gardening as well as hunting. By digging below historic Pawnee villages and reading the archaeological evidence in light of what was known about Pawnee life, Strong made an argument for long and culturally consistent occupation. Eventually, follow-up studies using radiocarbon dates revealed time gaps in the proto-Pawnee record and raised doubts that the excavations proved continuous occupation and descent, and the direct historical approach was then widely discredited. Nevertheless, in its time Strong's finding revolutionized the scientific view of the Plains culture area, which previously paid attention only to horse nomads, but afterward recognized the prevalence and longer time-depth of people on the Plains, and the long presence of gardeners as well as hunters.

It must be noted that some Indian people are among those who do not accept scientific theories about where Native Americans came from, and when. They rely instead on traditional accounts of the origin of humans and particular groups which have been handed down in narratives. Traditional explanations usually pose that Indians are the product of some kind of unique creation event which took place in their homeland. Thus, Indians today may hold the opinion that "we were always here." These explanations are explored in detail in Chapter 8. Vine Deloria, Jr. (Yankton; 1933–2005) outlined supposed weaknesses in various scientific arguments for Indian origins and pressed for an earlier presence of indigenous peoples (Deloria 1995). Deloria criticized the scientific view of Native American genesis, with its emphasis on in-migration and finite dates, and he contested the Pleistocene Overkill Theory, claiming that these constructs were simply another form of domination of Indians by non-Indians.

The Archaic

The climatic change that coincided with the late Paleoindian Period spawned a new repertoire of human adaptations which justify a different time designation, the Archaic. The change is denoted by the abrupt appearance in the artifact record of more triangular, side-notched stone points which replace the lanceolate shapes associated with the Paleoindians. The notches were a breakthrough allowing firmer binding to shafts. The Plains Archaic was a long period with many local manifestations and distinct point types. Archaeologists recognize Early, Middle, and Late Archaic traditions marked by innovations in projectile points. It will do here to discuss the period in general terms.

The climatic and vegetative variety that developed across the continent after the Ice Age was less pronounced on the Plains, and hence, Plains Archaic hunters pursued a lifestyle that was not severely different from that of the Paleoindians. Big game still played a major role in the diet, although the species remaining included a smaller modern version of the bison as well as deer and mountain sheep. There was, however, more inclusion in the diet of small game, fish, fowl, and gathered wild plant foods. People began using plant fibers to make baskets, nets, woven mats, and sandals. Other inventions of the Archaic include simple watercraft and domesticated dogs. These developments correspond to a proliferation of stone tools discernable as scrapers, drills, knives, net sinkers, and grinding stones for processing seeds. Roasting pits and middens of heated stones for cooking plants or acorns also reveal how vegetable foods were processed. Spears and atlatls were still the main hunting weapons, supplemented by snares and traps. There are numerous bison kill sites across the Plains dating to the Archaic, and together they suggest increasing sophistication over time, with human-built drive lanes marked by stone piles and even corrals supplanting simple natural jumps for the entrapment of the herds.

A burial discovered in 2001 on Coal Creek in Douglas County, Kansas, is typical of a number found across the Prairie and High Plains that date to the Middle Archaic. The grave was covered with a limestone slab. Beneath lay the bones of an older man, whose body was flexed, lying on its side, and oriented to a northwest–southeast alignment. The bones were covered in ochre, the red mineral pigment known to have sacred significance in Indian cultures past and present. Two implements, a stone drill and a side-notched projectile point, were found with the remains. Under the microscope, both artifacts showed wear from cutting and being hafted to wooden handles, indicating that these were not ceremonial treasures but rather everyday tools that accompanied the deceased. The man's teeth showed notable wear and a little decay, which fits with our understanding of the Archaic diet. Burials such as this one are usually solitary and never include more than four individuals in the same place, suggesting that Archaic groups were relatively small and nomadic.

Nonetheless, the population and density of settlements did increase during the Archaic in comparison to the Paleoindian Period, and some Archaic groups maintained camps in one spot year-round, although more frequently they moved among a series of sites according to a schedule, to take advantage of seasonal bounties of particular plants and animals. Leisure time allowed development of elaborate ceremonies and rock art. Numerous stone circles or "tipi rings" from the Middle Archaic appear on the surface of the Plains in Montana and Alberta, possibly indicating standardized rituals.

a.   b.   c.

0   1   2   3   4
centimeters

Figure 2.3   Archaic tools: Frio type side-notched dart point, hand-held drill, and flake knife from Kimble County, Texas.

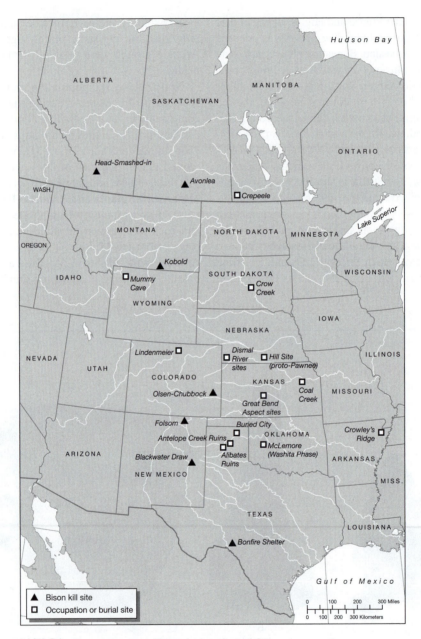

MAP 2.1 Some Important Plains Archaeological Sites.

During the portion of the Holocene geologic epoch that corresponds to Archaic times, there were fluctuations between warm and dry or cool and wet weather patterns. The Altithermal episode of 8,000 to 4,500 years ago was a peak dry spell that may have thwarted human occupation of the Plains to a great degree (its effect is a matter of continuing argument). Much of the Archaic archaeological record, which is ultimately scant given the long time frame, tells of human adjustments to these trends, in which there might have been greater reliance on either bison or plant foods depending on local conditions, and more concentrated or dispersed populations depending on the reliability of water, bison herds, or other resources.

The Late Prehistoric

The Archaic gives way to a new period called the Late Prehistoric with the advent of the bow and arrow, pottery, and, in some Plains areas, corn gardening and burial mounds. These developments begin to appear on the Plains roughly 2,000 years ago.

The presence of arrows, and thus bows, is indicated by small projectile points such as the side-notched Avonlea type from Saskatchewan and Harrell type of the Texas Panhandle, and others with notching in the base or corners, forming a stem and two barbs, like the Perdiz and Scallorn types. Bracelets made from antler that functioned as bowyer's wrist guards are also sometimes found. It is not clear whether the bow was invented independently in North America or diffused from Asia, although it seems to have spread across the Plains from the northwest. The crafting of bows and arrows, and necessary archery practice, was very labor intensive, but the payoff was greater hunting efficiency, and the bow was important as well in human conflict until the mid-nineteenth century.

Pottery from this period appears in several shapes and sizes. Coarse local clay was mixed with sand or granite grit for tempering, then molded to shape with the hands or a paddle, perhaps over an anvil-like stone, and baked. Pots were simple in design, only sometimes having collars or small handles. Some were decorated by marking the soft clay with cordage or the point of a stick, and a few have designs added around their rims with additional pieces of clay. Many styles of pottery are found and particular ones are diagnostic of specific time periods and cultural traditions.

Pottery is a clue for heavy use of plant foods, and in most cases for gardening. Another such clue is the frequency of ground stone tools, which show up in the Archaic and Late Prehistoric. Large, weighty implements made by abrading and polishing fine-grained sandstone, soapstone, or granite, quite different from chipped stone projectile points, were used to chop and pound plant foods. The mano (grinding stone) matched with a metate (slab or trough) is typical, and larger ones may indicate processing of corn rather than wild seed.

Burials in massive cemeteries or in mounds constructed from dry-stone masonry overlain with rocks and dirt are not uncommon in the Late Prehistoric. On the Plains, burial mounds are usually situated on high ground overlooking dwelling sites and arable floodplains. These features indicate large, relatively stable populations and a more sedentary, place-bound way of life. The mounds superficially resemble those constructed along the Ohio River and elsewhere in the Woodlands by the Hopewellian people, and mounds along with other artifacts and practices suggest some marginal relations with complex eastern societies.

Hunting still predominated across much of the Plains during the Late Prehistoric, and it is surmised that lifestyles of the period were similar to those pursued by earlier Archaic and later Protohistoric hunters. In general, and particularly in the south, reliance on bison intensified in the Late Prehistoric. Much of what we think of as Plains cultural life was probably in place. For example, the discovery of an altar fashioned from a buffalo skull, clay, and ochre at the Crepeele Site in southwestern Manitoba indicates the presence of ritual procedures that would be recognizable to historic and contemporary Plains Indians.

The first segment of the Late Prehistoric, circa 2,000 to 1,000 years ago, has been called Plains Woodland, marked by the presence of pottery which resembles that found to the east in the Woodlands area. Pottery in this case indicates some dependence on corn and squash and some intrusion of the technology for growing and storing plant food from the east. (The origin and spread of corn cultivation are examined in Chapter 3). Dependence on cultigens was still not heavy during this time, and in many ways the archaeological picture of the Plains Woodlands resembles that of the Archaic.

By about 1,000 years ago, however, some Indian people established settled villages that were highly dependent on the gardening of corn, beans, squash, and sunflowers, with hunting supplementary. This Plains Village Period lasted until the coming of Euro-Americans—until the 1600s or, in some places, as late as about 1850. During this period, villages were composed of clusters of earth lodges (in the north) or lodges made of grass or stone masonry (in the south) which each housed numerous extended family members, just as were found among some tribes by the first Euro-American visitors. Often the villages were fortified with earthen walls, wooden palisades, and trenches meant to help protect the populace and its food surplus stored in pits and ceramic vessels.

The gardening that sustained such large villages was best practiced along streams, and seminal developments took place along the rivers of the eastern north and central Plains. (Much information about the Plains Villagers was salvaged during the River Basin Surveys of 1946–1969, a series of archaeological projects along major Plains rivers prior to the construction of dams and reservoirs.) One concentration of villages grew along the Missouri River in North and South Dakota, giving rise to the Middle Missouri subtradition of archaeological patterning. A second subtradition, called Central Plains, flourished along the streams of eastern Nebraska, and a third, called Oneota, is found lying directly east of the other two. For some time these populations existed without much interaction, but about 550 years ago they appear to have begun merging. The resultant Coalescent tradition is thought to be ancestral to the historical Mandan, Hidatsa, Arikara, Pawnee, and Wichita tribes, which were living in villages upon the arrival of the Euro-Americans, and the Cheyennes and Crows, who abandoned villages for nomadic life on the open plains not long prior to the Euro-American arrival.

The occupational history of Crow Creek, a Middle Missouri site in south-central South Dakota, paints an intriguing picture of Plains Village life. The site, lying ideally on a high terrace above fertile floodplains where Wolf Creek and Crow Creek join the Missouri River, hosted human occupation for at least the past 1,000 years and yields abundant archaeological evidence which has been retrieved in several surveys and excavations. Some 48 houses protected by palisades and ditches are evident at the surface of the site. Repairs to the houses and renovations to the defenses, along with a huge accumulation of pottery shards, building debris, and other artifacts, show that the village was inhabited steadily for several centuries. The use of one ditch to receive trash suggests that at some point danger from attack subsided and the fortifications fell into disuse. A mass grave found on the northwestern end of the site, however, indicates that the village was attacked and burned and some of its inhabitants massacred after defenses flagged. Bone analysis of the victims reveals dietary stress, probably stemming from a regional drought. Cranial sampling suggests that they were indistinguishable from the historic Arikaras, which is to say, a people of southeastern,

Caddoan origin. Thus, the record at Crow Creek portrays a generally steady, secure way of life punctuated by environmental stress, migrations, and brutal warfare.

The Southern Plains saw distinctive versions of Plains Village life. Here, Caddoan people moved out onto the Plains from the east to establish villages and gardens during favorable climatic and groundwater conditions. Hunting of bison and deer and gathering of wild plants remained critical. A complex mosaic of village settlements spread across the south between Kansas and north-central Texas and only a few prominent examples will be mentioned.

One line of settlement followed the courses of the Canadian and upper Red rivers. During the Washita River Phase of about 800 to 550 years ago, Caddoans occupied central and western Oklahoma, tending gardens and dwelling in square or rectangular wattle-and-daub houses. Around the same time the Antelope Creek Phase developed directly west of the Washita River Phase in the Texas Panhandle. In this region, the Caddoan pioneer farmers built semi-subterranean, rectangular multi-room stone masonry dwellings as well as single-room houses and field huts. Remains of these buildings are found at numerous sites along the Red River, including the Antelope Creek Ruins and the Alibates Ruin. The variant Buried City site in Ochiltree County, Texas, has especially extensive ruins of single-room houses visible on the surface. The spotty distribution of rainfall and game led the Antelope Creek people to seek trade around the greater region to maximize their resource base, and sites from the later part of the phase produce notable amounts of pottery, turquoise beads, and obsidian that came from the northern Pueblos lying along the Pecos River and Rio Grande in New Mexico. (Because of these materials and the apartment-style dwellings, some archaeologists formerly thought that the Antelope Creek settlers were Puebloans rather than Caddoans.) This is an early manifestation of the Pueblo–Plains exchange system that

would remain important to Native people of both areas well into historical times. About 500 years ago, the Antelope Creek people suddenly dispersed from their large, dense settlements, first setting up scattered single-room houses near headwater springs and then eventually merging with neighboring populations or abandoning the region altogether.

One factor in the Antelope Creek decline may have been an invasion of new peoples from the north. The southward migration of Athapaskan-speaking peoples from northwestern Canada into the Plains and Southwest beginning around 500 years ago was a major event which introduced new populations and displaced others. These people were the forerunners of the Navajos and various Apache tribes. Though initially nomadic hunters, some Apachean migrants to western Kansas and Nebraska adopted a way of life with horticulture, pottery, and fixed villages like that of the Caddoans settlers from the east.

Another southern Plains Village manifestation is the Great Bend aspect. Taking its name from the huge curve in the Arkansas River in central Kansas, this aspect involved large river-terrace villages consisting of circular or oval houses that are assumed to have been of grass construction. The settlements were relatively late, dating from 550 to 300 years ago—into the Early Historical Period. Origins of this aspect are not clear, but the Great Bend people likely had ties to earlier local populations, the Coalescent traditions to the north, and the Washita River and Antelope Creek phases; and, southwestern ceramics found at Great Bend sites attest to their connection to the Pueblo trade. Most archaeologists regard the Great Bend people as ancestral to one or another of the subtribes of the historic Wichitas who inhabited Oklahoma and northern Texas in the 1700s and 1800s.

The Late Prehistoric is therefore of particular interest to students of the historical Plains tribes because of its potential for illuminating the near-term origins of the tribes. This interest has continued from the early days of Plains archaeology. In addition to the putative tribal origins noted above, some other widely accepted connections have been put forth, for example, that the Oneota tradition was ancestral to the Iowas and Missourias and that the Dismal River aspect of the Late Prehistoric found in Nebraska, Colorado, and New Mexico is attributable to Plains Apaches. Recently, there have been efforts to establish additional, very specific links between known historical tribes and Late Prehistoric and even Late Archaic populations, in essence reviving culture history and the direct historical approach. The methodology mingles Native oral traditions, theories of language evolution, and apparent continuities in religious symbolism along with archaeological data in order to read ethnicity backward into the prehistoric record. According to this method the Avonlea people of present Saskatchewan, previously associated with the Athapaskans, have been deemed ancestral to the Blackfeet. The Cheyennes are said to descend from the eastern Besant and the Kiowas from Northern Pelican Lake, both complexes found across the northwestern Plains. Many of these proposed connections are still considered conjectural or insupportable by the majority of archaeologists.

THE HISTORIC PERIOD

The Historic Period is defined as the span of time documented by written records. Technically speaking, this period begins on the Plains in A.D. 1541, when the expedition of Spanish explorer Francisco Vázquez de Coronado (1510–1554) ventured through present New Mexico, Texas, Oklahoma, and Kansas. Because the influences and observations of non-Indians were not intensive in the earliest decades of exploration, it is also helpful to recognize a loosely defined transitional period between prehistoric and historic times, the so-called Protohistoric Period.

After about A.D. 1600, the French and English fur trade in the north and Spanish mission system in the south introduced fairly consistent and sometimes highly detailed regimens of written documentation of Indian life. This was also the era in which Euro-Americans introduced manufactured trade goods and tied Indian populations into their expanding network of global trade. They brought guns and horses to the Plains Indians, as well as deadly germs causing devastating epidemics among Native peoples. For Indians, the Early Historic Period was a time of great upheaval. It was also a formative time when several of the tribes that are the subject of this book took shape, migrated onto the Plains, and set up their historical territories.

There are many sources of information for the historical Native American past. While archaeology developed primarily for the study of prehistory, its theories and methods are also applied in studying historical situations. For example, the battlefield where Sioux and Cheyenne warriors defeated U.S. Army troops under General George Armstrong Custer in 1868 has been studied intensively by archaeologists to add knowledge about the encounter (see Chapter 12). But other resources are usually more important in historical reconstruction. Indians' views about their own past are retrievable in oral traditions, in artwork, including pictorial histories drawn on hide or paper, and in memoirs and interviews recorded in writing or electronically. These sources, which are described or reproduced in subsequent chapters, are essential for understanding past migrations and tribal events. In fact, these Native sources can shed light on the Prehistoric Period as well as the historic era. Written and printed documents generated by non-Indians during the Indian past are also valuable, including the letters, diaries, reports, biographies, word lists, and business records of explorers, missionaries, traders, settlers, and government officials. The study of documentary evidence is largely the work of historians or those who, specializing in the pasts of small-scale or non-European societies, are termed *ethnohistorians* or *anthropological historians*.

Two enterprises of cultural anthropology conducted mainly by non-Indians contribute further data. *Ethnography*, the systematic description of particular cultures through field-work and participant observation, has produced many studies of Plains tribes at various points in time from the late 1800s up to the present. What is known about a culture from a particular ethnography may be carefully projected back in time, assuming a fair degree of cultural continuity, in a process known as *ethnographic analogy* or "upstreaming." This method is akin to the direct historical approach formerly practiced in Plains archaeology. Sometimes facts from many far-flung moments in time are combined into a composite ethnographic description and presented as if synchronic. This theoretical single time point, known as the *ethnographic present*, can be a convenience as long as the reader understands how it was really fashioned. *Ethnology*, the comparison of ethnographic data around larger questions of human history and behavior, also contributes to the picture of Plains life. An ethnological study might, for instance, draw upon several ethnographic reports to compare and contrast the incidence of the Sun Dance ceremony or capital punishment across multiple tribes.

Finally, *linguistics* is an essential discipline in the study of Plains Indians. Linguistic findings may pertain to the Prehistoric or Historic periods. The scholarly classification and comparison of languages can reveal past relations between groups and allow determination of when societies split, merged, or migrated. The degree of similarity or difference between two languages, which is often demonstrated by comparing lists of basic words like those for "mother" and "water," indicates the degree of separation in time between the two groups of language speakers. The Comanche language, for example, is very similar to Shoshone by such measures, indicating that the Comanches split off from the Shoshones relatively recently—around A.D. 1600. And even though the Arikaras of North Dakota and the Wichitas of Texas lived far away from each other in the Historical Period, they are known to be related because their languages are both of southeastern, Caddoan origin. Since the historical Plains tribes mostly originated outside of the Plains area, their linguistic connection to other tribes off the Plains shows the direction from which they came. The time and nature of contact between groups is also evident from vocabulary. Comanche clearly contains borrowed words of Siouan, Kiowa, Spanish, and English origin.

There are seven language families represented on the historic Plains. These are major groupings of languages that are related historically and structurally similar, although languages within these groupings are often not so similar as to be mutually intelligible. Variation between language families can be very great, equivalent to the difference between, for example, English and Chinese. The families include the following:

Algonquian—this family takes its name from the Algonquin tribes of northeastern North America and is associated with that region. Many tribes ranging from coastal Canada, New England, and the mid-Atlantic to the Great Lakes area speak Algonquian languages. Therefore, Plains Algonquian speakers have origins in the northeast. Tribes of this family that most closely neighbored the Plains include the Menominees, Sauk-Fox, and Illinois. The Plains Algonquians include the Plains Ojibwas, Plains Crees, Gros Ventres, Blackfoots, Cheyennes, and Arapahos.

Athapaskan—this family is the most widely distributed one in North America and includes all of the numerous tribes of western subarctic Canada and some in Washington, Oregon, and northern California, as well as those populations that migrated from the northwest into the Plains and desert southwest about 500 years ago. Northwestern tribes include the Carriers,

Chipwyans, and Beavers, while the Navajos and various Apache groups such as the Jicarillas and Mescaleros represent this family in the southwest. On the Plains, Athapaskans include the Sarcees in the north and those Apaches who occupied the Southern Plains, namely the Lipan Apaches and the Plains Apaches, also called Kiowa Apaches.

Caddoan—the southeast United States is the area of origination for this family, which takes its name from the Caddo tribe of Louisiana and East Texas. Caddoan tribes on the Plains migrated from this direction. They include the Wichitas, Kitsais, Pawnees, and Arikaras.

Kiowa-Tanoan—this family includes the languages of certain Pueblo villages along the Rio Grande in central New Mexico, plus that of the Kiowas of the Plains. It is not clearly understood how these two branches are connected historically, or how evident migration may have taken place.

Siouan—this is a large family whose members spread from a core area in either the Great Lakes–Ohio River Valley region or the Southeast. The Winnebagos of Wisconsin and Catawbas of South Carolina are Siouan tribes, but most tribes of this family in the Historic Period are found on the Prairie and High Plains. The family name is derived from the name "Sioux," which has been applied to three of the constituent tribes, the Tetons, Yanktons–Yanktonais, and Santees. Other Plains Siouans include the Assiniboines, Crows, Mandans, Hidatsas, Poncas, Omahas, Iowas, Otoes, Missourias, Kansas, Osages, and Quapaws. Although most of the language families have notable subgroupings, it is especially customary to refer to two within the Siouan family. The *Dhegiha speakers* include the Omahas, Poncas, Osages, Kansas, and Quapaws. The *Chiwere speakers* include the Iowas, Otoes, and Missourias. Members of both of these branches are also called *Southern Siouans.*

Tonkawa—the now extinct language of the Tonkawa tribe of central Texas was an isolate. Other member languages of a theoretical Tonkawan family may have been spoken by Southern Plains populations, but no positive reconstruction appears possible now.

Uto-Aztecan—this widespread family includes languages across Mexico and the western United States. Member tribes include the Aztecs of ancient Mexico and the Utes and Shoshones of the intermountain west. The Comanches are the only offshoot of this family to steadily occupy the Plains.

Knowing a tribe's language background can be a shorthand way of understanding other aspects of its history and culture. Although culture and language are not totally equivalent, and groups with common language origins can wind up having divergent cultures, on the Plains there is often good correlation between language and other customs. To say, for example, that the Omahas were speakers of a Southern Siouan language alerts us to other common customs among these speakers, such as particular ceremonies and types of houses. For this reason linguistic affiliation is often referred to and it is helpful to memorize the affiliation of every tribe.

One can see that all of these sources and processes for knowledge construction have limitations of accuracy and reliability. The best that can be done is the judicious cross-checking and combination of data from different viewpoints, with open acknowledgment of any uncertainty. In recent years, the methods and motives of non-Indian archaeologists, historians, and cultural anthropologists have been challenged from within and outside the disciplines. Their work has been said to be overly subjective, laden with assumptions, scientistic, and even racist. Indians and non-Indians alike, however, will continue to rely on the knowledge generated by professional scholars if the Native cultures of the Plains are to be understood and perpetuated, a responsibility that makes quality research all the more necessary.

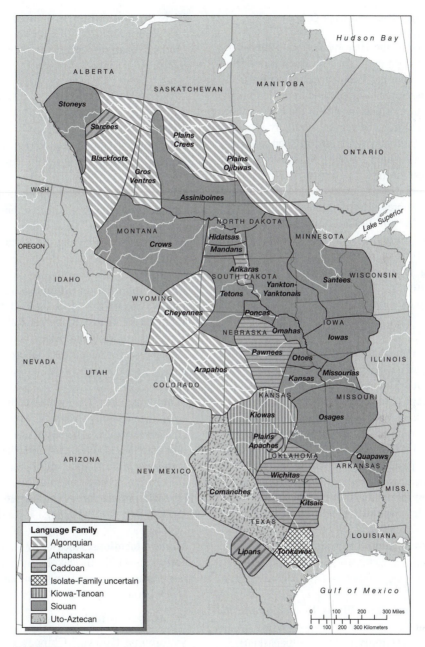

MAP 2.2 Linguistic Affiliations of Historical Plains Tribes.

The Historic Tribes and their Origins

At the dawn of the Historic Period, some of the tribes located on the Plains were descended from populations that had been in the region for many generations. Some of these parent populations are known to have origins outside of the Plains. Other tribes moved into the region relatively recently, during the Protohistoric or Historic periods. Once tribes were located on the Plains, some stayed more or less in the same territory all during the Historic Period, while others migrated within the region under pressure from other groups. During and after the non-Indian conquest of the area many tribes were relocated or restricted to much smaller portions of their historic territories. Following is a complete listing of the tribes, arranged from north to south, summarizing their origins and locations.

Stoneys (STŌN ēz)

Synonyms: Assiniboines, Nakoda Iyéska (self-designation)
Divisions: Mountain Stoney, Wood Stoney
Language (Family): Stoney (Siouan)
Origins: a small, closely related outgrowth of the Assiniboines, with a separate identity by the late 1700s
Range: plains along the North Saskatchewan River headwaters in west-central Alberta, and adjacent mountains into British Columbia
Historic population estimates: 1877:556; 1885:647; 1895:570; 1997:6,040
Modern location: five reserves in west-central Alberta

Sarcees (SÄR sēz)

Synonyms: Sarsi, Plains Beaver, *Tsuut'ina* (self-name)
Language (Family): Sarcee (Athapaskan)
Origins: offshoot the Beaver Indians of the subarctic woodlands
Range: headwaters of the South Saskatchewan River, southern Alberta
Historic population estimates: 1670:700; 1924:160; 1978:615; 1987:850
Modern location: Sarcee Reserve immediately southwest of Calgary, Alberta

Blackfoots (BLAK footz)

Synonyms: Blackfeet (in the United States), Siksika, *Siksikáwa* (self-name)
Divisions: Siksikas (northern), Kainahs or Bloods (middle), Piegans or Peigans (southern)
Language (Family): Blackfoot (Algonquian)
Origins: probably from the east, but otherwise uncertain
Range: North Saskatchewan River in Alberta south to the Missouri River headwaters in Montana
Historic population estimates: 1780:15,000; 1909:4,635; 1978:21,466; 1997:31,186
Modern locations: Blackfeet Reservation in northwestern Montana; Blackfoot, Blood, and Piegan reserves in southern Alberta

Plains Crees (crēz)

Synonyms: Cree, *Ne·hiyawak* (self-name)
Language (Family): Plains Cree (Algonquian)
Origins: western offshoot of the Cree of the subarctic boreal forest east of Lake Winnipeg
Range: southern and central Saskatchewan and contiguous east-central Alberta
Historic population estimates: 1670:15,000; 1894:6,766; 1950:10,000; 1973:43,761 in Canada
Modern locations: Rocky Boy Reservation in north-central North Dakota, numerous small reserves in central and southern Saskatchewan and Alberta

Plains Ojibwas (ō JIB wāz)

Synonyms: Ojibway, Chippewa, Saulteaux, Bungi
Language (Family): Saulteaux (Algonquian)
Origins: a mixed, formative Plains group descended from the Saulteaux tribe of Ontario

and the Ojibwas and other Algonquian tribes of the Great Lakes region

Range: southwest Manitoba and southeast Saskatchewan into northern North Dakota and Montana

Historic population estimates: 1650:35,000; 1910:20,214; 1970:8,400 in Canada; 1978:21,340 in the United States

Modern locations: Turtle Mountain Reservation in north-central North Dakota, Rocky Boy's Reservation in north-central Montana, numerous small reserves in southern Manitoba and Saskatchewan

Gros Ventres (GRŌ väntz)

Synonyms: Atsina, Fall Indians, Gros Ventres of the Prairie

Language (Family): Gros Ventre (Algonquian)

Origins: separated from the Arapahos at an unknown time and place

Range: circa A.D. 1750 between the North and South Saskatchewan rivers in central Alberta and Saskatchewan, circa A.D. 1850 on the Missouri River tributaries in north-central Montana

Historic population estimates: 1780:3,000; 1910:510; 1937:809; 1964:1,873; 1998:3,078

Modern location: Fort Belknap Reservation in north-central Montana

Assiniboines (ə SIN ə boinz)

Synonyms: Stoneys, Plains Stoneys, Stone Sioux, *Nakʰóta* (self-designation)

Language (Family): Assiniboine (Siouan)

Origins: westward expansion and offshoot from the Sioux by the 1600s

Range: Saskatchewan, Assiniboine, and Missouri River valleys in southern Saskatchewan and adjacent parts of Manitoba, Alberta, Montana, and North Dakota

Historic population estimates: 1780:10,000; 1904:2,605; 1998:5,500

Modern locations: Carry the Kettle Reserve, southern Saskatchewan and several other reserves across historic Canadian range, plus Fort Belknap and Fort Peck reservations in Montana

Crows (crōz)

Synonyms: Ravens, *Absáalooke* (self-designation)

Divisions: Mountain Crows, River Crows, Kicked in the Bellies

Language (Family): Crow (Siouan)

Origins: separation and westerly migration from the Hidatsas of North Dakota

Range: Montana on the Yellowstone River and three of its tributaries—the Powder, Wind, and Big Horn rivers

Historic population estimates: 1780:8,000; 1910:1,799; 1978:6,143; 1998:9,814

Modern location: Crow Reservation in southeastern Montana

Hidatsas (Hi DÄT səz)

Synonyms: Gros Ventres of the Missouri, Minitaris, Willow Indians, Fall Indians

Divisions: Hidatsas, Awatixas, Awaxawis

Language (Family): Hidatsa (Siouan)

Origins: from the east via the Middle Missouri to their historic location by the early 1500s

Range: three fixed villages at the junction of the Knife and Missouri rivers in North Dakota, plus hunting range over southwestern North Dakota

Historic population estimates: 1780:2,500; 1850:700; 1910:547; 1950:933; 1978:3,456 (combined with Arikara and Mandan on the Fort Berthold Reservation)

Modern location: Fort Berthold Reservation in west-central North Dakota

Mandans (MAN danz)

Synonyms: *Rųwą ʔka·ki, Rų ʔeta* (self-designations)

Divisions: Ruptare (East Bank), Nuweta (West Bank)

Language (Family): Mandan (Siouan)

Origins: from the east via the Middle Missouri to their historic location by the early 1500s

Range: several fixed villages at the junction of the Heart and Missouri rivers in North Dakota, plus hunting range over southwestern North Dakota

Historic population estimates: 1780:3,600; 1910:209; 1978:3,456 (combined with Arikara and Hidatsa on the Fort Berthold Reservation)

Modern location: Fort Berthold Reservation in west-central North Dakota

Arikaras (ə RIK ə rəz)

Synonyms: Rees, *Sáhniš* (self-designation)

Language (Family): Arikara (Caddoan)

Origins: a confederation of Caddoan bands closely related to the Pawnees, which moved up the Missouri River through South and North Dakota from Kansas and Nebraska during the Late Prehistoric

Range: on the Missouri River between the Cheyenne River in South Dakota and Fort Berthold in North Dakota

Historic population estimates: 1780:3,000; 1910:444; 1950:682; 1978:3,456 (combined with Mandan and Hidatsa on the Fort Berthold Reservation)

Modern location: Fort Berthold Reservation in west-central North Dakota

Santees (san TĒZ)

Synonyms: Sioux, Eastern Sioux, Dakota, *Dakʰóta* (self-designation)

Divisions: Mdewakantons, Wahpekutes, Sissetons, Wahpetons

Language (Family): Sioux (Siouan)

Origins: westward migration from region where Minnesota, Iowa, Wisconsin, and Illinois join, circa A.D. 1750–1800

Range: southwestern Minnesota and northern Iowa, later into the Dakotas and Canada

Historic population estimates (for all Sioux tribes): 1780:25,000; 1930:25,934; 1978:65,340

Modern locations: Santee Reservation, Nebraska; Lower Sioux, Upper Sioux Indian Commission, Prairie Island, and Prior Lake reservations, Minnesota; Sisseton Reservation and Flandreau, South Dakota; Fort Totten Reservation, North Dakota; Fort Peck Reservation, Montana; Sioux Valley, Bird Tail, and Oak Lakes reserves, Manitoba: Round Plain, Moose Woods, and Standing Buffalo reserves, Saskatchewan

Yankton–Yanktonais (YAŋKtən-YAŋKtə nā)

Synonyms: Sioux, Dakota, Nakota, *Dakʰóta* (self-designation)

Divisions: Upper Yanktons, Lower Yanktons, Upper Yanktonais, Lower Yanktonais

Language (Family): Sioux (Siouan)

Origins: westward migration from Minnesota, 1700s

Range: between the Red and Missouri rivers through eastern North and South Dakota

Historic population estimates: 1807:4,300; 1886:6,883; 1978:17,626

Modern locations: Yankton and Crow Creek reservations, South Dakota; Fort Totten and Standing Rock reservations, North Dakota; Fort Peck Reservation, Montana; Oak Lake Reserve, Manitoba; Standing Buffalo Reserve, Saskatchewan.

Tetons (TĒ tänz)

Synonyms: Sioux, Western Sioux, Dakota, Lakota, *Lakʰóta* (self-designation)

Divisions: Hunkpapas, Minneconjous, Sihasapas, Oohenonpas, Sans Arcs, Brules, Oglalas

Language (Family): Sioux (Siouan)

Origins: westward migration from Minnesota, 1700s

Range: western South Dakota and adjacent parts of North Dakota, Montana, Wyoming, and Nebraska

Historic population estimates: 1890:16,426; 1909:18,098; 1978:34,315

Modern locations: Cheyenne River, Lower Brule, Rosebud, and Pine Ridge reservations,

South Dakota; Standing Rock Reservation, North Dakota; Fort Peck Reservation, Montana; Wood Mountain Reserve, Saskatchewan.

Cheyennes (shī ANZ)

Synonyms: Tsistsistas (self-designation)
Divisions: Northern Cheyennes, Southern Cheyennes
Language (Family): Cheyenne (Algonquian)
Origins: from western Minnesota, into North and South Dakota (Black Hills) in the 1700s, during which time they absorbed the Sutaios, a closely related but dialectally distinct Algonquian group
Range: Upper Platte and Arkansas rivers, where Wyoming, Nebraska, Colorado, and Kansas join, with later centers in southeastern Montana and western Oklahoma
Historic population estimates: 1780:3,500; 1875:3,782; 1910:2,868; 1960:4,500; 1970:6,872; 1994:11,500; 2000:15,000
Modern locations: Northern Cheyenne Reservation, southeastern Montana; west-central Oklahoma

Arapahos (ə RAP ə hōz)

Synonyms: Hinóno?éíno? (self-designation)
Divisions: Gros Ventre, Besawunena, Hinanaeina, Ha'anahawunena, Nawathinehena; also organized as Northern Arapahoes and Southern Arapahos
Language (Family): Arapaho (Algonquian)
Origins: Red River Valley of northern Minnesota, 1600s
Range: central Wyoming to Oklahoma
Historic population estimates: 1780:3,000; 1835:3,600; 1861:2,150; 1910:1,419; 1923:1,754; 1989:6,894; 2000:10,433
Modern locations: Wind River Reservation, central Wyoming; west-central Oklahoma

Pawnees (pô NĒZ, PÔnēz)

Synonyms: Ckírihki kuru·riki (self-designation)
Divisions: Skiri, Chawi, Kitkahahki, Pitahariwata, latter three also called South Bands

Language (Family): Pawnee (Caddoan)
Origins: from the southeast, with definable identity by about A.D. 1550
Range: central and eastern Nebraska into adjacent Kansas
Historic population estimates: 1780:10,000; 1840:7,500; 1872:2,447; 1910:633; 1950:1,149; 1996:2,500
Modern location: north-central Oklahoma

Poncas (PÄŋ kəz)

Synonyms: Ppákka (self-designation)
Divisions: Northern Poncas and Southern Poncas (after A.D. 1878)
Language (Family): Omaha-Ponca (Siouan)
Origins: offshoot of the Omahas circa A.D. 1700
Range: between White and Niobrara rivers, southern South Dakota and northern Nebraska
Historic population estimates: 1780:800; 1847:1,600; 1910:875; 1939:1,237; 1978:2,022; 1998:4,387
Modern location: north-central Oklahoma

Omahas (Ō mə häz)

Synonyms: Umáha (self-designation)
Language (Family): Omaha-Ponca (Siouan)
Origins: Dhegiha-speaking Siouans from the Ohio River Valley
Range: northeastern Nebraska
Historic population estimates: 1780:2,800; 1829:1,900; 1883:1,226; 1910:1,105; 1978:1,168; 1984:2,188; 1998:4,950
Modern location: Omaha Indian Reservation, northeastern Nebraska

Iowas (Ī ə wəz)

Synonyms: Páxoǰe (self-designation)
Language (Family): Chiwere (Siouan)
Origins: offshoot of a Siouan population in Wisconsin during the Late Prehistoric, related to the Winnebagos
Range: various settlements across Iowa and adjacent fringes of Minnesota and Missouri,

generally trending southward between the A.D. 1600s and 1800s

Historic population estimates: 1780:1,200; 1848:669; 1880:222; 1910:358; 1940:649; 1978:2,386; 1996:2,608

Modern locations: Iowa Reservation in northeast Kansas and southeast Nebraska; north-central Oklahoma

Otoes (Ō tōz)

Synonyms: Oto, *Ĵiwére* (self-designation)
Language (Family): Chiwere (Siouan)
Origins: offshoot of a Siouan population in Wisconsin during the Late Prehistoric, related to the Winnebagos and united with the Missourias
Range: southwest Minnesota circa A.D. 1700, then along the Missouri River in southwestern Iowa and southeastern Nebraska
Historic population estimates (combined Otoe–Missouria): 1780:1,900; 1829:1,280; 1867:430; 1910:332; 1945:886; 1978:1,450; 1998:1,520
Modern location: north-central Oklahoma

Missourias (mi ZOOR ē əz)

Synonyms: Otoes (when discussing united Otoes and Missourias), *Ni-ú-t'-tcí* (self-designation)
Language (Family): Chiwere (Siouan)
Origins: offshoot of a Siouan population in Wisconsin during the Late Prehistoric, related to the Winnebagos and united with the Otoes
Range: northwestern Missouri circa A.D. 1700, then along the Missouri River in south-western Iowa and southeastern Nebraska
Historic population estimates (combined Otoe–Missouria): 1780:1,900; 1829:1,280; 1867:430; 1910:332; 1945:886; 1978:1,450; 1998:1,520
Modern location: north-central Oklahoma

Kansas (KAN zəz)

Synonyms: Kaws, *kká·ze* (self-designation)
Language (Family): Kansa (Siouan)

Origins: Dhegiha-speaking Siouans from the Ohio River Valley, most closely related to Osages
Range: along the Kansas River and tributaries, northern Kansas and small sections of adjacent Missouri, Nebraska, and Colorado
Historic population estimates: 1780:3,000; 1837:1,471; 1870:574; 1910:238; 1945:544; 1978:775; 1998:2,333
Modern location: north-central Oklahoma

Osages (Ō sā jez)

Synonyms: *Waźáźe* (self-designation)
Divisions: Great Osages, Little Osages, Arkansas Osages
Language (Family): Osage (Siouan)
Origins: Dhegiha-speaking Siouans from the Ohio River Valley, most closely related to Kansas
Range: between Missouri and Arkansas rivers, across region where Missouri, Arkansas, Kansas, and Oklahoma join
Historic population estimates: 1780:7,000; 1850:5,000; 1872:3,956; 1910:1,373; 1952:5,307; 1976:8,842; 1996:12,000
Modern location: Osage Reservation, north-eastern Oklahoma

Quapaws (KWÔ pôz)

Synonyms: Arkansas, *Okáxpa* (self-designation)
Language (Family): Quapaw (Siouan)
Origins: Dhegiha-speaking Siouans from the Ohio River Valley
Range: across central and southeastern Arkansas, into east-central Oklahoma, then on Quapaw Reservation in extreme northeastern Oklahoma A.D. 1833–1897
Historic population estimates: 1780:2,500; 1834:476; 1883:205; 1910:231; 1950:720; 1961:1,119; 1996:2,510
Modern location: extreme northeastern Oklahoma

Wichitas (WICH ə tôz)

Synonyms: Pawnee Picts, *Kirikir?i·s* (self-designation)
Divisions: Wichitas, Wacos, Tawakonis, Tawehashes, others
Language (Family): Wichita (Caddoan)
Origins: from the southeast, with definable identity by A.D. 1541
Range: south-central Kansas, central Oklahoma, north-central Texas, trending southward from A.D. 1700 to 1800; relocation from Texas to western Oklahoma in 1872
Historic population estimates: 1780:3,200; 1910:318; 1945:460; 1978:976; 1998:1,912
Modern location: western Oklahoma

Kitsais (KĒTS īz)

Synonyms: Kichais, *Kítsias* (self-designation)
Divisions: distinct northern and southern populations
Language (Family): Kitsai (Caddoan)
Origins: from the southeast, possibly via the central Plains; a small but linguistically distinct group closely associated with the Caddos and Wichitas and merged with the latter during the mid-1800s
Range: north-central Texas into western Oklahoma
Historic population estimates: 1849:300; 1893:52
Modern location: extinct as tribe; possible descendants among Wichitas in western Oklahoma

Kiowas (KĪ ə wəz)

Synonyms: *káygú* (self-designation)
Language (Family): Kiowa (Kiowa-Tanoan)
Origins: from the northwest or possibly the southwest, first known in southwestern Montana
Range: South Dakota (Black Hills) early; by 1850 centered at the junction of Colorado, Kansas, Oklahoma, Texas, and New Mexico

Historic population estimates: 1780:2,000; 1875:1,000; 1910:1,126; 1978:7,927; 1990:9,421; 2000:12,500
Modern location: southwestern Oklahoma

Plains Apaches (ə PACH ēz)

Synonyms: Apaches, Kiowa Apaches, Padoucas, *Na-I-Sha* (self-designation)
Language (Family): Plains Apache (Athapascan)
Origins: a small Apachean group from the northwest, separate from others, which often traveled and camped with the Kiowas
Range: South Dakota (Black Hills) early; by 1850 centered at the junction of Colorado, Kansas, Oklahoma, Texas, and New Mexico
Historic population estimates: 1780:300; 1910:139; 1930:184; 1951:400; 1992:1,342
Modern location: southwestern Oklahoma

Comanches (kə MAN chēz)

Synonyms: Padoucas, Ietans, Têtes Pelées, *Nɨmɨnɨ* (self-designation)
Divisions: Yamparika, Kotsatika, Penatika, Nokoni, Kwahada, Tenawa, others
Language (Family): Comanche (Uto-Aztecan)
Origins: separated from Shoshoneans in Wyoming about A.D. 1600 and migrated southward
Range: During the 1700s, their core area extended across eastern Colorado and New Mexico and western Nebraska, Kansas, and Oklahoma into Texas, and during the 1800s it centered in the Texas Panhandle
Historic population estimates: 1690:7,000; 1830:10,000; 1910:1,171; 1978:7,393; 1999:10,000
Modern location: southwestern Oklahoma

Lipan Apaches (LI pän ə PACH ēz)

Synonyms: Apaches, *Na'-izha'ñ, Čiší·hí* (self-designations)
Language (Family): Lipan Apache (Athapascan)

Origins: from the northwest, by the early 1700s or earlier

Range: central and southern Texas

Historic population estimates: 1690:500; 1910:28; 1970:150

Modern locations: Mescalero Apache Indian Reservation, south-central New Mexico; northern and western Oklahoma; population around Corpus Christi, Texas, recognized by State of Texas

Tonkawas (TÄŋK ə wəz)

Synonyms: *Tickanwa·tic* (self-designation)

Language (Family): Tonkawa (isolate—family uncertain)

Origins: presumed to be old inhabitants of the Southern Plains; first known in northern Oklahoma circa A.D. 1600

Range: central Texas

Historic population estimates: 1690:1,600; 1910:42; 1978:182; 2007:481

Modern location: northern Oklahoma

Sources: Ahler and Kay (2007); Bamforth (1988); Bamforth and Nepstad-Thornberry (2007); Burley (1996); Deloria (1995); Fagan (2005); Frison (1978); Gillam (1996); Hawley (2006); Hoard et al. (2001); Hoebel (1980); Johnson and Wood (1980); Kehoe (2002); Lyman and O'Brien (2001); Martin and Wright (1967); Meltzer (2006); Nicholson and Nicholson (2007); Parks et al. (1980); Reeves (1973); Schlesier (1994); Spielmann (1991); Strauss (2000); Strong (1933); Sturtevant (2001); Wade (2006); Wedel (1986); and Wood (1998).

CHAPTER SUMMARY

Humans have occupied the Great Plains for at least 11,000 years. The archaeological record, composed by excavating and dating artifacts, reconstructs Indian life in the region before written records. The earliest humans on the Plains are called Paleoindians. They lived in small, mobile groups as successful hunters of big game. Evidence points to an Asian origin for the Paleoindians, though the details of their arrival are debated. The disappearance of Paleoindians in the archaeological record by about 8,000 years ago is attributed to climate change. Warmer and more diverse climates gave rise to human adaptations termed Archaic. Archaic hunter-gatherers collected smaller game and plants using a greater range of inventions. Around 2,000 years ago the invention of the bow and arrow and pottery marked the next broad cultural period, called the Late Prehistoric. The succeeding Historic Period is defined by the arrival of Euro-Americans and their written records. Some of the Indian populations on the Plains during the Historic were there in some form during the Late Prehistoric. Other populations migrated onto the Plains during the Historic Period. In historic times, the Plains has been home to seven broad language families and 32 tribes.

QUESTIONS FOR REVIEW

1. Explain how the archaeological record is constructed, and what it can and cannot tell us about Indian life on the Plains before written records.
2. Summarize the theoretical debates surrounding the origins of the earliest Americans.
3. Detail the three broad Prehistoric periods on the Plains. Discuss their dates, artifact evidence, and inferences about the natural environment and human lifeways.
4. Explain the varied origins of the Indian populations that occupied the Plains in the Historic Period. Cite the origins of some specific tribes. How does language lend clues about tribal origins?

CHAPTER 3

BISON, HORSE, AND HOE

At the heart of any study of cultural ways must be some basic grasp of how people make their living. The repertoires of food- and shelter-getting techniques, and the knowledge of how to apply them, are referred to as subsistence practices. Four basic subsistence practices are commonly recognized, including foraging (hunting and gathering), horticulture (gardening), pastoralism (herding), and agriculture (farming), and all of these are relevant in some way to understanding Plains Indian life. Owing to the importance of horse and buffalo herds to their survival, Indians on the Plains developed cultures that in many ways resembled those of famous nomadic pastoralists like the Bedouins of Arabia and Mongols of central Asia. In strictest terms, however, the Plains Natives were hunters and gatherers, with some also practicing gardening. The best way to approach their subsistence practices is by examining the species that they depended on the most: the bison and other game, the horse and dog, and plants, domestic and wild.

THE BISON

Among the many strange and giant animals that roamed much of Eurasia and North America during the Pleistocene were some huge bovines

recognizable as ancestors of the buffalo. These animals included *Bison latifrons*, with horns like a Texas longhorn steer, only 6 feet or more from tip to tip, and *Bison antiquus*, a presumably shaggy monster with shorter, thicker, though still cattle-like horns. As the Ice Age drew to a close and climates and environments changed, the large herbivore species were forced to extinction. Yet another species of bison, however, had evolved late in the period, and this animal was able to survive and even flourish without competitors in the drier grasslands and woodlands that emerged. This smaller bison functioned as a "weed species," reproducing rapidly and expanding its range under conditions of ecological disturbance. Distinguished from its ancestors by its small, backward curving horns, the "dwarf" bison was still massive, in fact the largest land animal of its time in North America: males grew up to 12 feet long, $6\frac{1}{2}$ feet high at the hump, and weighed over a ton.

Two subspecies of this modern bison have been recognized in North America; these were once considered separate species. They are commonly called buffalo, although true buffalos are wild oxen native to Asia and Africa. The buffalo of the Plains is designated *Bison bison bison*, and the "wood buffalo" or "mountain buffalo" of the Rockies is labeled *B. b. athabascae*. The name "bison" is related to the German word "wisent" (pron. *vee-zunt*), used for the European counterpart *Bison bonasus*, which is now almost extinct and preserved only in a few parks and zoos.

The American bison is first reported in print as an inhabitant of back country Florida in a Spanish natural history dated 1535. A few years earlier, Cabeza de Vaca was the first European to witness Indian subsistence use of the animal somewhere south of Corpus Christi, Texas. In the early decades of Euro-American settlement, buffalos were found across the continent. English settlers saw them on the east slope of the Appalachians, from New York State and the present site of Washington, D.C. to Georgia, and exterminated them from these areas by the mid-1700s. The last herd to survive in the mountains of Pennsylvania was harried out of existence by 1801. In 1832, Indians in Wisconsin killed what were probably the last buffalo east of the Mississippi River. Further west, however, enormous numbers of buffalos persisted in the nineteenth century as they had for untold generations, providing a basis for the Plains economy.

European and American observers in the nineteenth century frequently guessed at numbers of 60–100 million. The naturalist Ernest Thompson Seton offered what was considered a rational and conservative estimate of 75 million animals across North America prior to European settlement, 40 million on the High Plains. To arrive at this figure, Seton projected from the range and forage needs of domestic cattle. Debate continues about exactly how to make such a projection, but this procedure is still at the heart of modern scientific estimates. Recent scholars have calculated that there were about 30 million buffalos on the Great Plains before widespread human-induced disruptions. Whatever the number, there were a lot of them. Judging from accounts of the time, the plenitude of buffalos in some areas almost defied description. Colonel Richard I. Dodge wrote of a 35-mile wagon trip between Fort Zarah and Fort Larned in Kansas during May 1871, 25 miles of which was spent passing through one herd of buffalos.

It is difficult to truly understand what these animals, in their vast numbers and sheer importance, must have meant to Native people on the Plains. The degree to which the buffalo was celebrated in story, song, and ritual can be reviewed briefly to heighten our appreciation. In Comanche myth, the appearance of the buffalo was equivalent to the beginning of human life. This idea was expressed in a story often titled "The Release of the Wild Animals," which existed in many versions. An ogre or old woman keeps all the buffalos penned in the mountains, sometimes in a cave, and the people are starving. "The people"—in this case a cast of animal characters, for humans and animals are yet to be differentiated from one another—conspire to release the buffalos. The trickster Coyote leads the planning, and he or his helpers gain entry into the ogre's lair on some pretext and succeed in stampeding them. Thus released, the buffalos populate the Plains, the hunting life of humans can begin, and starvation ends. In another Comanche story, a hunter sneaking upon a pair of buffalos overhears the animals talking to one another. They speak Comanche, and are discussing the names of the nearby rivers. In awe, the hunter returns to his camp without killing the buffalo, instead praising their medicine. The Comanches adopt the buffalo river names. In this tale very basic notions of the landscape are inherited from the buffalo, again signifying the animal's essential role in defining human life on the Plains.

Other stories from various tribes emphasize the family organization of buffalos, noting the complementary roles of the father, mother, and child and qualities of protection, nurturance, and playfulness. Or, a spunky young buffalo calf defeats an ogre, propelling her to the moon, exhibiting the frequently underestimated promise of youth. Buffalos were obstinate, courageous, and seemed to work to take care of each other.

The buffalo even seeks the blessings of the earth by throwing dust on himself. And, in their enormous numbers the buffalos were a successful population; they thrived as humans hoped to. In such observations, human values are represented as buffalo qualities and behaviors.

More evidence for the centrality of the buffalo is found in ceremonies. The Sun Dance, the annual major ritual for many tribes, usually included veneration of a buffalo effigy and prayers for increasing the herds (see Chapter 10). Buffalo dances, either to appease the buffalo guardian spirit or to harness buffalo medicine power for war protection, were widespread. In a version still done on the Southern Plains today, dancers hop in place so that their footprints in the dust resemble the tracks made by the buffalo's cloven hoof. Buffalo tongues were the food for ritual feasts, and a buffalo skull, symbolically brought to life by placing sage sprigs in the eye sockets, became an instant altar wherever it was set up.

Special respect was given to rare white buffalos when they were found. The painter and explorer George Catlin thought that perhaps less than 1 in 100,000 buffalos were white (modern geneticists, extrapolating from the rate of human albinism, say perhaps 1 in 15,000). Their skins were worn by the medicine men and raid leaders for power and protection among many tribes, including the Cheyennes, Mandans, Blackfoot, Kiowas, and Comanches. The Mandans sometimes sacrificed white buffalo skins to the Great Spirit, because they were the most uncommon and valuable, by leaving them outside to decay. In the mythology of the Oglalas (Tetons), the bringer of the seven sacred ceremonies and thus the founder of human society was portrayed as White Buffalo Calf Woman.

The human connection to buffalos was also represented in personal names. These names were often derived from a spiritual experience involving buffalos. Among the Crows in 1907 were elder men named Bull-chief and Gray-bull, for

example. Finally, there are some verbatim statements from Indian people about the importance of buffalos that were recorded when the buffalo hunting economy was still ongoing. These words were often delivered during treaty talks and were most directly about the necessities of survival, but even these statements indicate a profound relationship between people and animals. When the Penateka Comanche leader Buffalo Hump met with Sam Houston to negotiate the boundary between Indians and settlers in 1844, he insisted on a line that corresponded to the southern extent of buffalo migration in Texas: "It is on account of the buffalo: when they come down I want the privilege to come after them . . . I want the privilege to follow the buffalo on down. That country is full of bear, deer, wild horses and buffalo for my people to live on" (quoted in Winfrey and Day 1995, II: 109–110). The range of the buffalo and that of the Comanche people were simply inseparable in Buffalo Hump's way of thinking.

Successful buffalo hunting required knowledge of seasonal herding patterns. Generally, the animals congregated in large herds during the summer, ranging eastward on the High Plains, while during winter dividing into small herds and seeking shelter in the breaks or mountains, often in a westward direction. There was much variation depending on current climate, but nevertheless a good amount of predictability too.

Hunters and their families gathered or dispersed in rhythm with the herds. During the coldest months, single nuclear families or small bands, scattered widely, had the best chance of finding enough buffalo. In the warmth of the June sun, people gathered from far and wide to embark on cooperative hunts. They established huge camps, sometimes including entire tribes, as a base of operations for hunting and processing. Naturally, these camps became the site of group ceremonies and a place for trade and marriage as well. While the June hunts were meant to lay in supplies of meat, there were also large-scale hunts to obtain robes around November and December, when the hides were most heavily covered with fur.

Buffalo hunting method in the days before the horse often involved driving animals into some kind of trap. Paleoindians used this approach, and it persisted in various forms into the Historic Period. The Olsen-Chubbuck bison kill excavation in southeastern Colorado revealed a site where some 200 buffalos were stampeded and butchered about 10,500 years ago (see Map 2.1). Skeletons were all facing the same direction, and Scottsbluff points were found close by. The presence of calf skeletons indicated that the slaughter took place in late summer. The spread of bones around the site suggested butchering and sun-drying processes.

The typical method of killing with the buffalo jump required many men and women. Two parties would line up somewhat perpendicular to the edge of a cliff or bank, angling their lines to form a chute. A third group would emerge behind and across the herd, driving the buffalos into the chute. All worked at frightening the animals into a charge by hollering and waving hides. Once the lead animals took the plunge, the herd followed and a mass killing was all but assured. More people waited below to finish off any wounded animals and begin the butchering. If the drop-off was not severe, a corral could be built at its base to trap any animals not killed by the fall. Sometimes a precipice along a river or creek was chosen to make the fall even more lethal.

In a variation of the jump technique, an agile man donned a buffalo skin outfit complete with head and horns and acted as a decoy near the cliff edge while his companions closed in upon the herd from behind. Drawing the herd toward the

FIGURE 3.1 Indian hunters approach a buffalo herd disguised in white wolf skins in a painting circa 1832 by George Catlin (1796–1892).

edge, he ducked into a crevice while they teetered and tumbled around him.

Stalking on foot was also practiced—actually, on hands and knees. The hunters hid beneath buffalo or wolf skins and crept toward the herd from downwind. These disguises would permit them to get close, the buffalo skin allowing a friendly approach and the wolf skin prompting the bulls to stand their ground, in either case enabling several good shots with bow and arrow before the buffalos were startled.

Hunting methods were elaborated once the horse was available. Stalking on foot was still done, as was the jump—the Sioux called it *piskun*. But the horse also allowed surprise charges and extended chases. After scouts located a herd, a large number of riders could approach and speedily descend on their quarry. They might stampede the buffalos, forcing them through narrow draws, into lines of single or paired animals, with the hunters riding alongside and selecting individual animals to kill. A single hunter rode up behind a running animal at full gallop, clutching his horse with only his legs and aiming his bow or gun, and shot for the heart. If placed correctly, his arrow or bullet entered behind the ribs and deeply, perhaps even passing entirely through the body, and dropping the animal at once.

Something like an Indian perspective on this dramatic business comes from Herman Lehmann, who rode as an Apache and Comanche warrior for eight years after being kidnapped, at age 11, from his parents' Texas farmstead:

> We would mount our best horses and rush out when the herds passed near. The one who got the first shot usually brought down the biggest and fastest, so we raced to be first. We would ride right in among the animals and that would stampede them. After we had emptied our guns, we would work our way out of the herd, but if it proved to be too large and the pack too thick, we might be carried in the mad rush of the infuriated herd for miles. Nothing would turn buffalo when stampeded. They would go right off a bluff, into a river, or anywhere. I once knew two Indians carried over a bluff into a great hole of water who perished among thousands of buffalo.

> In one of these stampedes you could not see the source of danger, even if you might have been able to avoid it, for there was so much dust it was blinding, and those behind you would press you on. I was once caught in a stampeding herd. My horse ran against a mesquite and fell. I fell under him, but up near a large log. The herd trampled my horse into sausage meat. I was stunned, bruised and skinned, but I got over it. You lovers of excitement, how would you enjoy being among millions of buffalo, enveloped in dust, and traveling at the rate of thirty miles an hour and not permitted to select the ground over which you ran?

(Greene 1972:60)

Another tactic was to surround a segment of the herd with an arc of riders and then begin circling. Even a few riders moving rapidly could contain a herd with this method, though often many riders would participate. As the hunters tightened their ring, the bulls would run circles around the cows and calves to protect them, exposing their flanks to the hunters' arrows. Eventually all the animals would become disoriented and stationary, easy prey in a thorough if not frenzied finish. In such surrounds, and also sometimes in running buffalo hunts and bear hunts, the Apaches, Comanches, and Kiowas also used a lance. The lance, its long shaft suitable for work from horseback, and thrust underhand or stabbed with both hands from overhead, is distinct from a throwing spear. Lances were 7 feet or more long and tipped with stone or trade iron points or the broken blade from an old saber. Lancers aimed for the buffalo's heart or kidneys. Although much attention has been given to the spectacular communal efforts in both Indian and non-Indian portrayals of buffalo hunting, a solitary hunter on horseback with either bow or lance could also be very effective in providing food for his family during the times of year that the buffalos were scattered.

As soon as the fray was over, butchering was begun where the animals fell. A lone hunter had this task to himself, but in large communal hunts women in twos and threes mainly did the job, with men assisting in the initial heavy steps of skinning and dismembering among some of the tribes. Butchering was done in a careful order: the forequarters were removed; the hide was slit along the spine, the sinew along the spine stripped out, and the hide peeled away around the carcass; the hindquarters were removed, the flanks and brisket removed, the entrails removed, and the ribs and meat broken away from the spine. Anything not consumed immediately was wrapped in the hide and taken to camp for further processing.

Almost every part of the buffalo was useful to Indian people, and the people had strong convictions, reinforced by stories and religious teachings, that it was immoral to waste what the animals provided. Many parts of the animal were eaten raw and warm right after it was slain. The organs, marrow, and blood were rich in iron and vitamins, especially important to the diet in the absence of much vegetable food, and these parts could not be preserved. The blood was drunk from the veins; brains, kidneys, stomach, intestines, marrow, and fat were often eaten directly, though kidneys and marrowbones were also roasted back at camp. The raw liver sprinkled with gall was a choice part, and the milk mixed with blood a delicacy. A hunter might quench his thirst with the contents of the paunch or, if the kill was a pregnant cow, with the amniotic fluid.

The muscle meat of the buffalo came from the hump, flanks, and brisket, and lent itself well to preservation. It was hauled to camp, cut into strips, and hung from racks to dry in the sun, and thus lasted for months. Dried meat could be smoked, pounded to a granular or fluffy consistency, and mixed with different kinds of berries, nuts, and fat, to make pemmican, a light, nutritious food that lasted indefinitely and was perfect for snacking or travel.

The buffalo also provided a great deal of the stuff for Indian shelter, clothing, and tools. Skin and bone were the plentiful, important raw materials on the Plains, much more so than wood or stone. Of the many inventories of Indian uses of the buffalo, one of the best was published in 1885 by W. P. Clark, an army captain and authority on Plains Indian sign language. Clark's inventory is summarized in the following chart. More information about how these products were made and used appears in Chapter 6.

TABLE 3.1 **Uses of the Bison**

skin	tipi covers, beds, blankets, robes, shirts, boots, bridles, lariats, whips, ropes, saddles, parfleches, cradles, quivers, sleds, glue
hair	ropes, lariats, pillows
horn	spoons, cups, dishes, powder horns, arrowheads, bows
sinew	thread, rope, bowstrings, bow backing
bones	fleshing tools, arrow straighteners, arrowheads, axes, knives, deadfall traps
tail	scabbards, handles, rattles
dung	fuel, baby powder

EXTERMINATION OF THE BUFFALO

In light of the all-important role of the buffalo in Plains Indian life, it is easy to see how devastating the disappearance of the great buffalo herds in the 1800s was. Much has been written about this demise, and while the direct disturbances caused by whites that are so often discussed were indeed a driving factor, the ecological circumstances that contributed to the near extinction of the bison were complex.

To begin, the natural climatic cycles of the semiarid Plains left species vulnerable when other challenges came into play. This was the case in the 1840s and 1850s, when a prolonged drought on the central and southern Plains corresponded with the intensification of human disturbances of the bison herds. One human-introduced problem for buffalos was the horse. Horses spread rapidly across the Plains as another pre-adapted "weed species" and competed with bison for grass and water. This was true of mustangs and tamed horses too, since Indians and eventually whites sheltered their horse herds in the wet canyons that would have earlier hosted buffalos. Cattle were also harmful in that they carried diseases such as bovine tuberculosis and anthrax that appear to have been transmitted to bison. Stresses of competition and disease were compounded because the migration patterns of the buffalos were interrupted: the proximity of numerous settlements by the mid-1800s and the 1869 completion of the transcontinental railroad segment across the Plains diverted bison from their usual refuge places.

Hunting practices of both Indians and whites contributed most directly to the bison decline. Well before the slaughter waged by whites in the 1870s, Indian hunting was probably affecting the stability of bison populations. In the 1780s, New Mexican Spanish governor Juan Bautista de Anza warned the Comanches that bison were a finite resource and tried to persuade them to settle and become farmers. They were not convinced, but

Spanish observations were prophetic. By the mid-1800s, Spanish, French, and American trading posts had tied the Plains into a global market economy in which buffalo pelts were desirable commodities. Available in exchange to the Indians were coveted manufactured goods. The robe trade encouraged Indians to kill in excess of their immediate subsistence needs.

The removals of some 80,000 Indians of various eastern tribes to Oklahoma during the mid-1800s added to already mounting pressures on the southern buffalo herds. Periods of buffalo scarcity and starvation are recorded during the 1840s and 1850s. Even those Indians who continued to observe traditions of conservation may have added to the cycle of decline, for it was a practice when hunting to select buffalo cows of breeding age, because their meat was tender and their hides the best size and thickness for adult-size robes, and therefore natural reproduction rates were hindered.

During the robe trade era non-Indians also had an impact on buffalo populations. Hispanic hide hunters from New Mexico called *ciboleros* harvested thousands of animals each year from the Southern Plains, while travelers on the Santa Fe Trail also took a share. But the coup de grace was the white extermination campaign that accompanied the final expansion of settlement following the Civil War. Industrial trends from the east encouraged these great hunts. First, as railroads crept west, there was a demand for bison meat to feed the crews. Then, in the late 1860s commercial tanning processes were developed that allowed buffalo skin to be turned into leather for clothing, luggage, and machinery drive belts, creating an expanded market for hides. With the completion of the transcontinental railroad in 1869, sellers and buyers alike had a ready means for transporting the hides. The railroad also cut off the north–south migration routes of the buffalo, creating two great isolated herds on either side of the tracks. The larger southern herd was decimated between 1874 and 1878. The slaughter was repeated in the north between 1880 and 1884.

Several thousand non-Indian hide hunters and skinners flooded onto the Plains to make their fortunes. Working typically in outfits of 4–12 men, they set up camps for three months at a time, frequently in territory that had previously been assigned by treaty as Indian land. Armed with powerful and precise Sharps rifles, the hunters often shot from "stands" at some distance downwind from the herds, picking off the outer animals systematically, sometimes for hours, before the herd stampeded. In this manner, they might kill a hundred or more animals in a day. The skinners then went to work with their knives, using their horses and wagons to help rip the hides off the carcasses. The fresh hides were hauled to camp for drying and stacking. Some of the camps quickly evolved into "hide towns," centers for buyers and suppliers, and some hide towns in turn became major settlements.

Early on it became evident to frontier military commanders that the hunters were helping to weaken resistant tribes. In 1875, U.S. Army General Phil Sheridan appeared before the Texas Legislature to oppose a bill that would have protected the buffalo. His words (they have been recorded in different versions) are worth quoting in full:

> These men [the hide hunters] have done more in the last two years and will do more in the next year, to settle the vexed Indian question, than the entire regular army has done in the last thirty years. They are destroying the Indians' commissary; and it is a well-known fact that an army losing its base of supplies is placed at a great disadvantage. Send them powder and lead, if you will; but, for the sake of a lasting peace, let them kill, skin, and sell until the buffaloes are exterminated. Then your prairies can be covered with speckled cattle, and the festive cowboy, who follows the hunter as a second forerunner of advanced civilization.
>
> (quoted in Cook 1989:113)

Thus, Sheridan and his kind clearly understood the importance of the buffalo to Indian life, and the annihilation of the species became both a military imperative and a necessity before ranching and farming could be widely practiced. It is probably not accurate, however, as the historian Dan Flores has pointed out, to paint the buffalo demise as a well-planned military strategy. Rather, it was the result of ecological trends and unbridled market forces, and an absence of policies for the protection of the species and the Indian populations that depended on it.

It has been estimated that during 1872–1874, nearly 1.5 million buffalo hides were shipped east from Nebraska and Kansas railheads and that white hunters actually killed twice this number. In 1882, the peak year for hide prices and the coup de grace to the northern herds, 200,000 hides were shipped by rail out of the Dakotas and Montana. Apart from the hides, only salt tongues and cured hams could be safely sent to eastern markets, since refrigeration was still in its infancy. Thousands of animals were shot simply for sport. All told, the waste of animals was enormous and dramatically at odds with Indian ethic dictating the thorough use of resources.

Another big business on the Southern Plains involved the collection and shipping of buffalo bones. Beginning about 1870, but increasing markedly with the mid-1870s' buffalo slaughter, this trade supplied eastern industry with raw material for buttons, china, bone meal, and calcium phosphate used in sugar refining. Hundreds of bone pickers ranged over the South Plains, hauling the bones they gathered in huge wagon trains over "bone roads" to places along the railways that crossed Kansas or encroached from East Texas. Freighters bringing supplies to the frontier forts also hauled bone on their return trips. Enormous bone piles grew along the tracks, sad monuments to a mass extinction. The bone business did not affect Indian people directly, but it was another means by which non-Indian settlers survived during the critical period of

Plains occupation, and it hastened the growth of non-Indian travel routes across the area.

By 1884 the bison was virtually extinct. The disorientation and starvation imposed on Indian people were devastating. The apparent rapidity of the extinction must have seemed unbelievable to them. In tribal traditions, the story of the release of the buffalos was reversed, and the last tired animals were said to have been swallowed by the earth. Domestic cattle, of which there were never enough available in the early days of subjugation, made a poor but necessary substitute for the mighty bison. It would be more than a generation before the few remaining buffalos were propagated in captivity enough that total extinction was prevented.

By the mid-twentieth century buffalos were being raised in stable populations, either on game preserves or on commercial ranches for meat. Some of these enterprises have been managed by Indian people and tribes. In 1990, the Intertribal Bison Cooperative was formed to promote the reintroduction of bison to tribal lands, and by 2004 this co-op involved 42 tribes overseeing more than 8,000 animals. In 1997, the modern Wind River Shoshone Tribe was marketing buffalo meat and hides at Indian gatherings throughout the west.

Through such Indian and non-Indian sources, buffalo products are again available to support traditional practices. When a Comanche tribal delegation visited Fredericksburg, Texas, in May 1997 to commemorate an old treaty, it treated the entire community to a feast of buffalo, served out of the only practical container—a large blue plastic children's wading pool. And three years earlier, Indian people were treated to what many took to be an omen of cultural survival: the birth of a female white buffalo calf, the first known in the twentieth century. Traditionalists flocked to the farm of non-Indians Dave and Valerie Heider in Janesville, Wisconsin, to be in the presence of this tie with the Native practical and spiritual past. Some interpreted the birth as the prophesied return of White Buffalo Calf Woman. In these ways the buffalo survives as a potent symbol of Plains Indian life, long after its elimination as the principle source of food and shelter.

OTHER GAME ANIMALS

The significance of the buffalo should not overshadow the role of many other animals in Plains Indian subsistence. Deer, elk, and pronghorns were also major sources of meat and leather. They were taken with a variety of techniques similar to those used in hunting buffalos. For instance, pronghorns (technically not antelopes, though often called that) were chased down or surrounded by large parties under the direction of a medicine man with power to attract the curious, swift creatures. Grizzly and black bears were valued for their skins, oil, and claws, and bighorn sheep for their skins and also horn material, used to make bows and spoons. Small mammals such as rabbits, skunks, opossums, badgers, and porcupines made up a significant part of the diet when big game could not be found. These animals were often roasted whole, on a spit or simply by throwing them on hot embers, the fire singing off the hair. The peltries of foxes, beavers, otters, and muskrats were important as insulation and decoration, and even more so as trade items when the global fur trade was extended into the Plains by non-Indians, and ermine (white weasel) skins were valued as an emblem of chiefly achievement and suspended from the temples of war bonnets. Roasted grasshoppers were a snack for children, and wild honey was enjoyed whenever someone was willing to brave the process of smoking the bees away from their hive.

In general, the Plains tribes did not eat fish, reptiles, or amphibians. Though the "absence" of fishing has been often noted as a characteristic of Plains cultures, there were many exceptions. When game was scarce, the Plains Crees built V-shaped weirs of lashed, upright sticks across streams to funnel migrating fish into a basket trap. The Mandans, Hidatsas, and Arikaras regularly trapped catfish in this manner along the Upper Missouri River where their villages were located, and they considered the right to make a fish trap a ritual privilege. Tribes near the Rocky Mountains occasionally ate trout and whitefish. In addition to the basket trap, spears and arrows were used to kill fish, but nets and fishhooks were apparently not used prior to widespread contact with non-Indians. Another common exception to the fish-and-reptile ban was the roasting of turtles in their shells.

Birds also had an ambiguous place in the diet. While ducks and geese were hunted for food, land wildfowl such as turkeys and prairie chickens were considered off limits by most of the tribes, under the belief that the cowardly ways of these birds would be transmitted to someone who ate them. In times of hunger, however, nearly any food taboo might be suspended.

THE HORSE

The horse, along with the buffalo, was one of two natural factors that made the historic Plains Indian culture as we know it possible. The importance of the horse to Plains culture was certainly celebrated in Indian tradition and noted by numerous early observers, but it first received deep scholarly treatment in a 1914 article entitled "The Influence of the Horse in the Development of Plains Culture," by Clark Wissler, a prominent researcher at the American Museum of Natural History in New York. In his later writings, Wissler went so far as to define the historic era of Plains Indian life as the "Horse Culture Period." This period, Wissler proposed, spanned A.D. 1540–1880, though in fact the tribes in question did not receive the horse until well after 1540, and many had been forced to cease their nomadic, horse herding lifestyle before 1880.

Why was Wissler so enthusiastic about the influence of the horse? He understood, as Indian people did from direct experience, that the horse as an ecological and cultural element was fundamental to human life on the historic Plains. He further understood that the horse had caused dramatic alterations in human life. Wissler concluded that many of the cultural changes resulting from adoption of the horse were extensions or enhancements or prior practices, rather than entirely new cultural traits. Even so, the changes brought by the horse were remarkable, all the more so because they happened so quickly. In one sense, the horse spread across the Plains gradually, over several decades. Yet in relative historical terms, the adjustment of Indian people to this new form of technology was rapid and thorough.

The modern domestic horse, *Equus caballus*, evolved in Asia and Europe from a series of smaller animals that flourished in North America after 65 million years ago. One ancestor species migrated to Asia, Europe, and South America from North America during the Ice Age. In the New World, the horse then became extinct along with many other kinds of grass-eating animals on account of the climatic changes that accompanied the end of glaciation, and probably owing as well to human hunting. In the steppe grasslands of Eurasia, however, horses continued to thrive, and at some unknown point they were tamed for riding and later plowing.

The horse was reintroduced to the Americas by European explorers, beginning with Columbus in the 1490s. Spanish conquistadors brought horses to the mainland from breeding sites established in the Caribbean islands: Cortez in his campaigns against the natives of Mexico and Honduras beginning in 1519; Coronado and De Soto, the former exploring the present U.S. southwest and latter the southeast, both in 1541. Their horses were of a breed from the Andalusia region of southern Spain, derived from stock introduced from North Africa during the Islamic invasions, and known as Berbers or "barbs." Because of their evolutionary history, horses were pre-adapted to the New World grasslands, and barbs were right at home on the Southern Plains, which resembled the dry, rugged areas of Spain.

Earlier writers supposed that Indians first acquired horses that had been lost or abandoned

FIGURE 3.2 *Photo entitled* The Talk *by Edward S. Curtis (1868–1952) shows three typical Indian horses at rest with their Crow riders, 1905.*

by the Coronado and De Soto expeditions. That is why Wissler proposed that the "Horse Culture Period" began in 1540, and he then assumed that horses would have been widespread among the Plains Indians by 1600. This origin proved unlikely. A review of the muster roles of the Coronado expedition showed that, of 558 horses, only two were mares. The likelihood that these animals escaped to stock the Plains is extremely remote. Similar conclusions were reached about the De Soto foray. Also, there is no mention in Spanish records of stray horses or mounted Indians for 100 years after the great expeditions.

Evidence suggests instead that Indians started acquiring horses directly from the Spanish settlements around 1650. The earliest center of diffusion was Santa Fe/Pecos, New Mexico, and the first tribes to get horses, apart from the Pueblo Indians at the settlements, were the nearby Apaches and Utes, followed by the Comanches and Kiowas. They acquired the animals by trade and theft. The revolt of the New Mexico Pueblo communities against Spanish rule in 1680 and subsequent turmoil probably freed a large number of horses for Indian use. The Spanish settlements at San Antonio, Texas, became a second major source of Indian horses, supplying the Caddo villages of northeast Texas as well as the Apaches by the late 1600s.

As certain tribes moved south toward these sources during the 1600s and 1700s, they took up positions in a chain of distribution. One route ran directly north from Texas and New Mexico to the Upper Missouri. On this route, the Kiowas, Kiowa Apaches, Comanches, Cheyennes, and Arapahos took horse to the villages of the Mandans,

Hidatsas, and Arikaras, from whence they were further distributed to the Siouan and Algonquian tribes of the north. Another route with the same end points ran along the Rocky Mountains; this trade involved the Utes, Comanches, Shoshones, and Crows. The Shoshones diverted some of this trade to the far northwest, supplying such groups as the Nez Perce and Blackfoots. The Caddo and Wichita villages in Texas and Oklahoma also served a middleman role like that of the Upper Missouri villages.

Therefore, the diffusion of the horse was from south to north, and gradual; not until the late 1700s were the northern tribes supplied. When the French Canadian explorer La Vérendrye went with some Assiniboines to visit the Mandans in 1738, neither tribe had horses; but a few years later his son found that the Mandans had received some, probably from some Kiowas. Lewis and Clark reported that in 1805 the Shoshones had a large herd, but in 1806 it was observed that the more northerly Ojibwas were just learning to ride.

By the 1830s, once horses were widely adopted, another pattern of Indian horse trade emerged, in which animals were driven from the Spanish southwest to eager Anglo settlers waiting on the eastern fringes of the Plains. Horse taken from deep within Mexico, from Texas, or from New Mexico (these including animals which may have originated in California) were moved by intertribal trade and theft eastward to St. Louis, Missouri. From there they were ridden west again! Also, once this horse trading and raiding activity was widespread, escaped horses became more common, and wild horse herds became a source from which Indians could increase their stocks, although it was generally considered less work to buy or steal a tamed horse than to capture and break a wild one. Mustang herds, then, were at best a secondary source of Indian horses, and were not the main early source as was once supposed.

Before the horse, the only domesticated animal available to Plains Indians was the dog. It is presumed that dogs were brought to North America from Asia by the earliest human migrants. These were true domestic dogs (a descendant of some common wolf-dog ancestor of the Pliocene), not tamed wolves or coyotes, although there is some evidence that Plains Indians occasionally cross-bred their dogs with wild coyotes by tying female dogs in heat away from camp where they could be approached by the wild canids. It is difficult to reconstruct the breeds that possibly existed, but it is known that aside from the Eskimo dog, there were two general types of Indian dog—larger and smaller. The larger, less a pet and more of a work animal, was more common on the Plains. These animals were of medium to large size by modern standards, with large erect ears, a bushy curling tail, and a rough coat in gray, tan, black, and white, in various mixtures.

Dogs would have been very important for their work in hunting and hauling in prehistoric times, and they remained valuable well after the advent of the horse, as historic accounts and paintings of Indian camps still typically show a profusion of dogs. In pre-horse days, the Crows measured a man's wealth in the number of dogs he owned—as many as 100. Even in later times, dogs were helpful in hunting, for example, helping to tree porcupines. Cheyennes hunted beavers by breaking their dam to drain the pond, then sending dogs into the exposed entrances of the lodges to flush the beavers out, upon which they were clubbed. But dogs had perhaps the most impact on the Indian economy as beasts of burden. Indians applied dog power using two methods, both given names by the early French observers: *travois* and *pannier*. The travois was an A-frame of poles attached to the dog with a collar or harness and loaded with goods to be dragged. The pannier was a balanced pair of heavy packs hung over the dog's back. With these simple technologies, Indians significantly increased their ability to migrate and trade.

Dogs were also a source of human food. Archaeologists sometimes find their butchered remains amid the bison skeletons at ancient kill sites. In the Historic Period they were mainly eaten only in emergencies or in special feasts. George Catlin, writing while among the Sioux in the

FIGURE 3.3 Blackfoot woman and man with horse travois and dog.
Photo circa 1907 by Edward S. Curtis.

1830s, called the dog feast "the most undoubted evidence they could give us of their friendship" (1973, I:230). Among the Lakotas today, pet puppies are named to distinguish them from their anonymous brothers and sisters destined for the ceremonial stewpot, and it is assumed that a similar distinction between family and edible dogs was drawn in the old days. Catlin nevertheless believed that by serving such close animal companions as food in welcoming feasts, Indians were expressing the solemnity of their friendship vows in the most poignant way they knew. The Arapahos were another group known for eating dog flesh, such that their neighbors, the Comanches, called them the Sariteka, "Dog Eaters." Other tribes, such as the Comanches and Shoshones, held dog eating to be taboo, recognizing the close relationship between dogs and humans, and also the kinship of dogs with coyotes and wolves, which were seen as mythological characters.

Once the importance of the dog is recognized, it is easier to understand how the Plains Indians perceived the horse fitting into the animal kingdom and their own lives. Native names for the horse further this understanding, since some of the names—"medicine dog," "seven dogs," "elk dog"—cast the newer animal as a kind of super-dog, reflecting the function of horses in replacing dogs in facets of everyday work. The horse was better than the dog for pulling travois or carrying loads; it could subsist on grass and thus freed humans from the requirement to share hunted meat with their transportation animals; and, it yielded useful products of hide and hair, as well as more meat than the dog. The name "elk dog" and others like it, however, show that for many groups the horse appeared to resemble a giant elk or deer. The Comanches actually used three terms for "horse." Their general term, *tuhuya*, is traceable to the Shoshonean root language of Comanche, where it signifies a cervine (deer family) animal. Another word, *puuku*, meant a particular horse, such as one's own, favorite mount; in earlier Shoshonean use, this word meant "pet," as might be applied to a child's captive antelope. A third Comanche word, *kobe*, referred to a wild horse, and appears to have been derived from the Spanish word for horse, *cabello*.

The Comanche terms show that people found it useful to specify how close or distant the animal was in their personal experience. This practice was not unlike the Lakota distinction between familiar and distant (and thus edible) dogs.

The closeness that people felt toward horses was expressed in a number of ways. Brave Buffalo, a Teton, gave this introduction to a sequence of songs about horses that he recorded around 1911:

> Of all the animals, the horse is the best friend of the Indian, for without it he could not go on long journeys. A horse is the Indian's most valuable piece of property. If an Indian wishes to gain something, he promises his horse that if the horse will help him he will paint it with native dye, that all may see that help has come to him through the aid of his horse.
>
> (Densmore 1918:298)

Brave Buffalo and companions Two Shields and Śiyaka sang the following songs used "to make a horse swift and sure," which capture their sense of admiration in poetic terms:

friend
my horse
flies like a bird
as it runs

daybreak
appears
when
a horse
neighs

the four winds are blowing
some horses
are coming

see them
prancing
they come
neighing
they come
a Horse nation

see them
prancing
they come
neighing
they come

chasing
they walked
this
Horse nation
chasing
they walked

—*(Ibid.:299–303)*

Notwithstanding the kinship that people felt toward their mounts, there is no doubt that horses and mules were a significant food source for the Plains Indians. In this regard, again, the position of the horse resembled that of the dog. The food value of the horse has often been overlooked by scholars and downplayed within tribal cultures. The painted hide "calendar" or yearly history of Dohausan, a Kiowa, includes an icon for the summer of 1879 referred to as "the horse eating sun dance"; buffalos were extinct in Kiowa territory by this year, and Kiowas resorted to eating their horses. During journeys—camp movements, war expeditions, escapes after a raid—it often made sense to devour a horse from the herd instead of attempting to hunt. But wild horses were also taken for eating. Herman Lehmann and his Comanche captors " . . . killed a great many mustangs and roasted them. We would cut off a large slice, hair, hide and all, throw it on the coals and see it fry . . . .The part right under the hide was always nice and tender. Mustangs are very palatable . . . ." (Greene 1972:110).

Perhaps eating one's means of transportation was an especially obvious form of conspicuous consumption, for horsemeat was also considered a prestige food. Colonel Richard Dodge wrote, "The Comanches are extremely fond of horseflesh, preferring it to beef or even buffalo. The most delicate and delicious dish that a Comanche can set before his most distinguished guest is the foetus of a mare boiled in its own liquid" (1882:277). There are numerous other references about these practices in the accounts of white observers. Horse eating appears to have been more common in the south, owing no doubt to the easier availability of horses there. The Crows were so prone to accumulating what live horses they could, that they "never dreamt of milking mares or eating horseflesh" (Lowie 1983:223).

INDIAN HORSEMANSHIP

The elaborate repertoire of skills and knowledge that Indian people developed in order to make use

of the horse is amazing by itself, but even more so because it was firmly embedded in cultural practice within a few generations. A number of U.S. Army officers, who had been trained in a comparative perspective on the history of horsemanship, including Randolph B. Marcy and Richard I. Dodge, proclaimed in their writings that the Plains tribes were among the best light cavalry the world had known. Indian riding skills and tricks were admirable to outsiders, and within tribal culture they received much emphasis.

Men and women alike rode astride; they mounted from the right side (opposite European practice), the men by jumping and the women by climbing and sliding one foot over the middle of

FIGURE 3.4   Blackfoot man on horseback. Illustration circa 1833 by Karl Bodmer (1809–1893).

the seat. They practiced many options in saddling the horse. Often they used a simple pad saddle, made from three sections of stuffed hide sewn together front to back, the seams acting as joints so the pad would conform to the horse's back. The pad saddle had one strap to hold it around the horse's belly and two relatively short stirrup straps. Stirrups were fashioned from light wood covered in shrunken rawhide. Under the pad saddle, they placed a small piece of furred hide, from a buffalo for example, to act like a saddle blanket. Indians also rode on full saddles that appear to have been modeled from early Spanish ones. There were several styles, but all used a light frame of wood and sometimes elk or deer horn pieces, covered in shrunken rawhide and padded over and under with buffalo fur. The cantles and pommels were high, especially on women's saddles. Saddles crafted by non-Indians were welcomed when available, and people rode bareback with ease for short trips and in emergency situations.

Using short stirrups, the rider was able to steer the horse mainly with knee pressure, which freed the hands to use weapons in hunting or combat. If need be, the rider simply grasped the horse's mane to hold on. Bridles and reins were also used at times, however. The simplest rein was made by weaving lengths of extra horsehair into the horse's mane. Woven horsehair or leather was also fashioned into various kinds of bridles that looped around either the lower jaw or the nose of the animal, with one or two reins extending back to the rider. Indian tack did not include bits, but again, Indian riders accepted non-Indian tack when it was available. Metal spurs could be gotten in trade but were seldom worn; instead, most every rider carried a quirt for urging the horse on.

Indian riders were capable of remarkable maneuvers. Hanging with his arm through a loop woven into the horse's mane, a rider could totally shield himself behind his horse's body and even shoot arrows from beneath the horse's neck at a full gallop. From the same position, he could scoop up a fallen comrade. If knocked off in battle, he could remount by springing over the horse's hindquarters; if ahead during a horserace, he could flip around backwards in the saddle to jeer at his competitors. According to a Blackfoot elder, some Piegan warriors were adept at dismounting over the rear of their horse in a somersault, landing ready for armed combat on foot. Such skills were honed through continuous drilling and games. Learning began early, as children were placed in the saddle as soon as they could keep from falling off.

Indians developed a similarly rich set of skills for obtaining, breaking, and training horses. Trading for horses involved a good eye for horse qualities and temperament and clever bargaining. The horse raid was a specialized attack in which the raiders displayed incredible patience and stealth. The U.S. military reported thefts from guarded corrals and from bivouacs in which the horses were tied next to their sleeping owners. The capture and breaking of mustangs were less risky but required more work overall. Wild horses had to be tracked, spotted, and pursued over a long course. Their eyesight was phenomenally keen and their caution extreme, and they would usually bolt if humans got within a mile of them. But by charging upon them from a ravine or from behind a hill, Indian wranglers on horseback could wield a lasso; once the loop of this 15-foot rope was thrown over the mustang's neck, the rider dropped to the ground and choked the animal into submission. Keeping tension on the noose, and keeping the horse from rolling on its back to flail its hooves in defense, he gradually approached hand over hand, until he could hobble the animal, cover its face with his hands, and breathe into its nostrils. Pretty soon the horse was docile enough to lead back to camp.

Another capture technique, perhaps more a matter of legend than common practice, was called "creasing." Indian mustangers found that they could temporarily stun a horse by grazing its neck bones with a gunshot. Once the horse was down, paralyzed, they could rope and hobble it before it recovered. This procedure required exceptional aim, and it was not unusual for the horse to be killed by a bullet placed a little too low. Frontier artist George Catlin, stalking mustangs during his stay at a Comanche village in 1834, was ashamed when he broke the neck of one horse while attempting the technique. Catlin lamented that even when a horse did survive creasing, its spirit was destroyed. Creasing was tried mainly in the south, perhaps because wild horses were more plentiful there, while northern tribes like the Blackfoots seldom found it a worthwhile alternative to roping.

Boys or men would work at breaking horses that had reached the age of two or three. After mounting from another horse alongside, the wrangler would tire the horse by riding it into a creek or pond. If the horse was going to pull a travois, it might be trained by dragging a weighted buffalo hide. If destined for the hunt or battle, the horse had a long rope tied around its lower jaw, which would dangle between its feet and jerk its head every time it was stepped on; in this way the horse was conditioned not to step on anything trailing from itself, so that in the heat of action it would not yank its rider off. More conditioning was done by firing guns around the horse to get it used to the noise of battle. Special hunting horses called "buffalo runners" were trained to veer sideways when they heard the twang of a bowstring, to get out of the way of a falling buffalo. Once the horse was tamed and ready for work, extra measures were taken to increase its performance. Powered medicines intended to increase its speed were blown up its nostrils. Or, the nostrils were slit up to the gristle line to open them up more and make horse better winded.

Indian riders got much better speed and mileage out of their mounts than did their non-Indian adversaries. Their horses were small and scrappy to begin with and well adapted to eating Plains grasses. (U.S. Cavalry horses were large and strong, but they had to be fed grain, so that long trips with them had to be supported with slow-moving grain wagons.) Indians displayed a harsh attitude toward their animals, but at the same time it was clear that they greatly valued them. They preferred not to shoe their horses, except that tribes along the Upper Missouri made a rawhide boot for protection in the snow. A number of tribes hardened tender hooves by walking the horse over a dying fire or smoking its feet with sage. Ensuring that the horse herds had good grazing and water was a main concern, dictating travel and campsites perhaps as much as the availability of game. In the wintertime when grass was scarce or under snow cover, especially in the north, tree bark was an important secondary food for horses. Some tribes would even cut cottonwood boughs for feed, and the availability of trees was a factor influencing their herds' range and size.

THE HORSE AS AN INFLUENCE ON CULTURE

To summarize the significance of the horse in forming Plains Indian culture, it can be understood as a factor in three areas: migration, the economy, and human psychology.

Once people enjoyed the mobility that the horse provided, they were able to occupy the Plains more widely. Prior to the horse, the great distance between dependable water holes in some sections of the High Plains was a hindrance to travel and settlement. Journeying on horseback reduced the travel time between water sources and effectively shrunk the Plains for human travelers. The horse also permitted any group of people to make use of a wider range of environments across the Plains, maximizing the array of resources that they could exploit. Not only could the group travel readily among natural resource areas, but it could also launch quick, low-mortality raids to fend off competitors from its hunting or gardening territory, to disrupt competitive trade, or to plunder other settlements. The horse also gave a huge advantage in buffalo hunting, resulting in a more dependable food supply, and it was itself an emergency food when bison were scarce. Beyond allowing greater occupation of the Plains, the horse impelled it, for once groups became dedicated to horse use, they were drawn toward the sources of livestock, which for some were the Mexican settlements of New Mexico and Texas and for others the trade routes and trade centers of the central High Plains.

The horse also became a major economic factor within and between social groups. It became a standard of value and a means of exchange. The prowess in raiding and trading that allowed a man to accumulate many horses was evidenced by the size of his herd. Differences in horse wealth began to lead to distinctions between richer and poorer individuals, so that some tribes, such as the Comanches and Kiowas, had named categories that begin to look like social classes. Horse then became a common payment for other desired items such as firearms. Another well-known function was the transfer of horses from the groom's family to the bride's family to cement a marriage. Legal damages such as those collected for adultery or accidental homicide were also typically paid in horses. And when a man died, his horses were his main worldly possessions, to be distributed among his heirs, except some favorites that might be killed at his gravesite to accompany him in the afterlife.

The horse would ultimately influence people's attitudes and ways of thinking. Dedication to the growth and maintenance of the horse herds became a rallying point for societies, encouraging cooperation in other matters necessary for survival. When the Comanche elder Post Oak Jim told ethnographer Ad Hoebel in 1933 that some men loved their horses better than their wives, he was probably not denigrating women (or men) so much as trying to convey the sense of gratitude that people felt toward the basis of their lifestyle. Furthermore, the power that mounted people held over their neighbors and enemies who did not have horses must have been intoxicating. Horse

culture put a premium on daring and a love of freedom and mobility. Despite the hardships of the hunting life, horse Indians must have enjoyed a supreme sense of control over their lives and the land they wandered. "I am like the bird flying through the air," said the Comanche leader Buffalo Hump during an 1844 peace talk with Sam Houston, "I can travel and am always traveling . . . " (Winfrey and Day 1995, II:111).

Thus, the horse resulted in new technologies, new subsistence strategies, and new kinds of societies. Although Indians of the Plains were technically hunter-gatherers, they came to resemble people of another subsistence mode, the pastoralists. Pastoralists may be defined as people who either obtain the majority of their food from herd animals or center their activities around the needs and behaviors of their herd animals. Pastoralists are often nomadic, occupying grasslands or arid lands not well suited to agriculture and pursuing a raid-and-trade relationship with neighboring settled peoples. Because of their reliance on horse herds and the buffalo, the Plains Indians essentially matched this characterization.

WILD AND DOMESTIC PLANTS

My whole trust is in Mother Corn.

—Song of Roaming Chief, Pawnee singer
(Densmore 1929:92–93)

With all the attention given to the flash of the horse and buffalo lifestyle, it would be easy to overlook the importance of wild and cultivated plants in the lives of the Plains Indians. In fact, plant foods, whether gathered or grown, made up a critical part of every tribe's diet. Those who gardened raised corn, beans, pumpkins and other kinds of squash, and sunflowers. This gardening adaptation allowed early Indian populations to inhabit the High Plains along river courses, and although the importance of gardening waned somewhat as the buffalo, horse, and trading economy flourished in the 1800s, these old settlers persisted as important anchor populations. Those tribes that were fully nomadic and did not garden themselves still depended on vegetable foods, which they got from the semi-sedentary horticultural tribes through trade. And, all the tribes were also familiar with a large number of wild fruits, seeds, and tubers.

Corn was the primary crop. Since *corn* originally referred to any of a number of grains, some scholars have preferred the term *maize*, derived from the Taino (West Indies) Indian name *mahiz*, via Spanish. Either word is appropriate for the plant classified as *Zea mays*, a mutant version of an edible warm-weather grass called *teosinte*, first cultivated about 4,700 years ago in southern Mexico. So transformed was this species through selective breeding that the wild form no longer exists, and the domesticated version cannot survive and reproduce without human activity. Corn cultivation spread northward from Mexico very gradually and reached the Great Plains via adjacent regions to the southeast and southwest. Over the centuries, Indians bred a variety of strains that were adapted to various climate and soil types. On the Plains, they had all of the general types of corn recognized today, including flour, flint, dent, sweet or "sugar" corn, and popcorn. For most of these types, there were multiple varieties, sometimes seven or eight—of white, yellow, blue, red, and mixed coloration—maintained through selective breeding and by planting the varieties at a distance from each other.

Corn produces more grain per plant than wheat or rice, but compared to the other important cereal crops, it contains relatively little protein, niacin, or the amino acids that the body needs to make niacin. Indians found these essential nutrients instead in the beans they grew along with corn. Squash, also commonly cultivated in this setting, also brought nutrients to the mix, so that corn, beans, and squash have been referred to as the "three sisters." Meat from buffalo hunts was

another important source of complementary nutrients. Thus, corn fit well within the wider array of available foods.

Corn requires plenty of water, warm nights, and hot but not scorching daytime weather to produce maximum yields. The best conditions for growing corn without modern irrigation and fertilization are found east of the 100th meridian (roughly the east half of the Dakotas, Nebraska, and Texas). Approaching that line, periodic local droughts made farming chancy and led to boom and bust years for Native settlers; much beyond that line, Indian people sometimes pioneered garden settlements but did not have long-term success. Therefore, in the Historic Period it was mainly certain Siouan tribes, occupying the North and Central Plains from the east, and the Caddoans from the southeast, who relied on gardening. Their settlements were made along major rivers and their tributaries. The Arikaras, Mandans, and Hidatsas planted along the upper Missouri River, the Santees on the upper Mississippi, and the Pawnees along the Platte, Loup, Republican, and Blue rivers in Nebraska. The Wichitas were found by Coronado east of the Great Bend of the Arkansas River in Kansas, and later they occupied the river valleys of Oklahoma and north-central Texas. The Caddos planted on the Red, Sabine, and Angelina rivers in East Texas. Some Apaches also practiced gardening in the canyons of the Texas Hill Country, carrying forth with techniques developed in the southwest and encouraged by the Spanish.

Planting and harvesting was done on a seasonal schedule that fit with the timing of hunts and migrations. The cultivating tribes typically dispersed in winter camps away from their summer villages, so gardening began upon their return in April. The actual planting might be started according to some nature sign like the sight of returning geese; the Omahas planted their squashes when the wild plums blossomed. The land was cleared and planted during the spring, and then the crops were left to grow while the

FIGURE 3.5 In a rare image of Plains Indian gardening, a woman of the Fort Berthold Reservation in North Dakota demonstrates traditional techniques, tending her corn and squash garden high above the Missouri River with a bison scapula hoe, 1914.

villagers went off for several weeks of nomadic summer buffalo hunting. Harvest began when they returned late August or early September. First, green corn was picked. Next, into October, the beans and squashes were collected, and finally mature corn was harvested right before the cold weather set in.

The pattern is more accurately called horticulture rather than agriculture, because it required less than constant work and modification of the landscape, relatively low levels of human energy to clear and grow the crops, with no animal traction, and only simple tools. There was no known

fertilization or irrigation, except occasional scant ditching from springs in the Central Plains, thought to reveal old influence from the Pueblo southwest spread by the Apaches. Instead, gardeners selected the moist sandy loam deposited by streams. Along major rivers, such soil could sometimes be found well above the current floodplain as well as in the river bottoms. But arable soil was always limited, so gardens were established good distances out from the riverside villages along all connected streams, for as much as 10 miles. By planting in varied places, gardeners balanced risk and helped to protect their crops from a single catastrophe.

Crops planted in the main river bottoms were best shielded from the harsh winds that scoured the open Plains, while those on the higher tributaries might be less likely to be washed out in a flood.

Brush was usually thick in these areas, so the first step was to clear it off. Piles of cut brush were allowed to dry and then burned. Often the stream bank would form a natural border for the cleared area, otherwise some of the brush and sticks might be formed into a crude boundary fence. Each household owned and worked its own plot, generally in the 3- to 5-acre range, sometimes less or more. These family plots functioned much like the "kitchen gardens" of white settlers who later came to the Plains. They were larger than what modern people think of as a garden, and when viewed together were extensive. Around the present site of downtown Waco, Texas, in 1824 the Waco tribe had 400 acres of corn, beans, pumpkins, and melons under cultivation, supporting a village of 60 houses and several hundred people. Curiously, the assemblage of gardens at a Pawnee village in Nebraska in the early 1800s also totaled an estimated 400 acres, suggesting that the possibilities for garden and village size were fairly consistent across the Plains, given the landscape and available technology.

Women did most or all or the clearing and planting, by hand and without plows. Their tool kit was modest but effective: an ax, a hoe made from a buffalo shoulder blade mounted on a stick, a pointed stick for dibbling, and perhaps a rake made from antlers. They mounded the soft loam into small hills about a foot across, forming them in rows with a couple feet between each hill. A set number of corn kernels were placed in each hill. A ritual leader such as the owner of sacred corn bundles might be present to bless the first seeds planted. Beans were planted in the spaces between the hills so that their vines would wrap around the corn stalks. The other crops were planted in a similar way but in separate areas. As the corn began to grow, the fields were hoed twice to keep out weeds, but by the time the stalks were about a foot high it was time for buffalo hunting, and then the gardens were pretty much neglected until harvest.

In a successful year, the typical yield with these methods was 20–30 bushels of corn per acre. The aim was to make enough to feed the family for the year, plus extra for trading and some left over for next year's seed. This was usually possible, barring the odd drought or plague of grasshoppers, and despite disturbance by hungry buffalos, deer, and raccoons. In comparison, early white settlers in the same territory probably got similar yields. They had some technical advantages, including horse-drawn plows, but the strains of corn they brought with them from their Midwestern farms were less well adapted to the drier Plains than native varieties. Modern mechanized agriculture, with improved corn varieties and the key addition of irrigation, is more productive in absolute terms, often yielding over 100 bushels an acre. However, the Indians' method of cultivation was much more efficient. They expended much less time and energy in proportion to what they gained in return of food calories than do modern commercial farmers with their machinery, fossil fuel consumption, chemical fertilizers and pesticides, irrigation systems, and radical modification of the landscape.

A wide range of preparation techniques assured that the crops would be used to their fullest potential. Corn was fixed in several ways. Green corn was roasted or boiled on the husk or dried on racks and the kernels were stripped for storage. Ripe corn was pounded into meal to make mush or hoecakes, parched, or turned into hominy by hulling it with lye made from ashes. It could be mixed with beans or wild vegetables or cooked with meat in soup. (Today, Indian people in rural Oklahoma like "Dutch Treat" brand dried corn for making soup because it reminds them of old-time parched corn.) A favorite method for preserving pumpkin was to cut it into strips that were dried and then woven into mats, later to be broken off in convenient pieces for eating.

Storage pits or *caches* were essential for preserving vegetable surpluses. Caches were dug near the summer houses in a cube or bell shape and carefully lined and sealed with layers of dried grass, earth, and stone, in a way that effectively minimized losses to rodents, insects, and moisture-induced mold.

In addition to the food crops, several Plains tribes grew tobacco. This stimulant, native to the New World, exists in many wild and domesticated species. Indian people treasured it for ceremonial and recreational smoking, generally in pipes, but also, on the Southern Plains, in cigarettes rolled from oak leaves. Tobacco was frequently blended with other plant material such as sumac leaves to make a smoking mixture known as *kinnikinick*. The Mandans, Hidatsas, and Arikaras grew enough to trade with other tribes. Because of its ritual import, however, tobacco was planted and harvested by men rather than women. The Cheyennes also grew it before they became fully nomadic. Among the nomadic groups, only the Crows, Blackfoots, and Sarcees raised tobacco—as their sole crop—and this unusual bit of farming was a kind of ceremonial vestige from earlier days when the tribes' ancestors were settled; thus, the tobacco they grew themselves was reserved for ritual use. Most nomadic groups depended totally on traders for their tobacco and favored varieties grown outside the Plains.

In assessing the importance of wild plants, it can first be noted that there was very little use of plant fiber for making material items. Rawhide, sinew, and horsehair took the place of vegetable fibers when making footwear, containers, sewing thread, and rope, and there was little basketry on the Plains. Wood, though essential for making bows, saddles, and stirrups, was not plentiful enough in the proper form to be used as lumber. But for food and medicine, the tradition of wild plant use was quite rich. In fact, Native knowledge of wild plants on the Plains was so full that it is not possible here to do more than a little overview.

The most common trees across the Plains were the cottonwood, willow, and cedar (juniper). The cottonwood was so dominant that in the Shoshonean languages the same word is used for "cottonwood" and "tree" in the generic sense. Cottonwood boughs made good winter food for horses. The statuesque cottonwood, with "alive" leaves that rustle in the slightest breeze; the willow, always a sign of life-giving water; and the evergreen, fragrant cedar all were given mystical significance and used in various rituals. The most pervasive of these uses was the making of dried cedar leaves into incense. Some trees were important for their wood: lodgepole pine and cedar for dwelling poles and hackberry and hickory for saddle frames and weapon shafts. Mulberry and hackberry trees produce edible fruit and mesquite trees grow seed pods that were grounded to make a kind of flour. In the Southern Plains, pecans were a very important food. These nuts are very high in fat content and could be gathered in abundance along rivers. Several tribes, such as the Omahas and Pawnees, made sugar from the sap of maples or box elders. The inner bark of the slippery elm was one of several sources of chewing gum, used to slake the thirst of travelers between water holes.

Among the small trees and shrubs, the bois d'arc or Osage orange was favored for making bows, and light springy dogwood was the favorite wood for arrows. Many tribes ate the hips of wild roses. Edible hazelnuts grow on shrubs, as do serviceberries and buffalo berries, which were major foods among the Blackfoot and other northern tribes. Women throughout the Plains gathered various wild plums ("sand plums") and cherries ("chokecherries"). The latter were made into a soup valued in ceremonial meals or mixed with minced dried buffalo meat and tallow to form pemmican or *wasna*, as the Sioux call it. In the south, prickly pear fruits and leaf pads were cleaned of their spines and eaten.

Roots and tubers provided starch in the diet. Wild carrots, hog peanuts, groundnuts, poppy mallows, prairie turnips, buffalo gourd roots, Jerusalem artichokes, bush morning glory roots, wild licorice, prairie clover roots, and wild onions were some of many subsurface plants dug for food. Yucca roots make suds when agitated in water that were used for shampoo. Roots, along with tree bark, leaves, nuts, and berries, supplied various dyes and stains used to color leather, hair, feathers, quills, and cloth. For instance, the color red could be drawn from dogwood or alder bark, wild plums or currants, or bloodroot. Leafy low-growing plants and grasses, herbs, and seeds were less important in the diet, though pigweed, ragweed, goosefoot, and milkweed were prepared in various ways. Bee balm was widely used as seasoning and medicine. Sage and sweet grass were aromatics similar in function to cedar.

The food and medicinal uses of these and other plants will be mentioned again in context. At this point, it is important to appreciate the general importance of plants in Plains subsistence.

Sources: Allen (1920); Barnard (1941); Bongianni and Mori (1985); Bowers (1991, 1992); Canty (1986); Catlin (1973); Clark (1982); Cook (1989); Dary (1974); Densmore (1918, 1929); R. I. Dodge (1882, 1959); T. A. Dodge (1890); Ewers (1955); Flores (2001); Gilmore (1977); Greene (1972); Kindscher (1987); Koch (1977); Lowie (1982, 1983); McDonald (1981); n.a. (1994); Powers (1977); Powers and Powers (1984); Reed (1952); Roe (1955); Smith (1979); St. Clair and Lowie (1909); Wallace and Hoebel (1952); Wedel (1986); Weltfish (1965); "White Magic" (1994); Will and Hyde (1964); Wilson (1917); Winfrey and Day (1995); and Wissler (1914, 1974).

CHAPTER SUMMARY

Plains Indians obtained food, shelter, and clothing as hunter-gatherers. Some tribes also practiced gardening. Owing to their dependence on bison and horse herds, the Plains Indians also resembled nomadic pastoralists. Great herds of bison provided much of the Indians' meat, hides for dwellings and clothing, and bone and horn for tools. Indian customs and social life centered around buffalo hunting. Market hunters eradicated the bison by the early 1880s, causing a fundamental crisis in the Indian way of life. Other animals, such as deer, elk, antelope, and small mammals, were also important sources of meat, skins, and furs. The horse was instrumental in Indian hunting, migration, and warfare. It was an ideal vehicle for human travel over the vast grass-lands and an improvement over the domesticated dog as a beast of burden. Horses were also used for their meat, hide, and hair. Horses were acquired from the Spanish and circulated through the Plains in the Indian trade system. Indians developed superb methods of training and riding and imbued the horse with cultural significance. Domesticated and wild plants were also important to Indian survival. Corn, supplemented with beans and squash, was the main crop. Tribes in the wetter eastern portions of the region formed large fixed villages supported by extensive gardens. All the tribes of the region relied on wild trees, shrubs, and small plants for fruits, nuts, tubers, wood, dyes, and medicines.

QUESTIONS FOR REVIEW

1. Discuss the general categories of Plains Indian subsistence practice.
2. Describe the demise of the great buffalo herds and explain why it was such a profound blow to the Plains Indian way of life.
3. Reconstruct the diffusion of the horse on the Plains and its adoption as a defining cultural trait in the region.
4. How were plants important in Plains Indian life? Discuss major crops, gardening techniques, and the use of wild plants.

CHAPTER 4

TRIBAL ORGANIZATION

While we are used to thinking of Indian people as living in tribes with particular names, many of the common ways of describing human organization on the Plains actually mask the complex realities of social and political life. It is necessary to understand the true variety of social units that Plains Indians participated in, and their structure and purposes. Apart from the large-order groups usually termed "tribes," these units include kinship-based bands and clans, as well as associations or clubs formed by non-kinsmen. Special attention should be paid to the Native names for these units, the reasons for forming them, and the leadership positions that emerge in them.

TRIBES, BANDS, AND CLANS

The Notion of Tribe

The word *tribe* has been used in a number of different and often contradictory ways. Originally, it was applied to segments of ancient state societies in Israel, Greece, and Rome. The Roman historian Tacitus described the various groups of Germanic people that the Romans

encountered as "tribes," also extending the meaning to groups outside the state. Many subsequent writers have applied the term very broadly to non-European societies without exactness about their size or degree of integration, although normally with the implication that tribal societies were primitive and European ones civilized. Others have proposed a very specific, though ultimately difficult to support, evolutionary meaning for "tribe," reserving it for societies in the middle range of complexity, between small hunting and gathering societies organized in bands and large, complex chiefdoms and states. In this usage the term denotes people living by horticulture, simple agriculture, or pastoralism.

It was the broader application of "tribe" that led to its conventional use by non-Indian explorers, government officials, and the general public in describing the polities of Native North Americans. During the twentieth century, the governments formed by American Indians on reservations and in other Native communities also perpetuated this convention by frequently naming and referring to their organizations as "tribes," although more recently the term "nation" has often replaced "tribe" in self-designations. This

FIGURE 4.1   *Gros Ventre party approaching camp in Montana, 1908.*

kind of Native response to outsiders' expectations of structure and leadership was also common during the period of subjugation, when groups were essentially forced to represent themselves as "tribes" with "chiefs" in order to negotiate with colonizers. In recognition of this phenomenon, another proposed technical way of defining "tribe" is as a kind of organization produced from the interaction between large powerful state societies and the smaller societies they colonize. All of these uses of the term "tribe," however, tell us more about non-Indian perceptions of other people than about the people themselves.

Thus, American Indian people and those interested in their way of life are stuck with a term that has many meanings, no one of which can be supported theoretically. Still, it would be very difficult to avoid talking about Indian groups as

tribes because the word has become ingrained in our thinking and writing; this book will not avoid the word. But it is most useful to approach the term critically—to consider some of the supposed characteristics of tribes and ask whether they apply to particular Plains populations of the pre-reservation era. These criteria are both cultural and political in nature.

One idea is that members of a tribe share a common language. In general, common language is evident among most of the groups customarily recognized on the Plains as tribes. Sometimes, though, language is not uniform or totally distinctive. The wide-ranging Comanches displayed multiple dialects with different words and pronunciations. These differences were evident as late as World War II, when Comanche men were brought together in the U.S. Army to serve as "code talkers" (native-language radio operators) and had to agree on a fully common vocabulary. At the same time, the Comanche language is virtually identical to that of the Shoshones to the west of the Plains; on the basis of language alone, one might argue that the Comanches and Shoshones composed one tribe. Other measures of cultural homogeneity have also been attached to the idea of tribe, and again on the Plains, groups often display unity. The particulars of tipi construction, moccasin shape, arrow decoration, and the colors and designs of beadwork motifs are some of the many ways that people announced their group affiliation.

Geographic continuity is another common marker of the so-called tribe. Plains groups could be said to have contiguous territories but only in an artificial way. They generally maintained an internal sense of range and boundary, but the nomadic groups traveled far and wide and territories were subject to continual renegotiation. It has been argued that tribal groups derive their sense of spatial bounding because of conflict with outside groups, and it certainly was the case that warfare contributed to notions of border and group identity on the Plains.

Related to the idea of geographical connection is the qualification that a tribe unites all its members in some encampment or ceremony, at least occasionally. This standard was met by some Plains Indian groups, such as the Cheyennes and Kiowas, while other people we think of as constituting a tribe, such as the Comanches, never all gathered together in a single location. Even those groups with the custom of an annual meeting sometimes canceled them, during years when food was either too scarce to support a huge camp or, in a few cases, so plentiful that cooperation was considered unnecessary.

Other criteria for tribal status have to do with leadership and political unity. A single powerful leader in charge of a large group might suggest a "tribal" level of integration. Such leadership was only sometimes evident among the Plains groups.

Often, instead, there were multiple headmen leading smaller groups, and perhaps councils made up of these headmen. Councils were well institutionalized in some groups, while in other groups they were more temporary, convened only to deal with specific problems.

Integration across large numbers of people could also be achieved in other ways. Intermarriage among kin groups, as required by rules forbidding sex and marriage between relatives, achieved a measure of interconnection. Another means of unifying large groups was the non-kin association, a kind of club that potentially drew its membership from all families, and provided some service to all of them, and so functioned as an overarching and uniting structure. Yet another criterion for tribal integration, related to these others, was the presence of formal ways for limiting violence within the group. All of the Plains societies had customs for controlling disputes, and most had clubs whose members acted as temporary peace officers. One can imagine that all of the usual criteria for "tribal" organization would in fact emerge in any number of combinations and degrees in different groups, and that is what happens across Native North America and the Plains.

Bands

The notion of "band" rather than "tribe" is somewhat more helpful in understanding Plains human organization. Most everyday Indian thinking and activity about affiliation were directed at forging and maintaining bands rather than larger groups. The band is a small group of people who live and work together for mutual advantage. A single nuclear family (parents and their children) could function in this way, though normally the term indicates an extended group beyond the nuclear family; in the evolutionary schemes that have been put forth, the band is the primal social form beyond the family. Bands nevertheless grow along kinship lines. For example, a band could be started by two brothers who bring together their wives and children, and then other relatives. A group so formed might number 30, 50, or 200 people. Bands are flexible in their membership. There are no strong rules of heredity or work that keep people attached to the group, and they are free to come or go as they judge best. Therefore, bands are also flexible in size; members can gather or disperse as the local food supply grows and shrinks, and this makes them suitable for effective seasonal hunting and gathering.

Bands have a distinctive social character. Individual freedom and initiative are valued, but at the same time there is an emphasis on common obligation and equal access to the products of labor. There are relatively few social differences between band members. Differences that come about are the ones that appear most natural, those based on age, gender, and degree of personal ability. The leader that emerges in this egalitarian setting is someone who has an exceptional record as a provider and who gathers followers through personal reputation and charisma. His power rests on his ability to build consensus and inspire action, and he has neither the motivation nor the clout to physically force people to do what he wants.

Band organization often corresponds to bilateral descent. This pattern of tracing relatives through both the mother and father's sides of the family equally is the one familiar to modern Americans. In bilateral descent, a person need not be equally close to, or even like, all relatives on both the mother's and father's sides, but is nevertheless entitled to count them all as kin. Bilateral descent opens up maximum possibilities for developing supportive relationships with relatives, such as would be helpful in nomadic hunting and gathering. Whenever status is gained through individual work and achievement, and individuals can benefit from a wide network of helpful kin, bilateralism is favored. The majority of the groups occupying the Plains during the horse culture period exhibited an emphasis on band formation

and observed bilateral descent principles. Either their ancestors already had bilateral descent when they reached the Plains or they abandoned other principles and drifted into using bilateral descent as they became buffalo hunters.

Descent Groups: Lineages and Clans

While bilateral descent allows the widest options as hunters and gatherers seek to form support networks, it is less helpful when people's survival and personal status depend on passing down property and rights from one generation to the next. When the inheritance of garden land, for example, is important, a single, preestablished, direct line of descent is more likely to limit confusion. So, many societies practice unilineal descent, in which people are related either to their mother or father's family, but not both. In the version of unilineal descent called matrilineal descent, a person is related to others only through his or her mother and female relatives. In the version known as patrilineal descent, the person connects to relatives only through his or her father and father's male kin. It makes no difference whether people themselves are male or female, but it is who they trace their relatives through that determines whether descent is matrilineal or patrilineal.

When a unilineal descent principle is followed, the result can be the formation of a group of people with shared descent. This group exists through time, permanently and regardless of which individuals are born into it or die out of it. The unilineal descent group is therefore potentially much more stable than a family or band, which exists only as long as its members are alive and stay together, and this stability is desirable for the long-term possession of cropland and village sites associated with semi-sedentary horticulture. Descent groups that are organized from a known common ancestor are called lineages, and may be referred to as matrilineages or patrilineages depending on whether they trace the maternal or paternal line. An even larger encompassing unit can be formed, harkening back to a common ancestor so far in the past that the ancestor is no longer nameable or is represented as a mythological character. This larger-order descent group is called a clan, and may be termed matriclan or patriclan depending on the descent principle.

Clans are corporate groups, with common rights and responsibilities shared by all members. They may own hunting territory or garden land in common, or houses. They may own particular rituals that only they are allowed to practice. Often these rituals express a unique connection to the clan's ancestor figure. Associated with clan identity and rituals are taboos observed by the members as outward signs of ancestry. For example, a Bear Clan member would be prohibited from eating bear meat. Clans are also frequently corporate with respect to marriage; that is, all clan members observe the same rules about who to marry or not marry. Most often clans follow a rule of exogamy that requires that all members marry someone from a different clan than their own. Exogamous marriage has the effect of linking several clans together through intermarriage.

Membership in a clan is fixed at birth and does not change as the individual marries and has children. In a matrilineal society, the children belong to the clan of the mother, and in a patrilineal one, to the father's clan. The other parent normally lives with his or her spouse and children and functions as a close, supportive family member, but always belongs to his or her own clan and must devote his or her allegiance to that clan above all else. For instance, in a matrilineal society, one's father has a different structural position than one's mother and is more like an in-law who has married into, but not joined, his wife and children's clan. The father must continue to express allegiance to his own mother's clan by participating in its ceremonies and supporting the children born to that clan; that is, he has fatherly duties toward his sisters' children. His devotion to his own wife and offspring is still very important, though, not only for the well-being of his immediate family, but as a public expression of the desirable alliance between the father's and mother's clans, for it is these kinds of marriage and family connections in aggregate that tie all of the clans together into a larger, more powerful society.

Matrilineal exogamous clans were found among the Mandans, Hidatsas, and Crows. The Pawnees did not have clans, but their main social unit, the village population, was organized by matrilineal descent. Pawnee villages resembled clans in that they had mythological founders and distinguishing rituals, but they were also like large extended family bands, and they practiced endogamy (marriage within the group) rather than exogamy. Patrilineal clan societies on the Plains included the Osages, Omahas, Poncas, Kansas, and Iowas. Evidence about the Otoes and Missourias is more scant but indicates that they too were patrilineal. Note that the societies with unilineal descent are often linked to each other historically and linguistically, and are either semi-sedentary horticulturalists or have a background in gardening. Traces of matrilineality or patrilineality have been posited for other tribes by various researchers, either as leftovers from earlier periods or as emerging responses to white-induced trade and warfare, but the presence and causes of these tendencies are frequently debated.

Phratries and Moieties

There are a couple of other kinds of social units larger than the clan that are found in some Plains societies. Sometimes clans link together in pairs or trios to establish regular helpful relations with each other. These sets may or may not have names in the native language or reflect a sense of common descent among the member clans, but they are recognizable through the actions and attitudes of their members. Anthropologists call such a clan set a *phratry* (plural *phratries*).

It also happens sometimes that entire societies are split into two halves that play complementary roles to each other in rituals, games, or marriage. In a society with, say, 12 clans, 6 clans would compose one half, and 6 the other. This halving pattern can also sometimes be found in societies without clans. The halves may indicate some wide sense of common descent but are not very important outside of the rituals or games in which the differences are invoked. They have simple distinguishing names like the "Summer People" and the "Winter People" among the Pawnees and "Sky" and "Earth" among the Omahas. A unit of this kind is called a *moiety* (plural *moieties*) by anthropologists, after the French word meaning "half."

Native Naming

For the most accurate sense of how Native people organized, the names that various groups gave themselves must be considered. In general, Indian people recognized themselves as members of large groups with common language and history. The Native names for these large units usually mean something akin to "the people," "the real people," or something similar conveying a sense of ultimate humanness. These names have frequently come to be regarded as "tribal" names.

Many of the tribal names in common use today do not originate with the people who bear them, however. Often they are accidental corruptions or misapplied versions of Native names, or insulting nicknames from a neighboring tribe that were adopted into Euro-American speech. In several cases the names come to English through French or Spanish, adding another layer of distortion. "Sioux" is a French shortened version of the name employed by the Algonquian-speaking Indians for certain non-neighbors, possibly connoting "foreigner," and which is ultimately relatable to their term for the eastern massasauga, a small rattlesnake (leading to a common but imprecise conclusion that the Algonquians were purpose-fully referring to the Sioux as "snakes"). This name, as seen in Chapter 2, covers three major Plains political-linguistic units that are in turn each formed from multiple large, distinctive divisions made up of numerous bands. "Comanche," also applied to multiple divisions, comes, via Spanish, from the Ute Indian term meaning, roughly, "other" or "enemy." "Gros Ventres" and "Nez Perce" ("Big Bellies" and "Pierced Noses" in French, respectively) are other tribal names derived from uncomplimentary misnomers.

The outcomes in defining and naming groups were shaped by particular historical circumstances and the names now in use often disregard people's own sense of group identity. Naming people is a way of controlling perceptions about them, an act of political determination. The study of ethnonyms (the names of ethnic groups) therefore becomes a means of understanding the nature of interaction between groups.

The Cheyennes make a good case study in the intricacies behind tribal names (as reconstructed by ethnohistorian Douglas Parks, in Moore *et al.* 2001). The name *Cheyenne* has been used, first by French and then English speakers, since the late 1700s. The French had adopted the Sioux designation *sahiyena*, which also appears as *sahiyana* or *sahiyela*. In turn this name was derived from *sahiya*, which the Sioux applied to the Plains Cree; *sahiyana* includes the diminutive suffix *–na*, in effect meaning "little Plains Cree," probably indicating that from an early Sioux perspective, the Cheyennes appeared like another version of the Crees, who were also Algonquians. The name has been commonly translated as Sioux for "red talkers," supposedly a metaphor for "people of alien speech," but this derivation appears to be based only on a coincidental resemblance. Another mistaken derivation is from *chien*, French for "dog."

The Sioux name for the Cheyennes was widely adopted and modified by other tribes, including the Algonquian Foxes and Shawnees to the east of the Plains and the Caddoan Wichitas of

Oklahoma and Texas. Several other Plains tribes, however, including the Crows, Hidatsas, Mandans, and Comanches, referred to the Cheyennes by names in their own languages meaning "striped arrows." A variation of this idea in Comanche and Shoshone was "painted or striped feather." As this name idea diffused further it was modified in the receiving languages to mean "striped or spotted blanket" (an alternate name in Crow and Hidatsa), "spotted horse people" (Blackfoot), "striped people" (Blood and Piegan), "spotted eyes" (Flathead), and "scarred people" (Arapaho and Gros Ventre). A few tribes had yet other names. The Kiowas called the Cheyennes "pierced ears" and the Plains Crees, as if to confirm the Sioux characterization, called them "people with a language like Cree." Finally, the Cheyennes refer to themselves as Tsistsistas, to use the anglicized form, a name meaning "those who are from this (group)."

Much more relevant in everyday life were the divisions and bands. People generally identified first with these units and only secondarily with anything larger. Often the band names referred to stories about the groups, their alleged characteristics, and their position in the historical development of the larger society. The Cheyennes had 10 or 11 bands, or sometimes more, each with its proper location on the camp circle, called (in imperfect translation) Aortas, Hair Rope (or Hairy or Rope) Men, Eaters, Ridge Men, Scabby People, and so on. The Aortas were reportedly so named because of an episode in the past when they used a burnt aorta from a buffalo heart as a makeshift tobacco pipe. The Hairy Rope Men were said to prefer ropes of twisted hair instead of the usual rawhide, while the Eaters were said to be liable to eat anything, though they themselves claimed that the name indicated that their ancestors were the best hunters. Around the camp circle of the Kiowas, always in the same position, were divisions called the True Kiowas (presumably the original core), the Elk Men, Saynday's Son's Men

(Saynday was the trickster character of Kiowa myth), the Big Shields, the Biters, and others. The Plains Cree band names reflected a heritage of maintaining separate hunting territories, a continuation of eastern woodland practice, with environment and location titles such as Parklands People, Beaver Hills People, Prairie People, Calling River People, and Touchwood Hills People.

The names of clans are also revealing. The Omahas had a pattern of clan names seen in many cultures around the world, in which the descent groups were named for mythical ancestors in the form of animals or other elements of nature. Such ancestor emblems are called *totems*. Omaha patriclans had names alluding to the buffalo, buffalo calf, eagle, bird, deer, wolf, bear, elk, turtle, and wind. The mythological animal or element ancestor is an emblem of the solidarity shared by clan members, and it indicates the ancientness of the unit. Symbolically, the totem may stand for certain desirable qualities or behaviors in humans that are also seen in nature. Totemic naming also

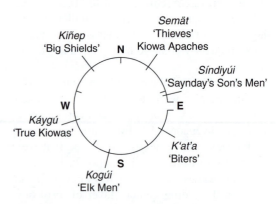

FIGURE 4.2   The Kiowa camp circle showing locations of bands, as recorded by James Mooney. The Kiowa Apaches (Plains Apaches) had a place among the Kiowa bands. The camp was shaped and oriented like a tipi, and thus was the symbolic house of the entire tribe.

has the symbolic effect of likening the differences among social groups to the differences among animals in nature. An extension of the idea of totemic naming is to call a clan after the taboo its members observe, such as the Do Not Touch Buffalo Tails and Do Not Touch Deerskin groups among the Poncas.

Where totemic clans are found, personal naming practices sometimes also reflect clan membership. The clans had stocks of personal names that were reused as children were born into each generation, all referring in imaginative and poetic ways to the characteristics of the totemic animal. Table 4.1 shows a sampling of the Elk Clan personal names among the Omahas.

The Omahas and other Southern Siouans carried this practice even further by giving ordinal birth names—names that indicated both a child's clan membership and its order of birth in the family. In the Elk Clan, a man's eldest son might be named Soft-horn, the second Yellow-horn, the third Branching-horns, and the fourth Four-horns.

Omaha and Osage boys also received distinctive haircuts in which most of the hair was shaved, with patches or locks left to create a design that represented some characteristic of their clan animal. A patch of hair in front and tail down the neck was the "head and tail of the elk"; other patterns represented buffalo horns, a shaggy wolf, or a turtle's appendages projecting from its shell. Such personal names and accompanying customs situated an individual in the realm of clan history and symbolic meaning. Names and customs also reminded people of the cooperative nature of the clan in matters of ritual and marriage.

Other clan naming systems did not make reference to totems. Instead, the clan names were nicknames or references to a supposed character trait of the members, and these names were often derogatory. They were thus like the Cheyenne and Kiowa band names. The Crows had this kind of naming, with clans called Bad War Honors, Greasy-inside-the-mouth, Sore-lip Lodge, and Without-shooting-they-bring-game.

TABLE 4.1   Personal Names of the Omaha Elk Clan

NAME	TRANSLATION	IMAGERY
Bi^{n}ç'tigthe	Sound of the elk's voice, heard at a distance	
Btho^{n}ti'	Smell comes	Scent borne by wind, discovering game
Çi^{n}dedo^{n}pa	Blunt tail	Refers to elk
He'çithi^{n}ke	Yellow horn sitting	Yellowish velvety skin on new antler growth of elk
Heço^{n}to^n	Antler white standing	Towering antlers of an elk
Ku'kuwi^{n}xe	Turning round and round	Bewildered elk when surprised
No^{n}mo^{m}mo^{n}tha	Foot action, walking with head thrown back	Peculiar manner in which the elk holds its head when walking
Nuga'xti	Real male	Refers to clan taboo against using meat or skin of male elk
O^{n}po^{n}çka	White elk	
Xaga'mo^{n}thi^n	Rough walking	Jagged outline of a herd of elk, their antlers rising like tree branches

Source: Fletcher and La Flesche (1972).

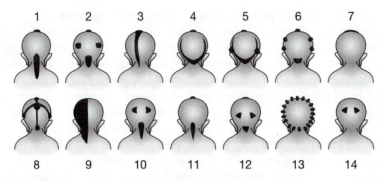

FIGURE 4.3   *Osage and Omaha boys' haircuts according to clan. (1) Head and tail of an elk; (2) Head, tail, and horns of a buffalo; (3) Line of buffalo's back as seen against the sky; (4) Head, tail, and body of a small bird; (5) Head, wings, and tail of an eagle; (6) Shell, head, feet, and tail of a turtle; (7) Head of a bear; (8) The four cardinal directions; (9) Shaggy side of a wolf; (10) Horns and tail of a buffalo; (11) Head and tail of a deer; (12) Head, tail, and growing horn knobs of a buffalo calf; (13) Reptile teeth; (14) Horns of buffalo*

ASSOCIATIONS

All of the sub-tribal level social groups discussed so far are formed of people who recognize common kinship, and with the main purpose of expressing common kinship. Plains Indian cultures were also notable for the degree to which they developed non-kin social groups. Non-kin groups are technically called associations or sodalities, but they have also been referred to as medicine societies, dance clubs, military or soldier societies, and craft guilds and by other similar names depending on the shared interest of the group. The key feature of these units is that membership is voluntary, meaning that it is not predetermined by kinship as clan membership would be. "Non-kin" groups might in fact recruit relatives, but members are not automatically born into them and membership is theoretically open beyond kin ties. Voluntary groups are important because they provide the structure for social relations that reach across kinship lines—they unite non-relatives in common purposes for the good of

all and counteract the tendency for kin groups to see themselves in competition with one another.

Since voluntary associations were formed around common interests of worship, work, and recreation, and those interests differed between men and women, the Plains associations were usually gender-specific, and men's associations were frequently the more prominent in social affairs. The reason for forming a group was often a blend of civil and religious duty, fellowship, and fun.

Men's Associations

Many of the men's associations were mainly military in nature. Even though every man was a warrior in Plains societies, associations were formed to promote valiant behavior and coordinate the efforts of raiding and defense. They were elite fighting units that took a special role in battle, perhaps as scouts or shock troops. Some were pledged to unceasing combat or continual patrol of the tribal perimeter.

Within the association, the members could be further distinguished. Commonly the ordinary members carried a strait lance and the smaller number of officers a lance with a crooked end like an umbrella handle. Long trailing sashes worn around the neck or over one shoulder also marked these warriors, with different colors for each rank. The no-flight warrior would take a position on the front lines of battle and pin his sash to the ground with his lance, a promise to hold his ground until relieved by a comrade who could join him in the fray and pull the lance to release him. The bravery of association warriors was proclaimed in special songs, some of which were referred to as "death songs," to be sung by a warrior as he faced his end while anchored to the ground. Following are some association songs, two from, respectively, the Teton Strong Heart and Fox societies and two from the Kiowa Koitsenko (Real Dogs); the Kiowa examples are death songs associated with nineteenth-century warriors Poor Buffalo and Satanta:

Friends
Whoever
Runs away
Shall not be admitted

The Fox
Whenever you propose to do anything
I consider myself foremost
But
A hard time
I am having

All brave men must die sometime,
The Koitsenko must die, too;
It is a great honor to die in battle.

No matter where my enemies destroy me,
Do not mourn me,
Because this is the end all great warriors face.

—*(Boyd 1981:76, 119; Densmore 1918:322)*

Contrary behavior was another widespread practice adopted by individuals or entire associations.

To demonstrate their unusual lack of fear, contrary warriors engaged in all sorts of backwards and illogical behavior. In camp, they plunged their hands into boiling soup and complained how cold it was or danced in the opposite direction of everyone else. In battle, they forsook common sense in pursuing the enemy, and the orders they took had to be given in the reverse. The *Heyoka* (Thunder Dreamers) of the Oglalas were well-known contrary warriors who could be bold and reckless because their spirit helpers were the powerful Thunder Beings. Among the Comanches were individuals called *pukutsi,* meaning someone who is crazy or stubborn. The *pukutsi* went around camp intruding on people's meals and singing at inappropriate times with the buffalo scrotum rattle he carried. He cried as the people did when mourning on a day when no one had died. Asked by an old woman to get her a buffalo skin, *pukutsi* came back with the skin of a Pawnee.

> One day the camp was attacked by Osages. Somebody said to *pukutsi,* "that's right—just sit there, don't do anything!" So he got on his horse and went after the Osages and killed all except one . . . didn't even have a bow, just a lance. He went to chase the last Osage, who was pretty far off. Somebody said, "That's right—go get that last one." He just reared back his horse, got off, and sat down. Those guys must have been real brave, though.

> (Ralph Kosechata, quoted in Gelo 1983)

The heightened coordination found in the military associations made them the logical groups to turn to when force was needed to control behavior within the tribe. Because the associations drew members from many kin groups, they could enforce the rule of law without creating conditions in which one kin group was trying to dominate others, that is, the kind of situation that would lead to a continual blood feud. Thus, military associations were often the temporary police force during tribal encampments, hunts, and marches. This method of social control worked well because it was precisely during the warmer months, when large groups of people were congregated, that police were needed and the associations were meeting; during winter the people in general were spread far and wide and the associations disbanded.

The Sun Dance gatherings in early summer required a good deal of regulation. Inconsiderate behavior, friction, and jealousies were more likely to erupt at this time. Tribal leaders would appoint one or more associations to serve as police as long as the people were convened (and it is important to note that the association members only had this coercive power when temporarily approved). Which association was appointed varied by tribal tradition; there might be random selection, a regular rotation of police duty among the associations, or the same association always appointed for this job. When it came time for the large communal buffalo hunt associated with the dance, it was imperative that no one ventured out ahead of everyone else to begin hunting, otherwise the herds could be scared off. Association members could patrol to prevent premature hunting. Long marches undertaken as the larger bands migrated also required policing. People had to be urged to keep up and not wander away from the main party in order to ensure the progress and safety of the whole group.

Association members were empowered in various ways. Often they carried quirts made with leather lashes attached to heavy wooden handles. These whips were not only a symbol of their authority, but were actually used to keep people in line. They could break up disputes with force and obtain restitution for the party that they determined had been wronged. To subdue a troublemaker, they might destroy his tipi and drive off his horses, ensuring that he would have to spend the rest of the encampment time getting his belonging back together. In more difficult cases, they were allowed to beat the offender or even deliver capital punishment. People who otherwise cherished individual freedoms welcomed this

measure of security during the large gatherings. The degree of force used by the association, however, was sometimes subject to controversy, and public opinion, delivered directly or through the commands of leaders, was always in play to influence the immediate and long-term behavior of the police.

Instances in which association members exceeded their authority are found, for example, in Cheyenne history. Some time in the mid-1830s the Cheyenne Bowstring Society members were eager to attack the Kiowas. They were instructed by the Keeper of the Sacred Arrows, a ritual leader with prophetic and advisory powers, not to go ahead with their plans. They disputed the Arrow Keeper's authority and beat him with their whips before setting off on the raid. According to oral tradition, when the 40 or more society members then encountered the Kiowas, they were surrounded and all massacred, as if under a curse.

Around the same time Porcupine Bear, a leader of the Dog Soldiers, was banished from the Cheyennes for stabbing to death another tribesman in a drunken tussle. Soon he was joined by a number of relatives and friends, many of them fellow Dog Soldiers, forming a residential band separate from the tribe. This Dog Soldier band existed for several years and pursued its existence quite apart from the other Cheyennes. They attacked the Kiowas in a stunning raid avenging the Bowstring Society massacre, although according to some accounts their victory was not celebrated by the main tribe because they were exiles. Gradually, the Dog Soldiers gained strength, taking up their own territory east of the Cheyenne area and intermarrying with similarly militant Sioux factions; they even staged their own Sun Dance. They became especially aggressive in tormenting non-Indian traders and raiding trains and settlements. Often the U.S. troops punished the other Cheyenne bands for the raids of the Dog Soldiers. The emergent Dog Soldier nation was annihilated by the Fifth U.S. Cavalry at the battle of Summit Springs, Colorado, in July 1869.

The foregoing examples show what could happen when associations stepped beyond the normal bounds of club behavior. In the first case, there was believed to be a supernatural punishment. In the second case, an association evolved into something different: the temporary, seasonal warrior's club evolved into a permanent military unit; it could also be said that the club became a band and, eventually, something approaching a distinct tribe. The balance between civic duty and military ambition could be fragile, and no doubt there were other unrecorded instances of association turmoil and transition in the earlier stages of Plains occupation.

Fellowship was also an important part of association life. Members often maintained their own lodge where they would retire to smoke, plan raids, and recite their war deeds. Even though the associations' duties were often secular rather than religious, they had their own origin myths along with ceremonies meant to seek the aid of their spiritual founder and guardian and to transmit whatever special spiritual power their guardian bestowed between members. They owned special songs and dances, unique shields, pipes, or medicine bundles, and insignia that required blessings in cedar smoke and other sacred techniques. Club dances and rituals were occasions for the public display of the warriors' ethos and accomplishments. There was a lot of good-natured teasing and practical joking in the association lodge as well. Common recreational activity during peacetime helped strengthen the bonds of friendship that unified the tribe.

Although the associations are described as voluntary and kinship was not the basis for belonging, membership was not totally random, but guided by social pressures. It was usually expected that a man would follow his father or older brothers in joining a particular club. Despite the risk of shame, young men were sometimes reluctant to join a no-flight society, and it is reported that among the Plains Apaches potential candidates often avoided camp during induction

time and had to be rounded up and pretty much forced into serving.

A few tribes had age-graded associations. These associations were like the grades in school through which succeeding classes pass. While age grades are considered voluntary associations because they are not constrained by kin ties, age-grade eligibility was defined automatically, and in some tribes these groups were so important as to include virtually all males. Among the Arapahos, Blackfeet, Gros Ventres, Mandans, and Hidatsas, the clubs represented a sequence that a man would graduate through with his age-mates as their lives progressed. After some years in one club, the generational group would buy its way into the next-ranked society, to displace the elder group and be replaced by a younger one. The elders were addressed as "fathers" or "grandfathers" and they demanded ritual payments and a feast before they would turn over the sacred knowledge, dances, songs, and insignia of the club to the younger men. The oldest men, having passed through all six or so associations, "retired" from warrior life.

Among the Arapahos, graded men's societies were known as lodges. Adolescent men joined the Kit-Fox Lodge together and proceeded through the Star, Tomahawk, Spear, Crazy, and Dog lodges. The Arapaho lodges were central to tribal integrity and highly ritualized. Each lodge involved elaborate initiations, special knowledge, ceremonies of prayer and sacrifice, and the bestowing of special honors or "degrees" with distinctive regalia. Younger men established mentorships with elders from the higher-order lodges. Women actually played an essential role in the system by receiving supernatural power from the elder mentors and transferring it to their husbands. Thus, Arapaho women were seen as progressing through the age grades along with their spouses.

More of the Plains tribes had ungraded associations. The Arikaras, Assiniboines, Cheyennes, Crows, Kiowas, Pawnees, and Sioux each had an array of unranked clubs that played a major part in tribal life. Virtually every man would belong to an association in these tribes. The Comanches, Sarsis, Shoshones, and Plains Crees also had ungraded societies, although they were less significant to the overall character of these tribes, at least during the periods for which we have information. Weak versions of military associations were also found among the Southern Siouans; in these tribes, strong clan and religious society structures took the place of military clubs in providing integration.

Membership in the ungraded clubs did not depend on age, although typically the core was formed of age-mates. And although the associations were not ranked chronologically, at any given time one or two might be more prominent in tribal affairs, and others moribund owing to war or disease fatalities. An association might disband for a time upon the death of one member, and occasionally a club was completely exterminated in battle and existed only "on paper" until an entire new membership could be established. In ungraded systems, there was sometimes a traditional competition between clubs to see who could accrue the most war honors. The competing clubs also played pranks on each other in camp. The Lumpwood and Foxes among the Crows had such a well-known rivalry. Retirement from the ungraded associations came with older age. Some offered a lifetime membership to elders, who continued as valued advisors, participating in club ceremonies and planning but not in combat.

Looking across the many plains tribes, whether they had graded or ungraded societies, there were only a limited number of club names in use. Most of the tribes had a Kit or Swift Fox society (named for small western fox species), and (Buffalo) Bulls, Wolves, Ravens (or Crow-Owners), and Dogs (with variations such as Crazy Dogs, Little Dogs, etc.) were also widespread names. Another name that shows up in various forms refers to a weapon: Tomahawks

among the Arapahos; Stone Hammers and Lumpwoods among the Hidatsa and Crow tribes. The Kiowas and Kiowa Apaches each had a Rabbit Society that introduced boys and girls between age 5 and 12 to the customs of society dancing and regalia and groomed them for adult club life.

The Kit Foxes in one tribe resembled their namesakes in the other tribes, sharing special details of dress and ceremony, to the extent that there must have been a common origin of the Kit Fox idea that was transmitted or imitated across tribal boundaries. The sale or ceremonial transmission of associations between tribes is recorded in some cases. In some instances too an association present in an ancient parent tribe might have spread as that tribe subdivided into the tribes known historically. Whatever the commonalities, each tribe added its own peculiarities over time and incorporated the basic society concepts in novel ways. The Kit Foxes of the Hidatsas and Arapahos were young men, while the Piegan Kit Fox society was made up of older married men. Societies might spawn junior counterparts; this process probably accounts for the occasional presence of Dogs and Little Dogs in the same tribe. Moreover, through time the rank of a particular club could change within the age-grade system of a particular tribe, if the system were disrupted and reorganized. Thus, a list of Hidatsa clubs from 1833 shows the Dogs as the sixth of 10 age-ranked clubs, while a list pertaining to around 1870 had the Dogs as the ninth club in the Hidatsa scheme. Lists and descriptions of associations in particular tribes that are found in historical writings and tribal oral traditions must be regarded as dated snapshots of a continuous process.

Women's Associations

Women also formed clubs around their interests, although these were not as prevalent or influential as those of men. One responsibility of adult women was to support the efforts of the male warriors in their families by providing material goods and comforts as well as the good wishes and spiritual protections that could be afforded by singing, dancing, and praying. An extension of these responsibilities across kin lines was achieved when women formed non-kin auxiliaries to the men's warrior associations. One or more women of such a group might be selected to gather food and cook for the men's club. On the night prior to the men's departure for battle, the women sang and danced to ensure their success. "Among the Kiowa a man starting out on a raid was likely to appeal to a body of possibly forty Old Women whom he feasted on his return in gratitude for their prayers" (Lowie 1982:97). It was also their job to spread sand in preparing the ground for the Sun Dance. At least in modern recollection, the Comanches had

similar women's groups that supported men's clubs such as the Crow Society. When the men came back from battle, the women donned the men's headdresses, took up their lances, and danced with scalps hanging from the lance tips in a victory celebration.

Other women's associations functioned ostensibly as craft guilds, although they promoted excellence in a wide range of female activities, such as midwifery. In these clubs, labor was combined to carry out intensive handwork in a helpful and friendly setting. Imagine all the hand stitching necessary to sew a watertight tipi cover of 14 buffalo hides, and it is easy to see the appeal of a group effort. A given project could be finished much more quickly, plus there was sharing of childcare and companionship all the while. Older women shared their expertise with younger ones,

FIGURE 4.4 Two members of the Cheyenne Warriors Society Auxiliary, a modern women's association, wearing the fringed shawls of the society at a powwow near Medicine Park, Oklahoma, 1982.

ensuring the continuance of techniques and gently enforcing "quality control."

Among the Cheyennes there was a single women's craft club, the Robe Quillers. Not a simple group of hobbyists, this club functioned as a true guild that owned the exclusive rights to the techniques of quillwork, the art of decorating clothes, bags, and tipi covers with dyed, woven, and sewn porcupine quills (a forerunner of decorative beadwork—see Chapter 6). The knowledge of quillwork was considered sacred, and it was practiced and imparted only in the most strictly ritualized ways. Every new decoration project was begun with a vow. Workers recited their past projects as if they were men proclaiming their great war deeds. If a novice was to be taught, she must first show respect by bringing food and materials for the club members. A camp crier announced the start of the new project, gifts were given away to celebrate it, and if a sewing mistake was made, an accomplished warrior would be summoned to cut away the bad part as if taking a scalp. Many of these ritual touches mirror those surrounding the pursuit of war honors by men; their use in relation to women's work was a way of recognizing the serious and complementary nature of women's contributions to tribal welfare.

Religious Societies

Although social life was infused with religion and all associations practiced some characteristic rituals, the main functions of the clubs were usually secular. There were, however, some non-kin associations with direct religious purposes. It is best to understand these societies as groups of medicine men and medicine women united in order to work their supernatural power collectively and to train novices, their successors in the next generation, in the ways of the spirits. People in these groups shared their knowledge and spirit power with each other and in effect sold or licensed it to younger people who aspired to follow them through often elaborate training rituals.

The line between military and religious societies is not entirely firm, since military club members typically shared some special ritual knowledge or supernatural power. Even outside the structure of the military clubs, power-sharing groups could form more or less spontaneously without turning into major tribal social units; the Comanches were known to have such short-lived cooperatives of power possessors. In the case of the Southern Siouans and Crows, however, religious societies became quite central.

Religious societies were the most important non-kin groups among the Southern Siouan tribes, and of the societies in these tribes, the Omaha Shell and Pebble societies are the best known. The Shell Society (*Washisk'ka Athi^n*, "shell-they have," "shell owners") was begun, according to tribal legend, by a mysterious stranger, actually a spirit from the animal world, who visited a worthy Omaha family and taught them the secrets of herbal medicines and magical powers, though taking the lives of the family's four children in exchange. The children are taken to a great lake, where they are engulfed by waves, and the grieving parents are left only with shells as reminders. This legend, ripe with symbolism about death and renewal in both the animal and human worlds, outlined a procedure whereby a select group of Omahas, including both men and women (in replication of the genders of the legendary family), could continue to pass down the bestowed supernatural knowledge in a prolonged series of initiation rituals.

Membership in the Shell Society was sold to new acolytes of the succeeding generation, usually along family lines. The members possessed a large assortment of ritual items, including a drum, special moccasins and face-paint patterns, a special board for cutting ritual tobacco, and hide packs containing pipes along with sticks to be handed out as invitations. Accompanying these items were numerous songs referring to episodes of the origin story. Regular meetings were held in May, June,

August, and September, signifying the respective mating times of the black bear, buffalo, elk, and deer. The dramatic apex of the rituals was the magical shooting of cowry shells into the novices, who feigned death and then, by coughing up the injected shells, rebirth—this capability attested to their mastery of supernatural power.

The Pebble Society used small translucent stones for the magical shooting but was otherwise similar to the Shell Society and may have been the older of the two. Whereas the Shell Society drew its members from chiefly families and emphasized group performances, the Pebble group recruited notable curers and focused more on doctoring. According to anthropologists such as Robert Lowie and Gloria Young, both were adaptations of a society prevalent among the Woodlands people to the northeast, the Grand Medicine Society (*Midewiwin*) of the Ojibwas, Sauk-Fox, and Winnebagos, which attests to the historical connection between the Southern Siouans and the Siouan peoples of the Great Lakes region (the great lake in the Shell Society legend is probably a reference to this connection). The Shell and Pebble societies have been referred to as secret societies because the knowledge transmitted was considered secret and the early segments of their rituals were closed to the public. However, the Omahas did not keep secret the identity of members with masks or totally private ceremonies, as is the practice in true secret societies in other cultures.

Religious observance was also the basis of a non-kin organization among the Crows called the Tobacco Society (*bacu'sua*, "soaking," a reference to the technique for sprouting tobacco seeds). This group, made up of several chapters and involving men and women both, oversaw the cultivation of the tribal sacred tobacco crop. The tobacco species they planted was not the same one they used for smoking, but another, considered holy and signifying the tribal past as a horticultural people. Members observed a complicated regimen of singing, dancing, planting, and harvesting to ensure the well-being of the

symbolic plant and, hence, the tribe. When the seasonal cycle was successfully completed, the tobacco itself was simply discarded in a ritual manner, by throwing it in a creek. The Crow Tobacco Society differed from the Omaha religious societies by focusing on gardening rather than animal power, but all were similar in their general intent to foster seasonal renewal and tribal welfare and in such details as initiation, special face-paint patterns, the selling of membership rights, and so on.

LEADERSHIP

Chiefs

Leaders of Plains Indian societies are normally referred to as chiefs, and this book will continue to use the term, but *chief* is very much like the word *tribe* in the conceptual problems it poses.

In some of the theoretical literature the term "chief" is reserved for the leader of a chiefdom, a specific kind of non-industrial society in which each individual member has a unique ranked position in relation to the top person, based on his or her kinship distance from that person. As the top person in the hierarchy, the chief is responsible for passing out the goods and services created by the group, but not everyone is treated equally. Here the leadership position is an inherited one, with a rule of succession placing a close kinsman of the chief in his office the moment he dies. Sometimes the chief is even thought of as a god on earth, which explains his privileged position. Societies in this proposed category are rare and transitional, standing in size and complexity between band and tribal societies, with their wide equality of members, and state societies, in which entire groups of people, rather than individuals, are ranked, forming castes or classes. Some societies that have been classified as chiefdoms include the Polynesians of the South Pacific islands and the prehistoric Mississippian Mound

Builders of the southeast United States. No Plains Indian society had this kind of organization, however, and Plains "chiefs" should be called "headman," the term used for band and tribal leaders, according to many of the theoretical schemes.

Whether the chief or headman name is applied on the Plains, it is more critical to understand the nature of the leadership role—how it was defined, what it was meant to do, how a person qualified for it. First, it must be noted that the role was variable. A careful look across the various Plains tribes through time shows that chiefs could have differing levels of responsibility, authority, and power. They might work alone or as members of a council. They might use physical force themselves, though usually they did not, and they might or might not get a military association to enforce their decisions.

It is also important to ask, in particular cases, whether the chief was fulfilling a role that was well defined and traditional in his own society or responding in an inventive way to new circumstances such as increasing trade or warfare, either with new Indian neighbors or with non-Indians. Non-Indians typically sought a single, authoritative leader with whom to do business and make treaties, even if such a strong figure was not normally part of the Native political structure. This approach could lead to non-Indian exaggeration of the degree of authority that was actually present, or else a new kind of leader might actually arise to meet non-Indian expectations. The early Spanish occupants of the Southern Plains, for example, thought in terms of their own military and civil patterns, and their reports refer to Native leaders as "generals" and "captains." American treaty negotiators frequently insisted on dealing with a "principal chief," even when no single leader had overarching authority from the Indian perspective. There is nothing less authentic about the non-traditional leadership roles—they result from very real circumstances—but they should be recognized as late developments in a dynamic process of adjustment to non-Indian influences.

One pattern that generally does hold true for the Plains was the distinction between military and civil authority; in other words, there were "war chiefs" and "peace chiefs." War chiefs were men who had enough of a reputation as fighters that they could repeatedly come up with convincing plans for raids, muster other warriors, and lead them in combat. Among the tribal leaders, they tended to be the younger, openly ambitious men. In tribes with well-developed military associations, the most prominent war chiefs might be the officers of the associations. War chiefs gained stature by the number of successful raids they led and the deeds of valor they committed. Success meant ensuring the safety of one's followers above all else, and not losing men in combat. It also meant returning with horses, captives, and other coveted goods. War booty was the property of the raid leader, but the good leader shared it freely with his followers, further enhancing his prestige and influence.

Except during times when a large part of a tribe was embattled, it was the peace chiefs who guided the day-to-day decision making. Peace chiefs were generally older but still vigorous men who had distinguished themselves as hunters and warriors but then wished to turn their efforts to domestic matters and the larger strategic issues of intertribal relations. In most tribes there was a clear distinction between war and peace chiefs, with different native terms for each, and it was necessary to abandon the first role for the second, although in some cases the difference has been overemphasized in non-Indian accounts, since Euro-Americans were liable to judge the purposes of Indian leaders categorically, while the formation of a leader's public persona was actually fluid.

The job of peace chief required a special personality:

> The personal requirements for a tribal chief, reiterated again and again by the Cheyennes, are an even-tempered good nature, energy, wisdom, kindliness, concern for the well-being

of others, courage, generosity, and altruism. These traits express the epitome of the Cheyenne ideal personality. In specific behavior this means that a tribal chief gives constantly to the poor. "Whatever you ask of a chief, he gives it to you. If someone wants to borrow something of a chief, he gives it to that person outright."

(Hoebel 1988:43)

Men with such qualities emerged frequently enough, and naturally. There were no campaigns or elections, nor were there rules of automatic succession. As the Comanche elder That's It explained in 1933, "I hardly know how to tell about them. They never had much to do except to hold the band together . . . . We did not *elect* [peace chiefs]. We were not like you white people, who have to have an election every four years to see who is going to be your leader. A peace chief just got that way" (Wallace and Hoebel 1952:209, 211).

While That's It's comments are useful in helping us contrast Comanche practice with the modern world of political electioneering, they do belie the marked degree of talent and effort that was necessary for a man to gain and hold a position of leadership. Universally on the Plains, chiefs were expected to be effective orators. They were supposed to be able to think through the pros and cons of a situation and to deliver persuasive speeches that spurred the formation of public opinion and roused the people to worthwhile action. Much of this effort was directed at making peace between potential or actual disputants, intervening, and soliciting peer pressure, without physical force and before violence erupted. The key concern was prevention of a blood feud, in which relatives of one complainant harmed relatives of another in an unending cycle of revenge that would tear apart the entire band or tribe. Calming talk was the essential step in defusing such a situation. The role of chief as "good talker" is indicated, for example, by the Comanche title

tekwawapi, *tekwa* referring to speech and *wapi* indicating an honored specialist.

To be effective, chiefs needed to maintain a commanding presence that would overcome doubt and shame those who were reluctant to do what was right for the group. Part of this demeanor was the ability not to reveal frustration over the kind of problems that bothered ordinary people. A chief would refuse the payments normally made to heal an insult or grievance, and even remained unperturbed upon hearing that his wife had run off with another man. "A dog has pissed on my tipi," a Cheyenne chief would say disdainfully when informed of such a problem.

Behind these public manners would have to be a keen understanding of human nature, applied both to those in the band and to outsiders—members of other bands and tribes, traders, potential and real enemies. This enhanced social sense had to be coupled with unusually good knowledge of natural factors affecting the future of the group, such as the climate and animal behavior. To gain all this understanding, the chief paid close attention to past practices and their outcomes, learning through personal experience, but also from oral traditions passed down by the elders. Thus, the chief was likely to be an expert student of tribal history.

It was sometimes easy for people to detect the character and wisdom of a chief in his offspring. Also, they became accustomed to relying on all the family members of such a public figure for leadership. Therefore, while there were no actual rules of succession, there were many instances in which a man was followed by his son or nephew in the chief's role, and sometimes the successor assumed the earlier chief's name.

Another common figure was the chief's assistant or camp crier who carried through with the chief's responsibility of announcing news, decisions, and policies throughout the village. His horse clopping among the tipis, the crier rode through camp and heralded the next migration, hunt, or ceremony, the outcome of a chiefs' meeting, or the approach of visitors. He would announce when lost objects had been found and return them to their owners. If a large council audience or greeting party was convened, it was up to the crier to arrange people in the proper order and positions. The crier was one of the few means by which a chief could extend his authority through the actions of another person. Among the Comanches, the herald could be referred to as *tekwawapi*, as a chief was. The Spanish found camp criers to be so prevalent among the Southern Plains tribes that they had their own words for them: *tlataleros*, derived from a Nahuatl (Aztec language) title, or *pregoneros*, Spanish for "proclaimers."

Councils

Chiefs worked in concert with, and shared authority in varying degrees with, councils made up of the headmen of smaller-order bands. The council structure ensured broad representation. In the serene setting of a large tipi at night, council members met, smoked, and engaged in slow and careful deliberations. On a warm evening, they rolled up the bottom of the tipi and people gathered outside to listen to the discussions. Councilors observed rules of etiquette that ensured that every representative had a turn to speak, or at least a chance to decline. Elder men spoke first, followed by successively younger male speakers and, occasionally, women. The talk was respectful and centered on the issues, not on individuals. Every effort was made to reach a full consensus, even if a decision required many meetings.

Usual matters for discussion included when and where to move camp, when and where to stage major rituals, and whether an association should be appointed as temporary police. The council also deliberated on the evidence and punishment in cases of crime within the tribe—adultery and murder. If there was a need for unified tribal policy on joining an intertribal alliance, declaring war, or establishing trade relations, the council handled these issues also, which were distinct from the organization of raiding parties by individual war leaders. In some cases, the council might even overrule the plans of a revenge or horse-raiding party because of worry for the safety of the participants or concern about the risk that enemy retaliation would pose to the tribe in general. Council decisions were proclaimed throughout the village by the camp crier.

The council concept reached its most involved form in the Cheyenne Council of Forty-Four. This council of 44 peace chiefs was considered more important to the survival of the people than any of the military associations or individual chiefs. As if to emphasize this importance, the Council of Forty-Four was said to have originated in a mythic episode older than the origins of all other tribal rituals. The Council origin story, an adventure about a captive girl who bestows traditions to the tribe, has several aspects: it makes the council superior to the tribal military associations; it creates an injunction against murder within the tribe, and thus against the anarchy that would result from such an act; and, it foretells the coming of other characteristic Cheyenne myth and rituals, again placing the council in a primal position within tribal tradition.

The Council of Forty-Four was more formal than usual on the Plains in that the number of members was fixed, and the membership term was a standard 10 years. Members were inducted in a special ritual. Normally at least four representatives were selected from every band. In a population of about 4,000 Cheyennes, this rule ensured quite thorough representation. Council members who lived through their whole term chose their own successor from their band, and although the office was not hereditary, they frequently chose their own sons. Five councilors who had already served at least one term were selected to return as sacred chiefs—a supreme chief and four assistants. These figures were each associated with particular rituals, spirits, cardinal directions, and seating places in the council lodge, in a web of symbolism.

CRIME, LAW, AND DISPUTE SETTLEMENT

A common question of social theory in earlier times was whether societies that lacked strong political authority figures and an alphabetic writing system could have law and order. The answer is a resounding "yes" once the Plains tribes are considered. The question is rooted in assumptions about how legal principles are recorded and enforced, based on practices in complex nations. But the rule of law should already be evident in the previous discussions of chiefs, councils, associations, and the importance of public opinion in shaping behavior. Further evidence of Native legal concepts and methods of enforcement can be seen by looking at individual cases which have been preserved through oral tradition and personal memory and recorded by anthropologists. Case studies show that Plains societies had clear ideas about crime and punishment, as well as a systematic approach to settling disputes and wrongs by looking at past precedents and seeking remedies that had worked before.

Theft was almost never a problem in an Indian camp. All men and women had essentially the same ability to make or obtain the basic tools and possessions so there was little incentive to take someone else's. A person who did feel the temptation to steal someone else's bow, saddle, or horse would not be able to hide it for very long anyway. Also, it was often thought that items like shields and regalia were imbued with the character or the personal spiritual power of the owner, so that it was believed that a thief could face supernatural backlash from the item itself if it were stolen. And the giving away of belongings merely for the asking was considered ideal behavior, so when someone coveted another's possession he or she could simply ask for it and expect to get it.

Consequently, no one needed to lock their homes or guard their property from tribe mates. (The one exception to the rule about intratribal theft was occasional and concerned horses: there are some Kiowa cases, for example, in which the theft of horses was prosecuted. In these cases the misappropriation was an act of revenge or was excused as "confusion" about ownership.)

Problems did arise, however, in the area of interpersonal relations. There were jealousies and arguments, tempers sometimes flared, and violence sometimes erupted. Wife stealing and adultery were not unknown. If a husband mistreated his wife, he might find himself in a fight with his brothers-in-law. Unsuccessful marriages also could result in a demand for the return of bride wealth—the husband of a divorcing woman might insist on the return of horses that he had given her brothers to recognize the union. The use of sorcery to cause illness to an antagonist was normally a matter between individuals and families, but if it was thought that a person used medicine power for evil on a regular basis, the problem was recognized as one affecting the entire group, and corrective action was taken against the sorcerer. There were also cases of accidental homicide and murder. Frequently, particular instances of such troubles were related to each other. There was a need to determine right from wrong, to assess and collect damages, and sometimes, to exact corporal or capital punishment.

When a man felt he had been wronged, he gathered what evidence and witnesses he could and sought out the offender. It was best to obtain a confession if possible. An accused man might simply own up to the wrong publicly, either to end the bad feelings with a humble admission or to challenge his antagonist further by boasting. Among the Comanches, men forced confessions from women by taking them to a lonely place and choking or whipping them, or threatening them with fire. The charges and outcome of an adultery or sorcery dispute could also be placed in the hands of the supernatural by invoking a conditional curse.

In the Comanche *tabepekat* ("sun-killing") ritual, an accuser presented the charges to the sun, earth, and moon, and the defendant swore his or her innocence in the same way, proclaiming, for example, "May I die when the geese fly from the south to the north if I have done the thing that he has charged me with" (Hoebel 1940:99). All then simply awaited the outcome; in some cases, it was believed, the guilt was indeed confirmed with the premature death of the accused. But frequently no confession or supernatural sanction was available, especially when individual men went against other men, and then dispute settlement was a matter of whether the accuser could build group consensus in order to isolate the accused, or else physically intimidate or force the accused to make restitution.

It was not unusual for a person to feel too weak to bring his case against a powerful warrior. He then had the option of enlisting a champion who would do so for him, selecting someone who could match the accused in strength and reputation. The champion went to work solely for the prestige of it, and if he collected damages they went all to the victim. In an odd twist on this tactic, an old woman that no honorable man would fight was put forward as the mediator. In one Comanche example of this method, the victim in a wife-stealing case did not get his spouse back but did receive a horse-load of goods as damages. Wives who were accused by their husbands of unfaithfulness were subject to severe beatings or the not uncommon punishment of disfigurement, the man cutting off part of the woman's nose and then disowning her.

Legal recourse in rape cases seems to have varied, if accounts are reliable. Several non-Indian observers have indicated that sexual relations were so free that unwanted advances were not a common social problem. One interpretation of these accounts might be that men acted with abandon and women had little power to bring formal complaints of rape, beyond attempting to drag a night-crawling assailant outside, calling attention to his misbehavior, and embarrassing

him. The Cheyennes, however, for whom there is an unusually detailed record, and who placed a high premium on women's chastity, punished even attempted rape severely by beating the offender nearly to death or destroying his property and killing his horses. If the violator was young, his parents might suffer the property destruction. In these cases it was normally the women relatives of the victim who meted justice. Women therefore had some legal protections beyond their brothers' oversight of their marriage situation. When a Cheyenne girl disemboweled her father as he tried to assault her, she was acquitted of murder charges, because the incestuous rape was considered so odious. By attempting it her father had become less than Cheyenne, less than human, so his killing was not considered a murder.

Murder was the most serious offense because, apart from the sorrow it imposed on the victim's family, it removed a needed person from the necessary work of survival and so posed a threat to the entire group. A murder also risked the beginning of a blood feud, a chain of revenge killings between the victim's and murderer's kin groups that could quickly disrupt normal work and take everyone, even bystanders, to the brink of starvation. Among the Cheyennes, the murderer was said to have the stink of death about him, as though his body were corrupting from within; this was a symbolic expression of his foul status. It would be said too that blood stained the feathers of the Sacred Arrows, an allusion that the murder was a blight on the entire tribe.

To help prevent blood feuds, banishment rather than execution was often the preferred punishment for murder. The offender was driven off for several years at least. Some refugees tried to be taken in by an alien tribe. Others struggled alone far from human company in a life of lonely hardship. Some eventually approached their former tribe laden with gifts and asked for forgiveness; if they appeared truly penitent and the memory and emotions of the crime had faded, they might be taken back. Though oral tradition records that some banished murderers were truly reformed, returnees had to tolerate stern warnings from the tribal council when readmitted and they remained stigmatized; some ritual act, like the reconsecration of sacred arrows or the bestowal of a peace pipe, was required as well. There were also cases in which a returned murderer killed again. In the one recorded Cheyenne case of a two-time killer, the murderer was executed in a clever ambush. The killer was shot dead by a kinsman of his two victims, wherein earlier he was summoned into the trap by members of his own military association. So while elements of blood feud were present, the non-kin association most closely responsible for the killer's public comportment stepped in to engineer his elimination, as part of its responsibility to impart justice and smooth over kinship-based antagonisms.

Intensive study of Comanche cases showed that this society granted the kin of a murder victim the right to kill in just retaliation, and that a strong collective will about this right combined with relatively weak kinship obligations among tribe members ensured that the case would then be considered closed without further feuding.

EXAMPLES OF ORGANIZATION: THE CROWS AND COMANCHES

Now that the many factors in tribal organization have been outlined, we can see how they are realized by comparing two Plains societies, the Crows of the northern Plains and the Comanches of the south.

The Crows

All Crows spoke a single language which was of the Siouan language family and related to Hidatsa. Those with this shared tongue called themselves *Absáalooke* (also spelled *Absiroke*, etc.), meaning the children of a large-beaked bird resembling a crow or kite. Despite the common language, the Crows lived in three distinct groups. The River Crows lived along the Yellowstone River, maintained contact with the Upper Missouri village tribes to the east, and had adopted the Horse Dance of the Assiniboines. The Mountain Crows lived in the Wind River region and had ties with the Shoshones in that part of Wyoming. A late offshoot of the Mountain Crows composed a third group, called Kicked-in-their-Bellies. The literature on the Crows refers to these units as bands or divisions, though they were relatively large and probably deserving the latter name.

Across the entire population was a system of 13 exogamous matrilineal clans. The Crow word for clan, *ashamamaléaxia*, meant "as driftwood lodges," a poetic image that likens the tightly woven social relations of the clan to a pile of tangled sticks found along a river. This metaphor of interconnection was also extended to other relations between people and between humans and the spirit world. The clans were grouped in pairs and threes to form nameless larger units for mutual aid, which anthropologists would call phratries. In general, clan membership dictated a person's main line of allegiance. In a feud, for example, one was expected to take the side of one's clansmen. In some matters, however, bilateral descent was recognized; this was the case for the inheritance of medicine bundles and the duties associated with them.

The Crows depended heavily on both military and religious associations to structure cooperation among non-kin. Their men's military associations were ungraded, and through the 1800s they included Stone Hammers, Foxes, Lumpwoods, Little Dogs, Big Dogs, Muddy Hands, Half-Shaved Heads, Black Mouths, Crazy Dogs, Ravens, and Bulls. Throughout the century, some of these units combined or divided, and the Crazy Dogs was imported from the Hidatsas around 1875; indeed most all of the units seem derived from the graded system of the Crow's Hidatsa relatives.

The Lumpwoods and Foxes were the dominant clubs and they participated in a famous rivalry in which they competed to make the first strike against enemies and even kidnapped each other's wives. One of the military clubs was appointed each summer to police the communal buffalo hunt, but there was no fixed rotation of service. We have also seen how the Tobacco Society functioned as a large non-kin religious order for both men and women. This group celebrated the common historic roots of the tribe as a gardening people related to the Hidatsas, by nurturing a purely representative strain of tobacco. Despite their key role in the Tobacco society and other rituals, and in the production of tipis, clothing, and baggage, Crow women apparently did not form craft guilds as women did in some other tribes, nor did they form war auxiliaries.

The Crow word for "chief," *batse'tse*, appears derived from words meaning a valiant man. Several such men of war accomplishment were available to form a council, with one rising above the others to enunciate policy. The Crow headman was typical for the Plains in assuming his role on the basis of charisma, a role with no coercive power but rather an obligation to figure out what was best for his followers and to persuade them of it. He was replaced once his luck gave out. His main functions included deciding on the movements of camps and the locations of individual lodges within the village and selecting the annual camp police. The Crow chief also had an aide, the *acipē'rira`*, or camp crier, who was also supposed to be a man of distinction.

The traditional legal system of the Crows has not been studied as an independent subject, but it appears that the presence of both clans and strong military associations worked to curb antisocial behavior very effectively. The dictates of inter-clan behavior emphasized mutual respect and the avoidance of insults. The police were empowered to punish troublemakers by destroying their property, banishing them, or confiscating illegally hunted game.

The Comanches

Like the Crows, the Comanches were also unified by a common language. It cannot be said that they had a unique language, however, because their language and that of the Shoshones are almost identical, indicating a relatively recent historical separation of the two groups. There were also dialectal differences among Comanche subgroups, as noted earlier in this chapter. But all Comanches recognized each other in common with the name *Numina*, meaning "our people." This term could mean "Comanche," or "Comanche-Shoshone" in the context of intertribal relations, or in the non-Indian world, "Indian."

Despite this common identity, in practice the Comanches organized in several large independent groups that have been called bands, divisions, or tribes; "divisions" is preferred here. Each division had its own territory, leadership, and patterns of external relations, as well as distinctive customs and words for things. The main Comanche divisions included the Kwahadi (Antelopes), Kotseteka (Buffalo Eaters), Nokoni (Wanderers), Penateka (Honey Eaters), and Yampareka (Root Eaters). Some of these division names continue the Shoshonean practice of naming groups by a stereotypic food. There were several other divisions, which over time appeared, split, combined, or vanished. The divisions in turn were made up from extended family bands called *numukahni* ("people-house"), which sought unity with others for mutual profit and protection.

The Comanches practiced bilateral descent and recognized no lineages or clans. Their organization favored freedom and flexibility rather than inheritance, and it reflected origins in the Shoshonean Great Basin, where small independent groups were the rule because of scarce hunting resources. There was never a gathering or coordinated effort of all Comanche divisions to indicate that there was one large tribe. Instead, the divisions themselves sometimes developed some of the characteristics that have been used to define tribes, such as strong leaders and associations.

Military associations were formed by the Comanches, but these units played a less essential role in social control and warfare than the clubs of some other Plains tribes, at least as far as the historical record indicates. They appear to be a late (after 1820) development, and the influences of Spanish military organization and the traditions of neighboring tribes like the Cheyennes, Kiowas, and Poncas are clearly evident. The Comanche associations included the Wolves (an early no-flight society), the Crows, Swift Foxes, Little Horses, and Big Horses. In addition, there were the *pukutsi* contrary warriors, but these men functioned as individuals, not as members of a club as in other tribes. While a Swift Fox association was found in both the Nokoni and Penateka divisions, most Comanche clubs were present in only one of the divisions, supporting the idea that the Comanche divisions were structured like tribes unto themselves. There was also a Buffalo Dance done in all the divisions, no doubt related to the widespread Bull association concept, but there was no distinct Comanche Bull association in historical times. Comanche women were active in war auxiliary dances—the Scalp and Victory dance—but appear not to have formed war clubs comparable to the Kiowa Old Women, or craft guilds.

An adult man who had accumulated war honors, called *tekwɨniwapɨ* ("brave man"), was eligible to become a leader. The Comanche word for a headman was *paraibo*, seemingly derived from words relating to the sun, the east, and a bright or shining quality. As we have seen, the *paraibo* was also regarded as *tekwawapɨ*, a "good talker," and he was assisted by another good talker, the camp crier. The Comanches did not observe a strict distinction between war and peace chiefs, although they recognized such specialties and could talk about them with modified terms such as *ɨrɨ? paraivo*, "good-hearted chief" or civil leader. Although the normal function of the headman was to guide a large extended family, in the face of Spanish and then Anglo trade and warfare, a number of powerful Comanche leaders emerged who forged cooperation across and between entire divisions.

Lacking clan structures or strong police associations, the Comanches relied mostly on interpersonal force and peer pressure to resolve disputes. Their law ways were studied intensively, and it is clear that they had a system for achieving an orderly society. Tribal law was "hammered out on the hard anvil of individual cases . . . in terms of Comanche notions of individual rights and tribal standards of right conduct" (Wallace and Hoebel 1952:224). A key feature in dispute settlement was the concept of *nanɨwokɨ*—"damages," or payments for the resolution of complaints with horses, guns, blankets, and clothing.

Further comparisons of other Plains tribes would extend the conclusion warranted by the Crow–Comanche contrast, that Plains social and political life was characterized by common patterns of organization and common methods of control, with each tribe developing a distinctive combination of emphases from this basic repertoire.

Sources: Berthrong (1986); Boyd (1981); DeMallie (2001a); Densmore (1918); Fletcher and LaFlesche (1972); Fortune (1932); Fowler (2001a); Frey (1987); Gamble (1967); Gelo (1983, 1986, 1999); Greene (2009); Hoebel (1940, 1988); John and Benavides (1994); Lévi-Strauss (1966); Llewellyn and Hoebel (1941); Lowie (1916, 1982); Mandelbaum (1979); Meadows (1999); Mooney (1979); Moore (1987); Moore et al. (2001); Wallace and Hoebel (1952); Whitman (1937); and Young (2001).

CHAPTER SUMMARY

Plains Indian societies were organized in tribes, bands, and sometimes in clans, and these terms have different meanings. The term "tribe" is commonly used for the largest groups, although the definition of "tribe" is variable. Bands, flexible groupings of relatives, were the more important organizational units in everyday life. Lineages and clans, groups which included people who shared common ancestors, were important in some Plains societies. Though kin ties were basic to group formation, the Plains Indians also developed associations, groups that brought together non-relatives, providing unity across families. Associations had various overt functions, such as combat, policing, craft work, or ritual duties, and were usually exclusively male or female. Plains leaders are commonly called "chiefs" but are more properly referred to as headmen. They were men known for their battle prowess or wisdom who motivated others to collective action in war and peace. Some tribes drew leadership from a council of several chiefs. Crimes were generally limited to sexual offenses and personal injury. Unwritten, customary laws were enforced by leaders, associations, and individuals with the support of their kin. Individuals or groups sometimes applied punitive force, but public opinion was the main factor in social control. A comparison of the Crows and Comanches shows typical similarities and differences in group structure, leadership, and conflict resolution.

QUESTIONS FOR REVIEW

1. What are the benefits and drawbacks of the terms "tribe" and "chief" as they have been applied to Plains Indian societies?
2. Compare and contrast the two social units called "band" and "clan."
3. Explain the role of associations in Plains Indian life.
4. Argue for or against the statement, "Plains Indian societies had no legal systems."

CHAPTER 5

FAMILY AND SOCIAL LIFE

Behind the intricacies of tribal organization lie the everyday matters of human interaction. Plains Indian people connected to each other through bonds of kinship and descent, family, age, marriage, mutual work and play, sex, and gender. All of these factors of social life presented characteristics that could be shared between individuals to unite them, or not shared, and thus marking differences between individuals in their roles and statuses.

KINSHIP

Kin Terms

Societies have different ways of naming and categorizing relatives. The study of kin terms lends clues to peoples' perceptions about relatedness, family organization, marriage, and other social matters. In turn, patterns of kinship and social organization mesh with particular subsistence practices.

In naming and addressing kin, Plains Indians in general employ certain practices that are not found to any great degree in Euro-American kin reckoning. First, Indian languages tend to distinguish older from younger siblings with different terms. Thus, one does not say "brother" or "sister" in Comanche, but "elder brother" (*pabi?*), "younger brother" (*tami?*), "elder sister" (*patsi?*), or "younger sister" (*nami?*). Interestingly, in Comanche the two older sibling terms appear to be derived from the same root word, as do the younger sibling terms, suggesting that relative age is as much a driving semantic concern as gender. The Sioux use seven or eight different sibling terms which indicate whether the sibling is older, younger, or youngest, as well as the sex of the sibling and the sex of the speaker. This emphasis on relative age and sex of siblings results from the differing status and roles of younger and older siblings—the older ones are respected by the younger ones, mentor them, and act as surrogate parents, with older sisters taking the lead. There are two Crow words for "elder sister"; one is reducible to "little mother" and the other to "little grandmother."

When an Indian person addresses others or refers to them in their presence, it is always considered preferable to use a kin term rather than the addressee's proper name. Although traditionally much thought and significance are given to proper names and they are changed over a person's life course, it is thought to be too direct and impolite to "wear out" a person's name by saying it in front of him or her. Kin terms, on the other hand, allow an expression of closeness or mutuality. The principle of fictive kinship is especially useful in conjunction with this practice because it allows the extension of kin terms to people not related by blood or marriage. Standardized kin terminologies also involve the designation of cousins as "brother" or "sister." So, one commonly addresses a non-relative as cousin or even sibling, or a cousin as sibling, to indicate a sense of closeness, as a pretext for cooperation. The opposite strategy can also work: using the more distant term can signal distance or dissatisfaction with the relationship. Speakers can move from one strategy to the other in a short time.

The Comanches in particular have been noted for manipulating the distance of relations through terminology as the circumstances dictate. The author experienced this control first hand in the Comanche home he lived in during fieldwork. The family matriarch called him by his first name, according to Anglo custom, during the early days of their friendship and in public contexts when their relationship was not an issue. After some time, however, she frequently called him "grandson," for example, when they were among Indian people in traditional settings, or when introducing him to old friends in the tribe, and the author reciprocated with the family sobriquet "gram." One day, however, when the author annoyed his "gram," she spoke of him to some other family members, in his own presence, as "that man," as if he was not even in the room! Overt familiarity through kin term manipulation can also be rejected. "Don't 'grandpa' me," an elder man told a younger non-relative whose attempt to tighten their relationship was unwelcome.

The boundary between kin and non-kin is softened also through the use of institutionalized friendship terms. These words connote a special friendship between two unrelated persons of the same age that approaches or even exceeds a sibling relationship in its mutual dedication, similar to the notion of "blood brothers." Such friendships were more common in the pre-reservation era. They involved constant companionship and were formed by two warriors of equal status, one of whom perhaps rescued the other, or between lower and higher status warriors in something of a servant–protector relationship. A Comanche man called such a special friend *haitsi*, a word that could also be used sometimes for male relatives or as a friendly greeting for a male stranger, that is, with much the same variability that the English word "buddy" is applied. Comanche men in a *haitsi* relationship might refer to each other as *nʉmʉkwʉhʉ?*, "our wife," an allusion to the wife sharing permissible between two brothers, or they might call each other *nʉmʉtʉi?*, "our girl friends," if they loved two girls who were friends. As this latter word indicates, two women could also form a special friends relation, signified with the term *tʉi?*. The Crows had very similar terms and usages, *ị'apa`tse* for male friends and *hị'ra* for females. These customs were widespread in the Plains tribes.

Another unusual pattern from the non-Indian perspective is the presence of reflexive kin terms across generations. Words of address that are the same for both speakers, like "cousin," are also used between grandparents and grandchildren and between great-grandparents and great-grandchildren. A Comanche boy calls his maternal grandmother *kaku?* and she calls him the same. The uniform term indicates the closeness and common interests shared between grandparent and grandchild, quite different from the formal relationship between parent and child, where the terms are not uniform but distinct. In Comanche, reciprocal terms do not extend beyond four generations; there is no great-great-grandparent-grandchild term. The probable reason for this lack is that in the old days life spans were shorter and few if any people actually knew their ancestors or descendants five generations distant. But the flexible Comanche system even accounts for this eventuality. The home in which the author lived during fieldwork at one point included five generations, from one of the oldest living Comanche women to her five-year-old great-great grandson. They simply addressed each other as "younger brother" and "elder sister." Everyone was amused and charmed by the fondness that the two expressed for each other in this way, and there was no chance of confusion that they were really siblings.

Relations with kin are also sometimes marked by either heightened familiarity or formality. The joking relationship involves expectation of teasing between certain relatives as a way of drawing friendly attention to their divergent interests and defusing animosity. Rivalry between brothers-in-law seems predictable, and brothers-in-law in some tribes are expected to tease each other mercilessly. Often the humor is obscene. A Comanche would greet his wife's brother with the fake salutation "your testicles!" On the other hand, Crow brothers-in-law are expected to make friendly, impersonal banter but avoid any off-color conversation. One time when the anthropologist Robert Lowie pretended to talk to a Crow consultant as a brother-in-law; his mispronunciation of a word, which sounded like a reference to his consultant's genitals, prompted the man to smack him, as was appropriate to the pretend relationship.

Extreme respect is indicated by an avoidance relationship, in which a person would not speak to or look at another out of deference. The Crows traditionally demanded an avoidance relationship between a man and his wife's mother and wife's mother's mother. He might avoid not only engaging her, addressing her, if at all, only through his wife, but he might avoid even saying her name or words that suggested the name. She was expected to act in the same way. The custom seems to have originated out of a desire to make an exaggerated

statement that the man was not sexually involved with kinswomen of preceding generations, thus minimizing any antagonism between men of those generations. A milder version of avoidance was observed between brother and sister after puberty, to prevent any intimation of incest, and also between a man and his father-in-law.

Kin Term Systems

There has been much study of the patterns in which kin terms are employed. Despite the many possible combinations of terming practices like those mentioned above that could logically occur, there are in fact only a limited number of patterns that are employed around the world. These patterns have been standardized in the anthropological literature by referring to a type society that exhibits each one, for example, the "Hawaiian," "Eskimo," and "Iroquoian" systems. (There is some variation in the total number of kin term systems as they have been classified by anthropologists, depending on whether certain minor distinctions are noted or ignored.) The standard patterns, however, do not account particularly well for Native American systems, which often look like combinations of the standardized forms. The discussion can become very complicated, but it is possible to focus on how certain Plains Indian kin term systems correspond to patterns of family and tribal organization, and how these social elements in turn match particular subsistence practices.

Hunter-gatherers—and all Plains societies relied on hunting and gathering to some extent—often find it advantageous to emphasize physical mobility, social flexibility, and cooperation. A successful hunter must be able to move about easily, unencumbered by a large interdependent group of relatives, but he also must count on help from as wide a network of relatives and friends as possible, both in sharing food and for mutual aid when he has wandered far from home. He must be able to associate freely with potential helpers and even change group membership or recombine the groups around him in new ways to maximize his chances of survival. Composition of the band and camp circle must easily change with the seasons. All of these needs encourage an outlook toward kin relations that could be called "horizontal," concerned mainly with the potential linkages between people of the same generation. This principal has also been referred to as "generational" because of the emphasis on uniting members of the same generation. On the other hand, hunter-gatherers are not concerned with the inheritance of material wealth or land (or accompanying ritual duties and ceremonial positions), so they are not prone to emphasize "vertical" kinship ties, those running between ancestors and descendants through the generations (the exception would be hunter-gatherers who pass down rights of ownership to hunting territories, but such strict territories did not take shape on the wide open Plains).

The kin term systems of the Cheyennes, Arapahos, Gros Ventres, Comanches, Plains Apaches, Wichitas, and most other High Plains groups show the "horizontal" outlook at work. Cousins are called by the same terms as brothers and sisters; in a symbolic way, the closely cooperative nuclear family is extended outward to include the more distant cousins. Also, by using sibling terms for cousins, the cousins are symbolically deemed not appropriate for marriage (since one never marries ones brother or sister), and thus marriage outside the local group is encouraged—another way of extending social ties outward, to the hunters' benefit. This idea is applied partly in the parental generation too, so that some aunts and uncles are called "father" and "mother." For example, among the Cheyennes, one's father, his brothers, and his male cousins are all called "father," and one's mother and all her female relatives in her generation are called "mother." The father's sister and mother's brother, however, are set apart as "aunt" and "uncle," respectively. The reason for this partial assimilation of aunts and

uncles to parents is not clear, but it may again be a statement about the cooperation necessary for hunting in the Plains environment. In terms of the systems recognized by anthropologists, the High Plains pattern looks like a combination of "Hawaiian" in ego's generation and "Iroquoian" in the parental generation. These terminological practices correspond to bilateral descent and band organization as described in Chapter 4.

A few of the High Plains tribes had gardening or hereditary hunting territories close enough in their background that the issue of land inheritance was still lurking in the kinship system, and their terminology preserves some interest in "vertical" or lineal relationships. The kin term systems of the Plains Crees, Assiniboines, Tetons, Yanktons, Santees, and a few others outline but do not activate separable lines of descent. Cousins are labeled in two ways: parallel cousins (father's brother's children and mother's sister's children) are called by sibling terms, while cross cousins (father's sister's children and mother's brother's children) are referred to as cousins. Their parents are correspondingly referred to alternatively with parent or aunt/uncle terms as in the Cheyenne pattern. Therefore, two lines of relatives are recognized on both the mother's and father's side, those that are assimilated to the nuclear family and those that are kept more distant. In general the term systems of these tribes conform to the pattern called "Dakota" by anthropologists. Even though there are vestiges of lineal organization in these terminological practices, the lines were not activated for inheritance on the High Plains, and the Dakota system corresponds to the characteristic bilateral descent and band organization described in Chapter 4.

Yet other tribes kept gardening in their subsistence regime and have a clear "vertical" orientation. The Crows, Pawnees, Mandans, Hidatsas, and probably Arikaras exhibited variants of a term system labeled Crow, which highlights the maternal lines of descent and corresponds to the presence of matrilineal clans, through which agricultural rights

FIGURE 5.1   *Portrait of a Cheyenne girl by Edward S. Curtis, 1911.*

or associated ceremonial obligations were passed from generation to generation. All of these tribes were semisedentary river villagers except the Crows, who were nevertheless an offshoot of the Hidatsas. In the case of the Crows, gardening was only superficial and ceremonial (only tobacco), and the function of the lineal ties evolved away from transmission of land rights and toward bonding among (matrilineally) related males for warfare. The Omahas, Osages, Poncas, Kansas, Iowas, and Otoes, who occupied the eastward prairies using some combination of horticulture and hunting, also had a vertical orientation, but theirs corresponds to the formation of patrilineal clans. Their terminology systems are labeled Omaha, essentially a mirror image of the matrilineal Crow pattern.

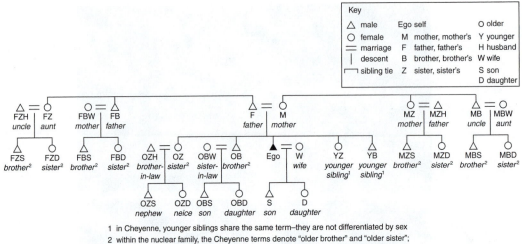

FIGURE 5.2   *Cheyenne kinship terminology. Using the closest equivalent English terms, this diagram shows how a Cheyenne man (Ego) refers to his relatives when using the Cheyenne language and traditional kinship system. This is a typical example; Cheyenne practices vary somewhat depending on time period, band composition, and sex of Ego.*

The Crow system is perhaps the most fascinating, or confusing, to non-Indian people because it involves the application of kin terms outside of their normal generational position. A Crow young man addresses as "father" his biological father and certain uncles, but also certain cousins and certain relatives in the grandparental generation. These practices make sense when two basic rules are kept in mind: first, in Crow I call my father's brother "father" (in the common way of extending the parental term outward); second, I call my mother's brother "elder brother" (the maternal uncle is indeed like a brother in that he is a nurturing elder member of my matriclan—a clan brother, so to speak). In conjunction these two rules play out in a curious way. Following the rules, my father's sister's son—my cousin—calls my father "elder brother." My father in turn calls my cousin "younger brother." Anyone who is my father's "younger brother" I call "father"; therefore, I call my cousin "father" even though he is in my generation and could even be younger than me.

Something similar happens in the generation above me too. Again following the rules, my father calls his mother's brother (my great-uncle) "elder brother"; anyone who is my father's older brother I call "father." There is in effect a diagonal skewing of the parental term through the generations.

The result is that in the Crow system I call "father" all the men of my father's matriclan regardless of their generation, a practice which emphasizes the perpetual fatherly relationship that men of my father's clan are supposed to adopt toward me and other offspring of my mother's clan, as part of the ongoing connection between the two clans. The connection is expressed first in the marriage of my parents and in my birth, but continually in other ritualized ways. For instance, my father's clan gives presents to me at special times in my life and may bestow my name. In turn, I will be among many matrilineally related men of several generations who call each other "brother" and are simultaneously all addressed as "father" by members of my wife's and children's matriclan, and this uniformity of

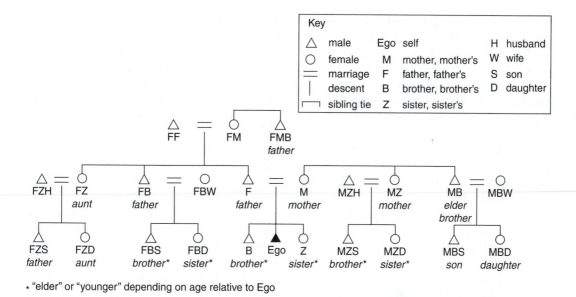

FIGURE 5.3 *Crow kinship terminology. Using the closest equivalent English terms, this diagram shows how a Crow man (Ego) refers to his relatives when using the Crow language and traditional kinship system.*

address expresses our internal solidarity and corporate obligations to other clans.

The Omaha system of the Southern Siouans has been called "Crow with a sex-change operation." In Omaha I apply the word "mother" to my mother, her sister, her brother's daughter, and her father's sister. The result is a skewed line of patrilineally related women.

FAMILY

The family, variously defined, remains a useful concept when exploring the social bonds among pairs of people and small groups that were made when kin ties were activated. For even though contemporary social scientists debate the definition of "family," as well as the question of whether "family" is a worthwhile category for social analysis, modern Indian people are very comfortable with the word. It reflects Native words and ideas. They use it to mean groupings of people centered on one or more parents and their children

who are living and working closely together, and also for the larger networks of people who are related to each other and have common interests.

It is also important to recognize the concept of family because, from an Indian viewpoint, this was a structure that defined in direct and powerful terms the primary social roles and responsibilities, such as "father" and "mother," that nearly all proper humans beings faced. The family embodied the moral principles governing social relations. These principles were fundamental and universal, so much so that even animals were believed to have families with roles and responsibilities for each member.

The smallest units of Indian society conformed to the standard ideas of the nuclear family and extended family. The nuclear family, as discussed in Chapter 4, consists of a man and woman and their children and is usually the smallest group of people living together—in one tipi or, as the children got older, in two or more adjacent lodges. A childless couple, or a single parent with his or her children, could also function as a minimal group, but would be regarded within the culture as an incomplete nuclear family. More common in Indian societies were extended families. An extended family included other relatives besides those in the nuclear family; it could be extended vertically to include grandparents or grandchildren, or it could broaden horizontally to join, for example, two men, their wives, and the children of both couples; or, it could reach in both directions at the same time. The Comanches use the word *nʉmʉnahkahni* ("people house," "people living together") to mean an extended family, and the Teton *tʰiyóšpaye* is a similar concept. An extended family could occupy a compound of adjacent tipis or a single large earth lodge or grass house.

Since bands were composed of multiple nuclear and extended families and stray individuals who affiliated with these groups, but there was no set number of families required to make a band, the definitional boundary between "family" and "band" can be uncertain to anthropologists and of little importance to the people who actually live in these units. The Comanche and Teton words for extended family connote something that can be combined into a larger unit, and can be used for the larger unit also. Indian people often use the English words "family" or "clan" loosely at different levels.

To add further complexity, men and women sometimes had more than one spouse at the same time, and the spouses and children occupied multiple tipis, stretching the usual notion of a nuclear arrangement but not meeting the definition of an extended family. To skirt these definitional questions when they do not matter to the discussion at hand, the neutral term "co-resident group" can be used.

Through an individual's lifetime, he or she typically participated in two or more families, at least one as a child, and at least one as a parent. All people, perhaps except in drastic instances when a population was nearly eradicated by disease or warfare, also had some sense of belonging to a wider network of relatives. A person's position in all these constellations of human interaction was determined by his or her place in the life cycle.

THE LIFE CYCLE

All Plains societies recognize some number of age grades, categories of people based on age brackets and associated statuses, roles, and responsibilities. Comanche grading, for example, is much like that in contemporary non-Indian practice, with teenagers distinguished from children and adults, and so on:

	Male		**Female**	
"baby"	*ohna?a?*		*ohna?a?*	
"child"	*tuinʉhpʉ?*	pre-teen boy	*tʉeput*	pre-teen girl
"adolescent"	*tuibihtsi?*	young man	*nai?pi*	young woman
"adult"	*tenahpʉ?*	man	*hʉbi*	middle-aged woman
"elder"	*sukuupʉ*	elderly man	*pʉetʉpʉ*	elderly woman
	narabʉ	"old man," joking	*hʉbi tsiitsi?*	"little old lady"

These grades are not actual groups of people "on the ground," but simply life stages with associated typical behaviors. Together they serve as an outline of the life cycle.

Birth, Infancy, and Childhood

Foregrounding the earliest life stages are attitudes about reproduction and childbearing. In general, the human capacity to reproduce is a theme that is celebrated in Plains culture, and children are highly valued. Some writers have speculated that the high rates of miscarriage, infant mortality, and women's death in childbirth that are characteristic of equestrian societies inspired pro-natal values and behaviors. Despite these cultural attitudes, before the reservation era birth and survival rates remained low and families were not large. In times of epidemic or when warfare was accelerated, the birth rate did not keep pace with replacement, one reason for the frequency of captivity and adoption.

There were also times when children were not wanted. To avoid burdening women with caring for multiple babies, a post-partum sex taboo was observed; a man avoided relations with a wife during the long period (up to four or five years) that she nursed their baby. The Cheyennes avowed that a couple should avoid sex with each other or anyone else until their first-born was well-grown, lest the child die. Other cultural beliefs reinforced this reliance on continence. Among the Sioux, sexual relations were valued mainly if not only for procreation. A man was supposed to control his desires during his wife's pregnancy by praying, taking sweat baths, and going to war. Babies born covered with mucous were thought to be the product of parents who had, inappropriately, continued to engage in sex throughout the pregnancy. The people scorned women who became pregnant frequently, especially those who became pregnant while they were still nursing a child, for not having their existing child's best interest at heart. They would say a baby who was weaned prematurely because of its mother's pregnancy was "rectum killed," because a pregnant mother's milk became watery, causing diarrhea in the baby.

Although herbs where regularly applied in promoting the health of women, it appears that medicines did not play much of a part in reproductive control. Sources on this subject are inconclusive: some mention the general Plains use of herbs in birth control and abortion or specific plants found on the Plains that have these properties, but without actual examples of use by Plains tribes. Contraception was a matter of abstinence, and abortion was induced with strong blows to the abdomen with fists or stones, an occasional procedure reported for the Comanches, Assiniboines, and others. The Cheyennes, however, who were relatively rigid in sexual and reproductive matters, reportedly viewed abortion as a crime. There is an account from the 1860s of the discovery of an aborted Cheyenne fetus. The council of headmen ordered all the women to appear with their breasts exposed. The breasts were inspected for signs of lactation, and one girl was then charged with the offense. She was banished from the tribe until after the annual renewal of the Sacred Arrows, a ritual which could erase misdeeds.

Infanticide executed by the mother is not unusual in traditional non-state societies and, like abortion, may be rationalized by those practicing it when the mother is unable to care for the baby or when the father will not take responsibility or is not considered socially acceptable. It is also employed in cases when a baby is deformed or severely ill. Probably in part on account of this practice, early non-Indian observers sometimes remarked on the absence of people with mental or physical impairments in Indian populations. Infanticide was usually committed through gradual neglect or abandonment rather than outright killing, although there are some accounts on the Plains of live burial. Twins, which placed an unusual burden on a mother in a highly mobile society, were perhaps more liable to infanticide, although they were not categorically condemned and in some cases were considered lucky and powerful—these attitudes varied even within the same tribe. In many cases unwanted children were adopted rather than killed, since adoption was extremely common and there was an overriding desire to maintain tribal populations, at least in the Historic Period.

Normally the prospect of a new child was a joyous one. Because babies in the womb and infants were considered both holy and vulnerable, a pregnant woman and those around her were careful to conduct themselves properly and not expose the baby to any dangerous influences. A lack of care at this critical time could cause the baby to return to the spirit world or to grow up with problems. Too much or too little exertion on the mother's part could alternately hurt the baby or make it lazy. If the mother was startled, it could cause a birthmark on the baby. She should stay close to home and make clothing for the child. Oglala women avoided eating rabbit and duck meat so the baby would not be born with a harelip or webbed feet. Women attending the mother should be of unimpeachable character.

A woman going into labor set up a pile of pillows and blankets and strode them on widely-spread knees while holding tight to two sticks planted in the ground. The father, and males in general, were kept out of the lodge during the delivery, as the conventional idea was that their presence would stall the birth. Instead, the woman was tended by one or more midwives who administered herbal medicines and massage. The emerging baby was received in the hands of the head midwife. She cut the navel cord to the width of three fingers and disposed of the placenta by wrapping it in hide and placing it high in a tree. When the attached part of the umbilicus fell off, it was sewn into a beaded leather container in the shape of a lizard or turtle (animals symbolizing long life) and also hung in a tree or on the child's cradle. Preservation of the afterbirth and cord from animals and sorcerers ensured good fortune.

The birth was proclaimed and celebrated around the camp, and in some tribes the arrival of a son or the woman's first born got special attention. Then the child was welcomed into the human world by having its ears pierced. The Crows pierced a baby's lobes two days after birth with an awl, though not in any special ceremony; the hole was kept open with greased sticks until the edges healed, then earrings were put through them. The Lakotas often did the piercing along

with naming, and as part of the Sun Dance or some other large ceremony.

The naming of a child was another symbolic step in granting human status, while also recognizing distinctive traits or instilling desired qualities. There were no surnames prior to the reservation period, when non-Indian practices were imposed, only singular names that denoted some personal quality or event in the life of the child, its family, or band. Affectionate nicknames were given to infants until more formal names were bestowed, at no particular point, but once it was apparent that the baby would survive the early days of life. The first formal name was given by the father or, preferably, by some person of distinction whom the father honored with the request. It was typical to call upon a noted warrior, who would give male or female alike a name referring in some oblique way to one of his exploits. Some kind of brief naming ceremony was staged in which the baby was declared to have the new name and lifted to the sun with prayers. Both among the Crows and Comanches, it was customary to lift the baby four times, a little higher each time. The Comanches believed that a baby's name could influence it, so that a sickly child would be named with a strong-sounding name, or even renamed if the first name was not sufficiently helpful. As males matured, their transitions through life were marked with the adoption of new names, ones referring to their own exploits rather than those of their mentors. Women's names typically did not change upon marriage to somehow incorporate their husband's name, nor were there titles akin to "Miss" and "Mrs."

Almost immediately after birth, the infant was placed in a baby carrier (described in Chapter 6), and it spent most of each day and the large part of its early years bound in its container. Non-Indian writers have speculated about the psychological and physical effects of restricting a baby in this way. Some thought that confinement led to pent-up aggression which exploded later in the adult Indian's "warlike" disposition, or that confinement slowed muscle development, leading to a need for compensatory regimens of exercise and ordeal for boys as they grew. Alternately, anthropologist Charles Hudson proposed that binding actually aided or accelerated the baby's muscle development by causing it to tense its muscles without moving its limbs, and thus perform isometric exercise, which can be an efficient and safe way of building strength. There is no conclusive evidence that tying babies into cradles had much effect on them, good or bad, beyond protecting them and ensuring that they were readily transported and thus more easily cared for.

Mothers were attentive and made sure their babies were dry, fed, and rested as much as possible. They made diapers from soft fawn skin stuffed with moss or fuzz from the cattail plant, washed the baby frequently with yucca root soap, powdered it with rotten cottonwood or the fungus that grows shelf-like on trees, and soothed its skin with a grease mixture such as marrow and wild bergamot. Many beliefs were held about how to optimize lactation and nursing. A nursing Arapaho mother avoided exposing her breasts to the heat of the sun and campfire, and even refused hot drinks, so her milk would not be "cooked." Newly formed milk was thought most healthful, so that a husband sometimes drew off his wife's early morning milk and spit it out, or a weaned child or puppy would be allowed to suckle, before the baby nursed. In addition to their own milk, mothers fed babies sips of soup and bits of meat which they chewed first. They rocked the children and sang soothing lullabies, softly intoning repeated phrases by humming or vibrating their lips, some with simple lyrics like this Southern Cheyenne example sung in 1990 by Wilma Blackowl Hamilton of Calumet, Oklahoma: "My little baby, my little boy, my little stinker" (Giglio 1994:54).

Childhood was a free and easy time so long as the band was not under stress from hunger or warfare. Children spent much of the day running, swimming, hurling mud, catching grasshoppers and butterflies. They were given a great deal of freedom and encouraged to be independent, curious, and even reckless. They were taught to mind themselves and not be an annoyance to their elders, but there was little direct supervision, and discipline was mild. Adults taught the rules for living by allowing children to have direct experiences, or through tales that described the experiences of others, and not through appeals to abstract statements about right and wrong. Their lessons about behavior were practical, focusing on how children should avoid getting themselves or someone else hurt. If they had to scare children into behaving, they warned them that some mythic creature would come get them, a possibility supported by the tales of careless children who got separated from camp, only to be imprisoned by a giant owl. This method shifted the role of disciplinarian from the parents or guardians to some imaginary being. There was little corporal punishment of children. Spanking was very rare. The Crows might pour water up the nose of a young child who refused to stop crying, but usually after one time just the threat of this punishment was enough. Discipline was often meted by the older sister who watched the children during the day or, among a matrilineal group like the Crows, by the mother's brother. Parents, though they had and exercised authority, were a little more distant; grandparents were indulgent teachers rather than disciplinarians. Any tone of authority was more than offset by the generous encouragement and treats given to children for their good behavior and little accomplishments.

The favorite child was a common custom. Parents might recognize one of their children in special ways. The favored one was lavished with presents and unusually fine clothing and honored in ceremonies at which the parents gave away gifts in the child's name. Girls as well as boys were selected for this treatment, and even adoptees were eligible. Singling out a child for special recognition was a way of highlighting the traits desired in all children, and a way for the parents to pursue prestige in public in a concentrated manner, when they could not afford to display wealth through all their children.

To some extent children lived a miniature adulthood. Kids of both sexes were put on horseback as soon as they could stay upright, so that they learned to ride by age four or five, and as they grew they helped tend the horses too, a task important to all in the camp. Though they could not do the heavy work of gardening, children in the sedentary tribes were also kept busy in the planted fields scaring birds. Girls played with dolls, set up miniature tipis, and pretended to cook, and they received small versions of their mothers' accessories, such as belts with scabbards and awl cases. Girls and boys played house together; the Crows called it *nā'xapāsu`a*, "calf-skin tipi." Boys were given toy bows and arrows and taught to aim at rolling hoops or stalk small birds and rabbits. Some tribes had boy's clubs that were lead-ins to the men's military societies, like the Kiowa *Pòláhyòp* or Rabbits for boys of age 8–12. At tribal gatherings, Rabbit society members wore small versions of adult regalia, camped apart from their parents in small tipis, and had a special dance in which they imitated their namesake by hopping with their hands held like ears. Childhood was also the time when some of the lifelong comradeships between pairs of boys or girls were first formed.

In rural Plains communities some of these methods of childrearing are still observable. Comanches still mention the giant owl to misbehaving children, or else a modern counterpart such as "the policeman." At a Kiowa powwow in 1983 a boy of perhaps age nine climbed so far up the pole used to support lights for the dance ground that if he fell he would surely have been injured, but though he was in plain view no one ordered him to climb down. The next evening two packs of boys amused themselves by throwing lit firecrackers at each other in a game of chicken, which was only halted by adults when one of the children was burned. When a child is hurt in these situations, provided there is not a true emergency, their discomfort is greeted with laughter and ridicule.

These approaches do not indicate laxness of parental care but rather a traditional emphasis on self-reliance and experiential learning, quite different from the doting witnessed in modern non-Indian suburbia. Modern parents still heap children with praise or give them candy for shooting a small bird or dancing well. And, they encourage children to imitate their elders in several traditionalist settings, most notably in the "tiny tots" category of powwow dance competition.

Puberty

The onset of the teen years marked a new status for boys and girls. The period around ages 13–16 was the point at which different gender identities were set more firmly. A boy would move out of his parent's dwelling and acquire a separate tipi, in order to observe strict avoidance of his sisters. Girls were approaching marriageable age and were carefully chaperoned. It is notable that the Comanche words for life stages above do not distinguish gender at the baby stage, since babies are not considered sexual or fully gendered beings. Normally the tribes had terms for the teen roles different from the words for male and female children. The Comanche *tuibitsi* or boy teenager is stereotyped within the tribe as someone who has discovered an interest in girls, likes to show off for them, sometimes foolishly, and is always primping and fixing his hair. In the old days, he would be seeking his first experiences in the hunt and battle or maybe going on a first vision quest. His female counterpart, called *naipi*, is also expected to be preoccupied with her appearance, but demure. Like her male counterpart, she should avoid siblings of the opposite sex, addressing her brothers and male parallel cousins only through a younger sibling. Her status is indicated most notably by menarche.

People across the area accord special significance to menstruation. They regard menstrual blood as the outward sign of a woman's procreative power, a kind of power that clashes (in Lakota, *ohakaya*—"to cause to be blocked or tangled") with the power of men, even medicine men. Although female procreative ability is culturally valued, and at times may even be characterized as superior to the power of men and post-menopausal women because it is inherent rather than begged from the spirits, menstruating women are thought of as impure, and their proximity capable of contaminating sacred objects. Even the odor of the menstrual flow may destroy the power that makes shields, other war implements, and ceremonial objects effective, or the medicine wielded by sacred men. Women do not have control over this power or its negative effects, and in some tribal traditions it is also thought that spirits lurking near menstruating women could also cause problems in men, such as palsy or madness.

These beliefs necessitate a number of taboos. Most pointedly, a woman is to have no sexual relations during her menses. In the old days, when camp was on the move, menstruating women had to march some distance from and downwind of the main party. It was paramount that a woman avoid touching a man's shield lest she spoil its protective function. The Crows kept menstruating women away from wounded men or men going to war. Among the Sioux, menstruating women were restricted to riding slow horses, as their power was thought to ruin fast ones. It was said that if a menstruating woman tanned a bear hide her skin would turn black and her face hairy, or that if she touched a weasel skin she might turn sick and die. Taboos also protected the woman from herself. She was supposed to avoid cooking or touching food, even her own, use special eating implements, and not even touch herself if avoidable—to this end menstruating women used special backscratchers.

Other people in the presence of menstruating women are also supposed to take precautions. Comanche medicine men and women must not open the satchel that holds their medicines when near a menstruating woman. To magically prevent themselves from inadvertently stepping in menstrual blood, Comanche men attach red mescal beans to the fringe of their moccasins.

To lessen chances of pollution, a bundle was made to catch the menstrual flow. Oglala bundles were made of soft buckskin lined with cattail down, held in place with a belt or breechclout. The bundle holding a young woman's first menstrual flow was tied up high in a tree, not unlike the cased umbilicus of a newborn, to keep it away from coyotes and other animals that might steal it in order to gain power over the woman. Medicine men and women also sought the discharge to make love potions. Perhaps to prevent this misuse, according to one report, among the Sioux a girl was seated over a hole in the ground to commingle her first flow with the earth in a positive magical statement of fertility.

In buffalo days, women in many tribes secluded themselves during their periods to further minimize the effects of their powerful state on those around them. Oglala women moved outside the camp to a special dwelling called *isnatipi* ("to dwell in alone"), generally referred to in English as a menstrual lodge. Anecdotes indicate that women did not feel stigmatized by this practice but accepted it as proper and actually enjoyed the respite from normal chores. Female relatives would wait on them with food, and they spent the time perfecting their crafts like quillwork and tanning and meditating on themes of womanhood as explored in myths about the moon and other female spirits. A young woman's character was thought to be particularly vulnerable during her first menses; the influences surrounding her at this time were thought to determine whether or not she would become virtuous. She would be attended to by a reputable, elderly woman who could instruct her in her duties as a future wife and mother. Nellie Zelda Star Boy Menard, a Lakota elder, recounted her memories of how she was taught during her first stay in the menstrual lodge in 1925:

> During the day all I did was sit and do either beadwork first. I have learned how to make the thread out of sinew then I sewed the beads on . . . .

She told me to think about a design in my mind and try to apply that design in my beading straight lines. When tired she taught me how to select the porcupine quills . . . . I had to take one quill at a time bite one end and flatten it with my fingernails . . . . I always have to work with quills in my mouth to keep it soft while sewing or wrap. Next I have started a pair of moccasins and within 4 days or as long as I can see without lamp I had to finish at least one side of moccasins . . . . My last day grandma taught me how to soften the rawhide and cut the soles . . . . Of course I was clean up every so often. Wash and eat. I cannot look outside or go near any men or boys.

(Bol and Menard 2000:26)

At the end of her seclusion, Nellie's grandmother bathed her with sage-infused water. Whatever dresses and underclothing Nellie wore during the four days were burned.

At least a few tribes lacked such firm traditions. Crow accounts vary as to whether women were isolated during their menses. A couple of reports refer to confinement for four days in a special tipi or willow shelter, with a diet of only wild roots, ending with purification through incensing and bathing or sweat-bathing. But Lowie maintained that most of the Crows he spoke with circa 1907 denied the use of any sort of menstrual hut. Plains Apaches did not practice isolation, but menstruating women were kept away from ritual settings unless they themselves were the subjects of a curing procedure.

As Menard's remembrance indicates, after reservations were established and through the twentieth century menstruating women continued to seek isolation from others either in traditional menstrual lodges or in some modified manner, for example, occupying separate tents, staying inside, and not looking out or going near males. Among the contemporary Oglalas, "it is still believed that menstruating women diminish the power of sacred things, and if they should accidentally come in contact with them, the objects must be taken into a sweat lodge and be prayed and sung over by the medicine man to restore their power" (M. Powers 1986:200–201). Sheryl Looking Elk of Pine Ridge Reservation (Sioux) writes, "My daughters received their Indian names after the Sun Dance four years ago . . . I didn't get a chance to see them in the ceremony as it was 'that time of month,' so out of respect for the Lakota way, I stayed in the car . . . " (Reyer 1991:40). At Southern Plains powwows today it is customary to make an announcement asking menstruating women to avoid the dance area.

Public ceremonies marking a person or group's transition to puberty or adulthood are common in societies around the world. They may involve boys or girls, but in societies in which only one sex has a puberty ritual, it is more often the males whose progress is highlighted in this way. It is often supposed that males have a greater need for such ceremonial recognition because their sexual maturation is less evident from observable physical changes. In Plains Indian society, however, boys do not undergo puberty rituals, but girls do, though still only in some tribes. It may be that because of the Plains emphasis on hunting and warfare, boys easily demonstrated their transition to manhood with a bison kill or war deed, whereas girls did not have a single episode or undertaking that announced womanhood. On the other hand, girls' physical maturation was evinced most suddenly with menarche, which could be the occasion for a public ceremony.

While an Oglala boy's transition received little notice, a girl's passage into adolescence was often marked by a public ritual. About 10 days after a young woman's first menses and after she had completed her time in the menstrual lodge, her parents sponsored a ritual called *Isnati awicalowan* ("they sing over her first menses"), also known as the Buffalo Ceremony. The buffalo was a common symbol of fecundity and family responsibility. The ritual was conducted by a sacred person at the father's request. The girl's passage to womanhood was celebrated in front of a large congregation as she was instructed in her responsibilities to her family and people, and in her relationship to the primordial female spirit White Buffalo Calf Woman. Her menstrual bundle was placed in a plum tree to keep it safe from Inktomi, the trickster spirit in spider form, and a new tipi was erected by the girl's mother and female relatives. All outstanding men and non-menstruating women were invited to the tipi, where the girl sat cross-legged, as a man or small child would. She sat between the fireplace and an altar topped with a buffalo skull, pipe, prayer wands, a bowl, and sage.

The presiding sacred person wore a buffalo headdress and a buffalo tail. He smoked the pipe and blew the smoke into the orifices of the buffalo skull and then painted a red line from the forehead of the skull to the back. The girl was then told how she was expected to behave as a woman: to be as industrious as a spider, as silent and wise as the turtle, and as cheerful as a meadowlark. After cautioning her about evil influences, the sacred person told her that she was now a buffalo cow and he a buffalo bull. He pantomimed a rutting bull in a dance by sidling up next to the girl as buffalo do in their mating rituals. The mother placed sage in the girl's lap and under her arms each time the sacred person approached. Finally, the sacred person placed a bowl with water and chokeberries on the ground and instructed the girl that this is a buffalo watering hole. She bent down and drank from it as a buffalo would and then the bowl was passed for all to drink from. When all had sipped from the bowl the girl was invited to sit as a grown woman, with both legs out to her side.

The last remaining vestiges of the girl's childhood were altered. She removed her dress and the sacred person offered it to someone needy. The girl's mother changed the style of her hair to allow it to fall to her shoulders and to the front, as a woman would wear it, rather than to the back as a child would. Then the sacred person drew upon her head as he had painted the buffalo skull, with a red line across her forehead and running back along the part. At this point the girl was proclaimed a woman and everyone exited the tipi to celebrate with a feast and a giveaway.

Anthropologists have observed that the Oglala girl's puberty rite sequence conforms to the pattern called "rite of passage" by theorist Arnold Van Gennep (1960). Van Gennep, writing circa 1909, noted that rituals marking the transfer of a person from one social status to another all had similar structures no matter the particulars. They unfolded in three stages, which he termed separation, liminality, and incorporation. Nellie Menard was first separated from the surroundings and contacts that were part of her childhood. She was then kept in a state of marginality, between the old and new, during her menstrual lodge seclusion (Van Gennep's term "liminality" is based on the Latin word for "threshold.") This was the phase of intensive instruction in her new role. Then, with the Buffalo Ceremony, Nellie was publicly reintroduced to society with a new status. All of these steps were denoted by such symbolic measures as ritual cleansing, clothing and cosmetic changes, and the acquisition of new, "adult" knowledge.

Details of the Oglala girl's puberty ceremony varied depending on the sacred person conducting it, the other actors, and on the time period. A few accounts associate another Lakota sacred ritual *Tapa Wankayeyapi* or the Throwing of the Ball Ceremony with the puberty transition sequence (others treat it and the puberty rite separately as two of the seven most sacred Lakota procedures). The ball is a beaded, stuffed buckskin globe enclosing an especially round stone of the kind that is so often valued in Sioux ritual, symbolizing the universe. A girl tossed the ball among a group of female age mates, and whoever caught it would receive great blessings and gifts from the thrower's family. When connected with the puberty sequence, it was the initiated girl who tossed the ball.

Not all Oglala girls could afford a puberty ceremony because the concluding feast and give-away were a burden on the family. It was up to girls who did not have one to demonstrate their virtue nevertheless, by working hard and attaining skills. Other tribes had much less involved rituals or none at all. A Comanche favorite daughter was sometimes set to run behind a spry horse, holding its tail, to mark her new womanhood. The Crows lacked any ritual, stating that girls often married around the onset of puberty, making further recognition of adulthood unnecessary. Puberty rites of any kind have been less reliably performed across the Plains since around the 1920s. As girl increasingly attended off-reservation boarding schools, as traditional forms of wealth gave way to reservation poverty, and as status relations between men and women shifted, the custom became less feasible or desirable.

Courtship and Marriage

A young man felt confident in taking the active role in courtship once he made some achievements as a hunter and warrior. Generally, this meant he waited until age 20–25, or later, before marrying. Women were thought to be marriageable at about age 16, sometimes earlier.

Courtship was conducted in much the same way across all the Plains tribes. The man took a liking to a particular woman and waited to encounter her some way off from her father's lodge; the places where women gathered wood and water were the likely spots. Initially the man might sit along the path to one of these places and play tunes on a "courting flute," a wooden flageolet, as a way of expressing his interest and, some would say, mesmerizing his intended. Or, he might ask her for a drink of the water she had

FIGURE 5.4 Colored pencil drawing by Big Back (Cheyenne) of courtship, circa 1870s. On the right the man approaches the woman, and on the left he enfolds her in his blanket.

collected or just tug on her dress or toss pebbles as she passed by. If she paid attention to him, they sought privacy to talk with one another. A common practice was for the man to appear wrapped in his buffalo robe or blanket and embrace the woman so that she was shrouded with him. Thus totally concealed, the two would talk, sometimes for hours, the man professing his love and vaunting his skills as a provider.

Lakota young women took control of the process by interviewing a succession of suitors under the blanket. A woman would wait outside her tipi at sunset, and soon a long line of suitors would form. Her kinfolk sat inside the lodge, out of sight but watching to size up the prospects. One by one the men stepped up and enveloped her in their blankets, intent on making quick, convincing pitches before it was the next man's turn.

Often the suitor enlisted a go-between such as older, distant female relative to talk on his behalf. The Crows called the practice of using a go-between *bĭ'a-kus-irāu*, "talking towards a woman." She attempted to arrange meetings for the lovers. Or, the suitor might befriend his intended's brother while on the warpath in a calculated way, treating him specially and giving him gifts so that he would put in a good word. Among the Comanches, an eager suitor might address his girlfriend's brother as *nɨmɨara*, "our children's uncle," as a further hint. If such communications were rebuffed by the girlfriend's family, the couple sometimes resorted to elopement. They rode off together and camped away for days or weeks, until their families had time to get used to the idea.

This emphasis on the backing of relatives is significant, for marriage was in many cases actually an agreement not only between the bride and groom, but between their kin groups. It was the consensus between their families that legitimized and supported their relationship and the offspring born from their relationship. In tribes with bilateral descent, such as the Arapahos, Cheyennes, and Comanches, marriage can be understood as an exchange relationship between two interest groups of related men. One group is formed by the groom's father (if still alive) and brothers, and the bride's father or brothers made up the opposite group. The bride's male relatives reviewed and approved of the groom by studying his character and the reputation of his family, and they authorized her to live with him. They essentially bestowed their sister on the groom.

Sometimes the woman left her kinsmen to live with the groom's people. This form of post-marital residence is known as patrilocal or virilocal residence. Those tribes with a matrilineal structure (e.g., Hidatsas, Pawnees), and some with patrilineal (e.g., Omahas) or bilateral (Cheyennes, Arapahos) descent, at least sometimes preferred that the groom move in with the bride's people, in the pattern called matrilocal or uxorilocal residence.

The groom's kinsmen completed the mutual exchange by providing gifts to the bride's family, usually horses, but sometimes blankets or other goods. (In elopement cases, the male's kinsmen hurried to provide such gifts even while the couple was still away to smooth over relations between the families.) The groom was also expected to provide meat to the bride's family, and in poorer times he might pledge his service as a hunter to her family for two or three years rather than give horses. Although Indian people sometimes have spoken of buying wives, these transfers of wealth, which symbolically cemented the relationship between the kin groups united behind the marriage, were more than simple purchases. Thus, the horses or goods that were exchanged are better called "bride wealth," which connotes strategic exchange, rather than by the older term "brideprice," which suggests buying and selling. The groom's labor on behalf of the bride's family is referred to by anthropologists as "bride service." The Mandans and Hidatsas added "dowry," goods transferred along with the bride from her family to the groom's, in their elaborate wedding productions. Marriages involving exchange between families were considered the most prestigious and stable. In poorer tribes, however, such as those to the far north that lacked many horses, exchange marriage was a difficult ideal to achieve with regularity, and the majority of couples united only by common consent.

Even though courtship was stylized, there were no fancy proposals and few wedding ceremonies to speak of. The suitor made his offer by presenting the gifts and the union was confirmed, or not, in the symbolic manner in which the presents were handled. If the woman's family took the tendered horses into their herd, the marriage was completed; if they drove them back to the man's herd, he was refused. This procedure spared everyone the potential humiliation of a rejected direct proposal. Other than the acceptance of the gifts, it was generally only the onset of cohabitation that marked the start of a marriage. The Mandans and Hidatsas were exceptional in holding a ceremonial feast in which the couple took center stage seated on a buffalo robe in the groom's earth lodge while horses and goods were transferred between the families in both directions. After the reservation period many people afforded themselves of Christian wedding ceremonies. Also, some Indian communities have developed modern nativistic wedding ceremonies based on the peyote ritual or other tribal rites, in which a medicine man publicly blesses the union.

People believed that arranged marriages between young women and older men were more lasting than unorchestrated unions between young age mates. The woman had some say about who she married but was bound by the decision of her male kinsmen. When a brother betrothed his sister to a man and she disobeyed the brother by eloping with someone else, she caused her brother great shame and was liable to be cut off from her family. It was her defiance of familial authority more than the elopement itself that was considered the offense. Old-time informants stated that men had the right to kill a sister who would not submit to their plans, though this outcome was rare. Or a woman so forced might commit suicide in protest, again, a rare occurrence, but definitely recorded. These severe customs may sound especially objectionable to contemporary people because the decisions were made by males and women were treated like chattels, but that was what was done.

The overriding concerns dictating marriage choice were the avoidance of incest and a desire to either marry within or outside the local group. Any recognizable degree of relatedness by blood would disqualify a potential mate. Young people often were not aware who their more distant relatives were, and it was up to the elders who watched over their courting to warn them, "he (or she) is your relative—stay away." Also, social groups had preferences about whether someone should marry within (endogamy) or outside (exogamy) the unit. Inhabitants of the Mandan, Hidatsa, and Pawnee villages typically married someone from the same village, to preserve the character and traditions of that settlement. A rule of exogamy, on the other hand, promoted the mixing of people and beneficial connections between groups. Clans like those found among the Osages, Omahas, and Iowas always practiced exogamy, and marriage between rather than within moieties was considered ideal. The residential bands of the fully nomadic tribes were also exogamous in general, although marriage within the band was allowed in some of these tribes, notably the Cheyennes, during certain periods of tribal structural change or for those men did not have the motivation or status to connect with women of other bands. There was also at times considerable intermarriage between neighboring tribes such as the Sioux and Cheyenne (see Chapter 11).

Many if not most married people had only one spouse, living as husband and wife in monogamy. But the Plains tribes all held plural marriage, or polygamy, to be the ideal. More prevalent was the form called polygyny, in which one man had more than one wife at the same time. Polyandry, in which a woman had multiple husbands at the same time, was also found in many groups, but secondarily to polygyny. Often, the co-spouses were siblings, resulting in the forms called sororal polygyny and fraternal polyandry. Old-time Comanches were fond of saying that sisters made good co-wives, because they were used to living and working together, and if a man liked a woman he was liable to like her sisters too. On the other hand, jealousy between non-related co-wives is a common theme in Plains oral tradition.

How were plural marriages made, and what was life like for those living in them? Typically, a man married one woman and then added one or more of her sisters to his co-resident group over time as they came of age and as he became more established as a provider. Recalling that marriage was an agreement between two male kin groups, it can be seen that the prospect of gaining additional wives was a kind of "incentive plan" for a new husband. In effect, his wife's brothers watched to make sure he took good care of their sister, and if so, he might expect them to bestow additional sisters. This expectation is actually embedded in many Plains languages. A man addresses his wife and her unmarried sisters all by the same term, which could be translated as "wife," but more precisely means "woman who is my wife or is likely to become my wife." Conversely, an unmarried woman calls her sister's husband "husband."

Polygyny also allowed a married man to bring a woman who lost her husband into a new domestic relationship, a form of social insurance for the woman and her children. Not all polygyny was sororal, though, and as men gained stature they could alternately marry women from different kin groups and multiply their connections with other groups in this way. In either case, men benefited from having multiple wives. There were more women in the co-resident group to process meat and make garments, and more children to tend the horses, so that a good hunter could maximize his prosperity. The number of wives was an outward sign of a man's abilities

and a mark of prestige, as was the number of children he fathered. And, a man who had multiple wives could have sexual relations within the bounds of marriage more continuously, an advantage that was especially appealing because of the post-partum sex taboo.

Most women actually considered life in a polygynous marriage preferable. They enjoyed the companionship and the mutual help in child-rearing, crafts, and chores. They also gained added prestige from participating in a large co-resident group. Some rivalries and jealousies erupted, but generally there was a willingness to cooperate. The husband gave increased attention and authority to one wife, frequently the first or oldest. The Blackfoots called this primary spouse "sits besides him wife." The other wives (Comanches have referred to them as "chore wives") were expected to take direction from the favorite wife. In a plural marriage group there were multiple adjacent tipis to accommodate each wife and her children, and the husband would spend his time among them.

Assuming a nearly equal rate of male to female births across the Plains tribes as in most human populations, some of the "extra" women needed to create polygynous marriages would have become available because of the imbalance in the adult sex ratio that resulted from higher male mortality in hunting and battle. But other women came, in effect, from the next generation. As a man aged and gained power, he was able to attract wives who were much younger than he was, actually members of the next generation. When the man died, his surviving younger wives were freed to marry again, this time to men of their own generation.

Especially in societies with plural marriage, there was a guiding sentiment that marriage and family relationships should be available to all. The option of remaining unmarried during middle age was virtually unknown in the Plains tribes and there were no social roles of bachelor or spinster. Only for older widows and widowers was it acceptable to remain single. An extension of this sentiment was the social rule called levirate. In the version of this rule practiced on the Plains, it was expected that if a married man died, his brother should take his place in the marriage. Naturally there were realistic factors that affected how and whether the rule could be followed in particular cases, such as whether the deceased man actually had living brothers and whether any of them could support the widow (if not, perhaps a cousin would be called in), but it was considered the optimal thing to do. A similar rule, the sororate, encouraged the replacement of a deceased wife with her sister. This practice was also widely found on the Plains. The upshot of these rules was that there was a scripted, though not totally automatic, way of ensuring the quick restructuring of domestic units after the death of an adult member so that men and women all continued to have spouses, and children parents of both sexes, and the economic and social benefits for all were not interrupted.

The expectation of a man replacing his deceased brother in the brother's marriage was so strongly established that a man might be offered sexual access to his brother's wife even while the brother was still alive. This arrangement has been variously viewed as "wife sharing," "the anticipatory levirate," or as a form of fraternal polyandry. Plains polyandry was not the mirror image of polygyny, with woman choosing multiple men, but rather multiple men sharing a woman. In any case, throughout the world polyandry is much rarer than polygyny, and so it was on the Plains.

Among the Pawnees, polyandry was the temporary result of a custom whereby a young man was taken as a sexual initiate and junior husband by his mother's brother's wife. Their relationship lasted four or five years, until the young man married someone from his own cohort. It provided companionship for the aunt while the uncle was off raiding, as well as a coming of age experience for the nephew. The woman might engage multiple brothers at the same time in this way. The spe-cific connection between a nephew and his aunt by marriage through the maternal line seems to have been an expression of Pawnee village organization, which was matrilineal. Alternately, a Pawnee boy could join his older brother in an "anticipatory levirate" arrangement. The maternal uncle and older brother were equated in Pawnee kin terminology (which followed the Crow pattern), so a young man's relations with the wives of either were structural 112 equivalents.

Absconding and Divorce

Men kidnapped the wives of other men and some-times kept them for their own. The practice was so frequent as to be customary, and it is noted in the ethnographic literature as wife-absconding. Absconding within tribes resembled the practice of taking women from other tribes during raiding but was distinct. Absconding was also considered to be different from adultery because the woman was at least on the face of it a passive participant, and the activity was out in the open. The Crows made wife kidnapping something of a national pastime. Members of the Crow Lumpwood and Fox men's societies often absconded with each other's wives as part of a general rivalry between the two clubs. So ingrained was the practice that Crow boys pretended to kidnap girls when playing house.

The proper reaction for a man whose wife was kidnapped varied across the tribes and was ambiguous within them. In theory, he should yield as a matter of sportsmanship and male dignity, though the episode might cause him heartache and spur him to kidnap another woman in revenge. In practice, the man felt pressure from his fellows to go after his opponent, especially in those cases in which the absconding was part of a longer feud between two men. In the resulting confrontation the aggrieved husband sometimes killed the woman, the absconder, or the rival's horses, but normally he pressed for damages—payment in horses or goods. Frequently the absconder headed off such demands by sending an offer of his own with an invitation to smoke the pipe and put the matter to rest. The Cheyennes appointed an impartial chief to handle such negotiations, thinking his prestige would force the parties to a quick and peaceful settlement. Often enough, however, a kidnapped wife was simply released after a short time, before any further contest. The man who lost her could not take her back without being shamed and ridiculed; she was free instead to marry someone else.

It is clear that in many cases of wife-absconding the woman was complicit, and in effect it was a means for her to gain a divorce and the protection of a new mate. A woman also had the option of walking away from a marriage of her own accord if her husband was cruel or committing adultery, or if she did not get along with a co-wife. She returned home to her parents or brothers, who listened to her complaints and decided if they were supportable. If so, they offered their protection and the woman's relatives publicly declared that she was divorced. If not, she was sent back to her husband on one of the brothers' horses. A man could also divorce a wife with even more ease, citing adultery, the compatibility of co-wives, her attitude, or his mood. He did not have to justify his cause to anyone. There was not necessarily any public announcement, although the Cheyennes, ever formal in matters of male–female relations, had a segment in their Omaha Dance in which men could "drum away" their wives, publicly shaming them as the dancing ended by beating the drum and proclaiming, "I throw her away." A woman divorced could not expect to reverse the decision, but her family was not obligated to return the bride wealth either. Her brothers and other relatives stood by to make sure that when she sought to remarry the divorcing husband could not renew his claims on her. No matter the reasons or means, divorces were very common.

Adultery cases could become highly charged. Perhaps for this reason, among the Cheyennes, it has been reported, absconding was more common than flagrant adultery; the turmoil surrounding it was less severe. In adultery cases the imbalance between women's and men's rights was especially evident and the dictates of male status especially compelling. A woman had grounds for divorce if her husband was unfaithful but could not punish him or his mistress, apart perhaps from shredding his clothes and baggage in anger. A man so offended, however, felt public pressure to pursue some outcome that restored his dignity. For a chief or prominent warrior, this might mean declaring to his friends that the whole matter was beneath him, and that he would not pay attention to it. Other men challenged their competitor to a fight or demanded compensation payments. Cheyenne men accused of adultery could swear their innocence on the Sacred Hat, a tribal holy relic, to forestall a fight. It was believed that if they lied, they would soon be struck dead, and certain deaths were cited as proof.

Besides confronting his competitor, a cuckold punished his wife. The Cheyennes did not allow a husband to force an admission from his wife, but among the Comanches the husband often began his case by extracting a confession, choking his wife or holding her over a fire. He then dealt her a severe whipping or some other cruelty. Sometimes the husband's rage led to homicide. In a study of traditional Comanche law, anthropologist E. Adamson Hoebel identified 23 adultery cases, and in 3 of these the adulterous woman was killed outright by her spouse (Hoebel 1940). The standard punishment for an adulterous wife was for the husband to cut off the tip of her nose or inflict multiple gashes in it. Severing of the ear is also mentioned. Actual examples of these mutilations were rarer in some tribes than others but the sanction was definitely in force. In the 23 Comanche adultery cases studied by Hoebel, 4 women had their noses cut. The sliced nose was an inescapable mark of social disgrace and it ruined the woman's chances of attracting another husband. There seems to have been an appreciation of just how severe a penalty mutilation was, so that it was not done frivolously, but even the threat of it must have been a potent preventive. The husband often made his point instead simply by cutting off one of the woman's braids.

Another dramatic penalty for an errant wife was socially sanctioned gang rape. The practice is most thoroughly recorded among the Cheyennes and also reported for the Blackfoots and Lakotas. The Cheyennes called the custom *noha'sɛwɜstan*, "any man's wife," or by a term meaning "on the prairie." The cuckold summoned the members of his military society or his cousins to a certain place on the prairie for "a feast," where he brought his unfaithful wife. Every unmarried man among them then had intercourse with her. In the account of Big Laughing Woman (Cheyenne; d. 1910) there were 40 or 50 men. Reports suggest that women did not always live through the ordeal. Big Laughing Woman survived and was never molested or moralized again, but no man would marry her afterwards. Thus, the aggrieved husband made a "free woman," as the Cheyennes said, of his adulterous wife. "On the prairie" was an ironic restatement of the limits on the woman's sexual activity, and a particularly violent expression of the primacy of male solidarity. Its prevalence among the Cheyennes seems to have increased with the rise in power of the male-centric military societies around the mid-1800s, corresponding in turn to the intensification of Indian–white warfare at that time. It was not uncontroversial or automatic, however, and there are several recorded instances in which the assault was interrupted, and the woman rescued, by her kinsmen. Public sympathy was frequently with the woman, as when she was found with her former sweetheart after being married off to an older man she did not love. And much public opinion was against the growing power of the soldier societies.

Once reservations were established, many of the traditional customs of marriage and divorce began to fade. Polygyny became expensive once buffalo hunting was replaced with farming and ranching, and there was no longer a disproportionate rate of male mortality from warfare. More to the point, plural marriage was illegal and actively discouraged by missionaries and civil authorities. The famous case concerns the Comanche leader Quanah Parker, who in the 1880s and afterward led his people on a course of cultural and economic assimilation, but who was still reluctant to dismiss his multiple wives. Pressed yet again by the Indian agent to select just one, he replied, "all right, but you tell them which have to go." That was enough to end any pressure on Quanah. But people beyond his generation found polygamy more and more impractical. During the twentieth century monogamous marriages became the norm, and these were made quietly in the traditional manner (but recognized by the dominant society as "common law" marriages), or else certified in civil or Christian services. Divorce also became a matter of common or civil law, and absconding was no longer a legal alternative. Today many Indian people continue to approach marriage as a fluid institution, expecting to be monogamous but to participate in more than one monogamous relationship through their lifetimes. The relatively high rate of adult mortality in poor Indian communities contributes to this outlook, but also there is less social stigma on divorce than in some sectors of non-Indian society. This pattern of normalized multiple monogamous marriages is recognized in the anthropological literature as "serial monogamy." While the label connotes a departure from the Euro-American ideal "till death do us part," serial monogamy is not really an exotic form of marriage, in view of the fact that half of all contemporary American marriages end in divorce, and the majority of divorced persons remarry.

Adulthood

Though the marital relationship was central in defining adult life, more general ideals of adult female and male demeanor also held sway. The ideal woman was said to be "virtuous, expert at feminine tasks, and physically attractive" (Lowie 1983:59). The Crow term was "*bīi'tsi*, 'a good woman,' the equivalent of our perfect lady, with the addition of good looks" (Ibid.). Attractiveness was at least partly a matter of grooming and dress, so the criteria of good looks and good skills were related. Similarly, notions of crafts expertise and virtue were connected: it was thought that a woman who worked hard and was good at cooking, preparing hides, and quilling, was a source of pride to her own family and her husband, and was therefore less likely to find herself in social difficulty. Hospitality is another admired quality for women, yet again related to their industry. In her work the ideal woman was thrifty. Omaha elder men would advise girls growing up in the following way, drawing a link between thrift and well-being:

> The thrifty woman has a good tent; all of her tools are of the best; so is her clothing.
>
> Hear what happens to the thriftless woman: She shall stop at a stranger's place; there are holes in her moccasins but she has nothing to patch them with, so she will cut a piece out of her robe to mend her moccasins with; then she will borrow her neighbor's workbag and from it take sinew stealthily and tuck in into her belt.
>
> If you are a thrifty woman, your husband will struggle hard to bring you the best of materials for your tent and clothing and the best of tools. If you have a good tent, men and women will desire to enter it. They will be glad to talk to you and your husband.
>
> If you are willing to remain in ignorance and not learn how to do the things a woman should know how to do, you will ask other women to cut your moccasins and fit them for you. You will go from bad to worse; you will leave your people, go into a strange tribe, fall into trouble, and die there friendless.
>
> If you are thrifty, build yourself a good tent or house [earth lodge], and people will like you and will assist your husband in all his undertakings.

(Fletcher and LaFlesche 1972:333)

In everyday behavior, women were supposed to be passive and quiet in the presence of men. Men did not look directly at them when they spoke. Women talked freely with other women but never loudly—loud laughter was associated with sexual promiscuity. Their native-language speech differed from that of men in some aspects of vocabulary, pronunciation, and inflection. After puberty, women sat with their legs to one side. They slept to the right of the tipi door.

The ideal man was a strong provider and protector. These traits he demonstrated with successful hunts, raids, and scouting expeditions, and by standing up for his kinsmen and family in tribal disputes. The model man was generous, sometimes giving away the fruits of his hunts and raids to build longer-term social ties and prestige. He was self-reliant but also comfortable with comradeship. He accepted the constant expectation that men were supposed to die in the service of their kinsmen, and that brave men died before reaching old age. The male ethos was largely about "honor" and "respect," concepts that were named explicitly in the native languages.

Men's behavior was a curious mixture. When among themselves, they needed at times to be aggressive, boastful, and boisterous. Whether tendering a joke or insult, or reporting on his war exploits, a man should be able to dish it out and take it too. But in touchy public situations or when dealing with their families, honorable men showed patience and restraint. These qualities were more and more expected from a man as he gained in age and experience, anticipating the transition to the status of elder. Men were supposed to avoid not only female speech patterns, maintaining their own forms of greeting, exclamation, commands, and questions, but also feminine subjects of conversation—even their own wives' pregnancies. A man sat cross-legged and slept to the left side of the tipi door.

The demands of work and gender identification did leave plenty of room for adults to enjoy themselves. Men had an inventive variety of archery contests, shooting for distance, speed, and accuracy. They also sharpened their hand–eye coordination with the hoop and pole game, throwing darts at a small rolling hoop. Other games promoted fitness and a tolerance for discomfort. Footraces over long distances were popular. The Arapaho Sherman Sage (circa 1843–1944) was in such good shape that he ran from Wyoming to Oklahoma to court his first wife. Lacrosse, the rugged team sport in which a ball is passed over a large field by players handling one or two netted sticks, originated in the Woodlands but was also known to the Cheyennes, Santees, Assiniboines, Iowas, and Otoes. More widespread was shinny, a form of field hockey for women. They drove a ball of hair-stuffed deerskin with curved sticks across a field the size of a football pitch, aiming at goals made from two stakes. Comanche women played *natsihtóo?etɬ* (ref. to cane or staff), a fast version of shinny. Instead of a ball, they passed a leather thong with their sticks, attempting to fling it to wrap around a single goal post. In other tribes the thong had a ball on each end, hence the English name "double ball." People enjoyed running for fitness and staging foot races. Horse racing was also popular, with high-stakes wagers. People throughout the region had a penchant for gambling games, with players betting all their possessions. Dice were made by marking bone pieces or plum pits, and they were cast with a basket or bowl. Painted sticks were also tossed in a variation of the dice concept. Dice and sticks were marked with distinct designs, and the ways that they fell in different combinations signified particular numeric scores. Another ubiquitous adult game was the hand game, in which two teams formed opposing lines; members of one team took turns guessing in which hand their opponent held one of two large cylindrical beads. The concealer threw his arms about and swayed to the singing and drumming that accompanied the game to confuse his rival. Hand games went on for hours at a time. The Dakotas, Omahas, and Iowas played a variation of the hand game that

was more popular in the Woodlands, in which moccasins were used to hide the markers. Further leisure time was spent in feasting, singing, dancing, and storytelling.

Old Age

Given life expectancies in the horse era, and the physical tolls of the nomadic life, persons were considered old beginning in their fifties. The prevalent ethos of "respect" ensured that in most cases older people were kept safe, accorded dignity, and involved in camp life in meaningful ways. The Hidatsas were even said to take in old women from other tribes to make sure they were cared for. Yet elders had to face the fact that society placed prime value on the young, the independent, and the fearless. "From infancy a Plains Indian boy had it dinned into his ears that bravery was the path to distinction, that old age was an evil, while it was a fine thing to die young in battle" (Lowie 1983:106). There was thus something of survivor's guilt when a person made it to the later years, and old age could be a sad and difficult time.

Changes in social role came with the advanced years. Elders of both sexes became valued for their capacity to remember the past and reconstruct it through the telling of myth, oral history, and ritual procedure. Older men were permitted to be more level-headed and forgiving rather than aggressive, and to take the part of wise consultant. One who still had enough energy to take an active role in internal tribal decisions could become a peace chief, as described in Chapter 4, though these opportunities were always limited. Older women were esteemed as the teachers of intricate crafts skills and advisors in personal and family matters. Also, women after menopause were allowed to enter public life and assume roles otherwise reserved for males, including healer and, occasionally, tribal councilor.

The end of a woman's childbearing years was fairly abrupt and physically obvious, so her change in status was well marked. The transition was harder for men because they usually saw only a gradual loss of vigor and prestige. To achieve some sense of closure, an aging warrior could publicly declare his retirement. He might do so by announcing that the next raid would be his last and that he would be giving away his battle name to a younger man. If the man belonged to the senior age-graded military society, he and his club mates would sell their memberships to the next cohort and retire from fighting together. These sales sometimes brought significant wealth and thus security for the elders. Ex-warriors found comfort in each other's company. Comanche men who were too old to go on raids met in the evening in a special tipi called the Smoke Lodge, where they smoked, boasted of past coups, and talked over the day's events. Smoke Lodge members were sometimes the butt of pranks played by the camp youngsters. In turn, they spoofed the young warrior's coup-counting bouts by reciting their own divorces and love affairs. It was thought that envy of the young caused elders to be especially prone to practicing sorcery. The wielder of malevolent magic in Plains tradition is usually an old man or woman.

The fate of people in old age rested ultimately on their conduct and reputation as middle-aged adults. Did they have caring offspring who would feed and shelter them as they grew less physically able? Were there enough such supporters that the elder did not become a burden on only a few? If they had been forthright and prosperous as adults, chances are they had accumulated enough of a family to take care of them.

The best outcome for an aging person was to die suddenly while still active as a mentor, surrounded by cherishing kin. In the worst cases, an elder suffered a long illness or lacked basic kin support and became too feeble to keep up with the mobile camp seeking game, water, and grazing. The person might then be left behind to die alone when the camp moved; or, he might walk off by himself to die, so as not to be a further hindrance

to the band. This sad ending was perhaps more common in the days before horses, for after that the food supply was more predictable, and it was possible to drag weak oldsters along on travois when they could no longer ride or walk. José Francisco Ruiz, a Tejano who lived with Comanches from 1813 to 1821, witnessed the abandonment of an elder only once.

Traditional attitudes about the aged are still quite evident in many Plains Indian communities. Elders may be accorded great respect during formal ceremonies and also through informal courtesies, such as when a young man walks around the powwow circle to say some kind words to an elder woman he spots across the dance ground. Individuals of different generations delight in talking in order to rediscover the kin connections or mutual family acquaintances they may have, and these exchanges help elders to remain feeling important and connected. The common practice of adoption provides an avenue for strengthening these bonds; an elderly woman who appreciates the kindness of a young man may "take him for a grandson." Traditional elder roles continue in contemporary versions such as member of the tribal government or consultant in oral history and language preservation programs, and the roles of ritual leader and curer still persist. Today older people may have accumulated enough wealth, through wage work and retirement benefits, land ownership, and such sources as farmland or oil leases, that they can have some financial security in their later years. There are also tribal programs that assist the elderly with meals, health care, and home repairs; these programs are promoted as modern expressions of the respect ethos. In some instances elders enjoy a good enough standard of living that they can help their younger kin with financial gifts and loans. Frequently, however, elders live as non-working poor members of low-income communities and their younger relatives spend much time and effort in struggling to support them.

Death and Burial

Berlandier, writing on the Southern Plains in the 1830s, commented that though he occasionally found an Indian who was reputedly aged 80 or 100, it was generally rare to find people in their sixties or seventies, and that individuals in these age brackets were less common than in the non-Indian populations of his time. Mortality was the ultimate fact of life. For those who did not meet their end in the most highly-valued circumstances—women in childbirth and men in battle—there were several other common causes of death. Berlandier noted "syphilis, smallpox, measles, pleurisy, asthma, rheumatic pains, and some forms of paralysis" as the most prevalent fatal diseases among the Texas tribes (Berlandier 1969:84). To this list of Plains scourges could be added diphtheria, influenza, tuberculosis, scrofula, cholera, scarlet fever, typhoid, malaria, and whooping cough, as well as diseases and accidents stemming from the overconsumption of alcohol. As most of these maladies were introduced by non-Indians and there were no vaccinations, there was virtually no natural resistance or prevention; the diseases caused great agony and were usually fatal. Other conditions like arthritis, cataracts, trachoma, malnutrition, and dental decay were not deadly but contributed to shorter life spans. Besides disease, there were fatal riding and hunting injuries and accidental shootings. Infanticide and geronticide were established practices, as noted, though not common. Plains Indians also occasionally committed suicide, typically by shooting or hanging. Sometimes a young woman took her own life in protest of an arranged marriage, as previously mentioned. Elders who were terminally ill or warriors crippled in battle sometimes killed themselves rather than face the humiliation of a reduced state. A sense of shame over some public incident might also drive a person to suicide, as in the recorded Comanche case of a man who was mortified when he accidentally whipped himself while trying to beat his horse.

A person's death was followed by four days or more of intense mourning. Women fell into a deep emotional state, crying, wailing, lopping off their hair, smearing themselves with white clay, and gashing their breasts, shins, and arms. The deceased's mother and sisters often cut off a finger joint. Men were less demonstrative but also sometimes cut their hair or flesh. Wounds were allowed to bleed to heighten the sympathetic sacrifice. Camp fires, normally kept burning continually, were allowed to die and be relit.

Burial was undertaken during this spell, generally two to four days after the death. People outside the immediate family handled the arrangements. In tribes with bilateral descent, relatives and close friends stepped in to help. In unilineal tribes, there would be a rule requiring either that the deceased's clan members stage the funeral or that the opposite clan (e.g., mother's clan in a patrilineal society) or opposite moiety take charge. They dressed the body in the deceased's finest clothes, often chosen by the person before he or she died, and painted the face. Attendants wrapped the body tightly in one or more robes or blankets, sometimes binding or stitching up the bundle. There was no embalming or mummification. After a brief period for viewing, the corpse was transported to the burial site balanced on horseback, by travois, or, in later days, in a horse-drawn wagon.

Several methods of burial coexisted across the region and within tribes. In the characteristic Plains burial practice, called "aerial sepulture" in some early ethnological writings, the body was left lying high in the branches of a tree or on a scaffold especially made for the burial. In tree burials, a large branching cottonwood was selected, and spare cross-framing was added if need be; sometimes a tree held more than one body. The built scaffold consisted of four stout upright logs with whatever supporting members were needed, holding up a narrow horizontal frame 2 or 3 feet overhead upon which the body rested. A tall, heavy tripod for holding the body has been noted as an alternate scaffold design for the Comanches. In whatever form of above-ground burial, the body was simply left to disintegrate. In some tribes the bones were later gathered and reburied in a practice termed "secondary burial." Secondary interment was the usual practice in some places, or else an option that some families chose if a loved one had been buried far from their village, in which case the bones were retrieved to be buried close to home. The gathered bones were painted and wrapped, and deposited in the ground or on the scaffold of a more recently deceased person, usually near the remains of relatives. The Hidatsas set up circles of retrieved skulls on the ground here and there that became places to fast for sacred visions. Though considered typical for the Plains,

elevated burial seems to have spread through the region replacing ground burial with the peaking of the horse and buffalo lifestyle. The Omahas, for example, adopted the elevated style only later in the course of the horse era. Several tribes continued to prefer ground burial and only used trees or scaffolds if the earth was frozen or no crevices could be found, and a few never used them.

Ground burial took different forms. Particularly in the southern and western parts of the region, a rock cleft, overhang, or cave was sought for depositing the body. In these partially hidden locales, no further effort was made to enclose the corpse. Away from large rock formations, the body was placed in a shallow natural depression and covered with brush, stones, and dirt to keep away scavengers. Tribes with eastern affiliations

FIGURE 5.5   Oglala tree burial near Fort Laramie, Wyoming.

frequently used a dug grave, sometimes shallow, other times deep, customarily prepared by an old man or old woman. Excavated graves were often covered with a low brush arbor or mounded with dirt.

The Kiowas and Comanches sought hills and canyons west of their usual campsites for crevice burials. The Wichitas favored hilltops near their villages for their shallow dug graves. The migratory tribes that preferred tree and scaffold burials located them away from non-Indian travel routes to hinder looting. The Hidatsas, who used all of the burial forms described so far, placed their dead around the edges of their villages. There were no cemeteries in the strict sense, but it was not unusual that burials were clustered. Indians began forsaking other forms for ground burial in wooden coffins after about 1870, as non-Indian funeral customs became influential. Until sawmills and carpentry shops were built near reservation communities, they used cast-off shipping crates and manufactured wooden travel trunks as caskets. Headstones were another non-Indian innovation, before which only the grave mound or perhaps a buffalo skull marked the resting place.

The nomadic tribes reserved yet another burial form for certain chiefs. The body was left inside the decedent's tipi, either seated or on a small scaffold; the tent was sealed up and everything abandoned as the camp moved away, and the funeral tipi left to decay under the elements. Cremation was also practiced when parties were traveling, but seems not to have been frequent.

Normally the corpse was laid on its back straight out or with the head slightly raised—this was the usual practice in platform burials and dug graves. Sometimes in a dug or crevice burial the body was instead laid on its side and bound in a fetal position. The sitting posture was used in some cave and excavated interments as well as in the chief's tipi burial. Orientation was deliberate and significant. Most often the body was laid with the head to the west so the deceased "faced east" to greet the sunrise. Kansa dead, however, were faced west to the setting sun, and Wichitas were similarly laid with the head to the east. Among some northern and eastern tribes such as the Plains Crees and Assiniboines, the head rested to the north, so the body appeared to watch the full daily path of the sun. Conversely, the Otoes faced their dead north to where they thought spirits traveled. A tribe observed the same principle of alignment even if it used more than one burial form or posture.

It was customary to leave some of the deceased person's favorite utensils, tools, weapons, or ornaments, and perhaps his or her saddle and bridle, in or on top of the grave. Typically these objects were broken when deposited. A baby was buried in its cradleboard. Also, the person's favorite dog or best horse was often slain by the graveside. The Comanche rationale was that the person should have this companion with him or her in the afterlife. In the case of a wealthy man numerous horses and mules were sometimes sacrificed. In a more economical version of this custom, one encouraged or demanded by white agents, the animals were shaved of their manes and tails and turned loose to fend for themselves, and all the hair was deposited at the grave. It could then be said that the animals were disfigured, made destitute, and had sacrificed their hair like human mourners. Texas Indian agent Robert S. Neighbors reported around 1850 that the Comanches had sometimes killed a favorite wife at her husband's grave, but had done away with this practice "from intercourse with the more civilized Indians" (Neighbors 1852:133). The extent of this custom is uncertain, though Neighbor's report corresponds to similar ones from the Great Basin culture area where the Comanches originated.

The dead person's remaining possessions were given away or destroyed in an elaborate manner. Goods were distributed among siblings and friends, as decided by the deceased or by surviving family members. The person who dressed the body might receive a horse in payment. Other band members not so closely associated with the dead person were sometimes invited by the family to take items in a show of generosity and anti-materialism. Usually the deceased's tipi was burned. The funerary giveaway was an important means of redistributing wealth and marking social obligations between the bereaved and other band members. As Neighbors wrote of the Comanches, "From the liberality with which they dispose of their effects on all occasions of the kind, it would induce the belief that they acquire property merely for the purpose of giving it to others" (Ibid.:134).

After the initial intense mourning period, the close family members of the deceased withdrew from normal life and lived in poverty for one to four years, sometimes longer. During this period they existed on the charity of their neighbors, another custom that reinforced social connections. In some tribal traditions the mourners were released from their duty once a scalp had been taken from an enemy tribe.

GENDER AND SEXUALITY

Stereotypes

Though much about Plains Indian gender construction is revealed in the foregoing discussions of family and social customs, the subject requires further specific treatment. Here it is first necessary to dismiss some dominant stereotypes of Indian people found in non-Indian literature and film. To summarize the observations of communication analyst Raymond William Stedman, Indian women and men have been typically portrayed each in one of two polar ways, one unrealistically positive and the other unrealistically negative (Stedman 1982). The more flattering stereotype of Indian womanhood is the *belle sauvage* (beautiful savage) or "Indian princess," a serene, sometimes heroic beauty, remote yet seductive, who is apt to be pictured partly naked. The princess image is perhaps best captured in some fanciful

depictions of the seventeenth-century Powhatan woman Pocahontas or Lewis and Clark's Shoshone guide Sacajawea. The derogatory female stereotype is the "squaw," a slovenly harpy and drudge. In the movies she tortures prisoners with fiendish delight, swarms to fight over the dress ripped off a white woman captive, and waits at the beck and call of her husband. (The term "squaw," once used as a general term for an Indian woman or wife, is today considered demeaning and its use is discouraged.) Indian men have fared no better in stereotype. The more positive image is the "brave" (another term that has come into disfavor), specifically one who is the faithful sidekick to a non-Indian hero. Type characters include Chingachgook in James Fenimore Cooper's *The Last of the Mohicans*, first published in 1826, and Tonto, companion to the Lone Ranger of radio and television serials circa 1933–1957. This Indian "man Friday" figure is taciturn and stalwart in taking the brunt of punishment when he helps his partner fight the bad guys, and he stands in contrast to other men, Indian and non-Indian, who are not so decent. The negative image of the Indian man is that of the "buck" (yet another contemptuous term), a crazed, animalistic predator who knows only wild dancing, drinking, pillaging, and scalping.

It is quickly evident that these images, no matter how invalid, have become deeply embedded in European and American popular culture and the public mind. They are seen in the earliest European woodcuts and map cartouches showing Native Americans and are pervasive in books and movies even today (see Chapter 13 for more on Indian stereotypes). They are founded on and perpetuate basic Euro-American cultural assumptions, including the dichotomy between the "noble savage" and "debased savage" developed in the writings of philosophers Jean Jacques Rousseau (1712–1778) and Thomas Hobbes (1588–1679). In these constructs Indians are thought to be more a part of nature than Euro-Americans, and thus the polar depiction of Indian genders also reflects the

Romantic concept that nature is alternately beautiful and dangerous. These stereotypes obscure the essential details of gender construction in Indian culture. It is on those details that we now focus.

Gender Roles and Relations

In hunter-gatherer societies, male and female roles are defined relatively strictly, according to the division of labor. Most simply, men hunt animals and women gather plant foods. Since the diet and trade economy during the horse era was heavily centered on the buffalo, which was killed by men but cut up, cooked, and tanned by women, the Plains division of labor has also been described as a combination of male procurers and female processors. Within tribal cultures these distinctions were drawn in very elaborate and specific ways, and the distinctions actually covered a great range of separate and overlapping tasks for each gender. Men's and women's distinct economic roles relate to their roles and relations in other spheres of life.

Hidatsa men, for example, spent most of their effort in preparing for and engaging in hunts and raids. Preparation involved some days of discussion, weapon-making, and religious ritual. Apart from concerted preparations, the periods between major work efforts were idle. (Of the related Crows, it has been noted, "To a transient visitor Crow men might easily convey the impression of laziness" [Lowie 1983:84].) The hunts, scouting expeditions, and raids which followed required intense, sometimes enormous, outputs of energy. So the pace of men's work was one in which there were periods of leisure or moderate activity alternated with times of extreme, often grueling and dangerous, action. While the more extreme activities featured individual exertion, many were ultimately team efforts, and men formed relatively large work groups, temporarily joining individuals from different lodges, camps, or even tribes, and assigning the tasks within the group by age and other status differences. Men's labor regularly took them far, often hundreds of

miles, from their camp and families. The reward for this hard and risky work was initial ownership of the meat, captives, horses, and other booty that was obtained, along with healthy doses of prestige.

Hidatsa women processed all the meat and skins obtained by men and collected and processed all small animal and plant foods, water, fuel wood, and bark and reeds for weaving. They did most of the work in building and maintaining the earth lodges and tipis, and the drying and storing racks and other furnishings in the lodges and around the camp. They made parfleches and did most of the decorative quilling and beadwork. Though the work could be physically demanding, its pace was steady and overall the energy expended was moderate. Women's work was conceived of as group work by nature—there was no strong recognition of individual accomplishments, but a social premium on the ability to cooperate. Women's work groups were more stable than men's, not formed for a single adventure as men's sometimes were, and smaller, normally involving the mothers and daughters of a single lodge. Tasks were mostly performed in and around the lodge, or in the gardens outside the village, but usually within a 1-mile radius of the lodge. A woman's reputation rested to some degree on her ability to work productively in this kind of collaborative domestic setting. And she had material wealth in that she owned all the items she created unless she gave them away.

Even with these clear differences, there was a fair amount of sharing of tasks and exceptions to the usual patterns. It was not unusual for women to accompany men into battle; they went along to cook, tend horses, and care for the wounded, but also found themselves fighting if the raiders' base camp or line of retreat was attacked. Hidatsa men sometimes assisted women in bringing in crops and processing tobacco, and they helped erect the four main poles when an earth lodge was built. Men of all tribes did the leatherwork for their own shirts, shields, ropes, and drums. Pawnee men made their own saddlebags. Interestingly, hide tanning fell to men or women depending on the animal and tribal custom. For example, the dressing of bear and beaver skins was widely thought to be a man's rather than woman's chore. Deer and elk skins were supposed to be tanned by women among the Blackfoots but by men among the Pawnees. The skins of white buffalos, which were rare and thought to be sacred, were tanned among the Cheyennes, Dakota, and Assiniboines only by notable women. When hide trading to non-Indian commercial markets was introduced in a tribal economy, the work on those hides was typically assumed by, or put upon, women. Though among the Pawnees women made wooden objects like pestles and bowls, among the Omahas men did this work. In the uncommon instances of Plains pottery making, women mostly were at work, but men were involved among the Assiniboines and Hidatsas. Women did most of the decorative painting, though men were likely to do the painting when adding pictures on their own tipis. Among the Omahas, men outlined the tipi designs and women and children colored them in.

These examples are sufficient to show that the Plains division of labor according to gender was actually complex, and so it may be expected that social, legal, and political rights and responsibilities pertaining to the genders were also not simply dichotomous. As in many areas of Plains culture, the total picture seems paradoxical. There were clear lines of difference enforced by custom, but also approved variations. Whatever the tribal pattern, it was consciously enforced. Men and women ridiculed any of their peers who were seen to be doing the work of the opposite sex. In the case of some women's crafts guilds, their techniques were often treated as secret and passed on carefully, preserving the work only in their domain. Men accrued prestige by openly showing their success in hunting and war, but women also had clear avenues of public confirmation. Sioux women kept a chart of their tanning accomplishment by marking their elk horn scraping tools

with black and red dots and circles denoting tanned robes and hides. Beyond such tallies, women gained renown for the beauty and durability of their handwork, qualities that were visible to all. By dressing, decorating, and grooming their husbands and children to look prosperous, women influenced the success of their family members and thus their own prestige and power, even beyond the acclaim they might receive directly for their craftwork skill. An Arapaho or Mandan woman robe quiller was able to exchange the robes she made in excess of her family's needs for horses, directly enhancing her wealth.

It followed then that a woman often began her performance in a religious ceremony by proclaiming the number and quality of robes she had made. The status that women enjoyed as contributors to the economy assured their position in religious affairs, and they complemented their brothers, husbands, and sons in ritual activities. First of all, post-menopausal women could be medicine women, counterparts to medicine men, and serve individual clients in curing ceremonies as men did. Such women received spiritual power in dreams and visions enabling them to understand how to cure with herbs, practice midwifery, protect children with charms, and execute quill and beadwork designs. Comanche medicine women sometimes passed their powers down to their daughters. A Comanche medicine woman enjoyed the highest social status and prestige available to a woman, and she was the social equal to a man. In large public rituals like the Sun Dance, it was usual to select certain virtuous women for key operations such as selecting the tree that would become the central pole of the dance ground. In other situations women served as assistants to male ritualists. A Crow woman could not herself unwrap the sacred bundle containing the Sun Dance doll for veneration, but she aided her husband in that part of the ceremony. Among the Blackfoots, women did unwrap medicine bundles and handed the contained holy objects to the men, functioning as intermediaries between men and the sacred powers. Blackfoot women were responsible for the daily care of the medicine bundles, including the one used in the Sun Dance. The Blackfoot trait of using women as spiritual mediators took a noteworthy form in the initiation rites of the Horns, a men's society among the Blood tribe. An initiate received spiritual power from his club sponsor by both men having sequent sexual intercourse with the sponsor's wife, a practice that may have been borrowed from the Mandans and Hidatsas.

Women also had some political and legal power. They acted as final authority on domestic questions in camp. Though not normally included in council gatherings that decided camp movements and trading or raiding trips, women kept informed about these matters and influenced decisions through their brothers, husbands, and sons. They owned personal property—all the goods they had made or accumulated, including tipis, and sometimes horses—which they were free to dispose of as they wanted. Food belonged to whoever collected it initially, but even if the collector was a man, it was women who took charge of it on behalf of the collector's family. And although men were quite free to use physical force against women, women could return it. Women's own force worked in concert with the protections offered by their male kinsmen. Some documented nineteenth-century Cheyenne disputes illustrate this right. Brave Wolf was set upon by nieces for beating his wife (the wife too then joined in), after which he gave his best horse to her brother to make amends. In another case, the man She Bear abused his wife, and while he was away on a trip she returned to her mother. When he got back She Bear went to the mother's lodge to retrieve his wife and struck her in the face. The wife's mother then attacked She Bear with a knife, stabbing him in the back, and then the daughter also beat on him with a club. They chased She Bear to his lodge with a hot branding iron and tore everything down, and the wife went home again with her mother. She Bear tried to

apologize as Brave Wolf did, but his horses were refused for a long time, until one day the wife's brother decided to give him another chance. The brother returned the sister (over their mother's objections) with a warning to She Bear to not abuse her again, and there was no further trouble.

The Cheyenne cases are interesting because, as noted earlier, that tribe experienced notable tension between female- and male-oriented factions under the stress of American expansion. These cases illustrate that, while there were general patterns in gender roles and relations, there were also shifts in these patterns as the horse culture period proceeded. Many tribes experienced such changes. The advent of the horse had set up the particular procurer/processor dichotomy and associated social statuses already described. In some parts of the Plains, the penetration of the northern fur trade caused some reshaping of the relative value of men's and women's work, as did the commerce in buffalo robes and horses with Americans later in the horse period. Warfare with non-Indians, a kind of fighting increasingly more intense than intertribal combat, especially after the 1850s, drove changes both in the relative contributions and power of men and in the importance of trade, in this case for horses, guns, and ammunition. The net effect was a trend toward polarization of men's and women's roles, and a trend toward the control and use of women's labor not only for family consumption and occasional intertribal trade, but to process furs and hides for steady and large-scale exchange in the penetrating national and global economies.

Additional dramatic changes in gender relations were brought about once Plains Indian people were confined on reservations and began joining the non-Indian wage economy. With the elimination of the traditional hunting role for men and the failure of government policies meant to transform them into prosperous farmers, male social power weakened. The domestic work of women continued, however (though no longer performed by co-wives in polygynous marriages), as did the traditional power stemming from that work. Initially on the reservations women's domestic tasks continued to evolve toward supplying distant markets in the last days of the buffalo robe trade, and then toward the production of Native objects for tourists and collectors, a source of income for many Indian women to the present day. But once the cash economy was established in Indian areas, it was often women who had more ability and inclination to become formally educated and go to work in stores, schools, offices, hospitals, and other wage work settings outside the home. The skills developed in these setting gave women greater ability to manage their households and often also better qualifications for serving in community leadership roles. And once reservation land was divided into individually-owned allotments and non-Indian inheritance laws were put into effect, women could accumulate independent wealth as landowners of their own allotments and acreage inherited from other women and men. By the late twentieth century it was not uncommon to find pre-menopausal Plains Indian women functioning in positions of social and political power that had no parallels during the horse period. Although modern Plains Indian culture continues to perpetuate and express traditional notions of the roles and relations between men and women, the underlying social structure exhibits more access to public power for women than ever before. This change stemmed directly from the Plains Indian historical experience, as well as from the general increase in women's rights in the American society that came to dominate the region.

Sexuality

The sexual lives of Plains Indian people living in the horse period can only be reconstructed cautiously. Sexual behavior was largely private and not observable. Reports by non-Indians were in many cases shaped by predispositions about the sexuality of "savage" as opposed to "civilized"

humans, a distinction that was especially acute during the Victorian era. Ethnographic studies and commentaries provided by Native peoples since the reservation period, however, provide some dependable information.

Public interactions between people of opposite sexes were guarded. The concerted separation of the sexes instituted in late childhood and through adolescence carried on into adulthood in a reduced form. The culturally configured attitude of adolescent shyness, called *scu* in Lakota, was believed to be directly related to sexual interest— it was the alternate side of sexual attraction. Lakotas believed that this attitude faded once a person had been married for a while and would only flare up again if there was a sexual interest outside the marriage. Thus, curiously, even affairs were thought to require shyness. Open expressions of affection were therefore rare. Husbands and wives did not hug in public, nor did adult mothers and sons. Ironically, actual instances of sexual contact between individuals were difficult to hide because true privacy was rare and not a realistic expectation. Couples had relations in close quarters with other people inside tipis, or they met on the outskirts of camp with at most a blanket to cover them. Other people created some sense of privacy by ignoring what could be seen or heard.

Despite all the emphasis on the reputation of males, or perhaps because of it, it was women who were seen as the instigators of sexual relations; they often made the advances and were usually held responsible for sexual indiscretions. For many teens, sexual life began with midnight visits between lodges, in a practice referred to as "tipi crawling" or "sleepcrawling." According to the Comanche Post Oak Jim, "Boys seemed to stay pretty much in their tipis. It was the girl's place to come to them" (Wallace and Hoebel 1952:133). Older unmarried girls crawled into boys' tipis at night to initiate them. The darkness helped protect their reputations. Boys did in fact make such nocturnal visits also. A young man might pull up the tipi pegs of the lodge where his sweetheart slept and attempt to touch her genitals, a custom which the Crow called *bī'arusce*. There is a humorous Comanche story of a young man who dons sunglasses one day, and thinking then it is nighttime, goes sleepcrawling, only to encounter his girlfriend's father.

In his remarkable memoir of Kiowa Apache life, Jim Whitewolf (circa 1878–1955) included this vivid description of initiation into love-making. At the time the Kiowa Apaches were located on a large reservation but still living in mobile camps.

One time, when I was a young boy, I went hunting with Big Alex's boy. He and I were just friends. There was a girl at the camp where he stayed. She was Apache Jack's wife's brother's daughter. When he and I decided to go raccoon hunting, she wanted to go along. She was older than us. I was a young fellow, just beginning to think about sex. Big Alex had a Mexican jack-mule. We rode it, and she walked. We went down by the creek. Our dog began to bark, and we saw three raccoons up in a tree. Big Alex's boy had a Winchester rifle, and he shot all three of them. We loaded them on the mule and went on. We sat down to rest, and this girl began talking nasty. She asked me if I knew anything about intercourse. I told her I didn't know where I could have any. She told me to come to the arbor near camp that night.

When I got back to camp, we skinned the raccoons and hung them up to dry. Big Alex's boy and I went down by the creek and he told me, "She's sure good. She'll show you all about it."

At sundown, we ate dinner. Apache Jack and his wife went away. There were just three of us in that camp—Big Alex's boy, that girl, and I. He went into the tipi, and she and I were left in the arbor. She lay down and raised up her dress. My penis was already stiff. I got on top of her. It didn't take long and I was through. Then I went to the tipi, and Big Alex's boy went there and had intercourse with her. He came back to the

tipi and we stayed there a while, telling stories. Every once in a while we would go in there and have intercourse with that girl. I don't know how many times I did it that night. Years ago, they used to tell a story that if you had intercourse when you were too young, your penis would be bitten off by the teeth in the woman's vagina. But after I did it that first time I was all right. I liked it. After that I used to go around to dances just looking for women to have intercourse with. My father used to tell me not to run around because some of the women might have a disease. But I never got a disease; I was lucky, I guess. After the country opened up, a lot of boys went to the hospital with that kind of disease, but they never would talk about it. Then I was more careful. I didn't go around just anywhere; I was careful which girls I went with.

One time I got caught right in the act of having intercourse with a woman. That time Henry Moon's wife was sick. I went to visit them. I took my buggy and went that way. Henry and his wife were staying with a certain woman. She fixed a bed on the north side of the room for me. Henry and his wife were on the other side. This woman lay down by me. During the night she wanted to have intercourse with me. I got on top of her. The bedsprings made a noise. Suddenly Henry came across the room with a lantern and called, "Hey, have you got a match?" This woman I was having intercourse with just yelled out, "No, I haven't got any match!" Henry didn't want a match; he just wanted to know what was going on with that woman and me.

(Brant 1969:99–100)

Although it was appropriate for women to make sexual advances, there were also mores about female chastity. These ideals addressed both virginity and marital fidelity. Virginity was broadly defined, and among the Tetons, a man could claim to have stolen a woman's virginity by seeing her naked or touching her privates. A Lakota saying held that if a girl participated in heavy petting her breasts would grow. The Cheyenne matched or surpassed the Tetons and all other Plains tribes in their concern about chastity. Among them an unmarried girl who yielded to seduction would afterwards have a very hard time securing a marriage proposal. Teenage girls of the Tetons, Cheyennes, Arapahos, and Crees slept with their feet toward the fire, or away from the outer edges of the tipi where a prowler could reach them, and wore what have been called "chastity belts" while sleeping or when away from their families. These consisted of a thin rawhide rope tied around the waist, run between the thighs, and then wrapped around both legs to the knees. Any attempted violation of the rope was grounds for the furious destruction of the offender's horses and all other belongings, and his parents' too if he were young, by the girl's relatives. A young Lakota woman always stayed in the company of a chaperone, usually a grandmother, to further safeguard her virginity.

Women's faithfulness after marriage was celebrated in a number of ways. A faithful wife was considered a "virgin" for ritual purposes, and a woman who lived her whole life only knowing one man sexually was especially admired. Throughout the region, married women took public oaths to swear their fidelity. The Tetons set up a special fire as the setting for women's oaths, or pledging on a pile of buffalo tongues was a widespread practice. In another common technique, the pledger held a knife blade in her mouth and was deemed honest if she remained uncut by it. (Lakota men could challenge a woman's claim to fidelity and prove their accusation by the same method.) The Crows tested a presumably virtuous woman by presenting her with the delicacy of a buffalo tongue; if she ate, she proclaimed her purity, otherwise she rejected the food with the saying "My moccasin has a hole in it." If a woman accepted special ritual responsibilities on the basis of her purity, it was the equivalent of one of these oaths. Public confirmation of women's virtue most commonly occurred preliminary to the Sun Dance—often a group of four virgins was selected to cut down the cottonwood tree that be-

came the dance ground center pole—but was made at men's military and medicine society dances as well.

In most tribes women who did not meet the purity test were not necessarily shunned, they simply failed to enjoy high esteem. But among the strict Cheyennes, a woman who had many affairs or had been divorced four times was tainted and would not be able to marry again until finding a single man who was willing to gain her purification by dancing in the Sun Dance. After this ceremony she could marry her champion and become respectable again, at least theoretically. The Cheyenne woman Calf Road, for example, had once served as a virgin in Elk Society ceremonies but then erred in several affairs and had her braids cut, only to be redeemed in the Sun Dance. After the ritual she remained faithful to her new husband but still suffered the insults of women and men alike.

Active promiscuity in adult women was tolerated under a few circumstances. A Comanche woman mourning over the death of her child was allowed a time of "roughing it out," a two- to three-year period in which she freely pursued sexual liaisons with different men. The husband accepted the behavior and waited it out, resuming a regular relationship with his wife when she had recovered. This mode of grieving was also allowed following the death of a loved husband. The Blackfoots used the term *matsaps* for a woman who was temporarily crazy with wanton urges. They blamed her condition on a certain type of dream and so did not hold her responsible. A promiscuous woman was one who was maximizing her chances of becoming pregnant. Allowed in response to the death of a child or husband, temporary promiscuity could have been a mechanism for population maintenance.

Men were largely ungoverned in their sexual activity. Unmarried men were not expected to be virgins. Comanche men wore a scant g-string called *tsa?nika?* around their genitals, but this was a magical protection of their potency, not a chastity device. Men in general were expected to be loose and their wives more often than not accepted their behavior without strong expressions of jealousy. They felt free to pursue their appetites and did so, thwarted only when women, their kinsmen, or rival men drove them off. A man who was long faithful to one wife could become the butt of teasing from his relatives, the Crows saying to such a person *dīwace' ro'ck-yusa`kēetak*, "you are as though next to a dead thing" (Lowie 1983:48).

A constant strain of ribald talk among adults was the soundtrack to everyday life. Men's banter with each other was laced with dirty jokes and double entendres such as the Comanche use of the word for vulture (*ekabapi*, "red head") to mean penis. Women were sometimes caught up in the jousting as their brothers-in-law followed the custom of the obligatory joking relationship; the nature of their remarks alluded to the sexual tension between people who might easily become spouses. Jim Whitewolf tells of his first attempts to participate in sex talk:

> Sometimes I talked dirty at home. When you were around your sisters, you weren't supposed to talk nasty. My mother was telling an old lady that I sure talked dirty sometimes. I talked that way when my mother's brother was around. One time my uncle was there, and I talked nasty. My mother went out and spoke to the old lady. This old lady got a sharp piece of glass and came over. She told me that she knew I was always talking dirty. She grabbed me and threw me down on my back. She cut my lip with the glass until it bled. Then she asked if I was going to talk that way anymore, and I said I wouldn't. They did that to a lot of kids who talked dirty.
>
> When I was small, I learned about how babies were born by listening to old women who talked about it. They were never ashamed to talk about those things in front of a small boy. It was only after you got older that they wouldn't talk like that in front of you.

(Brant 1969:48)

One of the common themes in sex joking was bestiality. Comanches, for example, liked to tell the story of a man who was humiliated by being dragged into camp by the horse with which he was trying to copulate. While such acts no doubt drew derision, sex with livestock and dogs was not unusual, with horses being used for gratification by men on war parties, according to some credible ethnographic reports.

Incest was one form of sexual behavior that was strongly renounced. Strict avoidance rules minimized interaction between siblings or sons and mothers. Father–daughter incest was probably the most common version, but it was still rare, and viewed as a wicked offense. Public disapproval was brought upon the offender, but protection of the girl was handled within the family. In one nineteenth-century case, the Cheyenne Long Jaw involved his daughter in incest. The girl's mother caught him and tried to get her daughter to take the first boy who showed interest as a husband, but Long Jaw ran off every boy who came to court her and threatened to kill the girl if she married. When the girl became pregnant, presumably by her father, the family broke up out of shame; the mother took the daughter away to live with the Sioux, knowing that she would no longer be marriageable in her own tribe. Another Cheyenne girl named Comes in Sight disemboweled her father, Bear Rope, with a knife as he was "trying to make a wife of her." The other people in her band understood her plight and she was not treated as a murderer.

As a rule homosexuality was acknowledged but not approved of in Plains societies. Negative attitudes were expressed in ridicule and continuous social pressure for males to avoid any behavior that could be considered feminine or submissive. Women were somewhat freer to engage in same-sex activity, and it can be supposed from modern comments that in the past the occasional coupling of females for sex and companionship was tolerated, although there is no evidence that lesbianism was frequent. Most notably, however, relations between people of the same sex were permitted, if not normalized, through the formation of two gender roles that were alternate to the ordinary male and female roles: the berdache and manly hearted woman.

Berdaches

Among most of the Plains tribes, as well as elsewhere in western North America, there was a distinct social role for anatomical males who dressed as women, associated with women, and spent most of their time performing women's tasks (see Table 5.1). These individuals, while never numerous, were accepted as functional members of society. They were not stigmatized but instead enjoyed a positive status, and often they were

TABLE 5.1 Tribes Known to Have Berdache Status During the Horse Era

Arapahos

Arikaras

Assiniboines

Blackfoots

Cheyennes

Crows

Iowas

Kansas

Lipan Apaches

Mandans

Omahas

Osages

Otoes

Pawnees

Plains Crees

Poncas

Quapaws

Shoshones

Tetons

Yanktons

Source: Callender and Kochems (1983:445).

celebrated for superior skills in sewing, beadwork, and cooking. The Indian male transvestite has usually been called *berdache*, a word introduced by the New World French and Spaniards, derived from Arabic and Persian terms meaning catamite. Modern terms that have been proposed to replace the word *berdache* because of its colonialist, lewd, and inaccurate connotations include *man-woman* and *two-spirits*.

Most berdaches fully cross-dressed for all activities, but this was not always a distinguishing characteristic. Some fulfilled the rest of the role without cross-dressing at all. Others wore a distinct combination of usual clothing items that was not clearly male or female. Berdaches might switch to the clothing appropriate to their sex when they were temporarily acting in the role of an ordinary male, such as when they traveled with men in a war party. Osh-Tisch or Finds-Them-and-Kills-Them (also known as Squaw Jim), a Crow berdache, donned men's clothes to fight in the 1876 Battle of Rosebud Creek, Montana.

It was considered good luck to have a berdache along on a war party. Some tribes sent them directly into combat, while others, like the Cheyennes, had them tend to the wounded or collect the scalps taken during the battle. It seems equally surprising that societies which placed such an overwhelming emphasis on the ideal of an aggressive male would institute a feminine role for men, and that the men who pursued the feminine role would then go to war. But, as earlier noted, women did go along on raids and sometimes took part in combat, so there is less inconsistency in these practices than first appears. Regarding the very presence of the berdache role, long ago Abram Kardiner, an anthropologist trained in psychoanalysis by Sigmund Freud, saw it as kind of release valve—indeed, the only honorable alternative—for the minority of males who were not psychologically fit to embrace the monolithic warrior role. In fact, however, there is no correlation between the prevalence of berdaches and the intensity of warfare across the North American tribes, as might be expected under Kardiner's thesis, nor were berdaches necessarily afraid to fight, as Finds-Them-and-Kills-Them's exploits demonstrate.

Some details about berdache sexual life are known, though the picture is clouded because Native informants were reticent and non-Indian reporters often prudish. There was probably great variability within and across tribes. To put a common preliminary question to rest, as far as is known, berdaches were not usually hermaphrodites; they had unambiguous male genitalia. Generally, though not always, berdaches were homosexual, taking a passive role in sex with ordinary males. Rare accounts mention supine receptive anal intercourse among the Cheyennes and fellatio among the Crows. Within the wider Plains attitudes concerning homosexuality, however, the berdache's situation was exceptional: he had a special calling and a sacred status. Not all men who participated in homosexual activity were berdaches—most were not. Conversely, an ordinary male who had sex with a berdache was not considered homosexual in the usual sense (although such activity was still sometimes discouraged of young men). Some berdaches, moreover, were clearly bisexual or heterosexual, and others probably asexual owing to impotence or weak sex drive. The sexual conduct of a berdache, as with any Plains Indian person, was not regarded as the defining feature of his social role, but rather as an accompaniment. Sexuality was not so determinant of identity as it has become in some modern non-Indian societies.

There was similar complexity on the question of berdache marriage. The Sioux expected a berdache to be promiscuous but not to marry. After a Lakota berdache's first sexual encounter, his parents would set up a tipi for him to live independently. Elsewhere berdaches were permitted to marry men and live and work among their husband's female wives, and were valued in the polygynous family for their industry. Berdache marriage was usually of some provisional kind.

Crow berdaches seldom married but were not prohibited from doing so. A Cheyenne berdache could only participate in a marriage as an auxiliary wife. The Hidatsa berdache most often married an older man who was childless and could not keep a female wife. If the husband already had other wives, the berdache took a separate lodge. The Hidatsa berdache was also able to build a family by adopting orphans or war captives and assuming the role of mother. A berdache marriage to a woman was recorded among the Osages, so that seems also to have been a possibility. There are no reports of Plains berdaches marrying or having sex with one another, though the latter may have taken place in light of information about berdaches in the Southwest.

The calling to become a berdache came subtly during childhood, as a boy grew interested in women's activities and began to try them, or it could come suddenly, later, in a dream or vision. There seems to have been some tribal patterning to these styles of inspiration. The Hidatsas and Crows stressed childhood inclinations and in most cases did not seem to need any supernatural validation of the choice. Other tribes, including the Plains Ojibwas, Tetons, Arapahos, Osages, and Omahas, thought that a sacred vision during adolescence or later was necessary, and for them the transformation to berdache status was a kind of religious event open to public attention. In Arapaho myth the original berdache (*haxu'xan*, "rotten bone") was the trickster who pretended to be a woman, married Mountain Lion, and bore him a false child. The Arapahos thought of the berdache calling as a supernatural gift from the animals and birds. The Omahas called the berdache *mexoga*, meaning "instructed by the moon," noting supernatural inspiration by the spirit patron of females. Similarly, the Ponca *míxuga* dreamt of being presented a choice between a bow and arrows and a pack strap by the moon spirit, and tricked into choosing the latter. Old Woman Above was the muse for Mandan berdaches, as was a similar female being among the related Hidatsas. In many of these stories the directive to become a berdache is considered unavoidable but unfortunate. The receiver should be reluctant, and should be pitied for having to depart from the usual warrior role expected of men. Thus, even though berdaches enjoyed supernatural approval and high status, there could be some ambivalence about their situation.

Other supernatural sanctions emphasized the combined nature of the berdache. The Lakota *winkte* ("woman would become") was said to follow the vision of Double Woman, a mythological figure symbolizing various sexual contrasts. The "double vision" entailed not only "female" dress, speech patterns, vocal tone, and economic and sexual functions, but also "male" attributes such as supernatural power acquisition. In one recorded instance of the death of a Lakota berdache, the people could not decide whether men or women should prepare the body for burial; finally it was decided that an old married couple would do it together, and in this way the body was disposed of honorably. It was acknowledged that berdaches could not bear children or breast feed, and that they were normally larger than women, so their female aspect was limited and balanced against male traits.

The combined character of the berdache made those in the role suitable as intermediaries between males and females and between humans and the spirits. Berdaches were renowned as matchmakers, love magicians, or as curers of venereal disease. It was a blessing to have a berdache name one's baby. The Cheyennes assigned a berdache to run the scalp dance, and the Crows designated one to chop down the first tree for the Sun Dance lodge. In all these instances the dual nature of berdaches made them unusual, suggestive of the sacred, and appropriate when dualities needed to be mediated symbolically in ceremony.

Ultimately, the berdache role amounted to a culturally accepted third gender. Theorists have pointed out that since gender is culturally constructed, the number of genders that a society defines is not necessarily limited to the two commonly based on the sexual distinction male: female. In fact, it is even possible to posit a fourth gender in some Plains tribes, because in some of them anatomical females assumed the appearance and work of men.

These so-called "manly hearted women" were not as prominent and widespread as berdaches but definitely known in some societies. The term derives from the Piegan (Canadian Blackfoot) word *ninauposkitzipxpe* and is used here generically. (Recently, the word *berdache* has been extended to include "women-men" as well as "men-women," but this usage masks the possibility of yet a fourth gender). Woman Chief was a Gros Ventre girl who was captured at age 12 and raised by the Crows. She distinguished herself in the 1850s by participating in horse raids and battles. Woman Chief used the horses obtained during her raids as marriage payments in order to establish a coresident group with several female wives. Running Eagle was the warrior name of a similar woman–man among the Piegan. She began life as Brown Weasel Woman and first made her mark by riding back in the midst of battle to rescue her dismounted father. Among her other exploits was a horse raid against the Crows.

Newspaper articles from northern Mexico circa 1850 tell of the region being terrorized by a band of Comanches under the female warrior called Tabe Peté or Arriba el Sol (*tabepa?atɨ*, "sun high," "above the sun," or *tabepitɨ*, "sun to arrive") and her two sons. One account describes her as 112 years of age; she was certainly a grandmother. After a career of raiding for livestock, scalps, and captives, in 1854 the Sols were ambushed and destroyed by Mexican forces while camped deep in Chihuahua. In a 1990 interview, Comanche elder Ned Timbo told of like adventures undertaken by his grandmother Waqueeta (*waako?itɨ* "trot return," "Trotting Into Camp") as a warrior in Mexico, and suggested that women fighters could be well organized: "They had a bunch that they called Woo-see. Woo-see Indians. They was nothing but womens. Women's corps, so to speak. They had their leaders, just like the army got their colonels; leaders of different small groups" (quoted in Pelon 1993:153).

Timbo's comment indicates that the Comanches at least may have had a fairly organized approach, but how manly hearted woman status was achieved and how firmly established it was in various tribes are not all that clear. It appears that, as in the case of the male berdache, childhood leanings and supernatural inspiration both played a part in the individual's decision to adopt the alternate role. As youngsters Woman Chief preferred boy's games and Running Eagle took up the bow and arrow. One report about Running Eagle says that she obtained warrior power from the sun in a vengeance pledge, as men would, after her husband was killed. The Tetons recognized members of two women's societies, Double Woman Dreamers and the Women's Medicine Society, as predisposed to dream about crossing over toward masculine behavior. They were likely to be aggressive and promiscuous, and unlikely to marry. It appears that manly hearted women were usually postmenopausal or perhaps experiencing amenorrhea. These conditions would fit with the roles of hunter or warrior, since menstrual blood was believed harmful to the supernatural power needed for successful hunting and warfare. Such women were distinguishable from those of childbearing years who partook in raiding and village defense without assuming a consistently different gender identification. Another question is the degree of transvestism associated with the manly hearted woman role. Running Eagle was said to have worn what sounds like a combination of clothing—men's leggings and shirt plus a women's dress. Whatever, for success in these pursuits, women-men were honored by the community as a man would be.

Table 5.1 lists the Plains cultures that included a berdache status. The Comanches stand out as one tribe that may have lacked a formalized berdache role, corresponding to a strong intolerance for male transvestism and male homosexuality, at least according to the scant and relatively late evidence. There is also no evidence of the custom among the neighboring Kiowas and Wichitas during the horse culture period. Women assuming male roles are definitely known for the Crows, Blackfoots, Assiniboines, Tetons, and Comanches, and probably appeared in other tribes also. It has been estimated that in the larger tribes there were no more than five or so berdaches at any one time, and fewer if any manly hearted women. In accounting for the greater proportion of berdaches, it has been argued that women's roles were less bounded to begin with, so there was less impetus for an anatomical female to assume an overtly masculine role.

Berdaches are still found in some present-day Plains societies. It is difficult to say when their presence results from an unbroken continuation of traditional roles, and when it results from a revivalism justified by the recent gay rights discourse. Both factors seem to be at work to different degrees depending on the tribe. In 1983 anthropologist William K. Powers reported that the berdache status survived in Lakota culture. Modern Lakota *winktes* were distinguished from homosexuals per se and were accorded respect instead of the ridicule that Lakota men typically addressed to ordinary homosexuals. Outright transvestism was less prevalent than in the past owing to non-Indian pressure against it, and the *winktes* mixed male and female dress and duties. Their sacred and matchmaking functions were still in evidence.

Since the later twentieth century, the emerging field of queer studies has drawn much scholarly attention to the berdache phenomenon. Some recent studies have moved away from understanding the traditional value of the role within American Indian cultures, and focused instead on arguments that homosexuality is natural and universal, and that Indian practices are a model for the social acceptance of gays, lesbians, bisexuals, transvestites, and transgendered persons everywhere. Popular gay rights imagery has also seized on the berdache as an example of tolerance. In turn, pop culture in general has picked up on the berdache as a "gay" figure; one memorable depiction was the comedic character Little Horse, a Cheyenne berdache, in the 1970 revisionist western movie *Little Big Man*. Many of these modern renderings reduce the complex gender role to a narrow version of its sexual facet, and once again impose non-Indian conceptualizations of sexuality, in this case "gay" or "queer" ones. Nevertheless, the Plains berdache tradition does deserve more study within the wider contexts of human gender identification and sexuality, particularly global patterns of transvestism and transgendering.

Sources: Anderson (2003); Barnard (1941); Berlandier (1969); Bol and Menard (2000); Bowers (1991, 1992); Boyd (1981); Brant (1969); Callender and Kochems (1983); Catches (1999); Culin (1975); DeMallie (1983); Denig (1930); Dodge (1882); Dorsey (1894); Dorsey and Murie (1940); Eggan (1955); Eggan and Maxwell (2001); Ewers (1958, 1997); Gelo (1986); Gladwin (1948); Grinnell (1891); Herdt (1994); Hoebel (1940, 1988); Hudson (1966); Hungry Wolf (1980); Jones (1972); Kardiner (1945); Kehoe (1983, 1995); Klein (1983); La Vere (1998); Lesser (1930); Lewis (1941, 1942); Linton (1936); Llewellyn and Hoebel (1941); Lowie (1983); Mandelbaum (1979); McFee (1972); Meadows (1999); Medicine (1983); Moore (1981, 1987); Neighbors (1852); Newcomb (1961); Pelon (1993); M. Powers (1986); W. Powers (1977, 1983); Reyer (1991); Roscoe (1998); Schneider (1983); Schweinfurth (2002); Simms (1903); Smith (1970); Spector (1983); Spier (1925); Stedman (1982); Van Gennep (1960); Walker (1980); Wallace and Hoebel (1952); Weist (1980); Whitehead (1994); Wissler (1986); and Yarrow (1881).

CHAPTER SUMMARY

The study of Plains social life must consider kinship and descent, family, age, marriage, mutual work and play, gender, and sex. Plains Indians had specific ways of naming and categorizing relatives. Their kin terminology systems conform to some general patterns. Nuclear and extended families were the basic social units. All Plains societies recognized age grades, categories of people based on age brackets and associated statuses, roles, and responsibilities. These grades included infancy, childhood, adolescence, adulthood, and old age. The phases of life were often separated by rites of passage, ceremonies that mark a change in status. Birth, naming, puberty rites, marriage (including plural marriage), divorce, and death all took characteristic forms among Plains Indians. Indian gender roles have frequently been stereotyped, but Plains roles, relationships, and sexual customs were complex. The berdache and manly hearted woman were alternatives to the usual male and female roles.

QUESTIONS FOR REVIEW

1. Explain how and why the ways of classifying and naming relatives among various Plains Indian tribes might vary from the practices employed by Euro-Americans.
2. Select a female or male age grade and describe the expectations that accompanied that role.
3. Explain how Plains customs of courtship, marriage, and divorce fit with other concepts of family and social organization.
4. Evaluate the statement, "Ultimately, the berdache role amounted to a culturally accepted third gender."

CHAPTER 6

MATERIAL CULTURE AND DECORATIVE ARTS

The tangible creations of Plains Indian people have been much admired for their ingenuity, color, and beauty. Indian houses, clothing, tools, weapons, crafts, arts, and other things made and modified for their survival and comfort have enjoyed a great deal of attention, and often non-Indians become interested in learning more about Indian cultures after an initial fascination with Indian material life. Besides appealing to the senses, Plains material items reveal a great deal about Indian people's capacity for invention, their deep understanding of the natural world, and, because so many items have symbolic value, their sense of place in the social and spiritual worlds too.

DWELLINGS

The Tipi

It would be hard to imagine a dwelling better suited to its environment than the Plains tipi. Known to English speakers by the Dakota term combining *ti*, "to dwell," and the indefinite suffix *pi* (thus, roughly, "something to dwell in"), the conical tent formed from poles and a hide cover was the sole house type for nomadic groups and a secondary travel lodge for groups that lived in fixed houses. Forerunners of the classic Plains tipi are observed among native peoples of the circumpolar regions, such as the northern Canadian Indians and Inuits, the Saami of Scandinavia, and Siberian tribes, all of whom have conical dwellings, though smaller and sometimes covered with bark or vegetable fiber matting instead of skin. The early occupants of the Plains must have had tipis that were smaller than those known historically, since horses were needed to regularly drag the longer poles and heavier covers of large tipis, and arguably horses made it easier to obtain larger numbers of buffalo hides for bigger covers.

The size of a tipi may be spoken of in terms of the number of buffalo skins used to make the cover. Fourteen to 18 skins were used for the average lodge, though as few as 7 or, for oversized ceremonial lodges, as many as 22. Closely

FIGURE 6.1   A woman walks among three painted tips in a camp of the blood division of the Blackfoot tribe. Photo circa 1913, by Roland Reed (1864–1934).

stitched together with sinew, the tanned hides were sewn flesh side out into a shape that wrapped perfectly around the supporting poles.

Initially, the builders made a foundation by lashing together a cluster of three or four poles at one end; this assembly was stood with the lashed end up, and the loose ends spread apart on the ground. The choice between the tripod and four-pole foundation was standardized by tribal tradition. Groups using three poles included the Crees, Gros Ventres, Assiniboines, Tetons, Mandans, Arikaras, Cheyennes, Arapahos, Poncas, Otoes, Wichitas, and Kiowas. The Sarsis, Blackfoots, Shoshones, Utes, Omahas, and Comanches preferred the four-pole base. (These preferences usually, but not always, reflect obvious linguistic and historical connections.) Once the foundation was set, several more poles were laid in the crotch formed by the base poles to create a conical framework. Depending on whether the foundation is three or four poles, how the additional poles rest and project above the crossing point varies: a tripod base produces a tidy swirl of pole tips, while the four-pole base causes the tips to lie in two bunches. Thus, a knowing observer might be able to tell, say, a Ponca from an Omaha lodge at a distance by the appearance of the tipi top. The kind and size of the poles used were also distinguishing. Peoples living on the northwest Plains, near the Rocky Mountains—most notably the Crows—had access to lodgepole pine, which produced timbers in excess of 30 feet. Crow tipis therefore have a particularly graceful hourglass appearance as the poles extend a good distance up beyond the crossing point. Elsewhere, other long, straight, and light timbers were used, such as yellow pine in the northwest, tamarack in the northeast, and white and red cedar.

Two people could put up this framework in a matter of minutes. Normally women owned the tipi components, largely the product of their labor, and were the ones to put it up. In another few minutes they could raise the cover into place with a lifting pole and lace it closed around the frame using hardwood pins; the lacer climbing up to do her work on rungs temporarily lashed between two poles, or standing on the shoulders of her companion. In joining the cover edges, parts of the seam were left open as a chimney at the top and a doorway at the bottom. At the top of the seam, the loose cover formed two lapel-like flaps. These were fitted with poles that allowed them to be closed or opened in varying ways from the ground outside, in order to direct the airflow inside the tipi, catching a breeze or drawing out smoke. The door might be a simple flap made by hanging a blanket or hairy skin from a lace pin, or a well-crafted oval of hide stretched over willow, with paint and beadwork. At the ground level, the cover was stretched and held taught with hardwood stakes or rocks. During hot spells, the cover could be rolled up from the ground to let air in along the floor. Drainage trenches or even snow fences made from brush were sometimes added around the tipi base for long stays in inclement weather. The tipi was usually set up so that the doorway faced east, away from the prevailing wind and in sacred alignment with the rising sun. To add more significance, the cover was often painted with colorful animal figures and patterns derived from the sacred dreams of the master. Generally, the finished lodge was about 15 feet in diameter and 15–25 feet high, standing elegant and ready for any condition.

Inside the tipi were a number of furnishings that helped create a comfortable living space. An important interior wall was formed by a "dew cloth" of skin tied to the frame from ground to about shoulder level, protecting the inhabitants from rain and condensation that would run down the poles. The liner also provided insulation and helped direct air flow. A fireplace was made on the floor near the center (actually west of center, directly beneath the smoke flap opening—the tipi cone tilts somewhat into the prevailing westerly winds, and the cone's footprint is not perfectly round but egg-shaped). Depending on the tribe, the fireplace might be on the ground surface or in a pit, and was normally small, only for heating—cooking was done outside whenever possible. A pile of buffalo chips or sticks was kept nearby to feed the flames. The floor was otherwise covered with sage and furs. Around the inside wall were the sleeping places. There might be a simple pallet and blanketing of buffalo robes, directly on the ground, or cots formed by suspending rawhide on low pegs. Beds were tucked into the angle of the cone and well below the smoke.

More comfort was provided with backrests. Ingenious in their portability, backrests were made from many willow rods strung together horizontally; they were suspended from stick tripod frames at the ends of the beds for sitting, and rolled up for travel. Around the lodge, other kinds of gear were hung from the poles or set on the floor. Large collapsible rawhide envelopes called parfleches, painted with bold geometric patterns, stored clothing and meat. A cylindrical rawhide case held the man's war bonnet. From the rafters, such items as a quiver and a green buffalo paunch water bag were hung. There were bowls, cups, and spoons made from wood, horn, and turtle shell. Various beaded bags and pillows stuffed with hair or grass completed the furnishings. Surrounding all within, the liner might be decorated with colorful scenes depicting the exploits of the lodge master.

Tipi residents and their visitors observed several points of etiquette that brought an air of respect and order to home life. While an open door permitted the unannounced entry of friends, a closed door required a polite request and an invitation to come in. It was correct for men to move around the north side and women the south, taking care not to pass between a seated person and the fire if possible. Kinship terms were used when begging pardon. The owner's place was opposite the door, with a place for an honored son or guest to his left—his heart side. Making and tending the lodge fire were activities governed by a sense of what was proper; for example, in keeping a wood fire the sticks were fed in endwise in a manner that regulated the heat

and light carefully. Often a small square of ground west of the fire was kept clear as an altar with cedar, sage, or sweet grass incense. The circular floor of the tipi, with this ritually cleared ground within, represented an orderly cosmos and a reverent attitude.

By 1900, canvas wall tents, log cabins, and frame houses had replaced the tipi as primary dwellings in most Plains Indian communities. Tipis were still valued for travel, ceremonies, and summer encampments, though canvas and muslin replaced bison skin and these materials required design changes such as sewn loops for the bottom pegs. Later tipis are generally a little larger than earlier ones, in the range of 20 feet across or more, because cloth is lighter than buffalo skin, making larger covers practical. The availability of cars and trailers in the twentieth century, with their better ability to transport long poles, plus the wider access to pole lumber they afforded, also contributed to the development of bigger lodges. Today, a trip to Crow Indian Fair south of Billings, Montana, during August to view the thousands of lodges will confirm the continuing importance of the design as both habitation and cultural icon. Perhaps the most interesting modern development has been the revived role of the tipi as a canvas for Plains painting. Traditional artists have recreated and reinterpreted patterns known from tribal history. In this way, the tipi, both architecture and art, lives on as a classic of form and function.

The Earth Lodge

In contrast to the light, portable tipi, the earth lodge of the Mandans, Hidatsas, and Arikaras, the Pawnees, and some Southern Siouans (Poncas, Otoes, Missourias) was a large, stationary structure meant for sedentary life. An earth lodge might last 15 years before the tolls of nature would require rebuilding, in which case a new lodge could be erected more or less on the same

FIGURE 6.2   *Members of a Pawnee family pose in front of their earth lodge, Loup, Nebraska, 1873. Bundled tipi poles rest atop the entrance.*

spot, if the villagers did not want to relocate to a better garden site.

Earth lodge construction plans and techniques varied even within tribes, but all were generally similar. Teams of women did the work, though the floor plan might first be laid out by some medicine men. A rawhide rope was set down to delineate a circle 30–90 feet in diameter, and the ground within was cleared. A dozen or more upright posts, about 6 feet high and thick as telephone poles, were placed around the circle, and more logs were added horizontally or vertically to form an outside wall. At the circle center, four to eight more heavy timbers, connected with cross members either lashed or joined in place, composed a framework about 10 feet high. Rafter poles connected the center frame to the outside wall, and the entire skeleton was packed with willow branches, sod, grass, and dirt in order to form an artificial hill-cavern. By excavating the

ground a few feet as the circle was first cleared, headroom could be added and a ledge was formed just inside the outer walls that served as a bench. Most earth lodges also had a low entrance extension, similar to the entryway of an Inuit igloo, though square rather than domed in cross-section, which prevented wind and rain from blowing directly into the house. Entrances often opened to the east or southeast, like a tipi door. An unlined pit about 3 feet around at the center of the floor contained the fire, and there was a sizeable hole in the center of the roof to let the smoke escape.

Within the central frame and around the fire was a bed for elders, seats for honored guests, and places for grinding and cooking. The main floor area was mostly open but could be divided with screens formed by upright logs. The spaces between the outer support posts formed bays dedicated to different functions: bed areas with platform cots enclosed with skin; pottery vessels and storage of food, firewood, or tools; an altar with ceremonial items such as a buffalo skull or medicine bundle, set up opposite the door; even corrals for horses. Some four dozen people, an extended family, plus their animals, could be housed in an earth lodge.

Villages of earth lodges were made up of houses built within feet of each other. These settlements typically featured enclosing defensive walls built up from sod, and numerous bell-shaped cache pits located among the houses to hold surplus from the harvest. Early photos often show many inhabitants sitting on top of their homes. The tribes living in earth lodges used tipis too for hunting trips.

The Grass Lodge

The grass lodge of the Wichitas and Kitsais was the third main dwelling type on the Plains. This distinctive house has been likened to a haystack or old-fashioned beehive. Predecessors of the Caddoan grass house dwellers on the plains built earth lodges, and it has been proposed that the grass lodge is an adaptation of the earth lodge design using different materials and techniques. Grass lodges were more graceful and symmetrical, standing about 30 feet high. A doorway so small that those entering had to stoop opened directly into a spacious but dark interior. Sometimes a smoke hole was located near the top. Other times no hole permitted the smoke of the central fire to escape; instead, it wafted into the eaves and seeped through the grass. The interior floor was packed with dirt. In the upper reaches of the structure, cross-poles supported stores of corn and pumpkin.

Erection of the grass lodge required many builders, mostly women, working together over a period of days. A square framework of logs similar to that used in the earth lodge center was built as basic support. Tapered poles, quite thick at one end, were set in the ground forming a circle around the base structure ("round like the sun," according to a Wichita origin myth) and their tops bent and lashed together with elm bark, somewhat like a curved tipi frame. To these vertical poles were lashed thinner horizontal members all around at intervals from the ground up, forming a basket-like frame, with the builders climbing their way up to lash each successive rung, sometimes with the help of a notched-log ladder. Next, they added bunches of little bluestem or buffalo grass in enormous quantity, held in place with light rods lashed to the framework. The bunches were overlapped like shingles. Like the earth lodge, the grass lodge was intended for long-term occupation by an extended family. After several years, as the grass rotted and became infested with insects and rodents, the lodge would simply be burned and a new one built.

The Wigwam

The term "wigwam" is sometimes used interchangeably with "tipi," but the two words refer to notably different structures. The wigwam, though found in various shapes and sizes, always involves a squat wooden framework of vertical and horizontal lashed poles covered with plant fiber matting, bark, or skins. It is characteristic of the eastern Woodlands of North America, and on the Plains it was used by some of the tribes with more recent eastern ancestry—mostly in the east-central Plains. The Osages, Iowas, Kansas, and Quapaws used the wigwam as their main dwelling. The Poncas, Otoes, and Missourias used the wigwam secondarily to the earth lodge, and the Plains Ojibwas sometimes built wigwams instead of tipis. Most of these groups built both round and rectangular styles of wigwam, from 30 to 100 feet long. Some preferred walnut, cypress, or elm bark, and others, hide or woven rush covering. The wigwams making up a village could be arranged regularly or not, and sometimes tribes built log palisades around the grouping.

FIGURE 6.3   Photo of Wichita settlement in Indian Territory, circa 1890, labeled "Ska-wa-cer's home," showing grass lodges, log cabins, arbors, storage platforms (some with canvas covers), wagons, and surrounding gardens. More grass lodges are visible on the far horizon, showing the dispersed nature of Wichita communities.

Often cache pits were dug directly in the wigwam floor rather than outside among the lodges to store supplies.

Other Structures

Regardless of the main house type, a village would also include other structures. Brush arbors or shades of various designs were common to all the tribes, set up adjacent to the main dwellings. Shades open to the breeze on one or more sides were more comfortable for working or napping in the heat of summer. The Crows favored a round arbor with a conical roof. On the South Plains, shades were made with uprights about 7 feet high and a flat roof of boughs, or a sapling hoop framework. The sweat lodge was a small dome also made from saplings and covered with brush and old hides. Six or so men huddled within

around a pile of rocks that had been heated in an outside fire and rolled in with large forked poles. Water was poured on the rocks to produce an intense steam for fitness and ceremonial purification. The sweat lodge was often built near a creek so that the participants could plunge into cool water after sweating. Similar small huts were built for women in which to seclude themselves during their menstrual period. Menstruating women were considered extra powerful and had to avoid contact with other people (see Chapter 5). Special tipis were erected solely for ritual, to house sacred pipes or accommodate curing ceremonies or peyote meetings, and occasionally long "medicine tipis" were built by joining two or more tipi frames and covers. The last notable structure type in pre-reservation times was the lodge built for the Sun Dance, which is described in Chapter 10.

Despite the persistence of grass houses in Oklahoma well into the twentieth century and the continuing special use of tipis, once reservations were established, Plains Indian people quickly adopted wall tents and cabins, and then frame and brick houses. These forms have posed difficulties for those adopting them. First of all, imagine how inconvenient it would be to talk about non-Indian architecture in an Indian language. A Comanche–Spanish dictionary published in 1865 shows the same Comanche word for wall, ceiling, and door, which makes perfect sense in a conical house, but not when the house is cubical. Rectangular spaces violate traditional ideas about the natural harmony or sacredness of circles. And, in practical terms, for people living in remote areas, non-Indian house types are expensive to build and maintain. Nevertheless, in Indian areas of Montana or southwest Oklahoma today one finds single-story brick homes built to Department of Housing and Urban Development specifications. These homes are small and crowded by non-Indian standards. Storage space is often a problem, necessitating sheds around the yard. The houses normally have electricity and indoor plumbing, though again it is hard to keep these features in working order. Indian domestic customs are carried on within the restriction of the modern structure. Occupants may prefer to use the house's side door rather than front door if it faces east, or line their closets with cedar to preserve their regalia, using the traditional material for pest control. An arbor or tipi may be set up nearby for sleeping to allow brick house dwellers some relief from the summer heat.

TOOLS AND WEAPONS

Garden Tools

In discussing material culture as in other matters, it is important not to forget the heritage of horticulture that enabled pioneering of the region by several of the long-standing Plains tribes. The basic gardening tool kit has been mentioned in Chapter 3. Women turned the soil with hoes made from buffalo shoulder blades. Sharpened sticks were enough for planting seeds and digging up roots. The digging stick was useful in gathering wild plants as well as cultivated ones. Rakes were fashioned from antlers mounted on handles. The Upper Missouri tribes built timber scaffolds upon which to dry corn, threshed the corn with hardwood flails, and pounded the grains with heavy wooden pestles in wood mortars.

Basketry and Pottery

Basketry and pottery are best considered in relation to gardening. These crafts may be useful to populations surviving on gathered plants, but they become more prevalent in societies relying on harvested surpluses of cultivated foods.

While tribes of the Southwest, California, and Northwest Coast are renowned for superbly woven fiber baskets, some so tightly made that they can hold water, others completely covered in gorgeous woodpecker scalps, only a few Plains groups had baskets and they devoted relatively little care to their construction. The Mandans, Hidatsas, Arikaras, and Pawnees made a distinctive style of burden basket for carrying corn at harvest. These were large, deep containers of willow bark, plaited to form geometric designs, on a framework of U-shaped bent sticks, complete with carrying strap. Small coiled basketry trays were made by the same tribes and some of their nomadic neighbors for gambling—dice made from stones or fruit pits were shuffled in them. The weaving of plant fibers to form mats, bags, and ropes can also be considered along with basketry, but these practices were similarly restricted. The Pawnees and Iowas made multipurpose reed mats; the Blackfoots made a kind of rope from bark fiber. Otherwise, no plant fiber weaving was found among the Plains tribes, except those Shoshones and Utes of the western margins who partook in the sophisticated basketry traditions of the Great Basin.

The ceramics of the Plains were also simple in comparison to those of neighboring culture areas. Influences in the design of earthenware came onto the Plains mainly from the Woodlands and only very tentatively from the Southwest. Again, it was the semi-sedentary peoples of Siouan and Caddoan background who relied on this technology. Pots were molded by hand from lumps of clay, not built up of clay coils or spun on a wheel. They tended to be collared, globular cooking vessels with no handles or a pair of small ear-like grips near the rim. Decoration was minimal, consisting at most of linear or triangular patterns pressed in the wet clay with cordage or a sharp stick. Tribal oral traditions and archaeology both support the notion that the quality of pottery on the Plains diminished after the Late Prehistoric Period, as horse culture and manufactured trade goods spread through the area.

It stands to reason that basketry and pottery skills would not be refined among horse cultures. With the dietary focus on buffalo, the kinds of plant processing aided by basket use became less important to many groups. A surprising number of nomadic peoples around the world do use pottery, but even so it is not very practical or efficient for nomads to drag or carry their surplus food in heavy breakable containers. Rawhide containers served better for food transportation on the Plains, or surpluses were simply cached and returned to later. Pots were not essential for cooking, since lighter animal paunches worked well as cooking vessels. Moreover, once contact was made with non-Indians, metal cookware became widespread—not so light as skin vessels, but more convenient, and more durable than clay pottery.

Cradles

In mobile societies the safe transportation of babies is a major concern. Plains tribes used several kinds of cradle to carry and protect young ones. While referred to as cradles, these devices were primarily carriers rather than beds.

The simplest design, called a cradleboard, consisted of a single plank somewhat wider and longer that its passenger. The baby was tied to the board with buckskin bands or cloth sashes wrapped around the plank. A hole near the top center accepted a thong for hanging the board. Cradleboards often included a small wooden shelf serving as a footrest, wooden side rails, and a face guard of squared or arched wood. The guard or "bow" allowed a cover to be draped over the baby's face to prevent sunburn, and from it dewclaw rattles or trade bells might be suspended to entertain the child. A soft animal pelt was added as cushioning. Though uncomplicated as a piece of equipment, the board held precious cargo and so was invested with spiritual power: Pawnee cradleboards were cut from the heartwood of a living tree and decorated with a carving of the sacred Morning Star to preserve the child's life. The board style of cradle was characteristic of the woodland east and so, in addition to the Pawnees, was found among the Southern Siouans.

Other cradles consisted of a leather container for the baby with an internal wooden support. In the style preferred by the Blackfoots, Crows, Nez Perce, Shoshones, and Utes, a roughly elliptical board stretched and backed a buckskin pocket that held the baby. The exact shape of the board varied; for example, Crow cradles had squarer tops than those of neighboring groups. Other types had multi-piece frames. Instead of a board, the Arapaho cradle employed an inverted U-shaped outer frame spread with a cross-piece to support the leather container. Wichita cradles used the U-shaped outer frame backed with two dozen vertical willow rods, the whole assembly held together with sinew. Apache models featured an oval outer frame filled in with horizontal wooden slats and a wide awning over the baby's face made from two bows joined by vertical slats.

Kiowa, Comanche, and some Sioux examples, known as lattice-backed cradles, utilized external frames made from two large planks joined by two cross members and set wider at the top than at the bottom. The pieces were joined not with nails or glue, but by burning small holes through them and tying them together with buckskin. A buckskin container resembling a giant shoe was tied onto the frame, laced up and down with the baby snug within. The pointed ends of the main planks projected several inches beyond the container top to protect the baby's head.

Various means were used to funnel off or absorb the baby's waste. Moss was the usual diaper material. After a day in the cradle, the child was unbound and dressed with bear or buffalo grease and powder made from decomposed cottonwood or dried buffalo dung.

The mother carried the cradle on her back by means of a strap around her upper arms and chest or with a tumpline around her forehead. But the cradle was especially handy for the mother when riding or doing chores in camp. Jean Louis Berlandier, a Swiss scientist observing Comanche ways in Texas around 1828, noted,

> Comanche cradles are packed on horseback on long journeys and the way they are carried is strange indeed. . . . When a rancheria [Indian camp] is on the march you may see the women on horseback with their babies swinging from the pommels of their saddles. . . . When they reach the day's campsite the mothers may swing the cradles from the branch of a tree, or prop them against a convenient rock, and so they nurse their babies.
>
> (Berlandier 1969:85–86)

The Comanche cradles described in Berlandier's report are actually cradleboards, suggesting that this tribe used more than one kind of cradle, a possibility with many of the groups.

At night Comanche babies were placed in a stiff rawhide tube, like the baby carrier container but without a frame. The rigid night cradle protected the baby should its parents roll over as it slept between them. Another sleeping contrivance for young ones was a small hammock suspended between trees or house posts, used by several tribes.

Much care was invested in cradle construction. Usually relatives of the parents were called upon to supply this item. Among the matrilineal Pawnees, the father's family made the cradle as an expression of mutual concern for the child. Normally a small, unadorned cradle was made for a newborn; if the infant survived the critical early months, another cradle of subsequent size was built, this one heavily decorated. Many larger cradles had casings entirely covered with quills or beads in an intensive labor of love, and the projecting planks of latticeback cradles were embellished with brass tacks in an hourglass pattern and red and blue paint. A fancy baby carrier was kept long after the child was grown as a family heirloom.

Boats and Rafts

On the open Plains, Indian people did not face the need to navigate large bodies of water, and voyaging on the rivers of the region was seldom a practical alternative to land travel. Crossing large streams with livestock or other belongings was sometimes necessary. Good descriptions of the Indian process for river crossing (and similar procedures of non-Indian cavalrymen and cowboys) were recorded by non-Indian observers. Swimming horses across the larger streams could be a harrowing undertaking during the springtime swells. Individuals were swept a long way downstream as they crossed, and it might take many anxious minutes for all members of a party to make the crossing safely. Generally, though, crossing on foot or horseback was sufficient.

Under these circumstances, only the most basic forms of watercraft were ever necessary. The typical Plains vessel was the bullboat built by the Mandans, Hidatsas, Omahas, Kansas, and Assiniboines and less regularly by most others.

FIGURE 6.4   Mandan woman paddling a bull boat, 1908. Photo by Edward S. Curtis.

This was a buffalo-skin boat with a simple framework of cross-lashed willow sticks; it was not a canoe, but round, with a flat bottom, like a tub. In structure the bullboat was very similar to the sealskin coracle used in the British Isles from ancient times into the twentieth century, although there is no historical connection. While the larger bullboats (about 5 feet in diameter) could contain a person, and were paddled by leaning over the rim and pulling the boat forward, many were smaller—enough to hold cargo but no passenger—and were pushed or towed by swimmers, usually women. If a bullboat was not available, as when men were away from home on a raid, a raft of sticks and hide could be improvised to keep weapons dry or transport a wounded warrior.

War and Hunting Gear

Among weapons, none was more essential than the bow and arrow. The same type of bow was used for both hunting and combat. It was relatively short—about 3 feet long—so as to be more easily handled from horseback. Some bows were straight, forming a simple arc when strung, while others had forward curves built in to produce more spring.

Any man was able to make his own bow, although among the Omahas and probably other tribes there were those known as specialists who built weapons for their companions in trade for tobacco and other goods. When fashioning a bow, the maker chose from a number of designs and materials. The so-called self-bow was made from a single piece of material, but it was also possible to glue and bind together different pieces for strength and flexibility to make a composite or "compound" bow. While only self-bows are found in the Woodlands and Mexico, the compound design is characteristic of western North America, suggesting that the concept diffused from Asia, where composite bows are the norm, but only part way. Both kinds were found on the Plains.

Wood was the usual bow material, and the species preferred on the Plains were ash and Osage orange (also called bois-d'arc, pronounced "bow-dark," French for "bow wood"), with other woods such as chokecherry finding secondary use in some areas. (Other trusty bow woods like hickory and yew were not native to the Plains, and obtained only infrequently.) Each of these woods had a good combination of requisite qualities: availability, strength, flexibility, shape memory, and workability with simple stone and metal tools. Long, straight, knotless sticks had to be found. They were seasoned, polished with fat or brains, and scraped into the desired profile. Sections of horn from the mountain sheep or elk could also be joined to make small elegant bows, though horn bows were not common, mostly found among the tribes near the Rockies, such as the Crows, Shoshones, and Nez Perce. Laminated horn-wood bows are found as well. To prevent cracking and perhaps to improve flexion, a bow stave was often wrapped with sinew chord or backed with a layer of sinew glued against it, and many or most Plains bows included this feature. The sinew was dressed with fat or paint made with mica or colored clay. Bowstrings were also made of sinew, normally from the buffalo, carefully rolled, twisted, noosed, and fortified with an application of thin glue.

Men took similar care in making their arrows. All knew how to do so, but old men with accumulated skill were highly respected, and a young Arapaho man might invite several elders to his tipi for a day of arrow making. Well before it was time to assemble some arrows, a maker looked for straight shoots growing off of dogwood, ash, plum, cherry, hackberry, mulberry, or serviceberry trees. These woods were tough but also had some flexibility, so that if a shot animal rolled over on the arrow it might spring and thrust itself more deeply instead of snapping. The shoots were collected, bundled, and dried in the lodge of many months. After seasoning, the blank shafts were cut and shaped. The maker determined the shaft length in relation to his body, for example, by measuring against his arm, combining the length from elbow to middle finger tip with the length from his wrist to the big knuckle of the middle finger. Thus, arrows were typically about 2 feet long.

The shafts were straightened with a bone tool resembling a box wrench or donut with a hole just big enough to work the shaft through, and then they were sanded to roundness using a pair of grooved sandstone slabs. Next, lengthwise grooves were scraped into the shafts. The Comanches reportedly used a tool like the arrow straightener, but with a sharp burr on the inside circumference, to cut arrow grooves. Different tribes employed distinctive groove patterns, but in general they were said to represent lightning, a magical appeal to power and fatality. Grooves may also have imparted spin to the arrows, improving accuracy, or sped the flow of blood out of the arrow's victim, although some modern archery authorities have questioned these explanations. Paint in some distinctive combination might be applied to identify the arrow with its owner. The shaft was then carefully fletched with two, three, or four rather long pieces of split feather, which helped the arrow to fly correctly. The shaft was grooved slightly to receive the feathers and they were fixed with glue and sinew thread. Feathers from wild turkey, owl, turkey vulture, hawks, or eagles were preferred; owl and vulture feathers were especially desired because they did not matte when wetted with blood. The feather end of the shaft was then notched for nocking, and the arrowhead glued and lashed to the other end.

Most arrowheads during the Historic Period were iron or steel rather than stone, obtained in manufactured form from non-Indian traders or made by the Indians from barrel hoops and frying pans.

The frontier observer Colonel Richard I. Dodge noted that even a skilful arrow maker could not hope to complete more than one arrow in a day's work. A man could use the product of an entire month of arrow making in only a brief skirmish or buffalo chase. Accordingly, arrows were very precious; they were not easily left behind in the field, and a good set of arrows might equal a horse in trade.

Arrows were housed in a quiver, which could be a simple tube of rawhide or an elaborate container made from the entire skin of a wolf, otter, or mountain lion. The fancier quivers had alongside the arrow compartment a separate, long narrow compartment of soft skin for storing the unstrung bow. Also stored within was a stick of dried hide glue, ready to be softened with hot water, to make repairs to the bow and arrows while in the field. The quiver had a strap and could be worn on the back for drawing arrows over the shoulder, but was often rested flat across the horse's back behind the rider, with the strap around his waist. The bowman drew, nocked, and shot his arrows very rapidly, such that until the advent of repeating firearms, an Indian archer could get off several accurate arrow shots in the time it took a gunman to reload and aim once. He held the bow at a tilt or almost horizontally, and pushed forward as the string was drawn back, in a quick, smooth motion. In battle or buffalo charge, he clutched extra arrows alongside the bow while firing.

Skill with the bow was acquired from an early age. As Colonel Dodge explained,

> The first childish plaything of which [an Indian boy] has recollection is the miniature bow and blunted arrows placed in his hands by his proud father, when he is scarcely four years old. Practicing incessantly, he is, when nine or ten years of age, able to bring in from his daily rambles quite a store of larks, doves, thrushes, sparrows, rabbits, gophers, ground-squirrels, and other "small deer," for which he is greatly praised, particularly by his mother, to whose especial delectation they are presently devoted. When sufficiently familiar and expert with this weapon as to warrant the experiment, he is furnished with arrows with iron points an epoch in his life ranking with the day of possession by the white boy of his first gun. He now quits the companionship of the smaller boys, and in company with lads armed as himself, makes wide excursions after larger game, sometimes being gone from his lodge for several days.

(Dodge 1882:415–416)

Archery practice continued throughout a man's lifetime. He sharpened his skills with games, such as firing off a batch of arrows as quickly as possible and shooting at a rolling wooden hoop target.

Along with his bow and arrows, a man placed great value on his shield. He selected the hide from the neck or shoulders of a bull buffalo, as that was the thickest available. The green hide was dried and shrunk using heat, cut in a circle about 2 feet across (measured to the width of the maker's body), and formed with a slightly convex or concave profile. The result had a texture and strength not unlike fiberglass. A single piece of hide thus prepared might be an inch thick and was all that was needed to make a basic shield. Sometimes multiple layers were laced on a wooden hoop frame. Buffalo hair added between the layers made the shield even more resilient, and in later days paper served this purpose. Texan colonist Stephen Austin relates in an 1822 letter how his party of settlers was detained by some Comanches north of Laredo. The Indians surrounded them and seized all their possessions. In a while the Comanches released them to go on their way, and returned all their property except for a few items, including Austin's grammar book. Austin seems puzzled by this transaction, since the Indians did not read, but one reason for

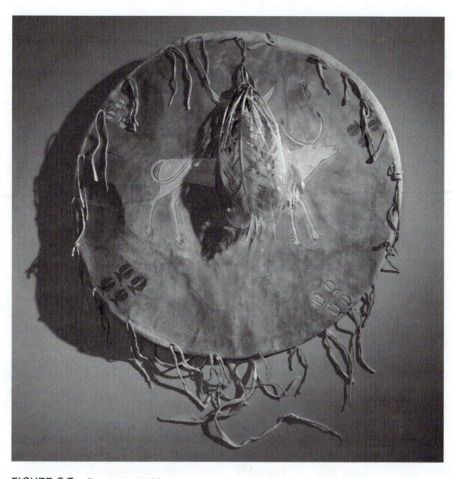

FIGURE 6.5   *Cheyenne shield.*

their liking books is apparent. Texas rancher Charles Goodnight found a complete history of Rome inside one Comanche shield.

The shield was reportedly tough enough to actually deflect arrows and low-velocity bullets fired from a distance. The warrior wore it strapped on his left forearm, leaving his hand free, and deftly angled it against incoming shots. Men practiced these moves by firing blunt arrows at each other.

A Comanche man set his shield on a tripod standing outside his lodge door and rotated it periodically throughout the day so it would continually face the sun and absorb its power. More power was endowed by attaching feathers, scalps, small medicine bundles, and the skins of small birds and animals around the rim, and painting the face with a visionary image such as a thunderbird, water monster, stars, or bear's paw. Especially powerful shields were stored far away from camp and the polluting influence of menstruating women, which would render the shields powerless and leave their owners in danger. To retrieve a distant shield, its owner approached it and returned home in a circular path analogous to the intact shield itself. The value of the shield was indicated by the high degree of ceremony attached to its decoration and storage. It is perhaps both ironic and understandable that, in a culture celebrating men's prowess as raiders above all else, the most valued material culture object was a defensive weapon.

Other tools of the warrior's trade were firearms, knives, lances, clubs, and tomahawks. Guns were obtained through trade, as battle trophies, and as implements handed out on the reservations to support subsistence hunting, scouting, and police work. Contemporary accounts and the holdings of museums confirm that many kinds of firearms were employed, including flintlock muskets and rifles of Spanish, French, English, and American manufacture, Sharps and Spencer carbines, an early German breechloader called a needle gun, elegant Ballard sporting rifles, and the famous repeating lever-action rifles made by Spencer, Henry, and Winchester. After the Civil War the better rifles were fairly well distributed, and revolvers were in wide use also.

Indians typically modified a long gun by cutting down the stock and filing off the end of the barrel to shorten it for better handling while riding, and the stock was adorned with brass tacks in decorative patterns. Guns might be housed in cases similar to those made for bows, carried across the saddle in front of the rider. A Comanche word for rifle, *pia eetu*, literally "big bow," gives some sense of how firearms were viewed and valued. Fancy guns became prestige possessions.

Notwithstanding their popularity and the high degree of Indian ingenuity applied to their maintenance, guns were not wholly practical. Ammunition was scarce and expensive, and any group was likely to have a mixture of different gun types, making it hard to stay supplied. Some Indians had the tools and materials to mold their own bullets and load cartridges, but lead and powder were not always dependably available. Indian ammo was often makeshift, with loose power and balls substituted

for the proper fixed rounds, or shells reloaded again and again with powder accumulated from numerous broken percussion caps. Though repairs to a gunstock could be made with rawhide and sinew, the fixing of metal parts was not something easily done in an Indian camp. In addition to these drawbacks, any advantage in firepower of the gun over the bow was dubious during most of the horse era. Even someone adept at reloading at full gallop could not get shots off as rapidly as a bowman, and the effective ranges of bow and gun were not much different until the advent of buffalo guns in the 1870s. Thus, the bow remained in favor all through the horse period and was often carried along with the gun even by enthusiastic gun owners.

Men and women both carried knives in scabbards. The knife was a basic, indispensable tool for many routine tasks, from skinning and butchering game to carving wooden tipi pegs. Though not a weapon of choice, if a man found himself locked in close combat he might resort to the knife, attacking with downward thrusts while parrying with his shield or tomahawk; the knife was also needed for scalping. Early knives were sharpened pieces of stone or bone; with the non-Indian trade came metal blades, either made by Indians from scrap or obtained whole. Leather scabbards, worn around the neck with a tether or on the belt, were typically large in relation to the blade they stored, and they received profuse ornamentation with quills, beads, and brass tacks.

Beside knives, other essential cutting tools were the implements used for scraping fat and loose flesh from the inside of hides as they were stretched and dried. In one version, the heavy cannon bone of a bison was toothed and sharpened at one end for scraping. Another kind of flesher resembled an adze, with a flat stone or metal blade mounted at right angle to a bone handle, allowing the tool to be drawn with both hands down a vertically mounted hide.

The lance was another bladed weapon. Indian lances were meant for thrusting and parrying and were only thrown as a last resort. Lances shorter than a man were wielded in hand-to-hand combat on the ground, while longer ones—7–12 feet or more—were thrust from horseback. These weapons consisted of a thin wooden shaft, decorated with fur or leather wrappings and feathers and tipped with a round point made from bone, stone, or iron (available in trade) or a blade made of a salvaged knife or sword. The Comanches, Kiowas, and Apaches favored a lance composed of a long, somewhat flexible yucca-stalk shaft with a saber blade. Lances were employed in hunting bison and bears as well as in battle.

Fearsome war clubs were made in several ways. Some terminated in a heavy wooden ball and others were shaped like a gunstock, either type sometimes having one or more metal blades projecting. Simpler clubs involved a rawhide covered stick as a handle, to which was lashed a rock or pair of horns. Rock heads could be lashed to swing freely from the end of the stick like the medieval European weapon called morning star. Clubs had leather wrist straps and were swung with great agility and effectiveness. Tomahawks were metal hatchet heads distributed by non-Indian traders and joined by the Indians to wooden handles, often with elaborate decoration. Swung or thrown, they were deadly as weapons, though often they were more valued as ceremonial items, exchanged as gifts, and buried to symbolize truces. In keeping with these ceremonial functions, some of the hatchet heads distributed by traders had a pipe bowl opposite the blade, such that the tomahawk handle also served as a pipe stem. Colonel Dodge suggested that clubs and tomahawks grew less important as actual weapons over the course of the 1800s, perhaps in relation to the spread of guns.

CLOTHING

The full-feathered headdress or "war bonnet" is perhaps the single most recognizable icon of Plains Indian identity. These headdresses are associated with chiefs, and indeed someone who deserved this role would qualify to own one, but they were considered appropriate wear for any accomplished warrior. The feathers signified important deeds, so that the bonnet was like the man's résumé. War bonnets were worn only in ceremonies or donned just prior to charging into battle. Other times they were rolled up tightly and stored in a tubular rawhide case that could be slung from one's horse or tipi rafters.

The bonnet was formed around a buckskin skullcap, or later, the crown cut out of a store-bought felt hat. To this base were added the tail feathers of the immature golden eagle, characteristically white with dark brown tips. Such feathers, the most highly regarded of all types, were attached securely in a radiating pattern around the edge of the crown by adding rawhide loops to their quills (or simply looping the quills) and tying them in with sinew and red yarn wrapping, somewhat loosely so that they would rake back and appear in dynamic motion as the wearer strode or rode. A long white plume of eagle down, receptive to the slightest breath of air, was placed amid the other feathers at the crown. For the man of many accomplishments, more feathers were added along one or two trailers of fabric down the neck and back. On some bonnets the trailer runs as far as the wearer's heels. Beadwork or quillwork banding was added around the forehead, and the temples were decorated with beaded medallions or hanging ermine (winter weasel, white with black-tipped tail) skins or ribbons of rawhide or fabric.

Every element of the bonnet held some significance. The main symbolic themes were the sun's rays and the lightness of the breeze, evoking ideas of spiritual strength and inspiration and agility in battle. Also, the feathers were decorated using a kind of code to indicate particular war deeds. The feather tips were decorated with dabs of paint or glued tufts of horsehair or eagle down, or cut with notches in various patterns. A feather with horsehair might count a stolen horse. Another coup indicator was the ermine skin hung from the temples of the hatband in some headdresses; among the Crows an ermine meant a captured enemy gun. Tribal affiliation is sometimes also shown in the bonnet's style. The feathers on Blackfoot bonnets are set more rigidly, forming an erect tube—this apparently the earliest form of the full-feathered headdress; on Crow bonnets, the feathers lay back very flat.

A similar kind of bonnet, though more rare and confined to certain tribes including the Sioux and Cheyennes, was made by attaching animal horns on the skullcap instead of the full complement of feathers. Entire or split buffalo horns were most common, and antelope horns are sometimes seen. On these hats, the trailer feathers are usually the long, uniformly dark wing feathers of the eagle rather than tail feathers. This horned bonnet is distinguished structurally from yet another kind of horned headdress, which was made simply by wearing the whole horned scalp and shoulder fur of a buffalo. Such headdresses were more typical among the Comanches than feather bonnets during pre-reservation times. In fact a range of other animal head and back skins were worn in this manner all around the Plains. Wolf, coyote, and bear were most common, the animal's snout projecting over the wearer's brow, assimilating him to his animal counterpart.

A favorite hat style of the Central and Southern Plains tribes was the open-topped turban made from a band of otter or beaver fur, with a trailer made from the animal's tail or cloth, both sections decorated with beadwork medallions. The Southern Siouans liked to add a large rawhide triangle projecting to one side of the turban. They also made cloth turbans. Through the twentieth century, the turban was considered a dignified look and part of formal dress in the south. Another headpiece of wide adoption in later years was the crest of stiff porcupine or deer tail bristles worn on the middle of the head, called a roach. An elaboration of the lock of hair left when the head was shaved in the style of Woodlands Indians like the Mohawks, the roach was introduced by tribes with eastern affiliations such as the Pawnees, Osages, Omahas, Poncas, and Tetons. The hair of the roach was spread and secured with a bone or metal plate called a roach spreader, tied around the chin with a thong. The spreader also might have a receptacle for the stem of one or two plumes. Roaches were sometimes accompanied by a cloth turban or headband. The stereotypic headband with a single feather standing from the rear was not part of Plains dress, though many people tied one or more loose feathers in their hair in lieu of any hat. Manufactured top hats and cowboy hats became very popular as soon as they were available, as many old pictures show, and Indian people develop their own styles for wearing these, refraining from adding creases and instead attaching feathers and beadwork or metal bands. While all the hat styles described were for men, contemporary Southern Plains women sometimes wear the turban in dances and there are photos from around 1900 showing Sioux women donning war bonnets.

Women's dresses exhibit several basic patterns. The simplest was a one-piece wrap-around skirt of deerskin, seen among the Pawnees, Osages, Caddos, and some other central and southern tribes. Simple open sleeves made from another skin could be worn above the wrap-around in a style called "jumper," of old and wide distribution, known among the Assiniboines, Plains Crees, Ojibwas, Blackfoots, Cheyennes, and Pawnees. Dresses were also made from two skins sewn together horizontally (top and bottom, as among the Cheyennes, Eastern Sioux, and Plains Crees) or, more commonly, vertically (front and back, among the Shoshones, Crows, Blackfoots, and Upper Missouri tribes). In some instances the two vertical pieces were joined at the neck and shoulders by a narrow third section, or yoke, through which a neck hole was cut. This yoke could be formed by folding the top part of the

FIGURE 6.6 This Photo of a Ponca delegation to Washington, DC shows a turban headdress, cloth shirts, pipe tomahawks, and bear claw necklaces typical of the prairie tribes.

back piece forward or sewing in a separate third piece. In parts of the central and southern Plains (among the Tetons, Poncas, Pawnees, Cheyennes, Arapahos, Utes, Kiowas, Comanches), the yoke developed as a large, third component, resembling a poncho or blouse, that was loosely laced to the two skirt pieces, or not joined to the skirt at all. Neck hole and sleeve cuts distinguished one tribal style from another. In sewing hide pieces together for clothing, the maker poked holes through the skins with an awl and then threaded a sinew strand through them, keeping the sinew end moist and pointed with her mouth.

Cloth, cotton thread, and eyed steel needles were used for dressmaking by the mid-1800s. At first stroud cloth, a woolen trade fabric, was the standard. Initially strouding was available only in dark red and dark blue, so these were the common dress colors and are still regarded today as traditional.

Later other colors of strouding were available, along with lighter calico and sateen fabrics. The cut of cloth dresses is somewhat boxier than that of skin dresses and may use separate gussets or side-pieces in addition to front and back sections. When modern dresses are made from buckskin, they often follow these cloth dress patterns rather than earlier skin dress forms.

Three other beautiful traditions of cloth craft emerged as Plains women adopted manufactured fabric, and, later, sewing machines. The first, ribbon appliqué work, is widespread, but most highly developed among the Osages and neighboring peoples along the eastern edge of the Plains area and, like many traditions there, reveals Woodlands influence. In this craft, women's shawls of dark-blue strouding are trimmed with borders composed of multiple overlain bands of colored satin ribbon, trimmed in ways that create diamonds and other shapes. A similar tradition of women's cloth dance shawls developed on the Southern Plains in the twentieth century. In this case large polyester rectangles are ornamented with appliqué geometric and naturalistic designs of felt or other fabric, and commercial chainette fringe. The shawls are required vestment for women as they join in powwow dancing, and the cumulative effect is a riot of color and motion. The corollary for men on the Southern Plains is the "red and blue," a blanket half in each color, worn over the shoulders during the Gourd Dance and peyote ceremony; these were originally stroud cloth but now employ materials and techniques like those used to make women's shawls. A third Plains cloth tradition is the sewing of "star quilts" (*owinja*, "quilt") among the Lakotas. Diamond- shaped patches in many colors of commercial cotton are combined in an eight-pointed starburst pattern, which forms the large central element of the quilt. Polyester batten is used to make the blanket warm but lightweight. Though the basic idea likely came to the Sioux through white missionaries, the Indians associate the quilted star with the Morning Star and cardinal directions of Native cosmology. Shawls and quilts function importantly as gifts at births, naming ceremonies, marriages, funerals, and memorial services as well as clothing.

In the old days men preferred to dress as lightly as circumstances would allow, often with only a breechclout and moccasins. The breechclout was a rectangle of deerskin or trade cloth about 1 foot wide and 6 feet long. The cloth was placed between the legs and drawn up and over a thin leather belt front and back, making two apron-like flaps that covered the man from his waist to about his knees. The length of the flaps overall and relative to each other was influenced by personal preference and tribal style. If more leg protection was desired, the man added leggings, separate tubes of deerskin or dark trade cloth hung with straps from the waist belt and covering thigh to ankle.

Leggings were cut and stitched in different ways according to tribal practice, some having flaps or fringes, and with seams running up the front or side.

Plains men's shirts have gotten much attention in books and museum displays but they were not everyday garb, rather special items worn by leaders in ceremonies only. Deer, antelope, and bighorn sheep were regarded as the only hides comfortable enough for wearing as shirts. From one of these skins, the section from the ribs back, including the hind legs, was cut to form the shirtfront; the two shoulder and foreleg parts of the skin were detached and sewn to either side of the front to make sleeve fronts. An identical fabrication was made as the shirt back and sewn to the front. Then a neck opening was made and on some shirts a decorative tab created below the neck front, both of these elements varying in shape by tribal custom. The erstwhile hind legs and (if left on) the tail of the animal hung below the wearer's waist, but otherwise the shirt stopped around his waist.

Shirts were variously dyed, painting with symbolic pictures, fringed, and decorated with long beadwork or quillwork bands running from the shoulders down the chest and sleeves. Most striking was the addition of ermine skins, plugs of horsehair, or numerous bunches of human hair, representing, respectively, stolen guns, captured horses, and scalps taken in battle. Shirts thus decorated are frequently called "war shirts" or "scalp shirts"; the shirt became another display of the man's war record, akin to the war bonnet.

Whereas earlier skin shirts preserve much of the natural contour of the donor animal and have only semi-closed sleeves, through the 1800s shirts become more tailored, reflecting non-Indian influence. Once calico and flannel, and ready-made shirts of these materials, became available from traders in the mid-1800s, cloth shirts were adopted and mated with other newer and older style items of clothing. Indian photo portraits from the late 1800s typically show a Victorian collarless, pinstripe cotton shirt along with cloth leggings and leather moccasins.

Footwear included moccasins and a type of boot derived from the moccasin. Moccasins occur in two main types: those in which a sheet of soft buckskin wraps the foot entirely, creating a soft sole; and those in which a separate hard rawhide sole is sewn to a soft buckskin upper. The soft-soled moccasin is found in the Woodlands, while the hard-soled form comes from the Southwest; both types occur on the Plains. The Assiniboines, Blackfoots, Crees, Crows, Gros Ventres, Sarsis, and Shoshones made their soft-sole shoes by cutting a single piece of skin according a pattern that would fold around the whole foot and sewing it closed around the toes and along the outside. Groups such as the Arapahos, Cheyennes, Comanches, Kiowas, and Tetons made their hard-soled versions by first tracing the foot on a stiff, flat piece of rawhide. This sole was joined to a soft upper cut on a tribally distinctive pattern. A tongue was made by slicing the upper in one of several ways or added as a separate piece. Slits around the ankle took a thong for lacing. The Comanches added a cuff around the ankle, short fringe in a line on the instep from ankle to toe, and long fringe trailing in a bunch from the heel. Cheyennes sometimes added a bison tail or beard on the heel. There is thus some truth to the notion, inspired by Hollywood westerns, that the footprint left with a moccasin allowed a tracker to guess the wearer's tribe. Sewing was done with the pattern turned inside out and the finished shoe then reversed on itself, to better protect the stitched seam.

In a variation on the soft-soled style, several tribes made moccasins of buffalo skin with the hair turned inward for winter wear. Winter shoes were cut oversized to allow wrapping the feet with cloth or stuffing extra hair or straw insulation, and they were thoroughly greased for waterproofing. Another trick for water repellency was to make the shoes from the top of an old hide tipi cover, which had been exposed to smoke for endless hours. Northward from Montana and North Dakota, women sometimes wore boots. Also, the Comanches are credited with originating a form of women's boot in the south, worn year-round, combining the ankle-height moccasin with leg extensions, an outgrowth of the practice of women sometimes wearing leggings under their dresses. Arapaho, Cheyenne, Kiowa, and Ute women also wore this style.

PERSONAL ADORNMENT

Body decoration supplemented dress in enhancing personal appearance. Much effort was devoted to hair styling, tattooing, painting, piercing, and the wearing of jewelry.

As a part of the body that grew continually, the hair was considered indicative of a person's life force or health of body and spirit. One's hair was ideally black and lustrous. Hair to shoulder length or longer was generally favored, and much attention was paid to grooming and styling it. Husbands and wives aided each other in keeping their hair free of lice and well groomed. Yucca root and other herbs were employed to make sudsy shampoos, some of which were thought to keep the hair black. It was brushed using a dried buffalo tongue, porcupine tail, or bunch of fibers, greased with bear oil, buffalo fat, or beaver oil, and perfumed with herbs. Sometimes artificial extensions were added, made from horsehair or the hair that a woman had cut off in mourning.

Women typically wore the hair parted in the middle and either loosely around the head or in two braids. A red ochre line was often painted down the part. Some tribes had distinctive men's coifs, so recognizable that they are drawn in pictographs to indicate tribal identities. The Blackfoots, Shoshones, and some Siouans wore a patch of bangs trimmed straight across the brow. The Crows similarly cut the hair over their foreheads short but pushed it upright in a "pompadour." Crow men grew their back hair so full and long that it might reach the ground. Or, to achieve the same length, they assembled elaborate falls by gluing strands of horsehair or discarded human hair together with globs of resin. Wichita men are shown in paintings from about 1828 with the front top of the head shaved and a horn-like lock curving back from the top center. This style was also reported for the early Pawnees. More familiar for the Pawnees and the Southern Siouans was a style in which both sides of the skull were shaved to leave a brush of hair in the center from front to back. From this center patch might emanate a long braided lock, as if to challenge enemies seeking scalps. Men of the Cheyenne, Brulé Sioux, and several other groups wore their hair parted either loosely or with two braids, not unlike women, but with a scalp lock also. Kiowa and Comanche men wore their braids wrapped in beaver or otter fur so that they resembled long furry tubes; the Comanche word for otter, *papiwuhtuma*, literally translates as "hair wrapper."

Except among some people in the south, where Mexican admixture was common, facial hair was considered undesirable. Indian men have relatively little facial hair to begin with, however, so shaving was not necessary to prevent beards and mustaches; they removed their scant whiskers by plucking. Both women and men plucked out their eyebrows also. They used pairs of mussel shells as tweezers, or in latter days, metal springs. For someone not used to seeing it, it is memorable to watch a person "shave" by rapidly and deftly running a spring over his face.

Tattoos were created by making numerous punctures in the skin with flint, cactus spines, porcupine quills, or steel needles, and rubbing charcoal into each wound. Healing produced a pattern of bluish-black bumps. Single dots, stripes, circles, triangles of multiple dots, and occasionally solid lines were applied to the forehead, cheeks, chin, chest, back, or arms of both men and women. Also, men with significant battle scars liked to highlight them with a tattooed outline. Tattooing was practiced throughout the Plains—among the Crees, Crows, Hidatsas, Comanches, Kiowas, and others—though the Wichitas and Southern Siouans relied most heavily on this form of expression. Nineteenth-century portraits show Wichita women covered with patterns on the face and around their breasts, and accordingly the Wichitas called themselves "Raccoon Eyes" and were called Panis Piqués ("Pricked Pawnees") by the French, while the Omahas and Osages displayed cosmological star and earth symbols on their foreheads and chests.

Body and face painting, though only temporary, was more prevalent than tattooing. Men's face painting is often referred to as "war paint," but preparation for combat was only one reason for desiring such embellishment. Painting oneself was a way of renewing the person and dedicating to some special situation, be it a battle, religious ceremony, or rite of passage. Red, yellow, blue, black, and green pigments mixed with grease were applied in vibrant patterns, creating pleasing symmetry in some cases, jarring transformations in others. Multiple stripes were applied to the face and body with the fingers, either by adding paint to the bare skin or by covering the whole surface in pigment and then subtracting some of it. Full handprints and spots were additionally common designs, as were the silhouettes of animal spirit patrons. Animal spirits were also brought to mind by painting the entire face in a mask-like pattern. Each color and shape was chosen with care to stand for some element of nature, perhaps revealed in a dream or vision, that inspired and blessed the person.

The wearing of rings in pierced ears was widespread. Multiple rings in holes all around the outside ear are frequently seen in old photos of adults. Ear piercing was done to both sexes in childhood and might be a casual practice or a ceremonial occasion. The Crows pierced babies' ears shortly after birth, the Cheyennes and Arapahos at about age five. Piercing often coincided with the formal bestowal of a personal name and was viewed as an act that conferred true human status on the child. It might be done at the Sun Dance. It was considered propitious for a medicine man or a distinguished warrior (who would recite a valiant deed during the operation) to do the piercing. The fresh holes were plugged with bits of rawhide so they would heal open. The child's family then gave away gifts in reciprocation.

Prior to trade with non-Indians, jewelry in the form of ear pendants and necklaces was fashioned

FIGURE 6.7   The cloth dress of this Arikara girl displays decoration of elk teeth and lazy stitch beadwork. Photo by Edward S. Curtis, 1909.

from bison bone and shells. Men were fond of wearing the claws of the grizzly bear, as a single item in the hair or strung in number on a necklace. Dentalium shells, narrow white tooth-shaped shells from the Pacific, and elk teeth were prized as dress ornaments and were sewn in rows across the front of a dress, increasing the value of the garment significantly. In later times, as elk became scarce, cowry shells gotten through trade were substituted for elk teeth, since they resemble them from a distance. Another decorative element from natural material was the hair pipe, a tubular white bead about 4 inches long and tapered toward both ends. Originally fashioned by the Indians from bone, hair pipes came into wide use when manufactured for trading by a company in New Jersey, which made them from the central columns of Caribbean conch shells that had been used as ships' ballast. Later, cow bone was used, and today they are made from plastic. As the name indicates, hair pipes were tied in the hair for decoration, but they were also strung end to end to make chokers, or in two long dangling rows to form a man's breastplate.

Metalwork

The Plains region is noteworthy for its absence of metals, and true silver, as used in the crafts of the southwestern Navajos and Pueblos, is not mined on the Plains. Silver in raw form and in finished trinkets was common in the trade between whites and eastern Indians during the 1700s and was also prevalent in Mexico, so some of this material made its way to the Plains. Brass kettles, brass and copper wire, and coins also furnished a lot of the raw material for early Plains experiments in metalworking. Simple armbands, bracelets, and rings were easily fashioned from wire. One of the earliest ornaments to become standardized on the Plains was the concha or cupped disk. These are commonly known on the Plains as hair plates

because they were often arrayed in diminishing sizes on the long hair queues that men wore, though they were also worn on belts and sewn to clothing. Another typical early ornament was an exaggerated crescent worn as a chest pendant or earring. This design was derived from horse bridle decorations like those introduced through early French trade. Also derived from bridle parts was the pectoral, a decorative plate in a roughly cloud or bird shape and with pendant crescents, about 6 inches across, worn by men on the upper chest. Large metal crosses worn on the chest were popular as well, inspired no doubt by missionary gifts or raids on Mexican churches.

Out of these earlier efforts, a distinct tradition of jewelry making in German silver emerged on the Southern Plains beginning in the 1860s. German silver, also called nickel silver, is a silvery alloy of nickel, copper, and zinc that became available in sheet form from white traders. Indian artisans found this material tough but malleable, and thin sheets could be pounded, cut, filed, and engraved (they did not melt or mold the metal). Along with the trade metal came hammers, files, and iron nails that could be used to engrave the metal. German silver techniques and designs developed around the same time as the peyote religion (see Chapter 10), and although earlier forms such as conchas and pectorals were continued in the newer material, emblems of the peyote religion became so characteristic that the craft is also known as "peyote jewelry." The shapes and engraving portray crosses, feathers, fans, water birds, tipis, and other things evocative of the peyote ceremony. These shapes give form to brooches, hatpins, earrings, combs, and crowns, which may be worn as badges of affiliation with the Native American Church. During the twentieth century a number of Oklahoma Indian metalsmiths became widely celebrated for their mastery of German silver work, including Julius Caesar, Pawnee (1910–1982), and George Silverhorn, Kiowa (1911–1969).

DECORATIVE AND FINE ARTS

Quillwork and Beadwork

Perhaps the most widespread and typical decorative art of the Plains was the adornment of skin clothing and containers with colored quills and beads. Quillwork was done earlier, though some work in quills continued after beads became commercially available, and is still done by some specialists today.

Prior to white contact, split bird quills were often sewn to clothing for decoration, but this practice faded and little is known about the bird species used. Porcupine quills became more prevalent, maybe because they are larger and easier to harvest in numbers. Bird quills absorbed Native plant and mineral dyes much better than porcupine ones, so richly colored early quillwork was likely done using bird quills. To create dark lines in the days before commercial dyes made it possible to stain porcupine quills darkly, blackish maidenhair fern stems were used as embroidery elements along with the quills. Grass and corn-husk were also substituted for quills, especially by the Cheyennes. Involved quillwork was most characteristic of the Upper Missouri and Central Plains. Although at least today porcupines are found as far south as Texas, they are generally more common in the north, and quillwork did not develop among the Southern Plains tribes.

One porcupine will yield 30,000 quills of different sizes, but a fair amount of work is necessary before quilling can begin. A creature has to be found, treed, and shot; quills are carefully plucked; then the quills are cleaned and sorted by size, the sharp tips are cut off, and the quills are boiled with dyes to color them. Imagine how a plastic drinking straw can be flattened and folded back on itself to create rectangular and triangular sections, and you can envision basic quilling technique. Indian women flatten the quills by drawing them through their teeth, one at a time.

FIGURE 6.8   *Omaha man, circa 1914, wearing eagle feather war bonnet, beaded pipe bag, stroud leggings, beaded moccasins, and holding an eagle feather fan and a pipe decorated with quill work wrapping.*

Then they fold the flattened quills in the desired pattern and stitch them in place on the skin surface to be decorated. Rows of stitched quills can readily cover large surfaces. Quills can also be woven together with only minimal sewing to cover three-dimensional surfaces such as the narrow bands of leather that are created by slitting a piece of hide.

Native bead making would have been similarly laborious. The archeological record shows that

Indian people did make and trade their own beads. But the time, effort, and precision needed to shape and drill small pieces of natural glass (sand fused by volcanic heat or lightning), wood, bone, shell, or stone made beads very precious. It is easy then to understand the appeal of manufactured glass beads to Indian people. White traders found a huge demand for glass beads imported from Italy or Bohemia and distributed through New York City, and rapidly factory beads replaced quills and native beads in much of the decorative work on the Plains.

The earliest trade beads were relatively large—more that $1/4$ inch in diameter—and were most suitable for stringing on necklaces. There are several kinds of early beads, such as the single-colored "Crow bead" and two-colored cornaline d'Aleppo. Large brass beads were also traded early on. During the early 1800s "pony beads" appeared, so-called because of the way they were transported by traders. These still relatively large beads were the first employed to cover skin surfaces en masse and are usually found in combinations of blue or black and white, though sometimes other colors appear. (Black, blue, and white have always been the cheapest colors for glassmakers to produce, so traders kept a higher profit margin by stocking these colors.) Pony beads lent themselves to bold contrasting patterns. Around 1830–1850 smaller beads became increasingly common. They may be tubular ("bugles"), donut-shaped ("seed beads"), or faceted ("cut beads") and come in over 80 colors and many sizes. Work in the tiny sizes like 16/0 ("sixteen ought") is especially prized.

The techniques used in beading, aside from simply stringing one or more beads in a necklace or pendant, have been termed sewing, netting, and weaving. The sewing techniques include overlay and lazy stitch. The former involves tacking or spot-stitching long strings of beads onto the surface to be decorated, and is especially useful in making curvilinear designs like floral decorations with stems and leaves. In the lazy stitch pattern,

short strings of perhaps seven beads are tacked continually alongside each other on a flat surface, producing bands that may stand alone or lie adjacent to other bands in a larger design. The lazy stitch lends itself to geometric patterns and allows large surfaces to be covered with relatively less labor than the other methods. The netting technique is commonly known as the gourd stitch, in which an initial row of beads is sewn to the leather or cloth foundation, but the succeeding rows are sewn to each other, one bead at a time, forming a network of interlocking beads. If sewn in with the proper tightness, the beads lie flat against the decorated material and cover it in mesh. The final row of beads is again sewn to the foundation to secure the mesh at both ends of the covered surface. This method is useful for covering curved surfaces such as the handles of rattles and fans, and is known as the gourd stitch because it is seen on gourd rattles. Weaving involved the square weave method on a simple loom. The loom could be a curved piece of springy horn or metal with several warp (standing) threads spread and tensioned from one of its ends to another. Weft (filler) threads containing beads are then interwoven at right angles using a needle. A band of beadwork several inches long can be created this way. The band is then stitched to a strip of cloth backing for stability, which in turn can be sewn on a belt or shirt for decoration. Weaving also lends itself to geometric patterning.

Watching skilled bead workers is a marvelous experience because they show great dexterity, but more so because often they achieve very complex color and shape patterns not by planning them in advance, but by making a continuous series of tiny decisions—bead by bead—so that the patterns unfold in unpredicted yet perfectly beautiful and symmetrical ways. It is customary for bead workers to include one tiny mistake in their work, an act of humility that reflects the idea that nothing made by humans is really perfect.

Over time, tribally distinctive styles of beadwork evolved. Sioux beadwork is characterized by large expanses of covered surface with a white background and patterns of small triangles and lines made with darker colors; only four or five different colors are usually employed together. Cheyenne beadwork is generally similar to that of the Sioux. These patterns are best executed in lazy stitch and show a clear derivation from quill-work. The Crows like to combine lots of different colors in pleasing matches to make large triangles and rectangles reminiscent of the designs painted on parfleches. Often the Crows enclose these designs in white borders in which the beads run in a different direction. For such patterns they prefer the overlay technique, and their method of over-lay is referred to as "Crow stitch." The Blackfeet and their neighbors in the northwest practiced another distinct style, also in overlay, but with a lot of stripes formed from rectangles, and marked color contrasts evoking the look of early pony beads, even when seed beads are used.

Abstract floral patterns of vines, leaves, and tulip-like blossoms betray a Woodlands influence and can be found in a number of tribes from north to south. The Plains Crees and Plains Ojibwas, with their obvious Woodlands heritage, prefer floral designs and have sometimes influenced their northern neighbors to the west across the Northern Plains. In the Central Plains, the Omahas, Osages, and Poncas adopted floral patterns under the early influence of the Otoes, Missourias, and Iowas, and that of more recently displaced east-erners like the Delawares and Sauk and Fox.

Under the influence of these same tribes in Oklahoma, the Kiowas too adopted a liking for floral designs, though theirs have a somewhat different look in the coloration and shape of the elements. More typical of the Kiowas and their Southern Plains neighbors the Comanches, how-ever, is a spare, elegant style in which narrow lanes of lazy stitch create borders of decoration. If the large surfaces of buckskin in between the bor-ders are decorated at all, they are pigmented with bright yellow or pale verdigris green rather than beaded. The exceptions to these practices are

Kiowa and Comanche moccasins and cradles, which are sometimes fully beaded with lazy stitch.

A look at the products from any tribe shows that each group has a finite vocabulary of accept-able beadwork design elements. There is a limited (though sometimes large) number of line and shape combinations which may be characterized by their makers as feathers, trees, dragonflies, arrows, mountains, crosses, whirlwinds, buffalo paths, tipis, and so on. Tribal color preferences are also obvious. Yet there was no total agreement about the pattern names and no common sym-bolic code of shapes and colors. The inspiration of the individual artisan was most important, and usually that remained private. Thus, in an exhaus-tive study of Arapaho beadwork patterns, anthro-pologist Alfred Kroeber was sometimes able to elicit explanations like the following about a pair of fully beaded moccasins:

> The white represents snow. The green . . . grass-covered earth. The blue and yellow figures consisting of three triangles represent the heart and lungs. The white stripe . . . is a dragon-fly. Groups of three light-blue squares near the instep were described as halves of stars . . . small green rectangles . . . represent caterpillars. The design on this moccasin was embroidered as it was previously seen in a dream.
>
> (Kroeber 1983:46)

Yet despite this kind of exactness about particular beaded and painted items, Kroeber concluded that overall " . . . there is no fixed system of symbolism in Arapaho decorative art. Any interpretation of a figure is personal. Often the interpretation is arbitrary" (Ibid.:144).

In addition to abstract linear and geometric designs, figurative representations are sometimes found in Plains beading beginning around the reser-vation period of the 1880s. Warriors on horseback, for example, are shown in pictures similar to those drawn in ledger book art. American flags are another common motif in late-nineteenth-century pictorial beadwork. The meanings of this American flag imagery are complex, reflecting contradictory feelings about allegiance to the tribe and the nation state as well as efforts, in some cases, to relate to non-Indian buyers of craftwork.

During the twentieth century a number of trends conspired to ensure that Plains Indian beadwork traditions would continue to flourish. Indian fairs, Wild West shows, and tourism at reservations and national parks all brought Indian craftsmanship to the eye of the general public. Non-Indian hobbyists and collectors provided a ready market and many bead workers even began filling orders by mail. The single biggest stimulus has been the intertribal powwow (see Chapter 7). The bulk of beadwork done today—and there is much of it—goes to decorating men's and women's dance outfits. But this most Indian of decorative forms is now also applied playfully, though with a serious message about the permanence of Native ways, to baseball caps and tennis shoes.

Carving in Wood and Stone

Three-dimensional carving in wood and stone was part of the Plains repertoire, though a minor art compared to what was done in the eastern forests. One of the more common items was a form of dance stick with one end curving and carved as a horse's head. Men carried these sticks, usually augmented with little horsehair manes and leather bridles, to honor the animals they lost in battle. Men also carried quirts or "war whips" with handles shaped like gunstocks, notched to tally battle deeds, while dancing, and mirrors set in carved wooden frames. The gunstock shape was used as well for a kind of hickory war club $2^1/_2$ feet long and about an inch thick. Ball-headed war clubs were made in the eastern Plains areas adjacent to the woodlands; the Otoes were known for a type carved in the shape of an otter. Humanlike figures carved from wood and representing spirits, often called "dolls," were wrapped in medicine bundles and treated by some tribes as fetishes at the Sun Dance. Miscellaneous decoratively carved wood items included bowls, drum stands, awl handles, and hair roach spreaders. Antler and bone were sometimes carved too to make handles and spreaders.

Wood and stone carving came together in the making of tobacco pipes known as calumets or peace pipes, which whether owned by individual men or venerated by an entire society, were considered among the most important of possessions. Their value was as instruments for establishing relations between people and between humans and the spirits. The ceremonial smoking of tobacco in calumets was part of every formal greeting and deliberation and a precursor to many rituals; and, pipes were solemn gifts bestowed on visiting strangers as a token of goodwill. The attention given to pipe making underscores their worth.

Pipes were formed from a wooden stem some 2 feet long and stone bowl segment of about 4 or 6 inches. The pipe owner carried these parts uncoupled in a special skin bag, and by joining them he consecrated the pipe, making it come alive spiritually. Stems were fashioned from a piece of green ash, sometimes round but more often flattish, carved in a spiral or with shallow-relief animal forms, or decorated with feathers or quillwork. The narrow stem had to be bored carefully with a red-hot poker. The bowl needed to be made from a stone that would not crack from the heat of the burning tobacco but which was soft and consistent enough to be shaped and drilled using hand tools. Calcite, limestone, and black steatite or soapstone fit this need, but the most widely favored material was the pink to brick-red soapstone called catlinite.

Catlinite, named for the frontier artist and explorer George Catlin, who described its use in 1836, was found in only certain locations in Minnesota and Wisconsin. Today the major source is protected at Pipestone National Monument in southwestern Minnesota. Here the red stone runs in narrow sheets under layers of earth and hard quartzite several feet below the surface, partly exposed through four centuries of quarrying. Although Dakotas controlled this area during the early Historic Period, access to the quarry was generally open to many tribes, members of which made trips there akin to pilgrimages. By tradition miners were only supposed to take what they could use for themselves, so although catlinite products were coveted trade commodities through much of the Plains and into the northeast, a big market in raw stone never developed. Even so, the seams have been depleted and today only Indians are permitted to dig or sell catlinite. Tribes living away from the catlinite sources came to depend on other stones. According to the Northern Arapaho elder Sage (circa 1843–1944), his people never used catlinite but liked black stone instead.

The pipe bowl segment was T- or L-shaped, with a horizontal section that mated to the stem and a vertical bowl like a smokestack. This piece was carved in the shape of a large animal, or a human face or figure in repose looking back at the smoker, accompanied by small animals such as birds, turtles, or otters. Occasionally the bowl stone was inlaid in a geometric pattern with other stone of differing color or lead. Regardless of these common elements, distinctive local and individual traditions of pipe making developed, for while Indian artisans were inspired by outside examples and borrowed materials and tools, they did not slavishly copy the work of others, nor did they think it polite to teach each other the "correct" way of making things. Thus, there are definable styles and sometimes pipes in different museums can be compared and confidently attributed to the same maker even when his identity has not been recorded.

Like many other traditional Indian arts, pipe making lives on in the work of some modern masters. One premier pipe carver and pipestone sculptor is Robert Rose-Bear, who is of Chippewa descent but conversant in Plains techniques and motifs. Rose-Bear digs catlinite himself from the famous quarry and shapes it with hand tools as well as power tools like the Dremel Moto-tool. Well versed in time-honored icons and the creation of miniature animal scenes, Rose-Bear also adds amusing innovations of technique, symbol, and theme. His works are thus identifiably his, in the manner of fine older pipes, and conventional yet contemporary, delighting traditionalists and art collectors alike.

Painting and Drawing

The oldest pictorial art on the Plains is found painted or scratched on rock. The terms used in dealing with such pictorial images have varied. *Pictograph* has been used to mean any pictorial expression of an idea, though in the context of rock art it has come to refer specifically to a painted image. *Petroglyph* has been used for any rock art image, but now normally means an image that is engraved (pecked or scratched) rather than painted. Regardless, Indians used a variety of natural mineral and plant pigments and stone gravers and chisels to leave their thoughts for others.

Some rock pictures were no doubt temporary messages for fellow travelers—images of game or foes, sometimes along with tally marks that might indicate number of enemies or days of travel. Hunting scenes are prevalent. Other pictures commemorate important events such as battles and were probably intended as permanent historical or biographical records. Still other pictograph panels portray abstract linear or geometric designs along with spiritual beings, relating mythic episodes or prescribing ritual. Such images were sometimes left in difficult to find places. In these cases the very act of painting could have been a ritual reenactment or a consecration of the locale.

Rock art is found widely across the region, sometimes as a single image on an isolated stone, more frequently in continuous arrays along cliff faces. Plains sites of notable size are most prevalent in the northwest, from Alberta to

Wyoming and South Dakota (around the Rocky Mountains and Black Hills), and in Texas. Since much of the rock art on the Plains dates to prehistoric times, art of the historic era is sometimes not discussed in connection with it, but the historic tribes did create pictographs, often next to or directly over more ancient pictures. The Historic Period in general is indicated by the inclusion of horses, guns, mission churches, and white men (recognizable by their brimmed hats).

Along the Milk River in southern Alberta is the site known as Writing-on-Stone, the densest concentration of rock art on the northwestern Plains. The site is preserved as a provincial park and visitor access to select pictures is allowed. Present here are 93 separate image clusters, including many prehistoric works and a huge, complex war scene, composed of roughly 350 distinct figures and thought to commemorate an 1866 battle near the river. There is a mystical character to the landscape at Writing-on-Stone, suggested by its caves, secretive alcoves, and fantastically shaped eroded sandstone formations called hoodoos. The prevalence of artwork at the site can be tied to the spiritual atmosphere that is created by its unusual geography. Even today, members of the Blackfoot tribe go to this place to seek visions.

A similarly remarkable concentration of rock pictures on the Southern Plains is found at the dramatic syenite outcroppings known as Hueco Tanks, 22 miles east of El Paso, Texas. Though strictly speaking in the desert southwest, Hueco Tanks was often visited by Kiowas, Comanches, and Plains Apaches, and these people left images amid pictures painted by earlier Puebloan and Mescalero Apache occupants. The Plains images are often clearly historic and include guns and horses, in contrast to the kachina spirit masks of the earlier Puebloans. For all the tribes, Hueco Tanks was undoubtedly an important refuge and a sacred landscape. Precious rainwater was stored naturally in hollows in the stone (hence the name), making the place a curious oasis, and the towering boulders offered both hidden passageways and inspiring views of the surrounding country. Like Writing-on-Stone, Hueco Tanks illustrates how rock art activity was often tied to spiritually significant places and notions of medicine power. Hueco Tanks is now a state park and it is possible to view some of the pictographs there.

In recent times anthropologists studying Plains rock art have proposed classifications similar to those used for artifact assemblages in archaeology, groupings that recognize stylistic conventions and imply a common time period and ethnic origin. The classification process also involves making sense of the meanings of recurring drawing elements. At present there is much controversy about the validity of rock art classifications and the reliability of modern explanations about rock art purpose and meaning. Experts argue whether the symbolic meanings of images were standardized and whether they can even be known today. Sometimes contemporary Indian people are enlisted to interpret prehistoric pictographs. Their input is not always conclusive, however, since it may be difficult to be sure that the meanings they report are really a continuation of ancient knowledge. When historic rock art is analyzed, judgments of meaning can sometimes be made more confidently, since there may be independent historical records that seem to match the events portrayed, or recorded Indian explanations of the pictographs or similar designs done in other media. Yet, even in the Historic Period, as we have seen in the case of beadwork designs, artistic meaning was variable and individualistic.

Despite these interpretive limitations, some recent rock art studies are not only convincing but also helpful in understanding Plains art more generally. One system, constructed by archaeologist James Keyser and Michael Klassen, has been developed for the northwestern Plains, though their classifications often account for art found over wider areas. Keyser and Klassen's categories, which they call "traditions," are summarized in Table 6.1. Note that these groupings can be

TABLE 6.1   Rock Art Traditions of the Northwest Plains

TRADITION	ESTIMATED DATES ON PLAINS	FEATURES	EXAMPLE SITE OR AREA	ETHNIC ASSOCIATION	REMARKS
Early Hunting Tradition	5800–500 B.C. or earlier	Mostly groupings of elk, mountain sheep, and other animals, portrayed in rounded shapes	Whoopup Canyon, east-central Wyoming	Archaic hunter-gatherers	Pecked pictographs only; intention seems to be sympathetic hunting magic
Columbia Plateau Tradition	1000 B.C.–A.D. 1850	Simple humans and animal figures in composition, and tally marks	Painted Rocks, western Montana	Flathead, Kutenai, Pend d'Oreille	Mostly red ochre finger paintings; associated with the vision quest or hunting
Dinwoody Tradition	1000 B.C.–A.D. 1775	Fantastic anthropomorphic spirit figures	Dinwoody Lake, west-central Wyoming	Shoshonean	Connected with shamanic visions and curing
En Toto Pecked Tradition	750 B.C.–A.D. 1000	Humans with exaggerated sex characteristics	Bighorn Basin, northwest Wyoming	Undetermined	Pecked sandstone exclusively
Pecked Abstract Tradition	500 B.C.–1000 A.D.	Complex, maze-like abstract designs	Black Hills, South Dakota	Undetermined	May depict the visual phenomena of shamanic trances
Foothills Abstract Tradition	1000 B.C.–A.D. 1000	Handprints plus outline figures of humans, animals, and zoomorphs	Rocky Mountain foothills, Montana and Alberta	Undetermined	Red finger-painting; bear symbolism; many private ritual sites in small caves
Hoofprint Tradition	A.D. 500–1800	Clusters of hoof-prints, animal and human heads	Roche Perée, southern Saskatchewan	Siouan	Pecked images
Ceremonial Tradition	A.D. 250–1850 or earlier	Shield-bearing warriors, human line figures with V-shaped neck-shoulder joints, boat-shaped animals	Writing-on-Stone, southern Alberta	Shoshone and others	Both pecked and painted images; widespread style, consistent over long period
Biographic Tradition	A.D. 1650–1900	Human, horse, and tipi line drawings arranged in narrative panels; also tallies of weapons	Writing-on-Stone, southern Alberta	Numerous Historic Period tribes	Usually incised, some painting; widespread from Canada to Mexico

(continued)

TABLE 6.1   Continued

TRADITION	ESTIMATED DATES ON PLAINS	FEATURES	EXAMPLE SITE OR AREA	ETHNIC ASSOCIATION	REMARKS
Robe and Ledger Art Tradition	As above	As above, but drawings done on hide or paper	Portable	As above	Included with rock art classifications to emphasize similarities across media
Vertical Series Tradition	undetermined, presumed from Historic Period	Multiple vertical columns of repeated non-representational symbols (e.g., crosses, crescents)	Pictograph Cave, south-central Montana	Sioux, perhaps others	Poorly known; widespread and discontinuous; usually painted, some incised; possibly a code for messaging or record-keeping

Source: Keyser and Klassen (2001).

defined according to distinctive features of the art, as well as dates, distribution, and in some cases the ancestral or historic tribes associated with exemplary sites. As such rock art classifications continue to be refined, they spur discussion that illuminates wider symbolic conventions. For instance, horseshoe shapes in historic rock art that are interpreted as signifying horses can be corresponded to similar signs used in the painting of war messages, tipis, and horses themselves (as when a warrior decorated his mount to proclaim how many horses he had captured).

While rock art is foundational to an understanding of Plains painting, graphic art of the Historic Period made on bone and hide is in a sense more typical of Plains culture, if only because it was portable. Portable paintings and drawings have much in common with rock art. For instance, the Comanches scratched picture messages on buffalo shoulder blade bones, which they left behind at their campsites to communicate with the next occupants. These scapula drawings might indicate the presence of game or the size of enemy parties in the area and action taken against them. One such drawing contained war-riors with shields and other devices that closely resemble the designs used in northwestern Plains rock art associated with the Comanches' Shoshonean ancestors. Similar pictorial communications were also incised into the bark of living trees. Thus, when comparing pictures across various media, it becomes apparent that there was some standardization of a graphic language.

Painting done on bison, elk, and deer hides was even more widespread. This work included both geometric designs and representational pictures of individual men's exploits and tribal history.

The tipi, whether made of hide or later cloth materials, presented an irresistibly large, portable "canvas" for proclaiming the head male occupant's personal record in vision questing or war. Tipis destined for special ceremonial use were also likely to be painted. Subjects were thus analogous to those expressed in biographical rock art. While tipi painting was practiced at least occasionally in most tribes, the Blackfoots and Kiowas were especially known for elaborating the tradition. The lodge cover was painted by spreading it flat on the ground. Large eagles, thunderbirds, water monsters, buffalos, and bears emblazoned around the lodge cover announced the occupant's guardian spirit or some mystical encounter he had with powerful beings. Animals with distinctive body parts like the bear were liable to alternate representation simply with pictures of claws or footprints. Such images were supplemented with colored stripes and shapes, symmetrically applied and representing elements of nature—earth, sky, rainbows, stars, vegetation, lightening, game trails—situating the occupant and his guardian alike in a balanced cosmos. Among the Blackfoots a large design called a "sun door" said that the occupant welcomed a visit from Sun during his daily travels. Every shape and color choice meant something. If the painter chose instead to show his war record, realistic images of himself, his foes, and horses unfolded across the cover to tell multiple episodes; feathers made up of black and white end-on-end isosceles triangles stood for coups. Tipi painting is one of the traditions from the horse era that was revived in the late twentieth century. Modern artists work on canvas covers in latex house paint.

Geometric painting reached its apex in the colorful ornamentation applied to parfleches. Women did most of this work. Their designs were not sketched out beforehand, but visualized or "dreamed." They prepared earth and vegetable pigments using involved processes of collecting, heating, and mixing, stored them in turtle shell containers, established strait lines using willow stick rulers, and applied the colors using bone "brushes" or disk-shaped crayons of solidified pigment. As in beadwork, the symbolic meanings were highly personal, though some designs had conventional interpretations. Groupings of small black triangles on Arapaho parfleches were called "bear hands"; the Crows associated the diamond shape with the sand lizard, a good luck omen. The Sioux had patterns called the "bravery design," with a red triangle standing for a turtle, a symbol of steadfastness, and another called the "distant view," with blue triangles representing the sacred Black Hills on the horizon. Also, tribes maintained preferences of style governing color choices, the kinds of shapes employed, and how they subdivided the decorated space. Beyond any of these emblematic meanings was the pure aesthetic effect produced by colors and shapes in wondrous combinations.

Apart from parfleches, the most common decorated hide objects were large complete bison skins worn like overcoats and called "robes." Paintings were therefore displayed across the wearer's back. The three prominent robe patterns were: a large circle composed of many radiating small feather shapes made from paired end-on-end isosceles triangles, called "feathered circle" by art historians; a design made up of a heavy border around the edge of the hide, enclosing a central rectangle; and a similar bordered design with an hourglass shape in the middle. The feathered circle was exclusive to the Sioux and their neighbors, while the bordered rectangle was typical for the Central Plains tribes, and the rectangle for the south. Striped patterns are also found. There are many nineteenth-century examples of these designs in museum collections throughout the world.

Although, as we have seen, realistic paintings of individuals' experiences similar to biographical rock art were sometimes rendered on tipi covers, they were also commonly done on robes, and such Native records painted on hide are referred to generally as "robe art." Occasionally realistic drawings are found together with geometric designs on one skin, but more usually one or the other appears alone. Geometric decorative painting was normally the work of women; men were the painters of realistic scenes. Robe art examples feature one of three kinds of information, conveyed by showing human and animal figures along with such objects as tipis and wagons: biographies, essentially the personal war records of individual men; "calendars," chronological histories of an entire tribe, found only among the Sioux and Kiowas; or portrayals of mystic visions.

After the mid-1800s, the same kinds of drawings were done on muslin, canvas, or paper rather than hide, often using pens, colored pencils, or crayons instead of paint. The cloth, paper, and pencils were obtained from traders, soldiers, and missionaries. Since much of the paper was lined paper from ledger books like those used by banks and stores, the style has become known as "ledger art." "Ledger art" is akin to "robe art" and thus also to late forms of rock art in its basic style and intent. (To emphasize this point, Keyser and Klassen include a "Robe and Ledger Art" tradition among their rock art classifications—see Table 6.1).

The "Exploits of Sun Boy" is a pictographic biography in paint, ink, and pencil on muslin (size 86 × 75 inches) by the Kiowa artist Silverhorn, circa 1880. The work shows 12 war adventure scenes of Sun Boy, a Kiowa chief in the 1800s. He is pictured on the right (indicating that he was the victor in the fight shown) in all but one of the scenes. Each picture reminded the muslin owners of a detailed story that would be told orally. Following are examples of the images and their meanings as far as they are known (Young 1986):

Sun Boy killing an Osage warrior. The Osage is identified by his roach headdress and black moccasins. This scene may place Sun Boy at the 1833 Cutthroat Gap massacre, though more likely it depicts some other fight, perhaps an act of revenge for that attack. In 1833 a large party of Kiowas was camped in a notch in the Wichita Mountains in southwestern Oklahoma when they were surprised at dawn and massacred by Osages. The victims were decapitated, their heads left in camp buckets. The Osages captured one of the Kiowa's sacred idols, a grave humiliation. This event and related ones drew the U.S. military into the southern plains for the first time.

Sun Boy fighting the Pawnees. The Pawnees were traditional enemies of the Kiowas. They

FIGURE 6.9A   Sun Boy Killing and Osage Warrior.

FIGURE 6.9B   *Sun Boy Fighting the Pawnees.*

are indicated with various colored shirts. Sun Boy is shown wearing a black (indicating dark blue) surplus military coat and brimmed felt hat like the ones he wears in a historic photo portrait. He carries a lance with a flag attached. This scene may refer to a fight in 1851, when the Kiowas defeated some Pawnees who had stolen a flag from the Kiowa sun dance lodge.

Sun Boy encounters General Sherman. This scene refers to the Warren wagon train attack in Young County, Texas, in May of 1871 (see Chapter 12). It shows Sun Boy counting coup (touching, but not killing) a coach with an army officer inside. It represents Sun Boy's presence when Kiowa warriors, led by Satanta and Dohate, lie in ambush on a hill over the Butterfield Trail. They let General William T. Sherman's frontier inspection party pass unaware and unmolested. A few hours later the raiders swooped down on

a wagon train, killing 7 of the drivers and capturing 41 mules.

The calendars of the Sioux and Kiowas are among the most sophisticated of all Plains pictorial works. They contain icons in a sequence, each standing for an important event of a year. Calendars are therefore also known as "winter counts," though the Kiowa versions have icons for both winter and summer of each year. Each icon prompted the calendar maker or his heirs to recall the key event as well as many occurrences surrounding it, so that the calendar functioned in the same way as the pictorial biography—as a mnemonic device to help perpetuate oral history.

The Sett'an Calendar is a pencil drawing on Manila paper by Sett'an ("Little Bear"), a Kiowa

FIGURE 6.9C   Sun Boy encounters General Sherman.

artist, circa 1892. This work records 60 years of Kiowa tribal history. Individual pictographs representing each winter and summer of the years 1833–1892, arranged chronologically in a spiral from the lower right corner to the center. Winters are indicated with a black bar, representing dead vegetation, and summers are usually indicated with a figure of the Sun Dance lodge. Icons are added to each of these marks representing the key event of that season. Following are some of the key events from Little Bear's viewpoint (Mooney 1979). Notice how some of these episodes correspond to Sun Boy's adventures.

Summer 1833. A Pictograph: Head with knife to neck, and blood. "They cut off their heads." This image refers to the Cutthroat Gap massacre described above for the Sun Boy muslin.

Winter 1833–34. B Pictograph: Stars and child above winter mark. "Winter that the Stars Fell." A spectacular meteorite shower before dawn on November 13, 1833, was witnessed across North America. The Kiowas, asleep in

camp north of Red River, were awakened and frightened by the eerie brightness. Indians across the Plains liked to use this event as a starting point when counting time. Sett'an was born the preceding summer, and shows himself in the pictograph as a baby beneath the stars.

Summer 1849. C Pictograph: Man with limbs drawn up in pain by the sun dance lodge. "Cramp sun dance." Kiowas called cholera "the cramp." It appeared just after their June Sun Dance, brought by the forty-niners crossing the plains for the California gold rush. People died within hours of showing symptoms, and perhaps half the tribe perished. The great cholera epidemic ravaged all the Texas tribes, and the Kiowas considered it the worst experience in their entire history.

Winter 1866–67. D Pictograph: Man with head against tree, bleeding from mouth, above winter mark. "Winter that Apamadalte was killed." Apamadalte was a Mexican captive among the Kiowas, whose Indian name means "Struck his head against a tree." He was riding with a raiding party under chief Big Bow when they encountered troops or militia near the Butterfield

FIGURE 6.10C

FIGURE 6.10D

FIGURE 6.10A   FIGURE 6.10B

FIGURE 6.10E   FIGURE 6.10F

stagecoach route in Texas. He was killed while trying to stampede the Texans' horses.

Summer 1871. E Pictograph: Indian man with war paint and soldier with rifle. "Summer that Satanta was arrested." The bold warrior Satanta (White Bear) helped lead the May 1871 Warren wagon train attack. He was soon arrested back on the Oklahoma reservation and stood trial in Jacksboro, Texas. Convicted of murder, he began serving a life sentence until paroled in 1873. After further raiding he was jailed again and committed suicide in the Huntsville, Texas prison in 1878.

Summer 1879. F Pictograph: Horse's head over the sun dance lodge. "Horse-eating sun dance." The Kiowas were permitted to go west from their reservation to hunt buffalo in Texas in the winter beginning 1879, but they found almost none. By summer they had to kill and eat their ponies to keep from starving. Here Sett'an records the date of the disappearance of the buffalo from the Southern Plains, signaling the end of the free-ranging Plains Indian cultures in that region.

In these samples of ledger art one can see many of the conventions of traditional Plains Indian painting. As the eminent historian of Indian art John Ewers pointed out, Plains realistic painting usually portrayed profile views of human and animal figures in flat colors, without backgrounds. The figures are done in outline and sometimes then filled in with a variety of colors, with a preference for primary colors. They are two-dimensional, having height and width but no depth or perspective. Colors are flat, without shading that would create a sense of roundness. When it is important to suggest perspective, it is shown in a shorthand way by placing the more distant element of a pair above the nearer one, but each the same size, rather than showing elements in different sizes to indicate foreshortening. Details of human and animal bodies like the shaping of the legs, use of dots for eyes, presence of horse's tails, and lack of manes have some variation but also much uniformity within and across examples. Actions are clearly indicated, though again by convention: running horses have stiff outstretched legs rather than accurately bent limbs.

It is important to note that all of these features are artistic choices and habits, not evidence of Indian artists' innate inability to deal with the devices of realistic coloring and perspective. These choices demonstrate that, even in representative painting, the overriding intent was to devote artistic energy to creating a narrative instead of replicating exactly what the eye sees. In fact, as Indian artists began drawing pictures that were intended for viewing by non-Indians as well as Indians, they readily employed more realistic figuration. This trend can be seen especially in Sioux, Cheyenne, and Kiowa ledger art created after reservations were established. Well-known examples come from the work of the Cheyenne and Kiowa artists who were among the 74 warriors and women rounded up by the U.S. Army in 1875 and imprisoned for three years at Fort Marion in St. Augustine, Florida. They made ledger drawings for sale to visitors, some of which use perspective to create panoramas almost like photographic souvenir postcards. The Fort Marion pictures also depart from the tradition of proclaiming war exploits, which is understandable given the prisoners' circumstances, and instead document the journey to prison and sometimes even express feelings of being torn between two worlds, as in the Kiowa Wohaw's drawing of himself standing between a buffalo and domestic cow, offering peace pipes to both.

Much more could be said of the painting styles that Plains artists executed after the reservation period. Increasingly artists from the region participated in the development of styles incorporating ideas from other Native American areas, notably the Pueblo southwest, as well as modern and postmodern trends of the non-Indian art world. The engagement of Plains tradition with southwestern and non-Indian fine art was pioneered by the famous group of painters called the Kiowa Five: James Auchiah (1906–1974), Spencer Asah (1906–1954), Jack Hokeah (1900–1969), Stephen Mopope (1898–1974), and Monroe Tsatoke (1904–1937). A sixth, female, painter, Lois Smoky (1907–1981), was also part of the group during its early days. As young people between 1914 and 1928, the Five studied easel painting with tutors in Anadarko, Oklahoma, and then at the University of Oklahoma. Steeped in tribal ways (Mopope was a nephew of Silverhorn and Ohettoint, a Fort Marion prisoner, and all the males were powwow contest dancers), the Five created sentimental watercolors of Indian camping, hunting, and dancing, taking care to preserve details of regalia and procedure in their pictures. Their human figures and animals, rendered in bold flat hues on a blank background, owe much to ledger art, but were modernistic at the same time.

The Kiowa Five earned international acclaim in the late 1920s and paved the way for subsequent artists of Plains cultural background, such as Acee Blue Eagle (Creek/Pawnee, 1907–1959), Dick West (Cheyenne, 1912–1996), Oscar Howe (Yanktonai, 1915–1983), and T. C. Cannon

(Caddo/Kiowa, 1946–1978). Some of the later twentieth-century artists continued the style developed by the Kiowa Five and their contemporaries, which became known as "Traditional," while others sought progressive, complicated integrations of their personal and cultural ideals with abstractionism and pop art. Thematically, later works often played with the acceptance, rejection, and even satirizing of established notions of what Indian art, and life, ought to be. Throughout the 1900s Indian painting gained widespread legitimacy beyond Native communities via promoting agencies like the U.S. Bureau of Indian Affairs Indian Arts and Crafts Board and institutions such as the Philbrook Museum in Tulsa, Oklahoma.

Paintings deliberately testing the definition of "Indian art" have not always found ready acceptance in museums and shows, including those having an express mission of exhibiting Indian art. When Oscar Howe wrote to protest the rejection of one of his abstract paintings from the 1958 Philbrook annual show, curators were moved to rethink the criteria and allow a greater variety of styles. Such conversations about inclusiveness, boundaries, and definitions continue. Photography, photomontage, and installation art now join easel painting as media for the exploration of Indian identity. At the start of the twenty-first century, pictorial art by Plains Indians runs the gamut from the perpetuation of centuries-old techniques of hide decoration to works that are deemed cutting-edge in the fine art world while nonetheless nativist in viewpoint, subject, and technique.

Sources: Adney and Chapelle (1983); Anderson (2003); Barker (1924); Berlandier (1969); Berlo and Phillips (1998); Boorman (2002); Dodge (1882, 1959); Dyke (1971); Ewers (1939); Feder (1962, 1964a, 1982); Finerty (1890); García Rejón and Gelo (1995); Gelo and Zesch (2003); Hill (1995); Keyser and Klassen (2001); Kirkland and Newcomb (1996); Koch (1977); Kroeber (1983); Laubin and Laubin (1957); Lowie (1982, 1983); Mooney (1979); Morrow (1975); Nabokov and Easton (1989); Nye (1969); Oklahoma Indian Arts and Crafts Cooperative (1973, 1976); Orchard (1975); Penney (2004); Sutherland (1995); Wallace and Hoebel (1952); Wedel (1986); and Young (1986).

CHAPTER SUMMARY

The material objects and art made by Plains Indians are appealing to the senses and reveal their world view. Dwellings, including the tipi, earth lodge, grass lodge, and other structures, were ingenious adaptations to the environment. Other characteristic objects include cradles and weapons. Plains Indians developed distinctive forms of clothing and adornment, such as particular styles of dresses, moccasins, hairstyles, and metal jewelry; and the war bonnet has become emblematic of Indian identity. Skilled decorative arts included quill embroidery, beadwork, and the carving of stone pipes. Painting and drawing took several forms, including rock art, paintings on hide, geometric decoration of rawhide containers, and annual histories called "calendars." Traditional pictorial art was meant to tell a story. Since the reservation era, Plains artists have explored new styles and media to contrast or reconcile Indian traditions with the standards of non-Indian art.

QUESTIONS FOR REVIEW

1. Select a Plains dwelling type. Note its distribution. Describe its construction, function, and suitability to the natural and human environment.

2. Select an object type such as cradle, bow, or moccasin and explain how the form of the object varied by tribe.

3. "Every element of the [war] bonnet held some significance." Explain.

4. Imagine that you are a Plains Indian artist around 1920. What are some of the past and present artistic conventions that inspire your work?

CHAPTER 7

MUSIC AND DANCE

Music and dance are probably the forms of expression that have come, more than any other, to emblemize Plains Indian cultural identity. Traditional songs, dances, and outfits are the main means by which Indians of the area actively represent their cultures to one another, to outside tribes, and to non-Indians. Mention Indian music to the uninitiated, however, and the same old stereotypes emerge: a drumbeat (one strong beat, three weak ones) that is heard in every second-rate Western movie and nowhere on the Plains, and a remark that the Indians are either dancing for rain or going on the warpath. There are in fact many kinds of music and dance, and they deserve the most serious attention ultimately because Indian concepts of history and core values of kinship, honor, and humor are perpetuated in musical performance.

The notion that there is a particular Indian music for the Plains rests on certain typological considerations. The music areas constructed by ethnomusicologists may not correspond exactly to general culture areas because the music specialists look at a smaller set of traits. One factor they consider is the degree of tension the voice is held to during singing. By this criterion,

the Plains area has been combined with the Pueblo Southwest, both regions favoring very tense singing. Common details of song structure further unite the regions on a gross level. On the other hand, the Pueblos prefer a low, growling vocal tone in some songs, while Plains singers value high-pitched, relatively loud singing in most cases; and the song forms of the Pueblos are greater in their variety and complexity. Plains music appears most distinct if viewed as an amalgam of many particular song and dance types, performance practices, clothing styles, and the historical and linguistic knowledge practitioners carry with them to make sense of it all; the sum of these characteristics may be referred to as *style*.

When the concept of style is carried further, it is apparent that there is more than one kind of Plains music. The most common differentiation is between Northern and Southern Plains styles. Northern singing is higher, much of it in the falsetto range, and the songs and dances are different than in the South, disregarding ongoing borrowing. Versions of the War Dance known as "Traditional" and "Grass Dance," and their specific songs, are dominant in the North, for example, while the "Fancy Dance" and different songs are

FIGURE 7.1   Men drumming and singing at the North American Indian Days annual powwow on the Blackfeet Reservation, Browning, Montana, July 2006.

standard in the South. Within the Northern style, authority William K. Powers (1990) identifies four sub-styles: one for the Blackfoots and their neighbors; one for the Crows; a North Dakota sub-style; and a South Dakota sub-style for the Sioux and Northern Arapahos and Cheyennes. On the Southern Plains (essentially Oklahoma) there are two sub-styles. That of Northern Oklahoma centers on the dignified "Straight Dance" type of war dancing and is associated with the Pawnees, Tonkawas, and Southern Siouans, notably the Poncas and Omahas. The Western Oklahoma sub-style favors the athletic "Fancy" War Dance and embraces music of the Comanches, Kiowas, Southern Cheyennes and Arapahos, and associated Caddoan and Apachean tribes. As with any such classification, care is taken to note that much sharing and change go on. For decades already the Straight Dance has been an integral part of

Western Oklahoma get-togethers, Fancy dancing is popular in the north, and in Oklahoma enthusiasts of the higher singing style form Northern singing groups.

Other musical characteristics of the Plains include a simple unvarying drumbeat (isorhythm) with any accents (sometimes called "honor beats") that might occur falling in fixed patterns. Along with the drum rhythm is a separable sung rhythm established by the placement of melody notes. The shape of the melody is normally "cascading," "terraced," "tumbling," or "stair"—starting high and stepping down to a low end. Melodies typically employ three to five different tones, at intervals of a major second or minor third, over a range, on average, of a tenth, and often within an octave. The intervals are essentially the same as those used in Western music, except that there is more frequent use of microtonal variation around a tone.

Microtones, or intervals of pitch difference that are smaller than those standardized in Western music—the sounds "between" the keys of the piano, so to speak—add dimension in Indian singing. Their employment was behind the insistence of one of my Comanche consultants that "you can't write Indian music." Standard Western notation is in fact often used to make transcriptions adequate for the study and reproduction of Plains song, though to reveal certain meaningful sound patterns, a graph is better. Few transcriptions do full justice, however, which was the point of my Comanche friend, and the best way to learn the tonal and rhythmic subtleties of a song may be to rehearse it under the direction of an Indian singer.

The form of Plains songs usually involves but a few brief phrases and is really a consequence of the way songs are performed. Although from the Indian viewpoint the phrases are not separable, they can be diagrammed using letters and it can be seen that they are repeated in set patterns. Common is the "incomplete repetition" pattern: AA^1BCBC, so-called because the AA^1 sequence is not repeated. Letter A stands for the introductory phrase sung by the song leader, which is followed or overlapped by A^1, called the "second," the same phrase sung by at least one other singer (in solo performance, singers "second" themselves). Letter B is the main body of the song, sung by all, and C is a cadence or resolution, sung by all. One pass through the sequence is considered an entire song, which is then rendered over again continuously for as long as the leader desires; four times is thought ideal unless the enthusiasm of the singers or dancers requires more. In actual practice, the leader begins the next A part while the previous C part is being completed by the rest of the singers, so the renditions are heard to overlap. Certain War Dance songs add one more final BC sequence after the renditions have apparently stopped, this coda referred to as a "tail" by Indian singers. Perhaps three-fourths of all songs show the incomplete

repetition pattern, and most of the rest are sung clear through without repetitions.

When there is more than one singer, the male voices sing in unison, and whatever female voices are added move in parallel an octave higher. Slight discrepancies among the singers are tolerated. Any further departure from monophony is extremely rare, though. Stark harmony singing appears in some Yankton peyote songs, introduced by worshippers who earlier learned to sing hymns in Protestant churches. Call-and-response singing is heard today in Stomp Dance songs in Oklahoma, but this dance is of southeastern origin and the songs probably reflect African American influence.

Generally, in public performances women sing by taking seats behind the men—their kinsmen—and adding their voices; their role is optional and considered supportive of the men's effort and is consistent with traditional ideas about female modesty and deference. Their performance itself is secondary in the sense that they wait for the melody to proceed downward enough for them to add their line one octave higher. In Oklahoma the women around the drum are sometimes referred to as "the chorus girls," indicating the secondary function in a way that is considered humorous (because it is an appropriation of an English phrase) but not derogatory. Exceptions to this pattern are important to note, however. Since the 1970s, several mixed-sex singing groups in which women perform like men have emerged on the Northern Plains, among the Blackfoots, Sarsis, Assiniboines, and Shoshones. There are also a few all-female singing groups in the region.

But if women's singing at public dances seems limited, there are other contexts in which it is more central: hand games, lullabies, children's games, and church hymns. Women have latitude as composers in these genres and in song types that traditionally take a female viewpoint, such as Round Dance songs lamenting an absent lover. In many Comanche church hymns composed in the Native idiom, women sing lead and the men second an octave lower, reversing the usual pattern. And women simply play an important role in perpetuating all kinds of songs by singing them around the house. This more hidden aspect of Indian music has been explored lately in excellent studies by Vander (1988) and Giglio (1994).

Notions of song origination and ownership can be complex. Plains singers may speak of "making songs," but as often talk about "receiving them," "hearing" or "catching" them. They may claim credit for composing or acknowledge learning from the singing of others. Remarkable events inspire songs, and though a song may come to have historical value for documenting an important battle or the first sighting of whites, the main intent is to capture and perpetuate the emotional essence of those living a dream-like experience. Songs are also learned from spirits during dreams and sought visions. A widespread belief is that one can learn new songs by sitting beneath a cottonwood tree and listening to the rustling leaves. Overall, songs are thought to be less the product of a rational, comprehensive creative process and more the result of the person being attuned and receptive. What is actually "heard" or "caught" is usually not specified; it could be an entire melody or lyric, the kernel of one or the other, or some mental image that prompts the singer to retrieve a defunct melody from their memory and reconstitute it. The foundational elements of songs are out there in the natural world for retrieval, and the Lakota word closest to "compose" suggests renewal or recreation.

Early collectors such as Alfred Kroeber among the Arapahos were baffled to find that different words sung to the same melody could be considered entirely different songs. Sometimes a "new" song would differ from some other only by the addition of a couple of notes. On what grounds a particular culture deems a song unique, when all songs are designed from a limited set of elements, is an intricate question illuminated by recent studies of Irish music, the blues, and other forms. We do know that as older Indian songs are

redone, the transformation may be incomplete, yielding lyrics that at first seem incongruous. An Arapaho song praising tribesmen who fought in World War I (WWI) reported, "The German got scared and ran and dragged his blanket along" (Densmore 1936:50–51), using an older melody and an old-fashioned metaphor for defeat.

The intensely personal nature of composition as Plains singers conceive it relates to the Native idea that song is virtually an extension of the person and therefore linkable to breath and personal life force. Ownership—the exclusive right to performance and transmission—might therefore seem to be a natural, obvious matter. There can still be disputes about song ownership and originality, however, and often are, particularly in modern days when musical sharing is accelerated via the car and tape recorder. As spirits may bestow songs to humans, song permission is properly bestowed from the original singer to others, and from one tribe to another, often in conjunction with matching dances or medicines. Songs can also be purchased when they accompany a curing procedure or medicine bundle that is being transferred, but the selling here is a kind of ritual exchange not to be confused with the marketing of commercialized popular music. Yet, overall, it would be difficult to show that the means and motivations for composing and singing are fundamentally different in Indian and non-Indian cultures.

There are several powerful social motivations for people in Indian communities to participate in musical activities. One is simply the appeal of visiting with neighbors, especially strong where households are spread apart. The companionship enjoyed by those who sing and dance together was summarized by a Comanche woman who told me, "I like to be where the people are." Singing and dancing are also ways of affirming one's social position. Kin ties are activated as a singer sits at the drum with his brothers and a dancer wears items patiently beaded by her aunts and mother; fellow participants who are not related by blood or marriage address each other with fictive kin terms. Even recently deceased persons are situated in the web of social relations, as their relatives sing certain songs in remembrance or refrain from dancing out of respect for the dead.

The bonds strengthened through music enable other kinds of mutual help, such as pooled work around the house or ranch, money lending, or traditional curing. And as musicians and dancers become proficient they gain prestige, bringing honor to themselves and their families—further social capital. Many cultural and political leaders begin developing their public image and influence at the dance ground. Cultivation of one's persona through singing and dancing must be done very subtly, however, because the spirit behind musical activity is more communal than individualistic, and the explicit cultural rule is that participants should not hold themselves above others.

A nascent professionalism in Plains music allows the better singers and dancers to earn money as well as stature. Dancing for payment and prize money goes back at least to the early 1900s, when Indian dancers were hired for rodeos, carnivals, and Wild West shows. Contest dancing grew along with the powwow movement after WWII, to the point where today the best dancers tour the Plains almost year-round competing for cash awards. Champion Jonathan Windy Boy makes up to $50,000 a year. The expenses of travel and outfits, and time away from wage work, have to be factored against the winnings, however.

Semiprofessional singing groups travel the powwow circuit too, while at the same time gaining renown with commercial tapes issued by Indian House, Indian Sounds, Canyon, and other companies. Commercial concerns prompt some singers to purposefully sequence, if not compose, songs for recording, and titles are invented for songs that never had names, so they can be listed on the tape insert. As previously suggested, when the music is transmitted by electronic means it is increasingly "disembodied," disassociated from the people who make it; this phenomenon is somewhat at odds with traditional ideas of personal and tribal song origin and ownership, so there is some risk of censure when one takes the music into the marketplace. The singer's humility can also be questioned. Yet, since they continue to serve social functions and often share their earnings with kin, it would be wrong to suggest that the semiprofessional musicians sing mainly for personal gain. And, of course, recordings preserve and disseminate songs, a fact appreciated by Indian singers more than anyone.

A good Indian singer has talents that are not obvious to someone used to Western art and popular music. Plains singers display a remarkable pitch sense, consistently starting a song in the same, optimal key without reference to a pitch pipe. They also have an impressive ability to keep steady time. The quavering of the voice that may sound like weakness, inaccuracy, or ornamentation appears according to preliminary study (Pantaleoni 1987) to be an extremely fast rhythmic pulse that meshes with the rhythm of the drumbeats. Nevertheless, the beats of voice and drum rhythm discerned by a Western ear do not always fall together, creating the illusion that the voice and drum are moving along at independent tempos. Certain combinations of melody, rhythm, and text are considered optimal, and talented singers know how to put them together correctly or else introduce small modifications in poorer songs to bring them into better balance. Beyond these feats, the good singer has a loud, high voice, knows many songs, and sings them without mistakes. The aesthetic has as much to do with power and dependability as with euphony.

From the Native viewpoint, the standards for good singing are set in reference to male singers, who dominate in public performance. Women sing more softly and less stridently, with a less obvious rhythmic pulse and smoother connection between tones. These vocal qualities are suited to the lullabies and children's songs that women sing at home, but carry over when women sing social and war songs outdoors except in some of the rare cases that women take on the male role.

In most songs, much or all of the melody is delivered using short syllables called vocables. Earlier these were called "burden" syllables, because they "carry" the melody, or "nonsense syllables" or "meaningless syllables." The latter terms are misleading because the syllables convey meaning even though they do not mean anything in and of themselves. Vocables are never strung together randomly; for any song, the sequence of vocables is set when the song is composed. When sequences are studied, it becomes apparent that vocables are used according to a host of rules that the singers must know at least subconsciously. Only certain vocables sounds may adjoin one another, and most are not repeated twice in a row. These rules promote an alteration of vowel and consonant sounds that aids delineation of the melody. Set sequences of various lengths which reoccur can be called vocabilic formulas. Certain formulas are only appropriate to certain melodic motions, or only for the beginning, middle, or end of a song; certain formulas are used only in peyote songs, others only in Round Dance songs, and so on. Some examples include *he yo wit si* or *he na yo we* in peyote ritual songs and *we ya hai ya we ya hai yo wen* at the end of Southern Plains Round Dance songs. The first few vocables sung by a head singer may therefore help cue everyone who will join him in singing and dancing as to which kind of song is starting. Because of all these notions of correct vocable use, vocables cannot be fully "meaningless"; they convey meaning by their grammatical arrangement, allowing communication among singers, dancers, and listeners. The concept of vocabilic meaning is not really profound; English-speakers know the ominous connotations of the old *Dragnet* television theme, "dum de dum dum," or the disdain behind "la de da" immediately, even if they cannot explain the meanings readily.

When worded text is used, the effect can be very interesting. Single words or short phrases can be included among the vocables to transmit the song's meaning, as in the following translation of a Yankton peyote song (Powers 1990:132):

Pray! *yo yo yo*
Pray! *yo yo yo*
Pray! *yo yo yo*
Pray! *yo yo yo*
Pray! *Ho*, you will live *he ya na he ye yo we*
There in heaven *ya ya*, there is life *ye ye haya hana yo*
Pray! *Ho*, you will live *he ya na he ye yo we*

Many performances alternate vocabilic and worded texts or replace vocables with words as the song is repeated. The Kiowa Flag Song, dating perhaps to WWI, conjures a respectful attitude with the texted phrases below (after Rhodes 1959:26), which are inserted in place of vocables as the song is repeated:

T'áhee gaw 'ohlt'ágaw
Raise the flag with care
Beyt'ágyah 'ohl hahyée
Go out and whip the enemy
Hóhndey 'óhndey bah'óhngyah
And be glad

Other songs are fully texted. The following Shoshone *Naraya* or Ghost Dance song (Vander 1988:19–20) illustrates the haiku-like or telegraphic quality of many Plains lyrics, and like others in the Ghost Dance genre, it is evocative of water, a symbol of life:

Buyuna durua buyuna durua gin
Duck's duckling duck's ducklings very small
Buyuna durua buyuna durua gin
Duck's duckling duck's ducklings very small
Tsa paran bangwavinora
Good in water swimming
Tsa paran bangwavinor
Good in water swimming

Certainly singers could compose long narrative lyrics if they wanted to, but it is the artistic effect of repetition or small incremental change and the ability to get at an idea across economically that are valued. "The absence of connecting words and phrases allows for a rich ambiguity of meanings" (Vander 1988:19–20).

Sometimes English lyrics appear. An early reaction of scholars was to view English words in Indian songs as evidence that authentic Native music was dying. But the English words are inserted in such a way that they follow the usual rules of song structure and vocable use, and either translate or stand in some playful semantic relation (parodic or poetic) to preexisting song elements. English is conventionalized in an Indian idiom, especially in love songs, with recurring references to "dearie," "snags" (trysts), and "one-eyed Fords," and allusions to American pop culture, all of which delight Indian listeners (Gelo 1988b:145):

Just because you left me for someone else
Don't think I'm sittin' here just missin' you
I've got all kinds of snags at all the Indian
    doins'
I don't need your love anymore

Go with me tonight, dear
Stay with me tonight, dear
Oh my darlin', stay with me tonight, dear
At the Motel Six, dear

The use of English is just another way of meeting Indian aesthetic expectations that singers enjoy in appropriate (generally secular) contexts. Sound effects are occasionally heard in Plains songs also, as in a South Dakota song describing a WWII air mission that has the singers imitate the whining of falling bombs. On the Fourth of July the commander of Ft. Sill, Oklahoma, sometimes details a bugler to a Kiowa powwow to blow "charge" during a particular Gourd Dance song; the song recalls a battle in which the Indians captured the bugle or bugler. Thus, the former foes remember their common history.

Instruments of the Plains include several kinds of drums, flutes, and rattles. Drums are played only to accompany singing and never by themselves. Only men play the drum, except among the few Northern groups in which women sing in the male role. The large wooden drum, 3 feet or more in diameter and having a head on both sides, can be homemade, though bass drums from commercial traps are acceptable. In precontact times a large rawhide sheet would have served the purpose. Thus, while the Comanche word for drum, *wobiaawotua*, translates literally as "wood cup [i.e., barrel] offspring," the Kiowa drum term, *pádl-k'á'-gá*, could be glossed as "hide for singing." The large drum is played horizontally, lashed to a four-armed wood frame (formerly forked sticks) that suspends it several inches off the ground. As many singers as can fit sit around it in folding chairs, sounding the drum in unison with long beaters made of wood or fiberglass shafts, the end pads covered with buckskin.

Set in the center of the dance ring, the drum is the first in a series of concentric circles symbolizing the community of humans and spirits. In form and function, the drum is analogous to a communal fire or cooking pot. The instrument is also a personality who deserves respect, so it is honored with a pinch of tobacco as the singers take their seats. The drum identity stands in place of the singers: gifts such as cigarettes and gas money to thank the singers are placed on the drum, the drum is beaten in a characteristic way to say "thank you" in return, and a crew of singers is referred to as a "drum." These customs direct attention away from the singers, who should not be celebrated for their talents, while still allowing recognition of their important role.

Two smaller membranophones are also found. One is the shallow, single-headed hand drum played by one person, essentially the same frame drum with cordage handle played around the Northern hemisphere, as among the Eskimos, Irish, and Saami. Frame drums are played on the vision quest, during hand games and some club functions, and by solo performers at non-Indian venues. The other type is the water drum used, on the Plains, exclusively in the peyote ceremony. By stretching a piece of buckskin over a small three-legged iron kettle partly filled with water, a drum is made that allows adjustment of tone. The head is softened periodically by splashing the water against it, or tightened by drying and thumb pressure. A single player uses a short stick to drums for a song leader seated next to him, creating a rapid, constant beat. Again the drum is full of symbolism, for the head bindings cross underneath the kettle in a pattern called the "Star of David" or the "Star of Bethlehem," the water inside represents rain, the sound thunder, and bits of charcoal are placed inside to signify lightening. The drum is assembled and taken apart as part of the ritual.

The Plains flute is, correctly speaking, a fipple flute because it is end-blown, is held vertically for playing, and contains a wooden divider within the tube that establishes two air chambers and generates vibrations. Flutes are made typically from two carved troughs of red cedar, about 2 feet long, glued together to make the tube. Sound results because the wooden divider inside the near end sends the airflow out of the tube through a small square aperture and against a block ("saddle") that is lashed on top, which in turn sends the air back through another aperture into the tube. The divider and the tube both vibrate. There are six finger holes along the tube for controlling the pitch. The block takes the form of a stylized bird, and often the lower end of the flute is carved into the head of a crane, a bird whose retracting neck is a phallic symbol appropriate to a courting instrument. Traditionally, a young man used the flute in courting, serenading a woman as she worked away from camp or signaling to her with a prearranged code while she sat in her parents' tipi. In recent years, the flute has become a concert instrument in the Indian community, used at exhibitions and funerals to play traditional tunes and hymns such as "Amazing Grace," and has also

gained a broad non-Indian following through its use in New Age compositions. Elders will make jokes if a married man plays one, remembering the flute's traditional purpose. The other common wind instrument is a "war whistle" made from the hollow wing bone of an eagle; these are piped by dancers during the powwow and Sun Dance and by the leader of a peyote ceremony.

Rattles and rasps of many kinds represent the idiophone family. Usually rattles are supposed to be shaken by male dancers in time with the song rhythm. Old-time societies often used a decorated stick with pendant dewclaws or a hard rawhide container with handle. Ghost dancers preferred a cow horn rattle. Gourd rattles, now called simply "gourds," were also common and have largely replaced the other types. A wooden spool plugs the gourd and accepts the handle, and feathers or horsehairs decorate the top. At times, trendy substitutes for the gourd have been Pet brand condensed milk cans and the large aluminum saltshakers sold in discount stores. An ingenious dance rattle is made for children from a tea strainer. Hollow rattles are "loaded" with seeds, BB's, buckshot, or small pebbles which ants or spiders have brought up from underground. How the rattle is held and shaken can be a matter of much discussion, with tribal styles noted and different methods for dances and peyote chanting. Initiation into a dance society may be marked by the presentation of a rattle along with regalia. A rare honor involves loaning one's rattle to a guest to dance with; so honored on one occasion, I was warned by the loaner not to "teach my gourd any bad habits," for an instrument can be thought to have its own personality. Notched wooden rasps, sounded with sticks, were also played in society and medicine dances. These take many forms, such as an animal with a ridged back.

The roots of Plains dance are ancient, and though exact details are often lacking, historical accounts and tribal lore give hints about the origins of the customs we know today. Animal impersonations to magically lure game animals, performed by medicine men and the public at large, were a regular part of hunter-gatherer life. The *Massaum*, a five-day rite of the ancestral Cheyennes, was one such animal festival (see Chapter 10). As shamanic and warrior societies developed to manage specific medicines, members might indicate their power by impersonating buffalos or crows. The Mandan Bull Society dancers wore buffalo head masks, while the Comanche *Tuu Wii* or Crow Society dance, with its hopping and cawing, recalls an episode in which a warrior left for dead was revived and given power by a crow. In fact, most ceremonial dances and songs are explained as having their origins in mythic encounters between humans and supernatural beings. Other early dances celebrating the prowess of warriors would have functioned essentially as male courtship displays and were undoubtedly rooted in Indian observation of the courtship dances performed by gallinaceous fowl of the prairie such as the greater prairie chicken and sharp-tailed grouse. The feather neck and back bustles worn by Plains dancers today imitate the plumage of these birds.

Once such dance customs were standardized within tribes, they would become the subject of intertribal sharing. The history of Plains dance is therefore one of constant diffusion and reinvention, consolidation and sharing, so that any dance likely has several possible "origins." The Grass Dance, forerunner of the modern War Dance, perhaps best illustrates this phenomenon. Sometime in the early 1800s, the Omahas combined elements of a declining men's society called the *Poogethun* with concepts from the Pawnee curing ceremony called *Iruska*. The *Poogethun* had been derived from the Chief's Society of the Oglala Sioux, and the *Iruska* was one of several similar shamanic societies that had developed among the Plains villagers and Sioux. The Omaha synthesis became known as the Hethushka Society (after "*Iruska*"). The Hethushka Society dance was then taken up around 1860 by the Yanktons and then the Tetons, and called the "Omaha Dance" or else

"Grass Dance," because the dancers wore tufts of grass under their belts to represent scalps. From here, the dance was transferred formally or informally through multiple paths to other Northern Plains tribes, so that between the 1870s and 1890s, it became very popular on several reservations. It fused with or replaced older dances in some places, and gained other names, such as "Wolf Dance" and "Hot Dance." "War Dance" is a later misnomer probably begun by non-Indian promoters, but the name has stuck as a handy one to describe many of the twentieth-century derivatives of the Grass Dance diffusion.

The War Dance is the centerpiece of the main contemporary musical gathering, the powwow. "Powwow" comes from an Algonquian word meaning a medicine man and was applied by the English settlers to curing ceremonies and eventually to any Indian gathering. In the 1950s it came to be used widely by whites and Indians to mean a festival of dance, feasting, gift giving, and other social activities of the kind derived from the old Grass Dance complex. The modern event takes place usually over a three-day weekend. Powwowgoers set up lawn chairs for onlookers and benches for the dancers, and many camp, around a circular arena. A "grand entry" procession leads participants into the ring as a flag song is sung, and the dancing begins. Activities are managed by an emcee, who keeps up a jovial patter while carefully regulating the dance schedule, and an arena director who sets up the dancer's benches and brings them water. Some dances honor elders, veterans, or visitors; some are for all participants in a particular style, others are exhibitory dances done by the host tribe or visitors, yet others are "intertribals" open to participants generally, and then there are contest dances too. Between dances, families host "give-aways," in which shawls, blankets, groceries, household items, and occasionally horses are distributed to friends and visitors. The sponsoring family or organization serves a big supper for all as a further gesture of generosity.

FIGURE 7.2 Two Assiniboine or Gros Ventre men perform an early version of the Grass Dance on the Fort Belknap Reservation, Montana, Fourth of July, 1906. They are feigning to spear dog meat from a kettle, an old custom in warrior dances. *Photo by Sumner W. Matteson (1867–1920).*

The basic War Dance step is a toe-heel step with knees flexed, left then right. The mass of dancers moves clockwise, within which individuals are free to go as their steps take them. There are then a number of variations with distinctive movements and clothing. Men's Straight dancing is done at a slow to moderate pace with a dignified bearing and little body movement. The dancer glances downward as if looking for tracks, cocks his head like a bird, or subtly suggests the motion of a man planting corn with a dibble. The dancer wears a loose cloth shirt with sleeves and ribbon trim called a "ribbon shirt," breechclout and leggings, and a deer or porcupine hair crest or "roach." The Men's Fancy Dance or Feather Dance is done in flamboyant outfits (dancers prefer the word "outfit" to "costume"), every part of which is calculated to add vibrancy. Belts, wrist cuffs, and decorative rosettes of colorful matching beadwork are common. Vivid, fluffy dyed chicken hackles make up bustles on the backside, upper back, and upper arms. The roach spreader, the plate that fixes the roach against the head, may be rigged so that it holds feathers which spin or rock in time with the dance steps. Angora goat hair anklets shimmer with each footfall. In keeping with this look, the dance itself is done with disjointed body movements at a frenetic pace. Spins, dips, splits, and hops are inserted in the routine.

The Men's Traditional style of War Dance requires an upright or bent posture with chest thrown forward and proud, alert expression, more than fancy footwork. Often Traditional dancers go counterclockwise, even against the flow of other dancers. They forsake shirts and dyed feathers for breastplates and raptor feather bustles, and they may carry clubs or shields. Body parts of animals are often conspicuous in these outfits, whether the pelt of a coyote worn over the head, or the dried head and tail of an eagle converted into a fan. An image is created of an old-time warrior whose dance movements tell the tale of a hunt or raid, and the Traditional dance is perhaps most like the Grass Dance of the later 1800s. The so-called Grass Dance is still done, with hanks of colorful flowing yarn suggesting the original tufts of grass, made to wave by the dancer's sinuous movements.

The basic women's War Dance is a toe-heel step so light that it looks like a flat-footed step with a slight bobbing. Women stand erect with eyes forward, striving for a graceful, dignified appearance and rhythmic swaying of the fringe on their dresses and handbags. They proceed clockwise among the male dancers. In the Fancy Shawl Dance, however, the woman clutches her shawl tightly over her shoulders, with elbows pointing out, stepping high, crossing and kicking her legs, and whirling completely, all the while moving forward at intervals. This style has spread slowly down from Canada since the 1970s, as has, more recently, the Ojibwa's Jingle Dress Dance, which requires an outfit covered with hundreds of metal cone tinklers. The woman moves energetically so that the cones sound in beat with the music. Occasionally women have done the Fancy Dance using men's dance steps and regalia, but this practice has yet to receive much acceptance.

War Dance competitions are held in various "divisions": Tiny Tots, Junior Girl's Buckskin [dress], Senior Women's Cloth [dress], Senior [men's] Straight Dance, and so on; a dozen divisions is not uncommon. The contests run each evening, with divisions ordered in increasing prestige, starting with the contest for little children of either sex and culminating on Saturday night with the final round for the Fancy Dance. Three or four judges stand at points around the arena while the contestants dance, watching them carefully and jotting down the numbers of those who impress them most with their comportment, timing, outfits, and, in the more athletic categories, ability to improvise movements within established limits. Closely rated dancers may be called back for an exciting one-on-one finale. Awards are made for first, second, and third place; often the winners are not announced until the closing hour of the powwow, to build suspense and hold the audience. For days afterward, onlookers reevaluate the contestants, talking about the dancing and outfits, and whether any of the judges were relatives of any of the winners.

A newer kind of competition is the drum contest pitting singing groups against one another. Powwows featuring a drum contest use a host drum which functions as the house band, occupying the center of the arena, but there are also contestant groups that set up around the edge of the dance circle. These singers must man their drums for the duration of the powwow, ever ready to sing a set of songs when called upon by the emcee. They are thus tested on a variety of song types and evaluated on their preparedness and repertoire as well as volume and endurance.

A quite different dance from the War Dance has become increasingly popular, especially in the south. There, in the 1950s, descendants of the Kiowa Skunkberry Society reactivated the exclusive society dance that had been forsaken 30 years earlier. Neighboring tribes had had similar dances, and the Kiowas' revival effort led quickly to sharing and imitation. The resultant Gourd Dance is an intertribal form that features dancing with rattles and a knee-flex step. Men dressed in street clothes plus a velvet sash and bandoleer of mescal beans grasp their "gourds" in their right hand and feather fans in their left. They face inward from the edge of the arena, dancing in place by shaking their rattles and bending their knees in time with the drum, and then advancing at intervals marked by an increase in drum volume. Women perform by dancing in place at the edge of the ring, wearing a shawl and perhaps holding a fan, but no rattle. The simple regalia and body movements invite participants who do not War dance as well as those who do. In the powwow program, the Gourd Dance is scheduled during the afternoon and early evening, before the War dancing.

Aside from these more serious dances, there are several social forms that are meant for having fun; many allow women and men to dance together and non-Indian onlookers to join in. The Round Dance has men, women, and children forming a circle facing inward and stepping sideways to the left in time with the drum. The Forty-Nine, which probably got its name from a risqué side show at an old county fair in Oklahoma, is similar in pattern but is held informally in the wee hours after the powwow closes, and is associated with rowdyism and sex play. Oklahoma Indians also enjoy the late-night Stomp Dance of the Creeks who relocated there from the southeast: men and women follow a leader in a serpentine shuffle, answering his shouted vocables with their own; the women have clusters of rattles strapped to their legs and the whole effect is like a chugging train. In the Two-Step, partners shuffle forward, hand in hand like ice skaters. Regional variations are called Owl and Rabbit Dance. The Snake Dance is a sinuous follow-the-leader maneuver, and the Buffalo Dance imitates the grazing bison and produces footprints like cloven hoof prints. The Eagle Dance, Hoop Dance, and Shield Dance are athletic exhibits sometimes offered between War dances for the crowd's entertainment.

Plains style music and dance, along with the powwow format, have been taken up by Native musicians throughout the hemisphere. Already in the 1950s, it was apparent that homogenization was taking place on the Plains and beyond, and that the intertribal forms of powwow music and dance were seizing the interest of Indian peoples, perhaps at the expense of their own local traditions. A seminal article by the ethnographer James H. Howard (1955) proposed the emergence of a super-tribal or "Pan-Indian" culture. Its characteristic features, Howard said, were the War Dance, Powwow, War Dance outfits, Stomp Dance, the Indian store where powwow supplies were bought, and the peyote religion, which had adherents from many tribes. Factors he saw contributing to homogenization in the post-war period were the shared socioeconomic status of Indians, marked by discrimination and poverty, and the commonalities resulting from increased intermarriage, English use, and attendance at intertribal Indian schools such as Haskell and Chilocco. Howard seemed to believe that Pan-Indianism was a last-ditch attempt to save Native culture through collective effort and "one of the final stages of progressive acculturation, just prior to complete assimilation" (Ibid.:220).

The concept of Pan-Indianism, grounded in useful observations of contemporary music and dance sharing, was applied by later scholars to explain all modern aspects Indian life, even while drawing criticism from many Indian and non-Indian authorities. Howard's model was based on activities in Oklahoma, when on the Northern Plains, sharing among tribes within that region was for some time more significant than any wider influence. But even in Oklahoma, reports of uniform acculturation were premature. Here the intertribal powwow increasingly became a venue for the revival of old dances and half-remembered songs, as descendants of the old societies strove to show the intertribal audience what was special about their own ways. It is possible that more traditional singers and dancers are active throughout the Plains today than at any time since the reservations were established, along with the versions of songs and dances they hold as tribally distinctive. Newly revived "tribal" traditions often make their way into the Pan-Indian program and become "intertribal"—examples include the Gourd Dance and Jingle Dress Dance.

In reality, a dialectic has been at work between sentiments that can be called "intertribalism" and "tribalism." This is the same old dynamic that has been at work since Grass Dance days and from time immemorial, and continuation of the reinvention and sharing process bodes well for Plains musical traditions and the values they encapsulate. And now, even as local revivalism intensifies, the influence of Plains music is approaching a scale that is truly global. Huge expositions such as the yearly Red Earth mega-powwow in Oklahoma City's Myriad convention center involve thousands of participants and onlookers from all over North America, while traveling groups like the American Indian Dance Theater bring Plains music and dance to eager audiences worldwide.

Sources: Beatty (1974); Callahan (1990); Densmore (1918; 1929; 1936); Feder (1964b); Fletcher (1994); Gamble (1967); Gelo (1986; 1988a; 1988b; 1999); Giglio (1994); Harrington (1928); Hatton (1986); Howard (1955, 1976); Koch (1977); McAllester (1949); Meadows (1999); Nettl (1954); Pantaleoni (1987); Parfit (1994); Powers (1980; 1990); Rhodes (1959); Titon (1984); Vander (1988); and Young (1981).

CHAPTER SUMMARY

Music and dance are strong emblems of Plains Indian identity. Plains music is a particular style of Indian music, with regional sub-styles. The overall style and sub-styles are defined according to such factors as vocal pitch, drum rhythm, melodic contour, song form, and associated dances. Singing and dancing provide enjoyment and strengthen social bonds. Songs are inspired by the spirits or historical events, or they may be composed by recombining common elements, or purchased from other song owners. Good singing requires a strong voice, knowledge of many songs, and impressive control of pitch and rhythm. Songs include sequences of vocables, brief word phrases, or both; modern songs may include English lyrics. Musical instruments include various types of drums, flutes, and rattles. Dances can generally be traced to animal imitation, acquisition of medicine power, and association customs. Dances undergo a constant process of diffusion and reinterpretation across the many Plains tribes. The evolution of the War Dance, the centerpiece of modern gatherings, is an example of this process. Intertribal sharing of songs and dances has been cited as evidence of a Pan-Indian culture. But sharing also stimulates the reinvention of specific traditions within tribes.

QUESTIONS FOR REVIEW

1. What characteristics are used to define the Plains style of Indian music and its regional sub-styles?
2. Explain the intricacies of song origination and ownership in Plains Indian music.
3. Examine the claim, "Plains Indian songs are made up of meaningless syllables."
4. Account for the origin of the modern War Dance, compare its different forms, and contrast the War Dance with other Plains dances.

CHAPTER 8

ORAL TRADITIONS

Before the world, the South Wind, and the North Wind and the West Wind and the East Wind, dwelt together in the far north in the land of the ghosts. They were brothers. The North Wind was the oldest. He was always cold and stern. The West Wind was the next oldest. He was always strong and noisy. The East Wind was the middle in age and he was always cross and disagreeable. The South Wind was the next to the youngest and he was always pleasant. With them dwelt a little brother, the Whirlwind. He was always full of fun and frolic. . . .

—(anonymous Lakota storyteller; Walker 1983:183)

Despite now centuries of disruption, oral traditions have been one of the more enduring aspects of culture on the Plains. The continuation of tribal stories is closely interrelated with the survival of native language, and no doubt the traditions have been eroded through language loss, although many of the stories are still retold by tribe members in English along with or instead of those in the original language. Consequently, scholars are able to continue collecting and analyzing traditional stories for linguistic and cultural studies, adding to a body of recorded material that has been accumulating since the late 1700s. In recent years a number of tribes have put oral traditions at the center of their own preservation efforts because of their value in maintaining language, history, and cultural knowledge. Several tribes now have programs for collecting tribal stories from elders, publishing them, and placing them in local school curricula.

For many Indian people the perpetuation of tribal stories is a critical matter of self-definition and self-determination. Roger C. Echo-Hawk (Pawnee) has rightly noted how the distinction between "history" and "prehistory," even as used in this volume, is an imposed non-Indian framework which suggests a strict divide between what is more or less knowable. But rather than thinking of their oral narratives as furnishing some less dependable vision of the remote past, Indians may see them as constituting their own authoritative ancient history, of equal value to the written records of non-Indian deep time (and a record which can and should be correlated with other records, such as those from archaeology). Indeed, many Indian storytellers regard their tales simply as history rather than, say, literature, art, religious doctrine, or folklore.

At least some non-Indian scholars have struggled with the historical value of Native oral traditions. The question of the retrieval of Native history has a long account on the Plains. As anthropologist Douglas Parks has pointed out (1996:1), anthropologist James Mooney's *Calendar History of the Kiowa Indians* (Mooney 1979 [orig. 1898]) was the first full attempt to combine Native and non-Indian sources to construct an American Indian tribal history. Mooney worked from two series of Kiowa pictographs rendered on hide and paper (described in Chapter 6). Each pictograph was a reminder that prompted stories, to be delivered orally by the elders, and the sequence of pictures in these cases provided a chronological order and degree of consistency to the storytelling. Mooney was able to reconcile information about the past generated by the pictographs with information from other sources, both Indian and non-Indian, toward an even more robust account of Kiowa history. Not all Plains tribes encoded their histories in so-called "winter counts," but all perpetuated a body of oral traditions that serves as a rich basis for understanding their past.

Notwithstanding the historical worth of Indians stories, they are also appreciated within and beyond Native cultures for their artistic qualities, as entertainment, and for their ability to condense and transmit life lessons, morals, and values. Indian narratives therefore may be regarded as oral literature as well as oral history.

Plains Indian stories conform to different types. Since the days of the German folklorists the Brothers Grimm, distinctions have been made between myths, legends, and folktales, and this typology captures some of the differences among Indian stories, though imperfectly. According to the folklorists' definition, a myth is a narrative that deals with some major existential question such as how the world was made or where people go when they die. Myths include characters and actions that are outside of normal experience; they take place in a different dimension of time and space, and while fantastic and improbable, these stories are regarded as serious and true by those who perpetuate them. Because myths concern creation and fate and demand belief, they are associated with the sacred and religious ideology.

Legends, on the other hand, tell of actual persons and events that are believed to have taken place in ordinary time in the past, though they may include exaggerations and unlikely outcomes. Legendary characters may have started out as real historical persons, but their exploits have become magnified. Therefore, legends can sometimes verge on the serious concerns and fantastic dimensions of time and space addressed in myth. Legends encapsulate the heroic history of a group of people. Believability of legends is negotiated—the listener is not quite sure if every part of the legend is true but is willing to go along.

A folktale is accepted by everyone as imaginary. In European folktales, for example, the beginning phrase "Once upon a time" actually cues the listener that what follows never actually took place, but is a made-up story for entertainment and perhaps moral education.

Other types of narratives can be added to this basic scheme. Sometimes people just tell others what happened to them in the recent or distant past in a conversational way. Such stories can be called unpolished reminiscences. If they relate the same episode repeatedly they may standardize the way they deliver it, forming a kind of narrative called a memorate. These kinds of stories are also extremely important in preserving and transmitting tribal knowledge, but have not been as systematically recorded as myths, legends, and folktales. One can also imagine how a legend or myth could form over time from a memorate, as the story is repeated by others over generations and becomes imbued with significance, more communal, and more remote from the original occurrence. Perhaps in some instances too a story that once had mythic significance could lose its importance over time and survive only in a reduced, more casual form.

Tribes have their own schemes for classifying stories. The Oglala Sioux recognize two genres, *ohunkanan*, which they liken to myths and fables, and *wicooyake*, the telling of war adventures and local events that are deemed "true" in the sense that they are part of immediate human experience. Similarly, Arikara storytellers note two classes, *naa'iikáWIš*, which they translate as "fairy tales," and "true stories" with no special native term. Both classes cover different kinds of stories, but generally Arikara fairy tales are stories about the trickster and other fanciful creatures, and true stories include those concerning mythic times, legends, historical and supernatural events, and the origins of ritual. The Comanches also use two different words to denote narratives. One, *narʉmu?ipʉ*, refers to any kind of narrative, while the other, *narukuyunapu*, is reserved, according to one storyteller, for "old time stories—some of it's facts, it may be something somebody saw in a vision, things that the people used to know that might be forgotten" (quoted in Gelo 1994:302). (The element *narʉ-* in both these words means "exchange," for that is how storytelling is conceived, and it is customary, though not mandatory, among the Comanches as among many Plains tribes for storytellers to receive small gifts in trade for their stories.) Each of these Native sets of categories, like the non-Indian distinction between myth and legend, grapples in its own way with the need to discern between the supernatural and everyday human domains.

Oral narratives have many essential qualities that can never be adequately captured by written transcription. Yet unfortunately so much of what remains of Plains Indian oral traditions is in the form of stories collected, printed, and reprinted over many years. And normally these stories have been saved in a form in which the native language has been translated freely into English. Free translations have varied greatly in quality, from those intent on making the story conform to English literary standards of grammar and plot sequence to those, more recently, rendered by

literary scholars trained to be sensitive to Native forms and meanings. For expediency, the present discussion does rely on free translations and summaries to illustrate features of narrative. It must be recognized, however, that narratives in these forms are highly imperfect and often at best rough approximations of what was originally being said and meant.

One practice that helps address the deficiency of the printed form is interlinear translation. The translation lines can be inserted directly between the native text lines or gathered in a parallel paragraph. For example, the following story told by Comanche elder Emily Riddles in the 1950s is rendered as she spoke it in Comanche with a literal English translation in parallel, numbered so that each sentence and word are directly glossed (after Canonge 1958:31–33):

1. soobe?sʉkʉtsa?_1 rʉa_2 ahtakíi?$_3$ tʉmʉʉmi?anʉ_4. 2.—ibu$_1$ nʉ?_2 tabe$_3$ ikahpetu$_4$ manakwʉhu$_5$ nana?atahpu$_6$ naboori$_7$ kwasu?i$_8$ tʉmʉʉkwatu?i_9, —mekʉ$_{10}$. 3. u$_1$ pía?kʉse?$_2$,—tua$_3$ ʉnʉ_4 o?ana$_5$ manakwʉ_6 miasuwaitu?i$_7$,—me$_8$ u$_9$ niikwiiy$\underline{u}_{10}$. 4. sitʉkʉse?$_1$ ahtakíi$_2$,—natsatsa$_3$ taa$_4$ nomia?eku$_5$, u?ana$_6$ esitsʉnʉ?ikatʉ_7, tahu$_8$ na?nʉmʉnʉʉka baiki$_9$ nʉ_{10} yʉtsʉmia?eek$\underline{u}_{11}$.—5. sitʉkʉse?$_1$ si?anetu$_2$ yʉtsʉhkwa$_3$ tʉmʉʉmi?atsi$_4$. 6. sitʉkʉse?$_1$ yʉtsiʉmi?arʉ_2, yʉtsiʉmi?arʉ_3, u$_4$ biarʉpinoo? karʉku$_5$, uma$_6$ karʉhúpiitʉ_7. 7. maa$_1$ ma$_2$ karʉkukʉse?$_3$ piawosa?áa?ra?$_4$ mawakatu$_5$ to?ihú piittʉ_6,—hina$_7$ ʉnʉ_8?—me$_9$ u$_{10}$ niikwiiy$\underline{u}_{11}$. 8. surʉkʉse?$_1$—tsaa$_2$ nʉ?$_3$ naboori$_4$ kwasu?i$_5$ suwa aitʉ_6—me$_7$ u$_8$ niikwiyiy$\underline{u}_9$. 9. sitʉkʉse?$_1$ nana? atahputi$_2$ tʉtʉetʉpihta$_3$ himan$\underline{u}_4$ uma$_5$ sihka$_6$ esi?ahtamúu?a$_7$ tʉ?ekan$\underline{u}_8$. 10.—meeku$_1$ nabuuni$_2$ —mekʉse?$_3$ surʉ_4 u$_5$ niikwiiy$\underline{u}_6$. 11. sitʉkʉse?$_1$ si?ana$_2$ wʉnʉrʉ_3, nabuihwʉnʉbuni$_4$. 12.—nohi?$_1$ tsaa$_2$ nabuniyu$_3$ nʉʉ_4—mekʉse?$_5$ surʉ_6 esi?ah-tamúu?$_7$. 13.—usʉ?$_1$ nʉ?$_2$ bʉesʉ_3 tsaa$_4$ naboori$_5$ nʉ_6 suwainihti$_7$ kwasu?utua?i$_8$ miaru?i$_9$ n$\text{ʉ}?_{10}$— usʉ?$_{11}$ mekʉse?$_{12}$ suurʉ_{13}. 14. si?anetʉkʉse?$_1$ surʉ_2 pitusʉ_3 yʉtsʉnʉkwa$_4$, so?ana$_5$ sehka$_6$ esi? ahtamúu?a$_7$ pʉkʉhu$_8$ sooyori?ikahtu$_9$ pitʉn$\underline{u}_{10}$. 15. surʉʉkʉse?$_1$ esi?ahtamúu?nʉʉ_2,—osʉ_3 hak arʉ_4 nan$\underline{i}$suyake$_5$ naboorʉ_6 ukʉ_7 tamʉkaba$_8$

kahtʉ$_9$—16. sʉmʉ?kuse?$_1$,—urʉ$_2$ u?$_3$ rʉmʉʉko? i?$_4$—me$_5$ yʉkwiiyu$_6$. 17. surʉkʉse?$_1$ pʉmi$_2$ urii$_3$ nasuyakeku$_4$, pʉnihku$_5$ uhka$_6$ pʉ$_7$ nara?urakʉ? iha$_8$ urii$_9$ tʉ?awekʉnu$_{10}$. 18. setʉkʉse?$_1$ esi?ah tamúu?$_2$ sebutu$_3$ tabe?ikahpetutu$_4$ sʉmʉyorinu kwa$_5$, tsu?nikatʉ$_6$, setʉ$_7$ sʉmʉkoyamanu$_8$, nanani suyake$_9$, setʉ$_{10}$ naboohka$_{11}$. 19. suku$_1$ sehka$_2$ naboori$_3$ ahtamúu?$_{a4}$ naahkaku$_5$, atanaihtʉ$_6$ urʉʉkʉ$_7$ bitʉnu$_8$. 20. surʉkʉse?$_1$,—mʉnʉ$_2$ esi?ahtamúu? nʉʉ$_3$ hakanihku$_4$ nananisuyakeku$_5$ naboohka$_6$?—me$_7$ urii$_8$ niikwiiyu$_9$. 21. surʉʉkʉse?$_1$,—tʉmʉʉy ʉkarʉ$_2$ nʉnʉ$_3$ usʉ$_4$ sube?sʉ$_5$ suhka$_6$ esi?ahtamúu? a$_7$ tʉmʉʉko?ikatʉ$_8$ nihánu$_9$, tsaa$_{10}$ naboori$_{11}$ u$_{12}$ kwasu?utʉmʉʉhka$_{13}$—me$_{14}$ yʉkwitʉ$_{15}$. 22. subetʉ$_1$.

1. Long ago$_1$, it is said$_2$, a grasshopper$_3$ went to buy$_4$. 2.—I$_2$ will go to buy$_9$ (a) different kind of$_6$ designed$_7$ coat$_8$ (I will go) far away$_5$ this way$_1$ towards (the) going down$_4$ (of the) sun$_3$,— (he) said$_{10}$. 3. His$_1$ mother$_2$ said to$_{8\ 10}$ him$_9$,— You$_4$ continually$_3$ want to go$_7$ over there$_5$ far away$_6$.—4. This$_1$ grasshopper$_2$ (said),—No matter$_3$? When$_5$ we$_4$ move$_5$, when$_{11}$ I$_{10}$ fly$_{11}$ among$_9$ our$_8$ relatives$_9$, there$_6$ (I) appear grey$_7$.—5. This one$_1$ at this place$_2$ flew off$_3$, / going/ to buy$_4$. 6. This one$_1$ goes flying$_2$, goes flying$_3$, where that big rock hill sits $_{4\ 5}$, (it) stopped and sat$_7$ on it$_6$. 7. As$_3$ he$_2$ sat$_3$ on it$_1$, (a) big grasshopper$_4$ climbed$_6$ towards him$_5$ and stopped$_6$,—What$_7$ (do) you$_8$ (want)?—(he) said to$_{9\ 11}$ him$_{10}$. 8. That one$_1$ said to$_{7\ 9}$ him$_8$—I$_3$ want$_6$ (a) nice$_2$ designed$_4$ coat$_5$.—9. This one$_1$ took$_4$ different kinds of$_2$ little stones$_3$ with it$_5$ [them] (he) painted$_8$ this$_6$ grey grasshopper$_7$. 10.—Now$_1$ look at yourself$_2$,—that one$_4$ said to$_3$ $_6$ him$_5$. 11. This one$_1$ stands$_3$ here$_2$ looking at himself much$_4$. 12.—I$_4$ look$_3$ very$_1$ nice$_2$,— said$_5$ that$_6$ grasshopper$_7$. 13.—Already$_3$ I$_2$ received$_8$ that$_1$ nice$_4$ designed$_5$ coat$_8$ (the) way I want$_{6\ 7}$. I$_{10}$ will go$_9$,—thus$_{11}$ said$_{12}$ that one$_{13}$. 14. At this place$_1$ that one$_2$ flew /off$_4$/ back$_3$; (and) arrived$_{10}$ there$_5$ (at the) place$_8$ (where) those various$_6$ grasshoppers$_7$ are flying a lot /to$_9$/. 15. Those$_1$ grasshoppers$_2$ (said),—Who$_4$ (is) that$_3$, (who) looks$_6$ pretty$_5$, (who) here$_7$ among us$_8$ /is/ sitting$_9$?—16. One$_1$ said$_{5\ 6}$,—It$_3$ (is) that one$_2$, returned from buying$_4$.—17. As$_4$ they$_3$ wished for$_4$ that$_2$, that one$_1$ told$_{10}$ them$_9$ in that way$_5$ [how] he$_7$ met$_8$ that one$_6$. 18. These various$_1$ grsshoppers$_2$ all flew off$_5$ (in) various ways$_3$ towards the going down (of the) sun$_4$ (and they) stay$_6$ (and when) these various ones$_7$ all returned$_8$, these various ones$_{10}$ are designed$_{11}$ pretty$_9$. 19. As$_5$ those various$_2$ designed$_3$ grasshoppers$_4$ are living$_5$ there$_1$, one from a different kind$_6$ came up$_8$ to them$_7$. 20. That one$_1$ said to$_{7\ 9}$ them$_8$,—How is it$_4$ all you$_2$ grey grasshoppers$_3$ are designed$_6$ pretty$_5$?—21. Those ones$_1$ are saying$_{14\ 15}$,—We$_3$ shopped around$_2$. Thus$_4$ at that time$_5$ when$_{13}$ he$_{12}$ bought$_{13}$ the nice$_{10}$ designed$_{11}$ coat$_{13}$ (someone) named$_9$ that$_6$ grey grasshopper$_7$ "Is Returned from Buying$_8$."—22. That is all$_1$.

Stories reproduced this way are more laborious to read than simple translations but provide a much richer sense of what is being communicated. First of all, a record of the Native voice is established, and even someone not conversant with the native language can see the vocabulary and grammar (word order), and thus gets some sense of pacing, vocal quality, and the nuances of meaning. In this case the conversational pace is highlighted by the transcriber using dashes to set off alternating quotations. Several narrative devices, in this case ones that are customary in Comanche storytelling, are also evident. The aforementioned quotations are important because Comanche stories, and indeed all Plains stories, rely heavily on character dialogue, even expressing the thoughts of characters as statements from them. There is very purposeful use of the pronouns "this" and "that" and the word "here" to distinguish between the first grasshopper and the other grasshopper he meets, making the main character and his experience more immediate to the listener. Repetition of words (Sentence 5, "goes flying, goes flying") is a common way of emphasizing extended or continuous action in Comanche, and Comanche storytellers use this device whether telling stories in Comanche or English. This practice may also be related to the Comanche linguistic trait of reduplicating initial sounds in motion verbs for emphasis. Here the teller creates a sense of significant distance by repeating the reference to flight.

The decisive moment for the adventurous grasshopper takes place as he sits on a "big rock hill"; such allusions to high landmarks as points of revelation are a common element in Comanche stories. Also notable are the opening and closing formula phrases, "Long ago, it is said . . . " and "That is all," which again are customary in Comanche storytelling. These are somewhat similar to the phrases "Once upon a time" and "happily ever after" in English fairytales in that they serve to mark off the story from other kinds of verbalization and cue the listener. The phrase "it is said" also places the narrator in a remote position with respect to the occurrences she is about to relate, in effect declaring "this is something I heard about, not saw directly," which is the common subject position for Indian storytellers.

Beyond these structural characteristics, it must be understood that a storyteller and listeners bring all manner of linguistic and cultural associations to the story by which they process its meaning, and which are not apparent to someone outside the culture. The Comanche story makes more sense if one knows that there is a great variety of grasshoppers found on the open plains of Comanche country (over 100 species) and that many of these types when viewed close up display distinguishing body features and colors, sometimes vivid markings arranged in marvelous geometric patterns. Although interesting in and of itself, the variation of grasshoppers may have been of special concern because in the past Comanches ate grasshoppers as an emergency food. But aside from this factor, variations in natural forms are important in teaching young people to be observant of their surroundings, a common concern in storytelling. In the story above, the main character is introduced as *ahtakíi?*, a generic grasshopper term reducible to "horn," in reference to the insect's horny face, and probably-*kíi* is an onomatopoeia element. The big grasshopper that he meets is a different kind, *piawosa?áa?ra?*. This name refers to a very large green variety and literally means "big suitcase uncle," after the notion that it wears large saddlebags or parfleches. Further along, the main character is called *esi?ahtamúu?a*, a more specific term for a grayish grasshopper, literally, "gray horny nose." This plain grasshopper is then transformed in the story into another recognized variety, the multicolored *tumuuko?ikatu*, "is returned from buying," also called *tumuuko?i?*, "to buy" or "to trade." In the traditional Comanche frame of reference, colorful textiles for clothing are acquired through trade. So the tale is in part a just-so story about the origin of one colorful variety of grasshopper. Listeners might know that the kinds of grasshoppers mentioned exist within an even larger semantic field that includes the red *ekawi*, the yellow *óhawi*, the *pásia* with yellow thighs, and the *kwasituna*, a type with a straight tail.

There is even more cultural significance in this story, however. The little grasshopper goes on a long, intentional journey to a hill to find what he is looking for. Hill landmarks such as Quitaque in Texas were used by the Comanches as the meeting places for trade with other tribes and the Comanchero merchants who brought colorful cloth from New Mexico. Moreover, the word for the "big rock hill" used in this story, *biarupinoo*, is also used as a proper noun in Comanche to name the sacred cliffs called Medicine Bluffs north of Lawton, Oklahoma, where people went on vision quests; so there is some suggestion of the supernatural in the grasshopper's adventure. This meaning is heightened by other details. The grasshopper flies toward the sun to obtain his colors. Throughout the Uto-Aztecan world (Comanche is a language in this family), the bright colors of flowers, birds, and insects are regarded as manifestations of the power of the shining sun. A sacred complement to this formula is the medicine power of the earth, as represented in mineral paints such as red and yellow ochre applied to the body, and indeed the little grasshopper is anointed by the big one with earthen paint ("different kinds of little stones"). Also inherent in the story are more general notions about the importance of trading and the value of beauty and personal adornment; and there is allusion to how personal names are best acquired—through notable deeds and adventures. Thus, the story touches on several aspects of Comanche natural history, religion, and social custom, and in doing so it teaches cultural knowledge in a way that is appealing to listeners, especially children. All this is not to say that a teller or listeners always have all of these significances in mind, but they are embedded there and perpetuated nonetheless.

Another aspect of narratives not easily captured in written form is the manner in which they are delivered and received. The performance of narratives as a communicative act involving the teller and audience is an important consideration in understanding their meaning and functions. On the Plains, performance practices are fairly standardized. Usually stories are told by one or more of the elders to a grouping of people. It is best not to tell them off the cuff, but always when the time and setting feel appropriate. It is a universal belief among the Plains tribes that traditional stories are supposed to be told during the winter and preferably after dark. This rule is especially applicable to myths, since stories having to do with the correct order of the cosmos must reflect the concern for order in the manner of their telling.

When a reason is given for this belief, it is usually said that winter evenings were when families were gathered for safety and warmth around the fireplace and had the leisure time away from buffalo hunting and related chores. It is often said that telling stories out of season can invite supernatural punishment; a summertime story might cause the sudden appearance of a dangerous snake. That the hearth is the idealized setting for storytelling further shows how the transmission of tribal knowledge is perceived to be a serious social duty nested in the family and kin group.

The techniques of oral narrative delivery are also typically not captured in written form, but in reading texts one should imagine how the storyteller uses body posture, gestures, tone of voice, abrupt shifts to signal dialogue, and sound effects to enhance the dramatic quality of the stories. The continuous reactions and responsive commentary interjected by listeners are also part of the total experience.

Another common belief among Indian storytellers is that they should not tell the same tale more than once in a season. This belief stems from the notion that the tales, myths in particular, are part of a long cycle of related stories that describe the continuing adventures of the main characters, and which should be delivered in sequence so as to complete the cycle. Viewed together, one can see that certain individual narratives can form a sequence. Often, however, in practice it is not possible or practical for storytellers and their listeners to complete a cycle, owing to time constraints, the mobility of individuals, incomplete story inventories among some storytellers, and the nature of the stories themselves. Particularly because parts of stories are recombined in various ways in a natural process of variation as they are heard and repeated within and between generations, a "correct" sequence of stories can become obscured or unimportant. In other instances story cycles are maintained with a strong commitment and respectful attitude.

The modular quality of oral narratives has led to the classification of narrative motifs. A motif can be any element that recurs across stories: a character, kind of character, object, action, concept, or structural feature of narrative. In the Comanche story given above, some of the motifs are the young adventurer, the mother, the journey of discovery, the anointing with earth pigments, and the visionary experience in a high place (which functions both as a location and plot apex). Such elements can be found in many other stories. Although Native storytellers typically do not think in terms of motifs when generating or discussing stories, the concept of motif has been useful to those studying a society's narratives from the outside, and for cross-cultural comparisons. Folklorists have given names and numbers to motifs and compiled them, most comprehensively in the *Motif-Index of Folk-Literature* (Thompson 1955–1958). A similar but distinguishable concept to motif is that of *type*, which refers to recurring overall plots. The story types that occur across North America and often beyond have also been named and indexed for comparative purposes. Some of the common story types found on the Plains include:

> The Eye-Juggler (coyote induces another animal to juggle its eyeballs, and they get stuck in a tree, blinding the animal; or, coyote imitates the stunt and blinds himself)
>
> The Star Husband (a girl looks longingly at a beautiful star and climbs heavenward on a rope to marry it; often used to explain the origin of the Pleiades or another constellation)
>
> The Earth-Diver (during a primordial flood a series of animals is dispatched to dive for mud; one succeeds and thereby establishes solid land)
>
> The Release of the Wild Animals (an ogress imprisons all the buffalos underground and a team of animals takes turns trying to release them, the last—the smallest one or the culture hero—successfully) (see Chapter 3)
>
> The Poor Boy (a small, poor boy who lives on the outskirts of camp with his grandmother perseveres and, sometimes with the help of miraculous powers, triumphs in war and wins the hand of a chief's beautiful daughter)
>
> The Deserted Children (children playing carelessly off at a distance are left behind by their camp; they encounter a malevolent old woman or ogre whose clutches they escape with tricks, magic, and the help of friendly animals)

How these themes are fleshed out with variations of detail and plot twists can vary tremendously,

yielding quite different narratives even among storytellers within the same tribe. (Indeed, there can be huge disagreement among tribe members about what is correct or admissible within their local tradition). The variations are themselves fascinating. Storytellers modify, substitute, and recombine motifs and tale types to create versions that in their minds are more entertaining, or more congruent with the specific natural and cultural environments of their tribe. Sometimes storytellers make changes on a whim or to add their personal flourish, or because they are not remembering exactly the story as they told it before or heard it from someone else. These changes have no larger intentional meaning. Other times, their changes are purposeful adjustments that reflect local notions about such matters as the economic and symbolic value of particular animals, how kinship and social relations are conceived, and how the supernatural world operates. Although it is possible to read too much significance into the differences, the study of oral narrative variations has stimulated much theorizing. Anthropologists, notably the French structuralist Claude Levi-Strauss (1908–2009), have drawn broad conclusions about how the human mind functions, and proposed regional and tribal cultural patterns, on the basis of the substitutions and inversions that have been introduced as tales were retold throughout South and North America, including the Plains.

Such transformation can be seen at work in the following four versions of the Deserted Children story:

> Version I: All the children of a camp are off playing. One man proposes that the adults abandon the children by moving camp, and they do so. The oldest girl leads the children in a search to find the camp. They are taken in by an old woman who is actually a ghost. She kills all but the youngest girl and her little brother, who promise to work for her fetching wood and water. The girl brings a series of different kinds of wood and water, and the old woman is only satisfied with the kind of twigs known as "ghost ropes" and stagnant water. The children escape by feigning

that they are just going outside; the girl leaves an awl in the ground as they get away which answers for them when the old woman calls after them. They come to a large river where a horned water monster demands to be loused. The boy louses him. The "lice" are frogs. The girl cracks a plum seed on her necklace four times to make the monster think that her brother has cracked a louse. The monster gives them a ride across the river. The old woman follows in pursuit. She refuses to louse the monster and he drowns and eats her. The children find the people who deserted them. Their parents and other relatives all deny knowing them. One man proposes that the children be tied and left hanging from a tree. A sick dog from the camp lingers behind and releases them. The children and dog find buffalos which the boy kills by gazing at them. They live prosperously. The girl dresses a pile of buffalo skins by sitting on them. She makes a tipi which is magically furnished. The dog becomes an old man. They find antelopes which the boy kills by gazing at them. Four bears arrive to guard their property. Their former campmates, now starving, attempt to rejoin them, and are driven away by the bears. The girl and her brother take spouses from the group, then the brother strikes the rest dead with his gaze.

(Gros Ventre; after Kroeber 1907:102–105)

Version II: While playing away from camp, two children, a brother and sister, call the chief an ugly name as he passes near. He directs the camp to move and abandon them. The children, forlorn, search for the camp and finally catch up. Their parents deny ever knowing them. The chief ties the children up and they are left to starve as he leads the camp to move again. An old dog releases the children. They find buffalos which the boy kills by gazing at them. The girl processes the meat and skins by sitting on them. They live prosperously and grow up. Their former campmates, now starving, attempt to rejoin them. The children deny ever knowing their parents.

(Arapaho; after Dorsey and Kroeber 1998:293–294)

Version III: Four children playing by a creek are joined by on older girl with a baby on her back. In the meantime their camp moves away without the children noticing. A succession of three of the children reports to the others that the camp has moved, but only the third is believed. They attempt to follow the camp's trail. Coyote comes along to warn them not to disturb the owl. As they pass the owl's house the baby cries and the owl hears him. The owl summons all the children and (implicitly) holds them captive with the intention of eating them. They escape by feigning to go to the creek to wash. As they get away they appeal to a frog for help, who answers for them when the owl calls after them. The owl comes upon the frog and attempts to kill him with his cane, but the frog jumps into the water, leaving the owl standing on the bank. The owl pursues the children. The children come upon a big creek and appeal to a fish-crane for help. The crane makes the oldest girl hold a louse in her mouth and bridges the creek with its leg, allowing the children to cross. The owl appeals to the crane for help crossing and is subject to the same condition, but the owl spits out the louse in mid-stream and falls into the creek. The owl, brandishing a stone club, continues pursuing the children and finds them on an open prairie. The children appeal to a buffalo calf for protection. As the owl approaches with its maul, the buffalo-calf charges him. The calf charges the owl and butts him up to the moon, where he can still be seen.

(Comanche; after St. Clair and Lowie 1909:275–276)

Version IV: Three children, a girl and her younger brother and sister, are mistreated and run away from home. They meet an old woman who is a child-eating ogress, and are invited to her tipi. The elder girl is aware of the danger and stays awake all night to guard her siblings. In the morning the children escape by feigning to go to a stream to fetch water. At the stream they appeal to a frog for help, who answers for them when the ogress calls after them. This explains the croaking of frogs. The ogress finally realizes the deception (and implicitly pursues the children). The children run to another stream and meet a crane. The crane lays down her neck for them to cross, but also does the same for the pursuing ogress. The children next come upon three buffaloes—a bull, cow, and a little red calf, whom they appeal to for protection. The cow and bull in turn charge the ogress but are killed. The calf charges the ogress and butts her up to the moon, where she can still be seen.

(Comanche; after Kardiner 1945:69)

In each example the main theme is child abandonment, but this arguably primal human worry is treated differently in each instance. In Version I children are purposely abandoned; in Version II, it is specifically done because they insult a chief. In Version III they are left behind accidentally, and in Version IV they are runaways. It seems that in the Gros Ventre and Arapaho tales the lesson is that parents should not be cruel, but in the Comanche versions the lesson is to children, not to play carelessly or run away. The number of children varies from an entire village's worth to a brother–sister pair. The older girl or sister, an important Plains social role (see Chapter 5), is a prominent character in Versions I, III, and IV, but not II. Only in Version I are any of the children killed, and in this case the protagonists are quickly reduced to a brother–sister pair. Versions I and II are different from the Comanche versions in that the parents are punished, by death in I and by rejection in II. Actually, Version I combines two episodes, the magic flight related in Versions III and IV followed by the mutual rejection of parents and children seen in Version II. Coyote makes an appearance only in Version III; perhaps he is relatable in a structural sense to the dog in Versions I and II. There are magical sequences in Version I (types of wood and water) and Version IV (the three buffalo defenders) analogous to the "three wishes" common in European fairy tales. The crossing of streams is important in all versions but varies in detail. The motif of the louse occurs in the Gros Ventre and

also one (but not both) of the Comanche versions, though in Version I the "lice" turn out to be frogs. The Comanche versions also have frogs, although here the frog makes its call to deceive the villain while the children escape, while in Gros Ventre it is an (animate) awl that aids the escape. In the Comanche versions live buffalos protect the children; in the Gros Ventre and Arapaho tales the buffalos are killed (give their lives) for food and shelter. The villains and their fates are similar but distinct in each telling. This dizzying list is only a partial accounting of the substitutions and inversions at work across the four versions, and this discussion will stop short of proposing specific tribal meanings for these variations, and just make the point that types and motifs are grist for a lively, endless process of narrative reinvention.

Meanings come alive most vividly through the personalities and activities of story characters. Chief among the character motifs is the one known to folklorists as the "trickster." Trickster figures are found in tales throughout the world but play a pronounced role in American Indian storytelling. This character is one who wanders aimlessly from one situation to another causing mischief for those he encounters. His hunger, bodily functions, and lechery are unbounded and uncontrolled. Many of the stories therefore include ridiculous scatological and bawdy situations which most tribes find acceptable and amusing, though non-Indians might consider them obscene. The trickster is selfish and ill-tempered; he has no conscience and seldom shows remorse. Often his tricks backfire.

In some tribal traditions the trickster never reforms, and listeners learn their lessons about bad behavior through the trickster's ongoing misfortune. In other traditions, as the trickster moves through a series of adventures he learns from his mistakes and becomes better behaved, more socially adept, and more humanlike. By following the trickster's conversion, listeners learn what is improper and proper behavior, and the origins of the etiquette and morals that make people social beings—human.

On the Plains, the trickster usually appears in animal guise, either as a spider, such as the Lakota *Inktomi* and Omaha *Iktinike*, or as a coyote; and he interacts with other animals. In rare instances spider and coyote even appear together as competing tricksters. Both the spider and the coyote are perceived of as having inherent trickster qualities. The spider appears knowing and clever in the way it hides underground, spins webs, and floats on invisible silk. Able to move easily among the lower, middle, and upper worlds, it exhibits potential as a sacred creature. Coyotes are notorious for their apparent cleverness and opportunism. Some Comanche names for the coyote highlight these traits: *káawosą* ("trick sack"); *káarena'pï?* ("tricky man"); *isapʉ* ("liar"); *tʉkʉwa?ra* ("food grabs"). Despite its unflattering reputation, the coyote earns attention as a potentially sacred creature because of its kinship with a noble sacred animal, the wolf. In the Algonquian northeast the trickster is a rabbit, and so it is among the Plains Crees and Plains Ojibwas; the rabbit also appears as an alternative to the spider sometimes in Lakota, Osage, and Omaha stories. The Plains Crees also feature another northern incarnation of the trickster named Wi-sak-a-chak (often Anglicized as Whiskey Jack), who is modeled on the Canada jay, another species thought to be mischievous.

Iktiniki meets Coyote on a walk. Coyote tells him of a dead horse he has found and suggests that they both drag it to Coyote's house to eat. Coyote ties Iktiniki's hands to the horse's tail and urges him to pull. But the horse is not dead; it stampedes and drags Iktiniki though the thorn bushes. Coyote laughs at his trick. Iktiniki plots his revenge and waits until winter. He takes Coyote out on a frozen lake and instructs him to put his tail through a hole in the ice to catch a fish. When the tail freezes in place, Coyote thinks he has caught a big fish. They both pull until they tear Coyote's tail off.

(Omaha; after Erdoes and Ortiz 1998:112–114)

Coyote is starving and goes along a creek bank. He repeatedly sees his reflection in the water and, thinking it is another coyote also trying to find food, becomes angry. He charges the "other" coyote and drowns because he cannot swim.

(Arikara; after Parks 1996:366)

Rabbit boasts to Squirrel that he can do anything with Buffalo. To prove it, he rides Buffalo to Squirrel's tree. He pretends to be sick so Buffalo will give him a ride. Rabbit saddles Buffalo, decorates him with a bell and feather, and whips him. As they approach Squirrel, Rabbit boasts, "See what I told you," and with that the Buffalo bucks and kicks, and the Rabbit jumps into the bush, with Buffalo chasing after him.

(Osage; after Dorsey 1904:9)

Wi-sak-a-chak eats many berries though the berries warn him that they will cause flatulence. Wi-sak-a-chak then goes hunting, but he breaks wind and scares the game and becomes angry at his anus. He burns his rump by sitting on hot stones. He comes upon a hill, and, too sore to climb, he walks around it instead. He walks in a circle thinking he is on someone else's trail. He finds a scab from his rump and thinks it is dried meat that his grandmother has lost. Hungry, he eats it. A little bird tells him he is eating himself but Wi-sak-a-chak calls him a liar.

(Plains Cree; after Dusenberry 1962:148–149)

While tricksters most frequently appear as animals, they are often described in ambiguous terms as animal-humans, because the stories involve their transformation from wild to social beings; or, they are described as fully human. Ambiguity may be expressed in phrases such as "Coyote was a man who . . . " and the appellation Old Man Coyote. As a human character, the trickster appears again as Inktomi (Sioux) and with such other names as Nihansan (Arapaho) or Nixant (Gros Ventre), Sitconski (Assiniboine), Saynday (Kiowa), Veeho (Cheyenne), and Old

Man Napi (Blackfoot). The last two are some-times explicitly associated with white men, reflecting a cultural stereotype that white people are deceitful.

Inktomi thinks only of copulating. He pursues a beautiful young girl. The girl is annoyed and complains to Inktomi's wife. They agree to change places. The young girl invites Inktomi to her tipi where his wife is waiting. In the dark-ness he believes he is making love to the girl and compares her to his old wife. In the morning he discovers who he is with. His wife beats him with a club.

(Lakota; after Erdoes and Ortiz 1998:123–125)

Inktomi marries at the age of 14 despite his parents' advice that he is too young. Before he moves in with his wife, his parents warn him that it would be wrong to speak directly or make love to his mother-in-law. But Inktomi lusts after his widowed mother-in-law and seduces her in an elaborate pretense.

(Lakota; Erdoes and Ortiz 1998:128–131)

Nihansan asks for the power to send his eyes up into a tree. He does not obey the directions not to repeat the trick more than four times. His eyes do not return and he is blinded. He asks a mole for his eyes and the mole agrees. Nihansan finds his own eyes and places them in their sockets again, and throws away the mole's eyes. That is why the mole is blind.

(Arapaho; after Dorsey and Kroeber 1998:51–52)

Veeho encounters a man with strange powers. The man is able to command stones and turn them over without touching them. Veeho begs the man for his power, and the man takes pity on him and decides to give it to him with the condition that he use the power no more than four times. Veeho displays the power four times to gain respect among his people. The people hail him as a chief, and he marries a chief's beautiful daughter. He forgets the injunction and

tries to impress the people a fifth time. A big rock chases him down and traps him. He appeals in turn to a buffalo, bear, and moose to release him but they are not able. He then tells an eagle that the rock has insulted him, and the enraged eagle breaks the rock, releasing Veeho. Veeho goes home bruised and broken, and his wife decides to leave him and declares him a fool.

(Northern Cheyenne; after Erdoes and Ortiz 1998:139–141)

Two other character motifs that often merge with each other and the trickster role are "creator" and "culture hero." The creator is the agent whose miraculous activity results in the universe as we know it: through a series of adventures and inter-actions with other characters, he differentiates life from death, day from night, summer from winter, humans from animals, and he imbues people and animals with their notable characteristics; and, he may make the mountains, rivers, stars, and so forth. The culture hero is similar in establishing particular tribal traditions, such as mourning cus-toms, ceremonies, dances, languages, and social divisions, by negotiating with other characters, performing miracles, and mentoring humans.

Old Man Coyote is cold. With a team of ani-mal accomplices, and by a sequence of tricks, Coyote steals summer from the Old Woman who possesses it. The Old Woman's children pursue and finally catch Coyote. Coyote refuses to give back summer and the children threaten to make war on him. Coyote proposes to share summer with them for half the year, and each accepts winter for the other half.

(Crow; after Erdoes and Ortiz 1998:13–15)

Saynday meets a (female) red ant. In those days the ant was round like a ball. He reduces his size to match hers. They debate the pros and cons of people dying. Saynday wishes that dead people should be reborn in four days; Ant argues that the world would get too full, and that dead people are tired and should be allowed to stay dead.

Saynday gives in to Ant's preference but warns her that she will have to live with the decision and mourn. Four days later Saynday finds the ant in the same place and she is sobbing. A buffalo has stepped on her boy and killed him. She begins cutting herself in two. Saynday stops her before she cuts off her head completely. Saynday then proclaims that from now on, when Kiowa women mourn, they should cut themselves but not kill themselves in sorrow.

(Kiowa; after Marriott and Rachlin 1968:223–225)

Besides the tricksters there are any number of animal characters who interact in tales, ranging from bear and bison to rabbit and prairie dog to turkey, quail, and chickadee. Rabbits, distinct from the Algonquian trickster figure, are also part of this cast. Normally these characters reflect some natural qualities of the animal. The bear and chickadee both figure in stories about seasonality, the former because of its habit of hibernating and the latter because it appears in numbers at the turn of the seasons, and because this bird has an unusual barbed tongue, and the number of barbs is thought to vary with passing months. The quail is often named Scares People on account of its habit of flushing suddenly from cover.

Often the animals who endure Coyote's antics are species that live and find safety in "communities" (prairie dog towns, quail coveys), and their social and timid nature contrasts with Coyote's solitary, selfish, and predatory ways; not to mention these animals are the natural prey of natural coyotes. They are also normally wary animals, and they fall victim to the coyote's tricks only when they let down their guard. These weaklings nevertheless often manage to turn the tables on their attacker. But just as the trickster is sometimes human, so may be his victims. There are plenty of tales in which he deals with people instead of animals. In some tales from the nineteenth century or later, Coyote plays his pranks on white cowboys, soldiers, and preachers. In these

tales, the trickster's chicanery becomes a Native defense against the supposed greater immorality of non-Indians. Coyote always triumphs in these stories.

Coyote commands Turkey to go to his house to be cooked by his wife. But when Turkey arrives at Coyote's house he tells the wife that Coyote sent him to copulate with her, and she complies. When Coyote gets home he realizes that Turkey had played a trick on him. Coyote sets out to kill Turkey. He fails at this task, and when he returns home, Coyote finds that his neglected family has starved to death. Whenever a coyote howls it is said he is crying over the death of his wife and children.

(Wichita; Dorsey 1995:289–290)

Coyote comes upon Rabbit with a leather pouch on his back. Coyote is curious and guesses that Rabbit has tobacco in the pouch. Rabbit tells Coyote that he has nothing that Coyote might want. But Coyote just thinks that Rabbit is being stingy. Insistent and then angry, he tears open the pouch. Lots of fleas are released and they infest Coyote. He runs off howling. This is why coyotes howl.

(Lakota; after Erdoes and Ortiz 1998:50–51).

A white man has heard about Coyote's trickery. He puts on fine cloths, mounts a good horse, and seeks Coyote, challenging him to cheat him right before his eyes. Coyote says he must go get his stuff for scheming. He borrows the man's horse, as well as his clothes so the horse will not be afraid of him. Coyote then gallops away, declaring "I have fooled you already."

(Comanche; after St. Clair and Lowie 1909:276)

The cast of animal and human characters may also appear in sundry combinations without the presence of the trickster. The resultant stories can be similar to, or derivative of, trickster tales in their structure and the way they explain origins or teach lessons about correct behavior. Others are simply stories about minor adventures. Sometimes they have been labeled "fables" because of their animal actors and moral purpose. The tale of the grasshopper given above is one example of an animal tale without trickster.

> Skunk and Opossum live together as sisters-in-law. Skunk proposes that they each eat their young. Opossum eats her young first. Skunk then proposes that they separate, and takes her young away. Skunk boasts that now only she has her young. Opossum becomes mad and defecates in Skunk's face and kills her.
>
> (Osage; after Dorsey 1904:11)

> A little boy steals a toy wagon when he and his mother go to a spring. He tries to conceal it from her. She makes him bring it back to the place he found it in the dark, scaring him, and tells him why he should not steal.
>
> (Comanche; after Canonge 1958:81–84).

> Four men returning from a war party come upon a big lake. They watch a panther and alligator battle in the water, killing each other.
>
> (Comanche; after Canonge 1958:93–94)

A class of myths that stands apart from the trickster cycle involves semi-deities, often female, who figure as alternate culture heroes in the origins of tribes and tribal customs. The Lakotas say that White Buffalo Calf Woman visited the people for four days and bestowed their seven major ceremonies. The character Corn (Silk) Woman or the similar Reed Woman appear in Mandan, Arikara, Omaha, and Sioux tales, as a spirit patron of horticulture. The Sioux explain *Anukite* (Double-Face, Double Woman, Two Face) either as a man who can change into a woman or as a beautiful woman who was punished for infidelity with a second, ugly face. She also appears as a duo of spirit women representing alternate answers in divination. In dreams

they inspire women to quillwork and tanning, or they inspire cross-gender behaviors among women and men (see Chapter 5). Various human old women and beautiful daughters are also standard characters, and along with the female spirits they evoke life stages and the presence or absence of fecundity, and signify the fundamental importance of women in survival, procreation, and social life.

> A young man goes hunting and finds a big buffalo. But there is nothing for him to hide behind in order to approach the game. Each morning he finds the buffalo again, facing a different cardinal direction, and each time fails to take a shot. One morning the buffalo is gone, and a strange plant is sprouting where it stood. He brings the holy men to see the plants. They decide to fence off the plants, discover at midsummer it is growing ears, and they learn to cook and eat the ears. They learn to plant the corn and grow more. A holy man is inspired to think of the ear of corn as a woman and instructs his wife to make a dress for it. She dresses the ear of corn, addresses it as mother, and sends it floating away in the river. Sometime later the woman arrives among them again and is recognized as Mother Corn, a counterpart of the Creator who helps people on earth.
>
> (Arikara; after Parks 1996:153–156)

Seemingly animate aspects of nature, including the sun, moon, stars, clouds, and winds, as well inanimate objects like mountains, stones, and even household items like the awl in the Deserted Children story given above, may serve as narrative characters. There are dwarves, giants, and monsters described by modern people as resembling dinosaurs and great snapping turtles. The standardized Plains water monster, like the one in the Deserted Children story, is a long saurian with horns. Its nemesis is the thunderbird, whose cry is thunder and eye flashes, lightning. A man with a sharpened leg is able to jump and stick himself in the trees. There are ogres, including the owl in the

FIGURE 8.1   *Anukite is depicted in this 1962 casein painting entitled* Double Woman *by Oscar Howe (Mazuha Hokshina, "Trader Boy," Yanktonai, 1915–1983).*

Deserted Children story, which some modern storytellers liken to the legendary Bigfoot; a blood clot that turns into a boy; a one-eyed bounding human head or skull; and an animated ball of pounded meat that bounces here and there.

> Meatball lopes along a road and comes upon Coyote lying in wait. Coyote professes to be starving and meatball offers him a bite of himself. Coyote moves ahead down the road repeatedly and secures more bites this way. The fourth time, meatball sees the meat between Coyote's teeth and realizes he is being tricked by the same Coyote. Then Coyote runs away.
>
> (Comanche; after Canonge 1958:21–23)

Plains legends, those stories situated in human time and space, have their own stock roles. The idea of the scout venturing forth in advance of his band to discover wonders is very common. Scouts are often able to become invisible in order to eavesdrop on talking buffalos or secretly witness the arrival of the first white men. Scouts exemplify the bold adventurous spirit that is the ideal for horse nomads. One version of this character among the Comanches is aptly named *Sokoweki*, "Land Seeker." In contrast to this adventurer are the contrary characters, braves who never leave their tipis. Another legendary figure is the poor, unpopular, sometimes deformed orphan boy, who though diminutive

FIGURE 8.2   Untitled 1939 painting by Acee Blue Eagle (Creek/Pawnee/Wichita, 1907–1959) showing thunderbirds attacking a water monster.

rises to the occasion in some tribal emergency and surprises everyone with his skill, bravery, and supernatural power. Little Brown Boy is the name given to this character in some Comanche stories; he is known as Wets the Bed among the Wichitas, Burnt Belly among the Pawnees, and Bloody Hands among the Arikaras. Little Brown Boy teaches about self-initiative and class mobility. Among the Upper Missouri tribes, many stories feature the Two Men, holy men who are also stars. Yet another figure of legend is the Scalped Man, the ghost of a scalped warrior who terrorizes the living.

Perhaps because so much significance can be invested in these memorable characters, Indian storytelling does not require elaborate plots, character development, or tidy story lines in which there is a clear outcome. For even though it is recognized that many of the stories that have been collected are fragmentary, still, Native stories need not conform to the structural expectations of non-Indian oral or written literature. Often trickster tales relate a sequence of interactions between coyote and other animals with no strong climax or resolution.

The lack of certain formal conventions may strike non-Indian listeners and readers as unusual. But such tales are understood as segments of a long ongoing series of situations (which are not only told in story form but then also explored further in conversation *about* the stories), and therefore they are regarded as meaningful and satisfying.

And, there are some stories that do have a definable structure of tension and resolution. There is also a tolerance for internal contradictions. In many tribal stories of the origination of the universe, the creator interacts with other beings who somehow already exist. The trickster character is especially capable of logically impossible activities. He can shift shape (an ability that supports the theme of personal transformation), or he is dismembered or dies, only to reassemble or resurrect himself within the same story or in a subsequent one.

Returning at last to the initial question of the historical value of oral narratives, we can see how some stories would provide very fanciful explanations of remote times. Thus, there are tales like the Plains Cree account of Wi-sak-a-chak's creating hills in Southern Alberta by sliding on his buttocks, the Comanche story in which the thunderbird crashed and produced a canyon in West Texas, and the myths of many tribes concerning the origins of the butte known as Bear's Lodge or Devils (*sic*) Tower in Wyoming. But the presence of these myths should not obscure the fact that Indian people also pass down stories about past events which are devoid of miraculous elements and which sometimes match very closely or exceed in precision the records produced by non-Indians. A host of stories from various tribes have been collected which relate genealogies, migrations, the fusion and fission of subtribal units, legal cases concerning murder and adultery, famous raids and battles, peace negotiations, descriptions of celebrated leaders, and other matters worth remembering. Many of these narratives are still in circulation in Indian communities today, and together they amount to a priceless resource for understanding the American past.

Apart from narratives there are other, briefer modes of traditional oral expression, though these have not been heavily documented on the Plains. Prayers appear to have been recited in standardized forms to the extent that several have been collected and presented as oral literature, as in this Omaha example:

Wa-kon'da [Great Spirit]
here needy he stands
and I am he
(Fletcher 1995:26)

Song texts along with prayers like this one make up a rich body of Native poetry. Additional examples of prayers and songs are given elsewhere in this book in context.

Joking has always played a part in maintaining cordial social relations and easing stress, and the capacity of Indian people for humor and wit is often noted. Older traditional humor mostly relies on riddles—enigmas posed for solution—or wordplay, or conundrums, which are riddles in which the solution depends on wordplay. Indian riddles often take a simple form, not involving wit or convoluted logic so much as just testing the listener's memory about local folk sayings or conventions. The oddest of these, from a non-Indian perspective, is the question "What am I thinking of?" which is common as a game throughout Native North America. Other riddles have standard answers:

There is a place cut up by gullies. What is it? (an old woman's face)

(Omaha; J. Dorsey 1884:334)

What is it that for one day has its own way? (a prairie fire)

(Comanche; McAllester 1964:254)

What is inside you like lightning? (meanness)

(Comanche; Ibid.:255)

What makes a cottonwood tree grow out of the top of your head? (telling a lie)

(Comanche; Ibid.)

Riddles sometimes appear as knowledge tests within myths or in ceremonies that promote healing or coax the arrival of summer. For example, in an Arapaho tale Blood Clot Boy defeats the evil White Owl in a riddle contest:

What is the most useful thing? (the eyes)
    Tell me what you live on mostly (buffalo meat)
    . . . tell me who are the parties who never get tired of motioning to come (the eyelids)

        (Dorsey and Kroeber 1998:306–307)

Closely related to these riddles are proverbs, terse sayings encapsulating some valued truth. The Omahas would say, "He is like an animal," meaning "he is obstinate," or "The raccoon wet his head," a figure of speech meaning that someone talks softly and smoothly when trying to persuade (Dorsey 1884:334). In Comanche to say "saddle the horses" is similar to using the English expression "go for broke," "go all-out," or "no holds barred" (Gelo 1983:7). Simile and metaphor are also employed, as in the Comanche phrase "long as a wolf's yawn," said of something taking too long, or the word *ekapabi* (vulture; literally "red head") for "penis" (McAllester 1964:257).

Nowadays Indian people tell jokes with Native themes principally in English and in forms that are familiar to Euro-Americans. The emcees at powwow arenas are a handy source for modern Indian jokes. As they manage the dancing and other activities, they punctuate their spoken directions with rehearsed jokes and improvised humorous asides. Their jokes and quips depend on wordplay in English and Indian languages, parody of non-Indian culture, and the stereotypes and dilemmas of modern Native American identity (Gelo 1999:52, 55):

These two Indians were driving along, and they see a loose pig. They look around, you know, then they grab that pig and put it between them in the front seat and put a hat and some sunglasses on it. Pretty soon they get stopped by the highway patrol. "Have you seen a loose pig?" "No." "Okay, go ahead." After the pickup drives off, one cop says to the other, "What do you suppose that pretty white woman was doing with those two ugly Indians?"

This man who was a real good dancer died. His best friend, who was a good singer, mourned and mourned. Then one day, the dead man visits his friend. "I've got good news. Heaven is wonderful. Every week they have a big powwow." His friend says, "That is wonderful!" A powwow every week? The ghost says, "Yeah, but the bad news is, you're the head singer next week."

Custer wear arrow shirt.

These kinds of jokes are in circulation throughout Indian communities and they are merely collected and recirculated at public events. In their joking patter, powwow emcees ridicule themselves, jest with people in the audience, and touch on topics that are not normally appropriate in polite or ethnically mixed company. In this way they test the boundaries of proper behavior and serve something like the trickster of traditional narrative.

Native oral traditions are likely to remain alive on the Plains as long as their social and cultural contexts remain relevant. As people tell and listen to the old stories today, they align their lives with the intentions of the spirits and the wisdom of the ancestors. In the next two chapters we will examine how the world established in myth by Coyote and Corn Woman, and sustained by legendary scouts and warriors, is renewed again and again by ordinary humans, through their personal and collective rituals.

Sources: Beckwith (1930, 1937); Bowers (1991); Brunvand (1968); Buller (1983); Canonge (1958); Deloria (2006); G. Dorsey (1904, 1995); Dorsey and Kroeber (1998); J. Dorsey 1884; Dusenberry (1962); Echo-Hawk (1997, 2000); Erdoes and Ortiz (1984, 1998); Fletcher (1995); Frey (1995); Gelo (1986, 1994, 1999); Kardiner (1945); Kroeber (1907); Lévi-Strauss

(1990a, 1990b); Marriott and Rachlin (1968); McAllester (1964); Mooney (1979); Parks (1996); Powers (1977); Schoen and Armagost (1992); Skinner (1916); St. Clair and Lowie (1909); Thompson (1955–1958); and Walker (1983).

CHAPTER SUMMARY

Oral traditions are one of the more enduring aspects of Plains Indian culture. The preservation of traditional stories has been a keen interest for Indians and non-Indians too. Such stories record history in the absence of written records, entertain, and encode cultural values. Non-Indians have used the categories myth, legend, and folktale to classify Indian stories. These categories correspond roughly to Native distinctions between stories as primarily mythical or historical. The translation of traditional narratives is always imperfect, although interlinear translation is a fairly thorough method. Storytellers and their audiences apply a host of meanings and interpretations to stories which are grounded in their native language and customs, but not always apparent to outsiders. Also, written translations are inadequate for capturing the performance of storytelling. Storytellers commonly recombine narrative elements. Folklorists have named the recurring motifs and plots to classify stories as they reappear through time and across many tribes. The trickster, an amorphous animal-human whose adventures define cultural norms, is a prominent Plains story character. Besides trickster tales, there are stories about the creation of the universe and tales that celebrate the exploits of historical figures, often in exaggerated form. The memories perpetuated through narrative are a valuable and often dependable source of historical information. Prayers, riddles, proverbs, and word-play are additional lively forms of Indian oral tradition.

QUESTIONS FOR REVIEW

1. Explain the relationship between traditional narratives and history as it has been understood by both Indians and non-Indians.
2. Name and define some of the common story types found on the Plains.
3. Using the "Deserted Children" story type as an example, explain how stories can vary in form and meaning as they are told in different tribes.
4. Discuss the trickster character type. What forms does it take on the Plains? What cultural concerns are explored in stories about the trickster?

CHAPTER 9

RELIGIOUS FUNDAMENTALS

It is a truism that Plains Indians life is infused with spirituality. Indian people are said to enjoy a sense of oneness with the natural world and its nonhuman inhabitants that gives them philosophical grounding and a serene outlook. They are further said to perceive no strict boundary between the natural and supernatural worlds, between the everyday and the mystic or holy. Although this image of Indian religiosity has been exaggerated in odd ways, it is basically accurate. It is also true that Indian religion places firm emphasis on people's active involvement with the world around them and the acquisition of knowledge from personal experience. In its ideal form, Indian religion is lived each moment—a religious attitude is pervasive and not restricted to occasional instances of worship: " . . . for the Plains Indian supernaturalism was not the equivalent of churchgoing of a Sunday, but something that profoundly affected his daily life and offered an explanation of extraordinary occurrences" (Lowie 1982:157). Some of the most profound statements of Native belief are the simple, daily expressions of honor and respect, as when the Lakota medicine man Peter S. Catches, Sr. (1912–1993) was instructed as a child by his uncle to always make his bed in the morning, out of reverence, because the blankets kept him warm at night. More obvious and equally important are the rich mythologies and glorious rituals found throughout the region.

As much as Indian religion has a distinctive character, in the end it deals with universal human concerns. Behind it there is the need for security in an uncertain and often dangerous world. Religion furnishes reasons for good fortune and bad and equips people to control or at least accept what the future may bring. Religion helps people understand how and why humans and the world around them came into existence and what happens to humans at the end of their earthly lives. And, it provides moral guidance as people attempt to get along and treat each other kindly for the mutual benefit of all.

The fundamentals of Plains religion are largely about supernatural power and beings, and the proper ways for humans to interact with these manifestations of the sacred. These beliefs and the basic rituals that derive from them are fairly uniform across the area, though there are sometimes interesting variations among the tribes owing to their different historical origins, subsistence practices, and records of cultural interaction. This chapter will explain the general ingredients of Plains religion and illustrate degrees of uniformity and variance with examples from different tribes.

In approaching the basic questions of religion, as in other areas of culture, there is no substitute for the translation of native-language words, and these will be a focus of the present discussion. It is first necessary, however, to briefly address some of the common social science terms used in discussing Indian belief. Although early theorists argued for a distinction between magic (manipulative techniques associated with "primitive" societies) and religion (prayer and submission practiced by "advanced" societies), it has since been recognized that all systems of belief about the supernatural contain both manipulative and submissive elements, and thus there is no absolute formal distinction between "primitive" and "advanced" belief. The present discussion will refer to Plains belief and worship as religion, recognizing the sophistication of Native traditions and proper respect due them, while occasionally referring to manipulative techniques within Plains religion as magical. It should be noted, however, that Native languages normally do not have a word equivalent to "religion," and some contemporary Indian people would reject the use of this term, which suggests churches, holy days, and hierarchical ministries, in reference to their own traditions, instead preferring the term "spirituality."

The anthropologist Robert Lowie gainsaid the separation of magic and religion and, following the theoretical lead of Robert Marrett (1866–1943), employed the overarching term "supernaturalism" when discussing Plains belief. This tack was not totally helpful from an analytic viewpoint because all magic and religious behaviors concern the supernatural. "Supernatural" is nonetheless a useful term for referring to that which is outside of normal experience, to the unseen dimension that is thought to parallel the usual order of experience, although as we will see, in Plains belief there is often no steady distinction between the normal and

supernatural—one gives way to the other, back and forth, fairly easily. A similar term, one much used by contemporary Indian people, is "sacred," again signifying something apart from the everyday, and also deeper or more important. In a famous formulation of the pioneering French sociologist Emile Durkheim (1858–1917), the "sacred" is contrasted with the "profane," which today often connotes that which is irreverent or disrespectful, but which more basically means "common" or "secular."

There are some other concepts from the anthropological study of religion that could be applied to Plains belief. Edward Tylor (1832–1917) called belief in spiritual beings *animism*, from the Latin *anima*, "soul." Marrett thought that belief in impersonal supernatural power was more basic than a belief in beings, and coined the term *animatism* for belief in power. Yet another term, *animalism*, was proposed by Åke Hultkrantz (1920–2006) for "the mysterious relationship between humans and animals in hunting cultures, manifested, for example, in the idea of spirits in animal form" (Hultkrantz 1987:137). These phenomena are all certainly common features in Plains religion. Their recognition, however, requires more than the application of a standardized term, but instead the careful consideration of cultural details, which in the end may call into question the utility or validity of the term. Also, terms like *animism* were developed in accordance with obsolete assumptions about the mentality of "primitive" peoples, and their employment can contribute to an oversimplified depiction of Plains culture as primal or static.

While sometimes calling into question particular anthropological terms and concepts, the following examination of Plains religion remains anthropological. That is, it is not concerned with the absolute truth or falsity of particular beliefs, but rather how they explain the world for Native people and how they help bond the people together in workable societies. The beliefs explored here are all regarded as true because they are true for those who hold them.

POWER

Regardless of whatever ritualists, ceremonies, or spiritual beings might be present in one tribal tradition or another, all Plains Indian religion is formed around one fundamental concept, that of *power.* "Power" is the English word used by Indians and non-Indians to refer to a phenomenon that is recognized in all Native languages. Algonquian speakers such as the Plains Crees and Cheyennes refer to it as *manitou.* The Numic-speaking Comanches and Shoshones call it *puha,* and the Kiowas say *d]y* (also written *dɑ-e;* pronounced *doy* or *dawe*). For the Pawnees, the term is *kawaharu.* The word is *baaxpée* among the Crows and *xupā* for the linguistically related Hidatsas. The term among the Lakotas is *wowaš'ake.*

Another common English gloss of all these terms is "medicine." The term appears in phrases such as "medicine man" and "making medicine." While this usage is also found among Indians, they do distinguish between medicine as power and as substance—tonic, salve, or herbal remedy—and have native-language words that keep this distinction. For instance, Comanches say *puha* when referring to power but *natsu* for medicinal substance, though they may use the English word "medicine" for either. Lakotas distinguish between *wowaš'ake,* power, and *pejuta,* medicinal substance, a word derived from the terms for "grass" and "root."

An initially helpful take on supernatural power is available by consulting the general scholarly literature on the subject. The power concept appears in cultures well beyond those of Native North America, and there is a longstanding practice of discussing it. One important synthesis was written by Durkheim, who compared power concepts found among natives of North America, Australia, and the South Pacific islands. Anthropologists came to use the Polynesian word *mana* as the generic term. *Mana* is defined as a supernatural or sacred force—outside of normal, everyday experience—and impersonal. It is likened to electricity, as a kind of energy which is itself invisible but evident from its effects, and which can flow from one location to another, dwell or be stored in variable amounts, and tapped. It can help or harm people.

In contrast to the prevalence of scholarly discussions, there are virtually no direct descriptions or analyses of power from Native Americans themselves. Their theories about power and its properties are instead evident only indirectly from myth and ritual, that is, from stories about humans and other beings acquiring and using power, and from their procedures for obtaining and manipulating it. From these sources of information, it is apparent that supernatural power has the attributes of energy that Durkheim and other scholars have identified. But rather than dwelling on the characteristics of power itself, Native discussions and activities are more likely to emphasize the conditions that are apparent when a being is receptive to power or possesses it.

The Lakotas go so far as to separate the idea of power (*wowas'ake*) from the condition of powerfulness and to emphasize the latter, terming the condition *wakan.* This condition is abstract and involved, though not impossible to explain or understand. A description by the Lakota George Sword circa 1908 provides a good start:

> *Wakan* means very many things. The Lakota understands what it means from the things that are considered *wakan;* yet sometimes its meaning must be explained to him. It is something that is hard to understand. . . . When a priest [Lakota religious leader] uses any object in performing a ceremony that object becomes endowed with a spirit, not exactly a spirit, but something like one, the priests call it *tonwan* or *ton.* Now anything that thus acquires *ton* is *wakan,* because it is the power of the spirit or quality that has been put into it. . . . The roots of certain plants are *wakan* because they are poisonous. Likewise some reptiles are *wakan* because if they bite they would kill. Again, some

birds are *wakan* because they do very strange things and some animals are *wakan* because the *wakan* beings make them so. In other words, anything may be *wakan* if a *wakan* spirit goes into it. Thus a crazy man is *wakan* because the bad spirit has gone into him. Again, if a person does something that cannot be understood, that is also *wakan*. Drinks that make one drunk are *wakan* because they make one crazy. Every object in the world has a spirit and that spirit is *wakan*. Thus, the spirit of the tree or things of that kind, while not like the spirit of man, are also *wakan*. . . . *Wakan* comes from the *wakan* beings. These *wakan* beings are greater than mankind in the same way that mankind is greater than animals. They are never born and never die. They can do many things that mankind cannot do. Mankind can pray to the *wakan* beings for help.

(Walker 1979:152)

What is Sword telling us in this passage? He uses the word *wakan* mainly if not totally as an adjective rather than as noun, emphasizing condition rather than power itself. As an adjective, *wakan* appears to mean "powerful," "sacred," or "holy." Sword indicates that this state and the underlying power are complex phenomena that are difficult to really to know about, evident only through their secondary manifestations. The nature of power itself (*wowaš'ake*) is for the most part only implicit in Sword's comments. We might gather from his remarks that power resides everywhere in the natural world, though not everywhere in equal amounts. Plants and animals often have it; anything may have it. It is possessed by nonhuman beings, which may be a good source of it, and their status as power possessors or holy beings is greater than that of ordinary humans. The *wakan* beings can help humans who approach them, presumably by transmitting power. It can also be inferred from Sword's statement that it is the fate and duty of humans to strive to understand and obtain power.

Most interesting is Sword's comment that the indwelling entity that makes something *wakan* is "not exactly a spirit, but something like one." He seems to conflate the ideas of supernatural being and supernatural force. While this is a distinction that has been a cornerstone of evolutionary theories of religion since the days of Tylor and Marrett, Native religionists should not necessarily be expected to espouse it. Instead they may recognize the ambiguous nature of the indwelling entity, which is a religious mystery comparable to the Catholic Trinity, in which one God exists simultaneously as three persons of varying corporality—Father, Son, and Holy Spirit.

A commonly noted aspect of power evident in Sword's comments is as a kind of knowledge or special intelligence, or as a mental state. It is therefore notable that the Indian sign language sign for "power" closely resembles the sign for "crazy" or "angry": the right hand makes an upward twisting motion from the forehead. Another aspect of power is potentiality. Anthropologist William K. Powers has translated the Lakota word *ton*, associated with *wakan* in Sword's passage above, to mean "To be born, to give rise to; one of the four aspects of 'soul'; potentiality" (Powers 1986:212). Similarly, the Kiowa term for power, *d]y,* appears to be related to words for "to be," "to be born," and "to sing." A Siouan child first beginning to walk or learning to speak early is said to be *wakandagi*, "manifesting or realizing its potential holiness." The Comanche woman in whose home the author lived during fieldwork in the 1980s expressed a similar idea when she remarked to her great-grandson that his mother was his "real first medicine." Other connotations are also made evident by analyzing the native terms. Powers has confirmed that the element *kan* in the Siouan *wakan* refers to an ancient or enduring quality. Defining the sacred as that which is old is a common human practice.

Many scholarly accounts, and even Sword's remarks, have contributed to the perception that Native ideas of power and potentiality are too complicated to be grasped. Stephen R. Riggs (1812–1883), a missionary and lexicographer among the Sioux after 1837, wrote of *wakan* that

FIGURE 9.1   The Lakota warrior and religious commentator
George Sword (center) circa 1891, when he was police chief on the
Pine Ridge Reservation. He also portrayed a scout in the Wild
West shows organized by William F. "Buffalo Bill" Cody, and poses
here with other members of Cody's troupe.

"No term can express the meaning of the word among the Dakota. It embraces all mystery, all secret power, all divinity" (Riggs, quoted in Durkheim 1995:195). Similarly, the anthropologists Alice Fletcher and Francis La Flesche wrote of the cognate Omaha *wakonda* that it is "not a modern term and does not lend itself to verbal analysis. . . . It is difficult to formulate the native idea expressed in this word" (Fletcher and La Flesche 1972, II:597). Care must always be taken in translating complex philosophical concepts, and oversimplifications and mistakes have been

made. Yet Sword, even while showing due respect for the intricacy of his people's power concept, was ultimately quite eloquent and informative about it. Too much caution among non-Indian analysts, born in some cases perhaps from romantic suppositions about the mysterious nature of Indian religion, is not warranted. Plains Indian power or medicine is clearly a version of the widespread *mana* phenomenon, and adjectives related to the power concept normally indicate something sacred or holy, which is easily understandable to most people.

SPIRITUAL BEINGS

If power is the foremost concept in Plains belief, spiritual beings play a close and important supporting role as guides to and sources of power. Nearly any object or creature in the natural world might be the form taken by a spirit. Most commonly, weather phenomena and animals are interpreted as spirits. In addition, some spirits take the form of fantastic creatures such as giants, elves, monsters, and ghosts.

Thunder

Today thunder is often simply another noise, but in the preindustrial world of the Plains, it was by far the loudest and most awe-inspiring of all sounds. Thunder contrasted dramatically with the near silence of everyday camp life and functioned as what communication theorist Murray Shafer called "the original *vox dei* and Sacred Noise" (Shafer 1980:179). As a high-intensity, low-frequency vibration, thunder was felt as well as heard, and it was often coupled with wind and rain, other very tangible effects of nature, and so it was logically characterized as a supernatural being.

The best known of such Plains beings is the thunderbird, a mythic depiction of thunder as an avian spirit presented in stories and beadwork designs, and its nest represented on the central pole of the Sun Dance ritual. The bird was most often described as like an eagle, only larger, though some tribes identified it with other birds such as the swan (Pawnees) or nighthawk (Plains Apaches). The portrayal of thunder as a bird made sense because migrating birds returned around the time of the first spring thundershowers. *Wakinyan*, a contraction of *wakan*, "sacred," and *kinyan*, "flying thing," is the Lakota name for the thunderbird, while the Comanche name appears to translate as "cloud talk" or "cloud beating." In typical accounts, the thunderbird lived in a tipi on a mountain to the west. Lightning was the flash of its eyes or arrows discharged from its talons; thunder was its cry or the flapping of its wings.

Among the Lakotas, if a person dreamed of the thunderbird or lightning, or of one of the thunderbird's messengers such as the swallow or dragonfly, they were liable to then be visited by a spirit called *Heyoka*. Taking the form of a shabbily dressed man, *Heyoka* did things in strange ways; his name meant "opposite to nature." The dreamer then himself was said to have become *heyoka* and was thereafter obligated to conduct his life in contrary fashion, doing things backwards and breaking the norms of society in a buffoonish and sometimes dangerous way. He was commanded by *Wakinyan* to talk backwards, wear his robe inside out, or rub mud all over his body, but also perhaps to murder someone. The dreamer lived in fearful obedience of *Wakinyan*, and his neighbors were both amused by him and afraid of him.

A thunder dreamer publicly accepted the role by acting out his dream in a ceremony called *Heyoka Kaga*, "Clown Making." In this enactment he played the fool and drew ridicule from his tribe mates, using antithesis to emphasize his newfound power. He might compose a song to recognize the honor of being chosen by the spirits, like this one made by Lone Man (Densmore 1918:165):

kola'	friends
waŋma'yaŋka yo	behold
wakaŋ	sacred
maka'ġa pelo'	I have been made
kola'	friends
waŋma'yaŋka yo	behold
wakaŋ'yaŋ	in a sacred manner
maka'ġa pelo'	I have been influenced
mahpi'ya ogli'naźiŋ ta	at the gathering of the clouds (before a thunderstorm)

Once in a while all *heyokas* staged a dance to demonstrate their power. They danced around a kettle of boiling dog soup and took turns plunging their hands in to grab chunks of meat, which they gave away to elder onlookers. Their power, enhanced with an application of the herb called prairie mallow to their hands, kept them from being scalded, and they boasted that the soup was too cold.

Thunder and lightning spirits were malicious and vengeful. Sometimes they granted a human who approached them the power to control rain and hail. But more often they struck down someone so bold. When thundering started, a person was supposed to stay quiet so as not to appear that she or he was challenging them. In any camp or community, however, there might be someone who felt powerful enough to try to dispel a storm. Among the Comanches in the 1980s, a medicine man or woman attempted to abate a mounting storm by throwing handfuls of dirt at the clouds while yelling at them to go away. If an ax was handy, its blade was swung into the ground in the direction of the storm to split it and make it go around (one elder told me that a sword was originally used for this purpose, and I once saw a bread knife—the only blade within reach at the moment—used this way). If these steps failed or the storm surprised the household at night, Comanches covered any mirrors in the house with sheets or towels, because it was believed that mirrors attracted lightning and reflected it to kill people. Then, the house was frantically fumigated with a burning hank of sweet grass to bless it and keep the harmful spirits away.

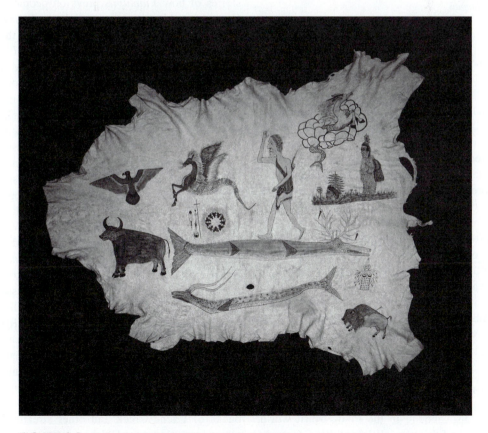

FIGURE 9.2 Painted buckskin by Silverhorn depicting Kiowa spiritual beings, including the thunderbird, Whirlwind (winged horses), Water Monsters, and trickster in human form.

Water Monsters

In Plains myth, the thunderbird is locked in ever-lasting combat with the Water Monster. James Walker, a doctor on Pine Ridge Reservation between 1896 and 1914, composed the following description from Sioux informants' accounts:

> *Unktehi* are like animals. They stay in the waters and live in swampy places. They have four legs and horns which they can draw in or extend them to the skies. They have long hair on the neck and head which is *wakan*. Their tails are strong and they can shoot or strike with them, and they use their tails as men use their hands. They are always at war with the *Wakinyan*.

> (Walker 1980:108)

Walker's report matches those from numerous other tribes about a horned saurian creature or snake found near water. For example, the Cheyenne creature called *mihn* looked "some-what like a very large lizard, with one or two horns on the head, and often covered, or partly covered with hair" (Grinnell 1972:97). These monsters waited to grab anything or anyone who ventured too close to their lair in a lake or river hole; they snatched and ate the thunderbird's fledglings and careless humans too. Devil's Lake in northeastern North Dakota, the largest natural body of water in the region, derives its name from the Sioux *Mini Wakan*, "Water Sacred," a reference to the water monster believed to live there. In the 1930s Kiowas identified Swan Lake on Cobb Creek, Caddo County, Oklahoma, as one place where a woman was grabbed and pulled under water while gathering water plants.

Giants and Dwarves

Giants also abound in the Plains spirit world. "Indians had their own 'Bigfoot' " a Comanche woman told me. According to another, "It look like a man . . . big, old monster. They said it got a face like a man. It's got hair all over its body and it got big feet. It's tall, you know" (Jones 1972:51). A Comanche captive in Mexico circa 1861 told of an "[i]maginary being that they suppose is in human form, gigantic, that carries an extraordi-narily large staff of wood, that eats men, that lives in some large caves that are in some mountains very far to the north; they believe that when he breaks the staff, they die" (García Rejón and Gelo 1995:37). The Comanche giant is called *Piamupits*. Some say that it has the facial features of an owl (its name translates as "big nose-creature," that is, "big owl") and it has been called "big cannibal owl" in English. There are many stories of how *Piamupits* preys on people, and Comanche children were scared into behaving with the threat that *Piamupits* would get them. A counterpart in Sioux tradition is named *Iya* or *Ibom*. He was said to be the first being created after the sky and earth were made. He is the chief of evil beings, a glutton notorious for having had incest with his mother. Like the Comanche ogre, *Iya* lived in the cold country to the north and he ate people.

Both the Water Monster and giant are associ-ated in tribal traditions with the fossil bones of extinct large animals that are found across the Plains. Walker wrote of the Sioux water monster: "Their females live on the dry land, and their bones are often found in the badlands" (Walker 1980:108). Thus, the Indians regarded the dinosaur bones commonly found in the heavily eroded badlands of southwestern South Dakota as the remains of the monster. Another site associ-ated with the Siouan female water monster lies in western Nebraska along the Niobrara River. Carnegie Hill, known by a Lakota name meaning "animal bones brutally scattered about," is densely packed with fossils from the Miocene. Similarly, the Comanches find evidence of the giant *Piamupits* in the petrified bones frequently exposed along the banks of Cache Creek and other streams and scarps in southwestern Oklahoma. Osage legends about a battle of monsters were based on the large concentration of mastodon bones found in Benton County, Missouri.

Fossil bones are prized as medicine for use in treating sprains and bone problems as well as skin lesions. A bone might be ground into powder and mixed with water for application, or simply held against the ailing body part. It is widely believed that fossil bone draws out the poisons that cause bodily illness. Fossil bone does exert capillary action; paleontologists like to test bones to see if they are ancient by licking them—the tongue sticks to fossil bone—and Comanche medicine collectors use the same procedure.

Given the connection between fossils and spirits, it is interesting to wonder whether some Native beliefs result from lore passed down from prehistoric times when monstrous Pleistocene mammals, such as mammoths, ground sloths, giant bison, camels, and short-faced bears, were actually encountered by Indian hunters.

Small humanoids are another kind of being described in similar terms across the various tribes. The Sioux tell of little people called *gica* who stand about 3 feet tall. They are usually males, wearing breechclouts and moccasins and carrying little bows and arrows. In some accounts, the Lakota contrary spirit *Heyoka* is also said to be a dwarf. Among the Shoshones and Comanches, elves called *nɨnapi* ("little men") are said to be about 1 foot high. They too are armed with little bows, arrows, shields, and miniature spears tipped with alligator spines. The Sioux say they are daubed with mud, and the Comanches picture them painted with red ochre, which they may bestow on humans who run across them. Sometimes they appear in the corner of one's eye, sitting perched on a boulder or shed looking down upon a person with a knowing grin. Or, they remain invisible and playfully slap someone who disturbs their haunts. Little people are most often encountered in lonely places, either hills or canyons, and are associated with the earth and water. The Plains Crees of the Rocky Boy Reservation in Montana claim that the *m-me-m-mege'-soo* live around Haystack Butte. Some of the Crow little

people or *awukkulé* are said to dwell south of Pryor, Montana, around a formation called Castle Rocks. Indians traveling nearby left them beads and other offerings to ensure safe passage. A common expression among the Crows is "strong as a dwarf," and all the tribes believe that they are very strong despite their size. They are also regarded as ancient, and they are said to have made the flint points and stone hammers that can be found here and there. Although they can impart medicine or advice to humans, mostly the little people should be avoided, because they are mischievous, if not malevolent, and deadly powerful.

Ghosts

A ghost is a particular kind of spirit, the soul of a human who is no longer alive. While other spirits are generally associated with the supernatural world and only periodically with the everyday realm, ghosts are spirits who are only recently on their way from the human domain to the supernatural. The Comanches, for example, distinguish between *atsabi*, "other-being," for "spirit," and *pɨe tɨyaai?*, "already dead," for "ghost." In Omaha, the term that differentiates ghosts from other powerful beings is *wano^n'xe*, translated as "a form that is transparent" (Fletcher and LaFlesche 1972, II:489). Further, the ghost per se may be distinguished from other aspects of the human soul. The Cheyennes differentiate between *tasoom*, a person's vital essence, and *mistai*, the night-wandering spirits of the dead. The Plains Crees likewise speak of a *tchi-pay* or ghost as distinct from the soul, *at'-tshak*, though the words are somewhat interchangeable. The Tetons consider the *wanagi* or ghost to be the fourth aspect of the soul. Three others, which could be termed "potential," "birth," and "breath," are previously evident in a person's conception, birth, and life, and the fourth aspect becomes apparent upon death. In turn, these 4 forms of soul are among the 16 manifestations of the sacred recognized by the Tetons, in a group that includes several other kinds of powerful beings.

Ghosts in Plains belief may take several shapes. Some are recognizable as specific people who are known to the living people who encounter them—they may be deceased relatives, friends, or acquaintances. Others are described in generic terms, such as "a handsome Indian boy." These descriptions usually add details about traditional appearance and dress and they closely resemble accounts of little people. One especially well-developed ghost character is the Scalped Man, legends of whom are heard among the Arikaras, Pawnees, Comanches, Wichitas, and probably other tribes. As his name suggests, this ghosts appears without his scalp, wielding a knife, bloodied and terrifying. He is a warrior who has been disgraced, doomed to wander around the outskirts of the people's camps. Ghosts may also assume nonhuman form. The small whirlwinds or "dust devils" that stir up on hot summer days are sometimes said to be ghosts. Or, ghosts take the form of owls; the interpretation of screech, barn, and great-horned owls as ghosts is probably universal among the Plains tribes.

Ghosts lurk at night around houses, in low lonely places like creek beds, and near where their corporeal forms died or were buried. They occupy abandoned homes and camps. In some accounts, ghostly visitors may show up in groups, making camp and going about their business like living people. Often their presence is felt rather than seen. One or more living people sense them, and even the dogs bark at them. When they are seen, it may be incompletely at first, with just the feet and legs showing and the rest of their image gradually becoming visible; or, like the little people, they appear suddenly in the corner of one's eye. Ghosts also make themselves know with sounds. The Blackfoots and Tetons say that they make strange whistling sounds. They make mournful noises and sing too. The hooting of an owl is said to be a ghost's call; one Comanche man told the author that a real owl's call comes

from above, but a ghost's comes from some low place, and that is how someone can tell the difference. Ghosts can also talk to people, though often they talk only in a way that is not clearly understandable, or they do not speak at all.

Hearing a ghost or seeing one can be dangerous, because ghosts are envious of those still living and take delight in tormenting them. They attempt to startle people in the dark, and the sudden scare is thought to cause strokes or the facial paralysis called "crooked mouth" or "twisted face," known clinically as Bell's palsy. The Scalped Man figure wrestles with his victims and can inflict tuberculosis. But ghosts are above all capricious, and sometimes they give the living warnings or help, and so it is good for people to attempt to understand them. They sing songs of victory or mourning that foretell the fate of a war party, and they predict the deaths of individuals, who may then take measures to postpone the inevitable. Ghosts also appear after someone dies to comfort the grieving kin, notably appearing after their own deaths for this purpose. And while it is extremely dangerous to seek medicine power from a ghost by, for instance, waiting by a grave and standing up to the frightening apparition, sometimes a ghost is impressed by the seeker or takes pity on him and gives them some medicine. If the Scalped Man's victim wins the wrestling match, he gains the power to cure tuberculosis.

A living person should be ready to deal with ghosts. It is most important for a person to eliminate any chance that a ghost can surprise them by being watchful in places where ghosts prowl. A ghost directly encountered is less able to cause trouble. A ghost should be confronted head-on and told in a firm voice to go away. They can be kept away altogether with a tobacco offering— even the light of a cigarette will do—or sage or cedar. Certain feathers also repel them. The Arapahos use a sympathetic principle, adorning medicine man's rattles with the feathers, skin, or claws of a screech owl. The Comanches take an antagonistic approach, decorating cradles and other items with crow feathers, because crows are the natural enemies of owls. The Crows use eagle feathers. The Omahas believed that a ghost would not fool with a knife, so that one could prevent them from tampering with food by laying a knife across the vessel. They also believed that a ghost would never cross any stream, so that if a person was being chased by a ghost, they only had to wade or jump across a creek to gain safety. Besides these techniques for keeping ghosts away, there are others for appeasing them. Normally a choice part of a slain animal or some bits of food are left for them. The Tetons spilled a little soup by the fire to keep the ghosts friendly, with the request "Ghosts, say for me 'I will live long' " (Walker 1980:164).

Some tribes observe a taboo on speaking the name of dead persons. The ban is a means of showing respect for the deceased, but ultimately it is in place so the living will avoid calling the ghost among them. When a dead person's name included everyday words, as it usually would, those words had to be replaced in conversation with synonyms or circumlocutions. A person with the same name or something similar would have to change his or her name. Ideally this avoidance would continue for several years, essentially the lifetime of the deceased's contemporaries. The practice is in place still today in some communities, although it is more difficult to observe because written records, bureaucratic settings such as schools and hospitals, and acquaintances from outside the Indian community all make it difficult to avoid using a decedent's name.

Ghosts exist forever. If a person dies by strangulation or is scalped, the soul is prevented from emerging. But under the usual circumstances, a deceased person's soul stays near his or her body for a time and then moves on to the spirit world. Generally it is thought that the ghost lingers for about one year, though the time is variable. Living people can recognize the ghost's presence during this period through ritual. The mourning period of one year, in which the decedent's rela-tives stay out of public life, observe special taboos, and depend on the generosity of their neighbors, corresponds to the ghost's presence nearby. During this period the Tetons sometimes "kept" the ghost in a rite called *Wanagi yuhapi* ("ghost they keep"), by placing a lock of the deceased's hair in a special tipi under the supervision of a sacred person and attending to it with food offerings. After a year or more, one day they marked the ghost's release by constructing an effigy from a carved wooden post, set inside the lodge on the south side, which women came to hug and lament over. The relatives then threw a huge feast and gave away all of their possessions to the needy in honor of the ghost, making themselves destitute until they received replacement clothing and lodging from their friends and relatives.

In modern times, traditionally oriented people still observe a year-long mourning period, with relatives coming out and staging a dance, feast, and giveaway to honor the deceased and thank their supporters around the time of the anniversary of a death. These observances are situated within the general round of tribal ceremonies and powwows and are explicitly to memorialize someone who has died. Though there may not be references to ghosts in these proceedings, they are clearly grounded in older beliefs about ghosts.

Both the name taboo and rituals which allow a prolonged state of mourning ending in a release event reveal a great deal about the emotional state of the survivors and how they deal with their sorrow. Upon the death of a loved one, a person seeks to avoid or at least control his or her exposure to memories of the deceased by not hearing the deceased's name and avoiding public social situations in which the dead person's absence would be conspicuous. The ritualized mourning period is a culturally constructed mechanism for the activation of communal support from friends and relatives and gradual emotional healing, and the mourners' eventual repayment of their supporters also contributes to a sense of closure.

Therefore, as the anthropologist David E. Jones has shown, another way to think of ghosts is as the poignant memories of loved ones lost.

The afterworld dimension where ghosts go is depicted in various ways by different tribes, and also variably within tribal traditions. Although often dismissed as a stereotype promulgated by whites, the idea of a "happy hunting ground" is not far off the mark, in that the destination for ghosts is often described as an encampment in a pretty landscape replete with shade, fresh water, and game, where the spirits of dead people will enjoy comfort. Life there is much like human life, but without the troubles. The location of this place may be regarded as unknowable, or it may be described as distant in a metaphorical way ("beyond the pines" according to one Teton elder, "downriver" in Hidatsa lore, or "west of the setting sun" in Comanche convention). It might be in the sky or, less frequently, underground. The Blackfoots said that souls traveled to a lonely area of sand hills near the Saskatchewan River in southeastern Alberta before assuming an existence like one on earth. In Teton tradition, after dwelling in the buttes west of the Sioux country for one year, the soul travels south along the Milky Way (which is called *wanagi tacanku* or "ghost road" in Lakota), where an old woman decides whether it will return to earth or go to the afterlife.

Apart from this Teton story, ideas of judgment, reward, and punishment in the afterlife are rare in Plains religion, and in most instances where they are reported it is very hard to be sure that they are not reflections of Christian influences. There are no concepts of heaven or hell strictly speaking; only in some cases there is an idea that the afterworld is more pleasant and easy for people who have been good, or that the souls of bad people are excluded from the afterworld and must return to earth. Commonly, it is said that murderers, suicides, and those who have been scalped, disfigured, or died in the dark are unable to enter the hereafter. Yet even where these beliefs seem to have currency, there is usually disagreement within the culture about them.

Because souls can travel between the human and spirit realms, reincarnation—a departed soul's return to occupy another life form—is sometimes acknowledged in Plains tribal traditions, as among the Blackfoots and Tetons. The idea is not strongly developed, however; reincarnation is thought of more as a theoretical possibility or a general phenomenon rather than as an inevitable process involving the reappearance of specific souls in specific new organisms. Thus, an implication of the Lakota soul concept is that freed souls come back perpetually to reanimate new life, but this possibility is not a focus of belief or ritual. Nor is Plains reincarnation ethicized; it is not a system of reward and punishment meant to influence the behavior of the living, as in the Hindu and Buddhist religions.

Animal Spirits

By far the most important everyday sources of supernatural power are not fantastic beings like monsters, dwarves, or ghosts, but the spirits of animals. When a man encounters an animal in the wild, it is always a matter of interpretation whether he sees the physical animal or an animal spirit. An animal spirit is likely to bestow medicine that in general is modeled on the natural abilities of the creature.

Both the buffalo and the bear are celebrated power donors owing to their habits and strength. The buffalo "anoints" itself with earth and so absorbs and transmits earth medicine, and its instinct for protecting its "family" and its formidable might are also bases for healing and battle power. Similarly, "[b]ears were considered [by the Hidatsas] to be the great doctors because they cared for their own young and because of their great strength" (Bowers 1992:357), and the Comanches said that a man with bear medicine could pass in front of the enemy with impunity to taunt them prior to a full engagement. The mountain lion is another creature that lends its great strength in the form of medicine. The elk gives medicine that is helpful in love magic because elks appear to be polygynous, the bulls mating with groups of females known as harems.

Wolves and coyotes are often viewed as messengers of the sacred. They grant the power of stealth, and guidance, and also give omens through their howling. According to the Lakota Thomas Tyon,

> In the beginning a man who dreamed of wolves always went towards the enemies' tipis like a wolf, it is said. He was, therefore, very inconspicuous, hence nobody was able to see him. This is right, so far. A man was wandering, lost in the wilderness, when a wolf came there and they went together towards the camp, it is said. Therefore they believe the wolf to be very *wakan.*

> (Walker 1980:160)

The author collected essentially the same tale from a Comanche elder in 1982 (Gelo 1986:118, 1994:305). When a Comanche runs across a coyote, he should greet the animal, saying, "tell me some good news, brother." Unlike these wild canids, domestic dogs are not thought of as power donors because they are closely associated with humans. Horses are similarly regarded.

Virtually any wild animal can bestow power. Some of the animal patrons are small or otherwise unlikely. The beaver is a great source of healing power because, like the buffalo, it is seen as a nurturing "family" animal and, like the bear, its body yields an oil that actually aids in physical healing. Otter medicine is used to ease childbirth, a reference to the river otter's habit of sliding down banks into the water. The mole, a denizen of the dark, helps babies to sleep. Lizards, dragonflies, ants . . . any creature can lend power fashioned after its particular habits.

The eagle is preeminent among powerful birds and is the equal if not the greatest of all powerful creatures. The focus of this belief is the golden eagle, especially the juvenile and immature

versions with white, black-tipped tail feathers. The Lakotas think of the immature bald eagle or *wanbligleška* ("eagle spotted") as a messenger who carries prayers upward to the supernatural. The mature bald eagle is held in less regard by the Cheyennes, because it eats carrion and steals fish from other birds. This unflattering image was reinforced when the Cheyennes found that the bald eagle was the U.S. national emblem. The crow is another very strong bird whose power is invoked in curing and martial success. It is a natural enemy of owls, which are associated with ghosts. The roadrunner bestows the ability to run and hide. The Comanches say that the meadowlark grants the power to go directly home. To protect its offspring from discovery, the meadowlark approaches its ground nest by landing many yards distant and walking through the grass. It leaves in the same manner. Well-defined paths radiate from its nest.

As a counterpart to these beliefs, certain birds are thought to impart undesirable qualities. Contact with doves will make a person lazy, and any of the gallinaceous birds such as turkeys, prairie chickens, grouse, quail, and domestic fowl are considered cowardly, and their cowardice contagious to humans. Although Indian people in the old days undoubtedly ate these birds sometimes when hunger demanded, they were supposed to avoid eating or touching them. Today the taboos are still known but not widely observed.

Although mystic animals are encountered by happenstance during hunts and war expeditions, in the old days power seekers might also run among buffalos or spend time in the known haunts of bears to raise their chances of acquiring medicine. These more active approaches were often recommended by a medicine man.

Thus, the distinction between hunting and medicine acquisition is not always clear, and this is especially the case regarding eagles, which are the most powerful creatures but not ones from which talismans are easily obtained. The Hidatsas,

Arikaras, and Crows, however, perfected an adventurous method of eagle trapping to obtain sacred feathers. Men set up trapping sites far from their main camps where they would go in the late summer or fall. These sites consisted of one or more small tipi-shaped wooden lodges adjacent to pits. Each pit contained a trapper underneath a lattice of branches and grass. A bait of a whole rabbit or fatty, bloody chunk of blacktail deer meat was left on the lattice. The trapper stared upward through the screen, watching patiently for eagles migrating on the west wind. The birds would appear first as tiny black spots far up in the sky, but soon enough one might be seen diving for the bait. As the eagle landed to take the meat, the trapper thrust his arms through the screen, grabbed the huge bird by its legs, and wrestled it into the pit, doing his best to avoid the sharp beak and talons. He briskly stripped off the dozen tail feathers and, once the bird was dazed, took it to the lodge and tied it up. In this way many feathers and a number of captive eagles, whose feathers would be harvested again when they grew back, could be collected in one season. Trapping sites were owned initially by their builders but became valuable over time and were inherited through clan lines.

Transcendent Spirits

In any Plains tribal religious tradition, certain spirits are considered to play an overarching role in the creation and continuing operation of the universe. Their role is celebrated in mythology and they are addressed in prayers and rituals meant to ensure the continuance of a secure life for humans. These spirits are more remote than those animal spirits and ghosts who are likely to be encountered in the course of everyday life. They have set the world in motion but now remain distant and largely disinterested in the common affairs of people. While they may be the ultimate source of supernatural power in the universe and individuals desire their blessings, they are not usually approached for personal power. Rather, they may be beseeched by groups of people for general aid, such as the appearance of game or the success of crops. Also, though they do not actively sit in judgment of humans and do not mete out rewards and punishments, because they are all-seeing and all-knowing they may represent a high order of moral authority, so that they receive the pledges of people intent on improving themselves and the oaths of those testifying in legal disputes.

In discussing these figures the term "transcendent spirits" seems preferable to anything else. It is difficult to talk about them as "deities" or "gods" without suggesting the intense veneration that such entities enjoy in other religions, although these terms are not unfounded and have been used in much of the academic literature and by Native ritualists as well. Similarly, it would be misleading to call them "supreme beings," for, though they may sit at the top of a hierarchy of spirits, they are of less immediate interest to humans than power and the common spirits who appear before them to grant it. Though Native people today often refer to transcendent spirits in English as Creator or Maker, and the general term "creator being" might be accurate in many cases, creation in some tribal mythologies is actually the work of one or more spirit agents under the transcendent spirit's direction, or else the question of whether the transcendent one and creator(s) are the same is left ambiguous. Ultimately, it may be inaccurate to define a Plain transcendent spirit solely as a being, for it may be personified sometimes, but other times thought of as an ultimate force or diffused impulse rather than being, all within the same tribal tradition. This dual characterization of being and force, also seen in George Sword's explanation of *wakan* quoted above, is a fundamental religious mystery in Plains belief.

Among the Crows, the transcendent spirit is called *Akbaatatdía*, "One Who Has Made Everything." Other Crow names for the spirit translate as "First Doer," "One Above," "Father," "Old Man Coyote," and "Old Man." This Maker (as the Crows say in English) is distinct and all-powerful. It is addressed in daily worship and is considered the ultimate source of all visions, cures, wisdom, and power. It is distinguishable, however, from the kind of supreme being envisioned in Judeo-Christian religions. "Unlike the Euro-American notion of a single, anthropomorphic deity, the Apsáalooke Maker is conceived of as more diffuse and less humanlike. . . . Akbaatatdía is more appropriately conceived of as a pervasive agent, omnipotent over all natural forces, yet part of all natural forces, the ultimate life-force, and the perennial meaning of the cosmos" (Frey 1987:63).

The Lakota *Wakantanka* (or *Wakandoga* among the Southern Siouans) is another complex transcendent spirit. The term means "great *wakan*," that is, "great sacred." *Wakantanka* embodies all the supernatural beings and powers in the universe, which exist in four ranked classes with four components each—(1) the superior *wakan*: Sun, Sky, Earth, Rock; (2) friends of the superior *wakan*: Moon, Wind, Falling Star, Thunder; (3) lesser *wakan*: buffalo, two-leggeds (bears and humans), the Four Winds, and the Whirlwind; (4) those similar to *wakan*, the aspects of soul: "potential," "birth," "breath," and "ghost." As George Sword explained, "Wakan Tanka is like sixteen different persons; but each person is *kan* ['ancient,' 'wonderful']. Therefore they are all only the same as one . . . " (Walker 117:153). Other supernatural beings and forces appear in Lakota belief, but often they are explained as the offspring of the sixteen aspects of *Wakantanka*.

A similar name among the Plains Crees is Kitchi Manitou or *Kiseimen'to*, "main sacred." In this case the name refers to a male creator being who is the source of all good things and the first to be addressed when prayers are sent to the spirits. Although the Crees normally view *Kiseimen'to* as a unitary figure, at times they present the idea that he exists in three phases, which have been labeled Master of Food, Master of Life, and Master of Death. These titles can be used as euphemisms for the creator, since it is considered disrespectful to refer to *Kiseimen'to* by name.

The Hidatsas recognize a transcendent spirit called *Itsikamahidiś*, "First Made," or *Itakatétaś*, "Old Man Immortal," also conceptualized as Coyote, the First Creator who made the earth. In some accounts this figure created everything, but in other Mandan stories and rituals other spirits are credited with forming the skies and under-world. To complicate matters, after about 1830 the Hidatsas adopted religious ideas from the neighboring Mandans, including the Mandan creator figure called Lone Man, so that their stories include two primal actors. The Hidatsa case reminds us that beliefs about transcendent spirits, like all cultural constructs, are dynamic and subject to change over time.

The all-pervading spirit of Cheyenne religion is named *Heammawihio*, "The Wise One Above." The stem *wihio* literally means spider, a creature which, like the coyote that the Hidatsas associate with the transcendent spirit, is a creator and trick-ster in Plains mythology. The Cheyennes perceive the spider as representing a higher order of intelligence because of its abilities to spin webs and walk up and down seemingly on nothing.

The Comanches do not seem at first glance to spend much effort reflecting about the nature of such a distant spirit, concentrating instead on power and its nearby donor spirits, and they have been contrasted with the other Plains tribes on this point. For their transcendent spirit, they use the name *Ta?ahpï*, "Our Father," and in earlier times also *Tatoco*, "Our Maternal Grandfather." These names do reveal some of the personality of the Comanche spirit, though, for the father in traditional Comanche family life is a relatively stern and distant figure, while the maternal grandfather is an affectionate guardian.

These examples from different tribes show that the transcendent spirit can be depicted with some variation, both within and across tribal traditions, being more or less active in creation and in the subsequent affairs of the universe, and taking any of several forms, described with much or little specificity.

The evil counterpart to the transcendent one is an interesting development in some tribes. As a match for Kitchi Manitou, the Crees recognize Matchi Manitou, "evil sacred," who is referred to with the euphemisms *Matasais*, "evil man," or *Hekakamiositmen'to*, "not good spirit." This figure may be a derivative of the creator *Kiseimen'to* in his role as Master of Death, but is probably also inspired by Christian concepts of Satan. A similar character is sometimes reported for the Comanches, but seems to be a projection of the Christian devil, whom they call *kwasi taiboo*, "tail white man." Lakota consultants have sometimes identified the mythological giant *Iya* as the chief evil spirit with an ability to take on different, dangerous sub-forms. There is, therefore, an impulse to attribute misfortune as well as good luck to certain spirits. Major evil beings have no prominent role in traditional Plains religion, however, and the workings of the spirit world are not reduced to a battle between good and evil main characters.

Cosmovision

The transcendent spirit is widely associated with the sun. Usually the sun is regarded as the most immediate manifestation of the spirit and is the focus of prayers and rituals meant to reach the transcendent one. In yet another religious mystery, statements may be ambivalent, even from within the same tribe, whether the sun is the embodiment of the transcendent spirit or whether the spirit lives in the sun or somewhere behind or beyond it. The sun is typically characterized as an all-seeing male who is responsible for life on earth, and is usually addressed as "Father." His life-giving power is obvious from the growth of vegetation, and his omniscience is evident from his relentlessly regular appearance each day and his ability to mark the passing of time and

disclose coming changes in the weather with his color and appearance. The Comanches have a rich vocabulary of terms for the sun which describe its different positions and appearances as it moves through the sky from dark to dark.

The earth is also regarded as a supernatural being, normally secondary to the sun but complementary. The earth is regarded as female and addressed as a mother or grandmother. Recently, the religionist Sam D. Gill (1991) has argued that the "mother earth" concept is largely an invention of non-Indian pioneers and writers. There is certainly evidence that the idea was amplified into a stereotype, and that earth was portrayed incorrectly, in a manner fitting with Christian presuppositions about non-Western religions, as a "goddess." But old Plains Indian language vocabularies, prayers, and folktales, as well as observations made in the early days of contact with non-Indians, leave little doubt that the basic concept of the earth as a mother figure is a Native one and that it was well established in tribal traditions prior to non-Indian misinterpretation.

Closely associated with the earth proper, rocks and even small stones can also be regarded as spirits or containers of sacred power. The Lakotas deem certain stones sacred, calling them *tunkan*, a term related to the word for "grandfather"; these stones contain their own soul aspect and perhaps additional ones inserted by a holy person. Their power can help in rituals meant to cure people or find lost objects, and small *tunkan* are carried on one's person in a leather pouch as protection. In at least some conceptualizations these stones are seen as surrogates of the earth: "When a child disappeared, *Maka* (the Earth) was invoked to help return them. The mysterious stones were consulted to learn what had become of the child" (Walker 1980:107). Similar ideas are found elsewhere. Today the Kiowas and Comanches collect the curiously round cobbles of pink granite found at certain places in the Wichita Mountains. The tiny stones that ants bring up from underground as they build their mounds are valued as sacred tokens among several groups. In 1982 the author was taken to a spot favored by the Comanches to collect such pebbles to place inside a dance rattle.

The moon, like the earth, is seen as a female complement to the sun, though it usually holds a less prominent place than earth in myth and ritual. In Lakota myth Sun and Moon were married but then separated, differentiating day and night. The Cheyenne name for the moon is *taesehe*, literally "night sun," and they believe it has a corresponding incarnation as a spiritual being called *Ameonito* who can appear in human form to help people. Similarly, the Crows regard the moon as *Káalixaalia*, "Old Woman," partner to *Isáahkaxaalia*, "Old Man," the sun. The moon is a protector of those traveling at night and others she may favor. According to the Comanche Post Oak Jim (b. circa 1869), Comanches preparing for a nighttime raid prayed and made smoke to the moon while sitting within a rope laid on the ground, saying "Mother, if it be your will, let this rope take many horses" (Wallace and Hoebel 1952:197). And like the sun, the moon shares valuable information with humans. The Crows read the position of the horns of the crescent moon with respect to the horizon in order to predict the severity of upcoming weather: the more they point away from the horizon, the worse the weather. Comanche elders say that an upward-facing crescent moon holds water, but one that is tilted or inverted will spill water, causing rain.

Meteorites and comets are sometimes accorded supernatural significance. "Shooting stars" are seen on the Plains on almost any clear night and the major showers such as the Perseids and Leonids make a dramatic impression on account of the wide horizon and lack of ambient light. Among all the tribes, 1833 was famous as "the year the stars fell" because of the spectacular meteor shower witnessed on November 13 of that year. In Lakota creation myth, Falling Star is the daughter of the Sun and Moon. The Pawnees and Comanches left sacrifices to a large meteorite that planted itself like a monument in the prairie turf near Albany, Texas, prior to 1808. The Comanches also venerated another meteorite near Elektra, Texas, in the 1850s. The Comanche name for these objects, which translates as "standing rock," appears to be the same name that their linguistic cousins the Shoshones used for the Grand Tetons, suggesting that the Comanche likened meteorites to sacred peaks. The Crows refer to a comet as *ihkachíishpishe*, "star with a tail," which has led to the alternate name "Devil Star," because of the Christian depiction of the devil as having a tail. Crow elders today still tell stories about the appearance of Halley's Comet in 1910, when tribe members dressed in their best clothes and sang all night, worried that the end of the world was at hand. The appearance of Coggia's Comet in early 1873 figured in the prophecies of the Comanche medicine man Isatai as he organized the 1874 Comanche Sun Dance and subsequent raid against white buffalo hunters at Adobe Walls, Texas.

The planets and stars are also often conceptualized as spirits, and astronomical systems must be regarded a part of Plains religious knowledge. Ethnoastronomers Ray Williamson and Claire Farrer have coined the useful term *cosmovision* for the domain of knowledge where astronomy and sacred beliefs about the origins and operations of the universe intersect. The star lore of the Plains tribes has been neglected by outsiders, at least until recently, under the mistaken assumption that hunting peoples would not have complicated astronomies. And only lately have tribe members themselves made concerted efforts to write down what the elders know about the night sky. Unfortunately, much of the traditional star knowledge of Plains people has probably been lost.

The information that does exist suggests that most if not all tribes maintained a healthy fund of celestial knowledge, not only for navigation and time-telling, but also as part of mythology about creation and the supernatural governance of human life on earth. For example, we have seen that the Sioux regard the Milky Way as a spirit trail; so did the Plains Crees and Cheyennes. The Cheyennes were dedicated sky watchers who scheduled their major midsummer ceremony according to the appearance of stars in the constellations that Euro-Americans call Taurus, Orion, and Canis Major. Most if not all tribes recognize the North Star as the "stationary star" (in Comanche, *kemiatatsanuupi,* literally "no-go-star"). The Kiowas, Comanches, and other tribes refer to the Pleiades constellation or, alternately, the Big Dipper, as the Star Girls or Seven Sisters, and maintain several variant stories linking these stars to human origins. In a related motif, the Crows refer to the Big Dipper as the Seven Brothers or Seven Buffalo Bulls. The buffalo bulls in this case are emblematic of brotherly love and cooperation, and they appear in a story about the origin of the Crow sweat lodge ritual, a gift of power from the star beings. More details of Crow astronomy are displayed in Table 9.1.

Like some other supernatural beings, stars and planets are conceived of alternately as natural objects and persons with the ability to act. Their activity takes place largely in the mythological period of creation rather than in the present, so they are mainly part of the supernatural backdrop. Occasionally, however, the stars mediate between the transcendent spirit and humans, playing a part in ritual or power transmission. They herald the proper dates for ceremonies and mark time during nighttime ritual, and once in a while they are donors of personal power. They communicate with people by their twinkling and even talk to people.

Overall, Plains cosmovision is more compli-cated than is often acknowledged, and notably among the tribes with a background in horticul-ture, lore about the stars and planets is situated within ambitious general theories of the structure of the universe. Groups including the Cheyennes, Sioux, and Plains Crees envision multiple levels of the universe. The Cheyenne schema includes five interrelated layers. The main ones are the earth's surface, the below, and the above. The thin strip of the earth's surface that supports life is distinct from the deep earth. The atmosphere directly above the surface, which provides air to make life possible, is one subzone; the larger earth's atmos-phere above that, home to the clouds and winds, is another, and deep space where the planets and stars dwell is yet another. All of these layers have specific Cheyenne names and particular religious significance.

The Pawnee system of beliefs about the stars, planets, and creation is frequently cited as the most complex of all on the Plains. The paramount figure is Tirawa, a father of all things who occupies the highest reaches of heaven. Three heavens below his are occupied by the the Stars, the Sun, and the Winds who along with thunder, lightning, rain, and the animals are the unseen Tirawa's messengers to the human world. Through them he sends down all things that people need. By the agency of his messengers, Tirawa created the land, its rivers, and its plants, especially corn. A union of the morning and evening stars, a warrior and maiden, respectively, produced the first girl, and the first boy was the son of the male Sun and female Moon. As humans populated the earth, stars were assigned as the patrons of each particular village.

All Pawnee mythology is an expansion of the story of Tirawa and his messengers, and all ritual is worship of some aspect of Tirawa's rule of the universe. The worship of Tirawa is largely communal rather than personal. As a totalizing entity expressed in many forms of nature, Tirawa is in one sense like the transcendent spirits in other Plains tribal religions. Yet Tirawa more than others approximates the definition of a supreme being and is therefore atypical. The unusually rich record of Pawnee myth and ceremonialism may skew the comparative perspective somewhat, but even so, the Pawnee system reflects more of the ancient religious orientation found among sedentary, horticultural Indians of the Southeastern culture area, rather than the usual beliefs of historic Plains hunter-gatherers, even those with gardening backgrounds.

TABLE 9.1 **Crow Stars and Constellations**

CROW NAME	EURO-AMERICAN NAME	NOTES
Bear Above	Part of Hercules	Constellation in the shape of a bear; rises in spring, indicates the best time for eagle trapping
Bright Star	Morning star—Sirius; also Mars, Mercury, Jupiter, Venus	Bright star or planet before sunrise; personified as Old Woman's Grandson; disappears during season of buffalo calving
Cougar Star	Undetermined	No information
Crazy Star	Venus	Its time of appearance and degree of brilliance are erratic
Day Star	Evening star—Venus	Bright planet shows before sunset; heralds nighttime ceremonies
Fire Star or Woman Star	Mars	Bright red, seen as a mythic woman, usually dangerous
Gathering of Stars	Pleiades	Perceived by Crows as a cluster of 10 stars; referenced during sweat lodge
Goose Above	Northern Cross—Cygnus	Cross- or bird-shaped constellation appearing in south; associated with geese migrating southward
Hand Star	Bottom of Orion	Shaped like a left hand from wrist to fingers; a symbol in myth of reaching for the sky, that is, an act of desperation; movement tells progress of winter
Old Campsite Star	Corona Borealis	Circular pattern looks like a camp circle; appears directly overhead at time of annual Crow Fair powwow (August)
Seven Brothers or Seven Bulls	Ursa Major—Big Dipper	Rotation around pole star indicates season
Star That Does Not Move	North Star—Pole Star— Polaris	Pivot point for rotating constellations that indicate time
Star With A Tail	Halley's comet, other comets	Once thought to predict end of world; people donned their best regalia during its appearance to await death
Turtle Above	Undetermined	Shaped like a snapping turtle described in myth
Weasel Star	Part of Draco; Cepheus; Cassiopeia; part of Perseus	A constellation that looks like a weasel in different postures as it rotates around pole star; rotation indicates season
Where They Take Women	Milky Way	The path by which Old Man Coyote, the culture hero, ran away with a man's wife

Source: McCleary (1997).

The Great Spirit

Since the beginnings of contact between Indians and non-Indians, it has become customary to characterize various transcendent spirits as the Great Spirit. Like the term "medicine" for power, "Great Spirit" is a coarse approximation of the Native concept. There is no term for a transcendent spirit in the Plains languages that literally translates as "Great Spirit." Modern Indian people nonetheless find the term convenient or useful to employ. Today, when the philosophical complexities of a phenomenon like the Lakota *wakantanka* are no longer as automatically transmitted to younger generations as they once were, the term "Great Spirit" provides tribal religious leaders with a handy gloss. It also allows them to compare the transcendent spirits of tribal religions with the one supreme being of Judeo-Christian tradition and to meld native beliefs with Christianity when they desire to do so. The Great Spirit concept has also been useful to Christian missionaries with the same goals. With it they equate Indian concepts such as the Lakota *wakantanka* or the Comanche *Ta?ahpï* with God and thus are able to claim that Christian beliefs are foreshadowed or prophesied within Native traditions, therefore rationalizing the incorporation of Indian elements in Christian ceremonies or the wholesale succession of Christianity.

In 1869 the lexicographer Stephen Riggs noted that, as far as he could tell, the Siouan *wakantanka* was a recent invention. Riggs thought that Dakota speakers came up with the image of a "great" *wakan* either to match or comprehend the Christian notion of a supreme creator. This claim would be controversial today because Sioux people now assume *wakantanka* to be a very ancient and central concept in their religion. There is really no way to test the age of the *wakantanka* concept, but Riggs's proposition remains interesting because it reminds us that even core religious concepts are constructed and changeable. We do know historically that the Great Spirit term is an introduced one, and that it continues to gain currency as an established element in traditional Plains religions. Its use leads to the simplification and homogenization of Plains religious concepts. In the future it well might totally replace older words and ideas about transcendent spirits.

SACRED SYMBOLS

Symbols are essential to the representation or expression of abstract ideas about the sacred. A symbol may be defined as an object or idea that stands for another object or idea. The connection between a symbol and what it represents is arbitrary, but it is shared among people by cultural convention. Not only is there wide agreement about the relation between a symbol and its referent (i.e., on the meaning of the symbol), but symbols also stand in systematic relations to each other, a quality which compounds their significance. The Plains Indians use a number of common symbols to represent ideas of the sacred.

Arguably the most prevalent representation on the Plains, a true "master symbol," is the circle. The circle reminds people of the cyclical nature of the seasons, eternal time without beginning or end, and a state of completeness or wholeness, all of which are diagnostic of the sacred. The holiness of this shape seems to be confirmed by nature, in the outline of the sun and moon. The harmonious and protective qualities of human social life are also outlined in circles, in the shape of the tipi floor, the circular arrangements of tipis when the people camp together, the sweat lodge, Sun Dance lodge, and dance grounds. Men's shields are another protective device in the form of a circle, and they are strengthened by absorbing the power of the circular sun. The Arapahos maintained one or more Sacred Wheels, wooden hoops about a foot and a half across, that were cared for by special keepers and included in curing ceremonies and the Sun Dance. The Sacred Wheel was said to denote the garter snake, an animal that formed the circumference of the earth in Arapaho myth. (The snake's apparent ability to regenerate by shedding its skin may have reinforced the significance of the wheel in representing a perpetual and complete cosmos.) Individual observances also include references to circles. The small wooden hoop is a familiar emblem carried by men dancers at powwows today as their personal sacred wheel. Comanches say that it always safest to travel in a circle, that is, by a circuit route rather than directly back and forth along the same path.

Sacred numbers are another device for signifying religious ideas. Certain numbers are "sacred" in that they express in a numerical way principles about how the cosmos is structured or how it works. The universally important sacred number among the Plains tribes and for much of North

America is the number four. Four is the formulaic count of items in virtually every enumeration of ritual objects or activities. It is represented in paintings and beadwork designs as a cross or a four-pointed star. It thus suggests a circle visually, connecting with that master symbol. Four summarizes the two-dimensional layout of the universe by combining the rising and setting points of the sun with the opposite axis, suggested, for example, by the swath of the Milky Way: the "four directions," east, west, north, and south. The directions may be described as winds, which in turn sets in place a series of climatic and life form associations. Colors are easily associated with these other elements as well to amplify the representational possibilities. Thus, a system of Lakota symbols can be outlined (Powers 1987:70):

1	2	3	4
West	North	East	South
Fall	Winter	Spring	Summer
Black	Red	Yellow	White
Blacktail deer	Buffalo	Whitetail deer	Elk
Swallow	Magpie	Crow	Meadowlark

The concept of nature organized in fours is so pervasive that it results in Indian classifications that vary from those created by non-Indians. For instance, non-Indian science recognizes two species of eagle inhabiting the Plains, the bald (*Haliaeetus leucocephalis*) and golden (*Aquila chrysaetos*). Indian schemes, however, often name four kinds of eagles. They may count the mature and immature versions of each of the two scientific species, which are discernable because the plumage differs between old and young birds, or else they include as "eagles" other species that scientists classify as "hawks." Since the eagle is considered the preeminent bird that bestows power, it makes sense that it would appear, from an Indian point of view, in four varieties.

Aspects of human life may also be counted in fours. The stages of human life from birth to death may be so counted. Anthropologist William K. Powers reports that modern young Lakotas extend the four directions and their associated colors to account for human racial differences, adopting the outdated notion that there are four races of humankind, "black," "red," "yellow," and "white" (Powers Ibid.).

The number five also occasionally appears as a sacred symbol. It is more common in the Great Basin west of the Plains, and among those tribes on the western edge of the Plains with Basin cultural affiliations—the Shoshones, Utes, and Comanches. Sometimes five may be expressed as the sacred number four plus an additional element. Or, elements can be arrayed in a pattern that includes five in relation to four, with one number as the primary organizing principle and the other as a secondary principle. This effect is evident in the Lakota symbol system outlined above, in which there are five kinds of elements organized in fours. Conversely, the Southern Ute universe can be expressed in a pattern of symbolic congruencies that includes both four and five, but here the dominant idea—that there are five zones of the universe—organizes four kinds of symbolic elements (after Goss 1990:17):

sky	zenith	eagle	white
mountain tops	upward	mountain lion	yellow
slopes	center	wolf/coyote	green/gray/blue
valleys	downward	weasel	red
underworld	nadir	rattlesnake	black

Once four and, to a lesser extent, five are established as symbolic numbers, multiples of these numbers also appear in mythic and ritual counts. The numbers 12 and 16 are the most common multiples, and occasionally 20. For instance, *wakantanka* in its 16 distinct forms, as described by George Sword, is known to Lakota ritualists as *Tobtob*, literally "four four."

Seven is the other prominent sacred number. Seven elaborates the circular connotations of four by adding zenith, nadir, and center to the four cardinal directions, and thus describing a sphere instead of a circle. In religious settings, center may be any place from which the ritualist stands to reckon the directions. Seven is also explicable as the sum of four, two, and one, a combination which may account for an array of elements appearing in myth or ritual. With these representational possibilities, seven shows up in many beliefs and practices. We have seen, for instance, how the stars in constellations with mythic import are counted as seven. This is interesting because there are numerous stars in the constellation Pleiades with varying visibility to the naked eye, but in Indian lore often the seven brightest are perceived. From among their numerous ceremonies, the Tetons consider seven as the major sacred rites.

William K. Powers points out that in Lakota practice seven often pertains to social organization, offered as the ideal number of political and social groups that comprise the tribal populace. Most notable is the characterization of the Sioux political divisions such as Teton, Yankton, and Sisseton as the *Oceti Śakowin* or "Seven Fireplaces." In turn, the Teton division is composed of seven subunits, such as Oglala and Hunkpapa. This tendency to count social units in sevens (even when the actual number of units "on the ground" varies from the ideal) is evident in many Plains tribal traditions. The Osages also referred to groupings of social units as "seven fireplaces," in their case the subdivisions of three major tribal divisions. The Poncas formed seven patrilineal clans for some time in their history (other times eight—two fours) and the Omaha council of chiefs had seven members, each of whom was promoted to the position through

seven grades. Expressing political order in terms of a sacred number amounts to a consecration of the society.

Powers also has illuminated how sacred numbers work logically. A number stands as a preset organizing principle in an otherwise chaotic universe. The act of counting presents worshippers with an orderly progression, as sense of control during the counting and, soon enough, as sense of completion. This predictability and finality is reassuring to humans as they attempt to deal with the supernatural. Even unfortunate events are made more sensible when they are perceived of as the unfolding of a sacred number sequence. The Comanches and other groups commonly say that deaths always come in fours. This observation helps them rationalize sad and otherwise senseless occurrences by comprehending them as steps in a natural order of fulfillment. The concept of completion is universally frequent in religious symbolism, apparent in the Christian formula of Alpha and Omega as well as in the etymological relationship in English between the words "holy" and "whole."

The most obvious and all-pervading symbol system is language. Words in the service of religious concepts may constitute a separate subsystem of communication, a "sacred language." There is evidence for sacred languages maintained by medicine men and women in many Plains cultures, although with a few exceptions they have not been well documented, in part because they are usually considered restricted if not secret. These idioms are spoken and sung during public rituals, curing ceremonies, and the initiation of novices. The invocation of sacred words corresponds to the employment of other sacred elements, such as numbers, movements, special foods, and ritual objects.

If the sacred is defined as that which is outside of ordinary experience, it stands to reason that words used to evoke the sacred would also be out of the ordinary. Sometimes the words used are in archaic forms, following the common premise that that which is old is sacred. Sacred words may also be unusual ones traceable to other languages. Or they may be circumlocutions in the form of descriptive terms. For example, in Comanche one might refer to the powerful animal spirits of the bear or coyote by one of several descriptive names. The usual word for "bear," *wasápe*, could be replaced with *tunayó*, "black oil," *piarapanakatʉ*, "big sole possessor," or *pʉhʉsoyo?*, "hair hanging down"; or, the coyote, *tseena*, might be called *kʉ?kwʉria*, "one who drools" or *ohaahnakatʉ*, "yellow arm pit possessor." The alternate words allow the ritualist to avoid using the spirit's "real" name, which would be impolite, and perhaps angering it. Another device for creating sacred language is the use of normal words but with agreed-upon meanings that are different than usual. Still other sacred words may not be translatable to anyone at all, even the ritual specialists, who just learn and perpetuate them as mystic or traditional. Whatever the origins, sacred words are usually considered incomprehensible to regular people, those who are not medicine men or women. But they are understandable to the spirits, and thus allow ritualists to converse with the spirits and mediate between the human and supernatural worlds.

Other symbols are useful in plainly showing the effects of ritual operations at work at the invisible or spiritual level. Universal on the Plains is the employment of flowing smoke, steam, and water to represent the infusion of good power, the washing away of negative influences, or the restoration of proper body operations in curing. Tobacco, cedar, and sweet grass are typically burned to produce sacralizing smoke. The Comanches prefer to make coals with pecan sticks on a small shovel or dustpan and sprinkle dried cedar on the coals. They waft the smoke over someone who is sick or fumigate the house to keep away ghosts. The aromatic sage, though not ignited, functions in a similar way. Steam is created by pouring water on super-heated rocks, as in the sweat lodge. Naturally flowing water also has this positive property. Old ritual items that have potentially harmful power are disposed of by throwing them in a flowing creek. In this regard it is notable that the Omahas believe that ghosts will not cross a stream, as noted above.

A host of other substances, objects, and images functioned as religious symbols. A man with bear medicine could represent his power with any of several parts of the bear—a claw, fang, or tail, not to mention pictures of entire bears or their parts painted on his shield or tipi; and even the bear's oil, which worked as an actual healing salve and insect repellent, could be regarded also as a sign of spiritual power. Similar emblems of other kinds of personal power were ubiquitous. In the ritual arena, poles, posts, saplings, sprigs or beds of sage, buffalo skulls, mounds of earth, shapes traced in the dirt, paint applied on bodies or surfaces, "dolls" (human effigies), and other like items commonly bore symbolic value. Many of these items are detailed in the descriptions of specific rituals which follow.

THE VISION QUEST

The ideal for Plains men is to establish a relationship with some donor of spiritual power. The spirit helper, or guardian spirit as it often called, is sought in a vision or dream, with the intention of making a lasting compact. The power seeker contacts the spirit by demonstrating his worthiness or neediness and assuming a dream-like state. The spirit may become sympathetic and provide personal protection, health, success in hunting, war, or love, wisdom, or perhaps an ability to cure or see into the future. The received power may also be in the form of knowledge, either the illumination of prior dreams or a prophecy about the outcome of a planned hunt or raid. In the present day, the vision may provide guidance about modern concerns, such as how to find work, take care of one's family, or deal with troubles such as alcoholism, drug addiction, or marital problems.

This procedure is commonly known as "vision quest" in English. The Sioux also refer to it as "pipefast," because the supplicant prepares and carries a pipe and also fasts while awaiting his vision. The Crow term *bilisshíissanne* means "to fast from water." Other native-language names indicate additional characteristics of the rite. The Lakota *hanbleceya*, "vision/dream-to cry," ("crying for a vision"), refers to the pitiable attitude that the seeker is supposed to adopt in order to gain the sympathy of a spirit. The Comanches do not place such an emphasis on the seeker's humility. Their term, *anahabi* or "hill-lie," ("to lie on a hill"), refers simply to the usual technique of waiting on a lonely knoll for the spirit's appearance.

The Plains vision quest is first undertaken by a young man at adolescence, though men continue to do them periodically through their adult lives, whenever they feel a need to revisit, change, or add spirit donors. The seeker first gets advice from an older man who is considered to be holy on account of his knowledge and personal experience about how to acquire power. To contract with this sacred person, the seeker offers a pipe that he has prepared especially for the ritual, and they both smoke. (Quests may also be undertaken by young women in some tribes, but this practice is unusual and generally a modern development. In these cases the tutor may be an older woman. For the sake of simplicity, this account will refer to male participants).

The sacred person teaches the seeker where to go and how to behave so that the spirits will appear. He teaches prayers or songs that will help encourage a spirit visit. And, he encourages the seeker to ready himself by cleansing his mind of negative thoughts.

When you have everything ready, you must prepare yourself, typically for an entire year. If you are prone to anger, you must stop. If you always have bad thoughts of others or if you are a womanizer, you must get these behaviors out of your system. If money has you by the nose and leads you around, get that out of your system.

(Catches 1999:150)

The seeker also begins making himself receptive to the spirits by detaching from his ordinary social roles. Even though his purpose in conducting the quest may be to strengthen relations with family and friends, for the time being he becomes, according to the Crows, like an orphan (*akéeleete*, "one who has nothing"). He becomes someone of whom it is said, "he is looking for something" (*baachichíilik*). This state further emphasizes his vulnerability and need for aid from the spirits as well as his fellow tribe members. To consolidate these preparations, just prior to the quest the seeker takes part in a sweat lodge. This ritual purifies him once more and also brings the seeker's relatives together in support of his quest, in effect beginning to mend his orphaned status.

The vision has to be obtained in seclusion, so the seeker is escorted or sent alone away from inhabited areas and left in a high place, which could be either a dramatic precipice or simply a knoll. Some of the celebrated vision quest sites on the Plains include Bear Butte north of Rapid City, South Dakota, Castle Rocks and other buttes in the Pryor Mountains of south-central Montana, Medicine Bluffs and several peaks in the neighboring Wichita Mountains in southwest Oklahoma, and Medicine Mounds in Hardeman County, Texas. Uncountable nameless hills have also served as vision quest sites.

Before departing, the seeker has pledged to stay out by himself for two to five days. The Lakotas may speak of each period of sunlight and darkness as a distinct "day," so that a 24-hour day in the non-Indian sense would be considered "two days" for ritual purposes. Whatever the details, the duration pledge as well as the promised starting date must be strictly kept for the ritual to work:

> When we pledge to go through a Pipefast, we are not saying things that we can change later on. If we say we are going to go on a Pipefast for four days and four nights, we must under no circumstances change the number of days. We have to go four days and four nights, because regardless of who you are—king, queen, president of the United States—you should not tell the Great Spirit you will do something one way and then slack off, or do it another way. When you talk to the Great Spirit on selecting a day, you have to do exactly what you have told Him; otherwise, the Pipefast is nothing at all, it is just time wasted. It is crucial for the Pipefast to be precise, even if one has to go through the heat of the day, the cold of the night, the wind, the rain, the hail, and whatever else.

(Catches 1999:147–148)

FIGURE 9.3   A Teton man undertaking the vision quest in a 1907 posed photo by Edward S. Curtis.

As the seeker is situated on top of the hill, he or his adviser, mindful of the direction of the rising sun, creates a ritual space, blessing the spot with smoke and perhaps marking the ground in some fashion. The Crows sometimes build a low stone wall. The Tetons create a rectangular area bounded with four colored flags and string holding small tobacco offerings, a device for indicating holy ground also used in some of their other rituals. Within this space is a smaller, shallow pit like a grave. The seeker wears only moccasins and a breechcloth. He sheds the moccasins as the quest begins, as an act of humility and nativism. In addition to his pipe, he carries a buffalo robe or its modern counterpart, a star quilt or sleeping bag, but he has no other protection and will have to endure the elements, however harsh.

Left alone, the seeker feels the growing sense of solitude and the cool air of night approaching. Then, the absolute darkness of night conjures dread, self-pity, and perhaps tears. He steps ever so slowly but continually within the boundaries of the ritual space. In an ultimately futile effort, he attempts to impose order by periodically praying and offering the pipe to the four directions and saluting the morning star and sun as they rise. He may rest—within the pit, if there is one—but strives not to fall into a long sleep. He has no food or drink with him the entire time. Pangs of hunger swell like waves through his body and his thirst becomes incessant. He meditates intensively. After a long while, a sense of timelessness or wonder overtakes him. At this point he has temporarily left the mundane world and has himself become spiritual. Birds and animals appear and talk to him, or perhaps a ghost, seductive women, or the thunder beings show up. Any of these beings may taunt or trick him, scare him, or share an important message. The spirits may try to chase the seeker from his post or carry him far away temporarily and instruct him in curing.

The appearance of some spirits may be subtle or momentary, but others materialize in the most astounding way, amid blinding lights and deafening sounds. In one description that reoccurs in Sioux accounts over time, the seeker is overcome by a colossal pounding noise, only to realize that the sound he hears is the steps of ants as they walk about at his feet. A larger-than-life eagle hovers before the supplicant; a stick turns into a rattlesnake; an elk rakes the pigmented earth with its antlers or a buffalo paws the dirt to suggest a mystic paint design for the seeker to wear; the thunder beings emerge from eerie cloud formations astride giant horses and rumble by.

Sometimes the vision is quite long and involved. The Crow chief Plenty-coups (d. 1932) told of a vision which he acquired as a young man at Two Buttes in south-central Montana. After fasting day and night, he heard a voice beckoning him eastward into the darkness and he followed, barefoot. He was aware of walking in the voice-person's tracks but had no sensation of his feet touching the rocky ground, and the person loomed ahead as a strange light. Coyotes began yelping around him and soon he was aware that many coyotes had encircled him and the person he was following, their circle progressing forward as the two trod along. The entire party then came upon a lodge that seemed to rise up out of the ground, and Plenty-coups was shown inside by the voice-person. The tipi interior was lighted, but there was no fire. Within were many old warriors sitting in two rows around the south and north sides. It appeared that they were counting coup (tallying war deeds) by sticking eagle feathers in the ground. Those on the south Plenty-coups recognized as the winds, thunder, moon, and stars. These spirits did not welcome Plenty-coups, but he was then invited to sit with those on the north, whom he recognized as the little people. The chief of the dwarves handed Plenty-coup some feathers and demanded that he count

coup. He was reluctant to lie, since he had no war deeds, but he stuck a feather in the ground, whereupon the dwarf chief spoke up and provided a coup account for his guest, detailing the slaying of a rider on a white horse. Upon demand Plenty-coups stuck another feather, and this time the dwarf chief described the killing of a man on a black horse. The dwarf chief then declared that Plenty-coups had great power within him and would someday be a chief.

A somewhat similar vision was reported by an Arapaho man between 1899 and 1901, suggesting that visions are culturally patterned across as well as within tribes:

> . . . he fasted on a hill near a lake on the Cimarron. It was the third night. As he was lying on the ground he heard footsteps. A man called to him to come to his tent. He thought someone was trying to deceive him, and he paid no attention. The person continued to call him. The fourth time he said, "Hurry and come. Other people are waiting for you." Then the informant consented. He went in his thoughts, but he himself did not get up from the ground. He went downward from where he was lying, into the ground. He followed the man who had called him, and entered a tent. On the right side of the tent sat four young men painted black with yellow streaks. On the left side of the tent sat three men painted yellow with red streaks. The man who had possessed the medicine sat at the back of the tent. He himself sat down at the left side, so that there were four on each side of the man at the back. This person was painted red. In front of him lay a pipe with its head to the north (the left). The head of the tent put mushrooms on the fire as incense, and then shook his rattle, in imitation of a rattlesnake, while the young men sang. Then he passed the pipe, and they smoked. After this, he rubbed and cleaned the pipe, and told the visitor that he must do in the same way. Then he folded his arms, bent his head, and two snakes came from his mouth, coiled on the ground, and darted their tongues. Then the man who had vomited the two snakes blew on then,

and they disappeared. At first the visitor did not know where they had gone. Then he realized that they were in his own body. He declares that he keeps them there now, one on each side. Through virtue of this dream he now cures rattlesnake-bites.

(Kroeber 1983:421)

In order to intensify the ordeal, especially if a vision was slow in coming or had eluded the seeker in previous attempts, in the old days members of certain tribes such as the Cheyennes, Crows, and Lakotas injured their own bodies, by themselves or with the help of their advisers. The common method involved the insertion of two wood or bone skewers through the chest or under the shoulder blades, by which the seeker was bound with a stout rawhide thong to a shoulder-high stake or a heavy buffalo skull. He pulled against the hindrance until his flesh tore and he broke free. Plenty-coups once chopped off the end of his left index finger with a knife so "some Person [spirit] would smell my blood and come aid me" (Linderman 1962:60), and the anthropologist Robert Lowie observed circa 1907 that several Crow men were missing digits. Cutting flesh from the arms was another common method.

As Plenty-coups's remark makes clear, the purpose in injuring oneself was to appear more pitiable, more humble or ignorant, in order to attract a spirit helper. Also, the flesh or blood removed from the body was offered as a sacrifice, a very personal gift to establish what was hoped to be an ongoing exchange relationship with the spirit. From a clinical perspective, the shock and physical pain of self-injury would enhance the unusual state of consciousness promoted in other ways by the quest procedure and more likely lead to a vision.

Even with such extreme techniques, a vision quest was not always successful. Either the seeker fell under the hardship and quit or he stuck it out but failed to have a visitation, suggesting that he was not quite prepared in his heart and mind. A failed quest was not always a cause for shame,

so long as the seeker made an honest effort. One simply tried again another time.

When the vision is received or the promised time is over, the seeker abandons the knoll or is retrieved by the sacred man and escorted home. During the quest the sacred man has led the seeker's relatives in prayer to support his effort. They all partake in another sweat lodge, reestablishing the seeker's membership in human society, and then the seeker talks about his experiences with the sacred man in private to get his interpretation. Together they fathom the significance of every aspect of the ordeal. Frequently the guardian spirit has granted one or more outward signs of the power that was conferred, such as a special song or taboo. The spirit may provide the seeker with an object symbolic of the guardian relationship such as a feather or part of an animal (the spirit either bestows the item magically during the vision or instructs the seeker to slay an animal and take the memento). The sacred man may advise the seeker how to care for this item. Visions can also spell a person's destiny, so afterwards they are carefully considered so that the seeker will be open to perceiving the fulfillment of the spirit's predictions or aware of additional signs about the future.

The successful visionary must apply whatever he has learned from the whole process to his daily life on an ongoing basis. He makes a talisman from the spirit object to either wear or put in safekeeping, and he records his power by painting his shield with a scene of the vision. He must sustain the attitude of sincerity and determination (called *díakaashe* in Crow, literally "he really did it") that attracted the spirits to his cause, and he must follow their directions. If he fails to follow through or finds other unexpected troubles that are not anticipated by his vision, he may seek another. When prophecies are delivered in the vision quest, it might take a long time for them to unfold, perhaps only through the accumulation of additional spiritual messages. Many years after his mystic visit to the little people, Plenty-coups had another vision, this time of a shield with two scalps suspended, and soon after he made his first two killings of enemies, the first riding a white horse and the second a black one, just as the dwarf chief had predicted long before.

In addition to the sought vision, Plains men and women also experience sacred apparitions involuntarily. Some writers have distinguished between visions and dreams by stating that the former are purposefully sought and the latter are not. In an influential dissertation on the guardian spirit concept (Benedict 1923), anthropologist Ruth Benedict concluded that sought visions were characteristic of the Plains culture area, while unsought dreams were the main means of inspiration for the tribes west of the Plains. A strict verbal distinction is not kept by Plains people, though, who frequently use the English term "dream" for both sought and involuntary experiences. The important thing to note is that Plains Indians report encounters with spirits when they are not on a vision quest—seeing an eagle that flies alongside and speaks to them while they are driving, for example. Also, dreams during sleep may be interpreted as messages from the spirits. Some contemporary Comanches believe that the ghost of a dead person will visit the widow or widower in a dream within four days of the death to bring comforting advice. A Comanche man took his car in to have the brakes checked the morning after he dreamed that an owl flew in front of his car. Whether a sleep dream is significant depends on the feelings and interpretation of the dreamer, though descriptions of unsought dreams and their meanings, like those of sought visions, are formulaic and obviously shaped by cultural expectations. There are also traditional narratives about involuntary encounters with spirits. A typical story describes a lost hunter or a warrior left for dead after a battle, who is visited by an animal spirit, usually a wolf, coyote, buffalo, or crow. The animal revives him, grants him medicine and a distinctive song or dance, and perhaps guides him back to his village. This story line is after all very much like the vision quest procedure.

Visions and dreams are the wellsprings of Plains religion, for all ceremonies, however small or large, are said to have originated with some individual's dream-like encounter with a spirit. The Lakotas regard the vision quest, along with the accompanying sweat lodge, as the original ritual among their seven fundamental rites, and esteem it as most basic because it is the only ritual that is for an individual alone.

MEDICINE MEN AND WOMEN

Sometimes a vision instructs the seeker to dedicate himself to studying the ways of power and the spirits, to "carry the pipe" as the Lakotas say. Or else a man may simply have a great deal of accumulated knowledge of these matters from his own questing. In either case he will gain a reputation for his expertise and be sought by others in the community for advice and help. He will be asked to coach others in the vision quest, to apply his power to cure the sick, and to run major ceremonies and lead the peoples' prayers to the spirits so they all can benefit from the special rapport he has established. The Comanches know this figure as *puhakatꞍ* "power possessor," and the Crows say *akbaalía*, "one who doctors." The Lakotas call him *wicaša wakan*, "man sacred" or "holy man." Such a person was described by the Lakota Little Wound around 1900:

> A *wakan* man is one who is wise. It is one who knows the spirits. It is one who has power with the spirits. It is one who communicates with the spirits. It is one who can do strange things. A *wakan* man knows things that the people do not know. He knows the ceremonies and the songs. He can tell the people what their visions mean. He can tell the people what the spirits wish them to do. He can tell what is to be in the future. He can talk with animals and with trees and with stones. He can talk with everything on earth.
>
> (Walker 1980:69)

Women as well as men may pursue the role of medicine practitioner, and many women have taken an important place in tribal society with this status, equivalent to that of senior men. The wives of medicine men are perhaps more disposed to this career, especially upon the death of their spouses, but there is no requirement that a woman apprentice with her husband. In any case, women do not take on the role until after menopause. A woman's ability to bear new life, evident in menstruation, is a great power that is antithetical to and supersedes any power acquired from spirits. It is only considered appropriate or necessary for women to seek and manipulate external power before or after the childbearing years. The Comanche woman known as Sanapia (1895–1979) trained and quested to be a doctor under the direction of her mother and other relatives from about age 14 to 17 then promptly married and had children, and only activated her status as a curer later in life.

Medicine practitioners in Plains cultures conform in some degree to the type of religious specialist called *shaman*. This term derives from *saman*, a word in the Tungus language of the Evenk people of Eastern Siberian, having to do with ecstasy and used for a charismatic person who specializes in engaging the sacred on behalf of fellow humans. There is much debate about how this term is defined and how widely it should be applied outside of the original Siberian context. It may be said to properly include only individuals who are chosen involuntary by the spirits to be mediators, or it might also include those who actively pursue a spirit connection or acquire power. The prototypic shaman is tutored by other ritualists but also has a first encounter with the spirits that amounts to a shocking initiation, after which he or she is set apart from normal society and regarded as eccentric though gifted. The shaman is able to move easily into a trance and uses this ability to hold community

FIGURE 9.4   A Blackfoot medicine man dressed in a bearskin attempts to cure a patient in a sketch by George Catlin.

séances in which spirit helpers are summoned to help everyone.

Whether the shaman is actually possessed by the spirits or simply communicates with them is another question of definition. In any case, the spirits grant the shaman extraordinary abilities. A shaman may be said to be able to read minds; see into the future; see through objects and hear with super acuity; find lost objects; become invisible; travel to the spirit world via the magical flight of his or her own spirit; produce disembodied spirit voices, vibrations, and flashes of light; withstand stabbings, extreme cold, or a walk on hot coals; escape from rope bindings; shift gender; and heal or harm people. The presence of these traits on the Plains is strong evidence for prehistoric cultural connections between Siberia and North America. On the other hand, there is no need to subscribe to the idea of a discrete and unified religion called shamanism characteristic of all "primitive" peoples, as some scholars have proposed.

Plains medicine men have also sometimes been called "priests," particularly when they are leading large rituals. As in the case of "shaman," use of the outside term raises definitional problems. "Priest" has been used casually to mean a celebrant of rituals and specifically for the clergymen of certain Christian denominations. Anthropologists instituted a difference between part-time specialists in small-scale societies ("shamans") versus full-time, professional religious leaders in complex societies ("priests"). This typology has been further expanded with terms such as "healer," "medium," "seer," "witch," and "sorcerer," to argue for the relevance of distinctions in function and degree of social integration and complexity. Subsequently other scholars have argued against these strict definitions, stressing the close similarities in function of religious specialists regardless of the local circumstances. Plains medicine men are part-time ritual specialists—they are not provided a living for the religious work they do.

The important matter from the Indian perspective is what a spiritually gifted person is able to do.

Little Wound remarks on the holy person's ability to talk to all creatures. Medicine practitioners are adept at communicating with animals and the spirits. They can talk to these beings to secure power and to express the wants of their fellow humans. Equally important as a basis for their authority is the ability to communicate with other people. Medicine men and women are good talkers who are talented at extemporizing prayers, good at remembering stories and songs, and effective in persuading people to behave themselves properly. They give advice to their fellow tribe members about how to handle everyday problems and how to live righteous lives. They direct rituals and instruct the participants on how to carry off their roles. And as part of their learning, they master the ancient, arcane words of sacred language handed down to make ritual procedures more successful. The medicine practitioner's speech is more than communication; it is an extension of his or her power, with causative force.

Medicine practitioners are also known for forecasting the future. They are always on the watch for unusual signs in the night sky, in the weather, or in animal behavior that might be omens. In addition to fortuitous signs from nature there are also prediction methods. Old-time Comanches thought that if you asked a horned lizard where the buffalo were, it would point its horns in the right direction. Or, someone would peek into the future by checking their reflection in badger blood. The Crows used a mixture of buffalo and badger blood. If a warrior saw his image as a white-haired old man in this mixture, he knew he would survive the next raid, but a scalped or bloodstained image meant trouble ahead. For this method of auguring, the Comanches split open the body of a badger that had been killed by chance. They sprinkled dirt on the blood and let the mess dry in the sun to create a shiny surface. Then they looked to read their fate in the same signs that the Crows recognized.

A related ability allows medicine practitioners to find lost and stolen things, including personal possessions, livestock, and people. Their supernatural power allows them to visualize the missing item in its current location and tell the owner how to retrieve it. While their power nominally grants this ability, the medicine man or woman is a keen student of human nature who knows the personalities and motives of people in the community, and can make educated guesses about the whereabouts of a stray child or "borrowed" item.

It is the curing ability of the medicine practitioner that most strongly defines his or her role in society. This ability hinges simultaneously on knowledge of pharmaceuticals and expertise in securing and applying supernatural power. Some curers work essentially as general practitioners, while others specialize in war wounds, snakebite, broken bones, or the illnesses imposed by ghosts. They may also be classified in Native terms by the kind of animal power they wield (i.e., "bear doctor") or the curing method they most prefer.

Usually a medicine practitioner secures abundant knowledge about plant and animal substances with actual healing properties, learning how to gather, prepare, and apply these medicines. There is much to know. Some plant medicines only have effective compounds at certain times of the year, or only work when harvested, dried, mashed, cooked, or combined in certain ways. The number of species in a medicine practitioner's kit is large and surprising in view of the common notion of the Plains as monotonous grassland. It is estimated that the Lakotas knew over 300 herbal remedies, such as ragweed, calamus, daisy fleabane, wild bergamot, mountain mint, and purple coneflower. The Comanche Sanapia had 16 species in her basic kit, including peyote, iris, milkweed, sneezeweed, broomweed, and prickly ash, plus the gummy amber-colored excrescence of mason bees.

I can just sit here and look at them bald prairies and see four kinds of medicines growing. I bet you can't even see them? Not many . . . even of my people, up to today, can even see them

growing early in the spring. I can because I've learned that way. There's lots of plants that can get you well, but they ain't many people who even know that anymore.

(quoted in Jones 1972:64)

The medicine practitioner applies these therapeutic substances using special techniques, like chewing a plant to release its medicinal compounds or brewing tea that can be swallowed by sick patients or massaged into their bodies. Such medicines are given in four doses or dispensed with four hand movements, and their effects are supplemented with prayers and the fanning of sage and cedar smoke over the patient to transmit supernatural power. These motions are intended to restore the normal flow of fluids or power within the body, which according to Native disease theory is disrupted by an unnatural blockage or by the presence of poisons or tiny, insect-like entities.

Medicine practitioners are well versed in creating illusions that they used to represent the effects of their power and the presence of the spirits they have summoned. Some of the abilities they exhibit are to make voices and other sounds appear in a disembodied manner, to make sparks fly in the dark, and to release themselves from tight bindings. A common device among the northern tribes is to somehow make a great din within a ceremonial tent and make it grow taught until it shakes as if it were energized. On the Southern Plains, it is said that medicine men sometimes make the image of a dead person appear on a hide or on the wall of a tipi. A Comanche elder once gave the author a vivid recollection of a ceremony he attended as a boy, in which the medicine man climbed up and down a tall, slender willow sapling that could not have normally supported a man's weight.

The Southern Plains is also home to a style of legerdemain employing a black handkerchief. Medicine men among the Plains Apaches, Kiowas, Comanches, and Wichitas sometimes wear a black scarf around their necks as a badge of power, which they take off to perform tricks. Under the cover of the black handkerchief, the nineteenth-century Apache ritualist Dävéko was able to fill an empty cup with sugar, turn a piece of paper into a stick of candy, and transform a white man's Stetson hat into a skull. Such displays no doubt bolstered confidence in Dävéko's power, so that he was more successful when he applied the handkerchief in curing. The scarf functions like an x-ray machine, the curer gazing through it at the patient to sight the illness. Then, it is used to rub or whisk away the cause of the affliction.

Another typical technique for representing remedial power, found throughout the entire region, is the sucking cure. The medicine practitioner draws out the illness of a sick person by sucking the object or substance that caused the trouble from the person's body. Arapahos call the intrusive object a "ghost arrow" and believe it to be a part of a dead person—a tooth, bone, hair, or piece of skin—shot into the victim by a ghost. Comanches refer to the item as a "boss" and describe it as a sharp stone or shard of glass. They believe that it has been inserted magically through the "blasting breath of some secret enemy," as one early observer of the tribe wrote, that is, by a jealous neighbor practicing witchcraft. Or else the illness is attributed to bad blood or poison that also must be removed. After singing, praying, and incensing the patient's body with cedar, sage, and tobacco, the medicine practitioner feels for the location of the "catch" or bump revealing the object or poison, and applies his mouth or a mouthpiece made from a hollow bone or drilled, conical section of horn to the spot and sucks until the object or poison is magically drawn into his mouth. He then spits it out in a bloody mass to show that he has achieved a cure.

Whether this performance is considered by the patient to be a physical operation or a metaphoric representation is hard to say, as attitudes are formed by the individual as part of the process.

The experience is preconditioned because it is a traditional teaching that a patient must believe in the medicine man's powers in order for his cure to work. Writing about the Crows, anthropologist Rodney Frey notes, "The efficacy of medicine is directly related to the recipient's 'belief' (*amm-aakalátche*). If a cure (*baalía*) is to be effective, the patient must 'believe' in it" (Frey 1987:141). In recent times, in a cultural context saturated by non-Indian science and popular culture, those seeking the sucking cure may choose not to confront the question of what actually happens, but instead simply focus on their faith in the possibility of a cure by traditional means, and whether the treatment appears to have an effect. In the 1980s a Comanche man began having severe pain in his left leg and several visits to the hospital failed to provide him with a diagnosis or relief. He then contracted with a medicine woman who told him that he had a boss in his leg that had been shot there by his ex-wife's relatives. She performed the sucking cure and produced a flint arrowhead. When asked if he thought that the medicine woman really withdrew a flint from his leg, he replied pensively, "I don't know. . . . All I know is I felt better."

Cases like this one reveal the possibility of witchcraft or sorcery, in which someone who possesses supernatural power uses it to injure rather than help a fellow human. In Plains custom the witch is pictured as an aging man or woman who is spiteful, soured on life, and envious of younger or more prosperous neighbors. The witch does his or her evil by shooting an intrusive object (projecting it, sometimes over long distances, with an intense stare, with the breath, or a buzzing sound), tricking the victim into violating a taboo or touching some polluting substance, or inflicting harm on a mud effigy of the target. The usual recourse is to have the witch's curse reversed by the work of a good medicine man. Those under repeated suspicion of practicing witchcraft, however, face shunning by other community members (a dire punishment when sharing is key to survival), and there are also recorded instances of the summary execution of witches by victims' families, their own families, or military societies. While witchcraft is a standard theme in Plains supernaturalism, it is not, as among the Navajos or Pueblos of the Southwest culture area, a continuous, inevitable counterpoint to beneficial sacred activity. Witchcraft cases are treated as aberrations on the Plains, and religious principles weigh heavily on the benevolent application of supernatural power.

Just as the successful vision quest requires purity of heart and mind, a medicine practitioner must continue to live righteously to keep his power, and this is a special burden for someone with a big reputation. He must remain respectful to the spirits, humble about his power, and scrupulous in observing taboos. Comanche medicine men believe that oil or grease is harmful to their power, so much so that they might prevent a car from parking in their yard lest the oil drip and spoil their power accidentally. If the man's power donor was an eagle, he must avoid allowing anyone to pass behind him while he is eating, in the same way that eagles instinctively protect themselves.

The medicine practitioner should never profit from his power but take pity on those less fortunate and use the power generously to help anyone who needs it. At the same time, the proper balance of the universe is maintained through reciprocity and some ceremonial exchange typically marks the medicine man's interaction with his power sources and his clients. For example, the Comanche medicine woman Sanapia customarily left bits of green cloth hanging in the bushes after collecting medicinal leaves. The doctor in turn receives a payment from his patient. Traditional media of exchange include tobacco, eagle feathers, peltries, and horses. Sometimes cash is used in payment, but in a small enough amount to serve only as a token. Some transactions even recognize that paper money is green, like the herbs whose benefits are being acquired. Among the Crows, the exchange between medicine practitioner and

patient is seen as one of an endless sequence of balanced transactions that perpetuate the natural and social worlds. After, or sometimes before, the curing ceremony, the Crow doctor receives cash, blankets, or something else of value, frequently in quantities of four. The patient must simultaneously provide a gift to the spirit who aids them in the cure. This gift is intangible but invaluable: *díakaashe*, the inner disposition of pride and sincerity that honors the spirit and ensures a successful transmission of curative power.

A medicine man who wields his power out of greed or with bad intent will eventually have it rebound on him and harm or perhaps even kill him. If merely careless about his attitude, he will fail to retain the power or obtain more, and his efficacy and reputation will quickly plummet. Even the most honorable of practitioners will face the eventual loss of power and prestige. The fate of a faded medicine man, one who has "lost the pipe," can be particularly harsh. His loss of power will seem stridently evident in his own physical aging and in the misfortunes that befall those close to him.

William K. Powers has written about the sad decline of Lakota spiritual leader George Plenty Wolf (1901–1977). Plenty Wolf's wife died, and around the same time he lost his two most cherished ritual rattles. His vision began to fail. Then his son-in-law, who worked as Plenty Wolf's chief singer in ceremonies, also passed away. Yet other relatives died or were injured, and each instance seemed to confirm publicly that Plenty Wolf's medicine was no more. Plenty Wolf gave up running rituals and no one in the community sought him out for advice or cures any more. The peoples' needs persisted, but they simply found a new medicine man. One evening some young toughs pulled Plenty Wolf from his pickup and beat him severely. Soon after he fell sick and died in the Public Health Service hospital. The fate of a medicine man is a reminder that no one is above the spirits, all humans are ultimately helpless, and the interests of the community as a whole always trump those of individuals, even those who have possessed great supernatural power.

The tension between individual and communal needs and interests is prominent in all aspects of traditional Plains Indian life, and religion is no exception. The fundamentals of Plains religion as outlined above, however, mainly concern individuals, either power seekers or power possessors. The anthropologist Anthony Wallace has pointed out the value of understanding religious activity that is organized at only minimal levels, noting that such activity may be the sole or principle means of addressing the supernatural in some societies, and remains important even where religious structures are large and complex.

Wallace refers to levels of organization as "cult institutions," using the term "cult" in its neutral, not pejorative, sense. In his most basic level, called "individualistic cult institutions," there is no distinction between lay person and religious specialist—every person is his or her own ritualist. This perfectly describes much of the basics of Plains religion, including the belief in power and its manipulation, taboo, the vision quest, and the notion of the guardian spirit. At the next level of complexity, called "shamanic cult institutions," there is a religious division of labor involving two individuals, the specialist who mediates with the supernatural on account of others and his or her client. The activity of Plains medicine men and women fits this description. The next chapter will examine the more complex outgrowths of visions and curing: group rituals that involve many worshippers at once.

Sources: Benedict (1923); Bowers (1992); Boyd (1981); Brown and Irwin (2001); Bucko (2005); Catches (1999); Densmore (1918); Dorsey (1995); Durkheim (1995); Dusenberry (1962); Ewers (1958, 1981); Fletcher and La Flesche (1972, I, II); Flores (1985); Forbush and May (1955); Frey (1987); García Rejón and Gelo (1995); Gelo (1986, 1994); Gill (1991); Goss (1990); Grinnell (1966, 1972); Harrington (1928); Harrod (1987); Hoebel (1988); Hultkrantz (1981, 1987); Jones (1972, 1980); Kardiner (1945); Kehoe (1996, 2000); Kracht (1997); Kroeber (1983); Linderman (1962); Lowie (1982); Marett (1909); Mayor (2005); McCleary (1997); Moore (1986); Murie (1989); Neighbours (1975); Nye (1935); Parks (1982, 1996); M. Powers (1986); W. Powers (1977, 1978, 1986, 1987); Schweinfurth (2002); Shafer (1980); Tylor (1877); Walker (1979, 1980); Wallace (1966); Wallace and Hoebel (1952); Watkins (1984); Williamson and Farrer (1992); and Wissler (1974).

CHAPTER SUMMARY

Plains Indian life is infused with religion. Plains religion concerns supernatural power and beings and how humans interact with them. Power or "medicine" is the most basic sacred concept. Power resides throughout the universe in spirits and natural objects and can be obtained and used by humans. Spirits include thunder, animals, giants, elves, monsters, ghosts, and celestial bodies. All tribes have a name for a transcendent spirit who is a pervasive creator. Such figures have given rise to the term "Great Spirit." Plains Indians use conventional symbols to represent the sacred, including circles, numbers, colors, and animals. Individuals seek power through the vision quest. Medicine men and women specialize in gaining power and using it to help others.

QUESTIONS FOR REVIEW

1. Interpret George Sword's explanation of the Lakota concept *wakan.*
2. Evaluate the term "Great Spirit" in relation to what is known about spirits as conceptualized among the Plains tribes.
3. Describe in detail the Plains vision quest.
4. How do Plains medicine men and women serve as religious specialists?

CHAPTER 10

GROUP RITUALS

Large stable populations such as those that came together on the Great Plains may develop a collective approach to the management of spiritual power, one in which a number of people work together to obtain, renew, and apply the power, and train and certify novices in religious matters. This group work is an alternative to healing or spiritual teaching performed one-on-one as each single case arises. Instead there is coordination of all interested parties, who meet regularly, according to a seasonal calendar. Their continual activity is considered beneficial to the entire tribe, for it may anticipate and prevent general misfortune and illness, or reestablish the proper workings of the universe, and the whole community comes to rely on it. The presence of a group approach to spirituality does not totally eliminate the activity of individual power seekers, or curers and their patients; individual, dyadic, and group patterns coexist in most societies. Thus, when proposing the "individual" (vision quester) and "shamanic" (medicine man–patient) cult institutions, anthropologist Anthony Wallace also identified the group approach as a next evolutionary step, and termed it "communal" cult institution.

Communal approaches to the spirit world are most easily examined through public rituals. Public rituals often involved nearly all tribe members at once as participants or spectators. On the Plains there were a number of these ceremonies, some specific to single tribes, others diffused through nearly all of the tribes. They present a wonderful opportunity to see, hear, and feel the expression of a community's deepest values, and group rituals have been studied extensively by non-Indians seeking cultural knowledge. Revealed are the common elements of Indian religion and the particulars of tribal worldviews. Along the way, the historical, social, and philosophical connections between different groups are often illuminated.

Some care is necessary when focusing on large-scale rituals; in the past, expositions of Native religion have done so to the detriment of full understanding. A false impression can be created, that people went to a few big ceremonies every year that totally satisfied their needs. But the large ceremonies were really points in a continual round of ritual activity. They meshed with each other and with less public and spectacular religious observances, and it was the entirety of this activity that was most important. From a Native viewpoint, a ritual might not be considered predominant simply because it was large. With these cautions in place, we can look at a number of public rituals that were, and are, characteristic of Plains religion.

THE MASSAUM

A bustling mass of dancers in fantastic animal spirit costumes characterized perhaps the earliest of the known Plains group rituals, the Cheyenne Massaum ("Crazy Lodge"). Properly speaking, the Massaum was a ceremony of the Tsistsistas, the larger of two known ethnic units that became the historical Cheyennes. Tsistsistas spirit impersonators convened at midsummer, as the blue star Rigel was about to rise in the southeast early morning sky, for a five-day rite. At stake was nothing less than the renewal of the Tsistsistas/Cheyenne world. The dancers reenacted the creation of the universe as recorded in myth, recharged the animal-based spiritual power that protected and guided them through the year, and restored their mastery of hunting, essential to their survival as Plains people.

The ritual itself was enormously complicated. The ceremony first had to be pledged by a woman, who upon completing it would function as instructor to women pledging in subsequent years. The pledging woman recruited three other women, who were former pledge makers, and a man to serve as both instructors and the main performers. The new pledge maker assumed the role of Ehyophstah (Yellow-Haired Girl), daughter of the thunder and earth spirits, and her fellow instructors represented other spirits described in myth. The pledge maker also decided upon a location for the ritual, most likely in consultation with a council of ceremonial leaders. Messages were sent to the dispersed bands to gather in the latter part of July at the chosen site. The camp was always oriented toward Bear Butte,

near present Sturgis, South Dakota, which the Cheyennes considered their sacred mountain. After they assembled the camp, the participants prepared for the ritual by purifying themselves in the sweat lodge. The main instructors and their assistants were painted red to transform them into spiritual actors.

During each of the next five days there were four or six main thematic activities, as summarized in Table 10.1. Each theme was developed through some combination of sacred procedures including prayer, song cycles, body painting, sand painting (creating images on the ground in colored sand), fasting, sign language performances, the smoking of tobacco with ancient-style straight bone pipes, and dancing. During the first day, a lodge was constructed which represented the universe before creation. Then this universe was inhabited by the five instructors/spirit impersonators. The Yellow-Haired Girl assumed a central role as the mythic teacher of the hunt. Next, the wolf spirits were brought alive as the master hunters, to exemplify the relation between predator and prey that order the natural world. The leaders of the wolves were Red Wolf and White Wolf, corresponding to the red star Aldebran and white star Sirius, whose appearances exactly framed, 28 days before and after, that of the blue star Rigel.

As a world renewal ceremony, the Massaum had much in common with rites held by tribes across the continent, from the Yuroks of California to the Algonquian Munsi and Mahicans of the East Coast. Given the Cheyenne's own background, the Massaum is seen as an outgrowth of ancient Algonquian ritualism. In turn, the Algonquian tradition has a great deal in common with Siberian shamanism. Anthropologist Karl Schlesier defined 134 traits comprised by the Massaum ceremony and was able to correlate 108 of these with shamanic practices in Siberia (Schlesier 1987). While some of the resemblances were of a very general kind that one would expect to find across any number of religions, such as the idea that the

TABLE 10.1   Main Ritual Activities of the Massaum

FIRST DAY	SECOND DAY	THIRD DAY	FOURTH DAY	FIFTH DAY
Sacred tree selected, cut down, and erected at ritual site	Four small mounds and directional lines added to lodge floor	Smoking and body painting symbolize the giving of Ehyophstah to the people	A second, interior camp circle is made, representing the abode of the animals	In the dark of early morning the five main performers paint themselves and prepare to emerge
Rafters set around central tree to form lodge	Male instructor paints sun and moon sign on lodge	The wolf skins are stuffed and painted, ritually enlivening these master hunters	In the animal abode participants prepare to reemerge as animals, with pairs of walking sticks representing animal forelegs	The five spirit impersonators come out to watch for the appearance of the star Rigel, which signals the start of a ceremonial hunt
Earth floor of lodge smoothed	Seating arrangement of main participants in lodge is established	At noon dog meat plus three types of plant food are served in a ritual meal	A crescent shaped shade is erected across from the lodge, representing a hunting pound	Many costumed animal impersonators emerge and a hunt is mimicked; the hunt is repeated four times
Fireplace constructed on east side of tree	Wolf and fox skins brought into lodge; more participants enter	At nightfall sacred songs are taught	The first animal impersonators, wolves, emerge from the lodge and are viewed by the public	Fractions of sacred meat are distributed to all in the camp to symbolize the outcome of the hunt
			The wolf impersonators move through the camp, making it a sacred universe	Led by Coyote, the animals process to a stream to drink, ending their fast
			At nightfall sacred songs are taught	Main performers return to the lodge and ritually disassemble the interior, ending the ceremony

Source: Schlesier (1987).

Supreme Being lives in the uppermost sky, others were quite specific, such as the sacrifice of albino animals and the making of seven marks on a ceremonial tree. Schlesier, therefore, made a case for the great ancientness, consistency, and durability of Cheyenne religious ideas as expressed in the Massaum.

Though they considered it fundamental, the Cheyennes could only stage the Massaum intermittently during the years of white intrusion into their territory, and they last performed it in an abbreviated ceremony in 1927. Reconstruction of the ritual and its underlying ideology at this late date is still important, not only for understanding the Cheyennes, but also because the Massaum contains many symbolic elements that reappear in other Plains group rituals, including the Sun Dance.

THE OKIPA

Another world renewal ritual that prefigures the Plains Sun Dance was the Okipa ceremony of the Mandans. The Okipa was also probably an influence on the Massaum, for the Cheyennes became acquainted with Mandan culture as they moved onto the High Plains, although the two rites are ultimately different in detail. A lively and sometimes lurid description of the Okipa, illustrated with four detailed oil paintings, was delivered by frontier artist George Catlin after his 1832 visit to the Mandan village near present-day Bismarck, North Dakota. Catlin was one of only a few non-Indians to witness a complete Okipa ceremony. Five years later the tribe was nearly wiped out by smallpox, and though the ceremony was continued until the 1880s, the later versions were diluted, and Catlin's account remains important.

The Okipa was a summer ceremony staged over four days. In general, the rite involved dancing, feasting, fasting, body painting, the giving away of presents, and physical ordeal. These activities took place inside a ceremonial earth lodge and also outside, in an adjacent village plaza marked with a central cedar pole. The lead ritualist was an impersonator of the primordial figure Nu-mohk-muck-a-nuh or Lone Man (First Man, Only Man). Lone Man was joined by other spiritual figures from creation myth to enact several vignettes illustrating the origins of the tribe and the restoration of spiritual power as derived from animals. In one segment, Lone Man chased away The Foolish One, a clown painted black with charcoal and bear grease, who pestered women with a large wooden phallus. This episode represented the establishment of an orderly society. Also enacted by costumed

FIGURE 10.1 *The Last Race, Mandan O-Kee-pa Ceremony, by George Catlin, 1832.*

participants was a sacred release of imprisoned animals, which functioned, like the hunt segment of the Massaum, to signify the origin and continuance of the hunter's way of life. The release of captive animals for human use is a nearly universal mythic theme on the Plains (see Chapter 3). According to Mandan belief, the actual release occurred at Dogden Butte, a glacial ridge about 60 miles north of present-day Bismarck. Men wearing full buffalo skins performed the Bull Dance in the plaza to summon the bison for human consumption.

The most sensational part of the Okipa was the ordeal that Catlin called the "cutting scene." Young male fasters submitted to having their chest or backs pierced in two places to accept splints. Supplicants were expected to suppress any show of pain when being pierced. Rawhide ropes were then tied to the skewers, and the men hoisted toward the rafters of the lodge. They remained suspended for many minutes until the pain caused them to pass out. Once they appeared dead, they were lowered to the ground and left alone until they came to. While unconscious, the men might have revelatory visions, and their revival symbolized a spiritual rebirth. Upon reviving, some men made even a greater sacrifice by having fingers chopped off. The small and index fingers of the left hand were amputated, leaving those most necessary for drawing a bow.

The Massaum and Okipa were unusual in their reliance on masked dancers, since masking and spirit impersonation were not prevalent on the Plains, even though these are common ritual devices in many parts of the world, including most of the adjacent North American culture areas. Otherwise, however, the Massaum and Okipa were typical, if not prototypical, of Plains communal ceremony. In this regard they can be considered along with other group rituals for the harnessing of medicine power, the initiating of new adepts, and the renewal of harmonious relations between humans and the spirits, including the rituals of the Omaha Shell and Pebble societies and the Crow Tobacco Society, as described in Chapter 4.

MEDICINE BUNDLE RENEWALS

Closely associated with the other organized rituals were the traditions, in many tribes, of renewing medicine bundles. Medicine bundle traditions span the realms of individual and group ritual; some bundles contained the personal medicine of a single owner, while others were thought to affect the destiny of the entire tribe. Bundle ceremonies might be staged by individuals with a few assistants in a relatively inconspicuous way that belied their importance, or included in the program of a large, multiday tribal ritual.

Simply defined, a medicine bundle is a set of objects kept in a wrapping of animal skin. The typical objects are stones, chunks of mineral paint, feathers, bird and small mammal skins, sprigs of sage or other herbs, and scalps. Sometimes pipes or arrows may be included. In a few cases, notably among the Kiowas, the main object is a simple male or female doll representing a primordial human. This collection of items functions as a repository and source of spiritual power and has its origin in one or more visions of an individual person or else in a tribally circulated body of myths; in either case, the underlying story includes directions for the ritual use and care of the items. The power of the bundle is often specific, the most common purposes being success in warfare, hunting, gardening, curing, or love. Depending on the guiding principles, a bundle and thus its power might be transferable from one owner to another through purchase or direct inheritance, or, in the case of tribally significant bundles, as a matter of public appointment, for instance, the tribal council might appoint a keeper from among members of an eligible family.

The bundle became a focus for ritual because it was supposed to be renewed at regular intervals. The skin was unwrapped and the items inside were examined and contemplated. The owner meditated on their origins and meanings. He smoked them in sweet grass or cedar incense as a blessing, prayed over them, and handled them in formal ways, for example, keeping them from touching the ground, as a show of reverence. Items might be cleaned, repaired, or repainted. The bundle renewal was the occasion for the performance of origin myths, sets of special songs, and dancing.

As a "complex" of tribal religious activity, the bundle tradition reached its most complicated development among the Mandans and Pawnees. While these tribes' bundle practices have faded from existence, there is abundant ethnohistorical information about them. The Mandans had a system of bundles that affected all aspects of tribal life. There were personal bundles, tribal bundles, and bundles that were subsidiary or auxiliary to the tribal bundles. Particular bundle ceremonies ensured the success of every important tribal enterprise, from fish and eagle trapping to buffalo hunting to garden fertility, warfare, and health. Rights to particular bundles were controlled by clans, and the ownership of bundle rights through inheritance or purchase was a prerequisite for anyone wanting a leadership position in the tribe.

The Pawnees had a similar complicated, ranked system involving both personal and tribal bundles. The higher-order Pawnee bundles were situated in villages rather than clans; they were inherited and owned by the village chiefs, though handled by a separate class of priests. A set of five Pawnee bundles superseded all others, four of which stood for the four semi-cardinal directions, and the last, the evening star (Venus shining brightly soon after sunset, called "female white star" in Pawnee). These five federation bundles, with the evening star bundle preeminent, integrated the various Pawnee villages and the cosmological world simultaneously and were tended by priests at the top of the religious hierarchy. They had to be renewed every year at the time when the first thunder of spring was heard, around the time of the spring equinox and appearance of the evening star. Priests of the Skidi band of Pawnees kept a large oval hide map of the night sky showing the position of numerous stars, which may have been used to schedule ceremonies or simply to illustrate the celestial myths reenacted through bundle rituals.

Anthropologist Jeffrey Hanson (1980) observed that the complexity of Plains bundle traditions mirrors organizational complexity, which in turn corresponds to ecological conditions and subsistence practice: semisedentary horticulturalists with more complicated forms of social and political organization had the more intricate and specialized bundle systems.

The Skidi Pawnee Morning Star Ceremony

The Pawnee bundle traditions correlated with the only example of human sacrifice on the Plains and one of only a few to ever develop among the North American tribes. Just as Pawnee rites associated with the spring equinox were marked by the appearance of the evening star, those celebrating the late April season of approaching warm weather were indicated by the morning star (Venus or possibly sometimes another planet, shining before dawn, conceived of as a male warrior) in conjunction with the moon and near the constellation Aries. The morning star ritual, not strictly required every year but held upon a sponsor's dream (which seems to have anticipated the required celestial alignments), involved the slaying of a captive to appease the mythic beings and ensure health, plentiful food, and success in battle.

Details of the sacrifice procedure and the sequence of steps differ among accounts and probably varied over time; following is a sample compilation. In the fall prior, the dreamer and some supporters went on a highly ritualized raid to obtain a girl captive about age 13 (or sometimes a boy) specifically for the rite. Not knowing her approaching fate, the captive was well treated while the time of sacrifice approached. When the morning star's appearance was imminent, the captive was honored over a three-day period with feasting and finery, and then anointed with sacred paint, with her body made half red and half black. Special songs described every step.

After midnight starting the fourth day, the captive was led to a scaffold of poles and tied to face the rising planet. In quick succession, executioners dashed from out of hiding around the scaffold and delivered the deathblows. One made a pantomime of torture by fire, singing the girl's groin and armpits. The next shot her once with an arrow in the heart, and a third delivered a blow with a club. A priest then cut out the victim's heart or at least made a chest incision allowing the free flow of blood. The priest marked his face with the blood, and blood was supposed to drip on an offering of buffalo meat set up under the scaffold. Next, every man and boy of the tribe emerged and fired an arrow into the back of the corpse to participate in the sacrifice and tap into the good fortune that was believed to result.

The sacrifice coincided with the renewal of the morning star bundle. Both during the planning of the dreamer's raid and as the captive was prepared for execution, the bundle was opened to reveal its contents—otter, hawk, and wildcat skins, feathers, scalps, tobacco, paint, a pipe, an arrow, two ears of sacred corn, and so on—and these items were prayed over and blessed with smoke. Some accounts indicate that the captor and executing priest wore some of the bundle items as they fulfilled their duties, that the captive was fed with a little bowl and spoon from the bundle, and that the fatal arrow was taken from the bundle and then returned.

The symbolism referred to fertility. One interpretation is that the executioner's arrow represented the act of planting. Another says that the arrow referred to hunting prosperity, and that women hacked the corpse with their hoes to similarly consecrate the gardening implements. Regardless, ultimately the procedure was a reenactment of creation myth. The peculiar means of injury were allusions to episodes in the Pawnee origin story. Even the scaffold embodied mythic ideas, in that it was built from different wood

species representing powerful animal spirits and their associated cardinal directions. The victim's role was that of evening star, whose death reunited her with morning star, personified by her captor and executioners, to begin life anew and ensure the return of the buffalos and the growth of crops.

The morning star sacrifice is known from instances in the early 1800s and presumably dated deep into the past. Only the Skidi band of Pawnees held the morning star sacrifice, although there is some indication that the related Arikaras of the Upper Missouri also had a sacrificial rite in earlier days. Other Pawnee bands rejected the idea of human sacrifice, at least during the Historic Period. White traders and agents who entered Pawnee territory abhorred and opposed it, and under their influence the Skidis lost their commitment to the sacrifice element. In 1816, the leader Lachelesharo (Knife Chief, Old Knife) and his handsome son Petalesharo (*Pitarésharu*, "chief of men," Man Chief) spoke out against the execution of a Comanche captive. Others in the tribe insisted that the sacrifice was needed to ensure prosperity. The daring Petalesharo cut the girl down at the last moment and rode off with her to send her home. The episode became legendary, and when Petalesharo visited Washington and other eastern cities in 1821 with a chiefs' delegation, he was feted and given a silver medal for the deed. The last known Skidi human sacrifice was made with an Oglala girl named Haxti on April 22, 1838. Afterward and into the twentieth century, the Skidis continued to renew the morning star bundle on the celestially determined dates, but without human sacrifices.

The early Plains Indian authority Clark Wissler supposed that Pawnee human sacrifice evinced influence from the Aztecs of central Mexico, since astronomy and sacrifice (including scaffold execution) were key features in the religion of the Aztec Empire circa A.D. 1500. And as Caddoans, the Pawnees shared in a general cultural heritage from the Southeast United States, where ritual cannibalism and the prehistoric presence of temple mounds and complex societies might also suggest ties to Mesoamerica. Later scholars have been more cautious in discussing such connections, however, citing the current dearth of archaeological evidence for contacts between the Aztecs and Indians of the Southeast or Plains.

Sacred Arrow and Pipe Ceremonies

Some of the most notable medicine bundles contained sacred arrows or pipes as their principle objects. (Rituals in which sacred pipes are renewed should be distinguished from the calumet or "peace pipe" ceremony, in which a pipe is passed around and smoked to call blessings on visitors or cement agreements between groups. The calumet ceremony is treated in Chapter 11.) The Arapahos kept a single flat pipe in a special tipi, always suspended off the ground, its proper care ensuring the prosperity of the entire tribe. The Blackfoots had 17 sacred pipe bundles distributed among tribe members and similarly venerated. Seven pipes were considered essential to the well-being of the Poncas. Each pipe stood for the particular powers and ritual responsibilities of one of the Ponca clans; six were kept together in one bundle to represent tribal unity, and the seventh was maintained separately by the chief's clan and used in chiefly matters such as the safeguarding of buffalo hunts and cursing of criminals.

The Cheyenne Sacred Arrows were bestowed on the tribe by Sweet Medicine, the culture hero and trickster figure. Sweet Medicine appears in Cheyenne myth as a young boy with amazing knowledge and powers who can shift shapes and assume the form of many animals. In some accounts it is said that he lived among the tribe for several generations. In one key episode, Sweet Medicine and his wife discover a mysterious hidden chamber within a mountain in the Black Hills, identified with Bear Butte northeast of Sturgis, South Dakota. There they find two sets of four arrows attended by sacred beings; the beings invite them to take one set, which is wrapped in coyote and buffalo skins, and instruct them in its meaning and care. Sweet Medicine and his wife emerged after four years within this holy lodge, and they passed the Arrows and sacred knowledge on to a succession of virtuous men—the Arrow Keepers—through the generations.

The Cheyenne Sacred Arrow renewal ceremony was pledged by an individual, and the scattered tribe members were summoned to gather for it at an appointed place, much as in other group rituals. Within the camp circle, a giant tipi reminiscent of the mystic mountain lodge was set up to contain the arrows. Over a four-day period the Arrows, and thus tribal fortunes, were restored through a series of procedures. The campers brought forth offerings of tobacco or valuables and laid them before the Arrow bundle by an altar in the tipi. Medicine men received the bundle from the Arrow Keeper, respectfully opened it, and repaired the feathers and sinew of the arrows. They blessed a large number of willow sticks representing each family in the tribe by passing them through smoke at the altar. The Arrows were placed temporarily in alignments signifying the directions of the cosmos and paired to stand for the complementary relationship between buffalos and humans. All the men of camp came through to witness the Arrows in their refreshed state before they were re-bundled and returned to the Arrow Keeper. The main participants sung four closing songs said to have been taught by Sweet Medicine, purified themselves in a sweat lodge, and the ceremony was closed; another year of tribal prosperity was assured. Versions of the Sacred Arrow renewal rite are still conducted among the Southern Cheyennes in Oklahoma, where the Arrows are now kept, and Northern Cheyennes may participate there or, infrequently, host the Arrows for renewal at their Montana reservation.

Arval Looking Horse, a Lakota Sioux, became the keeper of his people's Sacred Pipe in 1966, when he was only 12. At that time the prior keeper, his grandmother Lucy Looking Horse, died (women as well as men may keep the Pipe among the Lakotas), and she had had a vision that Arval should be the next in line—representing the nineteenth generation. Arval understood the origin of the Pipe from the following story. Long ago a man (implicitly a Cheyenne) was out scouting and he came upon the huge rock formation in northeast Wyoming, *Mato Tipila* (Bear Lodge), now called Devils Tower. It was a sacred mountain, with an entrance on the east, an interior like a tipi, and an exit on the west side. The man went inside, where he found the Sacred Pipe on the north side and a bow and arrows on the south side. He chose the bow and arrows and left with them, and since then the Cheyennes have had their Sacred Arrows. Later, a mysterious radiant woman delivered the Sacred Pipe in a bundle to the Lakotas and taught them how to pray with it and care for it. As she then disappeared over the western horizon, she assumed the shape of four animals, the last being a white buffalo calf. The Pipe is therefore known in Lakota as *Ptehincala hu cannunpa*, the Buffalo Calf Pipe.

The Buffalo Calf Pipe is considered the center or trunk of pipes, with all others its roots and branches. Its stem is equated with man and the bowl with woman, in a symbolic representation of procreative power. Believers attribute great powers to the Pipe for protecting forthright people or punishing wrongdoers. A story relates that once, when an Indian agent had the Pipe seized and brought to his agency, the Indian policeman involved in the seizure all died, and the agent had to ask the Pipe Keeper to come and take it away. Some also say that the Pipe grows shorter when times are bad, though Looking Horse himself disputes this belief.

Looking Horse keeps the Pipe in a red metal outbuilding in his yard at Green Grass, South Dakota on the Cheyenne River (Sioux) Reservation. Inside, the Pipe bundle is suspended off the ground and kept along with the drum and other ritual implements used in its veneration. Periodically, the Pipe is taken out for renewal. This blessing generally is held once a year, in conjunction with the Sun Dance, though Looking Horse once kept the Pipe put away for seven years, upon instruction from the spirits, who were displeased with people's bad behavior and lack of respect. When a ceremony is announced, hundreds of people come from far and wide. Numerous medicine men attend to help conduct the ritual and benefit from the blessings.

The ceremony for the Sioux Sacred Pipe is much like that for the Cheyenne Arrows. For presenting the Pipe, a square altar area is outlined on the ground near the outbuilding with stones (as a more permanent rendition of the traditional outline made with small tobacco bundles) and four cottonwood saplings decorated with flags in six colors that represent the four cardinal directions plus earth and sky. Worshippers, having first purified themselves in a sweat lodge, process to the altar barefoot and bearing sage. Singers drum and sing special songs. The Pipe is brought forth from its lodge, removed from the bundle, and placed on a tripod set up at the center of the altar area for all to see. People reverently approach the Pipe, pray to it, and touch it; some are overcome with emotion in its sacred presence. They may bring offerings in fulfillment of vows, or their own personal pipes to absorb the sacred power of the Buffalo Calf Pipe. To conclude the ceremony, all those with pipes at once fill them with kinnikinick, light them, and offer them to the six directions. Then the Pipe bundle is put away in its shed and the worshippers retire for a feast of buffalo meat, fry bread, and other Indian foods.

THE SUN DANCE

Of all the large-scale rituals on the Plains, the Sun Dance is the one that is most widespread and which has lasted the longest in the period of recorded history. Twenty tribes practiced it at the peak of the horse-and-buffalo economy in the early to mid-1800s, and many continue today. It is also the ritual that has gotten the most attention from non-Indian onlookers and writers. For these reasons, the Sun Dance has become iconic of Plains Indian life for many people. In one way at least, the Sun Dance is indeed very typical of the culture area, for like other aspects of Plains culture it is at once quite uniform over time and space, and yet takes on specific details and meanings in each tribe where it is found.

The term "Sun Dance" was coined by early non-Indian observers who seized on the Sioux dancers' custom of staring at the sun. This generic term is now in use even among Indian people when speaking English. But though the ceremony includes acknowledgment of the sun's power through ritual and symbol, it is not about sun worship.

The original tribal names better suggest Native perceptions of the ceremony. For many groups, the salient feature was the making of a special ritual lodge, and names among the Kiowas, Assiniboines, Crows, and others simply alluded to the lodge or some part of its structure. It may be that at least some of these names were metaphoric references likening the lodge construction to the assembling of the tribe. The Cheyennes recognized the idea of earth renewal, calling the ceremony New Life Lodge. A reference to sacrifice is found in the Arapaho name Offerings Lodge, and the Blackfoot term Medicine Lodge indicated power acquisition. The title Thirsting Dance among the Utes, Shoshones, Crees, and Ojibwas notes the dancers' practice of forsaking food and water. The Tetons and Poncas called it Sun-gazing Dance on account of the staring custom.

Behind these variable names and the general theme of renewal were different emphases. While the Cheyennes thought of the dance as a means of rekindling life, the Crows held the dance to vow revenge against a relative killed by tribal enemies through the agency of a sacred doll. In what amounted to a reversal of the Crow rationale, the Kiowas staged the dance ostensibly to honor their tribal medicine doll, though the doll veneration

was in turn a means of forecasting revenge and putting the world right. The main purpose of the Blackfoot version was to renew and transfer ownership of medicine bundles. Whatever the most explicit reason, the Sun Dance was a complete pageant, a gathering for survival and social purposes and the public expression of religious ideas.

The great gathering was made possible by the abundance of summer buffalo, and in turn the ceremony was a way of coordinating a maximally effective summer hunt. Bands that had been dispersed during the cooler weather met at an appointed place in June and joined in chasing the amassed herds. Large numbers of animals were slain and the meat was processed to feed the crowd and set up a surplus for later in the year.

Usually the bands camped around a huge circle, with each band's position on the circle indicating its status in the tribe or the point in past time when it originated. The gathering restored a sense of community across the entire tribe. Old family ties between siblings who had been scattered through marriage were renewed, and new friendships were made. The men's military associations that drew members from multiple bands were formed during this time of year, and they were pressed into service as police for crowd control—to make sure the hunt was run fairly and to curb rowdiness in camp. There was a festival atmosphere about the camp, with storytelling, gambling, horse races, feasting, secular singing and dancing, and an air of romance. It was the perfect time for courtship. The Lakotas have a saying: "Children are born nine months after the Sun Dance."

The religious ritual itself, unfolding over a week's time, loomed over all of this fertility and family life as if to sanctify it. In general the Sun Dance resembled, and grew out of, earlier large Plains earth renewal ceremonies such as the Massaum and Okipa, and was probably influenced as well by other rituals for calling game, healing, and initiating medicine men. It appears as a type of ceremony distinguishable from the others, and spreading through the Plains, after about 1800. There was great variability in the details, but a common description is possible. Like many Plains ceremonies, the Sun Dance was an annual event in principle, though sometimes, depending on local circumstances or tribal habit, one or more years could pass without one. The vision or vow of a male or female sponsor initiated preparations. In coordination with this inspiration, a medicine man was identified as leader, his assistants gathered, and individual dancers vowed to dance to fulfill some personal purpose. Men were the principal dancers and singers in all tribes, with some tribes including women in these roles also.

The dancers readied their regalia and sought elders to instruct them in the proper ways of dancing. Depending on the tribe, some ritual allusion to hunting was made; either the worshippers collected buffalo tongues, or they held a special hunt, or obtained a buffalo hide to be displayed in the ceremony. A place for the lodge had to be determined. A tree that would become the center pole of the lodge was found through an elaborate sequence. The tree might be revealed in a vision, and scouted and captured like an enemy, with multiple feints of attack. Often, virtuous women were selected to carry out some of these preliminary steps. More highly formalized activities followed: setting up and decorating the center pole with a buffalo effigy or thunderbird's nest, clearing the ground around it, building a circular lodge with rafters radiating from the pole and with a shade arbor around the edge, and making some kind of altar with earth, buffalo skulls, and other symbolic elements.

Dancers then occupied the lodge and began dancing to special songs. Men would be bare-chested, barefoot, and garbed only in a calf-length kilt of skin or cloth, perhaps with armlets and eagle plumes or a sage wreath worn on the head. More sprigs of sage were stuck in the dancers' waistbands. Cheyenne and Arapaho men added intricate painted designs on their chests, backs, and arms. Women wore special dresses and robes and sage wreaths too. The dance itself involved bobbing in place while focusing one's eyes on the top of the sacred pole. The dancer held between his lips a whistle made from the hollow wing bone of an eagle, which he sounded frequently to proclaim the intensity of his devotion. All during the event, dancers fasted. The leader's assistant might come before them with a paunch of water and callously splash it on the ground to test their determination. This very physical means of meditation was stopped from time to time so the dancer could rest, fix or modify his regalia and face paint, and perhaps drink a little chokecherry soup, just enough to keep going some more. Through this almost continuous dancing and concentration, it was believed, one became open to acquiring spiritual power.

In some tribes, however, some participants chose even harsher ordeals in order to make even more intense bids for power. The Oglalas, Canadian Sioux, and Poncas in particular emphasized these practices, which have often been referred to in written accounts as "self-torture." (On the other hand, the Kiowas disavowed injury in the Sun Dance, believing that bloodshed spoiled the mood of holiness.) Dancers and spectators alike might make flesh offerings by having half-inch bits of tissue cut from their arms by the dance leader or his assistant. At this time also, mothers who had vowed to see one of their children through some winter illness brought them forward to have their ears pierced, to fulfill the vow and unify the child's fortunes with those of the other sacrificers.

In particular, ear piercing made a symbolic bond between the child and those choosing the most dramatic form of ordeal: at the ceremony's climax, male dancers might have wooden skewers inserted through their breasts to accept tethers that tied them to the center pole. During the piercing and afterwards, the supplicants were not supposed to show any distress over the pain.

FIGURE 10.2   A magazine illustration from 1890 by Frederic Remington (1861–1909) showing a Blackfoot man pierced and suspended during the Sun Dance.

They leaned backward while dancing to place their weight against the ropes and sought eventually to break free by ripping their flesh, the release signifying ultimate achievement of their vow or bid for power. If the flesh did not give way after some time, supporters pushed the supplicant back or threw robes on them to add weight. Or, the dancer would move to the center pole, lay his head against it in a moment of prayerful resolve, and then dash backward as hard as he could to break loose.

An alternate method was to pierce the back below the shoulders as well as the breasts and hang from four poles about a foot off the ground until the flesh gave way. Or else only the back was pierced and the ropes were tied to one or more buffalo skulls. The supplicant dragged this heavy mass around the circle of the lodge, hoping to break free as the skulls tangled and their horns were caught in the dirt. If he had trouble breaking loose, a child might be sent out to sit on the skulls.

The dancing segment of the ceremony would last three or four days, from dawn to dark. Its end was marked by special closing songs, and for the dancers, it was marked by ritual cleansing in a sweat lodge and release from their fast. The camp dissolved and the Sun Dance lodge was abandoned and left to molder, a last sacrifice to Mother Earth. A tribe's old Sun Dance lodges marked its territory and stood as mute signposts of time passed. In the pictographic winter counts of the Kiowas, many of the years are actually named for some feature of those year's Sun Dances (see Chapter 6).

The meanings and teachings of the Sun Dance are rich and complex. When the ritual begins, the celebrants place evergreen sage in the eye and nasal sockets of the ceremonial buffalo skulls to symbolize the buffalos' coming to life. Other common colors of ceremonial paint and clothing are red for earth, blues for sky, red or white for day, blue or black for night, and yellow for the sun. Every object is invested with meaning. For example, the following explanation was given by the Lakota George Sword circa 1908:

> A hoop covered with otter skin ceremoniously is a symbol of the sun and the years. The years are a circle. An armlet of rabbit skin is an emblem of fleetness and of endurance on long journeys and during marches. A cape of otter skin is an emblem of power over land and water. A skirt of red worn by a man is an emblem of holiness. A blue skirt is an emblem of *Taku Shanskan*, that is, of the heavens, and indicates that the wearer is engaged in a sacred undertaking. Armlets and anklets are emblems of strength and of love and cunning in the chase.

(Walker 1980:182–183)

In Sword's words one can see how symbols elicit verbal explanations of the tribal belief system that then become learnable to members of the community, especially children. Participants and onlookers see examples of courage, self-sacrifice, endurance, and kinship unfold before them. Coupled with the stark drama of physical endurance and sacrifice, the shapes, sounds, smells, and colors of the Sun Dance contribute to a powerful, tangible enactment of core values.

The Study of Sun Dance Diffusion

In the early years of the twentieth century, anthropologists viewed the Great Plains as a vast natural laboratory for studying questions of cultural development. One of the main issues of interest at the time was diffusion, the process whereby cultural traits pass from one group to another. Anthropologists wondered whether diffusion proceeded in regular ways which could be described in general laws. Some also understood that the presence or absence of diffused traits within a given society would reveal something about that group's past, and thus that the study of trait distribution was important for reconstructing the history of a region which lacked Native-produced written records. Since the Sun Dance was widely shared across the culture area and was accessible to examination through Indian oral history, non-Indian historical records, and, in some cases still, direct observation, it became an obvious subject for diffusion studies.

Franz Boas (1858–1942), a founding figure of American anthropology, provided the inspiration for the Sun Dance diffusion study. Boas envisioned an approach to the study of cultural traits that was different from that put forth earlier. Prior theorists thought of traits primarily as indicators of a group's position on a presumed ladder of human cultural evolution. Pottery, for example, indicated that a group had progressed to the level of barbarism, midway in sophistication between savagery and civilization. It is now accepted that the sophistication or complexity of a culture cannot be appreciated only by the presence or absence of a few diagnostic traits, and at any rate, gross categories like savagery and barbarism are not sufficiently helpful to understanding. There was also early speculation of how traits originated and spread, but much of it was fanciful. For example, some theorists proposed that all major technological advances arose in ancient Egypt, a theory that defied the actual evidence. Boas advocated instead for the scientific documentation of traits in their particular tribal contexts. The focus was on understanding the local historical and psychological significance of the traits and their combinations. Part of this inquiry was to determine when a group got a trait, from whom, and how it fit with the other traits that the group already had in a configuration unique to that tribe. Only eventually, after much patient investigation of the particulars, Boas claimed, could general or universal patterns of human development be posited with any confidence. Put another way, before a grand history of cultural evolution could be discerned, a multitude of individual tribal histories had to be recorded. The Boasian program, in contrast to earlier, simplistic forms of diffusionism and cultural evolutionism, became known as historical particularism.

The actual work of this program as it was pursued on the Plains was organized by Clark Wissler of the American Museum of Natural History. Wissler assembled a group effort to study the Sun Dance (and military societies, another subject amenable to diffusionist questions) in many different tribes simultaneously, which would feed a composite picture. Alfred L. Kroeber conducted work on the Arapahos and Gros Ventres, while Robert H. Lowie undertook studies mainly of the Crows, with shorter visits to the Arikaras, Assiniboines, and Shoshones. Leslie Spier made a brief study of the Kiowas. Wissler himself conducted fieldwork with the Blackfoots.

Other studies undertaken independently of the American Museum effort were also included in the composite picture, including George A. Dorsey's reports on the Arapahos, Poncas, and Southern Cheyennes, George Bird Grinnell's study of the Northern Cheyennes, Alice Fletcher's work on the Oglalas, and the observations of Lieutenant Hugh L. Scott among the Kiowas.

It was Spier who then gathered the results of these contributing studies and charted the many traits associated with the Sun Dance, recording their presence or absence in 19 tribes, noting how traits were clustered within these tribes, and pairing the various tribes to see the number of traits shared between each pair. By arraying the data in these ways, Spier was able to see patterns in the development and spread of the Sun Dance. His interpretation relied on a concept promoted by Wissler, called the age-area hypothesis, which held that the more widely distributed traits were the older ones, under the supposition that they had been around longer and had more time to spread.

The traits in question included all kinds of details of ritual procedure that could be classified under broader features of the ceremony. For example, several traits had to do with the form of the dance lodge and its components: whether the lodge had a full or partial roof, whether the center pole was decorated with a buffalo hide, whether it was painted, whether there was an altar with buffalo skulls, and whether the altar was excavated. Other traits concerned the actual dancing, such as sun gazing, circling, flesh sacrifices, drumming on hide, and the blessing of spectators, among many others. Still other traits had to do with regalia details, such as the presence or absence of jackrabbit headdresses or white body paint, or whether sage sprigs were worn in the dancers' belts.

Spier determined that the Algonquian-speaking Arapahos and Cheyennes were at the center of the diffusion of the Sun Dance. These tribes had the highest trait counts—53 and 46, respectively. Not surprisingly, they were at the geographic center of the entire Sun Dance area. The nearby Oglalas had 40 traits, and the Blackfoots and Gros Ventres also had high trait counts, with 37 and 36, respectively. Tribes far from the center had fewer traits, with the Plains Ojibwas and Canadian Sioux possessing only 8 and 5 traits, respectively.

Ultimately the Sun Dance diffusion study was only a partial success. As some of the investigators became preoccupied with patterns of distribution and typicality, Boas's more basic agenda of recording tribal particulars was not carried out as thoroughly as it might have been. This was especially true for the tribes, such as the Comanches, that were quickly determined to be on the margin of the Sun Dance trait distribution area, at least as it appeared by the late 1800s. There were also problems in reconstructing tribal histories in the manner Boas recommended. Some of the investigators became frustrated because, often, different tribal elders possessed contradictory accounts of past events that could never be reconciled. And while Spier's reconstruction of the spread of the Sun Dance has not been significantly challenged, his effort failed to inspire similar studies elsewhere or contribute to larger theories of cultural development. All of the constituent tribal studies remain, however, providing rich detail about the Sun Dance and tribal life in general across the Plains, and they are valuable to later anthropologists as well as to modern Indian people who seek knowledge about their ancestors' religion.

A contemporary debate reexamines Spier's contributions and asks whether there is such a thing as the Sun Dance at all. Anthropologist Karl Schlesier (1990) and few other writers have argued that the Sun Dance as such is a fabrication made up by anthropologists to account for diverse tribal ceremonies with varying histories and purposes. This viewpoint looks at much of the same data that Spier observed, plus archaeological evidence of possible forerunner ceremonies, and emphasizes differences rather than similarities and connections. Schlesier's critique is instructive. It is unlikely that the Sun Dance construct will be abandoned, however, because it is convenient for describing numerous relatable ceremonies, and more importantly, because modern Indian people accept the category and use it in communicating about ritual among themselves and to the larger society.

Sun Dance Survival and Revival

Because the Sun Dance brought entire tribes together for traditional religious expression, it became a major target for government and church officials who wanted to break down tribal society and convert Indians to Christianity. The militarism, harsh ordeals, and authority of the medicine men were all aspects of the Sun Dance that troubled Indian agents and missionaries intent on assimilating their charges. During the Reservation Period and well into the twentieth century Sun Dances were outlawed and physically disrupted. During these times also some practitioners must have concluded that the dance was no longer possible to stage in its true form, since the buffalos were exterminated and other elements of the dance were difficult to include under reservation conditions; or, perhaps, some lost faith in the dance's ability to renew a desirable world. The newly formed Ghost Dance and peyote religions (see below) may have offered complete alternatives for some Sun Dance worshippers. The steep declines in tribal populations when reservations were first established compounded the effect of all these disincentives. Under such external and internal pressures, some people abandoned the dance. Others continued to practice it, but in secret. Still others were able to maintain occasional public ceremonies despite the disincentives.

By the late twentieth century it was possible to classify the Sun Dances of each tribe originally identified by Spier in four continuation categories (after Liberty 1980):

1. Old traditional ceremonies that had been continued
2. Ceremonies that had been adopted by tribes on the margins of the Plains late
3. Ceremonies among tribes where the Sun Dance had ceased and been revived or reintroduced
4. Ceremonies that were actually or apparently extinct

Six tribes that openly perpetuated the dance were the Arapahos, Assiniboines, Blackfoots, Cheyennes, Plains Crees, and Plains Ojibwas. Except for the Siouan-speaking Assiniboines, this group includes Algonquian speakers and so might be regarded as the resilient ancient core of Sun Dance practice. The presence of the Ojibwas on the list of retainers is interesting because they had relatively few of the ceremonial traits identified by Spier. From their case it is evident that other factors, such as how a ritual is integrated within a language and culture, and the degree of outside interference, can be more important than the number of traits in determining whether a ritual is retained or lost.

Among the Sioux tribes generally, it had appeared that the Sun Dance was extinct around 1900, but in fact some Oglalas (Tetons) did continue to hold dances. Theirs were mostly held in private to avoid persecution, deep in the Pine Ridge and Rosebud reservations. These hidden dances became the foundation for a revival inspired by the Cheyennes and Arapahos, whose dances the Oglalas visited regularly. By the 1960s pressure against the dance had lessened enough to allow frequent public ceremonies among the Tetons.

Two other tribes, the Shoshones and Utes, were able to sustain continuous Sun Dances. Unlike the ancient core continuators, however, the various Shoshone and Ute communities generally adopted the dance only in the late 1800s, and they developed versions that varied most from the typical form, especially through the inclusion of Christian elements.

A number of other tribes lost the dance but revived it from some combination of tribal memory and importation. The intertribal network of communication that developed during the twentieth century involved a lot of sharing of traditions, which helped some tribes restore their Sun Dance. The Crows, who ceased Sun dancing around 1874, sought out Sun Dance leaders among the Wind River Shoshones in 1941 to relearn the tradition, and they reinstituted a ceremony in their own tribe. The Kiowas quit Sun dancing, for good it seemed, in 1890, when Indian agents spread rumors of an impending police action by the army; yet in the late 1990s some Kiowas were experimenting with a revival. The Comanches, whose engagement with Sun dancing was late and experimental according to present evidence, staged some dances prior to 1878 but ceased after that year. Other tribes that appeared to have lost the ritual permanently were the Arikaras, Canadian Sioux, Gros Ventres, Hidatsas, Poncas, Sarsis, and Sissetons. However, as of 2001 only the Poncas, Sarsis, and Comanches had not pursued some kind of revival.

Among the Sioux, the Sun Dance became a powerful expression of cultural identity beginning in the 1970s. The resurgence of Sun dancing coincided with the rise of the American Indian Movement and native civil rights activism (see Chapter 12). Reservation youth previously detached from traditional religion became interested in their roots, and young Oglala men spoke of "wearing scars" from ceremonial piercing as a permanent marker of ethnic pride. If anything, the piercing ordeal became more common and severe in the modern Sun Dance than it had been in pre-reservation times. Urban Indians and Indians from tribes that did not traditionally practice the Sun Dance came to the Sioux reservations to participate in the revival. Tourists who had become accustomed to visiting pow-wows were attracted to the dance, as were non-Indian seekers of spiritual knowledge, including those associated with the cultural movement called New Age.

There was some backlash to this newfound popularity, as traditionalist ceremonial leaders sought to prevent outsiders' access to the dances, in some cases by canceling them. Overall, however, during the 1980s there was a proliferation of Sun Dance ceremonies on the Pine Ridge and Rosebud reservations. Rituals became privatized, with individual families or communities staging them, much like the way peyote meetings are sponsored (discussed below). These rituals focused on the well-being of the sponsoring group rather than on the traditional function of pan-tribal integration and welfare. Some Sioux leaders took an ecumenical outlook, advocating the spread of the Sun Dance as an equivalent to other widespread religions. Almost like evangelists, these leaders began staging Sun Dances off reservation, around the United States and in Europe, for participants and audiences that were mostly or all non-Indian. It remains to be seen what forms and functions the Sun Dance will take on in the near future, but it is safe to say that in some manner it will continue as a potent demonstration of the values associated with Indian culture.

THE GHOST DANCE

In 1889 word began spreading across the Plains reservations of an Indian prophet with extraordinary powers and teachings. Wovoka (Cutter), also named Jack Wilson after the white ranch family who employed him, was a Northern Paiute Indian living in Mason Valley, Nevada. There as elsewhere, Indian people were beset with disruptions to their lifeways on account of the influx of whites, and a feeling of desperation was taking hold. It had long been part of the cultural fabric among the tribes to the west of the Northern Plains to conduct ceremonies of world renewal, and Wovoka drew on these traditions as well as Christian teachings to formulate a messianic doctrine.

Wovoka preached of a way that the earth could be regenerated for the reuniting of all Indians. The tribes would live in harmony and the living would be joined again with their departed loved ones. Unhappiness, disease, and death would disappear. The land would be covered over with a new skin of greenery, full of buffalos and other game and devoid of white people. To bring about this change, Wovoka taught, all Indians should join together and repeatedly perform the *Naraya* or Ghost Dance, an old dance of the region meant to honor the ancestral spirits that had been neglected in recent years. This doctrine was inspired in Wovoka through a series of visions when he fell into a deep illness that coincided with a solar eclipse; he believed that he was taken to heaven and given the doctrine by Jesus and other supernatural figures.

"You must not fight. Do no harm to anyone. Do right always," Wovoka urged his followers (Mooney 1965:19). His message emphasized peaceful readjustment of the world order through hard work, clean living, obedience to movement leaders, and above all, fervent dancing. The dance itself was an adaptation of the common round dance, in which male and female dancers form a large circle (facing inward), hold hands, and step clockwise by opening and closing their legs in unison to the rhythm of songs. The hypnotic intensity of the dancing was unusual, however. Worshippers danced for hour upon hour, until they passed out. The dreams they had while collapsed provided further spiritual messages. Frequently they reported seeing their dead relatives, a preview of the new world to come. A host of new songs were composed for the dance, their lyrics expressing a sense of distress, alluding to key symbols of spiritual flight such as birds, and urging perseverance and optimism.

FIGURE 10.3 Shoshone Sun Dance, Wind River Reservation, Wyoming, August 1945.

The ceremonies were emotional and memorable. In 2005, Carney Saupitty, Sr. of the Comanche tribe described the dance to the author in vivid detail, in images handed down from his father and grandfather, who had witnessed many Ghost Dance sessions.

Throughout the Plains, conditions of defeat and reservation poverty made many tribal communities receptive to the new movement. The custom of intertribal visiting continued once the reservations were established, and word of Wovoka's teachings spread quickly. Sign language speeded intertribal communication, as did the new institutions of the railroad and the U.S. mail. As word spread, Wovoka's reputation and teachings were elaborated. Wovoka came to be regarded by some as the

FIGURE 10.4 *Arapaho Ghost Dance in Indian Territory. Painting circa 1893 by Mary Irvin Wright Gill (1867–1929), after a photo by James Mooney.*

Son of God, and it was said he bore the scars of the crucifixion on his hands and feet. He was credited with miracles. Some tribes sent emissaries to Nevada to see for themselves. The Tetons Short Bull and Kicking Bear were part of a large delegation from the Sioux, Shoshones, Cheyennes, and Arapahos. The Kiowa Apiatan (Wooden Lance) came back to his people reporting that the messiah was an ordinary man, and so a fraud, yet many Kiowas still became involved. In all, components of over 20 tribes took up the Ghost Dance, including the Shoshones, Assiniboines, Gros Ventres, Arikaras, Mandans, Sioux, Arapahos, Cheyennes, Comanches, Pawnees, Poncas, Otoes, Missourias, Kansas, Iowas, Osages, Kiowas, Kiowa Apaches, Caddos, and Wichitas, as well as displaced eastern tribes in Indian Territory and some tribes of the far west.

On the Northern Plains, Wovoka's message was transmuted and took on a militant tone. The spread of the Ghost Dance in the north coincided with growing hostility and resistance to non-Indian activities in the region, such as the invasion of gold miners and desperadoes in the Black Hills, the intrusion of rail lines, the extermination of the buffalo, and the general failure of the government to keep treaty promises and provide reservation supplies. A belief developed among the Sioux that if Ghost dancers wore special muslin shirts decorated with religious symbols, called ghost shirts, while they danced, they would be impervious to bullets. Soon the religious movement became conflated with political resistance in the minds of non-Indians, who became especially fearful about an uprising of Indians who were dancing themselves into trance en masse and who believed themselves bulletproof. U.S. Army leaders in particular were suspicious that the Ghost Dance fervor would contribute to an uprising. The annihilation of the Seventh Cavalry under General

George Armstrong Custer at Little Big Horn in 1876 was still on everyone's minds, and the northern reservations had not been settled to the extent that the army had developed stable relations with the Indians of the kind that would foster a detailed understanding of their motives.

Army troops moved into the five Sioux reservations in South Dakota in anticipation of an outbreak, while reservation agents began ordering a stop to the dancing and intertribal visiting. When the Sioux medicine man and Little Big Horn veteran Sitting Bull, a recent convert to the Ghost Dance religion, and his followers ignored these orders, Indian police and soldiers were sent to arrest him. The apprehenders went to Sitting Bull's cabin on the Standing Rock Reservation on December 15, 1890. One of Sitting Bull's group opened fire, killing an Indian policeman, and in the subsequent exchange of fire, Sitting Bull along with eight of his supporters and six more Indian police were killed.

In the days that followed, troops of the Seventh Cavalry marched on a camp of some 3,000 Indians who had assembled in the Badlands north of their homes on Pine Ridge Reservation in the hope that the deliverance promised by the Ghost Dance was imminent. The troops surrounded them and drove them back to the reservation, to a site on Wounded Knee Creek, where they were to be disarmed and dispersed. On the frigid morning of December 29, as the Indian men turned in their guns, one opened fired on the soldiers. A bloody melee erupted in which a number of Indians and soldiers were killed in close combat. The soldiers then trained their weapons, including four Hotchkiss mechanized light cannons, on the Indian women and children, mowing them down in the snow without mercy. Those fleeing were pursued into a ravine, where the havoc continued. Some 300 Indians were killed, the majority women and children, as well as 31 soldiers. The Wounded Knee massacre put an immediate end to the Ghost Dance religion among the Northern Plains tribes.

On the Southern Plains, circumstances were different and the Ghost Dance movement wound down peacefully. The reservations there had been relatively stable for about 15 years and military and civil authorities had close and frequent contact with the Indians. Some soldiers knew the Indians well; they conversed with them in different languages, including sign language, understood their cultures, and worked with them closely in Indian military units. As the Ghost Dance fervor grew, and news of the Wounded Knee tragedy came south to Indian Territory, non-Indians there did become alarmed and watchful. The leader of the dance among the Pawnees was jailed for several days in 1891. But key army officers, notably Lieutenant Hugh L. Scott at Fort Sill, urged their superiors not to overreact. Scott heard directly from I-see-o, a Kiowa scout, and other Indian contacts that the religion was teaching peaceful coexistence. He concluded, that many of those who were currently interested in Wovoka's message were likely to become jaded with the promises of the new belief system over time. Scott also learned that many of the Indians remained skeptical. While many Kiowas were embracing the dance enthusiastically, most of the Comanches were reluctant to get involved with the teachings of a new prophet, for a few years earlier some of them had followed a Comanche seer into battle and been severely beaten. Confident in his analysis of the situation, Scott persuaded the army not to use force. He prevented another tragedy and the movement eventually waned as he predicted.

The Ghost Dance faded in the south and far west over a long period. Dances were held through the 1890s and into the 1930s. During the same period, peyotism and Christianity came into prominence in Indian communities, offering different methods for imagining a better world. Gradually the Ghost Dance and related songs became disassociated from any expectation of imminent world renewal, and they simply became elements in more general worship and recreational activities.

In the 1990s, Ghost Dance songs could still be collected among the Cheyennes and Shoshones, and a distinctive cow horn Ghost Dance rattle from long ago hung on the wall for decoration in the Comanche home the author lived in during fieldwork. Wovoka himself desisted from his preaching after learning of the violence that had ensued. He repudiated the idea of protective shirts and discouraged further visits from tribal delegates. By the mid-1890s he had retired into a private existence, and he died in October 1932.

The Ghost Dance and the Origins of Religion

It has been observed that the pattern of development of the Ghost Dance resembles that of many other religions throughout human history. Because it had a relatively brief and definable period of development, the Ghost Dance has frequently been discussed not simply as a "religion" but as a "religious movement," this term emphasizing the dynamic rise and fall of the belief system in relation to changing social circumstances. In particular, viewing religious behavior as a movement draws focus on the ways in which social, political, or economic aims seek expression in religious form.

Defined as a movement, the Ghost Dance is easily likened to other cases. It could be classified as a "messianic movement" because, like many other religions, it was founded by a single charismatic prophet whose teachings provided a recipe for salvation. Or, the Ghost Dance could be referred to as "millenarian movement," one in which there is the promise of a second coming or world made new. With its focus on a return to aboriginal ways and rejection of introduced cultural elements, the Ghost Dance may be regarded as a "nativistic movement," or as a "revitalization movement" because of its purpose in regenerating the older cultural forms and ways of life. These categories themselves have a long history of development within the cross-cultural study of religion; they are related and somewhat overlapping. Each of the categories depicts

religion as a form of resistance to changing social, political, or economic circumstance.

The anthropologist James Mooney, who interviewed Wovoka and documented the rise of the Ghost Dance firsthand, was the first to draw similarities between the Ghost Dance and other movements throughout history. Mooney compared Wovoka to prior Indian resistance leaders, such as Popé, leader of the 1680 Pueblo Revolt, Pontiac, and Tecumseh. Mooney also drew comparisons with the Celtic King Arthur, Joan of Arc, and the Hebrew Messiah. In selecting such examples, Mooney reveals his opinion that messianic promises led inevitably to bloody confrontation and the dashing of millennial hopes. No doubt this opinion helped Mooney rationalize the violence he saw unfolding on the Plains. In fact, there are also cases in which a messianic message not only failed to stimulate violence, but also gave rise to stable and long-lasting belief systems. The religion founded by the Seneca prophet Handsome Lake in the 1700s, still practiced today among the Iroquois, is one such example.

A later theorist went forward with a more thoroughly developed version of Mooney's hypothesis, arguing that the Ghost Dance can be viewed as a template for understanding how all religions came into being. The psychological anthropologist Weston LaBarre amassed dozens of cases from throughout human history to demonstrate a recurring pattern of religious development. All religions, he concluded are born out of the tensions resulting from the collision of differing cultures. All offer other worldly explanations and solutions for these worldly stresses, become appealing to a downtrodden population, and take hold, some only temporarily but some with great durability. LaBarre's proposed pattern is very much like the concept of revitalization movement in highlighting religion's function of relieving psychological stress. LaBarre argued that even such a widespread and mainstream religion as Christianity, which is not normally likened to the belief systems of small-scale societies, actually conforms to the Ghost Dance pattern in the early days of its history, with its origins in military oppression (Romans over Jews), its messiah, and its promise of a second coming.

These comparisons should in no way demean the beliefs or experiences of the Ghost dancers or cause us to gloss over the unique aspects of the Native American religion. They do, however, lend understanding about the needs and motives of the Ghost dancers, by showing that they are ultimately very typical in human experience through the ages.

YUWIPI

Despite all kinds of introduced spiritual and medical beliefs, nativistic communal healing ceremonies have persisted to the present day. Healing rituals are not easily distinguished from those intended for world renewal, since the reestablishment of a person's physical wellness requires remaking of balance in the universe. Some group rituals, however, clearly use the healing of one or more individuals as their point of departure or main goal. A prominent example of a contemporary healing ritual is the *yuwipi* of the Teton Sioux. The *yuwipi* is a presumably ancient procedure that is still performed frequently, and it is elegant in the way it expresses Indian concepts of wellness and morality.

The Lakota term *yuwipi* refers to binding, for the pivotal activity of the ritual is the tying up and unbinding of a medicine man. Among the Sioux, the term "*yuwipi* man" is used more or less interchangeably with "medicine man." The yuwipi man is capable of prophesizing, finding lost objects, advising others how to live a proper life, restoring health, and convening the spirits to aid humans, much like curers throughout Indian America. These men frequently are leaders of other ceremonies too, such as the Sun Dance. But they are especially known for their ability to escape, with the aid of only the spirits, after being tightly bound in a wrapping of quilts and ropes. Frank Fools Crow (1890–1989) and George Plenty Wolf (1901–1977) were two of the most influential yuwipi men in the Lakota community during the twentieth century.

The setting for this operation is a one-room cabin cleared of its furnishings and darkened with blankets over the windows. Previously someone feeling sick or out of step with life has approached the yuwipi man with a humble plea for aid. They may be facing a serious illness, or uncertainty about school or their job, or perhaps something more mundane—their favorite horse and saddle have gone missing. Sometimes the patient is a young man who has pledged to conduct a vision quest at the same time as the *yuwipi*, to benefit from its supporting effect. The patient has brought a pipe to the healer four times and presented it, with a description of the problem, in a formalized appeal; in accepting the pipe, the *yuwipi* man has agreed to help. Now, as night falls (the rite is also called *hanhepi woecun* "night doings"), relatives and friends of the patient, from old people to children, gather in the cabin under the direction of the medicine man.

On the bare plank floor, the medicine man sets up an altar space outlined with flag-bearing willow wands planted in dirt-filled coffee cans, representing the six directions, and a string of small tobacco offerings (representing the numerous helpful spirits) that completely encloses the area. Within this zone a seventh willow wand marks the center of the universe, and here the *yuwipi* man makes his small altar by spreading dirt from a mole hole, symbolic of the uncontaminated sacredness of the subterranean world, on the floor. A pallet of sage sprigs is laid out by the altar and a smaller string of tobacco offerings, denoting the most powerful spirit helpers, encloses the altar and pallet. Also placed in this area are rattles that will be animated by the visiting spirits, and rawhide ropes and a star quilt for binding the *yuwipi* man. As the altar space is finished, participants sit down all around on chairs or blankets.

An assistant ties the *yuwipi* man's arms behind his back, wrapping the bindings carefully around his fingers, hands, wrists, and arms. Then he covers the leader head to toe with the quilt and ties it tightly. The bundled medicine man is lain face down on the bed of sage and the lights are put out. Designated singers, drummers, and the rest of the participants join together in a long sequence of songs which outline the unfolding spirit visit: preparation, calling the spirits, asking them for help, and asking them to leave in kindly fashion. They intone (Steinmetz 1990:66),

Tukasila wamayank uye yo eye	Grandfather, come to see me
Tukasila wamayank uye yo eye	Grandfather, come to see me
Mitakuye ob wani kte lo eya ya,	So that my relatives and I will live,
hoyewayelo eye ye	I am sending my voice

Soon the participants become aware of little flickering blue lights appearing here and there in the pitch-black room. Odd sounds begin erupting all around. They hear groans coming from different directions, and the sounds of the rattles and drum seem to bounce all about the room. Words of advice or inspiration are being whispered in their ears. Some of the talk is humorous. They feel pounding on the floor around their feet, and one or another might catch a slap to the side of the head. A breeze wafts through the room suddenly. The spirits who have been summoned have arrived and they are making their presence known.

The *yuwipi* man begins talking to the spirits—participants can hear his side of the conversation, but not the replies—and he informs the sacred visitors of the problems that need intervention. Participants interject "*hau*" to affirm his statements. When the *yuwipi* man has had his say, others in the room may also beseech the spirits, adding their own plights to those of the main patient.

After some time the commotion and talk subsides and the *yuwipi* man calls for the light to be turned on. He is found sitting calmly amid the strewn wreckage of his altar, the quilt and ropes neatly folded nearby, and the string of tobacco offerings rolled in a perfect ball. A feeling of relief comes over the group and the meeting disbands.

From an anthropological viewpoint, the *yuwipi* man has served as a mediator, bringing the spirits among the people by putting himself in a plight. As they rescue him, they become available to pity and help his followers. In the darkness of the cabin, the mischievous spirits make disorder from order, and then once again establish normality. The medicine man uses sleight of hand techniques and ventriloquism to enhance the feeling that the spirits are present, and his unbinding, also accomplished with the skills of an illusionist, is given as further evidence of their visit. The unbinding represents the peoples' release from their troubles. And whatever the specific cures that are effected, it is understood that the meeting has united the participants socially in a way that is lastingly beneficial to tribal well-being. The saying *Mitak' oyas'in*, "All my relations," proclaimed at various times throughout the meeting, draws attention to this integrating function.

PEYOTISM

The last major Native ceremony that became significant among the Plains tribes involves the ritualized eating of the hallucinogenic cactus peyote. Even though the present form of the peyote religion arose during the early reservation era and has thus been well documented, it remains clouded by misperception because it is practiced in private and uses a substance that outsiders have wrongly equated with dangerous drugs. It is important to understand the peyote religion in its own terms, as a richly meaningful expression of traditional Native values.

Origins of Plains Peyotism

One of the original scholars of the peyote ritual, Weston LaBarre, noted that while many psychoactive plant products were known to Indian peoples in South America, relatively few were found in the northern hemisphere, and most of these were found in Mexico and the southern United States. In these areas, drugs were sometimes used to sedate sacrificial victims and captives, to promote endurance during ceremonies, hunts, and ball games, and for making prophecies about where game or enemies would be found. Tobacco is the most common and widespread narcotic in Native North America, though a mild one. The Aztecs used *teonanacatl* ("divine mushroom"), a hallucinogenic mushroom. In the Southwest and California culture areas, parts of datura or jimson weed, though poisonous, were eaten or drank as tea by several tribes to achieve a ritualized delirium, and some Apache groups brewed corn beer. The so-called black drink, made by steeping the caffeine-rich leaves and twigs of the yaupon holly (*Ilex* sp.), was taken ritually by Indians in the southeast United States and eastern Texas for purging and to promote a nervous delirium conducive to visions.

Also in Texas, the red seeds of the Texas mountain laurel (*Sophora secundiflora*), called red beans, *frijolillos*, or mescal beans, were apparently an element in religious practice as far back as the Archaic Period—they are found in dry caves among prehistoric remains along the lower Pecos River. Mescal beans contain highly toxic alkaloids similar to nicotine that can cause severe nausea and death from respiratory failure. Curers may have known how to give controlled doses from the seeds, just enough to produce a feeling of exhilaration followed by a long sleep. Some kind of group mescal bean ritual was practiced among the Southern Siouans, Pawnees, Wichitas, Tonkawas, and possibly others during the 1800s. Descriptions of red bean use by these tribes mention both ingestion of the beans and their use in "shooting" procedures similar to those in the Omaha Shell Society. Some anthropologists have theorized that the ritual of red bean eating gave way to peyotism because peyote is not potentially deadly.

Peyote (*Lophophora williamsii*) is a small spineless cactus found in the Chihuahuan Desert and adjacent brush country covering southern Texas and north-central Mexico. Only a small portion of the plant appears above ground, and this part looks somewhat like the top of a carrot or turnip, though with noticeable segments and a center full of white fuzz. This top part, when harvested by slicing for ritual use, is called the "button," and is potent in either green or dried form. Concentrated in the peyote button are mescaline and numerous other alkaloids that affect the mind and bodily systems, and these compounds are released when the buttons are chewed or drank in tea form. The first compounds to take action produce a feeling of exhilaration, sometimes accompanied by color visions. Then other alkaloids exert their effects: wakefulness and endurance, concentration, a sense of timelessness, and lack of discomfort. As these effects in turn wear off, the user may fall into a long sleep. Other physical reactions include a reduction of skin sensitivity, heavy salivation and urination, and initially some nausea and possibly vomiting. Some studies suggest that peyote may also have antibiotic properties.

During the 1600s peyote was favored by several Indian groups of central and northern Mexico for achieving an altered state of consciousness in rituals. Today in Mexico the Huichols and Tarahumaras still practice peyote rituals that date at least to the times of the Spanish conquest.

Spanish Catholic friars preached against peyotism as the devil's work, yet they inadvertently aided its spread when they brought Mexican Indians northward to work in the Texas missions. The missions were intended to convert local tribes, and they attracted the Lipan Apaches among others. The Lipans and their neighbors to the north, such as the Kiowas and Comanches, probably had been acquainted with peyote as a means of prompting prophecies about war and hunting, but around the missions they learned about a more organized use of the plant. When some Lipans took up residence on the Kiowa-Apache-Comanche Reservation in Oklahoma around 1874, they formally taught their companions a group peyote ritual. Lipans named Chebatah and Pinero are remembered as the main transmitters, and it was Quanah Parker of the Comanches and his associates who standardized a ritual based on the Lipan example and began teaching it far and wide.

The new religion was a salve, a source of relief for those living in the atmosphere of defeat, oppression, and poverty that pervaded the reservation. Its teachings were optimistic and emphasized forgiveness, self-reliance, and dignity in the face of hardship. The doctrine and symbolism were influenced by Christianity, such that Jesus is mentioned in some peyote songs and teachings, though the ritual was considered to be an alternative to the church services of the missionaries, created by God specifically for Indians.

Peyotism offered a sense of promise, but it was clearly linked to old traditions too. The Kiowa-Comanche version of the peyote rite had been foreshadowed and influenced by some earlier ceremonies of the Southern Plains. It resembled the red bean ritual in some ways. There was also reportedly an old Kiowa medicine ceremony in which sacred stones were arranged on a crescent-shaped earthen altar inside a tipi. Another lesser-known peyote precursor was the Beaver Ceremony of the Nokoni and Yamparika Comanches, in which a medicine man with curing power from the beaver ministered to the sick. This rite required a special large tipi that had a symbolic floor plan with earthen features, group singing, and special rules for dressing and entering the lodge, much like the subsequent peyote ceremony. The red bean, sacred stone, and Beaver ceremonies in turn were like many group curing rituals found further north.

The peyote ritual is also understandable as a reduced version of the vision quest. Vision quests were much less practical once Indian people were restricted to reservations, but the new rite offered several aspects of the older practice, including tutoring by a medicine man, a period of fasting and intense surrender to an altered state of consciousness, a feeling a spiritual renewal; there is even a miniature hill built as part of the ritual layout in the form of an earthen altar. Thus, while the Plains rite was in one sense an important innovation, it also preserved many basic ritual elements. It was widely appealing because it seemed fresh and yet traditional.

Some Indians became ardent traveling missionaries of the new faith. Also, like the earlier Spanish missions, the Indian boarding schools established in the late 1800s brought together people from many different tribes to educate and Christianize them but provided a setting for the spread of peyotism. During the 1880s, many other Oklahoma tribes adopted the rite as taught by Comanche and Kiowa practitioners. Peyotism was then transmitted to the Prairie and Northern Plains tribes between 1890 and 1920, and by 1930 it had spread far to the north and into the Great Basin, Southwest, and California culture areas also. It was widely adopted, for instance, among the Navajos, who continue today to have many followers.

Along the way, the ritual was modified so that various tribes and regions differ in such details as the repertoire of songs and the layout of the ceremonial floor. Some tribes stage the ritual in wooden lodges or cabins instead of tipis or employ a concrete floor instead of the earthen altar. Versions also differ in the degree to which they include explicit Christian elements, such as the presence of a Bible on the altar or membership through baptism, most common among Siouan practitioners in the north. Differing versions have been called "Comanche Moon," "Half Moon," "Tipi Way," "Caddo Moon," and "Cross Fire" or "Big Moon," "moon" being a reference to the shape of the altar, which is varied along with other details of the setup and procedure. The variants are also known as "fireplaces." Though widespread and locally important, peyotism remains a minority religion among Native Americans, in that there is no tribe or group of tribes in which the majority of members practices it.

The Peyote Ritual

Notwithstanding the variations that have developed among different tribes, the peyote ritual is remarkably standardized, and within the orthodoxies of the particular fireplaces, the rituals are conducted with precise consistency, even though they are long and involved. Close attention to the detail of ritual procedure is one of the ways that the experience is made sacred.

The original Plains version of peyotism included a pilgrimage to the South Texas peyote grounds to gather buttons. The pilgrimage concept was basic to many of the Mexican predecessor rituals, and a collecting trip was usually necessary until a regular trade in peyote was established in the late 1800s. Since that time a pilgrimage has still been considered desirable if possible, as an act of pious dedication. Leaders especially have sought to make the trip with their families.

The long trip to South Texas or Coahuila takes on a special feeling as the pilgrim party approaches the peyote grounds. Menstruating women have been barred from the journey and the travelers observe a ban against sexual relations during the trip. There is also a taboo against the use of salt, which is a symbolic and practical way of anticipating the dehydrating effects of peyote ingestion. Upon arrival, a camp is set up and the

pilgrims rest before looking for the plants. Searching for the small, obscure cactus in the brush country is a deliberate process that requires sensitivity to local habitats. When the first plant is found, the party leader rolls a cigarette with loose Bull Durham tobacco, smokes it, and prays to this "father peyote" for help in discovering other plants. Some green peyote may be eaten at this point in an abbreviated version of the peyote ritual, as an aid to finding more. Sometimes pilgrims report the miraculous appearance or multiplication of peyote plants around them as they pray. The pilgrims may remain camped at the site for several days of harvesting.

The pilgrimage is in part an enactment of the peyote origin myth, which exists in many variations. Stories relate that the power of peyote was first revealed to Indians long ago in an episode in which a warrior, hunter, or woman was lost and near death, or actually dead. A powerful being, variously identified as Peyote Woman, the Great Spirit, or God, directs the unfortunate traveler to the plant, or else the plant itself calls out, and the traveler is revived by its power. In one variant of this tale, it was Quanah Parker himself who was stranded in Mexico and miraculously revived. The stories present several analogies, since the sighting and harvesting of peyote are like a hunt, and both the way peyote plants are discerned gradually in their natural setting and the visions afforded by peyote are kinds of revelation akin to the original revelation.

Whether or not a pilgrimage is conducted, the main ritual must be vowed and organized ahead of time. People promise to themselves and their associates that they will sponsor a peyote meeting at a given time, for one or more purposes: general spiritual renewal; in thanks for some past good fortune like the safe return of a loved one; to commemorate a death; to provide a sacred context in which to doctor a sick individual. The sponsor arranges for the grounds and tipi that will host the meeting and is responsible for financing the meeting, though he or she may receive donations from other worshippers. The next step is to arrange with a staff of ritual specialists who will run the meeting, for no meeting can be held without such leaders.

The staff includes the main leader, known as a road man, and assistants titled fire man, cedar man, and drummer. The road man oversees nearly all aspects of the ritual, from clearing the ground and setting up the tipi to the final putting away of the equipment, and the many hours of worship in between. He directs the ritual from a seated position behind the crest of the curved earth altar, on the west side of the tipi, opposite the door. Road men earn reputations for their knowledge of songs, prayers, curing, and procedural order, gained through apprenticeships and visions, and for their ability to deliver inspirational talks during the meetings, and they travel far and wide to stage meetings by request. The road man brings the bulk of the peyote eaten in the ceremony and normally travels with his own assistants. He does not charge for his services, but receives reimbursement for his expenses from the sponsor, and divides this money with his assistants. The fire man manages the fire and keeps order in the tipi. He builds the fire and feeds it by placing two sticks at a time in a V-shape and sweeps the ashes into a crescent shape. He sits on the north side of the tipi entrance, near the wood and water. The cedar man sits to the road man's left and is in charge of sacred incense, adding cedar needles to the fire and handling sage, tobacco, and the oak leaves used as cigarette wrappers. The drummer sits on the road man's right and drums while the leader sings. He puts together and takes apart the water drum, formed from a small iron kettle and skin, and takes care of these components between meetings. Sometimes one person carries off both the cedar man and drummer functions. The last specialist, called morning water woman or dawn lady, brings water to the celebrants at daybreak. She is not considered an officer like the male staff members and may not even attend the ritual, but simply awaits her job at sunrise. Usually

a postmenopausal woman related to the sponsor is honored with this role.

In the hours prior to the meeting, worshippers take other steps to prepare. For a period of ideally 24 hours they fast, avoiding all food, drink, and salt, in order to minimize the nauseating and dehydrating effects of the peyote. They partake in the sweat lodge or bathe in private, and don clothing that is considered traditional and appropriate—not feathered dance regalia, but clean non-Indian style dress clothes, though accessorized with Indian items such as mescal bead bandoliers, feathers, blankets, and German silver "peyote" jewelry (see Chapter 6), and devoid of reminders of the temporal, non-Indian world such as wristwatches and purses. Peyote men bring their special gear in varnished cedar boxes. A typical box might contain an eagle feather fan, a gourd rattle, a beaded staff made up of three jointed sections, small wooden drumsticks, sacks of Bull Durham tobacco, and jars containing peyote buttons, cedar, sage, and Indian perfume. Often the staff and handles of the fan and rattle have matching beadwork. Some of these items may be heirlooms, others crafted by the owner.

In the late afternoon, worshippers begin gathering near the tipi and socializing. The sponsor and road man greet the participants and the road man engages in avuncular conversation. Early on only men were allowed to participate in meetings, but over the course of the twentieth century women's participation became more acceptable and today it is not uncommon. Menstruating women are not supposed to attend, however, and the road man will issue a warning about this taboo before entering the tipi.

The meeting begins at sundown or at a set time thereabout, usually eight or nine o'clock. Entrance to the tipi may be made in a formal procession led by the road man, or else individuals go in after the fire man and wait for the leader to enter. People always move in a clockwise direction inside the tipi, following the path of the sun. The officers take their places and the others are free to sit with their friends anywhere around the lodge. Once the road man is settled in his place, latecomers must wait kneeling in the doorway for his permission to enter. The worshippers sit cross-legged or else kneel, leaning back on their heels; when singing or awaiting permission from the road man, they kneel upright on the right knee. Pillow and cushions may be brought in for comfort.

The meeting is officially started when the road man places his father peyote on its bed of sage on top of the crescent earth altar before him. He then rolls a cigarette and passes the tobacco and papers (black jack oak leaves or corn shucks) clockwise to the others. All smoke as the leader beseeches Peyote to hear everyone's prayers, and he offers the father peyote a smoke. The others focus their attention on the fetish button and pray silently or aloud. Then the cigarettes are put out and the butts stuck in the ground by the altar.

The fire man sprinkles cedar on the fire and the worshippers rub themselves with sage as a blessing, following the road man's example. During this incensing, the road man passes around a sack of buttons and the worshippers take from it and begin chewing. Each person takes a minimum of four buttons to begin, with the option of many more over the course of the night. The strength of the buttons varies naturally. It is virtually impossible to overdose. The peyote is bitter, with a corky texture. If someone vomits, it is interpreted as a sign that they were in a ready spiritual state to accept the blessing of peyote or, in some fireplaces, it is said that they have been purged of sin.

The road man sings an Opening Song and three others. Next, the drummer sings four songs, then he passes the drum to the left of the leader and on around to the other participants to sing in turn. The singing continues until midnight. Everyone eats more peyote and some people pray out loud to Peyote in unrestrained, suppliant tones. Participants are not supposed to leave the tipi during the singing, and if they must, they have to get permission from the road man and exit so as not to move between someone eating peyote at the moment, as it is improper to break the person's gaze on the altar area as he or she eats. When leaving in the middle of the proceedings, people turn clockwise in their places or make a clockwise circle with their right foot before moving.

Songs are normally sung in sets of four, and sometimes the songs in a set are thematically related. The singer shakes his gourd with his right hand and holds the staff and fan together in his left while the man to his right plays the drum. When he finishes his songs, the singer in turn drums for the man on his left, and so on. The rattle and staff always precede the drum as they are circulated, and they are handed over in a specific way. Women do not handle these ritual objects and they do not sing, except in soft accompaniment to the men.

The peyote ceremony has its own class of songs and special vocal and drumming styles. The singing is high-pitched, accompanied by the fast, insistent beat of rattles and the water drum, the pitch of which is manipulated by splashing the water inside onto the skin head and pressing the head with the thumb. Among the Yankton Sioux and some other tribes, songs include harmony singing, a rare feature in Indian music that shows an influence from Christian hymn singing. There are hundreds of different songs from many tribes in circulation; some correspond to certain points in the ritual, and others may be sung at any time in the meeting. The songs often contain brief lyric phrases that convey inspirational messages, nature imagery that is symbolic of a holy spiritual state, or imagery of the ceremony itself. The following examples, each a separate song, were sung by the Comanche Tekwaku in 1940 (McAllester 1949:30–32).

I got lost. My pipe, my hatchet. . . . [reference to the origin story]
Dawn I am bringing. You are coming from the east.
Male antelopes, breeding.

FIGURE 10.5 Modern Lakotas participating in a peyote ceremony.

Bird is circling, crying out. [possible
 reference to the anhinga, a sacred bird]
Rise up! We shall, when Jesus comes down.
He is standing, the wind is blowing [reference
 to participant standing up at the end of the
 ceremony at sunrise, when the prairie
 breeze often rises up]

The drumming and singing are essential,
adding to glow of the fire and the physical actions
of the peyote to produce a very powerful atmosphere of peacefulness, contemplation, and revelation. As the alkaloids take effect, the worshippers
become unaware of the discomfort that would
normally be felt from kneeling and sitting in the
same place for long periods. They feel a pleasant
sleeplessness that gives way to euphoria. They
may hear voices or visualize an animal spirit or
deceased relative. One common report in the
descriptions of Southern Plains meetings is the
appearance of a deceased person's silhouette on

the wall of the tipi. Or, they may perceive a
distortion of the ritual they are witnessing, such
as seeing the father peyote spinning, or seeing
colors and patterns in the smoke of the tipi fire, or
sensing a huge amount of time passing between
songs. Some get the feeling of being in the midst
of odd circumstances without normal control of
themselves, as in a dream. All of these images or
feelings are culturally patterned to some extent,
shaped subconsciously by the accounts of prior
ritualists, the teachings of road men, and the
traditional imagery of color and animal symbolism
that they have grown up with. Any of these sensa-
tions is subject to interpretation as a spiritual
message and may lead to deep transformations in
the person's way of thinking or in their lifestyle.
It is important, however, to understand that the
hallucinogenic effects of peyote are really only
one ingredient in the ritual. In fact, color visions
are not inevitable when taking peyote and they
are not considered vital for a successful

experience. Praying, singing, rhythmic drumming, the road man's gentle sermonizing, gazing at the tipi fire, the fragrances of the earth, sage, and cedar smoke—all of these sensory elements compound each other in contributing to the spiritual atmosphere that is so effectively developed in this ceremony.

Around midnight the road man interrupts the singing and there is a respite. The staff and drum are passed back to the leader. More cedar is put in the fire and the fire man tends to the ash crescent. The road man sings a Midnight Song and three others, and during these the fire man exits and returns with a bucket of water with a dipper. The water is passed among the officers in any one of a number of sequences and then on the others, all of whom may sip some. During this informal period the participants are free to talk, stretch, and go outside to relieve themselves. During this time also the road man talks at length. He makes a special effort to welcome newcomers by explaining to them some of what is signified in the ceremony. He may relate the origin story of peyote or advise individuals about how to deal with problems they are facing. Sometimes participants are invited to speak their feelings in a kind of testifying, and in some versions of the ritual there is a period of outright confession in which misdeeds are recited and forgiveness is begged from the father peyote and fellow community members. When the water is gone, the road man steps outside and blows his eagle bone whistle to each of the four directions to alert all the world that a meeting is taking place, effectively establishing the tipi as the center of the universe. A ritual smoke may open or close the midnight segment.

The singing resumes where it left off and the participants continue to eat peyote, gaze at the fire and altar, and reflect. They continue until daybreak, when water is brought in again, this time by the morning water woman. She waits outside with the bucket while the road man completes a Morning Song. The woman enters, smokes a cigarette and prays, and then passes around the water. In the meantime, some women outside the lodge prepare a ritual breakfast, and when it is ready the leader collects the ritual equipment and sings four songs, the last of which is called Quitting Song or Closing Song. The breakfast consists of four foods referred to as "poor Indian food," representing the major food types important to Indian people: water, parched corn, pounded meat, and canned fruit (formerly berries or plums). The foods are set in a line between the fire and door and prayers are made for thanks and future abundance. Thereupon the leader removes his father peyote from the altar and the worship is ended.

The ceremonial foods are distributed and shared, after which the participants may exit the tipi. Some linger inside; others rest nearby outside, sharing stories and songs and instructing each other in religious matters. The sponsor serves a secular dinner at noon, and then the participants leave for home.

Peyote Symbolism

Believers in the peyote religion rely on an intricate system of symbols to represent core concepts and values. The symbols are, not surprisingly, historically related to those used in nativistic curing, with some adaptations from Christianity as well. One of the prevalent themes is lightness, airiness, or flight as a way of describing the desired mental and spiritual state of the peyotist, and this idea is summoned with the body profiles and feathers of certain kinds of birds that are considered sacred because of their soaring abilities and distinctly colorful or iridescent plumage: the water bird (anhinga or water turkey), the scissor-tailed flycatcher, the sparrow hawk (kestrel), and the yellow-hammer (flicker), as well as the golden eagle. The crescent shape given to the swept ashes of the fire is said to represent the wings of the water bird, unifying aquatic and avian symbolism with celestial imagery. Crosses represent the four directions as well as, in some cases, Christ. These symbols, along with images of the implements of the ritual like the tipi and rattle, are portrayed as icons of the religion in several artistic media, such as beadwork, shawl appliqué work, and the shape and engraving of German silver jewelry (see Chapter 6).

Symbols are incorporated and connected in other ingenious ways. For example, when the hide head is bound to the iron kettle to form the peyote water drum, the binding thongs cross around the bottom of the kettle, forming a seven-pointed star configuration. This shape is called morning star, Star of David, or Star of Bethlehem. The water in the kettle is likened to precious rain, and bits of live coal are dropped in to stand for lightning, complementing the "thunder" that is the sound of the drum, in a condensed representation of the elements. The earth altar is like a miniature vision quest hill, with the father peyote sitting on its crest—the place for seeking visions or seat of knowledge. Inscribed in the dirt of the altar from tip to tip is a "path," a metaphor for the course of a person's life, which is also related to the title of the leader as "road man" and the general Indian depiction of a person's religious commitment as a road.

Peyote Politics and Law

From the outset, non-Indian authorities tried to suppress the peyote religion. Reservation agents and Christian clergy saw the new ritual as a return to Native ways that competed with their efforts to establish civilization, most alarming because it involved a hallucinogen. Other government officials aimed for the consistent development and thorough application of antidrug laws, and were not open to counterarguments of religious freedom in the case of peyote. In their zeal, opponents of peyote sometimes confused or conflated it with two other psychoactive plant products found in the southwest, mescal, a

Mexican liquor made from the agave plant, and the red bean of *Sophora secundiflora* (hence "mescal bean"). This confusion yielded the misnomer "mescal buttons" for peyote, which is still sometimes heard today. Some opponents mounted sensational and patently false accusations about the substance and its Indian users in order to have peyote use criminalized. They likened peyote to opium and heroin; it was said to be habit-forming, and peyotists were labeled as good-for-nothing addicts. Rumors were circulated that peyote meetings included orgies. In fact, there is no evidence that peyote is addictive or harmful, and the teachings of the peyote religion call for strict moral and behavioral standards.

Early efforts to make peyote illegal, beginning in the 1890s in Oklahoma, tried to control it at the territorial or state level by including peyote restrictions along with those prohibiting alcohol. Several worshippers were harassed and arrested to set up test cases in the courts. These tactics met with very limited success, however, so peyote opponents then began pressing for a national law. Congressional bills were introduced beginning in 1916, with the decisive hearings, involving hours of testimony and cross-examination, conducted in early 1918. Witnesses against peyote included Bureau of Indian Affairs agency officials, missionaries, Indian school superintendents and teachers, and two reformers who led national organizations promoting Indian temperance, S. M. Brosius, a white, and Gertrude Bonnin, a Yankton Sioux. Testimony in defense of peyote was organized by James Mooney, the dedicated ethnologist who worked closely with the Kiowas, among other tribes, on behalf of the Smithsonian Institution Bureau of American Ethnology. Mooney was joined by two other BAE anthropologists, Francis LaFlesche (himself a member of the Omaha tribe) and Truman Michelson, as well as peyote leaders from the Arapahos, Cheyennes, Comanches, Omahas, and Osages.

Mooney's group emphasized the beneficial effect of the religion in offering social stability and hope on the reservations, and they disputed the sordid characterizations of the plant and ritual. They likened peyote belief to the religions practiced in Christian churches. The bill banning peyote passed in the House but failed in the Senate. Mooney had succeeded in defeating this most serious attempt at a federal law, but anti-peyote officials in the Bureau of Indian Affairs vilified him as an interferer for his role in the hearings. The Smithsonian gave in to this criticism and withdrew Mooney from his Oklahoma fieldwork assignment. He died of a heart attack three years later.

Suppression efforts continued sporadically through the twentieth century. Canada outlawed peyote, and several states in the western United States passed anti-peyote laws, but these laws were not enforced steadily enough to interfere much with the development of the Indian religion. State-level regulation sometimes led to curious inconsistencies in public policy. For example, during the 1920s the state of South Dakota granted charters to several peyote churches (see following section) even though it had passed a law in 1923 prohibiting the transportation of peyote across state lines. The law was only repealed in 1962. Anthropologists continued to testify in defense of the religion; in 1951 five prominent ones signed a statement explaining and supporting peyotism in the journal *Science* (LaBarre et al. 1951).

Beginning in the 1950s and into the 1970s, certain non-Indian writers, artists, and intellectuals advocated widely the use of psychoactive drugs for mystic self-enlightenment or purely for recreation. The British novelist Aldous Huxley (1894–1963), American beat poet Allen Ginsberg (1926–1997), and Harvard psychologist Timothy Leary (1920–1996) were among those who drew public attention to mescaline and LSD, synthetic forms of the psychoactive compounds found in peyote and teonanacatl, and

consequently to peyote itself. Experimentation with peyote by non-Indians became prevalent. During this time non-Indians from far and wide began trespassing on the South Texas ranches where peyote grew and cutting buttons without the necessary care to ensure survival of the plants. The influx of recreational drug users to the peyote grounds drew more negative publicity about peyote, while the general populace remained largely unaware that the Indian religion teaches that the cactus is a sacrament with divine powers and that it is sacrilegious to eat peyote for secular reasons or personal amusement. Thus, two contrary aspects of non-Indian society, anti-drug legislation and recreational drug use, both had disruptive effects on Native religious practice.

Just as anti-peyote efforts in the early twentieth century were framed within the larger temperance movement under way at that time, efforts at the end of the century were mounted in the context of a national "war on drugs." The most recent significant court case began in 1984, when two American Indian peyotists in Oregon were fired from their jobs as drug rehabilitation counselors and denied unemployment benefits because they used peyote. They contended that their peyote use had not been prosecuted as criminal activity (the stated basis for denial of benefits) and that in any case they should be free to observe their religion even though their jobs required them to remain drug-free. While the Oregon appellate and supreme courts ruled in favor of the peyotists, the U.S. Supreme Court ruled against them, saying that their freedom to exercise religion did not override other laws. In effect, the court ruled that laws prohibiting drug use could take precedent over laws safeguarding religious exercise and that individual states could outlaw even the religious use of peyote. Congress passed the 1993 Religious Freedom Restoration Act extending free exercise rights as a direct response to the 1990 ruling, but the Act was struck down in another Supreme Court ruling in 1997.

The Native American Church

The 1918 fight against anti-peyote legislation was a tough one, and the Indian leaders present at the hearings concluded that in order to enjoy protection from further, inevitable, legal challenges, they had to confirm their claims that peyotism was like any other church by incorporating as one. In August of that year, Oklahoma peyote leaders convened at El Reno, Oklahoma, to charter a peyote church, the Native American Church of Oklahoma. Their articles of incorporation provide perhaps the most concise picture of peyote belief: " . . . the worship of a Heavenly Father . . . to promote morality, sobriety, industry, charity, and right living and cultivate a spirit of self respect and brotherly love and union among the members of the several Tribes of Indians throughout the United States . . . with and through the sacramental use of peyote" (cited in LaBarre et al. 1951:582).

In the ensuing years, a number of other state and tribal peyote churches were chartered in the Plains area and beyond, and in 1950 an organization for the entire United States and Canada, the Native American Church of North America, was born. Today the international Native American Church includes perhaps 300,000 members, although dependable numbers are not easily found. Some peyotists prefer membership in one of the state or tribally based churches, which are more or less affiliated in various combinations. The churches have had some success in promoting the rights of practitioners, and they issue membership cards, which help peyotists demonstrate their status as religious users when challenged by legal authorities. Other peyotists do not feel they need the validation or protection of an organized church and practice the religion without church membership.

The Peyote Trade

Demand for peyote by Native American ritualists has long sustained an industry of harvest and shipping based in and around Laredo, Texas. The harvest zone includes four south Texas counties: Starr, Jim Hogg, Webb, and Zapata; and small communities in this area such as Mirando City and Roma have been home to licensed professional collectors of Hispanic ethnic origin, known locally as *peyoteros*. Indian pilgrimages to the peyote grounds continued after Indian people were confined to reservations, but they became less practical because initially there were restrictions on travel from the reservations, travel was expensive, and the reservations were distant from South Texas. By the 1880s the *peyotero* business emerged, at first to have green and dried cut peyote ready when Indians visited. After 1881 a railroad line crossed the area, allowing the *peyoteros* to ship their harvest into Laredo, and from there, northward throughout the Plains and beyond. The *peyoteros* then began to fill orders by mail in addition to hosting Indian pilgrims, and the provision of peyote through mail order played a major role in the establishment, spread, and continuance of the religion.

Nine individuals were licensed by the State of Texas as peyote distributors in 1994, four in 2004. Annual sales during this period ranged from about $200,000 to $400,000. Earlier there were two dozen or more *peyoteros* licensed in a given year, but the profession seems to be vanishing, although the amount of peyote cut has remained constant—around two million buttons each year, except for 1,300,000 in 2004.

The future of the peyote religion is ultimately tied to the survival of the plant itself. Indian harvesters and the *peyoteros* know how to cut the buttons so as not to kill the plant. Careless harvesting by profiteers and drug experimenters since the 1960s, however, may be leading to a decline in the species (although decline does not seem clearly evident from recent State of Texas harvest records). Expert Omer Stewart felt that the long-run viability of the religion would require a system of legalized cultivation or steady legal importation from Mexico, which currently outlaws the trade or exportation of peyote.

INDIAN CHRISTIANITY

The introduction of Christianity to the Plains Indians by Spanish, French, and American frontiersmen and missionaries is discussed in Chapter 11. Here it is appropriate to emphasize that many thousands of Plains Indians have practiced various Christian religions either exclusively or in combination with Native religions, and Christianity continues to play a significant role in Indian social and cultural life.

Christianity made inroads among Plains tribes in different ways. On the Southern Plains, many populations were first exposed to Christian ideas through direct or indirect contact with Spanish explorers, missionaries, and settlers, and to a lesser degree, French traders; and perhaps Mexican captives among these tribes also played a role in transmission. But the greater effect came with a flurry of missionizing by many denominations in rapid succession once reservations were established in 1874 and for the rest of the nineteenth century. These efforts often involved establishing both a church and a school, either day or boarding. Thus, in the area where the Kiowas, Plains Apaches, and Comanches were settled, Quakers were first assigned to assimilate and convert the Indians. After an outbreak of reservation violence effectively drove off the Quakers, Methodist, Baptist, Episcopalian, Mennonite, Presbyterian, Roman Catholic, and Dutch Reformed missionaries came into the area. None of these religions was very successful in winning total converts in the early years, and their schools gained attendance only gradually, but together they created an atmosphere of Christian domination that stood as a counterpoint to traditional Indian belief.

On the Central and Northern Plains, Catholic missionaries coming from the northeast in league with the fur trade had some early influence, and then as reservations were set up Catholics and other denominations were assigned mission locations, but normally only one, two, or three competing denominations were thus started in any given tribe in the early years. The Anglican Church was especially active on some of the Canadian reserves. Table 10.2 shows the main sects affiliated with particular tribes.

During the twentieth century, the list of Christian sects engaged in any given Indian community tended to diversify. In the south, the strong orientation toward Methodist and Baptist churches among the general population meant that these mainline Protestant denominations began embracing more Indians also, so that, for example, the heavily Catholic Osages gradually included converts to the Protestant sects too. In the north, at Pine Ridge Reservation (Teton) for example, the earliest Episcopalian and Catholic churches were joined by Presbyterian and Congregationalist, and later Baptist, Church of God, Gospel Missionary Union, Lutheran, Seventh-Day Adventist, and the Church of Jesus Christ of Latter Day Saints (Mormons). Every summer on many western reservations, pairs of earnest young men in suits bicycle from house to house as Mormon missionaries. Mormons believe that American Indians hold a special place in human history and that their conversion is necessary for the salvation of all mankind.

Of increasing influence since the late twentieth century are fundamentalist Protestant organizations, which have the flexibility to develop individualized churches very much in keeping with local needs. Often they originate as splinter groups from the previously established Christian churches in an area, so that they concentrate not on conversion to Christianity but on reorientation of believers. These sects are effective in staging large public gatherings that are inviting to those who may simply be curious about spiritual matters. In Oklahoma, summertime Pentecostal camp meetings and stadium rallies draw significant numbers of Indian people who may participate by speaking in tongues or stepping forward to testify or receive a cure or blessing from the preacher. One well-documented example of a fundamentalist Indian church in the north is

TABLE 10.2   **Early Influential Christian Denominations Among Select Tribes**

Arapahos, Northern	Episcopalian, Roman Catholic
Arapahos, Southern	Baptist, Mennonite
Blackfoots	Anglican, Methodist, Roman Catholic
Cheyennes, Northern	Mennonite, Roman Catholic
Cheyennes, Southern	Baptist, Dutch Reformed, Mennonite
Crows	Baptist, Roman Catholic
Gros Ventres	Roman Catholic
Kansas	Roman Catholic
Mandan-Hidatsa-Arikara	Congregationalist
Osages	Roman Catholic
Pawnees	Methodist Episcopal
Plains Crees	Anglican, Methodist, Roman Catholic
Poncas	Baptist, Methodist
Quapaws	Roman Catholic
Santees	Roman Catholic
Stoneys	Methodist
Tetons	Congregationalist, Episcopalian, Presbyterian, Roman Catholic
Yanktons-Yanktonais	Congregationalist, Episcopalian, Presbyterian, Roman Catholic

Sources: Wright (1951) and Sturtevant (2001).

the Body of Christ Independent Church among the Oglalas at Pine Ridge. This congregation is described as "a small independent church that broke off from the traditional Christian churches. Members are typical Pentacostals who conduct prayer meetings including preaching, singing, clapping hands, spontaneous prayer, witnessing, and the laying on of hands for healing" (Steinmetz 1990:153).

In the course of these developments, several Plains Indians became notable leaders in Christian churches, and some assumed authority for non-Indian as well as Indian worshippers. The other side of this equation is that service in the Christian clergy and laity became a legitimate way for Indian men and women to pursue leadership roles in their communities. Philip Deloria (1853–1931), the son of a Yankton chief, was ordained as an Episcopalian priest and ran the mission church and school at Standing Rock Reservation (straddling North and South Dakota) for many years. His son Vine Deloria, Sr. was also a priest and missionary. Among the Pawnees, the adopted Sioux-French Reverend Adolphur Carrion and his Pawnee wife Marion C. Carrion led the establishment of the Methodist Episcopal Church. Lieutenant James Ottipoby, a Comanche leader in the Dutch Reformed Church, was the first American Indian commissioned by the Army Corps of Chaplains in World War II.

Christian priests and ministers play an active role in community affairs. In addition to running weekly services, they may oversee schools or foster homes, and they provide marriage counseling and advise in cases of adoption, alcohol abuse, and teen pregnancy. Some speak out stridently against competing practices, decrying the continuing influence of traditional Indian rituals and secular amusements and urging their followers to abandon them. Others, however, explore various fusions and accommodations between Christian and Native customs in order to offer a more relevant religious experience. It is important to note that these efforts most often result in changes in the supposedly "dominant" Christian religions rather than affecting traditional practices. The process of bringing Christian belief and ritual into conformity with Native culture has been referred to as *indigenization.*

One of many instances of indigenization is the development of Indian Christian hymns. The Comanches, Kiowas, Wichitas, Poncas, and other tribes have each developed large repertoires of native-language hymns for use in Christian services. Here is a Southern Cheyenne example sung in 1991 by Mary Lou Stone Road Prairie Chief and her grandson Jeremiah (Giglio 1994:171–172):

Ha hoo, Jesus,
Ni ya mi yo chi mi no do, hi yi
Ni Ma hi yo ni vi do vi
Na vi shi hi do da da no mo vi—, hi yi
Ha hoo, Jesus,
Nin shi va da mi mi no, hi.

Thank you, Jesus,
You carry us.
God's spirit makes us rejoice also.
Thank you, Jesus,
Have mercy on us.

The long Sunday morning service at the United Indian Methodist Church in the Dallas, Texas, suburb of Oak Cliff serves a congregation made up from many tribes. If Christendom ever devised a joyful answer to Babel's confusion of voices, it happens in Oak Cliff. The hymns are sung in many Indian languages, including Comanche, Kiowa, Ponca, and others, as well as in English. The worshippers sing strongly in their own languages and attempt to follow along in the others.

DUAL RELIGIOUS PARTICIPATION

Upon studying the variety of Plains Indian religious practices, it becomes apparent that individuals recognize threads of similar belief and symbolism across the various rituals and that these features allow practitioners to rationalize their involvement in many different ceremonies more or less concurrently. At the same time, Native religions commonly teach that revelation, and thus openness to new experiences, is a basic means of gaining spiritual knowledge and attaining a desirable spiritual state. It is not surprising, then, that Indian people would sometimes perceive resemblances between Indian and non-Indian religions and that they could be open to learning about and practicing religions introduced by non-Indians.

Anthropologist William K. Powers has emphasized that Indians also have pragmatic reasons for becoming involved in Christian religions, because there are social, political, and economic benefits to membership (Powers 1987). Powers notes that among the Oglala Sioux at Pine Ridge, Christian church membership is another way of expressing band affiliation and allegiance to particular Indian leaders, and that the churches provided an early form of welfare by issuing food, clothing, and some cash assistance. Powers has described the phenomenon of moving between Native and introduced religions as *dual religious participation*, although sometimes more than two definable religions are bridged.

The Lakota Black Elk (1863–1950) has often been regarded as a paragon of traditional Indian philosophy and religion. Black Elk lived through a period of profound cultural change and his memories of his early days were recorded by the poet laureate of Nebraska John Jacob Neihardt in the 1932 book *Black Elk Speaks* (reprinted in 1972), to preserve traditional Lakota worldview. More of Black Elk's knowledge was recorded in Joseph Epes Brown's *The Sacred Pipe* (1989; orig. 1953). Black Elk's memories and discussions of older traditions are indeed valuable, and

Neihardt and Brown's books have been relied upon as authoritative teachings of Indian worldview in countless high school and college classes. Ironically, however, Black Elk was known in his own community, for the last 46 years of his life, as Nicholas Black Elk, lay catechist in the Catholic Church. In 1904, Black Elk, then a medicine man in the *yuwipi* tradition, was forceably interrupted by a Catholic priest while doctoring a sick child. Black Elk was taken by the priest to the Holy Rosary Mission on the Pine Ridge Reservation and he accepted Catholic baptism two weeks later. This experience set him on a lifelong course of mediating between religions.

Black Elk and his children pioneered the incorporation of the Sacred Pipe in Catholic masses, dedications, and funerals on the reservation. He struggled intellectually with the validity of this combination. As well, Black Elk labored continually to make sense of his older beliefs in terms of newer ones, for example, reinterpreting one of his early visions, which he initially thought to be about the Ghost Dance, as a manifestation of the Christian messiah. Black Elk's persona as an explorer of multiple belief systems, and the life transitions that he experienced, were obscured by Neihardt and Brown's influential portrayals of an exclusively nativist holy man. But arguably he is an even greater exemplar of Indian religiosity because of his efforts to make sense of multiple traditions.

Black Elk's experience was not atypical. Comanche people living in rural Oklahoma in the 1980s moved easily among a number of religious settings. In the course of a week or two, an individual might attend a curing ceremony or wedding ceremony staged by a traditional medicine man, a peyote ceremony, a powwow (a "secular" dance event which nevertheless includes elements of curing the vision quest, and the Sun Dance), a Pentecostal camp meeting with fervent preaching and speaking in tongues, and a funeral service for a tribe member held under the auspices of the Methodist or Dutch Reformed church. The same individual might also keep Catholic statues in the car or home, for their beauty or protective power.

Comanche choices about religious participation were in part practical. For example, it would be illegal and very difficult in modern Oklahoma to conduct a traditional scaffold or crevice burial even if the mourners thought that this kind of interment was preferable, so Indian people there have come to rely on Christian churches and affiliated funeral homes when burying and honoring the dead. Church services and camp meetings also offered entertainment and socializing just as traditional Indian rituals do, and attending them enlivens rural life. But it would be a mistake to assume that participants in multiple religions have only shallow motives. Many Comanches are honestly intrigued by introduced religions, and some are totally committed to them. Most see no hypocrisy in moving among them and may feel both that doing so is in keeping with Native ideas of approaching the supernatural and that it results in a more intensive engagement with the supernatural than if they restricted themselves to one form of religion. With these attitudes afoot, there is much potential for the merging of religious ideas.

A few examples from Comanche culture illustrate how religious ideas meet and combine. "When I was raised we did not know when it was Saturday. One day was just like the others," explained Tekwaku, a Comanche elder and peyotist, in 1940 (McAllester 1949:19). Tekwaku was discussing how peyote meetings came to be held on Saturdays. The practice arose so that participants could use the second day of the weekend to recover from the meeting and return home. The weekend and workweek concepts are of course dictated ultimately by the Christian practice of resting and worshipping on Sunday. Comanches eventually devised a word in their language for this special day of worship: *Puha rabeni*, "power day," using the traditional Indian notion of power in the label. To designate Saturday, then, Comanches invented a derivative term, *Tueh puha rabeni*, "little power day" or "little Sunday." Similarly, they called Christmas *Waahima?*, which literally means "cedar getting." As the only prevalent evergreen in Comanche country, red cedar (juniper) is cut and dragged to the house if someone wants to set up a Christmas tree, although cedar is also a standard material in traditional Indian rituals, again on account of its evergreen and aromatic properties.

Such examples of Indian religious blending have sometimes been termed "syncretisms" by anthropologists. A syncretism is a combination or reconciliation of different and at times even opposing beliefs. Since any religious system can be analyzed as a combination of ideas coming from different times and places, the concept of syncretism is really of only limited explanatory value. It does, however, alert us to the varied origins and the blended nature of Indian beliefs and practices, and this is an important point, because non-Indians often assume that Native religion is hidebound or static.

This emphasis on the dynamic nature of Indian religion should not suggest that Indian believers lack commitment. Some may be highly enthusiastic about each of several belief systems they are participating in. There are certainly many people in the any Indian community who adhere devoutly to only one religion throughout their lives, be it the medicine way, the sacred pipe, peyotism, Pentecostalism, or Methodism, and vocally reject all the alternatives. There will also be a certain proportion of people who adhere to one faith at a time, but shift over the course of their lifetime, marking different stages in their lives with membership in contrasting religions. In all these cases there may be significant devotion.

RELIGION AND NATIVE IDENTITY

Organized religion is an effective vehicle for the formation and expression of ethnic identity. How a person feels or knows that he or she is an Indian or a member of a particular Indian group is often shaped and announced through belief and ritual. Myths, prayers, songs, dances, and verbal teachings encode and pass along the commonly shared values of the identifying group. Ritual actually brings the people together and functions as a public display of togetherness. At the same time, the group so unified appears distinct from other groups with different beliefs and rituals.

At the level of the individual, one's identity and reputation within an Indian community are partly forged through professed belief and ritual behavior. "He's a fisherman, he'll never be a powwow man," lamented a Comanche grandmother of her 10-year-old grandson, who was more interested in casting for bass than putting together a dance outfit and learning tribal traditions. The grandmother was concerned about her grandson's character, about the person who he would one day become, and if that person would be an Indian according to her sense of the term. In another Comanche example, the late Ralph Kosechata explained to the author how he became heavily involved in the peyote religion at about age 50 as a way of telling all those around him that he was now someone different—someone more sober and goodhearted, who exemplified the Indian ideal of an older man. It is also not unusual for families and bands collectively to maintain some distinguishing religious practices. These subunits within tribes may form around the varying religions that are available—one family may become known as peyotists, another as Episcopalians, a third as Sun dancers.

Tribal affiliation is another order of identity frequently served by religion. Often Plains rituals and their mythic charters explain how tribes began and became different from each other. For example, in comparing the Cheyenne story of Sweet Medicine and his acquisition of the Sacred Arrows with the Lakota Sacred Pipe origin myth, it can be seen that they are versions of the same story. The Cheyenne arrow and Lakota pipe thus stand for both the shared early historical experiences of the two groups (even the same geographic location is described in both stories) and their ultimate differentiation through the adoption of the contrasting key symbols of arrows and pipe.

However intense tribal pride may be, identity becomes an even more highly charged issue when Indian people distinguish themselves from non-Indians. Again, organized religion plays a large role. The rituals described in this chapter typically display values that Indian people regard as characteristic of Native ethnicity, such as generosity, personal and communal responsibility, respect for fellow humans, especially the elderly, and a cooperative relationship with nature. The Ghost Dance was an overt effort to reinstitute some of these values at a point when Indian people and their cultures were assumed to be doomed owing to white colonization. In modern times, religious activity continues to provide strong opportunities for the expression of indigenous values and ethnic pride, whether through full participation in rituals such as the peyote rite, *yuwipi*, or Sun Dance or through associated activities such as wearing peyote jewelry or a feather in one's hat, "wearing scars" from a Sun Dance, or taking part in peyote legalization efforts. Because of this identifying function, over and above its purpose in answering other basic human needs, group ritual will prove to be one of the most durable aspects of Indian culture.

Sources: Anderson (1996); Archambault (2001); Bowers (1991); Brown (1989); Catlin (1973, I); DeMallie (1984); DeMallie and Parks (1987); Gelo (1986, 1993); Gelo and Zesch (2003); Giglio (1994); Hanson (1980); Hanson and Chirinos (1997); Harris (1968); Harrod (1987); Hinojosa (2000); Hoebel (1980); Howard (1957, 1960); Hyde (1974); Kavanagh (1996); Kracht (1992); LaBarre (1970, 1989); LaBarre et al. (1951); Linton (1935); Marriott and Rachlin (1971); McAllester (1949); Mooney (1965); Morgan and Stewart (1984); Murie (1989); Powers (1977, 1982, 1987); Neihardt (1972); Nye (1969); Schlesier (1987, 1990); Steinmetz (1990); Steltenkamp (1993); Stewart (1980, 1987); Sturtevant (2001); Thurman (1983); Troike (1962); Tunnell (2000); Underhill (1965); Vander (1988); Voget (1984); Walker (1979, 1980); Wallace (1956, 1966, 1972); Weltfish (1965); Wissler and Spinden (1916); and Wright (1951).

CHAPTER SUMMARY

Group rituals are important as religious exercises and social gatherings. The Cheyenne Massaum and Mandan Okipa are examples of complex public rituals intended to renew the world. Many tribes also had rituals for renewing medicine bundles, collections of objects that were power repositories. Some bundles contained sacred arrows or pipes. A related ceremony, the Pawnee morning star rite, is the only example of human sacrifice on the Plains. The Sun Dance was the most widespread and definitive Plains ceremony, though its form varied from tribe to tribe. The spread of the Sun Dance has been studied to test theories of cultural development. The Sun Dance was suppressed by non-Indian authorities and in several cases has been revived. The Ghost Dance emerged in the late nineteenth century as a religious movement for reestablishing a Native world in the face of white conquest; it was suppressed by the military or faded on its own. The Lakota *yuwipi* is an example of a ceremony led by a medicine man for community healing. Peyote, a hallucinogenic cactus, is the sacrament in a religion that grew during the reservation era and is now organized as a church. Plains tribes have had long acquaintance with Christianity and many Indians belong to Christian denominations. Many participate in multiple religions. Organized religion remains a vehicle for the expression of Native identity.

QUESTIONS FOR REVIEW

1. Select a major ritual such as the Massaum, Sun Dance, or peyote ceremony, and describe its schedule, actors, symbols, and purposes.
2. Why has the Sun Dance been of interest to non-Indian scholars of cultural development?
3. How does the life of Black Elk exemplify dual religious participation?
4. Using Plains Indian examples, explain how "[o]rganized religion is an effective vehicle for the formation and expression of ethnic identity."

CHAPTER 11

EXTERNAL RELATIONS

Many descriptions of Plains Indian life leave the impression that tribal cultures were inward-looking and not widely aware of the large world around them. Certainly, early non-Indian perceptions were of relatively small, mobile, isolated, and often hostile populations with strange languages and customs. Even though several early observers lived and worked closely with Indian groups and witnessed or participated in armed conflicts, inter-tribal alliances, and treaty talks, there was not widespread or detailed grasp of how Indians dealt with outsiders. Often they have been portrayed as passive or incompetent when responding to outside forces. These images are tinged by the concept called primitivism—the idea that people in small-scale societies exhibit a simple or even naïve way of life, supposedly representative of the way all humans lived in ancient times.

It has taken a long time to put such notions to rest, but modern scholarship has shown that the Plains Indians were very conscious and capable strategists on their own account, pursing their own interests in a rapidly changing, global political and economic environment. There was nothing simplistic about their intentions or methods. They were not shy and retiring, but cosmopolitan,

taking an open and far-reaching view. They strove to understand and actively engage other tribes and non-Indian populations, and to affect the behavior of others to their own best advantage. They were adept in pursuing external relations through warfare, trade, and diplomacy.

WARFARE

Armed conflict was a continual reality in Plains life that defined so much of the distinctive social and cultural practices of the region. In prior chapters, we have seen how everything from childrearing and religious rituals to music and art reflected a preoccupation with war. The warlike tendencies of the Plains tribes are often cited as a key characteristic of the area. For example, Robert Lowie wrote, "Like the Eastern Indians, the Plains tribes were very warlike, thus again differing sharply from the natives of the Basin and the Plateau" (Lowie 1983:6). Early historian Frances Parkman, who lived for a few weeks during 1846 with Oglala Sioux, said succinctly, "War is the breath of their nostrils" (Parkman 1931:147). Why was the theme of warfare so pervasive?

FIGURE 11.1   *A frontiersman approaches an Indian for a parlay while his partners cover him with their rifles from behind their horses in this nineteenth-century lithograph.*

Was combat really as endemic as the cultural focus, and outsiders' portrayals, would seem to indicate? Why did the Plains Indians fight, and how? These and related questions lead once again through a complex array of facts, stereotypes, consistencies, and contradictions.

The term "warfare" has stood for a wide range of human activities and it is worthwhile to specify the particular nature of warfare on the Plains. It is easiest to say what Plains warfare was not. It was quite different from the combat waged by contemporary nation states. Sustained battles or campaigns were rare. There were no specialized, professional standing armies among the Indian tribes; instead, virtually all able-bodied adult men were soldiers, and they were activated as the need arose, though their service could become continuous in certain eras of severe competition. Concepts of military rank and its association with social status and power were found in all the tribes but in none were they highly elaborated, as they are in the armies of state societies. War itself was not about the submission of other people to the rule of the conquerors; captives were taken during battle, and some enslaved, but there was no wholesale subjugation of one population by another. Whether Plains fighting was about the permanent possession of territory is a little more complicated question. The overt purpose was not to gain ownership of land. War, however, did correspond to the expansion of some groups into the ranges of others, as well as defensive actions against such expansion, and the eventual displacement of tribes by other tribes. The motivation behind these population movements was control of a general territory that would allow dependable access to game (itself a variable proposition, especially because of the migratory tendencies of the buffalo herds), horse herds, river bottom camp and garden sites, and trade outlets.

Plains warfare was most like the kind of armed conflict that typically occurs in small-scale societies. It resembled the feuding that breaks out between groups of blood relatives within a tribal society, in which one revenge killing is followed by another, back and forth, sometimes for many generations, except that the feuding parties were distinct tribes whose enmity became a traditional rivalry. Much of Plains warfare could also be described as raiding, a practice characteristic of mobile pastoralists, involving surprise attacks and quick retreats for the acquisition of plunder. The literature on Plains war therefore often notes two basic kinds of combat, "revenge raids," or intertribal feuding, and "horse raids" in the pastoralist mold. These distinctions have some basis in the Native perspective. For instance, the Kiowas spoke of two kinds of war endeavor, the *ak'ataíd)mbanmá*, or revenge party, and the *ætsed)mbanmá*, or horse raid. Kiowa revenge parties involved more warriors than horse raids did and recruited members from beyond the organizer's residential band. They were launched in the summer at the close of the Sun Dance, imbued by the ceremony with a sacred purpose, and they lasted a brief time, until the need for vengeance was consummated in the death of an enemy. Horse raids were more casual, secular affairs, drawing on the organizer's close band mates, though horse-raiding parties might wander for an indefinite time. Similarly, the Osages distinguished between large-scale revenge raids organized in the summertime by two or more men, small revenge raids organized by an individual, and horse raids. In practice motives were sometimes mixed, since it was tempting enough to take some livestock during a revenge attack or to even an old score by killing during a horse raid.

Lasting rivalries were the framework for Plains combat. Often, however, particular intertribal feuds turned into alliances over the course of the Historic Period as the tribes migrated and the regional balance of power shifted. The Crows counted the Blackfoots, Sioux, Cheyennes, and Arapahos as their traditional enemies, but eventually allied with the Blackfoots and Gros Ventres against the others. The Santees customarily fought against the Assiniboines and Plains Ojibwas, later reconciling with the latter. The Kiowa Apaches named the Utes, Pawnees, Sioux, and Mexicans as their natural enemies. Wichitas held the Osages, Apaches, and Tonkawas to be their regular competitors. The Comanches, who were on good terms with the Wichitas, also generally viewed the Apaches, Osages, and Tonkawas as enemies, along with the Pawnees and Utes. Comanches initially fought the Kiowas, Cheyennes, and Arapahos too as those tribes moved southward, but then formed powerful ties with each. Even the most notorious rivalries were suspended at times by truces between groups who were eager to trade or weary of bloodshed.

Raiding is a low-intensity form of combat, with relatively few participants at once and light casualties. Though warriors were often merciless once caught up in the heat of battle, there was little tolerance for taking casualties or leaving comrades behind, and a war party was considered a failure if even one person was lost. Such attitudes were ironic given that death in battle was considered the most honorable fate for a man. And when an individual fighter took on an enemy, he well might dismount or forsake his gun for a club in order to even the match, as there was more honor in a fair fight. With its avoidance of mortality and displays of sportsmanship, Plains Indian warfare had a game-like quality. Warriors, it seemed, competed against their own tribe mates for glory, trophies, and booty, even more than they sought to harm the enemy.

Another curious trait of Plains warfare that has gotten less attention is the direct involvement of women in combat, beyond their role as encouragers of male warriors. According to one cross-cultural survey (Adams 1983), women were allowed to be active combatants in only 13 percent of the 70 worldwide societies sampled. Six such societies were found in Native North America, and three of them on the Plains: the Crows, the Gros Ventres, and the Comanches. This survey obviously took note of the famous manly hearted women as discussed in Chapter 5; however, some ordinary women, in most or all Plains tribes, also took a direct part in warfare. The wives of warriors frequently accompanied them on raids, and it was not uncommon to find two or more women among a war party. They went along to cook, sew, and tend the horses, and were especially interested in helping if the raid was meant to avenge the death of a relative. The women followed the men closely in battle and seized guns or other trophies from the enemy. At times, they even took up weapons. Conversely, male warriors considered women whom they encountered in battle to be worthy foes and took credit for killing them if the act required any daring.

There were some important exceptions to the usual pattern of small raids. Plains Indians mounted large-scale battles at certain historical transition points, and these engagements might involve alliances between members of different tribes. Naturally, tactics were different prior to the spread of horses and guns. In the northwest, early Shoshones and Blackfoots marched against each other in two opposing lines, carrying long bows, clubs, lances, and rawhide shields large enough to cover their whole bodies. Fatalities were actually rare in these engagements unless one side markedly outnumbered the other. In the south, the Plains Apaches and Caddoans wore body armor made from thick rawhide coated with glue and sand, which was very effective in repelling arrows and blows. This armor was inspired by the metal and leather plating of the Spanish, but also drew on Native traditions of protecting the body with hide or quilted cotton, practices that were prevalent west of the Plains from Canada to Mexico. Armored infantry shock troops with bows and lances formed long curved lines and attempted to encircle the enemy. As the fight progressed, one side either fully enclosed the other, borrowing the surround tactic from buffalo hunting, or the lines broke into smaller units for close combat. Again in this case an attack was only conclusive if one

side was much larger than the other. As the Apaches and Caddoans became among the first groups to have horses, they adopted their armor and tactics to cavalry maneuvers, and so dominated the South Plains in the late 1600s.

Once horses and guns were distributed fairly evenly over the area, the armor and line tactics became less practical, and armor was gradually abandoned in favor of the small leather shields suitable for riding, but there were still occasions for large war parties. In the spring of 1758 a combined force of 2,000 Wichitas, Tonkawas, and probably Comanches sacked and burned the Spanish mission at San Saba, Texas, in order to disrupt Spanish overtures to the Apaches. By 1786, the Spanish were allied with the Comanches when 347 warriors under 5 chiefs campaigned against Apaches south of Santa Fe, New Mexico. In the early 1800s, the tribes of the Southern High Plains assembled to attack the prairie and woodland tribes that were then pressing westward. Plains Indians also organized intertribal forces of 500 or more warriors with some regularity to fight against Anglo expansion. The Santees and Tetons in particular were successful in uniting the Sioux bands and their allies in the 1860s and 1870s to attack regular and volunteer cavalry units in their forts or on the hoof. A similar strategy was employed by the joint force of 700 Comanches, Kiowas, and Cheyennes that rode against the buffalo hunters' station at Adobe Walls in the Texas Panhandle in June 1874.

Mounted engagements ultimately looked much like the earlier pedestrian battles. If the opponents found each other without surprise, they lined up against one other at a distance, but encirclement was the main large-group tactic attempted as soon as possible. From there the action broke down into a muddle of charges, skirmishes, infiltrations, snipes, and hand-to-hand struggles between mounted and dismounted fighters. Squads of warriors tried to lure enemy parties into ambushes, stampeded the enemy's horses, and set the prairie on fire to trap them and create smoke screens.

Although Indian culture and those studying it have emphasized offensive action, defense was important too. In fact, horticultural tribes like the Poncas and Omahas were mainly defensive in their outlook. The Omahas spoke not only of *nú?attaðišą*, "pertaining to men," war expeditions for revenge or plunder, but also of *wa?ų?attaðišą*, "pertaining to women" or *ttíadi* "among the dwellings," village defense, and the Omaha word for "tribe" derived from the term for defensive warfare. For the fully nomadic tribes, dispersal was often the best means of defense, although if they knew an attack was pending they could surround their camp with trenches and breastworks of brush and timber. Parkman tells how some Blackfoots quickly erected a semicircular breastwork of logs 4–5 feet high at the foot of a cliff to defend against a Crow assault. The sedentary tribes normally built some sort of permanent fortification around their villages. The Pawnees and Poncas protected their towns with mounds and ditches creating a barrier several feet high. The Upper Missouri tribes did the same, adding a wooden wall along the embankment. Such defenses sometimes incorporated natural bluffs and ravines. In the 1750s, the Wichita tribes built fortified villages on opposite banks of the Red River in present Jefferson County, Oklahoma, and Montague County, Texas. One of these villages was described by a Spanish captive held there as enclosed by a palisade of vertical split logs, a rampart, and a ditch. It even contained underground chambers to protect elders, women, and children. From within this fort, in 1759, the Indians repelled a siege waged for four hours by a Spanish force of 1,600 men with two cannons; the defenders laughed and taunted their enemies all the while.

As to the overall frequency of fighting, there is disagreement among modern scholars. Recently, some historians have argued that the number of Indian battles, or at least Indian attacks against whites, was exaggerated by past non-Indian writers who wanted to emphasize the danger of the frontier and excuse the subjugation of the tribes. For some of these skeptical scholars, questioning the frequency of combat is part of a larger challenge to the negative stereotypes of Indian people, in this case the notion that they were "warlike." Undoubtedly, there have been mistakes in assessing the motives and details of Indian warfare because of the uncritical acceptance of contemporary non-Indian accounts. And, there has been a tendency to overlook violent acts initiated against Indians in favor of those started by them (this supposed contrast is itself sometimes problematic, given the cycles of revenge involved) and to view the activity of non-Indians as heroic and not itself aggressive or "warlike." Often today the basic facts behind historical confrontations can be reestablished by comparing non-Indian and Indian accounts of the engagements and the events that led up to them, and in some cases by adding information from the archaeological survey and excavation of the battle sites. But regardless of historical revisions, there is no question that a warrior ethos defined Plains culture and that during the Horse Era armed conflicts broke out continuously and numbered in the dozens if not hundreds annually.

Scouting and Trailing

The ability to move easily over the countryside while knowing the whereabouts of potentially hostile people was paramount to the security of every Plains population. Men with superior skills in tracking, navigating, and reconnaissance took on the specialized role of scout. Traveling parties, whether in combat or not, customarily sent one or a few scouts ahead to guide and forewarn the main group. Captain W. P. Clark, who commanded a corps of Indian scouts in 1876–1877, described their special methods:

> The object of scouting is to see and not be seen. An Indian, if mounted, carefully and slowly rises to the crest of every hill, and by a keen,

searching, sweeping glance takes in all the country stretched out below and beyond him. In ascending, if mounted, he dismounts just before reaching the top, and rises to the crest behind some rock, tree, or tuft of grass, and in going between divides, he moves as rapidly as possibly. In bivouacking, if it be not considered necessary to change camp after dark, the scouting-party moves over an eminence before going into camp, then anyone who may be following their trail will naturally be exposed to view before reaching the camp.

(Clark 1982:331–332)

In the symbolism of many tribes, scouts were called "wolves" in admiration of their stealth, and the sign language gesture for "scout" combines the ideas "wolf" and "look."

The scout was totally alert to his surroundings and knew how to glean information from many natural clues. A good record of these abilities was made by Colonel Richard I. Dodge, though he mistakenly attributed them to animal-like instinct. First, in the essential matter of navigating, every traveler relied on landmarks and constantly rode or walked in reference to some butte, knoll, creek bed, or other conspicuous landform. In the dullest stretches of the High Plains, the Indians erected stone cairns as markers in place of natural features. Cairns were also used to mark trails when the ground was covered by snow, while another means of marking trails under snow, in timbered country, was to place stones in tree branches on either side of the path.

Information about hundreds of landmarks was constantly discussed among travelers and memo-rized to renew and perpetuate the knowledge base. Dodge tells how a party of young Comanche warriors was given directions for their first raid from central Texas to Monterrey, Mexico. The older men presented them with a series of notched sticks, each representing a day of travel, and for each stick in the series they were taught, with the help of maps sketched in the dirt, to memorize a

sequence of key landmarks. Dodge's eyewitness to this instruction reported that the young warriors made a successful journey, some 1,000 miles roundtrip, though none had been to Monterrey before. The drawing of maps, either on the ground, or on sheets of tree bark, or later, on paper, is noted for several Plains tribes, including also the Assiniboines, Blackfoots, Kiowas, and Sioux. Several Indian paper maps exist today from the Horse Era, which show a good deal of correct detail and a tendency to picture the landscape in terms of days of travel rather than in units of linear distance.

Rivers, streams, springs, and lakes were always among the major landmarks, typically marked by stands of cottonwood, but the scout needed also to be able to locate drinking water in less obvious places. To do so, he read subtle trends in elevation, the soil, the vegetation, and animal behavior, such as the direction that doves were flying or whether wild horses seemed content or needy of water. It was possible to hear the presence of water in the chirping of frogs and insects, and smell it in the air.

Similar skills were applicable in trailing people. The scout read human footprints as he would animal tracks, feeling with his hands as well as viewing them to deduce the direction and age of the tracks (older tracks had insect trails across them or sand blown in them), the number and size of the individuals, their loads, and their tribal affiliations (sometimes indicated by moccasin shape). Other clues of human movement included scats, campfire remains, chance dropped objects, faint bends in the grass, displaced rocks, telltale traces of colored horsehair, distant dust clouds, startled animals, and birds reluctant to land. If a scout laid eyes on his quarry, he could then readily determine their tribe from their clothing, hair styles, or the form of tipi they had, three-pole or four-pole.

All of the skills of the scout could be wielded against him and his people by others with the same abilities. For this reason scouts were very cautious in approaching any landmark, knowing that enemies were navigating by the same points of reference and were most likely to be met near these markers. Also, travelers practiced tricks to confuse any enemy who was trailing them, such as riding in streams or on rocky ground, dividing and rejoining parties, doubling back, and setting up decoy fires and false camps. Dodge says that Indians felt safest when traveling alone, because they knew that a single person left a much less definable trail than a group would. He also noted that scouts were actually most important when riding behind the main party, lagging 3 or 4 miles to the rear to intercept a surprise attack by trailing enemies.

Indian scouts took a vital role in opening the Plains to non-Indian occupation. Scouts led the early Spanish, French, English, and American explorers and traders across the country. They also provided dependable maps. In particular, their knowledge of the most easily traveled gradients and the location of fresh water was essential. Some of the paths used by these scouts became the routes of major wagon trails used by non-Indian settlers, as well as of modern railroads and highways.

Groups of Indian scouts sided with the U.S. Army once settlement and combat with non-Indians increased, especially in the 1860s and afterward. Captain Clark commanded a mixed unit of Pawnees, Sioux, Crows, Cheyennes, Arapahos, and Shoshones. More usually units were made up of scouts from one to two tribes, whose main motivation was to guide their non-Indian allies in warfare against their tribal enemies. The Army scouting units also provided warriors with a sense of security and purpose at a time when established Native patterns of male status achievement were being disrupted. The Crows, who had struggled for territory between the larger and more powerful Sioux and Blackfoot nations, had developed great discipline in scouting on account of their dangerous position, and they were all too eager to furnish scouts for the Army

against their rivals. Eastern Shoshones, who had been bullied off the Plains by the Cheyennes, Arapahos, and Sioux, enlisted for similar reasons. Pawnees formed a celebrated battalion under Major Frank North which exploited their reputation as scouts (their tribal name in Indian languages is "Wolf"). The Pawnee scouts fought the Sioux and Cheyennes who had been encroaching on their buffalo grounds along the Republican and Platte rivers. They led the cavalry charge at Summit Springs, Colorado, in 1869, which decimated the Cheyenne Dog Soldiers; one Pawnee scout was awarded the Medal of Honor in this campaign. It was Osages who guided Colonel George Armstrong Custer the year before when he wiped out a Cheyenne village on the Washita River, Oklahoma. In the south, members of the beleaguered Lipan Apache and Tonkawa tribes led the way against the Comanches and Kiowas. Delawares, Shawnees, and Caddos displaced from the east also guided the Army on the Southern Plains, singly and in volunteer companies. Although excused from actual combat, once battle erupted the Indian scout units often joined the fight, and in some cases they played a decisive role in Army victories.

Signals and Signs

In order to coordinate dispersed groups when raiding, scouting, or hunting, Plains Indians devised a number of systems for long-distance signaling. Many of these methods took advantage of the open, rolling landscape and generally dry clear skies of the Plains. They were very effective in communicating specific information across distances of many miles.

The most well-known of these systems is smoke-signaling. This was a daytime technique. The signaler chose the most prominent rise in the area and built a fire with weeds, damp grass, or green cedar which would smolder and make a thick smoke. By choosing a high spot, he made sure not only that the smoke was visible from far away, but also that it would not be mistook for a campfire, since camps were usually set up in low places near water. Once the fire had burned long enough to attract attention, the signaler held his blanket over, and then off, the pile to collect and release defined puffs of smoke. The number and length of the puffs and the intervals between them were a code that relayed such messages as whether strangers or game were present, or if a returning war party had been successful, and whether the viewers should gather, disperse, approach, or flee in response. At night, fire signals were sometimes made, either on the ground or with firebrands—bunches of flaming grass tied to short poles for waving—though these lacked the precision possible with smoke. Many of the signaling hills were regular beacon points that formed a chain up and down the country for rapid and far-reaching communication. Bands selected their campsites close enough to these hills, or near others from where they could be viewed, so that they were always on the lookout.

A similar but quicker technique relied on the body motion of the signaler, either while on horseback or on foot, and magnified when possible with a blanket or lance. He took to the highest elevation in the area and reared his horse, or ran, in a tight circle or from side to side to indicate a discovery. Then he could send the details: a buffalo sign indicating game, made by holding his blanket up by the corners outstretched like horns, then lowered to the ground; an enemy sign made with frantic back-and-forth body motion, by running down the hillside in a zigzag, or with the blanket flapped rapidly overhead; an all-clear sign made with a gentle back-and-forth wave of the blanket; and so on. The position and thrusting motions of the lance also indicated various details. When a man found himself without horse, blanket, or lance, he could at least send a crude warning signal by throwing up handfuls of dirt.

Once shiny sheet metal and glass mirrors could be obtained, Indians used these for signaling also, reflecting sunlight in coded flash patterns. When Comanche riders intercepted a cavalry patrol under Lt. E. H. Bergmann out of Fort Bascom, New Mexico, in the summer of 1866, 12 miles outside their village, they transmitted over that distance to their camp mates the number and disposition of the soldiers and gained permission to bring them in for a visit, all with mirror signals. The Sioux and others were also adept in this method. Colonel Richard I. Dodge witnessed a Sioux war leader direct a drill of 100 mounted warriors for half an hour from a distant knoll by means of a signal mirror only. The historian Walter Prescott Webb maintained that Indian signaling inspired the invention of U.S. Army heliography, in which codes were sent by flashing sunlight with a mirror device, and the army's adoption of the semaphore system, which employed two flags held in different positions to spell messages.

With the advantage of long vistas for visual signaling, Plains Indians did not employ sound for sending long-distance messages. Western movies portraying drum telegraphs on the Plains are inaccurate. Hand drums, or simply sheets of hide, were beaten for drawing together a war party, but this was done around camp, not at any great distance. Sound signals came into play only in closely coordinated attacks and ambushes when the raiders needed to keep themselves concealed. In these cases animal and bird calls were employed with predetermined meanings. Boys became adept at imitating coyotes and whippoorwills for this purpose as part of their warrior training.

A different class of signs was used along trails to share information between divided parties. A bent twig or stick stuck in the ground leaning in the direction of travel served as basic trail markers for a larger party following its scouts. Sticks could also be arranged to leave more specific messages. A scout wishing to tell the main party behind him where their quarry was leaned a stick against a log across their path. The stick not only pointed in the direction of the quarry but also told how far ahead it was. The angle of the stick mimicked an arrow shot—a flatter stick suggested a longer trajectory or a distance of two or three days, while a more upright stick suggested a steep shot, or only one day's distance. In areas where there were large trees, the trunks were blazed to mark creek crossings and post warnings. Another imaginative technique was found on the Southern Plains, where it was customary to tie down saplings so they pointed in the direction of springs lying off the obvious trail. Over time these "turning trees" matured in their bent position, marking the way to precious water for several generations of travelers.

On the open prairie and deserts, scouts had to substitute pilings of stone or arrangements of bones or buffalo chips for wood markers. The broad, flat surface of a buffalo shoulder blade made a good tablet for tally marks and pictographic messages. Scapula drawings relayed military intelligence, the bones being left at trailside for others to find. Many recorded counts of armed enemies or horses, using line tallies and simple symbols such as stick figures or rifles for men and hoof prints for horses. Some portrayed complex narratives of the artist's exploits in battle akin to the commemorations found in hide paintings and pictographs.

The Face of Indian Battle

First-hand accounts relate that the Plains Indians had a large catalog of military drills and that the men practiced riding and shooting constantly. They rehearsed group tactics and the coordinated pickup of wounded comrades, but most of the skills were individual ones. Men were always prepared to fight.

A particular battle venture was usually inspired by a warrior's dream or vision. Medicine men were sometimes the receivers or interpreters of these messages, and on the Southern Plains, peyote was sometimes eaten to generate war prophecies. The revelation was typically very precise, at least as recounted after the fact. It gave a specific location for the action, the proper route of travel, the tactics to be used, and the exact

nature of the prizes—how many horses, their colors, the markings of the very best horse taken, and so on. Further supernatural direction to both begin and end a raid was given through omens such as the odd appearance of an animal or some sky sign.

With such a confident picture of what was possible, the inspired warrior invited other men to join him on the expedition. He relied on his brothers and special friends, the co-members in his residential group or military society if he belonged to one, and any others with a taste for adventure. The recruiter's success depended not only on the promise of his vision, but on his prior record. Had his earlier predictions come true? Was he a brave and dependable leader, and a good navigator in unfamiliar country? Was he a good judge of risk? Did he lose men in battle? In forging his team, the leader passed a pipe for all to smoke, confirming their commitment.

Together, then, the men sought purification in the sweat lodge, offered prayers for success, and perhaps made small flesh sacrifices also. As the time to leave approached, they packed their supplies: weapons, extra moccasins, war shirts, war bonnets in their cylindrical cases, more containers holding pemmican and war paint. In addition to their personal medicines, the men sometimes took along tribal medicine bundles which were unwrapped and prayed over on the eve of battle to bless the raid. The night before their departure, they danced and sang with abandon, along with their sisters, wives, and camp mates. War expedition songs such as the Kiowa *Gwoh-dawgyah* boosted their spirits (Boyd 1981:56):

> Going away on a war party
> That is the only thing to do,
> That is the only road (way)
> For a young man to gain fame and honor.

Warriors started out on revenge raids on horseback. When the raid was for horses, though, they usually left on foot, with the hope of stealing mounts to return on. The Kiowas and Comanches were atypical in starting all of their war expeditions on horseback. It was said that Comanches were ungainly on foot, but generally Plains men excelled at foot travel even after horses became common, and they covered vast distances in daily trots of 20 miles or more (the Arapaho Old Man Sage once ran from Wyoming to Oklahoma to court his first wife). Raiders on foot might carry their supplies with pack dogs, though there was some risk of a barking dog revealing the attackers' base camp before they could launch their surprise. In any case, they traveled single-file and kept out of sight once they entered enemy territory, moving through draws, over hard ground where tracks would not show, and often only at night.

For as long as the warriors were away from home, loved ones kept them in their thoughts and prayers. The Kiowa *Gomda-dawgyah* or Wind Songs was a typical class of songs expressing longing during a war expedition. They were sung by both the warriors and those they left behind (Boyd 1981:58):

> You young men sitting there,
> You have wealth and parents, relatives,
>   friends.
> But me, I am a poor and lonely boy.
> I will remain here and go on another
>   expedition,
> I know how to sleep and eat on the prairie
> away from home.
> This kind of life makes me happy and content.
> Idlers and cowards are here at home now.
> Whenever they wish, they see their loved ones.
> O idlers and cowards are here at home now,
> O idlers and cowards are here at home now,
> But the young man I love has gone to war, far
>   away.
> Weary, lonely, he longs for me.

As they closed on the enemy, warriors made final preparations. They painted their faces with black,

red, and yellow pigments in designs that would incite fear and impart magical offensive power or protection. They painted their horses in the same way. Weapons were checked and final consecrations made. Choices would be made about how much to wear and carry into the fight. Sometimes the best approach was to strip nearly naked and run in or ride bareback in a surprise attack, leaving most of the equipment to be picked up later. But when the war party was large and conspicuous, the warriors might take the time to don their war bonnets and other finery, to project the most fearsome appearance. Scouts reported their final information and it was shared among the attackers. A common element of raid accounts is that of the bold scout sneaking in and out of the enemy camp to learn where the horses were tied and how many defenders were present. At the brink of the assault, the party positioned itself in cover or on a hill crest from which to swoop. The leader gave his signal and the attack commenced.

Horse raiders might encroach ghost-like on the enemy camp to bridle and lead away a good number of animals, even cutting them loose while picketed closely to their sleeping owners, before any fighting erupted. Or else they intruded with a sudden noisy charge to drive away the horses en masse. In most of these instances the actual fighting was slapdash. In revenge raids the conflict was more prolonged. The raiders rode in circles around their enemies or sent repeated sallies from a safely distant observation point, ululating and attempting to overwhelm with numbers and ferocity, though at some point the fighting could devolve into a melee of flashing weapons. The Oglala Black Elk's vivid account of his first time in battle captures a sense of the action:

> Just after we camped on the War Bonnet [Creek], our scouts saw a wagon train of the Wasichus (whites) coming up the old road that caused the trouble before [the Bozeman Trail]. They had oxen hitched to their wagons and they were part of the river of Wasichus that was

running into the Black Hills. They shot at our scouts, and we decided we would attack them. When the war party was getting ready, I made up my mind that, small as I was, I might as well die there, and if I did, maybe I'd be known. I told Jumping Horse, a boy about my age, that I was going along to die, and he said he would too. So we went, and so did Crab and some other boys.

When the Wasichus saw us coming, they put their wagons in a circle and got inside with their oxen. We rode around and around them in a wide circle that kept getting narrower. That is the best way to fight, because it is hard to hit ponies running fast in a circle. And sometimes there would be two circles, one inside the other, going fast in opposite directions, which made us still harder to hit. The cavalry of the Wasichus did not know how to fight. They kept together, and when they came on, you could hardly miss them. We kept apart in the circle. While we were riding around the wagons, we were hanging low on the outside of the ponies and shooting under their necks. This was not easy to do, even when your legs were long, and mine were not yet very long. But I stuck tight and shot with the six-shooter my aunt gave me. Before we started the attack I was afraid, but Big Man told us we were brave boys, and I soon got over being frightened. The Wasichus shot fast at us from behind the wagons, and I could hear bullets whizzing, but they did not hit any of us. I kept thinking of my vision, and maybe that helped. I do not know whether we killed any Wasichus or not. We rode around several times, and once we got close, but there were not many of us and we could not get at the Wasichus behind their wagons; so we went away. This was my first fight.

(Neihardt 1972:78–79)

At another moment signaled by the war leader, the raiding party fled as quickly as it had appeared. Retreat was called for as soon as the enemy suffered harm, as soon as the attackers felt any casualties, or, as Black Elk relates, when there was a stalemate. If there was any chance of pursuit, the raiders rode continually and as fast as they could for two or three days until they felt

safe, and if they saw pursuers gaining on them, they jettisoned whatever they had to in order to increase their speed. Often the party split into smaller groups, and then individuals all went off in different directions, intending to rendezvous later or return to camp one by one. These tactics made it difficult to trail and confront the attackers, and as a result running counterattacks were usually not practical, leaving those seeking retaliation to mount their own raid later.

Non-Indian fighters had trouble adjusting to these tactics. Militias such as the Texas Rangers, once armed with repeating pistols, were nimble enough to have some success. The U.S. Cavalry, however, was much less effective in direct retaliation. Cavalry troops were based at fixed forts that might not be near the attack. It took time to mobilize the troops, and even when they got a good start, they were at a disadvantage because the troopers did not know how to live off the land as well as the Indians, and their large horses were grain fed, so the whole effort was tied to a slow train of supply wagons or pack mules. Over time the Army refined its pursuit tactics, but ultimately it shifted instead to a policy of total regional control, in which patrols policed Indian travel routes relentlessly and attacked Indian villages with overwhelming force.

Coup and Scalping

The term *coup* (from French, "blow") has come to mean any war deed, but specifically refers to touching an enemy. Ideally, the enemy was alive and dangerous. To "count coup," the warrior strode up to his opponent and defiantly touched him with his hand, a quirt, the end of his bow or lance, or with a special stick carried for the purpose (Cheyenne coup sticks were striped red and white like a candy cane). Performed in front of opposing battle lines, or in the thick of the fight, the coup was witnessed by other warriors as an act of extreme bravery and confidence. If the coup-counter walked away unscathed, it was evidence that his medicine was very powerful. The aptly named Crow chief Plenty Coups described the excitement of a coup bout during a fight with the Sioux:

> Inaction was beginning to fret me, when a young Sioux dashed from their line. He rode straight at us until he was within easy rifle range; then he turned his horse and rode him along our line, his feathered war-bonnet blowing open and shut, open and shut in the wind, as he swung his body from one side to the other on his horse. He was riding a beautiful bay, with a black mane and tail, and fast.
>
> Two shots spurted from our line, and down went the bay horse and the handsome Sioux. Both shots were as one; there was but one report, and Little Fire . . . lifted his gun high. "I killed him!" he cried. But Gun-chief, far along the line said, "No, no! It was my bullet that doubled that fellow up!"
>
> All this time the man was not killed at all. He was running by now, and Swan's-head was after him to count coup. The race was short. I saw a feather fly out of the Sioux's bonnet when Swan's-head struck with his quirt, saw the Sioux stagger under the blow, turn about and fire, with his gun's muzzle almost against Swan's-head's breast. The Crow reeled on his horse but did not fall, sticking to his horse to reach our line, with a big bullet through his breast. I saw a piece of his lung sticking out of the hole in his back, and he was bleeding so badly that his horse was red. His eyes were dead.
>
> With a yell that was good, He-is-brave-without-being-married darted after the running Sioux, who was now close to his friends. I saw the Crow strike him and count his coup fairly; but even as he struck him, the Sioux shot He-is-brave-without-being-married in the breast, just as he had shot Swan's-head. He was a brave man, that Sioux, and a good fighter.
>
> (Linderman 1962:257–259)

The kinds of war deeds were classified and sometimes ranked. The Poncas distinguished, in diminishing order of value, coup on an unwounded enemy, coup on a fallen foe, a second coup following someone else's, killing an enemy, taking a scalp, and capturing horses. The Crows recognized four deeds: the coup proper; leading a successful war party ("carrying the pipe"); theft of a picketed horse; and snatching the bow or gun of an opponent. The Iowas admitted three, in rank order of importance: leading a victorious war party; killing an enemy; and taking a scalp. In the prestige system of war deeds, the danger element was emphasized, and the riskier the deed the higher it was regarded. Touching was more highly valued than killing, and touching a live enemy ranked over touching a dead one. (The Santees called the coup *iyók`iheya kté*, "following the killing," indicating that usually coups were made on dead enemies). Clubbing outranked a gunshot, an exposed shot exceeded an ambush, and so forth. The variety of possibilities meant that there were many deeds in a typical encounter. The Cheyennes and Santees even allowed three men to count coup on a single enemy, while the Arapahos, Assiniboines, and Crows allowed four, in descending order of merit. "A man who had killed an enemy from a distance and raced to count coup but was outrun and forestalled by a tribesman had to content himself with the second honor" (Lowie 1982:108). Competition over coups among fellow tribesmen added to the game-like nature of Plains warfare.

Scalping was a widespread practice in the region. Contrary to some reports, scalping was not invented by whites as a form of bounty, although they sometimes promoted it as such. It was a Native practice common in the Eastern Woodlands, where many of the Plains tribes originated. Whereas in the East scalping became the main objective in combat and scalps the indicators of warrior prestige, on the Plains stolen horses or guns often served as alternate measures of raiding success. The significance of scalping among the Plains tribes was more variable, some tribes emphasizing it and others not, with no convincing pattern to this variation by area of tribal origin or language. The Crees and Tetons considered scalps important, while the Crows, Blackfoots, and Santees put more weight on horses, guns, or coups.

When a warrior took a scalp, he was taking a trophy of his victory. Scalps were keepsakes that could be brought back to camp and paraded by female kinfolk on the ends of sticks or displayed on a central pole. Women's celebration with scalps took the form of a special dance with its own class of songs, called Scalp Dance or Victory Dance in modern parlance. Scalps were dried and hung in the lodge, mounted on wooden hoops to carry and show off, or sewn onto shirts. The Santees buried the scalps they took once the Victory Dance was over so that the camp would not be haunted by the victims. The growing hair of one's enemy was symbolic of his life force, so taking it was a powerful affront. Scalping was an act of humiliation that defamed the enemy, marking him forever in the afterlife, and it struck fear in whoever found his body.

Beyond their function as tokens of bravery in intertribal raiding, scalps became a grim currency of interracial conflict. Tribes pitted against each other by Euro-American governments turned in Indian scalps for bounty, and Anglos and Mexicans also took up the practice of scalping against Indians. In the mid-1800s, an Indian scalp was worth 50–100 American dollars, a large sum then, paid by various state and local governments (though never by federal governments). The Anglos who ventured into Mexico against the Apaches and Comanches were not scrupulous about including Mexican scalps among the Indian ones they delivered. Bounty scalpers sometimes padded their totals by cutting scalps into halves and stretching the pieces.

The scalper approached his victim as he lay dead or wounded. If possible he rolled the body face down. While grasping the locks, he sliced along the front hairline if not all around, and, placing his foot on the head, gave one good yank to tear off the pate. If the victim was still breathing,

scalping was usually the last blow leading to death, but there were quite a few people who survived the horrendous experience. The Scalped Man character in Indian ghost lore, as described in Chapter 9, suggests widespread dread of this fate. The sad story of Josiah Wilbarger gives some further idea of what life held for Indian or white scalping survivors. Wilbarger was the first settler in Stephen Austin's colony along the middle Colorado River in Texas. In August 1833, Wilbarger and some friends were ambushed by Indians. He was temporarily paralyzed by a musket ball through the neck but did not lose consciousness, and he remembered later that as one of the attackers took his scalp it "sounded like distant thunder" (Wilbarger 1985:10). The Indians left Wilbarger for dead and he was found the next day by other settlers, wearing only a sock.

He had torn that from his foot, which was much swollen from an arrow wound in his leg, and had placed it on his naked skull from which the scalp had been taken. He was tenderly nursed at Hornsby's for some days. His scalp wound was dressed with bear's oil and when recovered sufficiently to move, he was placed in a sled, made by Billy Hornsby and Leman Barker (the father-in-law of Wilbarger) because he could not endure the motion of a wagon, and was thus conveyed several miles down the river to his own cabin. Josiah Wilbarger recovered and lived for eleven years. The scalp never grew entirely over the bone. A small spot in the middle of the wound remained bare, over which he always wore a covering. The bone became diseased and exfoliated, finally exposing the brain. His death was hastened, as Doctor Anderson, his physician, thought, by accidentally striking his head against the upper portion of a low door frame of his gin house many years after he was scalped.

(Ibid.:12)

There were so many survivors of scalping in the nineteenth century that medical journals of the time discussed their treatment.

Heads, hands, and other body parts were also taken as trophies and to inspire awe. Head-hunting was not a common practice in the region, but it was sometimes promoted with Spanish or Mexican bounties along with scalping. Beheading or dismemberment was used to terrorize the enemy, as when Osages massacred a Kiowa camp in 1833 in southwest Oklahoma, leaving the heads here and there in brass buckets. Warriors sometimes wore necklaces made up of the finger bones of their victims. On the battlefield, the fallen were stripped naked, lacerated, their genitals severed or mutilated, every orifice penetrated with spears, and their limbs and trunk left bristling with arrows. Women among the victors were as prone as the men to deliver these indignities, which again held symbolic meaning for the perpetrators. The Cheyenne women who came upon George Armstrong Custer's body on the Little Bighorn battlefield drove their sewing awls deep into his ears. Such a foolhardy leader, they reasoned, was like a reckless young warrior who had not listened to his elders, or perhaps he had failed to truly listen to the warnings of their chiefs; Custer "had no ears" according to the Indian idiom, so they made some for him. Their act was also an allusion to the Indian ritual of ear-piercing, by which a baby is transformed into a sapient human being.

Cannibalism

Anthropophagy, the eating of human flesh, is sometimes reported in connection with Plains warfare. In assessing these reports, it is important to understand that the terms "cannibal" and "cannibalism" have become highly controversial. Several contemporary scholars have pointed out that accusations of cannibalism are predictable when one opposing society seeks to dehumanize another, while actual evidence of anthropophagy as an firm cultural practice is quite rare throughout human history and arguably limited to a very few societies. In the case of American Indians, cannibalism was frequently cited by non-Indians

as a justification for conquest and extermination. The theme of cannibalism is also approachable from the Native viewpoint, and it is notable that Indian cultures have their own preoccupations with the subject. Their numerous myths and legends exploring the theme were rooted in anxieties about what it means to be truly human and how normal human behavior can be corrupted during times of starvation. Indian cannibalism tales are sensational, and their widespread occurrence suggests that no Plains culture regarded anthropophagy as normal or generally acceptable. Some, including the Hidatsas and Comanches, openly disavowed the practice.

But with all of these provisos, it is still probable that Plains warriors sometimes ingested the flesh, blood, heart, brains, or marrow of their enemies. Anthropophagy of this kind would have functioned, like trophy-taking, as an act of triumph, or as one of vengeance, or as a way of absorbing the enemy's supernatural power or desirable attributes. The ethnographer James Mooney was told of a pledge among certain warriors of the Kiowa tribe to eat the heart of the first enemy they killed, though Mooney did not establish whether the pledge was ever carried out. Possibly the pledge, or the warriors' reporting of it, was a statement of bravado rather than verification of cannibalism. There are also supposed eyewitness reports from both Indians and whites, from the mid-nineteenth century, stating that the Tonkawas ate the flesh of their enemies, and some of these reports suggest that the Tonkawas ate human flesh as meat and not just as ritual food. (The Kiowa and Comanche names for the Tonkawas, *Kiahipiago* and *Nꞟmꞟteka*, respectively, both mean "people eaters.") Even these accounts should be regarded with caution, since during the period the Tonkawas were being killed off by neighboring tribes and were scouting against them for the U.S. Army. At least one story, however, appears dependable, having originated from an Indian agent traveling with some Tonkawa refugees. There are other reports, usually traceable to French or Spanish accounts from the eighteenth century, of cannibalism among the Sioux, Osages, Lipan Apaches, Wichitas, and Comanches.

Captives

Taking live prisoners was a regular part of Plains warfare. The fate of captives is understood through such sources as tribal oral traditions, Indian autobiographies, military reports, and pioneer reminiscences. There are also numerous first-person narratives of white people who survived captivity among Indians, which form a large and controversial genre of American literature. Among these works are genuine accounts rich in poignancy and ethnographic detail, complete fabrications peddled by hucksters, and many that blend fact and fiction in varying degrees.

Raiders took captives to further distress the enemy, to collect ransom, or to add to their home population. They often avoided taking adult male prisoners, who were most able to resist or escape, but when they did it was in order to torture them to death as a means of revenge. Generally, it was the women of the camp who dealt the hideous regimen of pain that might include beating, cutting, gradual dismemberment, and burning with splints or directly on a fire, all compounded with exposure to the blazing sun and cold of night, blowfly maggots, and ants. The prisoner died after prolonged agony, and his cries were met with rejoicing and a sense of retribution. The only possible way of escaping was to act defiantly—many times a captive who stood up to the threat of pain or refused a demeaning command was let go without further harm, or even sent home on a fine horse, out of respect for his bravery.

Women and children were kidnapped for ransom or to live among their captors. They too were subject to brutal hardships when first seized. They were constantly beaten and threatened with execution to force them to keep up with the getaway and to discourage them from trying to escape. Women were raped, and those burdened with babies had to watch as their young ones were dashed against trees or thrown on lances. Prisoners were the property of the men who captured them, so they were put to work in their captors' camps or gifted to someone of the captor's choosing as slaves. They were given the worst tasks and mocked unmercifully as they went about them. Comanches sent the captive German Texan boy Herman Lehmann over the edge of a cliff on a rope to gather honey from a cave amid a cloud of stinging bees. Many months of such cruel treatment dulled the spirit of the captives and they resigned themselves to their new lives.

It often happened that over time a captive woman was taken by her captor or his designee as a wife (in Comanche the words for assimilated captive, *kwɨhɨpɨ*, and wife, *kwɨhɨ*, are closely related). Or, a captive child was given for adoption to a childless woman. And sometimes prisoners were pitied early on and taken care of by someone, and spared most of the usual hardship. Whereas those who were made into servants were given ridiculing names, those who were not burdened with menial tasks were given good names and other privileges. The Kiowa leader Big Bow took a Mexican captive named Kuitan as his personal servant on a war party and gave him first choice of the stolen horses. As captive children grew, they married Indian spouses. Captives who assimilated, and their offspring, achieved nearly full rights in the Native society and some became prominent tribe members. The Piegan headman Saukamappee was born a Cree, and the famous Shoshone chief Washakie was a Flathead by birth. Among the Comanche leaders who greeted artist and adventurer George Catlin in 1833 was His-oo-san-ches or The (Little) Spaniard, who was obviously originally named Jesus Sánchez and of Mexican descent. The most famous mixed-blood leader on the Plains was Quanah Parker (1852?–1911), the son of Comanche headman Peta Nocona and Anglo-Texan captive Cynthia Ann Parker.

The families of white captives sought to ransom them with the help of the military as well as civilian scouts, interpreters, and traders. The search for a captive could take months or years, all the while under the uncertainty of whether they were still alive. The son and daughter of John Babb of Wise County, Texas, were taken in a raid on the family ranch in September 1866. Babb enlisted the help of the commander of Fort Arbuckle, Indian Territory, as well as a civilian agent out of the fort and a sympathetic Indian headman, who found his children in April and June of the following year in two different Comanche camps and returned them to the fort; Babb paid $333 for the girl and $210 plus $23.75 worth of clothing for the boy. Other captives were returned to their families only after the military discovered them living in bands that had been forced onto reservations. Hermann Lehman was returned to his relatives in Texas this way, and went rather reluctantly. It was common for captives not to want to leave their adopted families. Often they only remembered their native language and birth names when reminded. Many captives continued to live with their adopted relatives once the reservations were established. For those who rejoined white society, some prospered in their personal and business lives and even enjoyed celebrity, but many never readjusted, and lived out their days as unhappy misfits.

Beyond the pathos and triumphs of individual captivity stories, it becomes apparent that the Plains hosted a sustained intertribal and interracial slave trade. Anthropologist John Ewers has speculated that early systematic raiding for captives may have provided the format for horse raiding. This thesis can be extended, for the patterns of trade in captives, furs, and horses were similar if not inseparable. Both on the Northern and Southern Plains, there was a general movement of enslaved people along the east–west axis. The Crees and Assiniboines kept numerous slaves from the Blackfoots and Gros Ventres to the west, while in the south by the early 1700s Plains Caddoans and Siouans were raided for captives by tribes east of the Plains, even while the Wichitas were transporting captives from neighboring tribes to New Mexico to be sold into the Spanish slave system. On the Southern Plains, there was also a movement of captives northward because of the forays of the Comanches and Kiowas against the Apaches, and of all three of these tribes against the peoples of Mexico.

The taking and trading of captives resulted in considerable ethnic admixture across the region. By the mid-nineteenth century, any tribe was bound to contain many individuals with parentage from other tribes, some of them far-flung and often some of Euro-American descent too. White Fox, an elderly Kiowa informant in 1935, estimated that captives made up 5 percent of his tribe, while the anthropologist James Mooney thought that at least one-fourth of all Kiowas had captive blood. Berlandier reported 500 Mexicans living among the Comanches by 1830, while his contemporary Jose Francisco Ruíz thought there were 1,000. Physical anthropologist Marcus Goldstein studied the Comanche population in 1931 and concluded that no more than 10 percent was full-blooded Comanche, largely because of the custom of taking Mexican captives.

Plains slave trading also gave rise to an enduring acculturated population living on the edge of the region, the *genízaros* of New Mexico. The name derives from the Spanish *Indios genízaros*, "Indian janissaries" or Indian slave-soldiers. Apache, Comanche, Kiowa, Pawnee, and Wichita prisoners brought to the Taos trade fairs of the late 1700s by their captors were frequently ransomed by the Spanish officials, who maintained a redemption fund for this purpose. The redeemed captives, many of them only children when rescued, paid off their ransom by working as indentured servants and citizen soldiers. They were settled largely in the Pecos River valley, where they became Christianized and blended with the Hispanic population, while maintaining some definably Plains Indian cultural traditions.

TRADE AND DIPLOMACY

Trade and raiding are like two sides of the same coin. Through trade, populations obtain resources from each other, only by peaceful contact instead of by violence. But while some cultural exchange may result from war because of captivities, trade is the more effective means of promoting this benefit. It creates a cooperative atmosphere for the movement not only of goods but also ideas, customs, and even people between different groups. The great degree of cultural sharing between Plains Indian populations of different backgrounds, which involved everything from clothing styles to myths, and which resulted in a fairly even culture across the area, was mainly a consequence of trade. Trade also promotes social change within groups, since the evolving demands for production of trade goods such as tanned buffalo robes, and the wealth brought through commerce, can alter the social roles of individuals and modify social structures, as discussed in Chapter 5. Also, trade forestalls war, by offering a way of obtaining needed resources that carries less risk of mortality than combat. Trade therefore can be understood as an aid to regional stability.

This discussion focuses on external exchange between members of different bands and tribes. The presentations and gift-giving that took place between members of the same band during religious ceremonies and marriages have already been described. The two kinds of exchange are related and often employ similar customs. But intertribal transactions did not assume mutual obligations between the parties for the common good over the long term; rather, they were hard bargains meant to acquire needed resources immediately.

Plains Indians had no markets in the technical sense. They had neither a full-blown economy of self-regulating markets or simple marketplaces. They did not regularly buy and sell goods and services within tribes. While various individuals were renowned for their skills in one craft or another, there were no highly specialized mass producers of the kind that characterize a true market economy (perhaps except for those people who participated heavily in the fur and buffalo robe trades which linked to world markets). They also lacked another feature of mature markets: money, a common currency that could be used to price or buy any and all goods or services. Money was introduced into the Plains economy by the Spanish, French, and Anglo-Americans, but Indian people did not adopt it to any significant degree until after they were forced onto reservations. There was nevertheless a good measure of organization and regularity in Indian trade. Commerce was often conducted at annual or seasonal trade fairs that were held, if not at the exact same campsite, in the same general location. These gatherings, along with incidental exchanges at other times and places, constituted a trade network of impressive scope linked by regular travel routes. This system was ancient and sophisticated, enabling the movement of goods all across Native North America.

Trade on the Northern Plains was executed mainly through centers along the Middle Missouri River in present North and South Dakota. The adjacent Mandan and Hidatsa villages, and the Arikara villages further south along the Missouri, formed two important trade centers, which actually functioned as a single regional locus. A third center, known as the Dakota Rendezvous, was the southernmost, along the James River near where it joins the Missouri. These three centers hosted vigorous trade among all of the Siouan tribes, and connected them with the Crees to the northeast and the Crows to the west, who in turn connected with tribes farther on. The Mandan and Hidatsa towns also attracted traders from the Southern Plains, including the Cheyennes, Arapahos, Kiowas, and Comanches. The nomadic tribes brought bison meat and hides to trade for corn, horses, and manufactured tools and trinkets.

The Crows connected the Middle Missouri trade centers with the Shoshone Rendezvous held in the spring in southwest Wyoming, thus tying the Northern Plains to the Great Basin. The Shoshones and other intermediate tribes further west then moved goods back and forth to The Dalles Rendezvous, a fall festival held at the site of salmon-laden rapids on the Columbia River, on the border of Washington and Oregon. In this manner, the Northwestern Plateau and Pacific Coast areas were connected to the Plains.

In a similar fashion, sedentary villages on the Southern Plains were trade centers for that region. The grass lodge towns of the Wichitas and Caddos along various Oklahoma and Texas rivers were the places where Kiowas and Comanches arrived to trade bison hides and deerskins for guns and other manufactured goods, and vegetable foods like corn and pumpkins. Horses were traded in both directions.

Supplementing the Wichita villages in the south was a trade center along the upper Arkansas River in present southeast Colorado, operated between 1740 and 1830 by the western divisions of the Comanches. Though itinerant, the Comanches camped recurrently in the Big Timbers, a long, dense grove of cottonwoods along the river, and regulated steady exchange there. Their customers early on included Kansas, Iowas, Pawnees, Wichitas, and Kiowas, as well as French and possibly British traders from the east and Hispanics from New Mexico. In its later phase this Comanche commerce hosted the Kiowas, Plains Apaches, Cheyennes, and Arapahos, who frequently went on to the Upper Missouri rendezvous, effectively linking the southwest Plains and New Mexican pueblos to the vast North American system. The goods named in accounts of this trade include bison hides, dried meat, tallow, deerskins, Indian slaves,

FIGURE 11.2 *Rendezvous on the Green River, southwest Wyoming. Painting by William Henry Jackson (1843–1942).*

salt gathered at plains deposits, corn, beans, squash, tobacco, Spanish knives, axes, bridles, horses, and mules.

The settlements along the Rio Grande in New Mexico, including the town of Santa Fe and surrounding pueblos, were additional trade centers linked with the Southern Plains. The trade out of this region in the Horse Era was a continuation of the prehistoric barter between the Pueblo Indians and Caddoans of 200 years or more earlier. Santa Fe was home base to the Comancheros, a rough-and-tumble class of Mexican and Pueblo Indian merchants. Their trade was licensed by the Spanish governors and the succeeding Mexican and American authorities in New Mexico, though at times many operated illicitly. The commodities they sought were buffalo robes and meat, horses, and mules. In return, they brought the Plains Indians flour and corn meal and hard, burned-black bread, which the Indians considered a delicacy. Other items from the Rio Grande valley were dried pumpkin, beans, onions, dried peppers, barley meal, blankets, saddles, dry goods, salt, and sugar. A few articles such as tobacco, guns, powder, and lead were traded in both directions.

To carry their goods, the Comancheros used pack animals as well as crude ox carts with squeaky wooden axles and uneven wheels made from the cross-sections of large logs, called *carretas*. They became experts at navigating across the vast and lonely Staked Plains. The Comancheros knew they could count on finding some Kiowas, Comanches, or Cheyennes along the breaks of the Canadian River in the northern Texas Panhandle, or they swung around or dropped off the steep eastern edge of the caprock to camp at Quitaque (Briscoe County, Texas) and Muchaque (Mushaway, Borden County, Texas), locations marked by curious hills visible from miles away on the Plains. Their camps at these sites were semipermanent, including caves dug out in the banks of the breaks. Once they arrived, the Comancheros sent up smoke signals which were often answered with the appearance of a wandering Indian band by the next morning. Oral histories say that the Indians were greatly excited when the Comancheros arrived. They made the gatherings into social events and enjoyed the goods they obtained. But for the New Mexicans it could be a hazardous business. Sometimes the horses that the Comancheros bought were soon stolen from them by the very people who had traded them, if not other Indians. Although most of the Comancheros' commerce was in northwest Texas, they also journeyed to the Wichita Mountains in southwest Oklahoma and the Davis Mountains near Big Bend, and sometimes far to the north, to the Platte River and beyond, to trade with the Crows, Arapahos, and Sioux.

As the non-Indian frontier solidified, attitudes about the Comancheros changed. While early on they were seen as a useful source of intelligence about Indian movements for the Euro-American governments that licensed them and contributors to regional stability because they promoted peaceful trade, in time they became the suppliers to Indian bands resisting colonization and the recipients of livestock stolen from white settlements. In these final days, the U.S. Army harassed the Comancheros, taking many of them prisoner and forcing some to guide the army to the last canyon hideouts of the Southern Plains Indians. The Comanchero trade was over by around 1875, once the southern buffalo herds were killed off and the Kiowas and Comanches were restricted to a reservation.

French and British traders entered the Plains from the northeast in the early 1700s with the fur trade and continued to play an influential role in Indian commerce as the Horse Era unfolded. The vast network of Indian trappers, non-Indian buyers, and middlemen from both groups spread westward and southward from Hudson's Bay to harvest enormous quantities of bear, wolf, fox, hare, martin, muskrat, and especially beaver for pelts for markets in Paris and London. Among the most active tribes were the Plains Ojibwas, Plains Crees, Tetons, Assiniboines, Crows, Flatheads,

Blackfoots, and Gros Ventres. A great deal of exploration and diplomacy was done through this network. Pierre Gaultier de Varennes de La Vérendrye and his sons Louis-Joseph and François were French-Canadian fur traders who encountered many of the Northern Plains tribes during the 1730s and 1740s while exploring the Upper Missouri and beyond in search of a route to the Pacific Ocean. The fur trade was also a pretext for the path-breaking expedition of Americans Meriwether Lewis and William Clark in 1803–1806. François (Francis A.) Chardon (d. 1848) was typical of the influential French and British adventurers who signed on with the American Fur Company out of St. Louis, Missouri, to work among the Mandans, Hidatsas, and Sioux in the early decades of the nineteenth century. French traders also opened commerce in the south, along the Arkansas River, introducing guns and ammunition to the region. Such traders from the east set up trading posts at the established rendezvous locations or at convenient alternate sites in the trade network. The posts or "forts" as they were often known were typically compounds of log, sod, or adobe houses and sheds for storing goods.

In the late 1820s, as it was extending into the Plains, the fur trade began a gradual decline. Changing fashions and the development of hats made from silk instead of beaver felt caused drops in the value of beaver pelts; at one point the price for one skin fell from six dollars to one dollar overnight. At the same time, the number of animals fluctuated, in part because of over-hunting. Plains tribes that had been involved in trapping were adopting the horse and focusing more on buffalo. Many traders therefore also shifted from furs to buffalo meat and robes.

The American brothers William and Charles Bent left the fur trade along the Upper Missouri and, beginning in 1828 or 1829, built a series of posts along the upper Arkansas River in southeastern Colorado. This was the first permanent non-Indian settlement in the Central Plains.

They quite purposefully located near the Big Timbers, where Comanches had been overseeing intertribal trade. One year Cheyennes traded an estimated 75,000–100,000 buffalo robes at Bent's Fort, valued at three dollars each. The Bents also ran a post on the South Canadian River in the Texas Panhandle in the 1820s through 1840s that served the Cheyennes, Arapahos, Kiowas, Comanches, and Apaches, with a focus on horse trading. William (1809–1869) was considered a member of the Cheyenne tribe, having married Owl Woman, daughter of White Thunder, keeper of the sacred medicine arrows. When Owl Woman died, Bent, following the custom of the sororate, married her sister. "Uncle John" Smith was another legendary American trader among the Cheyennes. When permitting Comancheros to barter in his area, he collected every third buffalo robe traded as a tax. Another team of American brothers, the three Torreys from Connecticut, built a string of posts in Texas that defined the line of westward settlement there in the early to mid 1800s. There were many other traders, named and unknown, both whites and Indians from more easterly tribes, who made trips onto the Plains and set up outposts for a year or so to participate in the fur and robe business.

Access to the trading posts was a factor prompting Indian migration and conflict. For example, the Bents drew the nomadic Cheyennes more regularly into southeast Colorado and the Texas Panhandle, and into competition, then alliance, with the Kiowas and Comanches. Traders at times stirred conflict, pitting rivals against each other for ever-scarcer hides and introducing guns and liquor into the volatile chemistry of intertribal relations. They did not always work in the best interests of the Indians or other whites. Bent's Fort at Big Timbers usurped the business that had been controlled by western Comanches. The Torreys were not above trading in goods stolen from Mexico. But since it was usually to their benefit to minimize the violent disruption of commerce, the white traders frequently took steps to promote peace and lawfulness. In some cases, they became official agents of their governments, hosting treaty parties at their posts, while other times they acted on their own. Comanche elders today tell an apocryphal story about how William Bent tricked a Comanche into meeting a Kiowa at his trading post by hiding the Kiowa behind a door, and when his two visitors got along it was the beginning of the alliance between the two previously rival tribes.

As the frontier caught up with the trading posts, the merchants adopted other roles. Sometimes their posts became the first banks or post offices in their region. They worked as guides and interpreters, and some, like William Bent, became Indian agents. At the close of the Plains Horse Era, they served as important sources about traditional Indian culture. George Bent (1843–1918), the son of William Bent and Owl Woman, for example, was one of the main informants in Cheyenne ethnology. His work joins that of Francis Chardon, whose 1830s diary is an indispensable eyewitness account of the Upper Missouri smallpox epidemic. The vocabulary notebooks that some of the later traders kept in order to converse with their Native customers are very valuable today for the preservation of Indian languages.

Regardless of the specific actors, trade during the Horse Era was essentially the same all across the Plains. Hides, meat, horses, and captives were exchanged for garden produce, wool blankets, bolts of cloth, handkerchiefs, glass beads, iron and brass, knives, sundries, paint, firearms, powder and lead, sugar, tobacco, flour, and coffee. Men traded with men and women with women. People did business with great zeal. Trade was even possible between such constant enemies as the Crows and Sioux, for if the general intertribal climate was not peaceful, traders would abide by a truce allowing enough time to visit and make a safe exit. Such agreements were predictable between village tribes and their nomadic enemies every year around the time when the village corn crops ripened. The calumet ceremony was the standard routine for marking these truce periods.

The Calumet Ceremony

The so-called calumet ceremony was the procedure used throughout the region when conducting intertribal visits and welcoming non-Indian visitors. In the stereotyping language of non-Indians, this procedure is often called "smoking the peace pipe," though sealing truces was only one function of the ceremony. The calumet was a tobacco pipe with a (usually red, elbow-shaped) stone bowl and separable wooden stem. The stem was typically decorated with long feathers. Its use in diplomacy is not easily differentiated from the religious ceremonies found in most of the Plains tribes in which sacred pipes were used to consecrate the proceedings or were themselves venerated. Nor was the calumet ceremony much different from the ritualized pipe smoking that opened tribal councils. The historical records, however, suggest the emergence of a common custom in which pipes were used to bless intertribal or non-Indian visitors and the negotiations that were made with them. This custom likely developed on the Plains prior to the Horse Era, and it became more frequent or visible with increased European contact and spread eastward into the Woodlands as contact between Indians and Europeans grew there.

The calumet ceremony was first recorded by Spanish traders out of New Mexico when visiting the Plains Apaches in 1634 and again in 1660. It may be assumed at this point that it was already widely diffused among the Plains tribes, and that the Apaches were probably not the originators (the red stone commonly used came from Minnesota— see Chapter 6). French explorers witnessed the calumet ceremony in the Mississippi Valley, among the Dakotas, Quapaws, and others, by the late 1600s and into the 1700s. In 1785, Comanche leaders in northern Texas welcomed the Spanish emissaries out of San Antonio, Pedro Vial and

Francisco Xavier Chaves, who knew to bring a pipe of their own. As Vial reported in his diary:

> Carrying the Spanish flag hoisted on a very tall pole, we presented it in a very large circle which all of the Indians had formed, seated on the ground as many as four deep, seeming in our opinion about 700. Surrounding the said circle were an infinity of young men, women, and children, who were standing. As soon as *capitanes* [chiefs] Camisa de Hierro, Cabeza Rapada, and the rest introduced us, with great civility and courtesy, they made us sit beside them in the first row of the center of the circle. We then brought out a large pipe which we took prepared with tobacco, and we and the *capitanes* Guersec and Eschas smoked it. We gave it to the *capitanes* Camisa de Hierro and Cabeza Rapada, who smoked from it, then passing it around to the ten *capitanes chiquitos* [band headmen], until the tobacco was finished. This indispensable ceremony concluded, the two *capitanes principales* asked us to tell them the reason for our coming so that all of those gathered might hear it.
>
> (John and Benavides 1994:38–39)

Vial documents one of the rules of Plains Indian hospitality, which is that it is impolite to inquire about a visitor's purpose until after he has been properly greeted. In this case, the purpose was to deliver gifts of tobacco, knives, beads, and vermillion on behalf of the Spanish governor of San Antonio and to propose ceasing mutual hostilities and aligning against the Apaches. The next day, after the Indians had a chance to discuss the aims of their guests, all assembled again and passed the pipe as before. Camisa del Hierro then made a speech in which he observed that the Spaniards must be true to their word, because the smoke from the pipe had not twisted.

The calumet ceremony commonly included other features. The hosts greeted their visitors with profuse expressions of happiness, firing guns into the air, whooping loudly, and hugging the guests tearfully. They might have them carried into camp on men's shoulders. They painted them with red ochre and decorated them with gorgeous feathers. Any flags, medals, or uniforms available were broken out to make the occasion special. A feast was put on, and the hosting men offered to share their wives as a further gesture of welcome. In some instances, the visitors were made to pantomime their death and rebirth, in a mock resurrection symbolizing new or renewed social relations, and many of the ceremonial traits lent overtones of mourning and adoption. Outright creation of a fictive father–son relationship between traders was one possible outcome. These customs, along with the smoking in a circle and long speeches, were very powerful in establishing an aura of good will. The exchange of presents in this context then opened the way for a peace agreement or bargaining to transfer larger quantities of merchandise. Retrieving captives was another frequent purpose behind the calumet ceremony, and it was also the procedure to use when striking a pact to fight together. "Accepting the pipe" was a metaphor for agreeing to take part in a joint raid.

Trade Languages

When Pedro Vial made his oration explaining the reason for his visit to the Comanches, he spoke "in the Tavoayaz language, which all of the Cumanches understand and speak perfectly well" (*sic*, Ibid.:39). The Caddoan dialect of the Taovaya or Tawehash, a tribe of the Wichita Confederacy, made perfect sense as a trade language because of the role that the Caddoan villages played as trade centers in the region. Use of Caddoan tongues for trade was probably an old practice in the area, picked up by relative newcomers like the Comanches. As the Comanches dominated the Southern Plains, their language in turn functioned as an intertribal medium. "Their language is the trade language of the region and is more or less understood by all the neighboring tribes," observed ethnologist James Mooney in the latter 1800s (Mooney 1907b:328). Other Indians considered Comanche an easy language to acquire. In turn, the Comanches were quite capable in Spanish, owing to their experience of many decades in dealing with Hispanic people in New Mexico, Texas, and Mexico. Presumably the Comanches could also have used Spanish to communicate with Indians who had come under Spanish domination, such as the Apachean, Puebloan, and Coahuiltecan groups they encountered. The Comanche language is laced with altered Spanish words and the majority of them signify items that the Comanches would have first obtained in trade, as well as some bywords like *weno* (from Spanish *bueno*, "good!") useful in negotiation. Table 11.1 lists some Comanche words of Spanish origin.

Spanish also penetrated to a surprising degree into the Northern Plains by the 1700s, owing probably to the significant mobility of individuals among the tribes from south to north. The Vérendryes apparently used it in some of their dealings. Plains Cree, however, was the most prominent lingua franca in the North. French and English were also established for commercial purposes through the fur trade. Other languages were shared more specifically in the North, allowing sufficient chains of translation. The senior Vérendrye noted that several Crees and Mandans had good command of Assiniboine. According to George Catlin, the Mandans were conversant in Hidatsa, but not vice versa. The Blackfoot language proper was shared across the Blackfoot Confederacy.

It is interesting that Plains tribes learned other societies' languages wholesale for trading, but pidgins (simple mixed languages used mainly in trade situations) did not develop, nor is there even much borrowing of individual words between Plains languages. Parkman mentions "a jargon of French and another of English" used by a Dakota leader along the Upper Missouri River in the 1840s (1931:126), but the details are not known and these tongues appear to have been formative at most. Perhaps definable pidgins would have emerged if there had been a longer period of contact between the linguistically diverse tribes on the Plains before

TABLE 11.1   *Comanche Words of Spanish Origin*

COMANCHE	SPANISH SOURCE	ENGLISH MEANING OF COMANCHE TERM
kabur̶u̶u̶?	cabra	goat, sheep, mutton
kamúta?	camote	yam, sweet potato
kobi	cabello	mustang
kupáre?	compadre	friend
kutsára?	cuchara	small spoon
more?	monte	monte (card game)
mura	mula	mule
naho?	navaja	knife
pan̶u̶	pan	bread loaf
papas̶i̶	papas	potatoes
pijura	frijole	bean
póro	barra	bar (of iron)
po?roo?	puerco	pig, bacon
supereyos	sombrero	hat
torosi?	toro	cattle
tomata?	tamate	tomato
totiya	tortilla	bread
tsaréku?	chaleco	vest
tsiira?	chili	pepper, chili
tu̶jano?	tejano	Texan
waratsi	huarache	sandal
weno	bueno	good

Sources: Casagrande (1954–1955), García Rejón and Gelo (1995), and Shimkin (1980).

the strong intrusion of non-Indian cultures. But there was no equivalent on the Plains to the pidgin called Mobilian Jargon, which eased exchange in the Southeast, or the Chinook Jargon, which would have been heard between traders at The Dalles and all through the Northwest.

Sign Language

The widespread use of Plains Indian sign language, a highly sophisticated method of communication with hand gestures, may have made verbal pidgin languages less necessary. Sign language was endemic to the Plains; during the Horse Era, it was not employed to any great degree in neighboring culture areas, although the Plains form may have been preceded by the earlier use of signs in the Northeast and Southeast Woodlands, the Northwest, and the Southwest. The elaborate version that developed on the Plains was not adopted by Indian populations east or west of the region, as suggested by the contemporaneous use of trade jargons in those areas, except to the extent that outside traders and hunters ventured onto the Plains.

Plains Indians used one or both hands to produce a vocabulary of several hundred signs. The hands were held in shapes, and sometimes moved also, in ways that imitated what was being indicated. These signs were more or less direct depictions, for example, an inverted V-shape of the fingers to indicate a tipi. Sometimes the sign was not an instantaneous shape, but a motion, as in the case of the sign for "hat," made by drawing the imaginary brim across one's forehead with the index finger. Hand-pictures conveyed meaning metaphorically as well as iconically, as in the sign for white man, which added the sign for hat with the upright index finger symbolizing a man. And as this example suggests, many signs were composite. A non-Indian type of house was indicated with the signs for tipi and white man; the moon was designated with the signs for sun and night. In addition to nouns, verbs could be expressed, as in the clutching and sweeping motion indicating "theft." Adjectives were also possible, through descriptive action, as in the sign for "bad," a motion of throwing away, or simply by pointing to something with the desired color or quality. Questions were posed by beginning the sign sequence with a wavering motion of the upright right hand indicating query. Counting, so important in trade and planning, was done with the fingers, with large quantities shown by flashing all the fingers at once to signify multiples of 10. To further illustrate the system, Table 11.2 lists the signs used for different tribes and their derivations.

TABLE 11.2   Sign Language Signs for Select Tribal Names

TRIBE	GESTURE	MEANING
Arapaho	Tap breast with tips of right-hand fingers	Reference to disfigurement of chief's chest by smallpox
Arikara	Twisting right-hand fingers around left thumb	Shucking corn
Blackfoot	Pass spread hands over feet, then point to something black	Moccasin plus black
Cheyenne	Slicing motion of right hand on left	Slashing arms and legs in mourning, or striping of arrows
Comanche	Right hand, pointing, drawn in with sinuous motion	Snake
Crow	Hands flapped outward slightly	Flying
Gros Ventre	Extend hands out from belly	Big belly
Kiowa	Right hand held upward and rotated	Rising, possibly a reference to the prairie
Mandan	Tap lower face with tips of right-hand fingers	Tattooed chin
Osage	Cutting motion along side of head with one or both hands	Shaved head
Pawnee	V-shape with first and second fingers of right hand	Wolf
Sioux	Draw right index finger across throat	Cutting off heads
Wichita	Curve drawn with right index finger	Tattoo rings

Source: Clark (1982).

The presence of such a well-developed gesture system should not be taken as evidence that Native oral languages were in any way substandard or inadequate. On the other hand, sign talking can be understood as a system with many linguistic properties and functions. And as the tribal names in Table 11.2 show, signs were often derived from verbal language. Study of the signs as well as words is enlightening from a cognitive standpoint because it shows which qualities and features of things in the world were seized upon by Indian people as salient for epitomizing and classifying those things. There are also interesting resemblances between hand signs and pictographs that indicate cognitive conventions. The brimmed hat indicates a non-Indian in Plains picture-writing as it does in sign language. Sign language has also been considered similar to Plains signaling as an inventive response to the concertedly visual environment of the open Plains. Some of the long-distance signals were nothing more than large-scale adaptations of gesture signs.

Sign-talkers combined their signs very quickly and fluently so that their gesture statements took hardly any longer than oral utterances would. They controlled their hands precisely so there was little or no misunderstanding. The give and take between two conversers in sign language is graceful and beautiful to watch. Sign-talkers accompanied their gestures with incidental facial expressions and body language which enhanced the primary medium. Most importantly, as they were signing, the talkers also spoke the meaning of their communication in their native oral language, even though the interlocutor did not understand it. Over time this practice must have contributed to intertribal language learning and would have sped the establishment of certain languages as trade languages. Ultimately, sign-talkers could transmit ideas with something very close to the exactness afforded by spoken language, and they were able to conduct complex negotiations, coordinate travel, hunts, and raids, and tell complicated myths and legends.

The same system of signs operated all across the Plains with very minor dialectal differences involving variant signs for some ideas. The center of invention for the Plains system is not known. Recent studies point to the Texas coastal area as the origin point, since many linguistically diverse groups lived there. The Plains tribes most often credited the Kiowas with starting sign language, though some tribal traditions identify the Cheyennes or Arapahos as the originators instead. These explanations were likely influenced by the central position of the three named tribes in Plains trade. The Kiowas and Cheyennes, along with the Crows, were uniformly acknowledged as the best sign-talkers, again perhaps a reflection of their middleman roles in north–south and east–west commerce. Tribes around the outskirts of the culture area, such as the Southern Siouans, Shoshones, and Utes, were said to be less proficient in sign language.

Sign language conversations can still be witnessed in some Plains Indian communities. Brenda Farnell has analyzed its use among contemporary Assiniboines at Fort Belknap Reservation, Montana (Farnell 1995a, 1995b). A common stylized presentation of sign language today is the performance of the Lord' Prayer in signs by powwow princess contestants. Several tribes are currently working to preserve sign talk along with their spoken languages through educational programs.

Indian Diplomats

In prior discussions of Indian social organization, we have seen how important band and tribal matters were regulated by people skillful in peace-making and oratory. These same talents were turned outward as bands and tribes sought to get along with other groups. Leading men and, occasionally, women proffered hospitality and made speeches to forge agreements for trade and peaceful coexistence. The pacts they made included the great tribal alliances previously mentioned, such as Sioux–Cheyenne and Comanche–Kiowa coalitions; major treaties with non-Indians, which will be detailed in the next chapter; and countless agreements of lesser scope between groups that gave shape to political relations across the Plains.

While there is seldom much record of what was said in intertribal negotiations, glimpses of Native diplomacy are provided in accounts of tribal talks with non-Indians such as in the Comanches' visit from Pedro Vial described above. Non-Indians fell in with Native practices quite easily. The colonials adjusted to Indian patterns of gift-giving and distributed tokens that at once symbolized friendship between Indians and non-Indians and the projected power and authority of the non-Indian governments. Such gifts were absolutely essential to any successful conference. The Spanish were unique in offering silver-headed wooden canes or *bastónes* as symbols of authority to Indian leaders, in effect making the recipients officers in the Spanish government. Other tokens were used by the French, English, and Americans as well as the Spanish, most notably large round silver medals worn with a colorful ribbon around the neck. These "peace medals," which came in two sizes for distribution to greater and lesser Indian leaders, usually showed a bust portrait of the current non-Indian leader, be it a European king or U.S. president. Many old photos show Plains Indian headmen proudly wearing these medals with their other regalia. Military uniforms for men were another favorite gift, along with flags for display in the Indian villages, as Pedro Vial related. And even though they did not read, Indian diplomats enjoyed receiving fancy commission letters. Indian people took these gifts very seriously. Such items were deeply venerated, sometimes treated like tribal fetishes with cedar smoke and displayed in ceremonies, for as long as the pacts they represented were in force.

Words of intent were more important than any gifts of friendship. Nowhere was the Indian genius for eloquence more dramatically exercised than in external affairs. Since diplomacy yielded alternatives to warfare, the most influential men had to be orators as well as warriors. As Captain W. P. Clark wrote, "With the Indians as with the Romans, the two professions, 'oratory and arms,' established men in the highest degree of personal consideration" (1982:107). The outstanding example of Plains Indian speechmaking was recorded in October, 1867, at Medicine Lodge Creek, Kansas, when Yamparika Comanche headman Paruasemena ("Ten Bears") made a heartfelt statement about his people's reluctance to accept the latest treaty terms presented by visiting U.S. commissioners. His words were taken down by the U.S. agents:

> My heart is filled with joy as I see you here, as the brooks fill with water when the snows melt in the spring; and I feel glad, as the ponies do when the fresh grass starts in the beginning of the year. I heard of your coming when I was many sleeps away, and I made but few camps before I met you. I knew that you had come to do good for me and my people. I looked for benefits which would last forever, and so my face shines with you as I look upon you. My people have never first drawn a bow or a gun against the whites. There has been trouble on the line between us, and my young men have danced the war dance. But it was not begun by us. It was you who sent out the first soldier and we who sent out the second. Two years ago I came up upon this road, following the buffalo, that my wives and children might have their cheeks plump and their bodies warm. But the soldiers fired on us and since that time there has been a noise like that of a thunderstorm, and we have not known which way to go. So it was upon the Canadian. Nor have we been made to cry once alone. The blue dressed soldiers and the Utes came out from the night when it was dark and still, and for camp fires they lit our lodges. Instead of hunting game, they killed my braves, and the warriors of the tribe cut short their hair for the dead. So it was in Texas.

They made sorrow come in our camps, and we went out like the buffalo bulls, when the cows are attacked. When we found them we killed them and their scalps hang in our lodges. The Comanches are not weak and blind, like pups of a dog when seven sleeps old. They are strong and farsighted, like grown horses. We took their road and we went on it. The white women cried and our women laughed.

But there are things which you have said which I do not like. They are not sweet like sugar, but bitter like gourds. You said that you wanted to put us upon a reservation, to build us houses and make us medicine lodges. I do not want them. I was born upon the prairie, where the wind blew free and there was nothing to break the light of the sun. I was born where there are no inclosures [sic] and where everything drew a free breath. I want to die there and not within walls. I know every stream and every wood between the Rio Grande and the Arkansas. I have hunted and lived over that country. I lived like my fathers before me, and, like them I lived happily.

When I was in Washington the Great Father told me that all the Comanche land was ours and that no one should hinder us in living upon it. So, why do you ask us to leave the rivers and the sun and the wind and live in houses? Do not ask us to give up the buffalo for the sheep. The young men have heard talk of this, and it has made them sad and angry. Do not speak of it more. I love to carry out the talk I get from the Great Father. When I get goods and presents I and my people feel glad, since it shows that he holds us in his eye.

If the Texans had kept out of my country there might have been peace. But that which you now say we must live on is too small. The Texans have taken away the places where the grass grew the thickest and the timber was the best. Had we kept that, we might have done the things you ask. But it is too late. The white man has the country which we loved, and we only wish to wander on the prairie until we die. Any good things you say to me shall not be forgotten. I shall carry it as near to my heart as my children, and it shall be as often upon my tongue as

the name of the Great Father. I want no more blood upon my land to stain the grass. I want it all clear and pure, and I wish it so that all who go through among my people may find peace when they come in and leave it when they go out.

(Taylor *et al.* 1910:59–60)

Ten Bear's masterful talk is rich with rhetorical devices, including: appeal to authority ("the Great Father told me"); metonymy ("the rivers and the sun"); metaphor ("We took their road . . . "); parallel construction ("The white women cried and our women laughed"); personification ("the first soldier"); rhetorical question ("why do you ask us . . . "); simile ("My heart is filled . . . as the brooks fill . . . "); and other colorful figures of speech ("for camp fires they lit our lodges"; "he holds us in his eye").

Indian diplomacy, then, rested heavily on oratory, along with rituals of welcome, gift-giving as a preliminary gesture, and the very act of sitting together and talking at length. These methods were uniform across the Plains and enabled tribes to establish lasting agreements. White approaches were somewhat different, emphasizing the signing of written documents and use of gifts as rewards at the conclusion of the negotiation. Both cultures tried to adapt to the each other's protocols.

Ten Bear's famous speech mentions his visit to Washington, D.C., which he had made in 1863. Trips to the nation's capital by tribal and inter-tribal delegations were a big part of Indian–white diplomacy. Each year several groups of Indian leaders, along with their white agents, visited the capital city. Indians considered an invitation to Washington as an honor and mark of status. The visits seldom gave the Indians much opportunity to make concrete negotiations on their own behalf; normally, they simply allowed them to hear confirmation from higher authorities of agreements they had already made at home. Sometimes the government attempted to broker peace between two tribes through their visiting delegations, as

FIGURE 11.3   Ten Bears (Comanche) in 1872, photographed in Washington, D.C. by Alexander Gardner (1821–1882).

was done in 1873 between the Arapahos and the Utes and Crows. The delegates were introduced to major non-Indian politicians, frequently even the president ("Great Father"), as Ten Bears testified. But from the white viewpoint, the visits were intended mainly to convey feelings of good will, to encourage whole Indian populations through their leaders to adopt white ways, and to impress the Indians with the size and power of white society. The visits gave Indians a chance to apply familiar methods of diplomacy, including speech-making, gifting, and feasting, while satisfying

their traditional love of travel, exploration, and learning about other people.

Intertribal Marriage

Marriage was an important tool in forging relations between different tribes. As noted in Chapter 5, marriage was a way of making alliances between families and bands within tribes. Marriages between people of different tribal groups could have the same effect. Sometimes, as we have seen earlier in the present chapter, intertribal marriage resulted when women were captured and taken as wives. This kind of intertribal connection was incidental to regional conflict, yet it could ultimately encourage a lessening of hostilities, because men might be less inclined to raid an opponent group if their sister and her children lived in that group. For the same reason, voluntary inter-tribal marriage could be a conscious step toward peace and cooperation. In intertribal marriages, normally the woman moved to live with her husband's people, though sometimes it was the man who relocated. These marriages could influence regional patterns of political alliance and cultural and linguistic sharing. Thus, for example, the great Kiowa–Comanche alliance coincided with the circa 1806 marriage between Kiowa head-man El Ronco and a daughter of the Yamparika Comanche headman Somiquaso, in which the Kiowa went to live with the Comanches.

To give some sense of the degree of intertribal marriage, Table 11.3 shows the number of women from other tribes living among the Southern Cheyennes in 1892. Fifty-two, or 8 percent, of the 652 adult women counted in the 1892 Southern Cheyenne allotment census were foreign-born. One might predict the high degree of intermarriage between Cheyennes and their close associates the Arapahos, but the other links with tribes of diver-gent linguistic background are remarkable.

At various points in the relatively brief history of the Horse-Era Plains, intertribal marriage was inten-sive enough to result in the formation of hybrid bands. These groups often affiliated with one of the contributor tribes as a subgroup and occasionally they functioned independently of either contributor tribe. Anthropologist John Moore notes that "the Cheyennes had a Ute band, a Ree band and 2 Sioux bands each of mixed parentage and containing a large proportion of bilingual people" (Moore 1994:20). Elders among the Comanches today claim the existence of an intertribal band called the Kiowa Comanches. Likewise, the Comanches and Kiowas each were heavily intermarried with Mexicans of pure or mixed Indian and European

TABLE 11.3 Number of Foreign-born Southern Cheyenne Women by Tribe According to the 1892 Allotment Census

TRIBE	NUMBER
Apache	2
Arapaho	17
Arikara	1
Blackfoot	1
Caddo	2
Creek	1
Crow	2
Kiowa	3
Oto	1
Pawnee	2
Ponca	3
Sioux	15
Ute	2

Source: Moore (1994:22).

descent, though Plains Indian–Mexican intermar-riage did not produce separate new nomadic bands. All told, Moore counts one or more hybrid bands existing between each of the 14 fully nomadic tribes of the High Plains (Ibid.). Hybrid Indian groups probably exemplify one kind of early stage in the evolution of the larger ethnic units ultimately recognized as tribes, and some of them would likely have continued to grow into distinct tribes if the process had not been interrupted by non-Indian expansion. The hybrid bands were so common that the usual view of tribes as insular, strictly bounded populations can once again be seriously challenged. But more to the present point, tribes were heavily intertwined and their relations with each other highly fluid. The Plains sociopolitical environment was one of cooperation as well as conflict.

With their refined ability to promote various kinds of relations with outside groups, the Plains Indians accrued a rich and complex history. Following chapters will chronicle the major episodes of Indian history in the region.

Sources: Adams (1983); Anderson (2003); Berlandier (1969); Blakeslee (1981); Bowers (1992); Boyd (1981); Brady (1996); Brooks (2002); Carlson (1998); Casagrande (1954–1955); Chardon (1970); Clark (1982); DeMallie (1993); Dodge (1882); Dunlay (1982); Ewers (1955, 1968, 1997); Farnell (1995a, 1995b); Fletcher and LaFlesche (1972); Foster (1960); García Rejón and Gelo (1995); Gelo (2000); Gelo and Zesch (2003); Greene (1972); Hämäläinen (1998); Hamilton (1988); Howard (1984); Hyde (1968); John (1975); John and Benavides (1994); Kenner (1969); Linderman (1962); Loomis and Nasitir (1967); Lowie (1982, 1983); Mallery (1881); Mishkin (1940); Mooney (1901, 1907b, 1907c, 1907d); Moore (1994); Neihardt (1972); Nye (1969); Otterbein (1985); Panzeri (1995); Parkman (1931); Ruíz (1972); Secoy (1953); Shimkin (1980); C. Smith (1980); R. Smith (1960); Tate (1994); Taylor et al. (1910); Thomas (1929); Viola (1995); Webb (1981); Wilbarger (1985); and Wood (1980).

CHAPTER SUMMARY

Plains tribes actively engaged outside groups and maintained external relations. Armed conflict and related methods such as tracking and signaling were highly developed as a means of dealing with outsiders. Scalping, cannibalism, and the taking of captives were corollaries of Plains combat. Trade and diplomacy were equal in importance to warfare as means of interaction. Plains Indians maintained vast networks linking trade centers. The calumet ceremony employed the "peace pipe" to greet visitors and seal agreements. Special verbal languages and a system of hand signs emerged to enable trade among different language speakers. The historical record includes many capable Indian diplomats and orators. Intertribal marriage was an important tool for promoting cooperation. Intensive intertribal marriage resulted in the formation of hybrid groups, forerunners of new tribes.

QUESTIONS FOR REVIEW

1. What Plains Indian cultural practices would have led Parkman to write, "War is the breath of their nostrils"?

2. Explain why the taking of live prisoners was a regular feature of Plains warfare.

3. Analyze trade centers, the calumet ceremony, trade languages, or sign language as evidence for the Indian interest in external relations.

4. Paraphrase Ten Bear's famous speech at the Medicine Lodge Treaty talks and identify the rhetorical devices employed.

CHAPTER 12

LIFE THROUGH THE TWENTIETH CENTURY

Indian concepts of time and its passing are traditionally cyclical rather than linear. Nevertheless, in learning about the cultural and social changes that accompanied non-Indian expansion into the Plains, a timeline framework is most efficient and, given the nature of historical sources, almost unavoidable. This chapter traces a sequence of events that epitomize the challenges and changes that Plains Indians faced because of the intrusion of non-Indians into their territories. Although the French from the northeast and southeast and the Spanish from the southeast and southwest introduced important changes in Plains Indian culture over long periods, it was the later relentless westward march of Anglo-American society that transformed and nearly extinguished the Indian way of life. Within the linear progression of American expansionism, however, there are constant alternations between war and peace, trust and betrayal, tribalism and assimilation, traditionalism and modernization, sovereignty and dependency, and thus the cyclical nature of time remains abundantly evident.

CONQUEST OF THE PLAINS

The early decades of the nineteenth century formed a prelude to total conquest. In these years the Plains tribes dealt mainly with each other in ever-shifting gambits for access to good hunting and trade. Though the Indians met white explorers and traders in increasing numbers, the influences of white society were mostly felt at a distance. But though remote, the forces of non-Indian presence could be profound. Differential access to white-introduced horses and firearms, we have seen, was a major early factor as tribes jockeyed for Plains territory. Ghastly pandemics such as the smallpox scourge of 1837–1839 and the cholera outbreak of 1849, moving in advance of the main body of white settlement, were also harbingers of the looming human invasion. The Corps of Discovery expedition led by Meriwether Lewis and William Clark, traveling from St. Louis along the Missouri River and across the Rockies to the Pacific and back during 1803–1806, had opened the world of the Plains

Indians to the American imagination and U.S. commerce. By the 1820s the U.S. Army was protecting white traders as they settled far up the Missouri, and by the 1830s a federal program of military expeditions, outposts, and roads was well under way throughout the Plains. Indian societies increasingly felt direct stresses by the 1840s and 1850s.

During these decades there began a cycle of treaties, land cessions, relocations, treaty violations and cancellations, and conflicts that would become full blown after the Civil War. From the Anglo-American viewpoint, treaties had multiple possible functions. Certainly they formalized or validated the transfer of control of land from Indians to non-Indians. They were also meant to guarantee the safety of non-Indians. Another sometimes over-looked intention of American treaties was to negotiate peace among competing tribes in order to reduce violence in a region and thus pave the way for the expansion of American commerce. For Indians also, treaties were a means of securing protection and regional peace. Specifically, they sought to retain or replace garden lands, hunting grounds, and trade networks; enhance trade with non-Indians for manufactured goods (or acquire presents outright); and limit the number of roads, rail lines, and settlements that disrupted their territories.

The Prairie Siouan and Pawnee tribes were the first among those of the Plains to engage heavy white encroachment on account of their easterly positions. As semisedentary gardeners, these groups could not prolong control of their territories by moving nimbly to avoid or attack intruders. They typically yielded their lands and moved west to reservations under treaty terms with little if any forceful resistance. Many of these tribes experienced multiple partial relocations over a few generations, which fragmented the groups and disrupted livelihoods to the extent that poverty became endemic, health plummeted, and death rates soared. For example, the Osages ceded about 100 million acres of their homelands in present

Missouri, Arkansas, and Oklahoma in three treaties dated 1808, 1818, and 1825, respectively. With this last treaty, they located on a reservation in southern Kansas. When the Kansas land was taken away in 1870, they moved to another reservation in northeastern Indian Territory. In 1824 the Iowas ceded all their territory in Missouri and in 1836 gained a small reservation on the Nebraska–Kansas border; small bands then moved away to better lands in Indian Territory, until an Iowa reservation was established there in 1883. The Poncas gave up their range in a treaty of 1858 for a Nebraska reservation, which within 10 years was reduced and mistakenly reassigned to their enemies the Sioux, then most were removed by force to Indian Territory, where they struggled further for many years to obtain suitable land. The plight of the Poncas gained much public sympathy and a special Congressional appropriation which enabled those inclined to return to live in Nebraska, permanently splitting the tribe. The Pawnees yielded all their lands in three treaties between 1833 and 1857 except for a 300-square-mile strip in Nebraska, which they sold in 1872 in order to move to Indian Territory, where they bought a new reservation in 1876. Once finally settled in Indian Territory, the surviving Prairie Indian communities struggled even more as Native lands there were turned over to whites and the State of Oklahoma was created. The Pawnee experience was typical: "Fully two-thirds of the reservation was rough country—rocky hills, ravines, and scrub timber. Lack of supplies, poor crops, epidemics, uncertainties about the government's Indian policies, and outside demands for opening Indian lands to white settlement caused a struggle for mere existence and a great decline in population" (Wright 1951:206).

On the Southern High Plains, the nomadic tribes were able to put off complete surrender by combining tactics of evasion, diplomacy, and armed attack and defense. Comanches and Kiowas, along with Wichitas, first met representatives of the federal government in July 1834, when the Dragoon Expedition under Colonel Henry

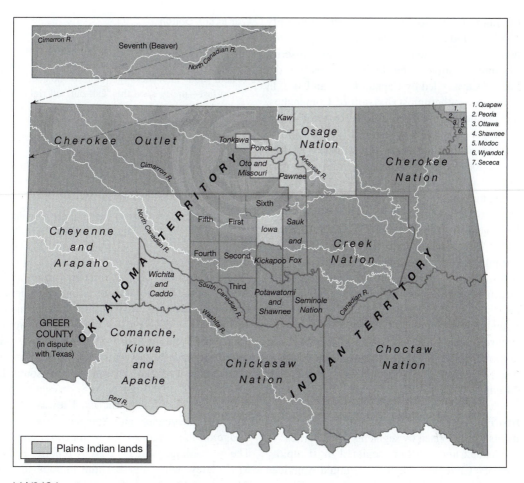

MAP 12.1 *Plains Indian Lands in Oklahoma and Indian Territories.*

Dodge visited their country. The Indian outlook toward the distant American regime was initially cordial. Their disposition toward the Anglo pioneers of Texas, however, grew ever more hostile as settlement increased and the friendly policies of Sam Houston gave way to those of the succeeding Texas president Mirabeau Lamar, an ardent Indian-hater. In the spring of 1840 some Comanches who came to the town square of San Antonio to trade captives were waylaid by the Texans in a bloody melee known as the Council House Fight. In revenge they attacked Victoria and Linnville, Texas (near present Port Lavaca), forever destroying the latter town, though the raiders took heavy losses from Texas militiamen when their retreat was ambushed at Plum Creek south of Austin. The Comanches also forayed deep into Mexico and trafficked in stolen livestock during the 1840s. They did accept the German settlers of the Texas Hill Country and struck a treaty with them in 1847 which was never substantively violated.

A broad treaty was made between Comanches, Kiowas, and Plains Apaches and the United States in 1853 at Fort Atkinson, Kansas, in which the Indians agreed to cease raids in Texas and Mexico and allow roads and forts in their range, in exchange for up to 15 years' worth of annuity goods. As Indian raiding and white transgressions nonetheless persisted, the tribes suffered a series of punitive attacks on their villages by the Second Cavalry led by Captain Earl Van Dorn. In 1855 the southernmost division of Comanches, the Penatekas, moved onto a reservation along the upper Brazos River in Texas. The Wichitas located on another reserve downstream. Both populations were then expelled to Indian Territory in 1859 as settlement pressure in Texas grew.

On the Northern High Plains, a critical moment came in 1851 when Americans established Fort Laramie at the site of a supply post on the North Platte River in eastern Wyoming. The Fort Laramie Treaty of that year (the earlier of two "Fort Laramie" treaties) set territories for all the area tribes. This treaty also formally recognized the division of the Cheyennes into Northern and Southern populations, a split which had actually occurred nearly 20 years earlier, when a large portion of the tribe went south from the Platte to live on the Arkansas River near the Bent's Fort trading post. The closely associated Arapahos had divided in the same fashion. As in the south, the first Fort Laramie Treaty and subsequent agreements were violated by segments of all parties.

Contact and conflict escalated most rapidly after the Civil War, when the reunited American nation turned its full attention to extending its sovereignty over the West. During this period a much greater volume of settlers moved onto the Plains. For frontier defense and offense, the state and federal governments shifted from reliance on militias to the regular army, and from infantry to cavalry. The Comanches and Kiowas took the lead role in mounting armed resistance in the south, and the Sioux led in the north. The divided Cheyennes fought intensely in both theaters. The battles of the 1860s to 1880s became known collectively, from the non-Indian perspective, as the Indian Wars. Native people plainly and accurately saw these clashes as their last, best attempts to oppose total conquest.

War in the South

> . . . we mount again and go until little light—pretty soon we make a line—the chiefs try to hold young men back—go too fast—no good go too fast—pretty soon they call out "all right to go ahead" we charge down on houses in wild charge—threw up the dust high. . . . I got on house with other Comanches and poked holes . . . to shoot—we killed two white men in wagon—the white men had big guns that kill a mile away—that pretty hard fight—from sunrise until 12 o'clock—then we go back. . . .
>
> (Comanche Quanah Parker, describing the 1874 Adobe Walls fight, quoted in Neely 1995:92–93)

At the start of the Civil War, federal troops withdrew from the frontier forts of Texas. Confederate forces took over only weakly, allowing Comanche and Kiowa raiding parties to harass the South Plains trails and drive off settlers. When the war ended, the federal government decided to quell hostilities and reopen settlement in the south. In October 1867 a 500-person U.S. delegation met with some 15,000 Comanches, Kiowas, Plains Apaches, Cheyennes, and Arapahos at Medicine Lodge on the Arkansas River in central Kansas. The proceedings were covered by reporter Henry M. Stanley, who later became famous for his African explorations. After much speechmaking from both sides, tribal leaders accepted on odd assortment of presents and signed a treaty which granted continued access to hunting grounds in the Texas Panhandle but which otherwise confined their followers to reservations in present western Oklahoma.

In the Medicine Lodge Treaty Indian leaders pledged to cease raiding, to attempt farming, and to send their children to schools. In exchange the government promised to send food and clothing, money to buy tools and seeds, and an agency for each reservation manned by a doctor, carpenter, miller, blacksmith, and teacher. But the leaders who signed at Medicine Lodge did not speak for all members of the Southern tribes, and not all the leaders who were present accepted the treaty terms. Those opposed to the treaty continued to hunt, raid, and live off the reservations. And those who did locate on the reservations soon found that the supplies and living conditions were inadequate, and many of them were prone to stray off and join with the still-wandering bands.

In response to continued Cheyenne attacks against settlers in Kansas, in 1868 the Army fielded an indiscriminate search-and-destroy force. In November, Seventh Cavalry troopers under Lieutenant Colonel George Armstrong Custer swarmed over Cheyenne Black Kettle's snowbound village on the Washita River, northwest Oklahoma, in a dawn surprise attack, killing over 100 Indians, including Black Kettle and his wife, taking 53 women and children hostage, and slaughtering about 900 horses. The following summer the Cheyenne Dog Soldiers suffered a final defeat in the Battle of Summit Springs, Colorado (see Chapters 4 and 11).

By the early 1870s white buffalo hunters were invading the Southern Plains in great numbers, killing off the Indians' traditional food supply and sparking further organized resistance. The Kiowas became especially fierce in their attacks, concentrating on isolated frontier ranches and travelers on the Butterfield Trail, a former stage and mail route connecting St. Louis and San Francisco, which ran across western Texas from Sherman to El Paso. Among their assaults was the famous Warren Wagon Train fight of May 1871. Some 100 Kiowas, Kiowa Apaches, and Comanches, led by Kiowas Mamanti, a medicine man, and headmen Satanta, Satank, and Big Tree, ambushed a train of supply wagons along the Butterfield road. The teamsters circled their wagons but were overrun, and all seven were killed and mutilated. The Indians lost three men and got away with 41 mules. Once back on the reservation, they boasted publicly of the raid. Ironically, General William T. Sherman had passed along the trail a few hours earlier on an inspection tour under the watchful eye of the hidden ambushers, who decided to let his small escort go and wait for the next party, in accordance with Mamanti's war prophecy (see Chapter 6). When Sherman learned of his near brush with fate, he resolved to step up army patrols in the region and catch the offenders. Kiowas under Big Bow made another similar wagon train attack in April 1872 at the lonely water hole called Howard Wells, Texas, killing 17 Mexican teamsters. Over the next few years, however, Kiowa opposition was broken as their principal headmen were jailed and some died resisting arrest or confinement.

Another crucial incident in the south was the June 1874 attack by several hundred Comanches and Cheyennes on the buffalo hunter's headquarters at Adobe Walls in the Texas Panhandle. The Indians besieged the post, but when the hunters were able to repel them with their long-range guns the Indians' leader, the medicine man Isatai, was discredited, and the assault fell apart. This offensive, following the Kiowa attacks, spurred a concerted response in which five U.S. Army columns converged from all directions on the heart of the southern High Plains, in a campaign known as the Red River War. It was a devastating sweep that culminated in September, when Colonel Ranald Mackenzie's Fourth U.S. Cavalry surprised the majority of off-reservation Comanches, Kiowas, and Cheyennes encamped in Palo Duro Canyon in the Texas Panhandle. As the troopers scrambled down the canyon wall and lined up to charge, the Indian families fled upstream, their men fighting a rear-guard action. Almost all of the hundreds of Indians made it up over the canyon edge and disappeared—only three were killed—but the army burned their lodges and captured 1,400 of their horses. The refugees endured a bitter winter on the Llano Estacado and surrendered the following spring. Thus, all Comanches and Kiowas were forced onto the reservation by 1875. That same spring, the last Southern Cheyenne holdouts were defeated at Sappa Creek, Kansas. Small raids and skirmishes continued in the region until 1878.

Seventy-four of the vanquished Cheyennes, Comanches, and Kiowas, those considered most responsible for white deaths and damages, were shipped to St. Augustine, Florida, to be held from 1875 until 1878 in the dungeons and yard of Fort Marion.

War in the North

The dust and smoke was black as evening. Once in a while we could see the soldiers through the dust, and finally we charged through them with our ponies. When we had done this . . . the fight was over.

(Chief Gall, describing the Battle of Little Bighorn, quoted in Utley 1988:191)

Take courage, the earth is all that lasts.

(Iron Hawk, exhorting his fellow warriors at Little Bighorn, quoted in Michno 1997:266)

The populous Sioux tribes, which had been aggressive against their Indian neighbors in staking territorial claims in the Dakotas and beyond, turned their might against white expansion in the 1860s. For seven days in August of 1862, Santee warriors rampaged on Minnesota towns, killing 737 settlers. Four hundred of the raiders were arrested and condemned to death; President Abraham Lincoln pardoned most, but 39 of the leaders were hung. The Santees were then driven westward into the Dakotas and joined with the Tetons, Cheyennes, and Arapahos, in a long series of raids and defensive fights against punitive Army expeditions. Red Cloud of the Oglalas (1822–1909) was the main Indian leader, along with the Cheyennes Dull Knife (?–1879) and Little Wolf, and this era of conflict became known as Red Cloud's War. Combat focused along the Platte River Trail in Nebraska and more so along the Bozeman Trail, which brought miners and garrisons from the Platte into Wyoming and Montana.

The most notable engagements in this period were the Sand Creek (Colorado) Massacre of November 1864, in which U.S. troops under Colonel John M. Chivington atrociously attacked a peaceful Cheyenne village under Black Kettle (he who was slain later in Custer's Washita raid), killing and mutilating about 150 Indian women, children, and elders, and the Fetterman Massacre in Wyoming in December 1866, in which 1,500 warriors completely annihilated a detachment of 84 troops and civilians. Northern Cheyennes under Roman Nose, smarting from the Sand Creek Massacre, trapped an elite force of civilian volunteers on a sandbar amid the Arikaree River on the east Colorado border in September 1868 in the legendary Beecher Island Fight. Several warriors, including Roman Nose, and 4 of the 50 soldiers, were killed in the nine-day standoff. But despite the success of Sioux and Cheyenne resistance, Red Cloud decided that the long-term odds were against him. He had effectively stalled use of the Bozeman Trail, and upon forcing the U.S. government to agree to quit all further attempts to establish the road and its forts, he signed a peace treaty at Fort Laramie in November 1868, and thereafter retired from fighting.

This second Fort Laramie Treaty defined large, exclusive reservation and hunting tracts for the tribes. Within five years, however, these territories were heavily violated as the Northern Pacific leg of the Transcontinental Railroad intruded into the region and an onslaught of gold prospectors and their ilk invaded the Black Hills. The Sioux rejected an outright purchase of the Black Hills and the region erupted in all-out conflict during 1876–1877, a period called the Sioux War. U.S. troops attempted a multipronged winter campaign like the one that had succeeded in 1874 on the Southern Plains, but the northern winter and the large numbers of Indian combatants proved difficult. Renewed resistance organized under the Sioux leaders Crazy Horse, Gall, Spotted Tail, and Sitting Bull was very effective.

In one of the most dramatic and controversial episodes in U.S. history, hundreds of Sioux and Cheyenne warriors wiped out the 210-man

FIGURE 12.1   Indian and U.S. federal negotiators, including General William T. Sherman (facing camera, third from left), planning the second Fort Laramie Treaty, November 1868.

command of George Armstrong Custer at the Little Big Horn River, southeastern Montana, on the afternoon of June 25, 1876. (Indian people refer to the location and battle as Greasy Grass, a translation of the Lakota name for the river.) Another 48 troopers died in related fighting, and the Indians lost an undetermined but apparently small number of warriors and noncombatants. It was a brief fight, "as long as it takes a hungry man to eat his dinner" according to Gall (Stewart 1955:358), not more than a few hours from first contact to "last stand" by the reckoning of modern scholars. News of Custer's utter defeat shocked and galvanized the non-Indian world, coming as it did on the eve of the celebration of the United States' 100th anniversary.

Historians and archaeologists have long struggled to account for such an overwhelming Indian triumph. Some maintain that Custer and his men, used to easy victories like the dawn surprise on the Washita, blundered onto a camp that was bigger than they realized. Others say that they arrived on tired horses, misread the tactical value of the terrain, failed to coordinate units properly to support each other, or underestimated the number of modern firearms available to the Indians. Another factor often cited is Custer's legendary arrogance, which, it is hypothesized, would have blinded him to the true dangers of the situation and drove him in an insane bid for glory. Ultimately the reasons for Custer's defeat may be much more straightforward: the Indians came out to defend their village with skill and valor; the soldiers fought well too, but were not able to maintain sufficient volume and accuracy of gunfire to keep from being overrun.

FIGURE 12.2 *Scene from the Battle of Little Big Horn drawn by a warrior who participated in the battle, White Bird (Northern Cheyenne).*

The Army carried on with a series of brisk actions that broke the powerful Sioux bands. In 1877 Crazy Horse was captured and bayoneted; Sitting Bull fled to Canada but surrendered in Dakota Territory in 1881. Sioux resistance was only fully quashed in 1890, with the shooting of Sitting Bull by Indian police and the massacre of Ghost dancers at Wounded Knee, South Dakota (see Chapter 10).

The Arapahos, in contrast to the Sioux and Cheyennes, did not fight, except in small groups that joined the other tribes. The Crows likewise did not put up a mass struggle against the U.S. government. Several Crow men scouted for the Army against their tribal enemies, at the Little Bighorn battle and elsewhere. The Crow reservation in Montana was, however, the scene of a minor outbreak in fall 1887, when an overeager agent tried to arrest some young warriors for stealing horses from the Blackfoots. The warriors shot up the agency and the First Cavalry was called in. A Crow policeman shot the rebels' leader and one trooper was killed in the fracas. The Blackfoots in Montana were generally hostile toward the Americans and launched raids on early encroachers, but after sustaining only one U.S. military action, a raid on an innocent village, they pled for peace.

Army operations on the Plains were bracketed by others against tribes to the west: the Nez Perce in Montana, the Utes in Colorado, the Bannocks in Idaho, the Modocs of the Oregon–California border area, and the Apaches who ranged from west Texas to Arizona. The result was a total subordination of the Native peoples in U.S. territory west of the Mississippi within a few decades.

While these events were taking place in U.S. territory, Plains Indians in Canada had to respond to somewhat similar circumstances. The Dominion of Canada was formed during 1867–1870 by combining British North America (the present eastern provinces) with the Hudson's Bay Company's holdings called Rupert's Land, which included the prairie regions of present Manitoba, Saskatchewan, and Alberta. To avoid the kind of strife that was raging in the United States because of white encroachment on Indian lands, the new Canadian government attempted to quickly establish Indian reservations (called reserves) and settle the Indians before whites arrived in numbers. Between 1871 and 1877 the government negotiated a series of seven treaties that confined the Plains Crees, Plains Ojibwas, Assiniboines, and Blackfoots to bounded lands. Numerous populations of these tribes were fragmented and assigned to small isolated reserves. As in the United States, relocation to the reserves was forced with limitations on hunting and encouraged with the provision of rations, farm tools, and seeds. And as in the United States, the supposed benefits of settled life gave way to starvation and despair within a generation.

Armed resistance to white expansion in Canada was not, however, organized primarily by tribal Indians, but by the Metís, the French-Indian mixed-blood traders of the prairie region who saw in the new Anglo-dominated Canadian government a loss of autonomy. Metís opposition came to a head in 1885, in what is known as the Northwest Rebellion, and at that point disaffected Plains Indians joined them in taking up arms against the government. The Cree leaders Big Bear and Poundmaker had first sued for a peaceful solution to the hunger of the reserves. But then Poundmaker's band terrorized the settlement of Battleford, Saskatchewan, and young Cree warriors under Wandering Spirit killed nine white settlers at Frog Lake, Alberta, confirming fears of an Indian uprising and prompting the dispatch of a large Canadian force of regular soldiers, militia, and mounted police. The Crees, along with Sioux, Assiniboines, and Metís, met and bloodied the troops at Fish Creek and Cut Knife Hill in west-central Saskatchewan. Soon after, though, the Metís capital of Batoche, Saskatchewan, fell to the Canadian forces and the Cree leaders

surrendered. Big Bear and Poundmaker were imprisoned, Wandering Spirit was hung, and the Crees were subjugated. The Blackfoots to the west, though an even more formidable force than the Crees, kept out of the rebellion and went on their Canadian reserves peaceably.

EARLY RESERVATION LIFE

The early reservation years spanning the late nineteenth and beginning twentieth century were grim times. Tribal populations, which had been on the decline since the great epidemics and eruption of all-out war, plummeted to historic lows once the remaining Plains peoples were concentrated and kept immobile. The combined effects of starvation, imbalanced nutrition, poor sanitation, disease, and depression took a huge toll. Plains Indian tribal populations reached their all-time lows between 1900 and 1910. Table 12.1 shows how tribal populations plunged. It was unrealistic to expect people with decades of nomadic skills to accept or adjust to settled life in short order. Moreover, the government support for this change was not delivered as promised in the various treaties.

For a few years Indian hunting parties were allowed to leave the reservations to search for buffalo, but by the early 1880s the great animals were all but gone. Beef, issued on the hoof, was the replacement; most Indians thought of it as inferior food. Typically the issued cattle were released one at a time to be chased down and butchered like buffalo. It was difficult for reservation Indians to develop their own beef herds because grazing was usually inadequate and they were prone to eating or selling off their stock to meet short-term emergencies. Besides beef, other staples such as white flour, corn meal, salt, sugar, coffee, and lard were supposed to be delivered. Some kinds of rations, such as bacon and rice, were foreign to the Indian diet. Comanches would not eat bacon because they thought pigs were dirty, and rice reminded them of

TABLE 12.1   Population Decline Among Plains Tribes

TRIBE	DATE	ESTIMATED POPULATION	DATE	CENSUS COUNT
Apaches, Lipan	1690	500	1910	28
Apaches, Plains	1670	700	1910	139
Arapahos	1780	3,000	1910	1,419
Arikaras	1780	3,000	1910	444
Assiniboines	1780	10,000	1904	2,605
Atsinas	1780	3,000	1910	510
Blackfoots	1780	15,000	1909	4,635
Cheyennes	1780	3,500	1910	3,055
Comanches	1690	7,000	1910	1,171
Crows	1780	4,000	1910	1,799
Hidatsas	1780	2,500	1910	547
Iowas	1780	1,200	1910	244
Kansas	1780	3,000	1910	238
Kiowas	1780	2,000	1910	1,126
Mandans	1780	3,600	1910	209
Omahas	1780	2,800	1910	1,105
Otoe–Missourias	1780	1,900	1910	332
Osages	1780	6,200	1910	1,373
Pawnees	1780	10,000	1910	633
Quapaws	1650	2,500	1910	231
Wichitas	1780	3,200	1910	318

Source: Parks et al. (1980).

maggots, hence their word for it, *wo?atuku*, "worm food." Whatever the suitability of the provisions, they were usually inadequate in quantity and quality. Congress cut the appropriations once the Indians actually surrendered. Supplies were often late owing to bad weather and poor wagon roads. Food arrived rancid; livestock were diseased. Agents and contractors sold off supplies to the black market for their own profit or ordered inferior ones with their allowances and pocketed the difference. And, the rations were meant only to supplement crops, so as Indians farming proved impossible there was never enough food. Annuity funds and other treaty items such as clothing were similarly in too short supply.

Overseeing the U.S. reservations with all the virtues and vices of a federal bureaucracy was the Office of Indian Affairs or Indian Office, known after 1947 as the Bureau of Indian Affairs (BIA). Formed in 1824, the office was a successor to government agencies dating to the time of the American Revolution for the negotiation of Indian treaties and management of the fur trade. Originally part of the War Department, the Indian Office was transferred to the Department of the Interior in 1849. Its main purposes since then have been management of Indian trust assets (land and money) and Indian education. In Canada, different agencies have overseen Indian affairs, notably the Department of the Interior

TABLE 12.2   Canadian Government Departments Responsible for Indian Affairs

DEPARTMENT	DATES
Department of the Secretary of State of Canada	to 1869
Department of the Secretary of State for the Provinces	1869–1873
Department of the Interior	1873–1880
Department of Indian Affairs	1880–1936
Department of Mines and Resources	1936–1950
Department of Citizenship and Immigration	1950–1965
Department of Northern Affairs and Natural Resources	1966
Department of Indian Affairs and Northern Development (a k a INAC)	1966–present

(1873–1880) and the Department of Indian Affairs (1880–1936). Indian and Northern Affairs Canada (INAC) is the modern Canadian counterpart to the BIA (see Table 12.2).

Reservations became the setting for intensive Christian missionary work, as detailed in Chapter 10. Non-Indian authorities considered Christian teachings to be a basic ingredient in the recipe for civilization. Soon after taking office in 1869, President Ulysses S. Grant instituted his "Quaker Policy." Worried about careerism and graft in the Indian Office, Grant decided, with much pressure from church leaders, that missionaries would make the most honest and effective Indian agents and superintendents, and so he invited Quaker clergymen to nominate them. Quakers took over the reservations of the Kiowas and Comanches, Pawnees, Otoes, and Omahas. Grant then expanded the program to involve other Protestant denominations and tribes, and soon each agency on the U.S. Plains was connected to one or another church. A very similar program was instituted on the Canadian reserves. Though Christianity contributed to tribal divisiveness and the erosion of Native traditions, it also gave some Indians a new frame of reference for the changes they were encountering, and Grant's sympathetic Quaker Policy bespoke a pacifist approach to assimilation which foreshadowed later Indian policy reforms.

Allotment

Although the lands set aside for reservations were deemed by whites to be the least desirable for farming and settlement, soon enough pressure mounted to open even these areas to non-Indian occupation. The Dawes Severalty Act, passed by Congress in 1887, authorized the federal government to purchase reservation land and open it to homesteaders. Under this act, each tribal member was to be given an individual parcel of 160 acres, then the "surplus" reservation land—anything which was not directly occupied by settled Indians, the majority of the reservation acreage—was given to non-Indian settlers. Aside from opening land for settlers, the Dawes Act was also an instrument for assimilation, turning Indians from collective into individual land owners and forcing them to live in more regular contact with non-Indians.

Consideration of the Dawes Act at the various reservations was a long process. A committee from Washington known as the Jerome Commission or Cherokee Commission traveled through Indian Territory (Oklahoma) to negotiate local agreements. Indians there debated the pros and cons of accepting allotment, and through the 1890s it was the major political issue, with leaders and factions lining up for or against it. Opponents spoke against the loss of traditional common land. They were suspicious of the proposed agreements because of past broken promises, and they sometimes tried in vain to revive old claims during the allotment hearings. Many were disturbed by the low prices offered for reservation acreage, which by law were not to exceed $1.25 per acre, and ultimately only about eight cents per acre in southwest Oklahoma, well below market value. The money would be held in trust and pay interest, not distributed in direct payments to the tribes or individuals. Also, the promise of Indian land ownership was exaggerated. The allotted land too was to be held in trust by the federal government, for 25 years, until the recipients could prove themselves, through appeals arbitrarily decided by their Indian agents, legally competent for fee patent ownership. Still, the offers of cash and land were tempting to many Indians, who were afraid for their survival because treaty agreements providing annuities and rations were about to expire. The commissioners pushed hard for acceptance and were not above using intimidation and possibly vote fraud.

Most Indian Territory tribes eventually yielded to the pressure and inevitability of the openings. By 1900 well over 15 million acres of reservation land were transferred to white ownership. Plains tribes whose reservations were abolished under the Jerome Commission included the Comanches, Kiowas, Apaches, Southern Cheyennes, Southern Arapahos, Pawnees, and Wichitas. The Kaws (Kansas) made a separate, slightly more advantageous allotment agreement in 1902, as did the Osages and Otoe–Missourias around 1906. Within a few years of the openings, whites outnumbered Indians in the opened areas by as much as 33 to 1. To this day the former reservation areas of these tribes remain a checkerboard of Indian and non-Indian landholdings. In 1907 the Poncas divided their reservation among themselves.

Beyond Oklahoma, other U.S. tribes also faced demands to allot, even though their reservations were not abolished as part of the allotment process. A few, like the Omahas, Santees, and Crows, actually began allotment before the Dawes

Act owing to local pressure. The Yanktons began taking allotments in 1890, the Northern Arapahos in 1900, the Tetons in 1905, the Montana Blackfoots in 1907, and the Gros Ventres in 1918. The Arikaras accepted allotments of their village site in 1891 but were able to keep ownership of the land not allotted for 25 years subsequent. Allotment was not practiced on the Canadian reserves, although the margins of the reserves were frequently reduced to allow white expansion.

It would turn out that allotment caused many problems. Conflicts erupted between full-bloods who received allotments and mixed-bloods who often were not eligible to receive them. The individual home sites set up by allotment required relatives to either accept isolation or crowd together in small, permanent compounds, disrupting traditional patterns of land use and social interaction. As the generation that received allotments grew older, land wealth became concentrated among the elderly, causing further economic and social imbalances. The comparatively meager trust funds obtained by the tribes in payment for the "surplus" lands did not improve local economies. The allotted parcels of 160 acres were actually not large enough for prosperous farming and ranching (on the sparse, dry plains it took 10 or more acres to graze a single cow). Within a few generations, these landholdings were further fragmented through inheritance. Also, when Indians assumed outright ownership, their land became taxable; unable to come up with the taxes, or in need of cash for other reasons, they frequently sold their parcels to whites and became destitute. Ironically allotment, coupled with the expiration of treaty annuities, initially made Indian people more dependent on the federal government than they had been prior.

Boarding Schools

White-run boarding schools for Indian children were established before and during the reservation era, and several of them have lasted through the twentieth century and up to the present day. These institutions were founded and funded by the federal government through the Office of Indian Affairs or by various Christian denominations, and they recruited students either from around the country or from local areas. Some of the prominent schools that enrolled Plains Indian children are listed in Table 12.3.

The first and most famous Indian Affairs boarding school was Carlisle Indian Industrial School in Carlisle, Pennsylvania. Carlisle was modeled on Hampton Normal and Agricultural Institute (now Hampton University), a school for African Americans in Virginia that combined book learning with manual training and Christian moral instruction. The one major difference was that Hampton prepared blacks to live among themselves in segregated communities, while Carlisle prepared Indians to live among whites. The founder and longtime superintendent of Carlisle was former frontier cavalry officer Richard Henry Pratt. Pratt had been in charge of the warriors imprisoned at Fort Marion. He found his prisoners trustworthy and interested in learning white ways,

and was encouraged by their adaptability. Pratt came to believe that the wisest course for Indian people was total assimilation into white society through education—"Kill the Indian, save the man," he was fond of saying.

Pratt initially recruited students from the Rosebud and Pine Ridge (Teton) reservations, then among the Cheyennes and Kiowas. Pratt especially enrolled the children of tribal leaders in the hope of demonstrating the advantages of white education to those who would be most influential in Native communities. The chiefs frequently agreed to send their children so they could learn how better to deal with whites. Soon many parents and the children themselves became interested. Luther Standing Bear (1863?–1939), son of prominent Lakotas (his father fought at Little Bighorn), volunteered to go with Pratt to prove his bravery.

Some parents, however, resisted the enrollment of their children in the boarding schools. Orphans under the charge of reservation authorities were more likely to be sent for schooling than children with relatives to protect them. Reservation agents sometimes sent Indian police to seize children

TABLE 12.3   Some Prominent Indian Boarding Schools Enrolling Plains Indians

SCHOOL	LOCATION	DATES OF OPERATION
Carlisle Indian Industrial	Carlisle, Pennsylvania	1879–1918
Chilocco Indian Agricultural	Kay County, Oklahoma	1884–1980
Flandreau Indian	Flandreau, South Dakota	1893–present
Fort Sill Indian	Lawton, Oklahoma	1871–1980
Genoa Indian Industrial	Nance County, Nebraska	1884–1934
Haskell Indian (now Haskell Indian Nations University)	Lawrence, Kansas	1884–present
Holy Rosary Mission (now Red Cloud Indian)	Pine Ridge, South Dakota	1888–present
Osage Mission	Neosho County, Kansas	1847–1895
Pierre Indian	Pierre, South Dakota	1891–present
Presbyterian Mission	Thurston County, Nebraska	1848–1906
Rapid City Indian	Rapid City, South Dakota	1989–1933
Riverside Indian	Anadarko, Oklahoma	1871–present

from their families and force them to attend, and they withheld rations from unwilling families until they surrendered their children to the schools. Forced recruitment was finally banned in 1908 by Indian Affairs commissioner Francis Leupp.

It was traumatic for Indian children to be taken from their homes, and further upsetting to have to deal with a strange new environment. Local whites came to gawk at them when they stopped en route or arrived at school. They were forbidden to speak their Native tongues even before they had any understanding of English. Conversely, the teachers had no preparation in Indian languages. School attendants cropped the children's hair close and, worse, cut off their braids, an act with strong symbolic and emotional effect. They banned moccasins and blankets and made the children dress in the tight, heavy boots and clothing of Victorian fashion or, for the boys, military tunics. Luther Standing Bear said red flannel underwear was the worst thing about Carlisle life, calling it "actual torture" (Standing Bear 1933:233). The children were drilled like soldiers to instill obedience and whipped for nearly any breach of school rules. No Native religious expression was allowed.

Teachers considered Native names pagan and unpronounceable, and gave the pupils new "Christian" names by some arbitrary method. They might list possible names on the chalkboard and dispense them at random (on tape stuck to the backs of the children's shirts), or read names from the Bible and proceed down the classroom rows to assign them. Or, the teacher left it up to the class: Francis LaFlesche (Omaha) tells how one newcomer to the Presbyterian Mission School was renamed William T. Sherman by proclamation of his classmates. Luther Standing Bear, originally called Ota Kte ("Plenty Kill"), was among those fortunate enough to select his own Christian name from the blackboard and retain a Native family name.

Half the students' day was spent in domestic or shop work. Girls learned sewing, cooking, baking,

canning, laundering, and typing; boys studied farming, dairying, millwork, blacksmithing, harness-making, and carpentry. This activity was not purely educational, for the schools were not well funded, requiring even young students to labor long hours growing and preparing their own food and building and maintaining the campus. Nutrition was often not adequate despite their efforts. Carlisle and some other schools had an "outing" program in which the students were sent off campus during the summer and following graduation to board and provide wage work for farms or businesses ("the best civilized environment," according to Pratt [1964:290]). Outings were intended to break down prejudices and give the students a chance to sharpen their English and pick up the nuances of white culture, while developing a work ethic. Luther Standing Bear worked at Wanamaker's department store in Philadelphia and was praised by Mr. Wanamaker for his quick advancement in the company.

Sanitation and health care at the schools were often substandard. They became major breeding grounds for tuberculosis of the lungs, scrofula (glandular tuberculosis causing festers), mumps, diphtheria, and influenza. Trachoma, a highly contagious bacterial infection of the eye that could lead to blindness, was also rampant.

School often seemed absurd to the children. Such basic white customs as eating only according to clock time were strange to them. Table 12.4 shows the incessant morning schedule at Carlisle. Indian students had little or no prior cultural context for many of the ideas they were taught in class. When ninth graders at Pierre Indian School grappled with the works of Shakespeare and Sir Walter Scott, these stories must have appeared unconnected not only to their natal traditions but to present-day white society as well. Similarly, students at Rapid City Indian School found themselves performing a musical based on the white fantasy of Pocahontas and speaking on such unfamiliar topics as "The Trouble with Rastus" and "The Necessity of War, 1775" in oratorical contests. Indian singing and dancing were banned

TABLE 12.4   Morning Schedule for Students at Carlisle Indian School

5:30	Rising bell
5:30–6:00	Dress and report for athletics
6:00	Warning bell
6:00–6:20	Setting-up exercise
6:20–6:25	Roll call
6:25	Breakfast bell; raise flag
6:25–6:30	Line up; march to dining hall
6:30–7:00	Breakfast
7:00–7:25	Care of rooms
7:15	Sick call; bugle
7:25	Work bell
7:25–7:30	Line up; detail reports
7:30–8:30	Industrial instruction
7:30–8:15	Academic division [breaking into grades]
8:15–8:25	Prepare for school
8:25	School bell or bugle
8:25–8:30	Line up. March to school building
8:30	School application industrial division
10:00–10:15	Recess; five minutes' breathing exercise
11:30	Recall bell; all departments
11:30–11:45	Recreation; details return to quarter
11:45	Warning bell
11:45–11:55	Prepare for dinner
11:55–12:00	Line up. Inspection. March to dining room
12:00–12:30	Dinner

Source: Fixico (2006:45–46).

in favor of choirs and brass bands. Baseball and football replaced familiar Indian pastimes, though Indian children came to excel in these sports, most famously in the nearly unbeatable football teams of Carlisle. As for the practical skills taught, many of them were not widely applicable in the reservation communities where most students returned, and the training was not sophisticated enough to prepare them for the better city jobs.

Given these stresses and shortcomings, it is not surprising that students frequently ran away, traveling on foot great distances or hopping trains. Their apprehension and return became a regular business for police in precincts near the schools and back on the reservations where the children usually tried to go. Some runaways simply disappeared. Others were found dead. One notorious tragedy took place in January 1891, when three Kiowa boys fled from school in Anadarko, Oklahoma, after one had been whipped. They got caught in a blizzard and froze to death. In 1909 two boys trying to get home to the Pine Ridge Reservation from the Rapid City School were similarly caught in a snowstorm and each lost both legs to amputation because of frostbite. Malnutrition, exhaustion, depression, illness, and the dangers of escape together meant that a high number of children at any school died. One hundred and ninety children lay in the Carlisle graveyard.

Retrospective analyses therefore often portray the Indian boarding school as a bleak institution of forced acculturation. K. Tsianina Lomawaima, an anthropologist and daughter of a former Chilocco student, summarized this view: "an institutional training ground for the subservice of the colonized" (Lomawaima 1994:xiv). Yet the recent scholarship of Lomawaima and others, based on interviews with former students, shows that the children were not simply passive victims of assimilation. Generally, they were aware of the forces of assimilation and disliked government agencies and policies, but they valued the experiences they had and the people they met at school. They had realistic purposes for attending. And, they were clever in subverting the schools' intentions of erasing Native identity.

Recall that a young Luther Standing Bear saw school attendance as a way of meeting the traditional expectation for acts of bravery. Anthropologist Sally McBeth interviewed many former boarding school students and heard six main motivations: children wanted to learn to cope in the white world; schools supplied food and clothing otherwise not available; schools provided foster care for children whose parents had died; children wanted to be with their friends; they were uncomfortable in integrated public schools; they wanted to be with other Indians (McBeth 1983:108–111). (For that matter, Indian adults considered the schools good places to work and were also drawn to them.) Children often forged fond relationships with their teachers and matrons. The strict, paternalistic Captain Pratt was admired by the students of Carlisle. "Oh Papa," wrote one Haskell student, "you do not know how much I love my teacher" (cited in Adams 1995:262). Schoolmates maintained friendships with letters and visits that spanned the distance between reservations and lasted lifetimes. And contrary to the aims of the schools, the students found solace in their shared Indian identity. They sang and danced their tribal traditions in secret, formed cliques along or across tribal lines, and much of the minor mischief they organized, like hunting on school grounds or tasting peyote, was Native in character. The common feelings and experiences that students recognized were a basis for a nationwide intertribal culture which blossomed during the twentieth century.

Ironically, the schools produced many eloquent Native critics of forced assimilation, including Luther Standing Bear:

The attempted transformation of the Indian by the white man and the chaos that has resulted are but the fruits of the white man's disobedience of a fundamental and spiritual law. The pressure that has been brought to bear upon the native people, since the cessation of armed conflict, in the attempt to force conformity of custom and habit has caused a reaction more destructive than war, and the injury has not only affected the Indian, but has extended to the white population as well. Tyranny, stupidity, and the lack of vision have brought about the situation now alluded to as the "Indian Problem."

(Standing Bear 1933:248)

Gertrude Simmons Bonnin (Zitkala-Ša; 1876–1938) was a Yankton student and later teacher at Carlisle:

At last, one weary day in the schoolroom, a new idea presented itself to me. It was a new way of solving the problem of my inner self. I liked it. Thus I resigned my position as teacher. . . . Now, as I look back upon the recent past, I see it from a distance, as a whole. I remember how, from morning till evening, many specimens of civilized peoples visited the Indian school. The city folks with canes and eyeglasses, the countrymen with sunburnt cheeks and clumsy feet, forgot their relative social ranks in an ignorant curiosity. Both sorts of these Christian palefaces were alike astounded at seeing the children of savage warriors so docile and industrious.

As answers to their shallow inquiries they received the students' sample work to look upon. Examining the neatly figured pages and gazing upon the Indian girls and boys bending over their books, the white visitors walked out of the schoolhouse well satisfied; they were educating the children of the red man! They were paying a liberal fee to the government employees in whose able hands lay the small forest of Indian timber.

In this fashion many have passed idly through the Indian schools during the last decade, afterward to boast of their charity to the North American Indian. But few there are who have paused to question whether real life or long-lasting death lies beneath this semblance of Civilization.

(Zitkala-Ša 1985 [orig. 1921]:97–99)

Commentaries like these were widely read by non-Indians and swayed public attitudes about how Indians were being treated in American society.

Another lasting effect of the boarding schools was the making of generations of younger Indians who returned to their home communities with different abilities and outlooks than the older tribal leaders. These people became active in community affairs and drove change. Sometimes they became advisors to tribal elders, and other times they opposed them. For example, during the 1920s Southern Cheyenne and Arapaho "school-boys" moved into positions of prestige formerly held by older chiefs and took over efforts to sue for land claims in Washington. Though their rising dominance in tribal affairs often caused discord, the white-educated young leaders contributed to a spirit of reform and progressivism that took hold in the early decades of the twentieth century.

A summary of the Indian boarding school in general might paraphrase historian Scott Riney's assessment of the Rapid City school: " . . . a place that was both good and bad, or neither, and in the end simply gone, living only in the memories of students who are fewer with each passing year" (Riney 1999:224). And whether good or bad, the boarding school experience became a regular part of Indian life during a time of significant social and cultural change.

PERIOD OF REFORM

By the 1920s growing public awareness of the dark side of the Indian boarding school experience led to reform measures that changed school practices and the agencies running the schools. Indian Service schools began offering more advanced instruction. Local public day schools increasingly became an alternative for Indian education, as racial prejudices faded by some degree and whites agreed to admit Indians despite quarrels about their contributions to the tax base. Around this same time, the establishment of the Native American Church (see Chapter 10) brought attention to the question of Native religious freedom. The most powerful influence on public thinking was the participation of numerous Indians in the U.S. military during the 1917–1918 American involvement in World War I (WWI). Over 10,000 Indians swore allegiance to the U.S. Constitution and served in the armed forces even though many were not citizens and were exempt from the draft. Non-Indians observed and appreciated this great show of patriotism.

As a result of such sympathetic public perceptions, a movement arose to grant blanket American citizenship for Native Americans. Previously citizenship had been granted only piecemeal. The 1906 Burke Act had allowed citizenship along with fee patent land ownership to tribal members of one-half or less Indian descent, and other Indians had received citizenship through marriage, military service, specific treaties, or declarations of legal competency. One-third of all Indians still lacked citizenship in the early 1920s. In 1924 Congress granted citizenship to all Indians born in U.S. territory. Many Indian people were ambivalent about this distinction, fearing it meant a loss of their tribal rights, although the citizenship statute stipulated that those rights should be preserved. Voting rights were granted separately, gradually, and in some cases grudgingly, by individual states, with Arizona and New Mexico the last to enfranchise Indians, not until 1948.

Poverty and poor health were still omnipresent in Plains Indian communities in the 1920s. During this era many Plains Indians still lived in canvas tents of the kind which had been issued to replace their tipis. The "Indian Problem" that Luther Standing Bear wrote about was outlined in the Brooking Institution's 1928 Merriam Report:

> The economic basis of the primitive culture of the Indians has been largely destroyed by the encroachment of white civilization. The Indians can no longer make a living as they did in the past. . . . This advancing tide of white civilization has as a rule largely destroyed the economic foundation upon which the Indian culture rested. . . . The price is a body of Indian citizens, unassimilated, poverty stricken, and diseased.
>
> (quoted in Nagel 1996:5)

The Merriam Report alerted Congress to the need for drastic improvements in reservation economies,

FIGURE 12.3 *American Horse (Oglala; 1840–1908) being certified as a United States citizen by allotment surveyor Charles Ash Bates (center) and interpreter Billy Garnett in 1907.*

sanitation, health care, and schooling. It heralded a progressive attitude that permeated the non-Indian public mind, government Indian policy, and Indian self-perceptions too. This attitude was accompanied by an awakening in the art world, as the fabled Kiowa Five artists traveled the country and beyond making known their visionary talents in painting, sculpture, and performance.

But in economic terms the decade of the 1920s was a period of uncertainty and false starts. As the white economy of the western states and provinces developed, there were moderately more local paying jobs for Plains Indians, though they tended to be seasonal—manual labor or, in the far north, work as hunting and fishing guides. Some households produced beadwork and souvenirs for railroad tourists, and those willing to travel found work as show dancers in Wild West exhibits and

Indian villages. Agricultural work was often more steady, but still tenuous. Plains Indian men had been reluctant to farm, since gardening and plant gathering were traditionally women's jobs. Men were also discouraged from agriculture because, in addition to the lack of a suitable land base, they were not able to get the necessary bank loans for equipment and seeds, and in some cases they were even prohibited by local law from owning farm equipment. Nevertheless, Comanches and Kiowas had gotten sizeable acreage under cultivation by about 1920, after which the post-WWI drop in commodity prices and the rise of mechanized farming rendered small Indian farmers uncompetitive. In the north ranching was the most practical course and by the 1920s the Blackfoots, Crows, and Sioux were invested in cattle and cowboy culture. The Crow chief Plenty Coups legitimized this new direction for his people by telling them of a vision he had of the mythic figure Chickadee, a harbinger of the future who is curious about everything around him. Plenty Coup's prophetic advice was for the Crows to learn new ways of survival by observing others. Yet again the fluctuations in national prices and also the severity of droughts and winter weather meant that Indian ranchers would have to ride boom and bust cycles. The Great Depression, which began in 1929 and lasted through most of the 1930s, did not affect Plains Indian communities very much directly simply because they were not yet heavily tied into the national economy. The prolonged drought and locusts of the Dust Bowl that corresponded with the Depression, however, further hurt the farming and ranching operations that Indians had begun.

One notable exception to the pattern of slow economic growth on the Plains was the rise of fossil fuel production in the early twentieth century. The Blackfoots, Crows, and Northern Cheyennes became involved in oil and coal, but the big oil boom was in Oklahoma, and the Osages were the tribe most famously affected. Their supposedly barren lands held huge reserves of oil and natural gas and members of the small tribe were shrewd in how they collectively and individually leased their property to the oil companies. As a result the Osage tribe became the world's wealthiest nation per capita. In 1924 alone Osage petroleum lease revenues exceeded $24 million. Between 1905 and 1945 the Osage Nation received $300 million; this money was divided among the 2,229 original allottees and their heirs. Such fabulous wealth was difficult to manage and very disruptive to the traditional community:

> . . . one person went through ten automobiles in one year . . . fancy houses were also purchased, and priceless china and silverware sat on shelves while the Osage ate with their fingers, as was their custom. Expensive vases were used to store vegetables rather than as decorative items, and grand pianos that served no useful purpose stood out on lawns in rain or shine. . . . The rich Osage lived in a world of illusion without incentives, a world whose values seriously disrupted their kinship society and affected their entire world view.
>
> (Fixico 1998:47)

Osage wealth and the seedy boomtowns attracted white swindlers who married into Indian families just long enough to collect inheritances, sometimes only a few days. During 1921–1923 henchmen of William K. Hale murdered 17 members of one rich extended family in an elaborate scheme to steal inheritances and insurance settlements, known as the "Osage Reign of Terror." Tribal elders called in the Federal Bureau of Investigation, whose agents worked undercover in Osage country for two years to break the case. Hale and his cronies were convicted and given life sentences.

Indian Reorganization Act

The Indian Reorganization Act (IRA) of June 18, 1934, also known as the Wheeler–Howard Act, had profound effects on the way Indian people governed themselves and related to the nation state. The act was promoted by John Collier, Commissioner of Indian Affairs under President Franklin Delano Roosevelt. Collier worried that Indians were loosing their collective identities as well as their ability to survive and prosper as assimilation and the long effects of economic deprivation continued. Collier envisioned a range of related remedies for the dire condition of most Indian communities. He wanted credit to be made available for economic development, the construction of vocational schools, and other strong commitments for conservation and development. He called for an immediate halt to any further allotment of communal land as had been permitted under the Dawes Act, and he wanted to see fragmented Indian landholdings put back together. Collier's list of reforms became known as the Indian New Deal.

The cornerstone of Collier's plan was his commitment to Indian self-determination. He spoke passionately of " . . . the power abiding within Indians, waiting for release through the enfranchisement or recreation of Indian grouphood" (Collier in Kelly 1954:5). Collier urged the formation of Native governments that could interact with state and federal governments on behalf of their constituents. He favored organization at the level of the tribe, even for populations in which clans and local bands were more meaningful units, because whites thought of Indians as existing in "tribes" and were not likely to engage them in smaller or more varied units. By the same token, Collier stressed that the tribal administrations should adopt features of non-Indian government, such as elections, representative bodies (tribal councils or business committees), and executives (chairpersons or presidents), in order to best mesh with outside governments. It was Collier's hope that these structures would not only allow better communication, but that they would take over many of the functions of the more alien state and federal bureaucracies, such as the receipt and management of funds and the delivery of social services.

During the 1930s most Plains reservations assumed some form of IRA government, either by direct adoption of the IRA or by some subsequent implementation of the IRA model. The adoption process typically took a number of years in which the pros and cons were weighed and votes were taken. On reservations housing more than one tribe, sometimes competing tribal interests were at stake (thus, for example, Fort Belknap Reservation, Montana, incorporated under the IRA in 1937 with Assiniboine approval but Gros Ventre opposition). Indians struggled to create governments with the forms they most desired, in some cases forms which allowed some continuance of traditional authority figures and decision-making processes and in other cases a departure from the older forms. They also sought to create governments that could be effective in addressing important issues such as treaty rights, land claims, economic development, and local crime and corruption. The adoption of an IRA government was not compulsory, however,

and some groups, such as the Shoshones and Northern Arapahos at Wind River Reservation in Wyoming and the Comanches, Kiowas, and Kiowa Apaches in Oklahoma, voted to continue with whatever council structure or chieftainship they already had.

Collier foresaw that tribal governments would be on par with state and federal ones, and indeed the tribal governments formed under the IRA have had a fair though imperfect degree of sovereignty, which has been upheld in several court cases. They may maintain their own courts, police forces, housing authorities, schools, and other governmental departments. The more immediate concern of the tribes was the effectiveness of the financial incentives that accompanied reorganization. On this score the Collier reforms were a mixed success. Indian communities sometimes split in arguments over how new resources would be distributed, and the federal government did not follow through in furnishing all of the funding and rights originally promised. Yet many reservations enjoyed improvements. Livestock cooperatives, irrigation projects, and housing consisting of wooden frame dwellings were set up using revolving credit. Indians gained employment while building valuable public works on the reservations, such as roads, bridges, dams, fences, wells, and community centers. Related measures included the Johnson–O'Malley Act of 1934, which provided federal aid to public schools to help them educate Native American children, and the 1935 establishment of the Indian Arts and Crafts Board, which supported traditional crafts through its co-ops, museums, and shops. All told, the Indian New Deal did set a new agenda for Native American–federal relations.

PERIOD OF TERMINATION

World War II (WWII) was another watershed in the history of Plains Indian cultural life. Indians joined the armed forces in proportions beyond those of all other ethnic groups, with Plains volunteers outnumbering draftees by two to one, and thousands saw combat and distinguished themselves in military service. Among them was Clarence L. Tinker (Osage), the first Indian in modern times to make the rank of general; Tinker was killed leading U.S. bomber squadrons in the Battle of Midway. Seventeen Comanche men were recruited as "code talkers," radio operators whose Native language transmissions could not be translated by the enemy, and they served bravely in the Normandy invasion and defeat of Germany in Europe. Many other Plains Indians fought in Europe and the Pacific, in the 45th Infantry ("Thunderbird") Division that recruited from Oklahoma and in other units.

There were some ironies in the Indian involvement in the war. Tribal governments published proclamations condemning the tyranny of Axis fascism even though Indians still did not enjoy full rights at home. Stereotypes of Indians as superhuman scouts and warriors became apparent in the hazardous duties they were habitually assigned and in the press coverage of the war. Yet there were also advantages to their participation, including employment and interesting opportunities to acculturate and demonstrate patriotism without having to forsake Native identity. Stereotypes aside, the conflict did provide a reason for Plains Indians to renew warrior traditions such as the Victory Dance, War Mother's societies, and the Kiowa Tiah-Piah society, a basis for the modern powwow Gourd Dance (see Chapter 7). At the same time, Indian servicemen and women were further exposed to the English language and American, not to mention European and Asian, cultural habits. Some acquired technical and managerial skills in the military that enabled them to get better jobs after the war, and all at least theoretically enjoyed veteran's status and benefits. Unlike African American soldiers, Indians were not kept together in segregated units, but assigned across predominantly white ones. Intermarriage between members of different tribes, and between Indians and

non-Indians, increased markedly. These experiences, coupled with postwar improvements in the nation's western infrastructure, notably rural electrification, telephones, and the interstate highway system, all combined to connect Plains Indian people more firmly to the outside world.

The late 1940s saw the beginning of another shift in government attitudes and policies. This shift was rationalized in part by Indian involvement in the war effort, through which Indian people appeared desirous and capable of participation in "mainstream" American culture. In addition, many of the New Deal enhancements to the reservations planned by Collier were canceled once the government turned its attention to the war, leaving the door open for alternative approaches when the war ended. A radically different philosophy of "termination" took hold which emphasized Indian self-sufficiency and the end of any special relationship between Indians and the federal government. For some, termination was the means by which Indians would come to fully exercise their citizenship rights and responsibilities. According to this view, reservations should be abolished because they perpetuated segregation. Others saw termination as a plan for backing out of treaty commitments and removing needed federal protections for Indian tribal rights. In either case it was a policy that fit with postwar trends of modernization and urbanization. Paradoxically, it was also a rejection of New Deal tribalism and a return to the assimilation model of the late nineteenth century.

Congress established the Indian Claims Commission in 1946 to settle any and all remaining treaty violation or other complaints filed by Indians against the federal government, as a first step to ending federal trust responsibilities. Then, in 1953 Congress passed a resolution allowing the termination of federal relations with individual tribes. To the extent that a tribe might continue to rely on government assistance, it was to come from the state rather than from Washington. Subsequently, bills were passed withdrawing federal support from several tribes around the country. On the Plains, the Osages, Iowas, and Quapaws fought off termination; only the Northern Poncas in Nebraska were terminated, and only between 1966 and 1990. But tribes across the Plains felt the general thrust of the policy. In a related measure, the BIA directed Indian students without special needs to attend public schools instead of boarding schools wherever possible. Also in 1953 an act of Congress lifted the ban on off-reservation sale of alcohol to Indians, and permitted liquor sales on Indian lands by local option; as government wards, Indians were previously not allowed to buy liquor, even after the 1933 repeal of Prohibition. Such "emancipating" steps were keenly debated by the National Congress of American Indians, which had been formed in 1944 largely of Plains veterans intent on balancing independence and civil rights with tribal rights.

As part of termination policy, during the 1950s the federal government started programs to relocate Indians from their former and current reservation lands to cities. An Indian urban migration had actually begun during WWII along with the general flow of rural people to the cities for work in the industries supporting the war effort—on some reservations an entire third of the population was away during the war years either in the military or in the defense plants of Los Angeles, Denver, Albuquerque, Tulsa, or Oklahoma City. After the war, relocation was promoted through government programs that assisted with moving, housing, job training, and placement. Destinations included Portland, San Francisco, Oakland, Phoenix, Dallas, Chicago, Milwaukee, Minneapolis, Billings, Montana, and Rapid City and Aberdeen, South Dakota, as well as the other cities named. Thus, today in several cities there are sizeable Indian populations and sometimes small Indian neighborhoods that include Lakotas, Poncas, Cheyennes, Kiowas, and other Plains people. These communities, which include churches, powwows, and social clubs, serve as safety nets for new migrants who initially find city life disorienting.

It was the intention of the relocation programs that Indians would return home from the cities and bring modern views and improvements to reservation life. There is typically continued movement between the cities and country, as urban Indians maintain family ties and visit their home areas. There is also something of a unified urban Indian culture stemming from the mixing of different tribes and common relocation experience. The urban culture is part of the larger phenomenon of "pan-Indianism" or "intertribalism" as described in Chapter 7. The postwar period saw a great deal of cultural sharing and mutual influence among the Plains tribes, and among Indians beyond the Plains, as a result of the greater mobility and communication. People remaining in the rural areas also participated in this sharing. The powwow, whether staged in the country or city, became a major venue for exchange. Oklahoma in particular was an incubator for intertribal identity because many tribes were thrown together there and their separate reservations then obliterated through allotment and state formation. As with prior government programs, the outcomes of termination and relocation were not totally consistent with expectations, since these assimilation efforts actually fostered a renewed sense of Indian cultural pride and identity.

Those Indians who remained in tribal homelands after WWII also sought to modernize by embracing various economic strategies. Tribal development enterprises, in which communal capital was invested in production from local resources, became common. The Montana Blackfoots developed a forest products industry and a famous product, the Blackfeet Indian pencil, which have evolved into the privately owned Blackfeet Writing Instruments, Inc. Other tribes invested in resorts and camps for tourists and scouting groups, gas stations, small garment factories, and other businesses. These concerns were often not successful or highly profitable, but they were the forerunners of some large contemporary tribal businesses, including gambling casinos (see Chapter 13). Another area of economic growth was oil and gas production, which increased across the Plains reservations during WWII. Oil and gas leases became a major source of income for many families in tribes besides the Osages, and the inheritance and retention of mineral rights became a widespread matter of interest. For most rural Plains Indians, the basic means of earning a living continued to be agriculture. In practicality this meant keeping up a small subsistence garden and some livestock while leasing most of one's land to white farmers and cattlemen, and then struggling to collect the lease money with some regularity. So regardless of the early attempts at economic development, the standard of living for most rural Indian families remained woefully low during the postwar period. Those who moved to the cities typically found themselves living below the poverty line too.

The Termination Period was a time when Plains Indians stressed over questions about their place in the modern world. They confronted strong pressure to abandon customary Native life ways as well as the federal trust relationship they had come to rely upon. Also, the wage work that Indians had increasingly adopted since the 1920s promoted individualistic thinking and tested traditional, communal ideals of cooperation and sharing. This was in many ways a gloomy hour in Indian history but repeatedly individuals demonstrated optimism, adaptability, and a willingness to take on the non-Indian world without ceasing to be Indian. Perhaps emblematic of this era, in the arts, was famed ballerina Maria Tallchief (b. 1925). In her career spanning 1949–1965 the Oklahoma-born dancer of mixed Osage/Scots/Irish ancestry achieved the highest levels in a non-Indian dance form, starring with the New York and Monte Carlo ballets.

PERIOD OF SELF-DETERMINATION

If the Indian New Deal was undone during the Termination Period, its spirit returned in modified form during the late 1960s. In this era Indian self-determination, the ability of Native people to control their own destiny, became the guiding principle. As the programs of termination came to

no decisive end, younger Indian leaders committed to greater degrees of collective activity in order to shape policy. Many of these leaders had grown up in urban Indian communities where they lived through the shortcomings of termination policy and learned how to organize for political action.

The larger context for Indian self-determination was an atmosphere of social change that swept the United States. The War on Poverty conceived by President John F. Kennedy and instituted by President Lyndon B. Johnson included a raft of legislation creating new agencies and funding lines to aid the poorest Americans. The civil rights movement that initially focused on the status of African Americans expanded and morphed to address the position of Chicanos, gays, and women in American society. American Indians were increasingly viewed as another oppressed segment of the American population deserving redress and affirmation of their basic rights. The environmentalist movement of the early 1970s also had an impact on the characterization of Native Americans, as Indians were held up as the original ecologists, living in harmony with nature. A memorable image of the period was provided by Iron Eyes Cody (b. 1904; Espera Oscar DeCorti of Italian parents; d. 1999), who acted in "Keep America Beautiful" television commercials, in which an Indian from the past, representing the environmentalist consciousness, starts to cry upon witnessing pollution and littering.

A number of key laws and court decisions were made on behalf of Indians during the 1960s and 1970s. The Indian Civil Rights Act of 1968 extended constitutional protections to those who lived under tribal governments. This was controversial legislation because it allowed Indian plaintiffs to sue for civil rights even against their own tribal governments, but it was step consistent with self-determination. Another provision of the Act was that state governments could not assume control over tribes without their consent, in effect nullifying the termination strategy of shifting federal obligations to the states. In 1978 the BIA modified its policy on schooling to support Indian students' individual choice of where to attend school, rather than advocating a preference for boarding schools, as in the early 1900s, or public schools, as in 1953. During his tenure, President Richard M. Nixon signed several laws that effectively ended termination. And up until 1978 the Indian Claims Commission, originally intended to enable termination, continued to hear cases and make settlements on behalf of Indian plaintiffs. Under this activity, for example, in 1964 the Gros Ventres were compensated for unfair prices paid for an 1888 land cession, and in 1974 the Comanche, Kiowa, and Plains Apache tribes got a $35 million award for unjust allotment dealings.

Indian reservations became eligible for War on Poverty funding and began dealing with numerous federal agencies, often directly rather than through the BIA, to secure grants for housing, job training, education, and economic development. Office of Economic Opportunity programs such as Head Start, which provided medical and dental care and educational programs for preschoolers, became commonplace on Plains reservations. Elementary schools, community colleges, health clinics, and tribal government buildings proliferated. Tribes began replacing the ramshackle wood frame houses that dotted the reservations with sturdy brick homes built under the auspices of the Department of Housing and Urban Development. Many tribes in both the United States and Canada also experienced an influx of wealth through increased oil and gas production during the 1960s and 1970s, particularly following the 1973 Arab oil embargo and 1979 Iranian Revolution, and they worked hard to manage this income and put it to constructive use.

There were also militant expressions of self-determination. Sioux and Omahas were among the 89 American Indians who took control of Alcatraz Island in San Francisco Bay for 19 months beginning in November 1969, citing an 1868 Sioux treaty granting Indians rights to unused federal property (the island was the site of an abandoned federal prison). The most radical and symbolic insurrection took place directly on the Plains. The American Indian Movement (AIM) was founded in 1968 by urban Indians in Minneapolis, including Russell Means (Oglala, b. 1939). Inspired by the civil rights movement, AIM advocated "Red Power" through watchdog activities and dramatic public protests. Means encouraged the group to become active on reservations. In February 1973 AIM members were called to the Pine Ridge Reservation in South Dakota to support a faction attempting to impeach the tribal president, whom it deemed corrupt and beholden to the BIA. The federal government, which viewed AIM as a subversive organization, sent marshals to Pine Ridge to defend the president, his supporters, and the BIA facilities on the reservation. In protest over 200 AIM members, men and women of various tribes including Teton and Kiowa, took up arms and occupied the reservation village of Wounded Knee, site of the infamous 1890 massacre. They kept up the siege for 71 days. In a series of shootouts two protesting Indians were killed and several people on both sides were wounded, and the village was ruined. Lakota medicine man Frank Fools Crow finally negotiated a truce. Some of the protesters became involved in other gunfights, and several went into exile or were jailed. The tribal president remained in office. Though AIM leaders called the siege a landmark event, Wounded Knee turned the feelings of many reservation Indians and the general public against those using violent tactics. As the 1970s progressed, Red Power advocates turned increasingly to legislation rather than forceful protest.

A positive effect of the Red Power movement was an increase in what has been called Red Pride. A fresh and lasting sensibility took hold in which Indian people became openly proud of their history and cultural heritage and committed to fostering Native identity on their own. As National Museum of the American Indian Senior Curator George Horse Capture (Gros Ventre, b. 1937) explains,

> Indian people can feel ashamed of themselves without reason. It all stems from racism. If you go to high school off reservation you have no friends, no girlfriends, you try to fit in, you give everything up. You sit in the back, keep quiet, try to go

FIGURE 12.4 American Indian Movement protesters stand guard outside the village church at Wounded Knee, South Dakota, during the 1973 occupation.

along, try to fit in, but something was missing. You know something is wrong. There's this empty void inside you. You coast along. Work 8-5 jobs. Life is not really worthwhile. But something is growing inside you all those years. Suddenly something like Alcatraz happens. All of those Indians coming together. Even if they didn't have any real goal, just a gathering, it's still very powerful. You realize you're not alone. You share the future, the same goals. Alcatraz—that gave me the strength. You realize that the white man is not going to do it. I have to do something myself. So it's been that way ever since.

(quoted in Nagel 1996:134)

Indians began in earnest to revive their ceremonial traditions and languages. The Sioux Sun Dance revival described in Chapter 10 took place during this period; young Comanches renewed the Tuu Wii (Crow) military society dance in 1976. Traditional arts of all kinds, from tipi painting to German silver metalwork, enjoyed resurgence. Indians started a host of new self-published newspapers and magazines on Native issues. They successfully urged the establishment of university degree programs specializing in American Indian studies. Many tribes began their own language preservation efforts, publishing dictionaries and sponsoring classes uniting elder speakers and young learners. More fundamentally, more people came to accept and admit their Indian heritage. Since 1960 the 10-year federal censuses show a continuous growth in the number of Native Americans. In Texas, for instance, the number of Indians counted has doubled each decade since 1970. Such increases not only are the result of natural increase, but show a greater willingness of people to identify as Indian.

Several Plains Indians stand out as influential in politics and the arts and letters during the rise of self-determination. Russell Means sought office in several state and national elections, albeit unsuccessfully, and later embarked on a film-acting career with some major roles. LaDonna Harris (Comanche; b. 1931), wife of Oklahoma senator Fred R. Harris, was a champion of the War on Poverty, as well as feminist and environmentalist causes, and stood as vice-presidential nominee for the Citizens' Party in the 1980 national election. The celebrated part-Kiowa novelist N. Scott Momaday (b. 1934) won the 1969 Pulitzer Prize for his story about an Indian veteran adjusting to the postwar world, *House Made of Dawn*. Momaday's work brought Native writing into the American and modernist literature mainstreams. The most persistent voice for American Indian rights was Vine Deloria, Jr. (1933–2005). Deloria, a descendant of a prominent family of Yankton tribal leaders and Episcopalian churchmen, headed the National Congress of American Indians during the pivotal mid-1960s. Later, as a lawyer and professor he authored some 20 books on Indian issues; he became best known for his first work, *Custer Died for Your Sins: An Indian Manifesto*, a gripping indictment of American expansionism and its effects on Indians.

The consolidation of Indian self-determination came almost exactly 200 years after the founding of the United States and a century beyond the Battle of the Greasy Grass. The span of Indian history from the early 1800s until the late twentieth century is a defining narrative for today's Native Americans of the Plains, as much an inheritance and charter for them as the traditional mythology which described the limits and opportunities of human existence in times past. In the next chapter we will examine contemporary life and the special issues and challenges that Plains Indian people face today.

FIGURE 12.5   N. Scott Momaday.

Sources: Adams (1995); Ahler (1980); Bernstein (1991); Berthrong (1992); Carlson (1998); Child (1998); Christafferson (2001); Clarkin (2001); Deloria (1969); Dempsey (2001); Eastman (1935); Ellis (1996); Fixico (1998, 2000, 2006); Foster (1991); Fowler (1982, 1987, 2001); Fox (1993); Frantz (1999); Grinnell (1956); Hagan (1976, 1979, 2003); Haley (1998); Hamill (2006); Harris (2000); Hoig (2006); Hosmer and O'Neill (2004); Hoxie (1984); Iverson (1985); Keim (1985); Kelly (1954); La Flesche (1963); Lear (2006); Lemont (2006); Linderman (1962); Lomawaima (1994); Macgregor (1946); McBeth (1983); McFee (1972); McNickle (1973); Meadows (1999, 2002); Means (1995); Michno (1997); Milner (1982); Momaday (2000); Mooney (1907a); Nagel (1996); Neely (1995); Nye (1969); Parks *et al.* (1980); Pratt (1964); Richardson (1933); Rickey (1963); Riney (1999); Stahl (1978); Standing Bear (1933, 1975); Stewart (1955); Szasz (1999); Townsend (2000); Utley (1988); Vandervort (2006); Waddell and Watson (1984); Washburn (1984); and Wright (1951).

CHAPTER SUMMARY

Plains Indian societies faced constant challenges resulting from the expansion of non-Indians into the Plains. After an era of early exploration by white traders and soldiers, there began a cycle of treaties, land cessions, relocations, treaty violations and cancellations, and conflicts. The Prairie tribes were relocated and placed on reservations prior to the Civil War. Following the Civil War, the U.S. government made a concerted drive to contain the nomadic tribes in a series of campaigns known as the Indian Wars. Comanches, Kiowas, and Cheyennes put up strong resistance in the south but were subjugated by 1874. Sioux and Cheyennes defended their northern homelands in an effort that did not fully end until 1890. The pattern of expansion and resistance was similar in Canada. Life on the reservations was a grim time of starvation and population decline. Some reservations were broken up by the early 1900s to allow further white settlement. Missionaries arrived and boarding schools were established to encourage assimilation. By the 1920s, public sympathy turned against assimilationist policies. Indians were granted citizenship and they entered the mainstream economy; some enjoyed oil revenues. The Indian Reorganization Act of 1934 provided for independent tribal governments. World War II encouraged further Indian assimilation. Thereafter the federal government sought to terminate its Indian treaty obligations and services. Many Plains Indians were settled in cities during this era. Since the 1960s, Indian policy has emphasized self-determination. Plains Indians participated in militant civil rights protests in the 1970s. More recently self-determination advocates have made an impact through cultural revival, politics, and the arts.

QUESTIONS FOR REVIEW

1. Reconstruct the Indian War campaigns on the Plains in either the northern or southern United States or Canada. Cite major battles and participants.
2. Support or dispute Lomawaima's statement that the Indian boarding school was "an institutional training ground for the subservience of the colonized." Provide details to sustain your position.
3. What was the Indian New Deal?
4. Trace the origins and evolution of the Red Power movement and explain George Horse Capture's assessment of this movement in his personal life.

CHAPTER 13

CONTEMPORARY PLAINS INDIAN LIFE

In reading most of the literature on Plains Indians, it is easy to form the impression that the people have been frozen in time. The heritage of nomadic horse and buffalo life, the dramatic story of dispossession, and the long struggles for Native rights all frame the image of the Indian in undeniably powerful ways. But contemporary Plains Indian people are not defined only by their heritage and history, but also in the ways they have continued to live as a distinctive part of American and Canadian society into the twenty-first century. This chapter focuses on the modern continuance of Plains Indian culture and examines a variety of issues having to do with acculturation, adjustment and resistance to the power of the nation state, and cultural identity maintenance.

LIFE IN INDIAN COUNTRY

What is daily life like for contemporary Plains Indians? How it is different from or the same as that of non-Indians? To examine these questions, we can visit "Indian Country." This term is often used by Indian people themselves for a composite of the many places in the rural western United States and Canada, including reservations and non-reservation lands, towns, and cities inhabited and frequented by Native Americans. It is a useful concept for discussing general patterns of present-day life.

Landscape

The landscape of the Indian Country is a wide expanse of countryside with occasional town centers and large and small cities. This pattern is essentially the same throughout the Plains region, with minor variation across the small Canadian reserves, the large U.S. northern reservations, and the former reservation lands of Oklahoma. The ratio of Indians to non-Indians in these areas will vary, with a large majority of Indians on some reserves and reservations, versus a proportion of one-fifth or less Indian in the Oklahoma counties.

The large cities of Indian Country include Calgary, Alberta, Omaha, Nebraska, and Oklahoma City, Oklahoma, each of which counts over one million people in its metropolitan area. Smaller cities include Bismarck, North Dakota (population 58,000), Rapid City, South Dakota (150,000), Billings, Montana (100,000), Cheyenne, Wyoming (55,000), and Lawton, Oklahoma (109,000).

Some Indian people live and work in these cities as a very small percentage of the overall population while keeping close ties with relatives in the country. Otherwise, for Indians the cities are occasional destinations for shopping or entertainment. Most of the small country towns have populations ranging from a few hundred to a few thousand, with a majority white population and some Indians. The town center is a white domain, with whites owning or operating the banks, churches, schools, post office, hardware stores, convenience stores, and cafes which form the nucleus of the community. Some Indians may live right in town, in the small houses lining the side streets, but most prefer to live off in the countryside, in homes clustered here and there along miles of latticework dirt and gravel roads.

The typical modern housing of Indian Country is introduced in Chapter 6. Modern dwellings are permanent rectangular structures of the non-Indian type. While many are single-story brick ranches, there are also older style wood frame houses and in some areas also log cabins. Mobile homes are another common alternative, and one source reports that Indians in the 1970s occupied mobile homes at almost twice the rate of whites (Fixico 2006:67). Modern houses are often laid out on a grid plan resembling a suburban neighborhood, without deference to traditional notions of dwelling placement which took into account protection from the prevailing weather, proximity to firewood and fresh water, and the clustering of relatives.

Indian houses seldom have a large amount of floor space or closet space though they may accommodate several people. They afford a lesser degree of privacy than is considered ideal in non-Indian households, but Native standards of privacy and personal space require less distance and seclusion. The dearth of closets and general absence of attics and basements promotes the storage of clothes and personal items in baskets and piles in room corners, not much different from the array of belongings in a tipi. Electric power,

propane, and indoor plumbing are the norms, though not universal. Home furnishings include the most comfortable furniture and nicest appliances that the owners can afford. A television with tape or CD player is often the central focus of the living area.

The yard, usually a rectangle enclosed in fencing, may feature one or more prefabricated metal storage sheds, and perhaps a car port (the houses seldom have garages, either attached or separate) and storm cellar. Sometimes a tradition-oriented family will have a rack in their backyard to store the poles of a tipi they set up for special occasions. The High Plains climate does not favor lush lawns or shrubbery, nor are these priorities in the regional aesthetic. The yard therefore contains dirt and native grasses, with perhaps some decoration of flowers, potted plants, and lawn ornaments. Driveways and parking areas are usually made of dirt of gravel rather than pavement. Cars, trucks, and tractors, working and dead, are parked around the yard. In these features Indian houses are not markedly different from those occupied by neighboring non-Indians of the same economic class.

Relatively few Indian people could afford to own automobiles prior to World War II, and most continued to use horses and wagons. After the war, as the road systems and earning power improved, cars became more common, and nowadays they are considered a necessity. They have fostered more widespread settlement across Native landholdings as well as the habits of far-flung travel that many Plains Indians are known for. Cars are a paradoxical element in Indian culture, because they contribute to materialism, individualism, and isolation, while also permitting congregation and perpetuating the mobility that horse Indians traditionally enjoyed.

In rural areas personal automobiles are the only modern means of transportation. Larger vehicles ride better and last longer on the rough roads of Indian country, and they carry enough people to achieve some of the desired sense of community during travel. The plush family vans that were stylish in the 1970s have been popular, as they ride comfortably on long trips and allow for several passengers plus the storage and changing of clothes necessary at powwows. Pickup trucks and station wagons have also been popular. People worry over the costs of buying and maintaining a car, and filling it with gas, and they typically keep the same vehicle as long as they can to economize. At powwows people make jokes about their dilapidated cars, and one old powwow song memorializes the "one-eyed Ford." New automobiles are sometimes prestige purchases or gifts, as when a family comes into oil money or a young adult receives his or her first share of tribal revenues.

Work and Play

If in the United States and Canada at large one's career is the defining characteristic, this is not so in Indian Country. The kind of work people do or the position they hold is not the primary emphasis in their lives. It is a person's web of relationships to kin and friends that situates him or her in the world, providing dignity and a sense of purpose and spiritual fulfillment. Work is more about feeding everybody and keeping warm. The jobs that Indian people typically take reflect this attitude as much as the kinds of opportunities that are available in Indian Country. In general, both men and women prefer manual labor, service work, or low-level white-collar jobs, in situations where work days are sporadic or workers can take time off without losing their jobs, to ensure that they can tend to family and tribal responsibilities. Men seek wage work as construction workers, agricultural and forestry workers, truck drivers, heavy equipment operators, mechanics, painters, and maintenance personnel. Women work as nurses, seamstresses, pressers, hairdressers, cooks, and custodians. For both genders, there are some other common options, such as school teaching and office work, including secretarial, clerking, and middle management. Military service is also a

highly regarded employment choice for both men and women; unlike the other common options it is an intensive commitment that takes people away from their families, but is consistent with Native values of valor and communal protection.

Throughout Indian Country a large percentage of people work for the government. They may work in various departments of their tribal government, in every capacity from administrators, clerical workers, and health providers to plumbers, foresters, and blackjack dealers. Many work for the state or federal agencies that provide economic and social services to the area. The Bureau of Indian Affairs (BIA) regional offices in particular employ mostly Indians.

Children in Indian Country normally spend their days in school. The reforms to Indian education outlined in Chapter 12 continue to unfold and shape schooling opportunities. One recent important trend is the emergence of tribal contract schools. These schools are financed by the Bureau of Indian Education (BIE) but administered directly by the tribes, in keeping with modern laws and policies for self-determination. (The BIE was formed in 2006 from the BIA Office of Indian Education Programs to function as a distinct and parallel branch of the Department of the Interior focusing on the education responsibilities.) Contract schools have been supplanting those run directly by the BIA. This trend has coupled with a notable increase in the number of public schools in or adjacent to Indian communities that have accepted federal funding to educate Indian students under the Johnson–O'Malley Act. As a result, Indian students find a variety of school settings. At Pine Ridge, for example, by 1982, half of the 22 schools were public, with the rest run by the BIA, the tribe, or religious missions. Almost one-third of the 364 teachers at Pine Ridge at that time were Sioux, trained at the tribal community college. The increase in Native teachers, along with the proliferation of Head Start programs that prepare preschoolers, is another important factor in Indian student success.

Contemporary Plains Indians take part in many of the same sports and games as their non-Indian neighbors. In many cases, these activities are organized in all-Indian leagues, though other times they are pursued in mixed social settings. On some reservations intramural basketball and softball are very popular. Kiowa and Comanche people living in Dallas participate in an Indian bowling league. The annual American Indian Exposition in Anadarko, Oklahoma, features an all-Indian golf tournament. Hunting and fishing are also common pastimes for Indian men, and though some still enjoy bow hunting and other traditional techniques, most use modern guns, rods, and reels. Horse racing is still a popular sport, for example, the racing of the American Paint Horse breed at the Crow Fair, and in southwest Oklahoma greyhound racing is fashionable. The most widespread and overtly "Native" recreational activity is powwow dancing, which has sacred as well as secular value, as described in Chapter 7. In recent years, with the advent of gambling in many Indian locales, the bingo halls and casinos also vie for peoples' time, as discussed below.

Almost every tribal community has a small rodeo, and there is also an all-Indian rodeo circuit that spans the western states and provinces with its own stars and events. The role of Indian cowboy dates to the late nineteenth century, when horse-savvy Indians began working on ranches and in the Wild West shows of Buffalo Bill Cody and Pawnee Bill. In 1912, Tom Three Persons (Blood) won the World Bucking Horse Championship at the Calgary Stampede in Alberta, Canada. Other Plains Indian rodeo champs have included Fred Gladstone (Blood), Cecil Currie, Sr. (Plains Cree), and Tom Reeves (Teton), who won the World Saddle Bronc Championship in 2001. Since the 1960s Indian rodeo has become more organized and professionalized, and regional events have been sequenced to avoid overlap and create a continuous circuit. In 1976, 11 regional associations joined to form the Indian National Finals Rodeo, with finals each year in Albuquerque, New Mexico. The circuit attracts major sponsors such as Ford Motor Company and Levi Strauss and awards over $1 million annually in prize money. The Calgary Stampede remains a major Indian rodeo venue on the Plains, along with the Crow Fair, Cheyenne Frontier Days in Cheyenne, Wyoming, and the Sarcee Indian Rodeo in Bragg Creek, Alberta.

Social Relations

Social life among Indian people today is regulated to some extent by traditional concepts. At home, people remain aware of Native kin structure and terminology, avoidance rules and joking relationships, institutionalized friendship patterns, gender roles, sexual mores, and proper stations of the life cycle, with many of these ideas encoded in the native language if it is spoken. There are many instances of continuation. For example, the strong grandparent–grandchild bond of old is activated in the care of children when parents separate or leave home to find work. Fictive kinship is still prevalent. Rules about mother-in-law avoidance and menstrual taboos are still in evidence. Public gatherings such as powwows, hand games, and church services provide settings for the reaffirmation of these ideas by ceremonial leaders and elders. In both private and public settings, however, one can see individuals continually deciding between older Native attitudes and practices and newer non-Indian ones that they have absorbed through observation, education, and the massive onslaught of print and electronic media.

Relations between Indians and whites in the small towns of Indian Country are characterized by mutual dependence and mild racial prejudice. Whites express resentment about the Indians' reliance on entitlement programs, their apparent reluctance to work and pay bills on time, and their seemingly aimless lifestyle. Indians hold themselves morally superior to the whites, whom they stereotype as profiteers determined to cheat Indians out of what little they have left. These attitudes are rarely expressed in confrontation, however. In business interactions, feelings engendered by stereotype are masked by a cordial formality, and interpersonal relations between Indians and whites are often truly cordial and caring.

The way that Indians and whites construct self-images and manage their interactions and impressions of each other has been called "face work," following the influential sociologist Erving Goffman (1959). Plains Indian face work has been examined in detail for the Plains Crees (Braroe 1975) and Comanches (Foster 1991). The premise for interaction is that Indian people feel that they are different and not fully part of the larger society. Reservations and boarding schools create administrative and physical forms of segregation. Older Indians remember that there were other places where Indians also suffered overt segregation. More recently subtle discrimination is more evident; for instance, Indians are frequently made to feel unwelcome in the local governments, businesses, and social events of white town centers.

The degree of separateness between Indian and white people who live in overlapping communities can seem startling to outsiders. I (author) experienced this reaction first-hand when beginning fieldwork in Oklahoma in 1982. During my first week living in a rural Comanche household, I went into the nearest small town to deposit my research grant funds. A friendly conversation ensued with the bank president, a young white man, about my background and reasons for being in the area. Some days later I was in town again and found myself talking with the woman who ran the five-and-ten-cent store, and who, it turned out, was the mother of the bank president and already had heard all about me. The Fourth of July was approaching and the woman asked about my plans for the day. I told her that I had been invited to attend a big powwow in the countryside; Fourth of July is a major powwow day and I (a non-Indian) was excited to be witnessing Indian culture. The woman seemed to assume that I was going to the powwow mainly out of courtesy to my Indian hosts. She appeared bothered that a non-Indian would have to spend the holiday with Indians. In a kindly if not pitying manner she invited me to the town celebration instead, which she noted as if to overcome any reluctance on my part, would feature fireworks and ice cream. It was apparent that this white town person had no sense of the richness of experience that a powwow could offer. I politely declined her invitation. At that moment, I realized that Indian and non-Indian neighbors could live in very separate worlds.

In such polarized settings, both Indians and whites often react to each other in ways that are culturally scripted and which tend to reaffirm notions of difference that each group holds of the other. These reactions are most often seen when Indians "trade at" (do business with) white-owned stores and services. Whites may adopt an authoritative tone that suggests that their Indian customer is not fully competent. They may make strong eye contact, ask direct questions which sound aggressive to the Indian ear, or insist on making small talk in the customary white manner of relieving social tension. Indians "push back" by adopting a stereotypically dour expression, remaining passive or silent to the point of discomfort, and purposefully disregarding other white conventions of politeness. Minor exchanges become performances in which representatives of each ethnic group live up to each other's worst expectations. (Again, however, there are many individual cases where antagonism is not evident).

These strategies of interaction are not applicable or necessary when Indians deal with each other, but the face work concept is also useful in looking at relations between Indians within their tribal communities. Here the traditional notion of honor persists, and one must live up to others' best expectations. A person appears honorable by respecting elders and nurturing children, by being generous, and by being available, active, and knowledgeable in family and tribal ceremonies and other cultural and recreational activities. Most of all, perhaps, the honorable person knows, and is seen as living in accordance with, the morals and values that underlie public expressions of tribal identity. Like the proverbial Cheyenne chief who dismisses most problems as petty annoyances beneath his attention (Chapter 4), the modern Indian person conducting face work ignores or suppresses conflict over minor disagreements so that everyone can get along and no one's self-interest is highlighted. In all matters there is a mentality of being under the scrutiny of one's neighbors. As Comanche elder Haddon Nauni put it in 1985,

> A Comanche, everything he does, he doesn't do it without basis or meaning. Whatever we do or are involved in has a purpose. If they can't do something that has meaning, then they just won't do it. He participates as one of us. He knows all the meanings. There's a purpose to everything. Respect the purpose by conducting yourself in a dignified manner. Your life was an open book to your people. You grew up in their sight. Your life is still an open book. It keeps you in line, if you care.
>
> (quoted in Foster 1991)

The Economic Picture

Even though the foregoing review of contemporary life reveals much similarity in the lifestyles of Indians and non-Indians, the general experience of Indian people is colored by a persistent underlying factor: grinding poverty. A comprehensive study by geographer Klaus Frantz (1999) shows that, although Indians have made great economic strides in recent decades, owing largely to increased federal assistance, they remain, along with African Americans, one of two most disadvantaged racial groups in the United States.

This position is evident from the figures for Indian life expectancy, health, housing, educational attainment, unemployment, and income.

Income statistics for Indians are cloudy because significant portions of their annual earnings may come from unreported sources such as giveaways, crafts sales, hunting, gathering, gardening, and church charities, as well as government food stamps and health assistance. But even with this caveat Indian income figures are strikingly low, with the average per-capita income in 1980 only 58 percent of that of non-Indians. The disparity is most severe on reservations, including those on the Plains, which show a poverty rate six times that for whites. Shannon County, South Dakota, which corresponds to the western half of the Pine Ridge (Sioux) Reservation, is consistently listed as the poorest county in the entire United States. Even on the most affluent Plains reservation, the Osage Reservation in Oklahoma, 16 percent of people lived below the poverty line in 1980, and the average income level for residents fell short of the U.S. average.

Traditional Indian values that put collective well-being before individual gain continue to influence the economies of reservations and other close-knit Indian communities. An emphasis on sharing among kin and friends contradicts the Euro-American standards of wealth accumulation, investment, and saving for the future with a definite purposes in mind, such as retirement or buying a larger house. Little value is placed on establishing good payment records or credit ratings. The individualism and independence that lead to competitive success in the money economy is antithetical to the collective sensibility; decisive action on the part of one person challenges both the authority of elders and the notion of communal consensus. If a person is seen to be energetically pursuing prosperity, it brings suspicion that he or she is not living up to traditional values and may even be planning to abandon his or her kin.

These attitudes, known in anthropological parlance as "leveling mechanisms," help explain many Indians' individual choices about jobs as noted above. They also explain the collective dynamic in Indian communities, where there is relatively little incentive for the planning, investment, or entrepreneurship necessary for private business development. A quite natural resistance to change and understandable fear that government subsidies would be discontinued also diminish ambition. In many places there is frequent turnover in the tribal government that reflects the lack of long-term perspective and makes economic development even less likely. Federal and tribal business development initiatives do not find fertile ground in such an atmosphere.

It would irresponsible simply to blame Indian economic hardship on Native attitudes alone, however. The limited resource base on many Indian lands, lack of collateral, dearth of outside capital, and great distances from major markets all play primary parts in discouraging business development in Indian Country. On the High Plains particularly, a region that is being abandoned by the non-Indian majority precisely because of these same limitations (Chapter 1), chances for Indian economic growth are not strong. Innovative development concepts such as ecotourism remain largely pipe dreams, with some notable exceptions, such as the reestablishment of tribal bison herds and grasslands. Perhaps the only viable trend has been the widespread establishment of gambling casinos on Indian lands (see below).

High unemployment is a scourge in Indian Country, with the rate for Indians in many areas much more than the U.S. and Canadian national averages, which are typically reported in the 4–7 percent range. According to Frantz (1999:128–130), exact unemployment numbers for Indians are difficult to come by. The U.S. census, BIA, and tribal governments may count people differently. For example, the census does not count as unemployed people who are able to work but have given up looking for jobs, while the BIA does. The BIA counts people with

occasional craft income as employed, while tribes may not. And, it is hard to distinguish between unemployed and underemployed people, especially in rural areas where much work is seasonal. Thus in 1980, when the U.S. national average was 7.1 percent, the overall unemployment rate for all rural Indians was 15 percent according to the U.S. census; however, in 1985, when the U.S. national average was 7.2 percent, unemployment on the Crow Indian Reservation in Montana was at 64 percent according to the BIA, or 80 percent according to the Crow Tribe. Other BIA unemployment rates for Plains reservations in 1985 included 17 percent for the Osage (Oklahoma), 27 percent for the Flathead (Montana), 72 percent at Pine Ridge (Sioux, South Dakota), and 86 percent at Rosebud (Sioux, South Dakota).

Wages and salaries therefore do not always play a big part in Indian household income. More income is derived from other sources. Non-Indians often think that Indians receive money from the federal or state government simply for being Indian, but this perception is inaccurate. Individuals may receive payments through their tribe made by the federal government to fulfill treaty obligations or to pay settlements for lost lands that have been adjudicated after the early treaties. They may collect rent on lands, and royalties on oil, gas, and timber, owned individually or tribally. If their tribe has any business enterprises, such as factories, shops, or casinos, they may receive per-capita payments that divide the profits among tribe members. In addition, those who qualify are eligible for essentially the same federal and state assistance programs available to low-income citizens generally, including welfare, unemployment insurance, and food stamps. Health care costs may be offset by Medicare, Medicaid, or services provided by the Indian Health Service (IHS), a branch of the U.S. Department of Health and Human Services. Any or all of these income sources may be available depending on

FIGURE 13.1 *Tribe member Elouise Cobell with oil pump on the Blackfeet Indian Reservation near Browning, Montana.*

the tribe and the individual, and whether the person lives on or off reservation.

Education is often cited as the avenue out of poverty. Federal and tribal governments spend a lot on schooling, and in 1985 one-fourth of all U.S. federal expenditures for American Indians went to education—only health programs received more funding. In recent decades, the numbers of Plains Indians completing elementary and high school have risen steadily, though they still lag behind national averages. The disincentives for Indians completing school are economic and cultural. Poor transportation and the need to contribute to the household economy, both reflections of rural or urban poverty, are sometimes cited as reasons for dropping out. Some young Indians find little interest in curricula that disregard Indian history and culture while reinforcing the languages and values of alien ethnicities. But the bases for these objections are being moderated. It is becoming increasingly easier for rural Indians to attend school, and classes are gradually being made more culturally relevant, so that the trend in Indian elementary and secondary education is guardedly positive.

Relatively few people in Indian Country attend college or obtain a college degree. Whereas 1 in 3 Asian Americans and 1 in 6 Euro-Americans completes at least four years of college, among American Indians the ratio is 1 in 13. Few major U.S. universities can boast an Indian student population of 1 percent, which would match the percentage of Native Americans in the total U.S. population. The smaller universities within Indian Country do a somewhat better job in enrolling Indians; for instance, Cameron University in Lawton, Oklahoma, the heart of Kiowa and Comanche country, enrolled 431 or 8 percent American Indians in 2007, where Indians make up 5–20 percent of the population in surrounding counties. In rural Canada some small non-tribal universities focus on Aboriginal culture and workforce development and draw heavy First Nations participation. And the old BIA colleges such as Haskell attract Indian students exclusively, though only in small total numbers. Overall, college is still not an option for the majority of Indian people.

There are many notable exceptions to the general pattern. The late Vine Deloria, Jr., earned a law degree from the University of Colorado. Filmmaker Lily Shangreaux (Oglala Lakota) holds a B.A. in psychology from Princeton, and Wallace Coffey, past Comanche Tribal Chairman, is a Harvard graduate. The rise in number of American Indian Studies programs and courses at major universities is sometimes cited as a factor promoting greater Indian participation in higher education, but while these programs signal commitment to including Native history and cultural perspectives in the curriculum, they have had little effect on the overall number of Indian graduates. There has, however, been an increase in college attendance at local institutions, mainly because many tribes or intertribal consortia have now established their own colleges with the assistance of the federal government. Others are in the process of doing so. This trend is analogous to the rise of tribal contract schools at the elementary and secondary levels.

Tribal and intertribal colleges are formed on the two-year community college model although some have expanded to offer four-year and graduate degrees. Fledgling institutions often partner with one or more non-Indian public universities to secure accreditation and extend their curricula beyond what they can offer locally. Indian-run colleges focus on degree programs that are thought to be most useful in promoting employment for their populations, such as agricultural science, natural resource management, business, education, nursing, social work, hospitality and gaming, museum management, and tribal administration.

They feature open admissions policies and make good use of distance learning technologies that allow students to complete courses from home. Indian-run colleges also offer degrees in tribal studies and take other measures to endorse Native history and culture. Little Big Horn College, for instance, conducts all student and business services in the Crow language. A list of Indian-run colleges on the Plains is provided in Table 13.1.

The net result of larger economic factors is that Indian household economies often have a boom-and-bust quality. Poverty is pervasive in preventing Indians from pursuing the basic level of security that many Americans take for granted, and they cannot afford the amenities that many Americans have come to think of as necessities. For example, the usual procedure of taking a bank loan to build a house is often not an option for Indians because tribal land cannot be put up for collateral. When they depend instead on federally subsidized housing, the houses are usually not well built and they find themselves trying to pay unusually high heating, cooling, and maintenance costs. One-fifth of all Indian households lacked a motor vehicle in 1980. In many rural Indian homes, there is no expectation of having steady telephone service, though people will contract for it during spells when they can pay the bills. In 1980, 41 percent of homes on the Crow Reservation and 63 percent on the Rosebud (Sioux) Reservation lacked telephones. In the same year one-fourth of homes on the Pine Ridge Reservation lacked running water. These conditions make it hard for people to stay healthy, to work, and to go to school, and thus is born a vicious cycle that makes it difficult if not impossible to rise out of poverty. So while Plains Indians are largely tied into the national economy and have access to technology and products as do non-Indians, the specter of despair hovers close by, and their participation in the "American Dream," to the extent they wish it, is at best incomplete.

TABLE 13.1   Indian-run Colleges on the Plains

INSTITUTION	MAIN CAMPUS LOCATION	DATE FOUNDED	HIGHEST DEGREE AWARDED	TRIBE(S) SERVED
Blackfeet Community College	Browning, MT	1974	Associate's	Blackfoot
Blue Quills First Nations College	St. Paul, AB	1971	Bachelor's	Plains Cree
Cankdeska Cikana Community College	Fort Totten, ND	1970	Associates	Yankton, Yanktonais
Chief Dull Knife College	Lame Deer, MT	1975	Associate's	Northern Cheyenne
First Nations University of Canada	Regina, SK	1976	Master's	Plains Cree
Fort Belknap Community College	Harlem, MT	1984	Associate's	Grow Ventre, Assiniboine
Fort Berthold Community College	New Town, ND	1973	Associate's	Mandan, Hidatsa, Arikara
Fort Peck Community College	Poplar, MT	1978	Associate's	Assiniboine, Sioux
Little Big Horn College	Crow Agency, MT	1980	Associate's	Crow
Nebraska Indian Community College	Macy, NE	1981	Associate's	Omaha, Santee
Oglala Lakota College	Kyle, SD	1971	Master's	Teton
Red Crow Community College	Cardston, AB	1986	Master's	Blood
Sitting Bull College	Fort Yates, ND	1973	Bachelor's	Teton, Yankton, Yanktonais
Sisseton Wahpeton College	Sisseton, SD	1979	Associate's	Santee
Stone Child College	Box Elder, MT	1984	Associate's	Plains Cree, Plains Ojibwa
Sinte Gleska University	Mission, SD	1970	Master's	Teton
Turtle Mountain Community College	Belcourt, ND	1972	Bachelor's	Plains Ojibwa
Yellowquill College	Winnipeg, MB	1984	Certificate	Plains Ojibwa

CONTEMPORARY ISSUES

Tribal Sovereignty

Remedies to social and economic disadvantages are often pursued through modern tribal governments. These governments gain some traction within state and national political spheres because, theoretically at least, they are sovereign nations within the larger nations of the United States and Canada. The inherent right of indigenous nations to govern themselves has been recognized and debated through philosophical argument from the earliest days of European intrusion into the New World. For contemporary Plains tribes, sovereignty is granted under federal law. In the United States, tribal sovereignty is established in the U.S Constitution, Article 1, Section 8, clause 3, which designates tribes along with the states and foreign nations as sovereign entities. This status is also confirmed in Article II of the Constitution, the part dealing with treaty-making.

The treaties actually signed by the U.S. government with various tribes further bear out the notion of tribal sovereignty. In Canada, sovereignty has been later in coming, and has a different character. The Royal Commission on Aboriginal Peoples (RCAP) convened between 1991 and 1996, recognized the inherent right of First Nations people to self-government, and recommended establishment and financing of a nationwide Aboriginal government to negotiate with the Canadian national and provincial governments. Specific steps to implement the RCAP plan are still underway.

As the sovereign power of tribal governments has grown, they have assumed more direct responsibility for the well-being of their constituents. Consequently, the BIA, INAC (Indian and Northern Affairs Canada), and other federal agencies have reduced their direct obligations, and increasingly they work with the tribes in consulting rather than management roles. Modern tribal governments take the lead in providing housing, social services, and education. They pursue organized action on behalf of their members in such matters as the settlement of land claims, repatriation of cultural materials, and protection of sacred sites. And they manage tribal affairs by negotiating with state and federal governments to determine the criteria for membership, tracking tribal enrollments, and running elections to furnish continuous leadership. Tribal governments also play a key role in economic planning and development.

Gaming

Many Plains tribes have participated in the trend of Indian tribal involvement in the gaming industry. Tribal sovereignty allows the establishment of bingo parlors and casinos whether or not gambling is legal in the surrounding area, and in fact where gambling is otherwise prohibited, Indian establishments have a monopoly. Gaming operations bring profits into Indian communities that are distributed in two ways: as wages for those working the games and associated restaurants and other businesses;

and in payments to tribe members according to tribal policy.

As mentioned in Chapter 5, wagering games were an essential part of traditional Indian life, and to some degree modern Indian gaming is a continuation of Native practice. The original Indian games such as plum-pit dice and the hand game, however, though they are still played, are not the basis for commercial gambling; instead, tribes have adopted non-Indian games for this purpose. Bingo is an American version of a game known as lotto that is traceable to renaissance Europe. Players receive cards with grids of numbers. An emcee draws and calls out numbers at random and the first player to mark a complete row of numbers and call out wins the game. Other games include slot machines, roulette, the dice game called craps, and the card games blackjack and poker.

Tribal bingo was pioneered by the Seminole tribe of Florida in 1979, and the idea quickly spread across the United States. By the early 1980s a number of tribes had sophisticated games. The small Otoe tribe, for example, managed a high-tech, high-stakes game in Red Rock, Oklahoma, by far Noble County's largest tourist attraction, which drew players from all over the region, who chartered buses, reserved motel rooms, and played for over $10,000 in prize money each night.

The author witnessed the advent of Comanche tribal bingo in July 1983 modeled on the big operations elsewhere in Oklahoma. On the opening night the grand prize was a new car, the first of many extravagant prizes offered periodically in addition to the usual cash winnings. The tribal complex gymnasium on Highway 44 north of Lawton, Oklahoma, was furnished with a podium, bingo machine (a blower that randomly releases numbered ping-pong balls), flashboard (large electric sign to show the numbers), many long tables with chairs, a concessions stand, a smoke shop, attendants in Las Vegas–style croupier outfits, armed security guards, and closed-circuit television monitors so that the players could watch the numbers being drawn from any seat in the house. A large sign advertised the game to those passing by on the highway, and when a car, truck, or boat was available as the grand prize, it was parked outside for all to admire. The game ran seven nights a week from 5:30 P.M. until 10:30 P.M., with afternoon sessions added on Sundays. The gym held 500 people and was filled nearly every night. Players bought a packet of "hard [cardboard] cards" and "paper cards" for 18 dollars, and experienced players bought as many extra cards as they could keep track of. Throughout the night players also tried their luck by peeling apart instant lottery cards called "rip-offs," purchased at a booth by the concessions stand for anywhere from 75 cents to several dollars, the prize commensurate with the price. Each week $120,000 in bingo prize money was available, though less than this was usually taken home. Each week the tribe earned thousands of dollars, all free of federal, state, and local tax. Tribal bingo games all around the Plains are still much the same as this, except that the "buy-ins" (price of basic card packet), "payouts" (prize

totals), and tribal revenues are appreciably larger than in 1983.

Since the mid-1980s, the big story in Indian gaming is the proliferation of tribal casinos from Canada to Oklahoma. These have varied from small installations of slot machines at crossroad convenience stores to multimillion-dollar resorts featuring poker, blackjack, craps, slots, bingo, a smoke shop, 24-hour grill, multiple bars, recreational vehicle hookups, truck parking, overnight accommodations, and shuttles to area hotels. Plains tribes now often operate three or more casinos in some combination of small and large facilities. In Oklahoma, where there is a dense concentration of different tribes, there is considerable competition, with some tribes, such as the Pawnees, pursuing vigorous development strategies to capture the largest share of gambling traffic. In Saskatchewan and Manitoba, where there are many small, scattered tribal communities, tribal or intertribal federations have been formed to manage casinos. Table 13.2 lists Native-run casinos on the Plains.

TABLE 13.2   Casinos Operated by Plains Indian Tribes

TRIBE OR CONSORTIUM	CASINO	LOCATION
Arapaho, Northern	Little Wind Casino	Ethete, WY
	Wind River Casino	Riverton, WY
Arikara, Hidatsa, Mandan	4 Bears Casino	New Town, ND
Assiniboine and Gros Ventre	Fort Belknap Casino	Fort Belknap, MT
Assiniboine and Sioux	Silverwolf Casino	Wolf Point. MT
Blackfoot	Blackfoot Satellite Casino	Blackfoot, ID
	Discovery Lodge Casino	Cut Bank, MT
	Glacier Peaks Casino	Browning, MT
	Park Lodge Casino	East Glacier Park, MT
Cheyenne, Northern	Charging Horse Casino	Lame Deer. MT
Cheyenne and Arapaho	Feather Warrior Casino	Canton, OK
	Feather Warrior Casino	Watonga, OK
	Lucky Star Casino	Concho, OK
Comanche	Comanche Nation Games	Lawton, OK
	Comanche Red River Casino	Devol, OK
	Comanche Spur Casino	Elgin, OK
	Comanche Star Casino	Walters, OK
Crow	Little Big Horn Casino	Crow Agency, MT

(continued)

TABLE 13.2   Continued

TRIBE OR CONSORTIUM	CASINO	LOCATION
Federation of Saskatchewan Indian Nations	Casino Moose Jaw	Moose Jaw, SK
Iowa	Casino White Cloud	White Cloud, KS
	Cimarron Casino	Perkins, OK
Kansas	Southwind Casino	Newkirk, OK
Kiowa	Kiowa Casino	Devol, OK
Osage	Million Dollar Elm Casino	Bartlesville, OK
	Million Dollar Elm Casino	Hominy, OK
	Million Dollar Elm Casino	Pawhuska, OK
	Million Dollar Elm Casino	Ponca City, OK
	Million Dollar Elm Casino	Sand Springs, OK
	Million Dollar Elm Casino	Skiatook, OK
	Million Dollar Elm Casino	Tulsa, OK
Otoe-Missouria	First Council Casino	Newkirk, OK
	Lil' Bit of Paradise Casino	Newkirk, OK
	7 Clans Paradise Casino	Red Rock, OK
Pawnee	Pawnee Nation Casino	Pawnee, OK
	Pawnee Nation Casino	Stillwater, OK
Plains Apache	Silver Buffalo Casino	Anadarko, OK
Plains Cree	River Cree Resort	Enoch, AB
Plains Cree and Plains Ojibwa	4C's Cafe and Casino	Box Elder, MT
	Northern Winz Casino	Box Elder, MT
Plains Ojibwa	Sky Dancer Casino	Belcourt, ND
Ponca	Blue Star Gaming and Casino	Ponca City, OK
	Fancy Dance Casino	Chilocco. OK
Santee	Dakota Connection Casino	Sisseton, SD
	Dakota Magic Casino	Hankinson, ND
	Dakota Sioux Casino	Watertown, SD
	Jackpot Junction Casino	Morton, MN
	Little Six Casino	Prior Lake, MN
	Mystic Lake Casino	Prior Lake, MN
	Ohiya Casino	Niobrara, NE
	Prairie's Edge Casino	Granite Falls, MN
	Royal River Casino	Flandreau, SD
	Spirit Lake Casino	St. Michael, ND
	Treasure Island Resort and Casino	Welch, MN
Santee and Teton	Lone Star Casino	Ft. Thompson, SD
Sarcee	Grey Eagle Casino	Calgary, AB
Saskatchewan Indian and Gaming Authority	Bear Claw Casino	Carlyle, SK
	Casino Regina	Regina, SK
	Dakota Dunes Casino	Saskatoon, SK
	Gold Eagle Casino	North Battleford, SK
	Northern Lights Casino	Prince Albert, SK
	Painted Hand Casino	Yorkton, SK

Stoney	Eagle River Casino	Whitecourt, AB
	Stoney Nakoda Resort Casino	Junction Hwy 1 and Hwy 40, AB
Teton	Golden Buffalo Casino	Lower Brule, SD
	Grand River Casino	Mobridge, SD
	Prairie Wind Casino	Pine Ridge, SD
	Rosebud Casino	Hwy 83 and SD/NE State Line
Tonkawa	Native Lights Casino	Newkirk, OK
	Tonkawa Indian Casino	Tonkawa, OK
Yankton-Yanktonais	Fort Randall Casino	Pickstown, SD
	Prairie Knights Casino	Fort Yates, ND
Wichita and Affiliated Tribes	Sugar Creek Casino	Hinton, OK

Gaming has been referred to as the "New Buffalo" because for many Plains Indian populations it has become the center of the economy. It is beneficial in bringing a steady tax-free income that is largely from outside the tribe and not based on limited natural resources. It also brings job opportunities for a cross-section of the tribal population, including teenagers and young adults. It provides the kind of local, semiskilled, flexible work that many Indian people prefer and pays relatively good wages. Gaming is also an economic and social context in which Indian people can remain in control while dealing with outsiders. Non-Indian supporters of tribal gaming often point to the prosperity that it can bring, its effect in promoting the acceptance of capitalism, and the progressive face it puts on tribal cultures as they seek to interact with the larger society.

There are, however, many opponents of Indian gaming enterprises. Within the tribes there are those who feel that gaming diverts people from important activities, such as family care, traditional pastimes such as the powwow, and other jobs that would be better for personal and spiritual development. Some worry that the per-capita payments that come from gambling are a disincentive to young people to work at all. Ironically, demands on entitlement programs sometimes increase with the advent of gaming: unemployment insurance claims actually go up because casinos provide more jobs that can be lost or left. Those influenced by Christianity feel that gambling is immoral, and many fear that it is addictive and causes people to spend beyond their means. And there are continual doubts about how much income is brought in and whether it is being distributed fairly. Advocates for the games counter that people spend beyond their means anyway, but at least in the case of Indian gaming the money stays within the tribe, and thus it is comparable to the powwow giveaway and other traditional forms of redistribution. Tribal gaming is a continual matter of controversy. In the 1984 Comanche tribal elections, bingo became the major issue; the candidates who vowed to stop the games lost the election. This scenario has played out again many times across the Plains, as gaming advocates almost always prevail.

Health

Health care accounts for the largest proportion of federal funding to Indian nations, and it is a major focus of the services provided by tribal governments. In the United States, the IHS provides medical and public health services to individuals and tribes. The IHS was established in 1955; prior to that, medical and health services were part of the BIA mission. The IHS runs a large network of

FIGURE 13.2 Mystic Lake Casino, owned and operated by the Shakopee Mdewakanton Sioux Community (Santees) at Prior Lake, Minnesota.

hospitals and clinics in tribal communities and urban Indian enclaves that are open to all members of federally recognized tribes, and also pursues sanitation projects and health education and training efforts around such themes as pre-natal care, well-baby care, and suicide prevention. In the same way that tribal governments may assume responsibility for services previously furnished by the BIA, they may also contract with IHS for specific services or take over those services. In Canada, the Medical Services Branch of the Department of Health and Welfare functions in the same manner. And similarly, a policy in Canada known as "health transfer" encourages First Nations communities to assume control of health care services as a matter of self-determination. Tribe members also often seek care from traditional medicine practitioners who have apprenticed to elders and learned about cures and supernatural power manipulation. Patients may partake in Euro-American medical

and health services and undergo traditional treatments either exclusively or in tandem.

The health problems that most trouble Indian people are those characteristic of poor rural and urban populations and include malnutrition, tuberculosis, sexually transmitted diseases, cancer, cardiovascular disease, liver disease, and diabetes. Though tuberculosis has been on the wane, most of these illnesses persist in Indian populations and appear among Indians at estimated rates of 2–10 times the national averages. Such diseases are often interrelated and individuals suffer from multiple problems; some are inherited conditions with genetic grounding that may be more prevalent among Native populations. There are also culturally specific conditions, including Windigo psychosis among the Crees and Ojibwas, which is a fear of turning into a cannibal monster that may manifest in anxiety and violent behavior, and ghost sickness—illness inflicted by a ghostly scare—prevalent in Southern Plains cultures, which results in facial paralysis (alternately identified as Bell's palsy) and general health decline. These culturally patterned illnesses have become rare as modernization proceeds, but where they still occur they are typically cured with traditional medicine practices.

Suicide, homicide, and fatal accidents are also more frequent among Native Americans than in the general population. These causes of death combine with disease to result in unusually negative patterns. Mortality rates from most causes are higher for Indians than for any other ethnic group. Life expectancy for Indians is notably shorter than for members of other groups. Therefore, even though Indians have higher birth rates than American whites or blacks, significantly fewer Indians survive past age 50, so that among Indians the elderly constitute a smaller percentage of the overall population. "If one takes these statistics into consideration, it would appear justifiable to compare the age structures of the aboriginal population of the United States with the population of a developing country" (Frantz 1999:104).

Substance abuse, especially alcoholism, is another major Indian health issue which correlates with maladies such as liver failure and also with high rates of suicide, homicide, and accidental death. Medical anthropologist Luis Kemnitzer, who worked among the Lakotas, maintained that Indian alcohol use should not be considered as a category of medical study, but is better understood as a cultural phenomenon that occurs in a broad context of oppression and revitalization. While there is merit to this argument, which brings due attention to social forces and implies the general question of whether alcoholism is truly a "disease," the fact remains that alcohol use is frequently intensive and a contributing factor to various health threats, and it is nowadays routinely addressed as a matter of health by non-Indian specialists and by tribal authorities as well.

Since colonial times, the image of the drunken Indian has been a persistent stereotype in American and Canadian culture. Most North American tribes, including those on the Plains, did not brew alcohol. Liquor was introduced to them by non-Indians, as a trade item, often with the purpose of disrupting their lives so that they could be more easily cheated and relocated. Today, alcoholism is a problem for individual Indians and certain Native communities and the issue requires serious study to separate fact from fiction.

The perceived prevalence of alcoholism in Indian society has led to many general theories of its causes. One theory poses that Indian people have a distinctive metabolism which makes them prone to the effects of alcohol. This theory cannot be rejected out of hand, because there are dietary studies suggesting that at least some Indians do have different metabolic patterns than non-Indians, owing to selective pressure on their hunter-gatherer ancestors for body types that store lots of food energy. It is also reasonable to speculate that there is a genetic makeup that allows the human body to process alcohol, and that Indians might not have developed and passed on this makeup because most did not have alcohol in their cultures over the long course of evolution. And alcoholism does run in families, again suggesting an inherited component. But at present there is no definitive evidence that genetic differences affect Indians' ability to metabolize alcohol, "hold their liquor," or resist addiction.

Other theories emphasize the social disadvantages of joblessness, boredom, poverty, and racial discrimination that would lead people to seek escape through intoxication. These ills are well documented in Plains Indian populations. Poverty and boredom, and sometimes discrimination, are prevalent in non-Indian populations in the rural west as well, and it is really an open question whether Indians seek escape through alcohol abuse in disproportionate numbers compared to non-Indians. It is, however, clear that there is a style of drinking behavior common among Indian people (as well as some non-Indians) which makes alcohol abuse conspicuous. Analysts distinguish between chronic alcoholism, marked by dependence and bodily deterioration, and binge drinking; more Indian alcohol abuse falls in the latter category. In the binge pattern, drinkers imbibe heavily for a few days at a time, interrupting their normal patterns of work and home life. They hide in a tavern, or travel over the countryside from bar to bar, or find some out-of-the-way place outside. During these spells, normally quiet individuals may become angry and outspoken. They get into brawls, are arrested, and suffer short jail terms and fines, and their names are listed in newspaper reports. Or, they simply turn up, passed out, in some public place. Much of the drinking and associated behavior therefore occurs in visible settings, which only reinforces the image of the drunken Indian.

In a frank and insightful assessment, ethnographer Niels Braroe, who worked in a Canadian Plains Cree community, sees Indian alcohol abuse as part of the complex script for Indian–white interaction. He explains public drunkenness as a means of social commentary in which contrasting ethnic values are highlighted through irony:

> For whatever reasons Indians drink, though, I think that one important element in their doing so openly is that they do not identify their behavior as specifically and exclusively Indian. Although Whites see Indians as a special group of congenital alcoholics, Indians themselves know that their behavior is little different from that of many White men. Indians are quick to cite the fact that on Saturday nights the Short Grass pubs are filled with drunken, boisterous cowboys, some of whom seek Indian company to continue drinking on the reserve or at the nuisance grounds [edge of town] after closing time. And there are always as many or more Whites mentioned in the police court [newspaper] column. Indians therefore see drinking as a sort of behavior learned from Whites, and even encouraged by some of them; indeed, until drinking rights were recently granted Indians had to rely on illegal White assistance to secure alcohol. In sum, Indians do not see their own behavior with regard to drinking as setting them apart from Whites.
>
> (Braroe 1975:139–140)

Various other studies have shed light on the characteristics of Indian alcohol abuse. Recall (Chapter 12) that alcohol sales on U.S. Indian land are permitted or banned by local option; several reservations still prohibit liquor. Prohibition on a reservation or in corresponding "dry" counties fosters particular attitudes and actions—secrecy and bootlegging—that stigmatize those who drink and cause those who want to drink to consume large quantities quickly to avoid detection. Prohibition also glamorizes drinking as a relatively nonconfrontational "outlaw" or resistance activity. This appeal is sometimes apparent in the common practice of peer-group drinking, in which age-mates, often young people, gather to get drunk as a form of rebellious recreation. Peer pressure makes it difficult for someone who wants to stop drinking to do so, especially since it is very hard to avoid other family members and friends who drink in the small, isolated rural communities or urban enclaves where Indians live. Other Indian drinkers match the profile termed "anxiety drinkers" by analysts, and tend to drink by themselves to forget their worries. So there are in fact a number of drinking styles and motivations.

Studies have also shown that the prevalence of drinking varies by tribe and by age within tribes. Another important line of inquiry concerns those people who have given up drinking altogether, and how they are able to do so. Some tribal populations show an unusually high number of individuals who have successfully stopped drinking for good. (Religious conversion, either to Christianity, or peyotism, or the Sun Dance, often plays a role when someone goes "on the wagon.") But ultimately many studies do suggest that among those Indians who drink alcohol at all, a higher proportion have problems with it than would be found in the general population.

Though the causes are not entirely understood, the effects of alcohol abuse are all too evident. Drunkenness limits peoples' ability to work and provide for themselves and their dependents. It can have serious long-term effects on a family's ability to deal with poverty and promote education. Alcoholism corresponds to crime, not only the violation of liquor laws, but also drunk driving and vehicular manslaughter, as well as theft, burglary, and prostitution to support the cost of addiction. Among the health problems resulting from alcohol abuse, fetal alcohol syndrome (FAS) has received much attention. FAS is a complex of permanent birth defects that results from maternal alcohol use during pregnancy. Defects include malformation of the face and skull, stunted limbs, cardiovascular defects, and defects of the central nervous system, including brain damage and its consequences of mental retardation and many other cognitive and behavioral problems. Chronic alcoholics face cirrhosis of the liver, heart disease, a compounding of diabetes if present, and many other ailments. Binge drinking also affects the body, but is most harmful in contributing to disease spread by unprotected sex, domestic violence, suicide, accidental shootings, and car accidents. In the rural west, mortality from alcohol-related accidents is relatively high because victims are often quite far from emergency health care facilities. Thus, statistically, Indian alcohol abuse looks especially grave as a health problem.

Alcohol abuse is therefore regarded as an issue for concern and action in contemporary Native communities. The IHS maintains numerous programs to combat alcoholism, including counseling and therapy services, information campaigns, and summits for tribal leaders. Other efforts to address the problem have been taken up by Native people directly. In September 2007, Native activists on the Pine Ridge Reservation appealed to the Anheuser-Busch Corporation to somehow keep its Budweiser beer from being sold to reservation residents. The reservation bans alcohol sales but four million cans of beer and malt liquor, a cheap beverage with twice the alcohol content as regular beer, are sold yearly in adjacent Whiteclay, Nebraska, mostly to the 16,500 people living on the reservation. Budweiser's products accounted for 86 percent of the area's alcohol sales, and for this reason they were the focus of the protest. Activists felt that the company bore some responsibility for alcohol abuse on the reservation and the resultant social problems, such as very high rates of youth suicide and drunken driving fatality. The company responded only by stating that a reduction of sales would be harmful to retailers and responsible adult consumers.

Other forms of substance abuse and their related social problems also plague certain Plains Indian communities. It is important not to sensationalize these problems or contribute to simplistic imagery of "reservations as the third world within the first world, but without any consideration of how the first world is implicated in the condition of the third world. . . ." (Biolsi 2007:xix). Therefore, it is recognized that drug problems tend to be only locally prevalent, are grounded in poverty, and are part of wider trends across the rural west and in urban neighborhoods, but they are present nonetheless. Casino money and the return of urban Indians to reservations are among the factors promoting the increased use of illegal drugs and networking with dealers. Cocaine, heroine, marijuana, and painkiller and inhalant abuse have become common in some areas. The national epidemic of methamphetamine addiction that swept eastward from the West Coast after the 1970s has also affected some Plains Indian communities. Methamphetamine addiction has been reported as rampant on the Blackfeet Reservation in Montana, a state with one of the highest rates of meth use in the nation. "It's destroying our culture, our way of life, killing our people. A lot of people, they feel sort of disempowered to do anything about it," states tribal drug counselor Darrel Rides at the Door (quoted in Kershaw 2006:A1). In some cases, Indians are partnering as drug traffickers with large-scale non-Indian criminal gangs and using the isolation and protection of the reservations to extend the reach of the drug underworld. The Blackfeet Reservation, bordering Canada and outside the jurisdiction of local non-Indian law enforcement, has been a haven for smugglers. Mexican drug dealers created a sophisticated business plan to market drugs on the Wind River, Pine Ridge, Rosebud, Yankton, and Santee reservations after observing the thriving alcohol business in Whiteclay, Nebraska. Authorities arrested 25 drug ring suspects, including a tribal court judge, on the Wind River Reservation in Wyoming in May 2005.

The treatment of all health problems in Indian Country remains a perplexing challenge for tribal leaders and medical professionals. It is clear that special insights and methods that take into account both the prevalence of diseases and their stubborn persistence within Indian communities will be necessary to overcome these problems. Approaches that consider the special historical, economic, and psychological circumstances effecting Indian people hold the most promise. The work of medical anthropologist Theresa O'Nell among the Flatheads, a Plateau tribe of western Montana, is exemplary of new approaches that can be applied on the Plains (O'Nell 1996). O'Nell's fieldwork probed the reported prevalence of depression among the Flatheads and their own concepts about the nature of this affliction. She found that the standard questions for studying depression did not lead anywhere with Flathead interviewees. Flatheads understood depression not as a personal mental state but as a communal response to the moral quandaries and struggles over identity inherent in the historical experience of the tribe. Flatheads even tended to see the feelings and behaviors associated with clinical depression as partly positive—as a dignified, traditional means of coping actively with the stresses of colonial domination. O'Nell's study is unable to reconcile psychiatric and cultural models of depression or recommend new treatments, but it illustrates the fundamental necessity of appreciating Indian cultural viewpoints before designing therapies. This lesson is equally important whether the health problem under consideration is (from the Western medical perspective) mental or physical.

Land Claims and Natural Resources

With sovereignty, tribes have taken an ever more active role in managing, protecting, and expanding the land bases available to their members. Particularly in the economically marginal environment of the Plains, how a tribe manages its land base, including water resources, grazing, timber, and mineral rights, is crucial. Many of the current controversies about resource management have been inherited from frontier days. The treaties from those times often contained loopholes or reflected inadequate planning, or they were simply violated, leaving Native populations with continuing struggles. Other problems are more immediate but still stem from the basic limitations of the Indian land base imposed through conquest. Tribal efforts to deal with land and natural resource problems are never without internal controversy—members of Native communities are seldom monolithic in their viewpoints—but several efforts have resulted in significant changes in tribal fortunes.

An illustrative case of this phenomenon has emerged on the Crow Reservation in Montana. In 1988, the U.S. Supreme Court ruled that Montana could not tax coal mined on Crow lands, and ordered that $30 million in protested taxes from the prior five years go to the tribe (although a similar ruling in 1998 went against the tribe, and the taxes it paid on coal between 1976 and 1982, plus interest, went to the state). In 1993, the tribal government levied its own railroad and utility property tax. And two years later it began collecting on a complicated settlement for land and coal denied to the tribe because of a surveyor's error in 1891 that placed a reservation boundary incorrectly. Part of the Congressional remedy was a trust fund of up to $85 million, the interest on which would fund tribal land acquisitions, economic development, and social and educational programs. The tribe also negotiated to open a new coal mine on its land in 1998 with the potential for millions more in royalties and taxes. These financial boons and extensions of tribal government authority corresponded with the opening of the first Crow casino, and together they forecast an era of unusual power and prosperity for this large tribe.

Another high-visibility case has been the Sioux efforts to reclaim the Black Hills region near their reservations in South Dakota. The region was overrun by white gold prospectors during 1875–1878 in violation of the second Fort Laramie Treaty (see Chapter 12), and rightful ownership was never restored. Starting in 1920 a coalition of Sioux tribes began a sustained effort to bring suit against the United States to regain the land. In July 1980, the U.S. Supreme Court ruled in favor of the tribes and awarded a cash settlement of $106 million, based on the land value in 1877 plus interest for the ensuing 103 years. The tribes, however, rejected the money, claiming that the Black Hills are not for sale, and have continued to insist on being awarded the land instead. "Money is like snow; it melts away," observed Pine Ridge tribal chairman Paul Iron Cloud, one of the coalition leaders (quoted in Fixico 1998:136). In the meantime, the awarded money sits in an account collecting interest, and the total now approaches $1 billion.

Religious Freedom

As Native revivals of traditional rituals such as the Sun Dance and y*uwipi* spread across the Plains in the late twentieth century (see Chapter 10), and as peyotism continued to suffer legal attacks, Congress enacted the American Indian Religious Freedom Act of 1978. The aim of this law was to recognize and protect the inherent right of American Indians to exercise traditional religions. In a related gesture, in 1996 President William Clinton issued Executive Order No. 13007, which declared the intent of protecting Indian sacred sites on federal lands. Such legislation raised public awareness about Indian religion and set the stage for further tribal efforts to exercise religious customs as much as possible in their former manner and at their former locations.

Sacred Sites

Concerns about land rights and religious freedom intersect when the preservation of Native sacred sites is at stake. One place that illustrates the many site preservation issues is Bear's Lodge, a magnificent column of gray igneous rock rising 1,267 feet above the surrounding terrain in northeastern Wyoming. The name of the rock refers to the Indian designation in several tribes, but to non-Indians it has been known since the 1800s as Devils (*sic*) Tower. Whereas the Indian names (e.g., Lakota *Mato Tipila*, Cheyenne *Na Kovea*) allude to the mythic creature Bear and have holy connotations, the non-Indian name associates the place with the evil spirit of Christianity and perhaps with pagan worship, and is derogatory of the rock's Indian religious significance. But the Lakotas, Cheyennes, Crows, Arapahos, Kiowas, and Eastern Shoshones were all familiar with the landmark owing to their residence and travels between the Black Hills and Bighorn Mountains, and all profess some sacred relationship to the place. Among these tribes the formation is the subject of creation stories, and it has been a location for vision quests, Sun Dances, and *yuwipi* ceremonies.

In 1906, Bear's Lodge was declared America's first National Monument by President Theodore Roosevelt and placed under the control of the National Park Service (NPS). In recent years the NPS has begun to take Native perspectives into account as part of its charge to manage and protect sites. When seeking information about how Bear's Lodge has been used by Native people, however, the agency found that Indians often feel it is not appropriate to reveal the details of their religious customs. This paradox suggests that Indians should have some direct authority in site management, so they can influence decisions without having to discuss ritual secrets. A major Indian concern is that large numbers of non-Indians use the site for the sport of rock climbing. Indian traditionalists regard this use as disrespectful and, potentially, spiritually dangerous. They also worry about non-Indian visitors intruding on the privacy and ritual space of Native worshippers and desecrating the offerings left at the site. Climbing is now banned in June, the time of the Sun Dance.

Other Plains sites are subject to similar concerns. The Black Hills of southwestern South Dakota have been a focal point for many tribes through the years, and some of the formations there have religious significance. Harney Peak, the highest mountain in the range, is considered by Lakotas to be the center of the universe, and has been a vision quest site. *Mato Paha* (Lakota, "Bear Mountain") or *Noahvose* (Cheyenne, "holy/sacred/teaching mountain"), also called Bear Butte, near Sturgis, South Dakota, is a sacred place where Native worshippers must tolerate non-Indian recreational visitors. Nearby Mount Rushmore, sculpted to depict four U.S. presidents Washington, Jefferson, Lincoln, and Theodore Roosevelt, is considered an affront by many Indian people, a brazen statement of racial superiority gazing over the land they once owned. The Lakotas knew the mountain as "Six Grandfathers." In Hardeman County, Texas, four distinctive hills known as Medicine Mounds were once used for vision questing by the Comanches and perhaps others. The mounds had been privately owned by non-Indian ranchers since the 1880s, until the land went up for sale in the early 1990s. The Summerlee Foundation, a Dallas-based trust for historic preservation, purchased the property and sometimes opens it to Indian visitors. Another Southern Plains site, Medicine Bluffs (Comanche: *Puha Rupanʉtʉ*) north of Lawton, Oklahoma, is generally protected as part of the Fort Sill military reservation, though the Comanche Nation is negotiating with the U.S. Army for better access and more sensitive management. The ownership and use rights of sacred sites will continue to spark controversies and renegotiations, as well as cooperative preservation efforts, in the foreseeable future.

An important related matter is the preservation of Native concepts of geography. Indian people had their own systems of geographic knowledge, and names for places and pathways, that amount to alternative cultural views of the Plains. Unfortunately, these conceptual systems have largely been eradicated as Native people were driven from their territories and Indian place names were replaced with non-Indian names. In Texas, for example, there are startlingly few locations with Indian-derived names even though the entire state was populated by numerous tribes. Occasionally, an Indian name remains via a Spanish or English translation, though the origin is not widely recognized. Some of this information is still retrievable in the memories of older Indian people. Over a century after their ouster from Texas, Comanche speakers still know the Native names for all of the major river drainages in the state. But the tribes and their supporters must move fast to preserve such knowledge, otherwise the loss of Native territory is compounded in yet another way.

Graves Protection and Repatriation

Indian people have long decried the retention of tribal historical and sacred objects, as well as the skeletal remains of their direct or collective ancestors, by non-Indian museums and scientific institutions. Much of this material was obtained during times when Indians were assumed to be vanishing and were not accorded the rights of normal citizens. It was also a common assumption that scientists, as educated members of the dominant society and class, were privileged in deciding how Native material culture should be valued and owned. Ritual objects, grave goods, and skeletons were sometimes obtained by archaeologists directly from digs or purchased from their Indian owners in open transactions, but other times they were acquired dishonestly—either bought from looters or taken from their owners without permission or under duress; and in at least one case, an Army commander had his men cut off the heads of Plains Indian battle casualties and shipped them back east for use as scientific specimens. Senate testimony in 1989 revealed that 163 museums held 43,306 skeletal remains of Indian people. Arguments that these materials were critical to the advancement of science did not prove persuasive, since most of them had never been analyzed in the many years they were stored. Some Indian advocates argued that scientists had no right to possess these materials no matter what the reason.

Indian tribes and organizations lobbied intensely to press these concerns, and in 1990 Congress passed the Native American Graves Protection and Repatriation Act (NAGPRA). The Act, which applies to federally funded museums and agencies (except the Smithsonian Institution, which is governed by a separate, similar law), calls for the return of human remains, funerary objects, sacred objects, and culturally significant objects to the lineal descendants of the original owners, or to tribes that are culturally affiliated to the original owners, upon request. If an item can be said to be vital to scientific study, the current possessors have 90 days to analyze it before returning it. The Act requires that institutions publish lists of all the artifacts they possess to enable Indian claims. Grants may be made to tribes to assist them in processing their claims. Another section of the law governs archaeological investigation. If they expect that a survey or dig will uncover Indian burials, archaeologists are required to consult with potential descendants or tribes when planning their research. If they find protected materials unexpectedly, they must consult with the descendant or tribes within a short time of the discovery. And, the Act provides guidelines for demonstrating the tribal provenience of items; for example, an ancient skeleton may be reclaimed by the contemporary tribal population whose historic ancestors occupied the area where the skeleton was found. Finally, the Act imposes financial penalties on museums and agencies that do not comply with the law, as well as fines or jail time on anyone convicted of buying or selling protected Indian human remains or cultural items. Since the enactment of NAGPRA,

hundreds of thousands of articles have been de-accessioned (taken out of collections) and repatriated (given back legally and physically).

The return of the Omaha Sacred Pole is one exemplary case of repatriation on the Plains. This episode actually took place while the NAGPRA laws were still being written. The "Real Omaha" or Umo^n'ho^n'ti is sacred person in the form of a cottonwood pole with miraculous beginnings that had accompanied the Omahas in their migrations and hunts and safeguarded their well-being. In 1888, after the Omahas were impoverished and forced onto a reservation, the Omaha anthropologist Francis LaFlesche persuaded the pole keeper Yellow Smoke to send the "Venerable Man" to an eastern city for safekeeping. He thus came into the possession of the Peabody Museum in Cambridge, Massachusetts. Exactly a century later the Omaha tribal chairman, a descendant of Yellow Smoke, and another tribe member visited the Sacred Pole at the museum; they wept for his long confinement and separation from his people. They negotiated with museum officials, who agreed to return the Real Omaha to his tribe, and in July of 1989 he was home again. While the tribe was building a suitable dwelling for the Sacred Pole, the University of Nebraska at Lincoln offered to keep him safely in their museum. This gesture eased tensions between the Omahas and the university over another matter, the tribe's request for the return of numerous skeletal remains from an old Omaha village that the university museum had collected. Both parties agreed that the university could conduct intensive study of the skeletons to report about the diet and health of the ancestral Omahas, and when the study was finished in October 1991 the remains were reburied on the Omaha reservation. Some Omahas believe that the Real Omaha purposefully presided over this happy outcome in order to join with the remains of the people who tended to him long ago.

In the years since there have numerous other cases of repatriation and reburial, some even reaching beyond the United States. In 1998, Lakotas at Pine Ridge Reservation took ownership of a

Ghost Dance shirt from the municipal museum in Glasgow, Scotland, where it had been since 1891. The shirt had been stripped from a victim of the Wounded Knee massacre and somehow came into the possession of a cowboy who gifted it to the city during a visit of Buffalo Bill's Wild West Show. In 2000, U.S. senator Ben Nighthorse Campbell (Northern Cheyenne/Portuguese) wrote and sponsored a bill creating a National Historical Site at the place of the infamous Sand Creek massacre. The Cheyenne and Arapaho tribes in Montana and Oklahoma located human remains from the massacre in several museums and pursued reburial.

NAGPRA has not totally stopped exploitation of Native artifacts and burial grounds but it has lessened desecrations and sensitized people to the issues. And as the Omaha case suggests, repatriation efforts can evince a spirit of cooperation and mutual respect. More scientists are now sympathetic to Indian rights of ownership and spiritual needs and are eager to assist not only in repatriation but also in the preservation of sites and objects after they are delivered to Indian hands. There are, however, many non-Indians who feel that Indian materials should be retained in scientific collections under the possibility that yet-undiscovered analytic techniques will reveal important clues to human prehistory that are relevant to all humankind. These pro-science advocates worry about tribal communities' abilities to care for the artifacts in anticipation of some greater good, and they question the claims of current Indians to ownership that are based on remote ancestral connections. In any case, NAGPRA has amounted to a renegotiation of the power relationship between Indian people and the people who would study them or otherwise possess their cultural patrimony.

Mascots

The depiction of Indians in commercial emblems has become a subject of widespread dispute and activism. Sports mascots have been at the center of some of the most notable controversies. There are several national professional sports teams in the United States with Indian names. In 1992, an unsuccessful lawsuit was mounted to force team owners to change the name of the National Football League Washington Redskins. The Cleveland Indians of Major League Baseball's American League have retained their red-faced cartoon Indian mascot Chief Wahoo despite occasional protests. The Atlanta Braves of the National League abandoned their screaming Indian logo and Chief Noc-A-Homa ("Knock a Homer") stadium mascot in 1986 but have remained under fire for the "tomahawk chop," a cheering motion made by fans in the bleachers that critics say contributes to a stereotype of violence. At the collegiate level, the most prolonged and publicized case involved the University of Illinois at Urbana-Champaign, whose symbol, the fictitious Chief Illiniwek, portrayed by a white student in Sioux regalia, was deplored by critics for his bastardized fancy dance performed at half time; this symbol was dropped in 2007.

There have been similar protests involving Plains schools. Following complaints from neighboring tribes, the National Collegiate Athletic Association (NCAA) in 2005 censured the University of North Dakota for its Fighting Sioux nickname and mascot, saying the imagery created a "hostile or abusive environment." Under the same NCAA ruling, Northeastern State (Oklahoma) University changed its nickname from Redmen to River Hawks. While these revisions were prompted by concerned Native people, not all Indians oppose all Indian mascot names. Florida State University uses the Seminole name with official consent from tribal governments in Florida and Oklahoma. Similarly, West Texas High School in Stinnett, Texas, obtained tribal approval to continue using the name "Comanches." At some schools on the Plains the student body includes Indians and the community regards their Indian mascot as a source of pride rather than as an act of appropriation or offense.

Controversies over the use of the word "squaw" in place names and the English language generally have also become commonplace. The U.S. Geological Survey counted 1,050 place

FIGURE 13.3 *Powwow attendee Sonny Hensley with an anti-mascot button.*

names around the United States that included the word as of 1996. Upon the urging of Comanche tribe members, in 2005 the city of Lawton, Oklahoma, changed the signage on a creek running through town from Squaw Creek to Numu Creek, using an Anglicized form of the Comanche word for "Comanche" or "Indian." Many Indians have embraced the theory that "squaw" derives from an Algonquian word for vagina and was therefore originally an obscene slur, even though this derivation is disputed among professional linguists and historians. Regardless of its origin, the word is known to have taken on derogatory meaning by the nineteenth century, and it evokes the stereotype of the servile Native woman that is offensive to modern Indian people.

Media Imagery and Cultural Florescence

Modern Indian people live within a national society whose mental image of their culture has been shaped largely by hours of Hollywood movies and television shows. Whether noble or debased, Plains Indians are usually portrayed as savages in these works and there is little or no effort to fully explain their cultures or humanize them.

The 1956 film *The Searchers*, directed by John Ford and starring John Wayne, illustrates typical characteristics of the western genre even while attempting to move beyond them. It is a powerful drama and well crafted in some ways. The novel by Alan LeMay from which the screenplay was adapted draws closely on the real-life experiences of Comanches and Texans in the 1860s, in particular the sagas of white captive Cynthia Ann Parker and African American teamster Britt Johnson, who ransomed his captured family after searching for several months in 1864–1865 across Indian Territory and the Llano Estacado. John Wayne's character in the film, Ethan Edwards, undertakes a five-year search for his two young captive nieces. Many of the scenes are realistic and the dialogue contains a smattering of authentic Comanche words. Yet the action was filmed not in

Texas but in Monument Valley, Utah, a grander landscape that Ford preferred for its mythic atmosphere; and the Indians in some scenes, when not non-Indian actors, are clearly Navajos from the filming location. The moral dilemma facing Ethan Edwards is whether to rescue his surviving niece when he finds her or else execute her because she has been sullied by marriage to her captor, the demonic Chief Scar. As the plot climaxes Edwards decides to spare the girl, but this act of mercy toward a white girl does nothing to outweigh his blatant hatred of Indians, which culminates in his scalping of Scar. Ford successfully caused audiences to consider miscegenation, racism, and genocide, and with these themes *The Searchers* was an ambitious departure from more simplistic cowboy-and-Indian formulas, but still the film portrays Plains Indians without any depth and in a totally negative light.

Revisionist westerns like *Little Big Man* (1970; see Chapter 5) and *Soldier Blue* (1970) attempted to retell the story of the American frontier with sympathy for Indians but were not primarily concerned with the accurate portrayal of Native culture. *A Man Called Horse* (1970) includes a fantastic scene in which an aristocratic white captive (Richard Harris) is initiated into the Sioux tribe by ordeal before taking the most beautiful woman of the tribe as his wife. This popular movie has been described as "a pseudo-factual mélange of anthropological blunders and white supremacy" (Stedman 1982:260).

The 1990 film *Dances with Wolves* was significant in proclaiming a different Hollywood sensibility about Plains Indians. The movie was a very literal adaptation of the novel of the same title by Michael Blake, with the important exception that the protagonists are Lakotas instead of Comanches. This relocation was needed because the producers wanted to include Native language in the film and Lakota has many more fluent speakers (and semi-professional actors) than Comanche; and the largest herd of buffalos was available for filming near the Lakota reservations. In fact, a good part of the film dialogue is spoken in rudimentary Lakota with

English subtitles, and the movie was the first in a series of modern major releases that included extensive Native language. The relocation produces a few historical inaccuracies: Ten Bears, the name of one of the Lakota characters, was the name of an actual Comanche headman (see Chapter 11); and in one scene, the Indians possess an old Spanish helmet, which would be more probable on the Southern Plains than in the Lakota country. The story follows the adventures of a federal cavalry officer and inadvertent Civil War hero (played by Kevin Costner) who is sent to man an abandoned frontier post, is assimilated by a Lakota band, and fights with them against encroaching whites. Although influential critic Pauline Kael dismissed the film as a cloying naturist fantasy, it was enthusiastically received by the public. *Dances with Wolves* became the all-time most successful western, reportedly grossing $500 million and garnering seven Academy Awards. The film was widely praised by non-Indians and Indians for its sensitive and authentic treatment of Native culture. Costner, who also directed the film, was ceremonially adopted by a Lakota family at the Washington, D.C. opening. Afterward, however, many Lakotas spoke out against Costner because of his investments to develop a luxury resort, named "Dunbar" after his movie role, with casino and golf course in the Black Hills.

Indian imagery today is global in reach. It frequently emerges in Europe, where, in addition to much serious scholarship and excellent museums documenting Indian culture, there has been a long tradition of "playing Indian" in various manners. The enormously popular dime novels of German writer Karl May (1842–1912) tapped into the European romantic fascination with native peoples and the American wilderness. The first-person narrator in May's novels is Old Shatterhand, a white man who becomes blood brothers with a noble Apache chief named Winnetou. Such stories have provided a template for the ways Plains Indian history and culture can serve as raw material for non-Indian fantasy. Among contemporary Europeans are numerous hobbyists who gather at powwows to pitch tipis and dress in Indian regalia (many with a fanatical devotion to authenticity in materials and styling), and some go so far as to invent alternate "Indian" personal and tribal identities for themselves. There is also a lecture circuit throughout Europe which hosts a parade of medicine men, many of dubious Native credentials, who dispense their mystic wisdom and blessings. In 1986, the Legoland theme park in Billund, Denmark featured a 14-meter-high sculpture of the Sioux leader Sitting Bull made from 1.5 million plastic toy blocks.

Modern Indian artists and writers, and their audiences, have been adroit in promoting more sophisticated views of Indian history and culture. *Native Peoples* is a slick bimonthly magazine started in 1987, which brings colorful articles about Indian life-ways to a newsstand readership of 155,000. The 500th anniversary of Columbus's arrival in the Western Hemisphere in 1992 provided a large opportunity for Native commentary and satire, and the quincentennary became less a celebration than a critical reexamination of U.S. social history. N. Scott Momaday issued one of the more polite calls for revision:

> I think that it's a wonderfully important time to reflect on the meaning of Columbus's voyages to America, and the following establishment of colonial settlements in the world. The whole history of Indian/white relations from 1492 to the present is a large subject to get at, but is eminently worth thinking about. I would hope that the question would produce greater awareness of Native cultures, the importance of those cultures, and indeed the indispensable importance of them in the light of the twenty-first century.
>
> (Nabokov 1991:436–437)

The 1998 independent film *Smoke Signals*, written by Sherman Alexie (Spokane/Coeur d'Alene), was the first movie produced exclusively by American Indians. The film earned widespread critical acclaim for its portrayal of the life of young adults on a reservation, and though the story takes place in Idaho and Arizona, it resonated with Indians in the Plains communities. A constant element of this film and other recent Indian commentaries is the use of gentle but incisive humor. Vine Deloria, Jr., among others, has emphasized the importance of humor to Indian people as a defense against acculturative pressure: "When a people can laugh at themselves and laugh at others and hold all aspects of life together without letting anybody drive them to extremes, then it seems to me that people can survive" (Deloria 1969:168).

At the same time that Indians are pushing back against stereotype, they are also earnestly involved in the preservation of Native language and culture. Their efforts correspond to population increases in many tribes, a trend that is both problematic and promising, since the numerous recently born tribe members are more likely to be disconnected from tribal traditions yet potentially interested in them as they age. Despite the continuous and warranted fear that Native traditions are eroding, it is arguable that the number of people participating in tribally sanctioned dances and rituals is at an all-time high. And, most tribes sponsor language and cultural preservation committees that record traditional stories, offer language classes in which young people learn from elders, and publish dictionaries. Thus, where the survival of Native languages and oral traditions was once largely in the hands of anthropologists and dedicated lexicographers like the missionary Stephen R. Riggs among the Santees, and these specialists played a crucial role in bridging knowledge, nowadays tribe members themselves have taken ownership of these processes.

Identity

The overriding question facing Plains Indian people in the foreseeable future may well be "Who exactly is an Indian?"

Blood quantum is the term used to refer to an individual's degree of Native biological descent. The term uses the common metaphor of "blood" to signify biological inheritance. The concept of blood quantum has been put to multiple uses. It is a way of quantifying a person's degree of Indian descent that can be used to differentiate among people for social or legal purposes—for example, to determine who may or may not belong to a recognized tribe, or who may be eligible for particular protections or entitlements. Attendance at Indian schools, federal grants to attend college, and the right to possess peyote and eagle feathers for religious purposes are some of the issues that have been determined by blood quantum. Also, membership in a recognized tribe by virtue of blood quantum may also dictate subsidiary rights, such as the ability to join certain branches of the Native American Church. Blood quantum is also used more causally as a shorthand way of talking about a person's racial identity.

Some view the blood quantum concept as another bureaucratic imposition and management tool of the non-Indian government, a vain attempt to quantify the intangible quality of Indian-ness. Or worse, they feel it is a tool of racism or genocide, which constricts the rights of tribal groups to define their memberships, and assumes the disappearance of Native Americans, because fractionalization of Indian descent toward the point of insignificance can only increase with the passing of time. Employment of the concept by both the federal government and tribal governments, however, has become ingrained and perhaps inescapable.

The blood quantum idea was mainly used at first in the United States to distinguish between whites and Negroes (African Americans), with various state laws declaring that anyone with one-fourth or more African American descent was to be classified as Negro. Blood quantum was thus used to promote *hypodescent*, the principle that a person of mixed descent should be classified as belonging to the group of lower status.

It is a social device for discouraging interracial sexual relations and marriage and promoting the purity of the dominant race. Indian descent was also sometimes included in these early laws. The Dawes Act and subsequent allotment process introduced blood quantum as a basic measure of Indian identity on the Plains. As an outgrowth of the Dawes Act, blood quantum was also used as a measure of "whiteness" and thus competency when bestowing legal rights and releasing individuals of Native descent from government ward status. Blood quantum became firmly instituted in federal and tribal policies during the reorganization and termination periods (see Chapter 12).

Blood quantum is sometimes combined or replaced with another measure of Indian descent, *lineal descendency*. Under this principle, a person must demonstrate with birth certificates and other documents direct descent from someone who appears in a past written record of tribal membership. Typically descent is traced to someone on a roll or census dating to some significant moment in the tribe's history, in the nineteenth or early twentieth century.

The BIA used one-fourth blood quantum in establishing eligibility for many of its Indian programs, but has come under increased pressure from Congress and its constituents to abandon blood quantum and instead use membership in a recognized tribe as the criterion for program eligibility. Individual tribal governments continue to use blood quantum, and they set their own percent requirements according to whether they wish to restrict or expand membership. Most tribes on the Plains and elsewhere in the United States use the old standard one-fourth measure. The Arapahos, Assiniboines, Blackfoots, Cheyennes, Iowas of Oklahoma, Otoe–Missourias, Pawnees, Poncas, and Sioux are among those observing the one-fourth standard. The Wichitas allow one-eighth, and the Comanches changed from one-fourth to one-eighth in 2002. The Kiowas are also considering a reduction from one-fourth to one-eighth. The Iowas of Kansas and Nebraska and the Osages are unusual in allowing membership to persons with any demonstrable degree of descent. Because blood quantum continues to be a common criterion, the BIA issues a Certificate of Degree of Indian Blood in the form of an identity card to individuals who apply and furnish evidence of descent.

The rules of tribal enrollment prohibit people from holding membership in more than one tribe. In intertribal Oklahoma it is not uncommon for people of mixed tribal heritage who may qualify by blood quantum for membership in more than one tribe to register with the one that provides the most desired benefits. Under this strategy children may even be enrolled in different tribes than their parents. Enrollment status is a legal matter and does not necessarily determine how, or with whom, a person participates in social and cultural activities on an everyday basis.

Contemporary Indian people struggle with the need to prove indigenous identity. On the one hand, they may reject the demands of the dominant society to account for their biological makeup and family history. Yet many also desire some requirements and see no easy alternative to the measures currently in use. Tribe members wish to conserve the tribal resource base and protect it from those who would fraudulently claim to be Native Americans in order to share in tribal benefits. Disputable claims to tribal membership have been made since reservation land was being allotted to individuals, and in modern times revenues from oil and casinos are attractive to imposters, along with access to care at Indian hospitals and other valuable services. Also at issue is the perceived destruction of "real" Indian culture by people who insert themselves in tribal communities and activities even though they lack personal knowledge of Native traditions. Persons of questionable Native heritage are derided by registered tribe members as "pretendians," "wannabes," or "members of the Wannabe tribe." Critics of accountability measures, however,

would say that the present requirements deny tribal membership or indigenous identity to many who deserve it, and that the resultant antagonism among tribe members, and between registered tribe members and those who cannot technically attain membership, amounts to another racist tactic for the ruination of Native society.

Despite government efforts to strictly certify Indian identity, at any given time living Plains Indian communities are made up of a variety of people, some who satisfy legal requirements and others who merely acknowledge or claim Native ancestry. The most salient criterion for Indian identity to some people is simply the will to participate in the Indian sociocultural community. This attitude is quite consistent with traditional Indian approaches to group membership, which were inclusive and not overly race-conscious, as evidenced in past practices of adoption and intermarriage. On the other hand, there are individuals who qualify for tribal membership according to blood quantum and lineal descendancy but who choose to live totally outside the Native community. Tina Emhoolah (Comanche, b. 1970) eloquently summarized the different levels of identity for the author by describing an onion and its many layers. On the outside are people who know that they are of Indian descent and that is as far as their consciousness of identity goes. Then, there are those who participate as Indians by carrying an identification card and using the IHS, but their Native identity is still relatively superficial. The many degrees of identity proceed in this way. At the center are those who have intensively learned and practice Native language and traditions throughout their lives.

It is ironic that concerns about indigenous identity are intensifying at a time when the absolute number of self-identifying American Indians is growing. According to the U.S. Census the number of American Indians grew from 552,000 in 1960 to 1,959,000 in 1990, an increase of 255 percent. The Canadian census of 2006 counted 698,025 Indians, revealing an increase of more than 100 percent over the prior two decades. The increases results from high birth rates and lower mortality rates because of better health care. But only about half of the growth is attributable to natural increase and survival. It also results simply because more people want to claim Indian identity, which has become culturally fashionable and in some cases financially enticing. Plains tribal enrollments have generally grown in proportion to the national census figures. At the same time, it is evident that fewer and fewer people will be able to meet blood quantum requirements as the years pass.

The recent Comanche Nation's diminishment of its blood quantum requirement is a stopgap response to this dilemma, one that other tribes have also pursued or are contemplating. But there are only a limited number of times this strategy can help. New ways of measuring indigenous biological heritage, such as the use of DNA analysis, do not offer a solution either. Intermarriage between members of different tribes or with non-Indians will continue to erode tribal and indigenous identity. Identity will increasingly be gauged as inter-tribal or undifferentiated Indian biological heritage rather than in terms of tribal affiliation. And without tribal identities and tribal social structures, the long-term persistence of Plains Indian societies as we know them is questionable. But the demise of these societies has been predicted many times before. The great resiliency of Native cultures, the growing political and economic strength of many tribal governments, and the pluralistic tendencies within the larger American and Canadian nations may yet combine in powerful new ways to perpetuate Plains Indian societies well into the future.

Sources: Biolsi (2007); Blake (1988); Braroe (1975); Brightman (1988); Comeau and Santin (1995); Cutler (2002); Deloria (1969); Fixico (1998, 2006); Foster (1991); Frantz (1999); Gelo (1986, 2000); Goffman (1959); Hanson and Chirinos (1997); Jawory (2003); Jones (1972); Kael (1991); Kemnitzer (1980); Kenmotsu et al. (1994, 1995); Kershaw (2006); Larner (2002); Lazarus (1991); May (1999); N.A. (1987); Nabokov (1991); O'Nell (1996); Passel (1996); Ridington (1993); Robinson and Armagost (1990); Ruibal (2005); Stedman (1982); Strickland (1980); Voget (2001); Vollers (1996); Wagner (2007); Walker (2007); Wernitznig (2007); and Woomavoyah (2006).

CHAPTER SUMMARY

Life in contemporary "Indian Country" is both similar to and different from life in mainstream United States and Canada. Indian Country is a definable landscape of rural lands, towns, and cities where there are significant Native populations. Limited work opportunities in these areas, when coupled with Native values and discrimination, result in severe poverty for many Indian people. Education is promoted as an avenue out of poverty, with mixed results. Pressing contemporary issues also include continuing struggles for tribal sovereignty; the pros and cons of legalized gambling on Indian lands; health (including substance abuse); land claims; stewardship of natural resources; religious freedom; protection of sacred sites and Indian graves; and controversies over Indian mascots and derogatory language. Media representations of Plains Indians continue to shape the larger public imagination. Indian writers and artists have been energetic in countering simplistic depictions of Native ways. Owing to continued biological and cultural assimilation, the ultimate question for the future is how Indian identity will be defined.

QUESTIONS FOR REVIEW

1. Describe the physical landscape of Indian Country.
2. What is "face work"? How does the concept illuminate interactions between modern Indians and non-Indians?
3. Explain the economic and social impacts of legalized gambling on Indian lands.
4. What factors are relevant in deciding "[w]ho exactly is an Indian"?

BIBLIOGRAPHY

Adams, David B. 1983 Why There Are So Few Women Warriors. *Behavior Science Research* 18:196–212.

Adams, David Wallace 1995 *Education for Extinction.* Lawrence, KS: University of Kansas Press.

Adney, Edwin Tappan, and Howard I. Chapelle 1983 *The Bark Canoes and Skin Boats of North America.* Washington, DC: Smithsonian Institution Press.

Ahler, Janet Goldenstein 1980 The Formal Education of Plains Indians. In *Anthropology on the Great Plains.* W. Raymond Wood and Margot Liberty, eds. Pp. 245–254. Lincoln, NE: University of Nebraska Press.

Ahler, Stanley A., and Marvin Kay, eds. 2007 *Plains Village Archaeology.* Salt Lake City, UT: University of Utah Press.

Allan, Tony, and Andrew Warren 1993 *Deserts: The Encroaching Wilderness.* New York: Oxford University Press.

Allen, Glover M. 1920 Dogs of the American Aborigines. *Bulletin of the Museum of Comparative Zoology at Harvard College*, Vol. 63, No. 9. Cambridge, MA.

Anderson, Edward F. 1996 *Peyote: The Divine Cactus.* Second edition. Tucson, AZ: University of Arizona Press.

Anderson, Jeffrey D. 2003 *One Hundred Years of Old Man Sage: An Arapaho Life.* Lincoln, NE: University of Nebraska Press.

Archambault, JoAllyn 2001 Sun Dance. In *Handbook of North American Indians*, Vol. 13, Part 2. William C. Sturtevant, ed. Pp. 983–995. Washington, DC: Smithsonian Institution.

Bamforth, Douglas B. 1988 *Ecology and Human Organization on the Great Plains.* New York: Plenum Press.

Bamforth, Douglas B., and Curtis Nepstad-Thornberry 2007 Reconsidering the Occupational History of the Crow Creek Site (39BF11). *Plains Anthropologist* 52:153–173.

Barker, Eugene, ed. 1924 The Austin Papers. *Annual Report of the American Historical Association for the Year 1919.* Washington, DC: U.S. Government Printing Office.

Barnard, Herwanna Becker 1941 *The Comanche and His Literature.* Unpublished M.A. thesis, English Department, University of Oklahoma.

Baumgartner, Frederick M., and A. Marguerite Baumgartner 1992 *Oklahoma Bird Life.* Norman, OK: University of Oklahoma Press.

Beatty, John Joseph 1974 Kiowa-Apache Music and Dance. *University of Northern Colorado Museum of Anthropology, Ethnology Series* No. 31. Greeley, CO: University of Northern Colorado.

Beck, Warren E., and Ynez D. Haase 1989 *Historical Atlas of the American West.* Norman, OK: University of Oklahoma Press.

Beckwith, Martha W. 1930 Mythology of the Oglala Dakota. *Journal of American Folklore* 43:338–442. 1937 Mandan-Hidatsa Myths and Ceremonies. *Memoirs of the American Folklore Society* 32. New York: J. J. Augustin.

Benedict, Ruth 1923 The Concept of the Guardian Spirit in North America. *Memoirs of the American Anthropological Association* 29. Menasha, WI.

Berlandier, Jean Louis 1969 *The Indians of Texas in 1830.* Washington, DC: Smithsonian Institution Press.

Berlo, Jane, and Ruth B. Phillips 1998 *Native North American Art.* New York: Oxford University Press.

Bernstein, Alison R. 1991 *American Indians and World War II: Toward a New Era in Indian Affairs.* Norman, OK: University of Oklahoma Press.

Berthrong, Donald J. 1986 *The Southern Cheyennes.* Norman, OK: University of Oklahoma Press.
1992 Struggle for Power: The Impact of Southern Cheyenne and Arapaho "Schoolboys" on Tribal Politics. *American Indian Quarterly* 16:1–24.

Biolsi, Thomas 2007 *Deadliest Enemy: Law and Race Relations On and Off Rosebud Reservation.* Minneapolis, MN: University of Minnesota Press.

Blake, Michael 1988 *Dances with Wolves.* New York: Fawcett.

Blakeslee, Donald J. 1981 The Origin and Spread of the Calumet Ceremony. *American Antiquity* 46:759–768.

Bol, Marsha C., and Nellie Z. Star Boy Menard 2000 "I Saw All That": A Lakota Girl's Puberty Ceremony. *American Indian Culture and Research Journal* 24:25–42.

Bongianni, Maurizio, and Concetta Mori 1985 *Horses of the World.* New York: Gallery Books.

Boorman, Dean K. 2002 *Guns of the Old West: An Illustrated History.* Guilford, CT: The Lyons Press.

Bowers, Alfred W. 1991 *Mandan Social and Ceremonial Organization.* Moscow: University of Idaho Press.
1992 *Hidatsa Social and Ceremonial Organization.* Lincoln, NE: University of Nebraska Press.

Boyd, Maurice 1981 *Kiowa Voices: Ceremonial Dance, Ritual and Song*, Vol. I. Fort Worth, TX: Texas Christian University Press.

Brady, Ivan 1996 Cannibalism. In *Encyclopedia of Cultural Anthropology.* David Levinson and Melvin Ember, eds. Pp. 163–167. New York: Henry Holt.

Brant, Charles S., ed. 1969 *Jim Whitewolf: The Life of a Kiowa Apache Indian.* New York: Dover.

Braroe, Niels Winther 1975 *Indian and White.* Stanford, CA: Stanford University Press.

Brightman, Robert A. 1988 The Windigo in the Material World. *Ethnohistory* 35:337–379.

Brooks, James F. 2002 *Captives and Cousins.* Chapel Hill, NC: University of North Carolina Press.

Brown, Donald N., and Lee Irwin 2001 Ponca. In *Handbook of North American Indians*, Vol. 13, Part 2.

William C. Sturtevant, ed. Pp. 416–431. Washington, DC: Smithsonian Institution.

Brown, Joseph Epes 1989 *The Sacred Pipe.* Norman, OK: University of Oklahoma Press.

Brunvand, Jan Harold 1968 *The Study of American Folklore.* New York: W. W. Norton.

Bucko, Raymond A. 2005 Lakota. In *The Encyclopedia of Religion and Nature*, Vol. 2. Bron R. Taylor, ed. Pp. 983–985. New York: Thoemmes Continuum.

Buller, Galen 1983 Comanche and Coyote, the Culture Maker. In *Smoothing the Ground: Essays in Native American Oral Literature.* Brian Swann, ed. Pp. 245–258. Berkeley, CA: University of California Press.

Burley, David V. 1996 Review of Schlesier's Plains Indians, A.D. 500–1500: The Archaeological Past of Historic Groups. *Plains Anthropologist* 41:312–314.

Caire, William, Jack D. Tyler, Bryan P. Glass, and Michael A. Mares 1989 *Mammals of Oklahoma.* Norman, OK: University of Oklahoma Press.

Callahan, Alice Anne 1990 *The Osage Ceremonial Dance I'n-Lon-Schka.* Norman, OK: University of Oklahoma Press.

Callenbach, Ernest 1996 *Bring Back the Buffalo! A Sustainable Future for America's Great Plains.* Washington, DC: Island Press.

Callender, Charles, and Lee M. Kochems 1983 The North American Berdache. *Current Anthropology* 24:443–470.

Canty, Carol Shannon 1986 *New World Pastoralism: A Study of the Comanche Indians.* Unpublished M.A. thesis, University of Texas at San Antonio Department of Anthropology.

Canonge, Elliot 1958 *Comanche Texts.* Norman, OK, Oklahoma: Summer Institute of Linguistics.

Carlson, Paul H. 1998 *The Plains Indians.* College Station, TX: Texas A&M University Press.

Casagrande, Joseph B. 1954–1955 Comanche Linguistic Acculturation I, II, III. *International Journal of American Linguistics* 20(2):140–151, 20(3):217–237, 21:8–25.

Catches, Pete S., Sr. 1999 *Sacred Fireplace (Oceti Wakan): Life and Teachings of a Lakota Medicine Man.* Santa Fe: Clear Light Publishers.

Catlin, George 1973 *Letters and Notes on the Manners, Customs, and Conditions of the North American Indians.* 2 vols. New York: Dover.

Chadwick, Douglas 1995 What Good is a Prairie? *Audubon* 97(6):36–46.

Chardon, Francis A. 1970 *Chardon's Journal at Fort Clark, 1834–1839.* Freeport, NY: Books for Libraries Press.

Child, Brenda J. 1998 *Boarding School Seasons.* Lincoln, NE: University of Nebraska Press.

Christafferson, Dennis M. 2001 Sioux, 1930–2000. In *Handbook of North American Indians*, Vol. 13, Part 1. William C. Sturtevant, ed. Pp. 821–840. Washington, DC: Smithsonian Institution.

Clark, W. P. 1982 *The Indian Sign Language.* Lincoln, NE: University of Nebraska Press.

Clarkin, Thomas 2001 *Federal Indian Policy in the Kennedy and Johnson Administrations, 1961–1969.* Albuquerque, NM: University of New Mexico Press.

Comeau, Pauline, and Aldo Santin 1995 *The First Canadians.* Toronto: James Lorimer and Company.

Cook, John R. 1989 *The Border and the Buffalo.* Austin, TX: State House Press.

Costello, David F. 1969 *The Prairie World.* New York: Thomas Y. Crowell.

Culin, Stewart 1975 *Games of the North American Indians.* New York: Dover.

Cutler, Charles L. 2002 *Tracks That Speak.* New York: Houghton Mifflin.

Dary, David 1974 *The Buffalo Book.* New York: Avon.

Deloria, Ella C. 2006 *Dakota Texts.* Lincoln, NE: University of Nebraska Press.

Deloria, Vine, Jr. 1969 *Custer Died for Your Sins: An Indian Manifesto.* New York: Macmillan.
1995 *Red Earth, White Lies: Native Americans and the Myth of Scientific Fact.* New York: Scribner.

DeMallie, Raymond J. 1983 Male and Female in Traditional Lakota Culture. In *The Hidden Half: Studies of Plains Indian Women.* Patricia Albers and Beatrice Medicine, eds. Pp. 237–265. Lanham, MD: University Press of America.
1993 "These Have No Ears": Narrative and the Ethnohistorical Method. *Ethnohistory* 40:515–538.
2001a Introduction. In *Handbook of North American Indians*, Vol. 13, Part 1. William C. Sturtevant, ed. Pp. 1–13. Washington, DC: Smithsonian Institution.
2001b Sioux Until 1850. In *Handbook of North American Indians*, Vol. 13, Part 2. William C. Sturtevant, ed. Pp. 718–760. Washington, DC: Smithsonian Institution.

DeMallie, Raymond J., ed. 1984 *The Sixth Grandfather.* Lincoln, NE: University of Nebraska Press.

DeMallie, Raymond J., and Douglas R. Parks, eds. 1987 *Sioux Indian Religion.* Norman, OK: University of Oklahoma Press.

Dempsey, Hugh A. 2001 Blackfoot. In *Handbook of North American Indians*, Vol. 13, Part 1. William C. Sturtevant, ed. Pp. 604–628. Washington, DC: Smithsonian Institution.

Denig, Edwin Thompson 1930 Indian Tribes of the Upper Missouri. In *Forty-Sixth Annual Report of the Bureau of American Ethnology.* Pp. 375–628. Washington, DC: U.S. Government Printing Office.

Densmore, Frances 1918 Teton Sioux Music. *Bureau of American Ethnology Bulletin* 61. Washington, DC: U.S. Government Printing Office.
1929 Pawnee Music. *Bureau of American Ethnology Bulletin* 93. Washington, DC: U.S. Government Printing Office. 1936 Cheyenne and Arapaho Music. *Southwest Museum Papers* 10. Los Angeles, CA.

Dodge, Richard Irving 1882 *Our Wild Indians.* Hartford, CT: A. D. Worthington and Company.
1959 *The Plains of the Great West.* New York: Archer House.

Dodge, Theodore Ayrault 1890 Some American Riders. *Harper's New Monthly Magazine* 82(December–May): 849–862.

Dorsey, George A. 1904 Traditions of the Osage. *Field Columbian Museum Publication* 88. Chicago, IL.
1995 *The Mythology of the Wichita.* Norman, OK: University of Oklahoma Press.

Dorsey, George A., and Alfred L. Kroeber 1997 *Traditions of the Arapaho.* Lincoln, NE: University of Nebraska Press.

Dorsey, George A., and James R. Murie 1940 Notes on Skidi Pawnee Society. *Field Museum of Natural History Anthropological Series* 27(2), Publication 479. Chicago, IL.

Dorsey, James Owen 1884 Omaha Sociology. In *Third Annual Report of the Bureau of American Ethnology.* Pp. 205–370. Washington, DC: U.S. Government Printing Office.
1894 A Study of Siouan Cults. In *Eleventh Annual Report of the Bureau of American Ethnology.* Pp. 351–544. Washington, DC: U.S. Government Printing Office.

Driver, Harold E. 1962 The Contribution of A. L. Kroeber to Culture Area Theory and Practice. *International Journal of American Linguistics Memoir* 18. Baltimore, MD: Waverly Press.

Driver, Harold E., and J. L. Coffin 1975 Classification and Development of North American Indian Cultures: A Statistical Analysis of the Driver-Massey Sample. *Transactions of the American Philosophical Society* 65(3), Philadelphia, PA.

Driver, Harold E., J. A. Kenny, H. C. Hudson, and O. M. Engle 1972 Statistical Classification of North American Indian Ethnic Units. *Ethnology* 11:311–339.

Dunlay, Thomas W. 1982 *Wolves for the Blue Soldiers.* Lincoln, NE: University of Nebraska Press.

Durkheim, Emile 1995 *The Elementary Forms of Religious Life.* New York: The Free Press.

Dusenberry, Vernon 1962 The Montana Cree: A Study in Religious Persistence. *Stockholm Studies in Comparative Religion* 3. Stockholm: Almqvist and Wiksell.

Dyke, Paul 1971 *Brulé: The Sioux People of the Rosebud.* Flagstaff, AZ: Northland Press.

Eastman, Elaine Goodale 1935 *Pratt: The Red Man's Moses.* Norman, OK: University of Oklahoma Press.

Echo-Hawk, Roger C. 1997 Forging a New Ancient History for Native America. In *Native Americans and Archaeologists: Stepping Stones to Common Ground.* Nina Swindler, Kurt Dongoske, Alan Downer, and Roger Anyan, eds. Pp. 88–102. Walnut Creek, CA: Alta Mira Press.

2000 Ancient History in the New World: Integrating Oral Traditions and the Archaeological Record in Deep Time. *American Antiquity* 65:267–290.

Eggan, Fred, ed. 1955 *Social Anthropology of North American Tribes.* Chicago, IL: University of Chicago Press.

Eggan, Fred, and Joseph A. Maxwell 2001 Kinship and Social Organization. In *Handbook of North American Indians*, Vol. 13, Part 2. William C. Sturtevant, ed. Pp. 974–982. Washington, DC: Smithsonian Institution.

Ehrich, Robert W., and G. M. Henderson 1968 Culture Area. In *International Encyclopedia of the Social Sciences,* Vol. 3. David L. Sills, ed. Pp. 563–566. New York: Free Press.

Ellis, Clyde 1996 *To Change Them Forever.* Norman, OK: University of Oklahoma Press.

Erdoes, Richard, and Alfonso Ortiz 1984 *American Indian Myths and Legends.* New York: Pantheon Books.

1998 *American Indian Trickster Tales.* New York: Viking.

Ewers, John Canfield 1939 *Plains Indian Painting.* Stanford University, CA: Stanford University Press. 1955 The Horse in Blackfoot Indian Culture. *Bureau of American Ethnology Bulletin* 159. Washington, DC: U.S. Government Printing Office.

1958 *The Blackfeet: Raiders on the Northwestern Plains.* Norman, OK: University of Oklahoma Press.

1968 *Indian Life on the Upper Missouri.* Norman, OK: University of Oklahoma Press. 1981 Water Monsters in Plains Indian Art. *American Indian Art* 6(4):38–45.

1997 *Plains Indian History and Culture.* Norman, OK: University of Oklahoma Press.

Fagan, Brian M. 2005 *Ancient North America.* Fourth edition. New York: Thames and Hudson

Farnell, Brenda M. 1995a *Can You See What I Mean?: Plains Indian Sign Talk and the Embodiment of Action.* Austin, TX: University of Texas Press. 1995b *Wiyuta: Assiniboine Storytelling with Signs.* Austin, TX: University of Texas Press.

Feder, Norman 1962 Plains Indian Metalworking with Emphasis on Hair Plates. *American Indian Tradition* 8(2):55–76.

1964a *Art of the Eastern Plains Indians: The Nathan Sturges Jarvis Collection.* New York: The Brooklyn Museum.

1964b Origin of the Oklahoma Forty Nine Dance. *Ethnomusicology* 8:290–294.

1982 *American Indian Art.* New York: Harrison House/Harry N. Abrams.

Finerty, John F. 1890 *War-Path and Bivouac.* Chicago, IL: M. A. Donohue.

Fixico, Donald L. 1998 *The Invasion of Indian Country in the Twentieth Century.* Niwot, CO: University of Colorado Press.

2000 *The Urban Indian Experience in America.* Albuquerque, NM: University of New Mexico Press. 2006 *Daily Life of Native Americans in the Twentieth Century.* Westport, CT: Greenwood Press.

Fletcher, Alice C. 1994 *A Study of Omaha Indian Music.* Lincoln, NE: University of Nebraska Press. 1995 *Indian Story and Song from North America.* Lincoln, NE: University of Nebraska Press.

Fletcher, Alice C., and Francis La Flesche 1972 *The Omaha Tribe.* 2 vols. Lincoln, NE: University of Nebraska Press.

Flores, Dan 1985 *Journal of an Indian Trader: Anthony Glass and the Texas Trading Frontier, 1790–1810.* College Station, TX: Texas A&M University Press.

1990 *Caprock Canyonlands.* Austin, TX: University of Texas Press.

2001 *The Natural West.* Norman, OK: University of Oklahoma Press.

Flores, Dan L., ed. 1984 *Jefferson and Southwest Exploration: The Freeman and Custis Accounts of the Red River Expedition of 1806.* Norman, OK: University of Oklahoma Press.

Forbush, Edward Howe, and John Bichard May 1955 *Natural History of American Birds of East and Central North America.* New York: Bramhall House.

Fortune, Reo F. 1932 Omaha Secret Societies. *Columbia University Contributions to Anthropology* 14. New York.

Foster, James Monroe, Jr. 1960 Fort Bascom, New Mexico. *New Mexico Historical Review* 35:30–62.

Foster, Morris W. 1991 *Being Comanche.* Tucson, AZ: University of Arizona Press.

Fowler, Loretta 1982 *Arapaho Politics, 1851–1978.* Lincoln, NE: University of Nebraska Press.

1987 *Shared Symbols, Contested Meanings: Gros Ventre Culture and History, 1778–1984.* Ithaca, New York: Cornell University Press.

2001a History of the United States Plains Since 1850. In *Handbook of North American Indians*, Vol. 13, Part 1. William C. Sturtevant, ed. Pp. 280–299. Washington, DC: Smithsonian Institution.

2001b Arapaho. In *Handbook of North American Indians*, Vol. 13, Part 2. William C. Sturtevant, ed. Pp. 840–862. Washington, DC: Smithsonian Institution.

Fox, Richard A., Jr. 1993 *Archaeology, History, and Custer's Last Battle: The Little Big Horn Reexamined.* Norman, OK: University of Oklahoma Press.

Frantz, Klaus 1999 *Indian Reservations in the United States.* Chicago, IL: University of Chicago Press.

Frey, Rodney 1987 *The World of The Crow Indians: As Driftwood Lodges.* Norman, OK: University of Oklahoma Press.

1995 *Stories That Make the World.* Norman, OK: University of Oklahoma Press.

Frison, George C. 1978 *Prehistoric Hunters of the High Plains.* New York: Academic Press.

Gallatin, Albert 1973 *A Synopsis of the Indian Tribes within the United States East of the Rocky Mountains, and in the British and Russian Possessions of North America.* New York: AMS Press.

Gamble, John I. 1967 Changing Patterns of Kiowa Indian Dances. In *Acculturation in the America. Proceedings and Selected Papers of the 29th International Congress of Americanists.* Sol Tax, ed. Pp. 94–104. New York: Cooper Square Publishers.

García Rejón, Manuel, and Daniel J. Gelo 1995 *Comanche Vocabulary: Trilingual Edition.* Austin, TX: University of Texas Press.

Gelo, Daniel J. 1983 *Comanche Field Notes.* Unpublished manuscript in author's possession.

1986 *Comanche Belief and Ritual.* Unpublished Ph.D. dissertation, Rutgers University Department of Anthropology.

1988a Comanche Songs, English Lyrics, and Cultural Continuity. *European Review of Native American Studies* 2:3–7.

1988b Comanche Songs with English Lyrics: Context, Imagery, and Continuity. *Storia Nordamericana* 5:137–146.

1993 The Comanches as Aboriginal Skeptics. *American Indian Quarterly* 17:69–82.

1994 Recalling the Past in Creating the Present: Topographic References in Comanche Narrative. *Western Folklore* 53:295–312.

1999 Powwow Patter: Indian Emcee Discourse on Power and Identity. *Journal of American Folklore* 112:40–57.

2000 "Comanche Land and Ever Has Been": A Native Geography of the Nineteenth-Century Comanchería. *Southwestern Historical Quarterly* 103:273–308.

Gelo, Daniel J., and Scott Zesch 2003 "Every Day Seemed to be a Holiday": The Captivity of Bianca Babb. *Southwestern Historical Quarterly* 107:35–68.

Giglio, Virginia 1994 *Southern Cheyenne Women's Songs.* Norman, OK: University of Oklahoma Press.

Gilbert, B. Miles 1980 The Plains Setting. In *Anthropology on the Great Plains.* W. Raymond Wood and Margot Liberty, eds. Pp. 8–15. Lincoln, NE: University of Nebraska Press.

Gill, Sam D. 1991 *Mother Earth: An American Story.* Chicago, IL: University of Chicago Press.

Gillam, J. Christopher 1996 A View of Paleoindian Settlement from Crowley's Ridge. *Plains Anthropologist* 41:273–286.

Gilmore, Melvin R. 1977 *Uses of Plants by the Indians of the Missouri River Region.* Lincoln, NE: University of Nebraska Press.

Gladwin, Thomas 1948 Comanche Kin Behavior. *American Anthropologist* 50:73–94.

Goffman, Erving 1959 *The Presentation of Self in Everyday Life.* Garden City, NY: Doubleday.

Goss, James A. 1990 *Ute Myth as Cultural Charter.* Paper presented at the 22nd Great Basin Anthropological Conference, Reno, Nevada.

Greene, A. C. 1972 *The Last Captive.* Austin, TX: The Encino Press.

Greene, Candace S. 2009 *One Hundred Summers: A Kiowa Calendar Record.* Lincoln, NE: University of Nebraska Press.

Gregg, Josiah 1967 *The Commerce of the Prairies.* Lincoln, NE: University of Nebraska Press.

Grinnell, George Bird 1891 Marriage Among the Pawnees. *American Anthropologist* 4(3):275–282.
1956 *The Fighting Cheyennes.* Norman, OK: University of Oklahoma Press.
1966 *When Buffalos Ran.* Norman, OK: University of Oklahoma Press.
1972 *The Cheyenne Indians.* 2 vols. Lincoln, NE: University of Nebraska Press.

Hagan, William T. 1976 *United States—Comanche Relations: The Reservation Years.* New Haven: Yale University Press.
1979 *American Indians.* Chicago, IL: University of Chicago Press.
2003 *Taking Indian Lands.* Norman, OK: University of Oklahoma Press.

Haley, James L. 1998 *The Buffalo War.* Austin, TX: State House Press.

Hämäläinen, Pekka 1998 The Western Comanche Trade Center: Rethinking the Plains Trade System. *Western Historical Quarterly* 29:485–513.

Hamill, James 2006 *Going Indian.* Urbana, IL: University of Illinois Press.

Hamilton, Allen Lee 1988 *Sentinel of the Southern Plains: Fort Richardson and the Northwest Texas Frontier 1866–1878.* Fort Worth, TX: Texas Christian University Press.

Hanson, Jeffrey R. 1980 Structure and Complexity of Medicine Bundle Systems of Selected Plains Indian Tribes. *Plains Anthropologist* 25:199–216.

Hanson, Jeffrey R., and Sally Chirinos 1997 *Ethnographic Overview and Assessment of Devils Tower National Monument, Wyoming.* National Parks Service Report NPS D-36. Denver, Colorado.

Harrington, John P. 1928 Vocabulary of the Kiowa Language. *Bureau of American Ethnology Bulletin* 84. Washington, DC: U.S. Government Printing Office.

Harris, LaDonna 2000 *LaDonna Harris: A Comanche Life.* Lincoln, NE: University of Nebraska Press.

Harris, Marvin 1968 *The Rise of Anthropological Theory.* New York: Harper Collins.

Harrod, Howard L. 1987 *Renewing the World: Plains Indian Religion and Morality.* Tucson, AZ: University of Arizona Press.

Hatton, Orin T. 1986 In the Tradition: Grass Dance Musical Style and Female Pow-wow Singers. *Ethnomusicology* 30:197–222.

Hawley, Marlin F. 2006 Introduction. In *Plains Archaeology's Past: A Collection of Personal Narratives.* Martin F. Hawley and Virginia A. Wulfkuhle, eds. Plains Anthropologist (Special Issue) 51:487–520.

Herdt, Gilbert, ed. 1994 *Third Sex, Third Gender Beyond Sexual Dimorphism in Culture and History.* New York: Zone Books.

Hill, Robert M. 1995 *The Pipestone Art of Robert Rose-Bear.* Paper presented at the Tenth Biennial Conference, Native American Art Studies Association, Tulsa, OK, October 18–21.

Hinojosa, Servando 2000 Human-Peyote Interaction in South Texas. *Culture and Agriculture* 22:29–35.

Hoard, Robert J., William E. Banks, Rolfe D. Mandel, Michael Finnigan, and Jennifer E. Epperson 2001 A Middle Archaic Burial from East Central Kansas. *American Antiquity* 69:717–739.

Hoebel, E. Adamson 1940 The Political Organization and Law-Ways of the Comanche Indians. *American Anthropological Association Memoir* 54. Menasha, WI: American Anthropological Association.
1980 The Influence of Plains Ethnography on the Development of Anthropological Theory. In *Anthropology on the Great Plains.* W. Raymond Wood and Margot Liberty, eds. Pp. 16–22. Lincoln, NE: University of Nebraska Press.
1988 *The Cheyennes: Indians of the Great Plains.* New York: Harcourt Brace.

Hoig, Stan 2006 *A Travel Guide to the Plains Indian Wars.* Albuquerque, NM: University of New Mexico Press.

Horgan, Paul 1979 *Josiah Gregg and His Vision of the Early West.* New York: Farrar Strauss Giroux.

Hosmer, Brian, and Colleen O'Neill, eds. 2004 *Native Pathways: American Indian Culture and Economic Development in the Twentieth Century.* Boulder, CO: University of Colorado Press.

Howard, James H. 1955 The Pan-Indian Culture of Oklahoma. *The Scientific Monthly* 18(5):215–220.
1957 The Mescal Bean Cult of the Central and Southern Plains: An Ancestor of the Peyote Cult? *American Anthropologist* 59:75–89.
1960 Mescalism and Peyotism Once Again. *Plains Anthropologist* 51:84–85.
1975 The Culture-Area Concept: Does it Diffract Anthropological Light? *The Indian Historian* 8:22–26.

1976 The Plains Gourd Dance as a Revitalization Movement. *American Ethnologist* 243–258.

1984 *The Canadian Sioux.* Lincoln, NE: University of Nebraska Press.

Hoxie, Frederick E. 1984 *A Final Promise: The Campaign to Assimilate the Indians, 1880–1920.* Lincoln, NE: University of Nebraska Press.

Hudson, Charles M. 1966 Isometric Advantages of the Cradleboard: A Hypothesis. *American Anthropologist* 68:470–474.

1976 *The Southeastern Indians.* Knoxville, TN: University of Tennessee Press.

Hultkrantz, Åke 1981 *Belief and Worship in Native North America.* Syracuse, NY: Syracuse University Press.

1987 *Native Religions of North America.* San Francisco, CA: Harper and Row.

Hungry Wolf, Beverly 1980 *The Ways of My Grandmothers.* New York: William Morrow.

Hyde, George E. 1968 *Life of George Bent.* Norman, OK: University of Oklahoma Press.

1974 *The Pawnee Indians.* Norman, OK: University of Oklahoma Press.

Iverson, Peter, ed. 1985 *The Plains Indians of the Twentieth Century.* Norman, OK: University of Oklahoma Press.

Jawory, Adrian 2003 Rodeo! Cowboys in Indian Country. *Native Peoples* 16(5):42–47.

John, Elizabeth A. H. 1975 *Storms Brewed in Other Men's Worlds.* College Station, TX: Texas A&M Press.

John, Elizabeth A. H., and Adán Benavides 1994 Inside the Comanchería, 1785: The Diary of Pedro Vial and Francisco Xavier Chaves. *Southwestern Historical Quarterly* 158:26–56.

Johnson, Alfred E., and W. Raymond Wood 1980 Prehistoric Studies on the Plains. In *Anthropology on the Great Plains.* W. Raymond Wood and Margot Liberty, eds. Pp. 35–47. Lincoln, NE: University of Nebraska Press.

Jones, David E. 1972 *Sanapia: Comanche Medicine Woman.* New York: Holt, Rinehart and Winston.

1980 Face the Ghost. *Phoenix* 4:53–57.

Kael, Pauline 1991 *Movie Love: Complete Reviews 1988–1991.* New York: Plume.

Kardiner, Abram 1945 *The Psychological Frontiers of Society.* New York: Columbia University Press.

Kavanagh, Thomas W. 1996 *Comanche Political History.* Lincoln, NE: University of Nebraska Press.

Kehoe, Alice Beck 1983 The Shackles of Tradition. In *The Hidden Half: Studies of Plains Indian Women.*

Patricia Albers and Beatrice Medicine, eds. Pp. 53–76. Lanham, MD: University Press of America.

1995 Blackfoot Persons. In *Women and Power in Native North America.* Laura E. Klein and Lillian A. Ackerman, eds. Pp. 113–125. Norman, OK: University of Oklahoma Press.

1996 Eliade and Hultkrantz: The European Primitivist Tradition. *American Indian Quarterly* 20:377–392.

2000 *Shamans and Religion: An Anthropological Exploration in Critical Thinking.* Prospect Heights, IL: Waveland Press.

2002 *America Before the European Invasion.* New York: Longman.

Keim, De B. Randolph 1985 *Sheridan's Troopers on the Borders.* Lincoln, NE: University of Nebraska Press.

Kelly, William H., ed. 1954 *The Indian Reorganization Act: the Twenty Year Record.* Tucson, AZ: University of Arizona.

Kemnitzer, Luis 1980 Research in Health and Healing. In *Anthropology on the Great Plains.* W. Raymond Wood and Margot Liberty, eds. Pp. 272–283. Lincoln, NE: University of Nebraska Press.

Kenmotsu, Nancy A., Timothy K. Perttula, Patricia Mercado-Allinger, James E. Bruseth, Sergio Iruegas, and Curtis Tunnell 1994 *Archaeological and Documentary Research at Medicine Mounds Ranch, Hardeman County, Texas.* Texas Historical Commission, Department of Antiquities Protection, Cultural Resource Management Report 4. Austin, TX.

Kenmotsu, Nancy A., Timothy K. Perttula, Patricia Mercado-Allinger, Thomas Hester, James E. Bruseth, Sergio Iruegas, and Curtis Tunnell 1995 Medicine Mounds Ranch: The Identification of a Possible Comanche Traditional Cultural Property in the Rolling Plains of Texas. *Plains Anthropologist* 40:237–250.

Kenner, Charles L. 1969 *The Comanchero Frontier.* Norman, OK: University of Oklahoma Press.

Kershaw, Sarah 2006 Through Indian Lands, Drugs' Shadowy Trail. *New York Times*, February 19, p. 1.1.

Keyser, James D., and Michael A. Klassen 2001 *Plains Indian Rock Art.* Seattle, WA: University of Washington Press.

Kindscher, Kelly 1987 *Edible Wild Plants of the Prairie.* Lawrence, KS: University Press of Kansas.

Kirkland, Forrest, and W. W. Newcomb, Jr. 1996 *The Rock Art of Texas Indians.* Austin, TX: University of Texas Press.

Klein, Alan 1983 The Political-economy of Gender: A 19th Century Plains Indian Case Study. In *The*

Hidden Half: Studies of Plains Indian Women. Patricia Albers and Beatrice Medicine, eds. Pp. 143–174. Lanham, MD: University Press of America.

Koch, Ronald P. 1977 *Dress Clothing of the Plains Indians.* Norman, OK: University of Oklahoma Press.

Kracht, Benjamin R. 1992 Kiowa Ghost Dance, 1894–1916: An Unheralded Revitalization Movement. *Ethnohistory* 39:452–477.

1997 Kiowa Religion in Historical Perspective. *American Indian Quarterly* 21:15–33.

Kroeber, Alfred L. 1907 Gros Ventre Myths and Tales. *American Museum of Natural History Anthropological Papers* 1(3):55–139. New York.

1939 Cultural and Natural Areas of Native North America. *University of California Publications in American Archaeology and Ethnology* 38. Berkeley, CA.

1983 *The Arapaho.* Lincoln, NE: University of Nebraska Press.

La Vere, David 1998 *Life among the Texas Indians.* College Station, TX: Texas A&M Press.

LaBarre, Weston 1970 *The Ghost Dance: Origins of Religion.* Garden City, NY: Doubleday.

1989 *The Peyote Cult.* Fifth edition, enlarged. Norman, OK: University of Oklahoma Press.

LaBarre, Weston, David P. McAllester, J. S. Slotkin, Omer C. Stewart, and Sol Tax 1951 Statement on Peyote. *Science* 114:582.

La Flesche, Frances 1963 *The Middle Five.* Madison, WI: University of Wisconsin Press.

Larner, Jesse 2002 *Mount Rushmore: An Icon Reconsidered.* New York: Nation Books.

Laubin, Reginald, and Gladys Laubin 1957 *The Indian Tipi: Its History, Construction, and Use.* New York: Ballentine.

Lazarus, Edward 1991 *Black Hills/White Justice: The Sioux Nation Versus the United States, 1775 to the Present.* New York: Harper Collins.

Lear, Jonathan 2006 *Radical Hope: Ethics in the Face of Cultural Devastation.* Cambridge, MA: Harvard University Press.

Lemont, Eric 2006 *American Indian Constitutional Reform and the Rebuilding of Native Nations.* Austin, TX: University of Texas Press.

Lesser, Alexander 1930 Levirate and Fraternal Polyandry Among the Pawnees. *Man* 30:98–101.

Lévi-Strauss, Claude 1966 *The Savage Mind.* Chicago, IL: University of Chicago Press.

1990a *The Origin of Table Manners.* Chicago, IL: University of Chicago Press.

1990b *The Naked Man.* Chicago, IL: University of Chicago Press.

Lewis, Oscar 1941 Manly-Hearted Women Among the North Piegan. *American Anthropologist* 43:173–187.

1942 *The Effects of White Contact Upon Blackfoot Culture with Special Reference to the Role of the Fur Trade.* American Ethnological Society Monograph 6. New York: J. J. Augustin.

Liberty, Margot 1980 The Sun Dance. In *Anthropology on the Great Plains.* W. Raymond Wood and Margot Liberty, eds. Pp. 164–178. Lincoln, NE: University of Nebraska Press.

Linderman, Frank B. 1962 *Plenty-coups: Chief of the Crows.* Lincoln, NE: University of Nebraska Press.

Linton, Ralph 1935 The Comanche Sun Dance. *American Anthropologist* 37:420–428.

1936 *The Study of Man.* New York: D. Appleton-Century.

1943 Nativistic Movements. *American Anthropologist* 45:230–240.

Llewellyn, Karl N., and E. Adamson Hoebel 1941 *The Cheyenne Way.* Norman, OK: University of Oklahoma Press.

Lomawaima, K. Tsianina 1994 *They Called in Prairie Light.* Lincoln, NE: University of Nebraska Press.

Loomis, Noel H., and Abram P. Nasitir 1967 *Pedro Vial and the Roads to Santa Fe.* Norman, OK: University of Oklahoma Press.

Lowie, Robert H. 1916 Plains Indian Age-Societies: Historical and Comparative Summary. *Anthropological Papers of the American Museum of Natural History,* Vol. 11, Part 13. New York.

1982 *Indians of the Plains.* Lincoln, NE: University of Nebraska Press.

1983 *The Crow Indians.* Lincoln, NE: University of Nebraska Press.

Lyman, R. Lee, and Michael J. O'Brien 2001 The Direct Historical Approach, Analogical Reasoning, and Theory in Americanist Archaeology. *Journal of Archaeological Method and Theory* 8:303–342.

Lynch, Dudley 1970 *Tornado: Texas Demon in the Wind.* Waco, TX: Texian Press.

Macgregor, Gordon 1946 *Warriors without Weapons: A Study of the Society and Personality Development of the Pine Ridge Sioux.* Chicago, IL: University of Chicago Press.

Mallery, Garrick 1881 Sign Language Among North American Indians. In *First Annual Report of the Bureau of American Ethnology.* Pp. 269–552. Washington, DC: U.S. Government Printing Office.

Mandelbaum, David G. 1979 The Plains Cree: An Ethnographic, Historical, and Comparative Study. *Canadian Plains Studies* 9. Regina, SK: Canadian Plains Research Center.

Marett, Robert R. 1909 *The Threshold of Religion*. London: Methuen.

Marriott, Alice, and Carol K. Rachlin 1968 *American Indian Mythology*. New York: New American Library. 1971 *Peyote*. New York: Mentor.

Martin, Paul S., and H. E. Wright, eds. 1967 *Prehistoric Extinctions: The Search for a Cause*. New Haven: Yale University Press.

Mason, Otis T. 1896 Influences of Environment upon Human Industries or Arts. In *Annual Report of the Board of Regents of the Smithsonian Institution [. . . .] to July, 1895*. Pp. 639–665. Washington, DC: U.S. Government Printing Office.
1907 Environment. In *Handbook of American Indians North of Mexico. Bureau of American Ethnology Bulletin*, Vol. 30, Part 2. Frederick W. Hodge, ed. Pp. 427–430. Washington, DC: U.S. Government Printing Office.

May, Philip A. 1999 The Epidemiology of Alcohol Abuse among American Indians: The Mythical and Real Properties. In *Contemporary Native American Cultural Issues*. Duane Champagne, ed. Pp. 227–244. Walnut Creek, CA: Altamira Press.

Mayor, Adrienne 2005 *Fossil Legends of the First Americans*. Princeton, NJ: Princeton University Press.

McAllester, David P. 1949 Peyote Music. *Viking Fund Publications in Anthropology* 13. New York.
1964 Riddles and Other Verbal Play Among the Comanches. *Journal of American Folklore* 77:251–257.

McBeth, Sally 1983 *Ethnic Identity and the Boarding School Experience*. Washington, DC: University Press of America.

McCleary, Timothy P. 1997 *The Stars We Know: Crow Indian Astronomy and Lifeways*. Prospect Heights, IL: Waveland Press.

McDonald, Jerry N. 1981 *North American Bison*. Berkeley, CA: University of California Press.

McFee, Malcolm 1972 *Modern Blackfeet: Montanans on a Reservation*. New York: Holt, Rinehart and Winston.

McNickle, D'Arcy 1973 *Native American Tribalism*. New York: Oxford University Press.

Meadows, William C. 1999 *Kiowa, Apache, and Comanche Military Societies*. Austin, TX: University of Texas Press.

2002 *The Comanche Code Talkers of World War II*. Austin, TX: University of Texas Press.

Means, Russell 1995 *Where White Men Fear to Tread*. New York: St. Martin's Press.

Medicine, Beatrice 1983 "Warrior Women"—Sex Role Alternatives for Plains Indian Women. In *The Hidden Half: Studies of Plains Indian Women*. Patricia Albers and Beatrice Medicine, eds. Pp. 267–280. Lanham, MD: University Press of America.

Meltzer, David J. 2006 *Folsom*. Berkeley, CA: University of California Press.

Michno, Gregory F. 1997 *Lakota Noon: The Indian Narrative of Custer's Defeat*. Missoula, MT: Mountain Press.

Milner, Clyde A., II 1982 *With Good Intentions: Quaker Work among the Pawnees, Otos, and Omahas in the 1870s*. Lincoln, NE: University of Nebraska Press.

Mishkin, Bernard 1940 *Rank and Warfare Among the Plains Indians*. American Ethnological Society Monograph 3. New York: J. J. Augustin.

Momaday, N. Scott 2000 *House Made of Dawn*. New York: McGraw-Hill.

Mooney, James 1901 Our Last Cannibal Tribe. *Harper's Monthly Magazine* 103(June/November):550–555.
1907a Cheyenne. In *Handbook of American Indians North of Mexico. Bureau of American Ethnology Bulletin*, Vol. 30, Part 1. Frederick W. Hodge, ed. Pp. 250–257. Washington, DC: U.S. Government Printing Office.
1907b Comanche. In *Handbook of American Indians North of Mexico. Bureau of American Ethnology Bulletin* 30, Part 1. Frederick W. Hodge, ed. Pp. 327–328. Washington, DC: U.S. Government Printing Office.
1907c Signals. In *Handbook of American Indians North of Mexico. Bureau of American Ethnology Bulletin* 30, Part 2. Frederick W. Hodge, ed. Pp. 565–567. Washington, DC: U.S. Government Printing Office.
1907d Sign Language. In *Handbook of American Indians North of Mexico. Bureau of American Ethnology Bulletin* 30, Part 2. Frederick W. Hodge, ed. Pp. 567–568. Washington, DC: U.S. Government Printing Office.
1965 *The Ghost-Dance Religion and the Sioux Outbreak of 1890*. Chicago, IL: University of Chicago Press.
1979 *Calendar History of the Kiowa Indians*. Washington, DC: Smithsonian Institution Press.

Moore, John H. 1981 Evolution and Historical Reductionism. *Plains Anthropologist* 26:261–269.
1986 The Ornithology of Cheyenne Religionists. *Plains Anthropologist* 31:177–192.
1987 *The Cheyenne Nation: A Social and Demographic History.* Lincoln, NE: University of Nebraska Press.
1994 Ethnogenetic Theory. *Research and Exploration* 10(1):11–23.

Moore, John H., Margot P. Liberty, and A. Terry Straus 2001 Cheyenne. In *Handbook of North American Indians*, Vol. 13, Part 2. William C. Sturtevant, ed. Pp. 863–886. Washington, DC: Smithsonian Institution.

Morgan, George R., and Omer C. Stewart 1984 The Peyote Trade in South Texas. *Southwestern Historical Quarterly* 86:269–296.

Morrow, Mable 1975 *Indian Rawhide: An American Folk Art.* Norman, OK: University of Oklahoma Press.

Murdock, George Peter 1967 *Ethnographic Atlas.* Pittsburgh, PA: University of Pittsburgh Press.

Murie, James R. 1989 *Ceremonies of the Pawnee.* Douglas R. Parks, ed. Lincoln, NE: University of Nebraska Press.

N.A. 1987 Giant Plastic Medicine Man. *European Review of Native American Studies* 1(1):54.
1994 White Magic. *People Weekly* 42(14):53.

Nabokov, Peter, ed. 1991 *Native American Testimony.* New York: Viking.

Nabokov, Peter, and Robert Easton 1989 *Native American Architecture.* New York: Oxford University Press.

Nagel, Joane 1996 *American Indian Ethnic Renewal.* New York: Oxford University Press.

Neighbors, Robert S. 1852 The Na-ü-ni or Comanches of Texas. In *Information Respecting the History, Condition and Prospects of the Indian tribes of the United States*, Vol. 2. Henry Rowe Schoolcraft, ed. Pp. 125–134. Philadelphia, PA: Lippincott, Grambo.

Neighbours, Kenneth Franklin 1975 *Robert Simpson Neighbors and the Texas Frontier, 1836–1859.* Waco, TX: Texian Press.

Neely, Bill 1995 *The Last Comanche Chief.* New York: John Wiley and Sons.

Neihardt, John G. 1972 *Black Elk Speaks.* New York: Pocket Books.

Nettl, Bruno 1954 *North American Indian Musical Styles.* Philadelphia, PA: American Folklore Society.

Newcomb, William W., Jr. 1961 *The Indians of Texas.* Austin, TX: University of Texas Press.

Nicholson, B. A., and Sylvia Nicholson 2007 Late Prehistoric Treatment of a Bison Skull in Southwestern Manitoba. *Plains Anthropologist* 52:317–324.

Nye, William Sturtevant 1935 *Notes.* Manuscript Collection, Fort Sill Museum Library. Lawton, Oklahoma.
1969 *Carbine and Lance: The Story of Old Fort Sill.* Norman, OK: University of Oklahoma Press.

Oklahoma Indian Arts and Crafts Cooperative 1973 *Painted Tipis by Contemporary Plains Indian Artists.* Anadarko, OK
1976 *Contemporary Southern Plains Indian Metalwork.* Anadarko, OK

O'Nell, Theresa DeLeane 1996 *Disciplined Hearts: History, Identity, and Depression in an American Indian Community.* Berkeley, CA: University of California Press.

Orchard, W. C. 1975 Beads and Beadwork of the American Indians. *Contributions of the Museum of the American Indian, Heye Foundation* 11. New York.

Otterbein, Keith 1985 *The Evolution of War: A Cross-Cultural Study.* New Haven, CT: Human Relations Area Files Press.

Pantaleoni, Hewlitt 1987 One of Densmore's Dakota Rhythms Reconsidered. *Ethnomusicology* 31:35–55.

Panzeri, Peter 1995 *Little Big Horn 1876: Custer's Last Stand.* Oxford: Osprey Publishing.

Parfit, Michael 1994 Powwow: A Gathering of Tribes. *National Geographic* 185(6):88–113.

Parkman, Frances 1931 *The Oregon Trail.* Chicago, IL: The John C. Winston Company.

Parks, Douglas R. 1982 An Historical Character Mythologized: The Scalped Man in Arikara and Pawnee Folklore. In *Plains Indian Studies. Smithsonian Contributions to Anthropology* 10. Douglas H. Ubelaker and Herman J. Viola, eds. Pp. 47–58. Washington, DC: Smithsonian Institution Press.
1996 *Myths and Traditions of the Arikara Indians.* Lincoln, NE: University of Nebraska Press.

Parks, Douglas R., Margot Liberty, and Andrea Ferenci, compilers 1980 Peoples of the Plains. In *Anthropology on the Great Plains*. W. Raymond Wood and Margot Liberty, eds. Pp. 284–295. Lincoln, NE: University of Nebraska Press.

Passel, Jeffrey S. 1996 The Growing American Indian Population, 1960–1990: Beyond Demography. In

Changing Numbers, Changing Needs: American Indian Demography and Public Health. Gary D. Sandefur, Ronald R. Rindfuss, and Barney Cohen, eds. Pp. 79–102. Washington, DC: National Academy Press.

Pelon, Linda Nash 1993 *Issues in Penatuhkah Comanche Ethnohistory.* Unpublished M.A. thesis, University of Texas at Arlington Department of Anthropology.

Penney, David W. 2004 *North American Indian Art.* New York: Thames and Hudson.

Pirkle, E. C., and W. H. Yoho 1985 *Natural Landscapes of the United States.* Dubuque, IA: Kendall/Hunt.

Popper, Frank J. 1992 Thinking Globally, Acting Regionally. *Technology Review* (April):46–53.

Popper, Deborah Epstein, and Frank J. Popper 1987 A Daring Proposal for Dealing with an Inevitable Disaster. *Planning* (December):12–18.

1988 The Fate of the Plains. *High Country News* 20(September 26):15–19.

Powers, Marla N. 1986 *Oglala Women.* Chicago, IL: University of Chicago Press.

Powers, William K. 1977 *Oglala Religion.* Lincoln, NE: University of Nebraska Press.

1978 The Art of Courtship Among the Oglala. *American Indian Art* 5(2):40–47.

1980 Plains Indian Music and Dance. In *Anthropology on the Great Plains.* W. Raymond Wood and Margot Liberty, eds. Pp. 212–229. Lincoln, NE: University of Nebraska Press.

1982 *Yuwipi: Vision and Experience in Oglala Ritual.* Lincoln, NE: University of Nebraska Press.

1983 Comment on "The North American Berdache." *Current Anthropology* 24:461–462.

1986 *Sacred Language: The Nature of Supernatural Discourse in Lakota.* Norman, OK: University of Oklahoma Press.

1987 *Beyond the Vision: Essays on American Indian Culture.* Norman, OK: University of Oklahoma Press.

1990 *War Dance: Plains Indian Musical Performance.* Tucson, AZ: University of Arizona Press.

Powers, William K., and Marla M. N. Powers 1984 Metaphysical Aspects of an Oglala Food System. In *Food in the Social Order.* Mary Douglas, ed. Pp. 40–96. New York: Russell Sage Foundation.

Pratt, Richard Henry 1964 *Battlefield and Classroom.* Lincoln, NE: University of Nebraska Press.

Reed, Erik K. 1952 The Myth of Montezuma's Bison and the Type Locality of the Species. *Journal of Mammalogy* 33:390–392.

Reeves, Brian 1973 The Concept of an Altithermal Cultural Hiatus in Northern Plains Prehistory. *American Anthropologist* 75:1221–1253.

Reid, T. K. 1998 Sioux Tribe Wins Return of Famous Ghost Shirt from Scottish Museum. *Houston Chronicle,* November 20, p. A14.

Reyer, Carolyn 1991 *Cante ohitika Win (Brave-hearted Women): Images of Lakota Women from the Pine Ridge Reservation, South Dakota.* Vermillion: University of South Dakota Press.

Rhodes, Willard 1959 *Music of the American Indian: Kiowa.* Booklet accompanying phonograph album AAFS-L35. Washington, DC: Library of Congress, Archives of Folk Song in cooperation with the Bureau of Indian Affairs.

Richardson, Rupert Norval 1933 *The Comanche Barrier to South Plains Settlement.* Glendale, CA: Arthur H. Clark.

Rickey, Don, Jr. 1963 *Forty Miles a Day on Beans and Hay.* Norman, OK: University of Oklahoma Press.

Ridington, Robin 1993 A Sacred Object as Text: Reclaiming the Sacred Pole of the Omaha Tribe. *American Indian Quarterly* 17:83–99.

Riney, Scott 1999 *The Rapid City Indian School, 1898–1933.* Norman, OK: University of Oklahoma Press.

Robinson, Lila Wistrand, and James Armagost 1990 *Comanche Dictionary and Grammar.* Dallas, TX: Summer Institute of Linguistics and the University of Texas at Arlington.

Roe, Frank Gilbert 1955 *The Indian and the Horse.* Norman, OK: University of Oklahoma Press.

Roscoe, Will 1998 *Changing Ones: Third and Fourth Genders in Native North America.* New York: St. Martin's Press.

Ruibal, Sal 2005 NCAA Upholds Fighting Sioux as Abusive Nickname. *USA Today,* September 29, p. 1c.

Ruíz, Jose Francisco 1972 *Report on the Indian Tribes of Texas.* New Haven: Yale University Press.

Scaglion, Richard 1980 The Plains Culture Area Concept. In *Anthropology on the Great Plains.* W. Raymond Wood and Margot Liberty, eds. Pp. 23–34. Lincoln, NE: University of Nebraska Press.

Schlesier, Karl H. 1987 *The Wolves of Heaven.* Norman, OK: University of Oklahoma Press.

1990 Rethinking the Midewiwin and the Plains Ceremonial Called the Sun Dance. *Plains Anthropologist* 35:1–26.

Schlesier, Karl H., ed. 1994 *Plains Indians, A.D. 500–1500: The Archaeological Past of Historic Groups.* Norman, OK: University of Oklahoma Press.

Schneider, Mary Jane 1983 Women's Work: An Examination of Women's Roles in Plains Indian Arts and Crafts. In *The Hidden Half: Studies of Plains Indian Women.* Patricia Albers and Beatrice Medicine, eds. Pp. 101–122. Lanham, MD: University Press of America.

Schoen, Lawrence M., and James L. Armagost 1992 Coyote as Cheat in Comanche Folktales. *Western Folklore* 51:202–207.

Schweinfurth, Kay Parker 2002 *Prayer on Top of the Earth: The Spiritual Universe of the Plains Apaches.* Boulder, CO: University Press of Colorado.

Secoy, Frank Raymond 1953 *Changing Military Patterns on the Great Plains.* American Ethnological Society Monograph 21. Locust Valley, NY: J. J. Augustin.

Shafer, R. Murray 1980 *The Tuning of the World: Toward a Theory of Soundscape Design.* Philadelphia, PA: University of Pennsylvania Press.

Shimkin, Demitri B. 1980 Comanche-Shoshone Words of Acculturation. *Journal of the Steward Anthropological Society* 11:195–247.

Simms, S. C. 1903 Crow Indian Hermaphrodites. *American Anthropologist* 5:580–581.

Skinner, Alanson 1916 Plains Cree Tales. *Journal of American Folklore* 29:341–367.

Smith, C. Hubert 1980 *The Explorations of the La Vérendryes in the Northern Plains, 1738–1743.* Lincoln, NE: University of Nebraska Press.

Smith, Ralph A. 1960 Mexican and Anglo-Saxon Traffic in Scalps, Slaves, and Livestock, 1835–1841. *West Texas Historical Association Year Book* 36:98–115.

1970 The Comanche Sun over Mexico. *West Texas Historical Association Year Book* 46:25–62.

1979 The West Texas Bone Business. *West Texas Historical Association Year Book* 55:111–134.

Spector, Janet 1983 Male/Female Task Differentiation Among the Hidatsa: Toward the Development of an Archaeological Approach to the Study of Gender. In *The Hidden Half: Studies of Plains Indian Women.* Patricia Albers and Beatrice Medicine, eds. Pp. 101–122. Lanham, MD: University Press of America.

Spielmann, Katherine A., ed. 1991 *Farmers, Hunters, and Colonists: Interaction Between the Southwest and the Southern Plains.* Tucson, AZ: University of Arizona Press.

Spier, Leslie 1925 The Distribution of Kinship Systems in North America. *University of Washington Publications in Anthropology* 1(2):69–88. Seattle, WA: University of Washington Press.

St. Clair, H. H., and Robert H. Lowie 1909 Shoshone and Comanche Tales. *Journal of American Folklore* 22:265–282.

Stahl, Robert J. 1978 *Farming Among the Kiowa, Comanche, Kiowa Apache, and Wichita.* Unpublished Ph.D. dissertation, University of Oklahoma Department of Anthropology.

Standing Bear, Luther 1933 *Land of the Spotted Eagle.* Boston, MA: Houghton-Mifflin.

1975 *My People the Sioux.* Lincoln, NE: University of Nebraska Press.

Stedman, Raymond William 1982 *Shadows of the Indian.* Norman, OK: University of Oklahoma Press.

Steinmetz, Paul B. 1990 *Pipe, Bible, and Peyote Among the Oglala Lakota.* Knoxville, TN: University of Tennessee Press.

Steltenkamp, Michael F. 1993 *Black Elk: Holy Man of the Oglala.* Norman, OK: University of Oklahoma Press.

Stewart, Edgar I. 1955 *Custer's Luck.* Norman, OK: University of Oklahoma Press.

Stewart, Omer C. 1980 The Ghost Dance. In *Anthropology on the Great Plains.* W. Raymond Wood and Margot Liberty, eds. Pp. 179–187. Lincoln, NE: University of Nebraska Press.

1987 *Peyote Religion: A History.* Norman, OK: University of Oklahoma Press.

Strauss, Lawrence Guy 2000 Solutrean Settlement in North America? A Review of Reality. *American Antiquity* 65:219–226.

Strickland, Rennard 1980 *The Indians in Oklahoma.* Norman, OK: University of Oklahoma Press.

Strong, William Duncan 1933 The Plains Culture Area in the Light of Archaeology. *American Anthropologist* 35:271–287.

Sturtevant, William C., ed. 2001 *Handbook of North American Indians*, Vol. 13. Washington, DC: Smithsonian Institution.

Sutherland, Kay 1995 *Rock Painting at Hueco Tanks Historical State Park.* Austin, TX: Texas Parks and Wildlife Press.

Szasz, Margaret Connell 1999 *Education and the American Indian.* Albuquerque, NM: University of New Mexico Press.

Tate, Michael I. 1994 Comanche Captives: People between Two Worlds. *Chronicles of Oklahoma* 72:228–263.

Taylor, Nathaniel G., John B. Henderson, Samuel F. Tappan, John B. Sanborn, William S. Harney, Alfred H. Terry, William T. Sherman, and Christopher C. Augur 1910 *Papers relating to Talks and Councils Held with the Indians in Dakota and Montana in the years 1866–1869.* Washington, DC: U.S. Government Printing Office.

Thomas, Alfred B. 1929 An Eighteenth Century Comanche Document. *American Anthropologist* 31:289–298.

Thompson, Stith 1955–1958 *Motif-Index of Folk-Literature.* Bloomington, IN: Indiana University Press.
1966 *Tales of the North American Indians.* Bloomington, IN: Indiana University Press.

Thurman, Melburn D. 1983 The Timing of the Skidi-Pawnee Morning Star Sacrifice. *Ethnohistory* 30:155–163.

Titon, Jeff Todd, ed. 1984 *Worlds of Music.* New York: Schirmer Books.

Townsend, Kenneth W. 2000 *World War II and the American Indian.* Albuquerque, NM: University of New Mexico Press.

Troike, Rudolph C. 1962 The Origins of Plains Mescalism. *American Anthropologist* 64(5, Part 1):946–963.

Tunnell, Curtis D. 2000 *A Landmark Court Decision in Southern Texas on Peyote and the Native American Church.* San Antonio, TX: Southern Texas Archeological Association.

Tylor, Edward B. 1877 *Primitive Culture.* New York: H. Holt.

Underhill, Ruth M. 1965 *Red Man's Religion.* Chicago, IL: University of Chicago Press.

U.S. Department of Commerce 1980 *Red River Valley Tornadoes of April 10, 1979.* Natural Disaster Survey Report 80-1. Rockville, MD.

Utley, Robert M. 1988 *Cavalier in Buckskin.* Norman, OK: University of Oklahoma Press.

Van Gennep, Arnold 1960 *The Rites of Passage.* Chicago, IL: University of Chicago Press.

Vander, Judith 1988 *Songprints; The Musical Experience of Five Shoshone Women.* Urbana, IL: University of Illinois Press.

Vandervort, Bruce 2006 *Indian Wars of Mexico, Canada and the United States, 1812–1900.* New York: Routledge.

Viola, Herman J. 1995 *Diplomats in Buckskins.* Bluffton, SC: Rivolo Books.

Voget, Fred W. 1984 *The Shoshoni-Crow Sun Dance.* Norman, OK: University of Oklahoma Press. 2001 Crow. In *Handbook of North American Indians*, Vol. 13, Part 1. William C. Sturtevant, ed. Pp. 695–717. Washington, DC: Smithsonian Institution.

Vollers, Maryanne 1996 Costner's Last Stand. *Esquire* 125(6):100–107.

Waddell, Jack O., and O. Michael Watson, eds. 1984 *The American Indian in Urban Society.* Washington, DC: University Press of America.

Wade, Dale A. 2006 Avonlea and Athapaskan Migrations: A Reconsideration. *Plains Anthropologist* 51:185–197.

Wagner, Angie 2007 On Reservation, Dealers Found a Market for Meth; Gang Compounded Poverty with Crime. *Washington Post*, May 6, p. A3.

Walker, Carson 2007 Budweiser's Help Sought on Reservation. *Associated Press*, September 18.

Walker, James R. 1979 *The Sun Dance and Other Ceremonies of the Oglala Division of the Teton Dakota.* New York: AMS Press.
1980 *Lakota Belief and Ritual.* Raymond J. DeMallie and Elaine A. Jahner, eds. Lincoln, NE: University of Nebraska Press.
1983 *Lakota Myth.* Elaine A. Jahner, ed. Lincoln, NE: University of Nebraska Press.

Wallace, A. F. C. 1956 Revitalization Movements. *American Anthropologist* 58:264–281.
1966 *Religion: An Anthropological View.* New York: Random House.
1972 *The Death and Rebirth of the Seneca.* New York: Vintage Books.

Wallace, Ernest, and E. Adamson Hoebel 1952 *The Comanches: Lords of the South Plains.* Norman, OK: University of Oklahoma Press.

Washburn, Wilcolm E. 1984 A Fifty-Year Perspective on the Indian Reorganization Act. *American Anthropologist* 86:279–289.

Watkins, Laurel J. 1984 *A Grammar of Kiowa.* Lincoln, NE: University of Nebraska Press.

Webb, Walter Prescott 1981 *The Great Plains.* Lincoln, NE: University of Nebraska Press.

Wedel, Waldo R. 1986 *Central Plains Prehistory.* Lincoln, NE: University of Nebraska Press.

Weeks, John B., Edwin D. Gutentag, Frederick J. Heimes, and Richard R. Luckey 1988 Summary of the High Plains Regional Aquifer-System Analysis in Parts of Colorado, Kansas, Nebraska, New Mexico,

Oklahoma, South Dakota, Texas, and Wyoming. *U.S. Geological Survey Professional Paper* 1400-A. Washington, DC: U.S. Government Printing Office.

Weist, Katherine M. 1980 Plains Indian Women: An Assessment. In *Anthropology on the Great Plains*. W. Raymond Wood and Margot Liberty, eds. Pp. 255–271. Lincoln, NE: University of Nebraska Press.

Weltfish, Gene 1965 *The Lost Universe: Pawnee Life and Culture*. Lincoln, NE: University of Nebraska Press.

Wernitznig, Dagmar 2007 *Europe's Indians, Indians in Europe*. Lanham, MD: University Press of America.

Whitehead, Harriet 1994 The Bow and the Burden Strap: A New Look at Institutionalized Homosexuality in Native North America. In *Sexual Meanings: The Cultural Construction of Gender and Sexuality*. Sherry B. Ortner and Harriet Whitehead, eds. Pp. 80–115. New York: Cambridge University Press.

Whitman, William 1937 The Oto. *Columbia University Contributions to Anthropology* 28. New York.

Wilbarger, J. W. 1985 *Indian Depredations in Texas*. Austin, TX: Eakins Press.

Will, George F., and George E. Hyde 1964 *Corn Among the Indians of the Upper Missouri*. Lincoln, NE: University of Nebraska Press.

Williamson, Ray A., and Claire R. Farrer, eds. 1992 *Earth and Sky: Visions of the Cosmos in Native America Folklore*. Albuquerque, NM: University of New Mexico Press.

Wilson, Gilbert L. 1917 Agriculture of the Hidatsa Indians: An Indian Interpretation. *University of Minnesota Studies in the Social Sciences* 9. Minneapolis, MN.

Winfrey, Dorman H., and James M. Day 1995 *The Indian Papers of Texas and the Southwest, 1825–1916*. 5 vols. Austin, TX: Texas State Historical Association.

Wissler, Clark 1914 The Influence of the Horse in the Development of Plains Culture. *American Anthropologist* 16:1–25.

1917 *The American Indian*. New York: McMurtrie.

1974 *North American Indians of the Plains*. New York: Burt Franklin Reprints.

1986 *A Blackfoot Source Book*. New York: Garland.

Wissler, Clark, and Herbert J. Spinden 1916 The Pawnee Human Sacrifice to the Morning Star. *American Museum Journal* 16(1):49–55.

Wood, W. Raymond 1980 Plains Trade in Prehistoric and Protohistoric Intertribal Relations. In *Anthropology on the Great Plains*. W. Raymond Wood and Margot Liberty, eds. Pp. 98–109. Lincoln, NE: University of Nebraska Press.

Wood, W. Raymond, ed. 1998 *Archaeology on the Great Plains*. Lawrence, KS: University of Kansas Press.

Woomavoyah, Jan 2006 No More Squaw Creek!! *Numu Tekwapuha Nomneekatu Newsletter* 9(1):6–7.

Wright, Muriel 1951 *A Guide to the Indian Tribes of Oklahoma*. Norman, OK: University of Oklahoma Press.

Yarrow, H. C. 1881 A Further Contribution to the Study of the Mortuary Customs of the North American Indians. In *First Annual Report of the Bureau of [American] Ethnology, 1879–1880*. J. W. Powell, ed. Pp. 87–203. Washington, DC: U.S. Government Printing Office.

Young, Gloria A. 1981 *Powwow Power: Perspectives on Historic and Contemporary Intertribalism*. Unpublished Ph.D. dissertation, Indiana University Department of Anthropology.

1986 Aesthetic Archives: The Visual Language of Plains Ledger Art. In *The Arts of the North American Indian: Native Traditions and Evolution*. Edwin L. Wade, ed. New York: Hudson Hills Press in Association with Philbrook Art Center.

2001 Intertribal Religious Movements. In *Handbook of North American Indians*, Vol. 13, Part 2. William C. Sturtevant, ed. Pp. 996–1010. Washington, DC: Smithsonian Institution.

Zitkala-Ša 1985 *American Indian Stories*. Lincoln, NE: University of Nebraska Press.

CREDITS

Chapter 1: *p. 1*:Kiowa Gomda Dawgyah ("Wind Songs") by Maurice Boyd, Texas Christian University Press; *p. 4:* Daniel J. Gelo; *p. 5*: National Archives [557189]; Edward S. Curtis/Library of Congress Prints and Photographs Division[LC-USZ62-90821]; *p. 6*: Roger Coulam/Alamy; *p. 8:* David Hiser/Stone/Getty Images.

Chapter 2: *p. 22*: All Rights Reserved, Image Archives, Denver Museum of Nature and Science; *p. 24* Chase Studio/Photo Researchers, Inc.; *p. 27*: Daniel J. Gelo/University of Texas at San Antonio.

Chapter 3: *p. 46*: Catlin, George (1794–1872)/The Art Gallery Collection / Alamy; *p. 53* Edward S. Curtis/ Library of Congress Prints and Photographs Division [LC-USZ62-130189]; *p. 55*: The Library of Congress Prints and Photograph Division [LC-USZ62-61937]; *p. 57*: National Archives [530974]; *p. 62*: State Historical Society of North Dakota 0086-0281.

Chapter 4: *p. 67*: MPI/Archive Photos/Getty Images; *p. 75*: "Death Songs" by Maurice Boyd, Texas Christian University Press; *p. 79*: Daniel J. Gelo.

Chapter 5: *p. 95*: Edward S. Curtis/The Library of Congress Prints and Photograph Division [LC-USZC4-8814]7]; *p. 106*: Daniel J. Gelo; *p. 117*: National Archives [530913]; *p. 124*: "One time, when I was a young boy ..." by Charles S. Brandt, Dover Publications, Inc.

Chapter 6: *p. 133*: National Archives [530913]; *p. 136*: William Henry Jackson/Bettmann/Corbis; *p. 138*: Institute of Texan Cultures, UTSA, #089-0140, Courtesy of Private Collection; *p. 142*: Edward S. Curtis/Library of Congress Prints and Photographs Division [LC-USCZ62-46966]; *p. 145*: shield, Southern Cheyenne, 1870 Denver Art Museum Collection: Native Arts Acquisition Funds, 1968.330; Photo © Denver Art Museum. All Rights Reserved; *p. 149*: Paris Pierce/Alamy; *p. 153*: Edward S. Curtis/Library of Congress Prints and Photographs Division[LC-USCZ62-136594]; *p. 155*: Ivy Close Images/Alamy; *p. 164*: Silverhorn (James Silverhorn; Haungooah) "The Exploits of Sun Boy," c. 1880-1900, Gift of Muskogee Public Library, 1982.6 © 2011 Philbrook Museum of Art, Inc. Tulsa, Oklahoma; *p. 165*: Silverhorn (James Silverhorn; Haungooah) "The Exploits of Sun Boy," c. 1880–1900, Gift of Muskogee Public Library, 1982.6 © 2011 Philbrook Museum of Art, Inc. Tulsa, Oklahoma; *p. 166*: Silverhorn (James Silverhorn; Haungooah) "The Exploits of Sun Boy," c. 1880-1900, Gift of Muskogee Public Library, 1982.6 © 2011 Philbrook Museum of Art, Inc. Tulsa, Oklahoma; *p. 167*: Daniel J. Gelo.

Chapter 7: *p. 171*: John Reddy/Alamy; *p. 176*: Yankton peyote song "Pray! yo, yo ..." by William K. Powers, Powers William; "The Kiowa Flag Song" after Rhodes 1959:26; "Shoshone Naraya" or "Ghost Dance" song, by Judith Vander, UCLA; *p. 176* "Just because you left me ..." Daniel J. Gelo 1988b, by Tom Mauchahahty-Ware; Millard Clark, Daniel J. Gelo; *p. 179*: Photograph courtesy of the Milwaukee Public Museum.

Chapter 8: *p. 190*: "Deserted Children Story, ..." Version 2., Arapaho by Dorsey; Kroeber, University of Nebraska Press; *pp. 190-91*: "Deserted Children" by Kardiner, Columbia University Press; *pp. 190-91*: "Deserted Children Story" by Kardiner, Curley, Ellin; *p. 192*: "Iktiniki meets Coyote on a walk ..." Viking Penguin, Inc.; "Coyote is starving and goes, ..." University of Nebraska Press; "Wi-sak-a-chak eats many berries ..." by Dusenberry, Acta Universitatis Stockholmieusis; *p. 193*: "Inktomi thinks only of copulating ..." by Erdoes; Ortiz, Viking Penguin, Inc.; "Inktomi marries at the age of 14 ..." "Forbidden Fruit ..." by Erdoes; Ortiz, Viking Penguin, Inc.; "Nihansan asks for the power ..." by Dorsey; Kroeber, University of Nebraska Press; "Veeho encounters a man ..." by Erdoes; Ortiz, Viking Penguin; "Old Man Coyote is cold ..." by Erdoes; Ortiz, Viking Penguin; "Saynday meets a (female) ant" by Marriott, Harper Collins Publishers, Inc.; *p. 194*: "Coyote commands Turkey ..." by Dorsey, University of Oklahoma Press; "Coyote comes" by Erdoes; Ortiz, Viking Penguin, Inc.; *p. 195*: A young man goes hunting University of Nebraska Press; *p. 196*: Double Woman, 1971 casein on paper 18 1/8 x 22 1/2 University Art Galleries at the University of South Dakota on loan from the Howe Family; *p. 197*: Manuscript Acee Blue Eagle Papers: "Painting and Drawings" by Blue Eagle, National Anthropological Archives, Smithsonian Institution; *p. 198*: "Wa-kon'da ... here needy he stands ..." by Fletcher, University of Nebraska Press; *p. 199*: "What is the most ..." by Dorsey; Kroeber, Powers, William.

Chapter 9: *p. 205* William R. Cross/Library of Congress Prints and Photographs Division [LC-USZ62-104571]; *p. 207*: Smithsonian Institution Catalog No. 229,900; *p. 221*: System of Lakota symbols by Willliam K. Powers, William Powers; *p. 225*: Interfoto/Alamy; *p. 229*: Edward S. Curtis/ Library of Congress Prints and Photographs Division [LC-USCZ62-99611].

Chapter 10: *p. 238*: Smithsonian American Art Museum, Washington, D C/Art Resource, NY; *p. 246*: MPI/Getty Images; *p. 247*: Lakota George Sword circa 1908. "A hoop covered ..." by James R Walker; Raymond J. DeMallie; Elaine A Jahner, University of Nebraska Press; *p. 252*: B. Anthony Stewart/National Geographic Image Collection/ Alamy; *p. 253*: National Archives [530915]; *p. 263*: Allen Russell/Alamy; *p.270*: "Mary Lou Stone Road Prairie Chief ..." by Giglio. Virginia.

Chapter 11: *p. 276*: MPI/Archive Photos/Getty Images; *p. 283*: Kiowa Gwoh-dawgyah. "Going away on a war ..." by Boyd, Texas Christian University Press; *p. 284*: Kiowa Gwoh-dawgyah. "You young men sitting ..." by Boyd, Texas Christian University Press; *pp. 284-85*: "The Oglala Black Elk, ..." by Neihardt, John G. Neihardt Trust; *p. 292*: MPI/Archive Photos/Getty Images; *p. 302*: SPC BAE 4420 Vol. 6 01003705, National Anthropological Archives, Smithsonian Institution.

Chapter 12: *p. 311*: National Archives[531079]; *p. 312*: Walter Rawlings/Robert Harding Picture Library Ltd/Alamy; *p.314*: "Population Decline Among" by Raymond Wood; Margot Liberty; Parks, Liberty Margot; *p.314*: "Population Decline Among Plains ..." by Raymond Wood; Margot Liberty; Parks, Liberty, Margot; *p.319*: "Morning Schedule ..." by Fixico, Greenwood Publishing Group; *p. 322*; Denver Public Library, Western History Collection; *p. 329*: Bettmann/Corbis; *p. 330*: Jacques Brinon/AP Images.

Chapter 13: *p. 339*: Ray Ozman/AP Images; *p. 346*: Greg Ryan/Alamy; *p. 355*: Mike Simons/Getty Images.

375

INDEX

Note: Page numbers followed by *f, t,* and *m* indicate figures, tables and maps respectively.

Babb, John, 290
Badlands, 5f, 6, 9m
Badlands National Monument, 10
Balcones Escarpment, 11, 9m
Bands
  of Cheyennes, 72
  of Kiowas, 72f
  and tribal organization, 68–69
Basin, 13–14
Basketry, 139–140
Bates, Charles Ash, 322f
Battle of Summit Springs, 309
Beadwork, 155–158
Beans 60, 61
Bear Paw Mountains, 10, 9m
Bear's Lodge, 198, 351
Beaver Ceremony, 259
Beecher Island Fight, 310
Belle sauvage (beautiful savage), 119
Benedict, Ruth, 228
Bent, Charles, 294
Bent, George, 295
Bent, William, 294, 295
Berdaches, 127–131
  definition of, 127
  Finds-Them-and- Kills-Them 127
  marriage and, 128
  Osh-Tisch as, 127
  sexual life of, 128
  tribe gender roles and, 129
  tribes with, 127t
  war parties and, 127
Bergmann, E. H., 282
Beringia, 24
Berlandier, Jean Louis, 141
Big Back, 106f
Big Laughing Woman, 112
Bilateral descent, 69
Bird quills, 15
Birds, 12
Birth, infancy, and childhood, 98–102
  Birth control, 99
  child delivery, 100
  disciplinarians, 101
  ear piercing, 100
  favorite child custom, 101–102
  games, 102
  naming of child, 100
  nursing and care, 101
  survival rates, 99
  unwanted children, 99
Bison (buffalo), 11, 13, 43–51
  antiquus, 43
  bonasus, 44
  bones, 50–51
  butchering of, 48
  commercial tanning processes
    and, 49–50
  extermination of, 49–51
  horse and, 49
  hunting of, 45–48, 50
  importance of, 45

Indian stories/ceremonies about,
  44–45
kill sites of, 28m
Late Prehistoric period and, 29
latifrons, 43
subspecies of, 43–44
types of, 43
uses for, 48, 48t
Black Elk (Lakota), 271
Black Elk Speaks (Neihardt), 271
Blackfoots, 36
  beadwork of, 157
  berdache status and, 127t
  Christian denominations among, 269t
  music styles of, 171
  sign language signs of, 298t
  Sun Dance and, 244
  tipi painting and, 162–163
  women and medicine, 121–122
Black handkerchief legerdemain,
  231–232
Black Hills, 10, 9m
Black Kettle (Cheyenne), 309, 310
Black Mesa, 10, 9m
Blake, Michael, 356
Blood quantum, concept of, 358–360
Blue Eagle, Acee, 168, 197f
Blue grama grass, 2
Boarding schools, 316–321
  forced recruitment in, 317–318
  Indian singing/dancing in, 318–319
  list of, 317t
  Native names and, 318
  Office of Indian Affairs and, 317
  outing programs of, 318
Boas, Franz, 15, 247
Boats and rafts, 141–142
Bodmer, Karl, 57f
Body/face painting, 152
Body of Christ Independent Church, 269
Bointy, Sallie Hokeah, 1
Bonnin, Gertrude Simmons, 265, 320
Bow and arrow, 142–144
  making of, 142–143
  types of wood used in, 143
Bowstrings, making, 143
Braroe, Niels, 348
Brave, as stereotype, 119
Brazos River, 8, 9m
Breaks, 6
Breechclout, 150
Brideprice, 107
Bride service, 107
Bride wealth, 107
Brosius, S. M., 265
Brown, Joseph Epes, 270
Brush arbors/shades, 138
Buffalo Calf Pipe, 243
Buffalo Ceremony, 105
Buffalo Commons concept, 13
Buffalo Hump (Penateka Comanche
  leader), 45, 60

Buffalo runners, 59
Bull boat, 142, 142f
Bureau of Indian Affairs (BIA), 265,
  314, 334
Bureau of Indian Education (BIE), 334
Burial, 116–119
  aerial sepulture practice of, 116
  arrangements, 116
  corpse positioning and, 118
  cremation as, 118
  funeral tipi for, 118
  funerary giveaway after, 118–119
  ground, 117–118
  methods of, 116–117
  secondary, 117
Buried City, 31

Caches, 64
Caddoan
  dance types, 171
  grass houses of, 137
  horses and, 278
  language family, 34, 35m
  people, 31
  trade language of, 296
Caesar, Julius, 154
Calendar History of the Kiowa Indians
  (Mooney), 184
Calgary Stampede, 335
California, 14
Calumet ceremony, 295–296, 304
Calumets (peace pipes), 158, 242
Campbell, Ben Nighthorse, 354
Camp crier, 83–84
Canadian River, 8, 9m
Canadian Sioux, Sun Dance and, 245
Cannibalism, 288–289
Cannon, T. C., 168
Canyon (recording company), 174
Carbon-14 (^{14}C) dating, 20
Carlisle Indian Industrial School, 317
  morning schedule for, 319t
Carretas, 293
Carrion, Adolphur, 269
Carrion, Marion C., 269
Casinos, 338, 343, 343t–345t, 345
Catches, Peter S., Sr., 201
Catlin, George, 45, 54–55, 59, 158, 225f,
  238, 238f, 289, 297
Catlinite, 158–159
Cedar trees, 64
Central Lowland, 2
Central Plains, 9m
  defined, 2
  subtradition, 30
Character motifs, narrative, 191–197
  animal characters as, 194–195
  creator as, 193–194
  culture hero as, 193–194
  trickster as, 191–193
Chardon, François (Francis A.), 294, 295
Chastity belts, 125